Knowledge and Postmodernism

in Historical Perspective

Knowledge and Postmodernism

in Historical Perspective

edited by
Joyce Appleby
Elizabeth Covington
David Hoyt
Michael Latham
Allison Sneider

Routledge
New York and London

Published in 1996 by

Routledge
29 West 35TH Street
New York, NY 10001

Published in Great Britain in 1996 by

Routledge
11 New Fetter Lane
London EC4P 4EE

Library of Congress Cataloging-in-Publication Data

Knowledge and postmodernism in historical perspective / edited by Joyce Appleby ... [et al.].
     p.   cm.
  Includes bibliographical references.
  ISBN 0–415–91382–9 — ISBN 0–415–91383–7 (pbk.)
  1. Knowledge, Sociology of. 2. Postmodernism. I. Appleby, Joyce Oldham.
  BD175.K62   1996
  121—dc20   95–35192
                                                                       CIP

Contents

Acknowledgments

We would like to thank the Andrew W. Mellon Foundation for initiating and supporting the summer seminar in which this book of readings was developed. We would also like to thank the History Department of the University of California, Los Angeles for its support of the undergraduate seminars in which these readings were first used. We are also grateful to Jasamin Rostam-Kolayi, Bob Myers, Stephen Miller, Arleen de Vera, William van Benschoten, Augusto Espiritu, Michael Mahoney, and Kimberly Garmoe for helping us refine our thoughts in the Mellon graduate seminar of 1994.

Timeline

1500		1550		1600

Copernicus (1473–1543)

Francis Bacon (1561–1626)
Johannes Kepler (1571–1630)
Galileo (1564–1642)
Thomas Hobbes (1588–1679)

1600		1650		1700

John Locke (1632–1704)
Isaac Newton (1642–1727)
René Descartes (1596–1650)

Montesquieu (1689–1755)
Voltaire (1694–1778)

American Revolution (1776)
French Revolution (1789)

1700		1750		1800

David Hume (1711–1776)
Adam Smith (1723–1790)

G. W. F. Hegel (1770–1831)
Immanuel Kant (1724–1804)
Jean=Antoine Condorcet (1743–1794)

THE MODERN AGE

End of Napoleonic Empire (1815)

(1848) European Revolutions

1800		1850		1900

Alexis de Tocqueville (1805–1859)
Leopold von Ranke (1795–1886)
Auguste Comte (1798–1857)
Karl Marx (1818–1883)
Charles Darwin (1809–1882)

Franz Boas (1858–1942)
Friedrich Nietzsche (1844–1900)
Ferdinand de Saussure (1857–1913)
Max Weber (1864–1920)

(1914) World War One

(1939) World War Two

1900		1950		present

Ruth Benedict (1887–1948)   Claude Lévi-Strauss (1908–   )   Max Horkheimer (1895–1973)
Theodor Adorno (1903–1969)

Knowledge
and Postmodernism
in Historical Perspective

I am sure that it has not escaped your notice that we live in an era of *posts*. The buildings going up around us are postmodern; our age is postindustrial; our literary criticism, poststructural; our sociology, postpositivist; our political science, postbehavioral; our philosophy, postanalytical. Clearly, ours is an age that knows where it has been and needs to assert that it is no longer there.

To label our art, our science, and our economic life with the prefix *post* suggests both sequence and dependency—first came modernism, positivism, industrialism; then postmodernism, postpositivism, postindustrialism. Our rejected antecedents supply the identification for these times. We do not have a new name for our period as eighteenth-century Westerners did when they began talking about the modern era. Rather, we identify our age by the distance it has moved away from a style, a mode of reasoning, a production system. Never has it been so starkly apparent how indebted one era is to its predecessors.

This would seem to be an historian's paradise were it not for the fact that historians have become postempirical. That is, there is now a general recognition that history is more important as a literate people's way of finding meaning in the present than as a compilation of true statements about the past. Of course, scholars who make new findings or uncover long-buried evidence are still rewarded while those who distort the facts are criticized. It is not that accuracy has lost its value, but rather that the emphasis has shifted away from documentation to interpretation, away from reconstructing a chain of events to exploring their significance.

Using a conceptual shorthand, we could say that meaning has replaced cause as the central focus of attention. This book will trace this dramatic shift of interest. We will begin with the emergence of causal explanations and follow the arc of science from its first exhilarating aspiration of representing the physical universe accurately to the vaulting ambition of applying the scientific understanding of cause and effect relations to the affairs of human beings. Riding high in the nineteenth century, the social sciences raised expectations that were not—perhaps could not be—met. When we reach the end of the twentieth century, and the end of this text, we find scholars withdrawing from the outward-looking search for causes in favor of an introspective probing that turns their inquiries in upon themselves. The world around them appears less a free-standing reality and more a social construction, known to us not through our five senses but rather by our proliferating interpretations. This, in the proverbial nutshell, has been the trajectory of knowledge and postmodernism from the seventeenth through the twentieth centuries.

Like the past itself, written history changes in style and content. The study of these changes is called historiography. These shifts remind us that history belongs to a people's intellectual life. Like life itself, its truths are cumulative; like life, it is subject to abrupt shifts of direction. In all intellectual productions—whether in literature or law-making or scientific theory—authors bring to their subjects the presuppositions that form their cultural heritage as well as their own personal idiosyncrasies. Historians also respond to the traditions within their discipline, to the problems set and the opportunities opened up by their predecessors. Historiography involves first studying the social milieu in which a historical work was written and then connecting that to the intellectual links that bind the author to his or her cohort. This book follows the history of knowledge-production in the modern West.

A very convenient and psychologically satisfying way to present a history is to tell a story. That is exactly what we will do. We have created a narrative that deliberately joins contemporary thought about knowledge to the scientific revolution of the seventeenth century, the Enlightenment of the eighteenth century, the grand social theorizing of the nineteenth century, and the growing skepticism about objective truths which has flowered in the postmodernist movement of the last quarter century. The connecting links in this narrative are the explorations of the physical world, the application of science to the study of society, and the discovery of culture, followed by the contemplation of these philosophical developments as objects in themselves. Much of the material included here is pointed towards postmodernism—an intellectual phenomenon of recent decades. We close, however, with critics of postmodernism who summon us back to the "Enlightenment Project," as the eighteenth-century faith in reason, progress, and individual autonomy is often called.

In this reader you will find writings that represent critical philosophical benchmarks along the path of our narrative. They are significant because they introduce or summarize key understandings about human nature, cosmic design, what constitutes the good, the true and the beautiful, political authority, and the relations between past, present, and future. Such concepts form the foundations of the building of knowledge; they hold the edifice up, but are hidden from sight. It will be no small part of our task in studying "knowledge and postmodernism in historical perspective" to expose the assumptions that act as unseen foundations for the intellectual productions we've included.

It is also worth recognizing that the narrative we are presenting is one of many that could be constructed about the transformation of Western intellectual traditions between the seventeenth century and the present. This does not mean that our selections are arbitrary. Rather, it points to the fact that the choices made are open to question—indeed, should be questioned. These choices also reflect considerable thought about what is going on in the contentious debates about knowledge in our time.

THE MODERN ERA

We begin our story with knowledge because the publication in the seventeenth century of novel findings about the universe ushered in the modern era. The natural philosophy and Aristotelian ideas of the ancient Greeks were repudiated, signalling what historians refer to as the scientific revolution because it involved the radical idea of interrogating nature directly and forever changed how inquirers thought about reality. Accompanying this major intellectual transformation were startling changes in the material world as seventeenth-century merchants created patterns of exchange that linked the newly-explored parts of the globe with metropolitan Europe. New goods, new labor systems, new levels of population, greater wealth, and denser systems of transportation and communication literally redrew the face of the earth. Somewhere between Galileo Galilei's looking into his telescope and European investors pouring money and slaves into the commercial cultivation of sugar in the West Indies, the modern era began.[1]

A good way to begin our exploration of modernity is to take stock of the impact of the scientific revolution. When writers began to popularize ideas about the new learning, they did so within a world that took its values from custom, its political order from monarchies, its religion from established churches, and its understanding of human purpose from the Bible. Hierarchical, orthodox, and traditional, seventeenth-century Europeans feared change, and they were on the verge of the greatest changes the world has ever seen. The proponents of the new science had a difficult time convincing their contemporaries that Copernicus's theory of the earth's revolution around the sun and Galileo's use of the telescope to confirm this theory were not threatening to everything they held dear.

When Francis Bacon began urging his king and fellow Englishmen to look upon Galileo's findings as a blessing for mankind, he offered a new understanding of knowledge. Science—or natural philosophy, as it was then called—could benefit mankind; it could be turned to useful purposes. The state-established churches of Europe, whether Catholic or Protestant, exercised great power over public discussions. Recognizing this, Bacon made a critical distinction between first causes which came from the will of God and second causes which represented the natural mechanisms through which that will was exercised. God's creation of women as helpmates to men would be a first cause in contrast to the secondary causes which would be the effects of the anatomy that differentiates women from men. This emphasis upon secondary causes turned scientific inquiry away from speculations about God's intentions and towards descriptions and analyses of how things worked. A great popularizer of the new learning, Bacon set forth a program for experiments that would reveal the causal relations presumed to underlie all natural phenomena.

Deeply satisfying to those who were refashioning old Aristotelian pictures of nature, the new science also had an impact upon Western European political life. Where earlier investigators had approached the "secrets of the universe" with the reverence befitting the penetration of divine mysteries, the neo-Baconians discussed their findings with unbounded enthusiasm. Their lively disputes and public demonstrations aroused the intellectual curiosity of a reading public which had steadily grown larger, in part because of cheaper forms of printing.

Experimentation provided criteria for evaluating scientific opinions while the use of mathematics offered an even more demanding kind of proof for the multiplying hypotheses about the behavior of gases, the movement of planets, and the circulation of blood. Bacon held up this testable reality as a check on the self-serving opinions about the world that human beings loved to spin. Nature, he said, fought back; self-flattering notions collapsed if they failed to account for the reality outside human contrivance. With exacting tests of how things worked, scientific investigators could leave behind the dark chambers of Hermetic mysteries and closed Aristotelian systems.

René Descartes, a French mathematician, chose a more rational road to truth. Probing for certainty about what he could know, he fell back upon his own capacity to reason. *Cogito ergo sum,* "I think therefore I am," was his enduringly quotable statement that reason was the essence of humanity. From this radical subjectivity, Descartes divided the world between human beings who had volition and the rest of the material world which moved according to mechanical laws. He believed that mathematics provided a certain foundation for all metaphysical thinking and that scientists could accurately predict what would happen in the external world. His thorough skepticism, elaborated by others, formed another major stream of seventeenth-century thought pouring into that great river of cumulative intellectual accomplishment we call the Enlightenment.

Descartes' long sojourns in the Netherlands and Sweden also remind us of the risks that the new natural philosophers took in challenging the monopoly of the Church and its claim to be the sole authority on truth and the creation of the universe. Indeed, because of the initial resistance of European Christendom to the new learning, science became indelibly identified with secularism, and secularism, in turn, with modernity. There was, however, a profoundly spiritual component to the idea that divinity was revealed in the orderliness of the universe.

The seventeenth century which had opened with Bacon's summons to investigate nature ended with Isaac Newton's publication of the Principia. With his elegant mathematical formulation of the laws of gravity, cast within an explanation of the entire solar system, Newton vindicated Bacon's faith. Although only a dozen or so people in all the world could follow Newtonian mathematics, the impact of the Principia was phenomenally large. His conspicuous genius elevated the reputation of all human beings. Human reasoning in general stood revealed as capable of mastering the most fundamental cause-and-effect relations of the physical world.

During the ensuing century, the Enlightenment project formed the agenda for a succession of thinkers and reformers. And it is the sweeping triumph of the scientific revolution and its collateral intellectual enterprises that have caused postmodernist thinkers in our own time to recoil. Following the trajectory first marked out by the enthusiasts of modernity—and subsequently by a growing chorus of modernity's critics—will enable us to put postmodernism in historical perspective. But we must understand first why the changes associated with modernity stirred people's imagination for nearly three centuries.

Scientific enterprise came to be associated with the qualities of openness, criticism, and experimentation. It relied on accessibility, encouraged dissent, promoted the quest for greater knowledge, replaced divine intention with instrumental reasoning, and offered outcomes as a standard for judgment. In other words, it had acquired a style, a form of life markedly different from the reverence, loyalty, and secrecy promoted by other institutions. Outside of Great Britain, its American colonies, Switzerland, and the Netherlands, European absolutist monarchs and their established churches opposed the radical thrust of the new science and combatted it through persecution and repression. This opposition brought to light the deep incompatibility of the new science and the old political authoritarianism.

Blocked in their effort to promote free inquiry, the enthusiasts of science—particularly on the Continent—began to attack those in power who impeded the exchange of ideas. Like a pebble thrown into a pond, this call for the reform of existing religious and political institutions reached wider and wider circles. Scientific inquiry had acquired an activist partner, the philosophical reformer. In France, publicists of the new science like Voltaire and Denis Diderot came to view the Old Regime as a kind of outrage. Fascinated by John Locke's idea that human beings were born as blank slates upon which the sensual traces of experience shaped one's destiny, they imagined a reformed world where constructive early experiences could open humankind to endless improvement. With reform, the power of reason could become the source of emancipation from ignorance, superstition, disease, and oppression. They even imagined a new type of community built around an affinity for philosophic inquiry, unmarred by racial and religious prejudices which stirred the passions of their countrymen.

If science was the knowledge of consequences, as Thomas Hobbes had said, and human beings learned through experience, as Locke had concluded, then the progressive acquisition of knowledge could usher in a new era for mankind. Until this time, Europeans had looked backwards for their notions of the ideal—either to the Golden Age of Greece or to the Garden of Eden of the Bible. It now occurred to some radical thinkers that the future might be dramatically different from everything that had gone before. The human past was quickly resequenced. First there was the Classical Era, then a lapse into the Dark Ages—an eighteenth-century term referring to the period stretching from the fifth-century Fall of Rome to the Renaissance—after which the Enlightenment brought forth the Modern Era.

Here the pilots of the ship of science acquired their first barnacle of hypocrisy, for Western prosperity, which nourished these expectations of marvelous change, was built in part on the labor of kidnapped Africans. Modern slavery, which began with the European colonization in the New World, mocked the claims of a new dispensation for mankind. Even as dedicated an Enlightenment thinker as Thomas Jefferson could only proceed in his idealization of the new age of natural rights by blinkering himself to the degradation of that ideal in his own home. Like many others, he fixed his attention upon the idea that the future would be different, that the Enlightenment which replaced the Dark Ages would itself be followed by an even more humane era. Like a conceptual magic wand, future expectations made existing inhumanities disappear.

An interesting feature of the time scheme of Enlightenment thinkers is that it imposed Western chronology upon the whole human race. In their narrative accounts, philosophers connected only a part of humanity—specifically the Hebraic tribes that settled in Judea and the Hellenic and Roman peoples of the Ancient World with the Germanic tribes who settled in Western Europe—and called this universal history. While all societies tend to promote an ethnocentric view of the world, this European formula went further and incorporated all of the world in its own history. Since the links between contemporary Europe and the ancient and medieval world were actually composed of texts—the Bible, Greek philosophy, Roman history—an enormous importance was attached to reading. From the eighteenth century on, a science of interpretation, called hermeneutics, emerged and formalized methods of studying texts which distinguished understanding from knowledge. As we shall see, this distinction became the pivot for shifting in the early twentieth century from a fixation on cause to a fascination with meaning.

The centrality of texts to Western ways of reasoning can be seen in Thomas Paine's *Common Sense*. Writing to convince the American colonists that they should declare their independence from Great Britain, Paine moved through the mental library of his contemporaries, selecting here a passage from the Scriptures, there a reference to Roman history, and using them all to gain assent to the radical concepts propagated by the *philosophes*. He said of the vaunted English Constitution that "it was noble for the dark and slavish times in which it was erected" and he drew his idea of government from the principles of nature. Rejecting the arbitrary distinctions of monarchy and aristocracy, he announced that male and female were the distinctions of nature and good and bad the distinctions of heaven. The continued subordination of America to England was, he maintained, "repugnant to reason" and to "the universal order of things." When Jefferson later wrote in the Declaration of Independence that "we hold these truths to be self-evident that all men are created equal, that they are endowed by their creator with certain unalienable rights," he gave vivid proof that the activity which led men and women to question the fundamental ideas about the cosmic order could lead to subversive action in the political realm.

Implicit in the Enlightenment appeal to reason over reverence was the belief that human beings were capable of restraining their passions for their own good rather than doing so out of fear of punishment from family, church, or state. Unexpectedly, seventeenth-century writings on commerce actually helped shape a new conception of human nature. Originally seeking to explain the complicated trading patterns which linked Africa, Asia and the New World to the metropolis of Europe, observers developed analytical models that explained the regularities in prices. Writers in England—freed from governmental restraint because of the civil disorders—drastically revised ways of looking at human behavior. Whereas Christian sermons stressed man's degenerate condition—"in Adam's Fall did sin we all"—and popular drama emphasized the fickleness and impulsive behavior of men and women, economic analyzers saw constancy and reasonableness and began tracing the spring of economic life to what they called natural human predispositions.

SCHOLARLY EXPLANATIONS OF THE MARKET

The market—a word that slowly changed from a reference to local sites for selling farm produce to an indicator of the dense circuitry of goods and payments crisscrossing the globe—appeared as a new phenomenon because it had broken out of the interstices of traditional society. Observing men and women in their commercial transactions, economic writers reported that people knew what they wanted in the market and approached their ends rationally. Prompted by self-interest, people carefully calculated their own advantage and sought out the best bargains. Moreover, they all responded in the same fashion, suggesting a uniformity that challenged the traditional view of human difference. Pursuing these observations, analyzers of world trade came up with a description of human nature that emphasized its constancy and self-improving character. The growing conviction that these human attributes were fundamental made conservative writings about the sinfulness and irrationality of men and women appear self-serving. Promoters of commercial development ranged themselves on the side of reform.

Growing with the rapidly increasing complexity of world trade in processed foods and fibers, the new economic commentary put into circulation ideas about the uniformity of human responses that grated offensively with those who believed that the world was divided between the noble few and the ignominious many. Thus, alongside the other contentious discourses about modernity there grew an analysis of economics that pivoted around the new concept of the similarities of reasonable men. In *The Wealth of Nations*, the Scottish philosopher Adam Smith brought to fruition a century of observations in a magisterial description of the economy as a natural system. Human beings whom he described as inherently disposed to truck and barter sought their self-interest in market bargains. Their profit-maximizing efforts were regulated not by well-crafted regulations or the wisdom of magistrates, but rather through the competitive striving of profit-maximizing market participants. As Smith dryly commented, it was not from the benevolence of the butcher and baker that we got our good, cheap meat and bread, but rather from their own self-interested drive to secure as much trade for themselves as possible.

Similarly indirect, according to Smith, was the accumulation of savings that enabled manufacturers to introduce the division of labor into their production systems. "The principle that prompts to save, is the desire of bettering our condition, a desire which . . . comes with us from the womb, and never leaves us till we go into the grave. In the whole interval which separates those two moments, there is scarce perhaps a single instant in which any man is so perfectly and completely satisfied with his situation, as to be without any wish of alteration or improvement of any kind."[2] As one commentator remarked, "being of a Newtonian disposition to use his imagination and systematize his thought . . . Smith perceived order beneath the seeming chaos in man's affairs in nature."[3]

This discovery of order underneath the chaos in men and women's affairs totally redirected scholarly investigations about social action. Prior to the eighteenth century, events were variously attributed to Providence—that is, God's personal interference in human affairs—or contingencies, like the outbreak of plague or the invasion of a foreign army, or personal intention such as the will of the monarch or conspiracies of ill-intentioned groups. The school of Scottish philosophers graced by Adam Smith and David Hume developed the idea of unintended consequences as exemplified in Smith's observation that the competition of bakers and butchers produces the social benefit of good bread at low prices despite their simple desire to profit from their endeavors. This paradox of unintended consequences shifted the questions from "Who did it?" to "How does it work?"[4]

Two important components in the eighteenth-century science of man, as it came to be called, came from the Scots. The first was the assertion that there exist invisible social forces producing effects independent of willed action; and the second was their creation of what they called conjectural history, a larger interpretive frame for explaining the development of private property and the growth of trade. They imagined an evolution of social development starting with hunters and gatherers, progressing through a pastoral stage to agricultural societies and then to their own commercial era. Within this conjectural evolutionary process, private property secured the sanction of law, the family became sanctified, and savings from past labor accumulated for investment in productive enterprises. One of the bitterest ironies of the Modern Era was that the same profit-making impulses that fueled Western material prosperity also promoted the expansion of the slave trade which eventually brought ten million coerced Africans to the New World. No stranger to this irony, nor to the fact that the factory system imposed grueling work routines upon children and adults, Smith reckoned these among the losses in a general progress that had lifted Europe out of the famine-stricken centuries of the Dark Ages.

Through their analysis of the voluntary realm of commercial economic life, the thinkers of the so-called Scottish Enlightenment imagined an entity called society—an informal realm of being and action which, as one scholar noted, was not subject to the laws of the state, but "on the contrary, subjected the state to its own laws."[5] Whereas Christian divines and political philosophers alike had depicted the state of nature as a horrible place where, in Hobbes's words, "life was solitary, poor, nasty, brutish, and short," the new theorists stressed men and women's cooperative capacities and their ability to get along through their own exertions, undisturbed by the now-deemed unwarranted intrusions of government.

THE LIBERAL PARADIGM

Fueled by these pathbreaking reconceptions of social action, radical thinkers came to believe that the scientific method was as applicable to the social order as it was to the physical universe. Reacting to this, conservatives defended those different rhythms of human life stemming from people's attachment to the familiar and their varying emotions. When they opposed the new agenda for social engineering based upon newly-discovered laws of society, a century-long battle began. Looking backward we can see that the Enlightenment's favorable orientation to social reform and to the scientific exploitation of nature converged at the end of the eighteenth century in an assault upon absolutism. The American Revolution, followed by the French Revolution, took philosophical speculations out of the study and salon and thrust them into the roads and streets where ordinary men and women engaged in mortal combat against their governments.

It is this campaign for the reconstruction of Europe's ancient regime, following the successful drive for independence of the American colonies, that created the high drama of the Enlightenment. It also brought to the center of our historical narratives the heroes of science, the martyrs of tolerance, the trumpeters of new inquiries to slug it out with the manipulators of superstition, the defenders of privilege, and the oppressors of the unwashed multitude. This is the conflict that ushered in our modern age; the first cultural war that gives us the frame of reference for the cultural wars of our own time. Men, Voltaire commented, would not be free until the last priest had been strangled with the entrails of the last prince. (Women presumably would have to await some further act of desecration.)

For many generations people explained the wars of the French Revolution, lasting until Napoleon's defeat in 1815, as part of a Titanic struggle between the defenders of the status quo and the champions of enlightened liberty. This rendering of the conflict acquired a mythic quality over time, encouraging a general amnesia about the bloodletting attributable to vengeance, anger, and zealotry.

The Enlightenment's focus upon positive change, the untapped human potential, and the idealization of nature construed as an orderly, knowable system gave direction to nineteenth-century reformers, even as it drove others into furious criticism. Reformers committed themselves to working out institutionally the implications of the stunning intellectual breakthroughs of the late seventeenth and eighteenth centuries. In the United States the Enlightenment became a national creed and more. From the time of Jefferson's election, in 1800, liberal tenets shed their character as scientific propositions or theoretical assumptions and came to represent the face of reality itself.

For most Americans, nationalism lost its connection with ethnicity and attached itself to a universal destiny for mankind adumbrated in the Declaration of Independence. American universalism, however, remained stained with racism because the credo "all men ... created equal" invariably excluded Africans and native Americans. Nature was also summoned to disqualify women from full participation in the new liberal universe.

Liberalism projected onto the future in a peculiarly forceful way its optimistic vision of possibility. The contrast, of course, was with venerable ideas about the inexorable organic cycle of the human life—birth, vigorous growth to maturity, inevitable decay, and death. To project fresh, good positive change as always lying in the near future was to imagine society poised at the threshold of accomplishment, as having a collective life in a perpetual adolescence. This favorable attitude towards change also transformed the relationship between past, present, and future.

The expectation of positive improvement in the future denigrated both past and present. To a large extent, the past lost its attraction and the present became a mere springboard. Change became development; random events were turned into processes. A host of human problems could be ignored because their solution was anticipated in the future. To domesticate the future, which after all is the dreaded unknown, required robust images to quell the anxiety of possible disasters. Success in doing this represented an extraordinary reach of human confidence and persuasive power. From this liberal orientation towards changes came the drive for reform—personal reform, social reform, even the reform of nature. In vain did conservatives inveigh against the hubris of the liberals in assuming that they had brought the ineffable and unpredictable, the imprecise and irrational, under the control of their analytic categories.

Liberalism's second positive orientation was towards human nature—only now conceived not as an impulse to sin, but as an endowment. Here the debt is to Locke, whose sensational psychology suggested the importance of the environment in determining how infants develop. The idea that a baby is born with a blank mind contrasted sharply with earlier assumptions of human corruption, dependency, wickedness, and original sin. Posited in a different intellectual milieu, Locke's notion of a tabula rasa might have remained with philosophy, but combined with the positive orientation towards change, this hypothesis about the unfolding human potential produced the underpinnings for an enormously popular belief in progress. The engine of reform was going to be education, for the road to modern utopias generally ran through the classroom.

A final defining element of Western liberalism was its positive orientation towards nature, an orientation which has produced the modern West's symbiotic relationship with science. In its long, arduous overcoming of tradition and the status quo, liberalism battened off nature. Nature delivered an alternative ordering mechanism to customary authorities; nature supplied proofs of subversive new propositions about government, society, the human makeup; nature furnished models for reform. Of course this "nature" referred to was also a Western invention— the nature of seventeenth- and eighteenth-century natural philosophers who had changed it from a mysterious, divinely inspired creation to a grand object of human curiosity, a secular realm of explication and experimentation.

Once the belief in progress infected the brain cells of the west, the world as a given to be understood, accepted—even cherished—yielded to the spirit of inventiveness, to the drive to plan, improve, and replace. With this restless prompting towards ingenuity came the unavoidable conclusion that society was a human invention. Science, more than ever, had to play the role of religion, explaining the ways of natural design to man, for nature had become the new law-maker. It was an older and wiser philosopher, Frederich Nietzsche, who remarked late in the century that to look upon nature "as if it were a proof of the goodness and care of God and to interpret history as a constant testimony to a moral order was now past because it had conscience against it."[6]

THE SCIENCE OF SOCIETY

One of the most astute of the new students of society was Alexis de Tocqueville, a man who cherished much of the aristocratic order which lay in ruins across the face of Europe after the wars of the French Revolution. Thoroughly modern in his understanding of social processes, Tocqueville came to the United States in 1833 in order to study the effect of "the condition of equality." Certain that democracy would soon triumph in all of Europe, and by no means thrilled by this prospect, he brought social theorizing to a new peak of interpretive brilliance with his exploration of the myriad ways that equality affected the popular attitudes, the institutions, the relation between the sexes, and the public values in the United States. Sociology had gained its first and most classic expression in Tocqueville's *Democracy in America*.

Looking back, one can see that from rather modest seventeenth-century inquiries into the nature of plants and planets came a cascade of theories ricocheting from the physical to the social world: the formidable *isms* and *tions*—positivism, functionalism, behavioralism, dialectical materialism, evolution, and finally modernization itself, all of them totalizing descriptions of the human enterprise rendered as inexorable processes. The paradox of unintended consequences yielded to full-blown historical explanations based on impersonal political, economic, or social laws. Like a new modern litany, historians invoked the power of tendencies, processes, developments, objective forces, and dominant ideas to explain the momentum of change overtaking Europe, the United States, and most of the world drawn or forced into their orbit.

MODERNITY'S FIRST CRITICS

Nineteenth-century enthusiasts of science and reform took enormous pride in the technological triumphs of their day: steam boats, water power, textile factories, cotton gins, and railroads. The wonderful array of machines, engines, and pumps that did the work of human strain and sweat spoke more eloquently than words about the progress of the age. The traditional economies marked by customary practices, threats of famine, local trade, and the conspicuous spending of rulers, prelates, and noble families had finally yielded to commercial economies of disciplined consumption, wealth turned into investment, improved standards of living, and above all the emergence of the productive ideal, which summoned everyone to think of himself as a resource. British observers thought of the new order which began in Great Britain as naturally evolving. For Europeans, industrialization came so fast that it was hard to see it as a natural phenomenon. Different explanations were required to make sense of the sudden disruption of the old agrarian order and the cruel wrenching of men and women from their farms to fill the jobs in urban factories. For some, the entire Enlightenment story of natural progress began to ring hollow as they watched it play out in rural communities across the land.

The most important critic produced by industrialization was Karl Marx, who confronted the whole Enlightenment Project as a massive mystification generated by the wealthy few to justify the immiseration of the poverty-stricken many. His immediate task was to unmask the natural-rights philosophy, with its democratic overtones, so that workers could see who were the sole beneficiaries of the new capitalist system. Rejecting the Scots' description of evolutionary social change, Marx attacked Smith's account of the accumulation of capital with ferocious scorn: "The spoilation of the church's property, the fraudulent alienation of state domains, the robbery of the common lands, the usurpation of feudal property and clan property and its transformation into modern private property, under circumstances of reckless terrorism, were just so many idyllic methods of primary accumulation."[7]

Although he cared most about revolutionizing society, Marx sought first to establish an accurate account of Europe's history, one that would liberate people from Enlightenment fantasies and direct attention to the conflict between classes which, he said, fueled the engine of history. He maintained that the economy, not men's reasoning minds, formed the foundation on which rose all legal, artistic, and intellectual constructions. "The mode of production in material life," he wrote uncompromisingly, "determines the general character of the social, political, and spiritual processes of life. It is not the consciousness of men that determines their existence, but, on the contrary, their social existence determines their consciousness."[8]

Embodying much of the Enlightenment outlook that he mocked—including an appreciation of the enormous material progress which capitalism had wrought—Marx presented his improved science of society as believable because it had been cleansed of the self-serving explanations of an exploiting ruling class. He replaced the Scots' conjectural history of evolutionary stages of social development with a grand theory of Revolution. As a prophet, Marx believed that the triumph of the dispossessed proletariat over the profit-maximizing capitalist class would bring about a new era. Sounding very much like a latter-day *philosophe*, he predicted that in the future world of communism, men and women would recover their true calling as the creators of value rather than the alienated producers of marketable goods for a world gone mad over commodities.

A different critique of the modern world came from Frederich Nietzsche, another German disenchanted with the world that science and industry had made. Far more interested in sensibilities, tastes, and values than Marx, Nietzsche rejected the claims of Western thinkers that they could represent the reality of the physical and human worlds. Hitting the Enlightenment in its scientific solar plexus, Nietzsche scoffed at those from Bacon onward who had assumed that they had access to nature unmediated by subjective influences. He challenged their conviction that minds, like mirrors trained on objects, could register objective facts. Nietzsche insisted that the realm of human knowledge was primarily artistic and personal rather than scientific and impersonal. People did not discover nature; they imagined and interpreted it.

Nietzsche was equally dismissive of modern political philosophy. What is the difference, he asked, between saying "'I want x' and 'I have a right to x?'"[9] Convinced of the bad faith and obfuscation in modern systems of knowledge, he was in no way thrilled by triumphs of science, for he accounted it a victory of mediocrity over excellence, in which the banality of comfortable bourgeois living was traded for the intrepidity of the aristocratic spirit. In Nietzsche's view, it was not democracy for the masses that held hope for social salvation, but rather the overcoming of the crass materialism of his age through the imaginative powers of a superman bringing a new myth, an idea that remains somewhat obscure in his aphoristic prose.

SOCIAL DARWINISM

The devastating critiques of the Modern Era from Nietzsche and Marx coincided with a scientific achievement that matched Newton's Principia. This was Charles Darwin's *The Origins of*

Species, which appeared in 1859. A member of the educated English upper class, Darwin was steeped in the speculative writings of the Scots as well as those of Thomas Malthus, who had made dire predictions about a population debacle when the human capacity to procreate outran its capacity to produce food. These advanced social theories gave Darwin the intellectual tools to explain the fossil evidence of species replacing species and of global variations in species. Long awaited, Darwin's masterpiece swept into one grand synthesis decades of observation on the forms of life encoded in plants and animals, both fossil and living. Molding this enormous mass of detail into one grand explanation of the origin of homo sapiens, Darwin joined the fact of spontaneous and inheritable variations within species to a theory about how certain of these fortuitous mutations enhanced the chances of survival. Calling this process "natural selection," he showed how the struggle for survival could lead to new life forms or species.

Darwin's theory shocked those who believed that God had created Adam and Eve and all other living creatures. As the Harvard zoologist Alexander Agassiz remarked, "The resources of the deity cannot be so meagre that in order to create a human being endowed with reason, he must change a monkey into a man."[10] Indeed, Darwin offended almost everyone by highlighting the randomness of changes which demonstrated the paradox of unintended consequences rather than the awesomeness of the divinity's creative power. A runaway best-seller for a scholarly work, *The Origin of Species* gave scientific validation to other contemporary ideas about evolution. Here was progress marked out in the grandest scope imaginable.

Change had long been recognized, but Darwin's made constant, regular variation and adaptation a central feature of nature. Demonstrating how advantages associated with a mutation that could improve life prospects would come to dominate when the carriers of the mutation outproduced those without it, Darwin developed a theory which both reflected and encouraged social theories about the importance of individual competition for the progress of the whole. Later dubbed "the survival of the fittest," this explanation of the slow evolution of man from primates could easily be analogized to the society of Darwin's day, when successful industrialists grew mightier and richer in the face of mounting poverty. Very quickly his ideas were absorbed by social theorists, particularly Herbert Spencer in England and William Graham Sumner in America, whose hypotheses about changes in society became known as Social Darwinism.

Picked up and elaborated by anthropologists, Social Darwinism suggested that the peoples of the world might be arrayed along a spectrum of development, from the most primitive tribes to the civilized nations of the world, with the technologically superior West representing eons of successful adaptation. Thus, despite the influential criticism of the West's scientistic culture by Marx and Nietzsche, Darwin's powerful and original scientific theory gave fresh life to the empirical approach first discussed by Francis Bacon. The grand evolutionary scheme, in which society passed through savagery and barbarism to attain civilization, seemed to find a place for every known fact, but it did so by denigrating those people without written languages who lived outside the commercial sway of the West. Evolutionary thinking swept into popularity. New work in genetics, and the use of statistics to measure critical differences between the sexes and various human groupings, led Darwin's cousin to develop eugenics, which the Nazis exploited in their campaign to promote so-called Aryan people over non-Aryans. Where science appears, scientism is never far behind.

In the United States, these new theories about superior and inferior races came to dominance at the same time that a flood of immigrants arrived from Eastern and Central Europe. Social Darwinism offered a ready explanation of why they appeared so strange in appearance, habits, and speech. At the same time, social scientists in America's universities furnished respectable scientific terms for discussing the inferiority of Negroes, Jews, and the entire female sex. Economists, goaded in part by Marx's savage attack on capitalism, began discussing the free enterprise system as a natural environment that promoted the survival of the fittest in industrial society. As Herbert Spencer said of social failures, "The whole effort of nature is to get rid of such, to clear the world of them, and make room for better. Progress is not an accident but a necessity," a sentiment echoed by Sumner when he wrote that the "law of the survival of the fittest was not written by man and cannot be abrogated by man. We can only, by interfering with it, produce the survival of the unfittest."[11]

THE CONCEPT OF CULTURE

The linchpin of social evolutionary theory was that all forms of life go from the simple to the complex through natural deterministic processes. Culture in this view was restricted to the civilized races and referred to their polished manners, refined tastes, and artistic accomplishments. Franz Boas, a German anthropologist who came to the United States in 1886, gave culture a new meaning that took the sting out of Western superiority and laid the foundation for a turning away from Social Darwinism. Boasian definitions of culture still resonate in American social science. His study of the Eskimos convinced him that all societies produced complicated understandings of reality; the idea of tribal societies being closer to nature was a reflection of Western ignorance. All people have a culture; creating meaning is a central function of social existence. With these insights, Boas fashioned a methodology for studying non-Western societies that challenged the West's self-serving biological determinism and ethnocentric standards for judging others. The West's absorption with science and technology was its cultural expression. Using culture in the plural, Boas also demonstrated that only local studies could yield useful information about other peoples because cultures were socially specific.

The work of Boas's students at Columbia University, particularly Margaret Mead and Ruth Benedict, introduced American readers to the fruits of anthropological field research and opened up the intellectual possibility that values were relative to particular societies. Benedict's *Patterns of Culture*, published in 1934, became a best-seller, opening American readers to the fascinating variety in human systems of meaning. Cultural anthropology, with its detailed explorations of how values attach themselves to the stuff of social practices—to marriage patterns, work routines, and child rearing—led the way to a new appreciation of the power of the particular, and hence challenged the Enlightenment ideal of the universal. Boas had turned culture into a concept powerful enough to undermine the deterministic evolutionary schemes of his predecessors.

Following the anthropologists' lead, other scholars in the humanities and social sciences have explored the dynamics of culture. Now defined as a complex of invisible and elusive influences, culture, we say, gets inside us when we are too young to know what is happening. Culture fills up the tabula rasa that Locke described. Once there, its hidden promptings dictate the behavior that differentiates us from people born into other societies. At the level of personal psychology, we see culture mobilizing the raw material of emotion into enthusiasms, commitments, and prejudices. Its signs—symbolic, lexical, and conceptual—provide human beings with vehicles for expressing their religion, their science, their laws, and their fantasies. Deeply private, culture ministers to the individual's struggle to find value. Functionally power- ful, culture provides the repertoire of collective norms and forms that make coherent social action possible. This social-scientific view of culture has now found a place in ordinary conver- sation, as the debates on multiculturalism indicate.

The one distinctive American school of philosophy—that of pragmatism—emerged in the same years as Boasian anthropology. For its proponents—Charles Peirce, William James, and John Dewey—pragmatism offered a way of socializing scientific proof. Dissatisfied with both idealism and positivism for their inherently one-sided views of certitude, pragmatists looked for the proof of scientific statements in their practical consequences. In their eyes, rigorous examination, systematic experimentation, and vigorous debate among all comers would do a better job of verifying knowledge than formal systems of logic or the objectification of social phenomena. Dewey in particular rejected the mind's-mirror-of-nature metaphor in favor of experience, which for him meant an engagement with objects seen as both things and goals. Dewey's stress on the collective, interactive aspect of knowledge-production fit nicely with his concern for revitalizing American democracy, which had foundered under the racist attacks against immigrants and the political corruption emanating from the industrial tycoons. For Dewey, pragmatism took on moral overtones as a philosophy that accepted the provisional nature of truth without abandoning belief in the reality science sought to know. Pragmatism, with its commitment to improving the future and expanding the universe of participants, also offered a template for political reform.

THE IMPACT OF MAX WEBER

After the Second World War, American sociologists discovered Max Weber, a German thinker who had sought to reconcile a number of conflicting tendencies in social thought, pushed as it had been by Darwin's natural determinism yet compelled to take account of the profusion of values created by human beings. In his classic study *The Protestant Ethic and the Spirit of Capitalism*, Weber wrenched "ethic" and "spirit" from their well-understood context and threw them into an utterly unexpected frame of reference. Ethics had heretofore belonged to secular inquiry about proper behavior, while "spirit" had evoked either religious or poetic thoughts. Neither seemed appropriate for discussing capitalism, which referred to a system of exploiting labor, land, raw materials, and money for profitable exchange.

The human predispositions that animated economic action were taken for granted in both liberal and Marxist interpretations. Either capitalism gave expression to a universal drive for self-improvement expressed through the urge to truck and barter, as Smith had said, or it reflected the will of a ruling class to mold working men and women to new modes of produc- tion. Capitalism had also been the object of study of the most positivistic of the social sciences, economics, which gave mathematical precision to the setting of rates and prices. Yet Weber provocatively maintained that the values of precapitalist societies had acted as impediments to economic change. Hence scholars had to ask: how had men (women do not figure into his analysis), reared to respond to a traditional set of social imperatives, been able to take on the exotic values of the free-market system? As Weber had written in an effort to defamiliarize the profit motive, "A man does not by nature wish to earn more and more money, but simply to live as he is accustomed and to earn as much as is necessary for that purpose."[12]

Weber answered his own question by pointing to the economic advance of Protestant coun-tries. Tracing their break with traditional values to their ardent embrace of a calling, their plea-sure-deferring self-discipline, their obsessive rationality, and their stern defiance of customary norms, he saw that all of these cultural forces had enabled them to work, save, invest, and produce. Weber, whose conclusions were extremely compatible with those of Boas's students, redirected attention to the invisible realm of social norms and human motivations. Giving to human beings what Peter Berger once called "a craving for meaning," Weber asserted that human beings have "an inner necessity to comprehend the world as a meaningful cosmos and to know what attitude to take before it."[13] These were the factors that held the key to understand-ing that most striking of social transformations: the passage of Western nations into modernity. Rejecting Adam Smith's claim that people sought self-improvement, Weber asserted that human nature does not manifest itself in universal drives, but rather varies according to membership in a particular society. One cannot explain capitalism by invoking behavior patterns that are them-selves the consequences of the capitalist era. The historical sequence is out of order.

Weber, however, had great respect for the force of external causes at work in the world and sought to develop a social theory that would maintain a multifaceted explanation of action. Responsive to Marx's elegant explanation of how material factors structured thought, he wanted to explain how things happened as well as how the interpretation of those happenings entered into social action. His *The Protestant Ethic and the Spirit of Capitalism* was actually a concrete example of how a system of meaning became a cause. Working with a more complex understanding of human nature, Weber had introduced the centrality and particularity of values to social action, but he had not abandoned the Enlightenment aspiration to develop a theoretical grasp of all phenomena.

English-speaking scholars, introducing Weber to their colleagues after the Second World War, had to contend with an Anglo-American audience unused to considering the concept of culture in relation to the practical enactments of their own society. Uncivilized peoples had culture; modern Western ones followed reason. Convinced of the centrality of values in making coherent social action possible, America's leading social scientist, Talcott Parsons, wrote about society as a system of systems in which the system of meaning subtly shaped concrete economic and political practices. Enormously influential from the 1950s onward, Weber's work endowed American social sciences with a complex picture of society which recognized the elements of autonomy in the state, in religion, and in the economy.

Culture, redefined as a system through which all societies give meaning to life, inculcated respect for the array of mores, religions, and institutional arrangements that human beings had created. The effect was to highlight the importance of society, exchanging, you might say, social determinism for natural determinism. Where Darwinian analogies inspired an awe of nature, twen-tieth-century scholars focussed upon the predominating force of society.

In France the power of society was frequently studied under the rubric of structuralism, a strain of thought emanating from the work of Ferdinand de Saussure, a Swiss linguist. Saussure transformed the study of language by treating it as a social system of signs. In Saussure's view, the relationship between a sound and the object that it seeks to represent is entirely arbitrary, but once it is established, it remains fixed. The sign, for Saussure, combines a sound with an object of signification. Most importantly, the sign, or word, takes its meaning from other words in a sentence. Saussure viewed language as fundamentally social—indeed, as both chisel and glue for human communities. Individuals are bound by language and have no ability to change it, even though language changes over time. But paradoxically, no definitions are ever absolute, since they shift with usage.

Saussure's structural approach to language had a great impact on scholars trying to systematize their understanding of social influences. Claude Lévi-Strauss, a French anthropologist, used Saussure's work to study culture as a system of symbolic meanings, many of them originating in the subconscious. Lévi-Strauss opened up the deep structuring of the human mind to speculation, if not empirical testing. By exploring the symbolic significance of the most practical actions—whether one ate food cooked or raw, for instance—Lévi-Strauss greatly expanded what could be considered cultural and therefore part of the anthropological domain. Yet despite his wide-ranging curiosity about the specific symbolic systems, Lévi-Strauss believed that uniform symbolic functions could be detected in the unconscious activities of human beings. His structuralism tended to downplay the importance of changing political and economic situations—the things historians study—in its search for the fundamental character of human nature. After two hundred years of addressing society as an object for analysis, scholars had passed from straightforward representations of external behavior to elusive theories about the wellsprings of the human imagination.

BEYOND THE CRITICS OF MODERNISM: THE POSTMODERNISTS

In *The Advancement of Learning*, Francis Bacon wrote that "God hath framed the mind of man as a mirror or glass capable of the image of the universal world, and joyful to receive the impression thereof." This conviction about the mind as a mirror has sustained the scientific enterprise for four centuries. For much of that time, philosophers and social scientists shared this scientific faith. In recent decades, however, those who study society have grown less certain of the mind's ability to mirror the objective world. They have even raised questions about the capacity of language to act as a neutral conveyor of information. Acting on these doubts, they have put the whole Enlightenment project on trial, giving to our era a name—postmodernism—that advertises the distance we have travelled since Bacon framed his ambitious program around the curious investigator.

Surveying the breakdown of consensus about what constitutes knowledge, David Harvey concluded that "the moral crisis of our day is a 'crisis of Enlightenment thought.'"[14] As we have seen, the cascade of new scientific inquiries, new reform aspirations, and new social formations that marked the closing decades of the eighteenth century became known as the Enlightenment project. The phrase was apt because European reformers wanted very much to take ideas out of their cloistered security in libraries and studies and put them to work, inspiring and guiding a massive transformation of the human condition.

Like all reform movements, the Enlightenment was deeply enmeshed in its immediate past. The "infamy" that it sought to erase was that of the old regime with its absolutist monarchies, church-dominated education, and institutionalized cruelty. Enlightenment leaders sought a total break with their inheritance, casting off hereditary privileges, local attachments, and venerable customs in a truly heroic effort to release the pristine human spirit epitomized by the free and independent individual. Especially important to them was the idea of universal human aspirations. Philosophers and revolutionaries wrote and acted for all mankind, and occasionally even for womankind. The stirring conviction that all men were equal in their rights expressed itself as a commitment to the potential of the whole human race.

It was one of the most profound convictions of eighteenth-century reform that nature offered a better guide to the proper ordering of human affairs than any institution prescribed by social authorities. At one level exhilaratingly liberating, this reliance upon nature bristled with hidden tyrannies of its own. First of all, it gave to scientists a privileged position as the explicators of natural relations. Second, by connecting human similarities to natural law, it opened up the possibility of construing difference as deviance. And finally, men and women newly liberated from the authority of church, state, and family were delivered over to the impersonal discipline of reason and natural order. The purposefulness imposed by the imperatives of progress placed a high premium on instrumental reasoning and utilitarian justifications, both enemies to the free play of imagination and the arbitrary impulses of the heart.

What is pertinent to our postmodern situation is that the Enlightenment, more than any other body of social thought, hid its roots and denied its historical genesis. It is the one ideology whose partisans—often ranging themselves behind the protective shield of science—resisted seeing the moral and historical components of their world view. Whether in the study of the elements, the organization of politics, or the rearing of children, Western scholars have insisted until very recently upon the objectivity of their observations of reality, the neutrality of their findings, and above all, the impartiality of their standards.

From within strongholds of the modern West, there was a clear consensus during the nineteenth century that its knowledge came from the liberation of reason, indeed, that truth and falsehood were stamped upon the universe waiting for the discerning discriminator to make the distinctions public. Like a heat-seeking missile, the human curiosity was presented honing in on reality and detonating its protective cover. Completely absent from this account of how the West built its formidable fortress of information was the play of human passion, of prejudice, of power, of reason in the service of the collective ego.

With the incessant progress of technology came jarring shocks from what Joseph Schumpeter benignly labeled capitalism's "creative destruction," by which he meant the constant replacement of old devices with new techniques. From the realm of production in the nineteenth century, this dynamic passed to consumption patterns marked by early obsolescence, and will in all probability assert itself next in hypercommunication. These relentless transformations have endowed the entire Modern Era with a nervous agitation punctuated by business cycles of boom and bust triggering the cyclical emotions of hope and disappointment. In many ways, the nineteenth-century heirs of the Enlightenment put mind over matter when they spoke of a natural order in the presence of an unremitting disordering of social arrangements.

By the second half of the nineteenth century, the underside of modernization—the deracinated individuals, the massification of taste, and the mindless pursuit of gain—spawned a movement in the arts called modernism. Modernism got its name from its avant-garde position, but it was actually propelled by an anti-modernist outrage at the cost of progress. Dada, Surrealism, and Cubism all drew on the growing feeling that the more concrete the technological accomplishments of the West, the more abstract its commitment to real personal satisfactions. Although retrospectively we can see clear links between modernism and postmodernism, there are significant differences. Where modernism played with the elements of reality, juxtaposing them in an aesthetic of surprise and puzzlement, it did not challenge the concept of reality itself, which has become the principal postmodernist target. In architecture the clean, glass and concrete lines of modernism signalled the affirmation of truth and beauty, whereas the pastiches and pop art of the postmodernists signal a levelling of aesthetic values.

While much in modernism shaped the way contemporary critics think about late-twentieth-century society, it was not until the 1970s that a comprehensive challenge to modernity in all its forms emerged, with its own center of philosophical and aesthetic gravity. The rubric post-modernism announced the passing of the Modern Age, but many postmodernists went well beyond a notice of death to an exhuming of the body itself. Four old Enlightenment bones, in particular, have attracted attention: rational inquiry as a prelude to reform (the critique), the free development of liberated persons (the autonomous individual), the mastery of the cause-and-effect relations that run the world (the idea of progress), and the capacity of language to describe the external world (representation).

The individual was the pivotal force in the Enlightenment project. Postmodernists have been indefatigable in reconstructing the omniscient power of the social. Around these two charged poles have gathered almost all of the filings in this grand dispute about the Enlightenment project. Two French philosophers, Michel Foucault and Jacques Derrida, come to everyone's mind when postmodernism is mentioned. Foucault, who worked primarily with historical materials, used them to detonate a whole gallery of icons: the credibility of reforms effected under the banner of Enlightenment, the independence of individual thinkers, the continuity of human efforts, the idea of progress. Wishing to reveal the arbitrary aspect of Enlightenment science, Foucault reversed Bacon's claim that knowledge is power to make the point that only those with power have the right to say what is knowledge.

The celebrated postmodernist statements about the deprivileging of authors and the death of the subject are basically assertions that the concept of individuality is spurious because men and women are actually the repositories of their cultural systems. We do not speak language, say the postmodernists; language speaks us, imposing as it does a particular logic, aesthetics, and morality, or as Foucault would say, a discourse. Discourses, not impartial scientific investi-gations, define our world, as it is social constructions of reality, not reality, that we encounter when we speak and act. More concerned with language, Derrida has subjected the texts upon which Western civilization has relied for its understanding of the world to a process called deconstruction, in which imaginative exposures of gaps, transgressive possibilities, or unin-tended indicators lead to a multiplicity of readings. Having rendered communication unstable, Derrida then answers the classic epistemological question "What can I know?" with "Nothing for certain."

Where modernity promoted rational discourse, postmodernists have rained down upon the claims of rationality showers of ridicule, mockery, neologisms, and word plays. They have felt compelled to upend nearly every modern conviction. Enlightenment hopes were based upon the newly-discovered capacities of scientists to represent the external world, but postmod-ernists have denied that we have access to objects except through human paradigms and discourses. The social glue of language has become unstuck. Words are now presented as changelings and texts, as the sites for an endless succession of interpretations. Even the univer-sal affirmations of the Enlightenment have been relocated as part of the hypocritical strategies of a small elite in the West.

Just as modern thinkers conceived of time in new ways with their lexicon of process and development, so postmodernists proclaim a new understanding of time as discontinuous, open to rupture and capable of multifarious arrangements. Another striking contrast between the two cultural forms is the way postmodernism parodies the seriousness of the Enlightenment agenda, insisting upon the edification of the trivial and the unintended disclosures of all communication. Not only do postmodernist literary critics rail against the academic establishment's canon of major works of literature or philosophy, but postmodernist social critics insist that marginal observers have as much of value to say as licensed experts. For postmodernists, any effort to fix meaning will and should yield in time to the power of the repressed, the disclosures from the edge, and the surprises that come from the decoded and disinterred. Very much influenced by Nietzsche's effort to tear the veil of illusion from modern society, postmodernists have returned inquiry to its Baconian starting point: is the objective world accessible to human inquiry, and are language and reason up to the task of representing such a nature?

Our reliance on posts, as in postindustrial or postmodern, to locate ourselves in cultural times indicates that we still identify ourselves through old beliefs. We have not so much rejected modern values as lost the old certainty about modernization. Like the eighteenth-century *philosophes*, postmodernists often feel a kind of exhilaration in having routed a soul-diminishing absolutism, but unlike our predecessors of two centuries ago, we do not have a new program to deflect us from the contemplation of the misery, pain, and failure in the human condition. Postmodernism in this view might be taken as the messenger of our disappointment, and characteristically people have tried to shoot the messenger, blaming postmodernist thought for promoting nihilism and relativism.

It will be part of our task to sort out these issues, remembering that discrediting one view of human reason is not the same as denying reason's role in human affairs. As Joseph Rouse so aptly put it, "the world is always interpreted through language and practice. An uninterpreted world would be unintelligible. But the interpretation does not make the world the way it is; it allows it to show itself the way it is."

The pessimism that the postmodernist critique generates can be mitigated by the defenders of the Enlightenment project, led by Jürgen Habermas. We shall give the last word to these critics and commentators, who have engaged with the issues raised by postmodernists with increasing fervor in the last decade. They have shown what is at stake and what is involved in giving up on the representation of reality and the capacity of people to communicate, in hopes of changing it. What remains to be seen is how much of our world rests on modern footings. Here, the American postmodernist philosopher Richard Rorty has posed the critical question: "Can free societies prevail without the philosophical foundation upon which they have rested for two hundred years? Can the Enlightenment project survive Enlightenment fantasies?"[15] We won't know until we move into that unknown future, accepting its unknowability.

NOTES

1. While it would be more consistent to oppose postmodernism with modernism, it would also be misleading because modernism has a variety of referents. We wish to contrast postmodernism with the whole of the intellectual and institutional changes associated with the Enlightenment and their elaboration during the nineteenth century, so we shall use the terms *modernity* and *the Modern Era* to designate the forerunner of postmodernism.
2. Adam Smith, *The Wealth of Nations* (New York: Random House, 1937), pp. 324–25.

3. Joseph J. Spengler, "The Invisible Hand and Other Matters," *American Economic Review* 67 (1977).

4. Gordon Wood, "Conspiracy and the Paranoid Style: Causality and Deceit in the Eighteenth Century," *William and Mary Quarterly* 39 (July 1982), p. 401–41.

5. Karl Polanyi, *The Great Transformation: The Political and Economic Origins of Our Time* (Boston: Farrar & Rinehart, Inc. 1944), p. iii.

6. Karl Loewith, *Meaning in History* (Chicago: University of Chicago Press, 1949), p. vii.

7. Karl Marx, *Capital*, trans. Samuel Moore and Edward Aveling (London: Glaisher, 1920), p. 805.

8. Karl Marx, *A Contribution to the Critique of Political Economy*, trans. N. I. Stone (New York: 1904), p. 24.

9. As quoted in Thomas Haskell, "The Paradoxical Persistence of Rights Talk in the 'Age of Interpretation'," *Journal of American History* 74 (1987), p. 1003.

10. As quoted in Bruce Kuklick, *The Rise of American Philosophy, Cambridge, Massachussetts, 1860–1930* (New Haven: Yale University Press, 1977), pp. 22–3.

11. Ibid., pp. 161ff.

12. Max Weber, The Protestant Ethic and the Spirit of Capitalism, trans. Talcott Parsons (New York: 1958), p. 60.

13. Max Weber, Wirtschaft und Gesellschaft (Tubingen, 1947), as translated and quoted by Norman Birnbaum, "Conflicting Interpretations of the Rise of Capitalism: Marx and Weber," *British Journal of Sociology* 4 (1953), p. 134.

14. David Harvey, *The Condition of Postmodernity: An Enquiry into the Signs of Cultural Change* (Oxford: Blackwell, 1989), p. 4.

15. Richard Rorty, *Knowledge and Power* (Ithaca: Cornell University Press, 1987), p. 159; *Philosophy and the Mirror of Nature* (Princeton: Princeton University Press, 1979), pp. 330–31.

The Scientific Revolution

and Enlightenment Thought

Introduction

"Nature and Nature's laws lay hid in night,
God said, 'Let Newton be!' and all was light."
—Alexander Pope

As the historian Norman Hampson has pointed out, Pope exaggerated.[1] Not all was light, but in the seventeenth and eighteenth centuries many enjoyed an increasing confidence that more and more of the world around them would become accessible to human understanding. The discoveries made by thinkers like Newton in the seventeenth century profoundly changed the frameworks through which people understood both their immediate environment and the wider universe in which they lived. Where there once appeared only impenetrable, divine mysteries, it suddenly seemed that the frontiers of knowledge were open wide and rapidly expanding. By the eighteenth century, the implications of the increased knowledge of nature made themselves felt in the social arena as well. If universal physical and chemical laws could be determined, why not explore the principles of economics, politics, and international relations in the same way? Why not apply those insights in order to perfect the structures of society itself? Human understanding, in this sense, passed through two overlapping stages as the groundbreaking achievements of the seventeenth-century Scientific Revolution contributed to the increasing confidence in the possibilities of human progress that characterized the eighteenth-century Enlightenment.

In this context, the thinkers of the Scientific Revolution and the Enlightenment credited human knowledge with unlimited potential. Using nothing more than rational faculties, they believed they could unveil the principles of the natural environment and manipulate them to their advantage. Turning towards the problems of society, they could both determine and forge the forms of government best suited to the essential qualities of human beings. The world, it seemed, had entered an exciting, new, and limitless age. Knowledge promised rapid growth in understanding and, ultimately, heralded a coming human perfection.

Isaac Newton's *Principia* (Mathematical Principles of Natural Philosophy), published in 1687, certainly had revolutionary implications and clearly reflected the power of the seventeenth-century scientific advances. Its full significance becomes clear, however, only in the context of the changing understandings expressed by those before Newton. Newton's universal law of gravity ordered the complexity of both celestial and earthly movement with a single, simple, beautiful equation. Dramatic as that development was, however, it rested on a changing understanding of the crucial relationship between mathematical reason and experimental observation, a relationship that had been building since the middle of the previous century.

Nicholas Copernicus (1473–1543) and Johannes Kepler (1571–1630) applied mathematics to observation and provided two of the most famous new understandings of the natural universe. Copernicus, born in Poland and educated in Italy, directly challenged the received wisdom that defined the cosmos as a set of concentric spheres originating with the earth and moving outward to encompass the various planets, the sun, and the fixed stars. Using mathematical hypotheses, Copernicus found that he could explain the observed world more readily by placing the sun at the center of the solar system, and in a book published just after his death, he argued for a heliocentric model. Kepler, a German, took that formulation a step further, and where Copernicus had hypothesized circular orbits, Kepler built on observations that suggested elliptical ones. Kepler also found that the motion he observed could be expressed in terms of a mathematical relationship between the time of each planet's revolution and its distance from the sun. The nature of observed phenomena, it seemed, could be understood and expressed through the power of human reason, in this case, in simple, elegant equations.

Where Kepler's mathematics refined the Copernican hypothesis, Galileo (1564–1642) used technological applications to provide sensory, experiential evidence. An Italian enjoying the patronage of the powerful Medici family, Galileo invented a telescope in 1609 that allowed him to observe the rough surfaces of the moon, the planets, and, most significantly, other planetary moons. Far from being fixed points of light or massless "luminous orbs," the planets and their satellites had density and revolved just as the earth did. Reason, it seemed, could be verified by direct, sensory observation.

Newton's *Principia*, therefore, represented the most stunning advance in a long chain of breakthroughs that employed theory and reason to explain the reality of nature. Investigation of the world, moreover, confirmed the accuracy of the theoretical expressions. With the founding of England's Royal Society in 1660, a community of gentlemen practitioners set about the task of determining universal principles with great optimism. Their expectations were met in a number of ways as scientific organizations published written journals, and research institutions developed standards of evidence and proof. If methods and results were expressed in a clear and honest manner, the new scientists believed, any reasonably skilled individual should be able to reproduce an experiment and evaluate its conclusions. Through that type of replication, the constancy of nature and the power of universal laws could be revealed to all. Any clear-minded observer or subject, it seemed, could focus on the distinct object of study to reveal and confirm the truth. Though mathematical principles and theories were often derived in isolated studies and tested in private laboratories, the knowledge produced became increasingly public.

Many also expected that the new knowledge would enable both the prediction of future events and an increasing control over the environment itself, key elements in the transition to "modern" ways of thinking. Formulations like Newton's law of universal gravity did not remain inert, trapped within the covers of books and the shelves of archives. They profoundly affected the ways in which people interacted with the world around them. Mathematics, chemistry, and mechanics established abstract principles that, over time, became powerful tools with which to manipulate the world itself. The law of gravity allowed the prediction of tidal patterns based on the interaction of forces produced by the sun, earth, and moon. Newton himself served as an advisor to a group attempting to establish methods by which ships could determine their longitudinal positions while on the open ocean, far from the reference points of land. Better understandings of magnetism also led to the use of more accurate compasses. Along with these improvements in navigation, improved cartographic techniques facilitated European voyages of exploration and exploitation of the land and peoples in Africa, Asia, and the Americas. Knowledge of trajectories and artillery, gained through the applications of calculus, also provided Europe with a decisive enhancement of military technology. By experimenting with an air pump and creating a vacuum in a carefully constructed glass chamber, Englishman Robert Boyle discerned a mathematical relationship between pressure and volume that provided a key link in the eventual development of the steam engine and its applications for both the industrial and transportation revolutions. Though often coming at the expense of other regions and on the backs of impoverished laborers, these advances gave many Europeans a sense that scientific advance brought with it substantial material progress.

These confident, new models of the universe and man's position within it, however, did not meet with unrestrained praise from all quarters. For those adhering to "traditional" sources of authority, the expressions of "modern" science seemed to threaten the very foundations of faith and security. During the Renaissance, thinkers placed classical philosophers of antiquity like Plato and Aristotle at the summit of human achievement and many still claimed that the new "scientists" enjoyed nothing more than the vision of "dwarves standing on the shoulders of giants." While living in Athens from 384 to 322 B.C., Aristotle analyzed natural forms in terms of immutable, unchanging essences. Considered authoritative by Renaissance thinkers, his views contrasted sharply with ways of thinking that sought to move beyond description and classification to laws explaining dynamic processes. Where ancient understandings stressed the composition of matter in terms of a combination of earth, air, water, and fire, new models pursued analyses based on pressure, magnetism, acceleration, mass, and gravity. For those believing that man had continually degenerated from the "Golden Age" of the past, the new achievements lacked credibility and threatened to undermine the secure base of knowledge passed down through generations.

Conflict with religious authority also meant that modernity was born fighting against older traditions that stressed radically different understandings of human knowledge. The Protestant Reformation of the sixteenth century had opened the way for sharp challenges to Catholic doctrine, but the faithful of many different sects still held that the Book of Genesis revealed that God created the cosmos and placed the earth at its center where humans lived, died, and ultimately faced divine judgement that would cast them into heaven or hell. It was the pursuit of knowledge, after all, that had resulted in the Fall of Adam and Eve. It appeared to many that attempts to determine the laws of the universe through mathematical reason and mere sensory observation denied the power and mystery of God's perfect plan. Moreover, they ran the risk of sinful pride. Protestant practices of Bible reading did open up possibilities for individual interpretation of God's truths in ways that subverted the sanctioned explanations of Catholic clerics. Yet in an era when people believed in the power of witchcraft, the presence of occult forces, and the proximity of the Last Judgement, the line between accepted discovery and intolerable heresy remained unclear. Rather than take the chance of transgression, many thinkers kept their opinions to themselves. In 1609, Galileo's telescope had provided evidence confirming that the earth did revolve around the sun, but many professors of his time refused to look through it in fear that their senses might lead them to conclusions in direct opposition to the teachings of their faith. Before long, Church inquisitors forced Galileo to officially recant his conclusion. Though he maintained his views privately, the chilling effect of heresy slowed their dissemination. For those insistent on the presence of a living God who acted directly in human affairs, new notions of God as a type of "clock-maker" setting a mechanical universe in motion and retreating to distant and passive observation seemed particularly threatening.

These tensions often prompted the new scientists to try to distinguish between the phenomena they observed and evaluated and the causes that produced them. Newton himself spent much of his time producing treatises in defense of his ecclesiastical belief and traditional faith, and his *Principia* reflects an attempt to control the implications of his work. As he explained it, the universal laws he determined "would not have arisen without the design and dominion of an intelligent and powerful being."[2] As many scientists expressed it, their findings did not remove God from the universe, they merely revealed the glory of His creation.

The work of William Harvey, a member of the growing community of English scientists in the mid-seventeenth century, provides a striking example of the ways that increases in natural knowledge challenged political authority as well. Using mathematical skills, Harvey was able to estimate the capacity of the heart and the number of its beats per day to determine the quantity of blood circulated through the body. These studies led him to revise his earlier opinions and conclude that the heart, the highest organ in the human body, did not serve as the foundation of human life. It merely worked to circulate the vast quantity of blood that carried vital nutrients. Because the heart was associated by metaphor with the rule of an absolute monarch over a kingdom, the publication of Harvey's discovery in the midst of a long struggle between King and Parliament added credence to the demands of republicans opposing the rule of a supreme monarch over the "body" of the state. During times of political unrest like the English Civil War and the Glorious Revolution of 1688, those illustrations of the natural world carried wider significance.[3]

No matter how scientists tempered the expression of their discoveries, the knowledge produced by the Scientific Revolution of the seventeenth century often led to unforeseen effects and changes. Most significantly, many began to conclude that if thinkers could identify universal laws for the natural world, they should be able to do the same for human society. That application of reason and observation to the realms of economic and political structure provided a crucial bridge to the Enlightenment of the eighteenth century. As educated elites came into contact with the new forces of scientific learning, they questioned the institutions and systems in which they lived. The scientists also considered themselves philosophers, historians, and theologians. During the Enlightenment, they asserted that the knowledge they gained in one realm of thought produced valid conclusions for others as well.

In many ways the work of Thomas Hobbes (1588–1679) and John Locke (1632–1704) reveals two different versions of a common approach to the connections between scientific thinking and the new theories of society that would soon emerge with the Enlightenment. Arguing that human nature was essentially combative and evil, but giving human beings the capacity to think through their situation, Hobbes concluded that men would erect governments to impose order on the inherently dangerous human qualities he saw expressed in the violence of the English Civil War and its struggle between the king and Parliament. In his *Leviathan*, published in 1651, Hobbes argued that only a monarch with absolute power could solve the problems inherent in enforcing civil peace on a contentious society.

An Englishman with interests both in medicine and politics, Locke also used an analysis of human nature to argue for a particular form of government. Although his approach was similar to

Hobbes's, Locke arrived at very different conclusions. First, in his *Essay on Human Understanding* (1690), he argued that true knowledge was derived from human experience. Because human minds at birth were like blank slates (*tabula rasa*), the process of education and the manipulation of the environment would decisively influence the development of an individual. The sense that humans had the power to change these factors and to arrive at accurate knowledge of the world around them contributed to a growing faith in the potential for the perfection of human institutions in ways that would improve the quality of life.

Locke carried that optimism into his political thinking, where he applied ideas of natural law to determine the optimum forms of government. Arguing that all individuals were entitled to natural rights of life, liberty, and property, Locke concluded that the main obligation of government was to secure these rights, not to impose peace at their expense. Written in the midst of England's Glorious Revolution of Parliament against royal authority, Locke's *Two Treatises of Government* (1688–1689) applied that reasoning to work out a theory of contractual agreement between rulers and ruled that would serve as a universal model.

Locke's conclusions challenged those that went before him, and his work provides an example of the type of thinking that gained increasing credibility during the eighteenth century. Confident in the power of reason and the potential for progress, Enlightenment thinkers understood society less as an instrument of Providence or a set of institutions frozen in traditional forms than as a human invention that could be shaped to improve the quality of life. That hopeful spirit led to the articulation of a number of new political and social theories.

In France, political theorizing became part of a widespread discontentment with traditional institutions. Writers like Montesquieu (1689–1755), a judge and nobleman, attempted to improve the state of society through understandings of human nature. In his *Spirit of the Laws* (1748), Montesquieu reasoned that democracies could only work well in small countries where civic virtue could flourish. Elsewhere the love of honor and fear of authority regulated order. In the best government, he said, power should be divided and balanced to prevent the abuse of authority by rulers that, given total control, inevitably oppressed their subjects. Voltaire (1694–1778), another famous French writer and critic, differed from Montesquieu because he supported the authority of powerful monarchs he considered "enlightened," yet he too sought to change the shape of society and argued that religious toleration and intellectual freedom served the purposes of increasing moral understanding and promoting material progress. During the middle of the eighteenth century a group of men known as *philosophes* also began to publish pamphlets that were eagerly read by a growing middle-class public. Between 1751 and 1772, Denis Diderot completed their most ambitious project by editing and publishing the *Encyclopédie*, a seventeen-volume collection of historical, scientific, and technical knowledge that also contained elements of social criticism.

Other thinkers directed their understandings of human nature towards the effects of Europe's growing trade relationships with the rest of the world and the links between politics and economy. In Scotland, Adam Smith and David Hume attempted to explain how significant increases in material wealth had come about. Why did ordinary workers in Britain live better than kings in other parts of the world? Answers to these questions focused on the question of social development. How had a society moved from "traditional" forms of production and consumption to "modern" ones? What were the implications of this change?

The writers of the Scottish Enlightenment came up with a "conjectural history" that retraced human society as it passed in succession from forms dominated by hunters and gatherers to those composed of shepherds, then farmers, and, finally, merchants. This historical typology contained a number of intellectual breakthroughs. For the thinkers of the Scottish Enlightenment, economic, political, and social change were linked together in a complex system that often resulted in larger social effects not directly related to the different goals of individual actors. Human beings, the Scottish thinkers argued, acted on their self-interest within a structure of social mores and material constraints, and behaved in ways that produced complex patterns of social interaction. In the absence of government interference, Smith held that individual trading led to the highest levels of wealth possible for society as a whole. This focus on unintended consequences of human action played a key role in future attempts to study society in terms of larger systemic processes and common principles independent of the actions of particular rulers or individual events. The Scottish Enlightenment, in this sense, redirected understandings of historical change to processes and away from events.

The Enlightenment was not a period without conflict. Locke's conclusions clashed directly with the earlier ones formulated by Hobbes and took on added significance in the context of turbulent political struggles. Even thinkers like Montesquieu and Voltaire did not agree on the forms of government most certain to lead to the amelioration of society. But the possibilities implicit in Locke's social contract theory and Smith's emphasis on the evolutionary advance of material wealth had a decisive impact both in Europe and across the Atlantic in the new American nation. Building on the faith in reason and expanded human understanding that characterized the Scientific Revolution, Enlightenment thinkers urged upon their contemporaries a crowded reform agenda aimed at no less than perfecting human society. Many of the new ideas met stiff resistance, and all did not suddenly "become light." For many, however, knowledge and human achievement seemed to have limitless potential. In the context of American and French revolutionary aspirations, moreover, it seemed that the knowledge and advances of the present might finally sweep away the fallacies and injustices of the past.

NOTES

1. Norman Hampson, *The Enlightenment* (New York: Penguin Books, 1968), p. 38.
2. Newton, as cited in I. Bernard Cohen, *The Newtonian Revolution* (Cambridge: Cambridge University Press, 1980), p. 5.
3. Christopher Hill, "William Harvey and the Idea of Monarchy," in Charles Webster, ed., *The Intellectual Revolution of the Seventeenth Century* (London: Routledge and Kegan Paul, 1974) pp. 160–81.

Francis Bacon

The work of Francis Bacon (1561–1626) reflected both faith in the promise of knowledge and an attempt to justify its pursuit in light of traditional opposition. Appointed to serve the English crown as an ambassador and legal advisor, Bacon soon turned his attention to philosophical questions and, along with others of his time, developed a method of experiment and induction that suggested a new relationship between knowing and doing.[1] Mere observation of an object's essential qualities or form no longer sufficed. To gain knowledge, one had to use manual labor and mechanical skill in conducting experiments. Rather than deducing knowledge of particulars from commonly accepted general principles, the investigator induced larger laws from smaller pieces.

Building on that framework, Bacon's *The Advancement of Learning* (1605) laid out a plan for proper study and a defense of the value of disciplined inquiry. Stressing the virtues of knowledge for the "improvement of man's estate," Bacon argued that the scholar should strive for universality of conclusions, mature deliberation, and a suspension of rash judgement until the facts themselves are proven secure. Rather than become embroiled in "vain altercations," the altruistic scientist guides the intellect in ways that benefit from self-criticism and promote moral development.

Most significant is the fact that Bacon actually had to *justify* learning, a value that we often take for granted today. Using historical examples, Bacon argued that learned men do not necessarily become soft and unfit for political leadership or military command in the service of the monarchy. Instead of catching men up in endless circular arguments of no real substance, well-directed learning can make valuable contributions to the quality of life and improve the character of those pursuing knowledge. Subjective senses, Bacon believed, could reveal objective reality and facts in a world that had, until then, remained dominated by unsupported speculation, conjecture, or enforced opinion.

Aware of the subversive implications of his conclusions and his position as an advisor to the crown, Bacon also sought to temper his account and argue that independent pursuit of knowledge did not necessarily imply a rejection of secular or theological authority. Emphasizing the virtues of glorifying God by revealing the wonders of the world He had created, Bacon took great pains to distinguish his endeavor from the proud pursuit of an irreverent knowledge of good and evil. In Bacon's universe, God remains the primary cause of all phenomena. Man simply studies the secondary effects He produces. In a similar sense, Bacon dedicated the work to King James I for reasons that go beyond a personal attempt to climb the ranks of royal authority.

Bacon's work also carried definite public and social implications. Proclaiming the virtue of published, accessible, written knowledge, Bacon broke with older traditions of aristocratic privilege and guilds that attempted to keep their specialized skills secret. Clear, open information delivered with candor made learning accessible to more of the population at a time when documents were increasingly published in common vernacular language instead of formal Latin. In this sense, Bacon's work stands as an invitation for all possessing reason to learn from their own experiences, perfect themselves, and enjoy the possibility of progress.

1 Paolo Rossi, "Hermeticism, Rationality and the Scientific Revolution," in William R. Shea and M. L. Righini Bonelli, eds., *Reason, Experiment and Mysticism in the Scientific Revolution* (New York: Science History Publications, 1975), p. 255.

FRANCIS BACON
(1605)

The

Advancement

of Learning

1. In the entrance to the former of these, to clear the way, and as it were to make silence, to have the true testimonies concerning the dignity of learning to be better heard, without the interruption of tacit objections; I think good to deliver it from the discredits and disgraces which it hath received, all from ignorance; but ignorance severally disguised; appearing sometimes in the zeal and jealousy of divines; sometimes in the severity and arrogancy of politiques; and sometimes in the errors and imperfections of learned men themselves.

2. I hear the former sort say, that knowledge is of those things which are to be accepted of with great limitation and caution: that the aspiring to overmuch knowledge was the original temptation and sin whereupon ensued the fall of man: that knowledge hath in it somewhat of the serpent, and therefore where it entereth into a man it makes him swell; *Scientia inflat*: that Salomon gives a censure, *That there is no end of making books, and that much reading is weariness of the flesh*; and again in another place, *That in spacious knowledge there is much contristation, and that he that increaseth knowledge increaseth anxiety*: that Saint Paul gives a caveat, *That we be not spoiled through vain philosophy*: that experience demonstrates how learned men have been arch-heretics, how learned times have been inclined to atheism, and how the contemplation of second causes doth derogate from our dependence upon God, who is the first cause.

3. To discover then the ignorance and error of this opinion, and the misunderstanding in the grounds thereof it may well appear these men do not observe or consider that it was not the pure knowledge of nature and universality, a knowledge by the light whereof man did give names unto other creatures in Paradise, as they were brought before him, according unto their

Clarendon Press, Oxford, 1920, I:5–43.

properties, which gave the occasion to the fall: but it was the proud knowledge of good and evil, with an intent in man to give law unto himself, and to depend no more upon God's commandments, which was the form of the temptation. Neither is it any quantity of knowledge, how great soever, that can make the mind of man to swell; for nothing can fill, much less extend the soul of man, but God and the contemplation of God; and therefore Salomon, speaking of the two principal senses of inquisition, the eye and the ear, affirmeth that *the eye is never satisfied with seeing, nor the ear with hearing;* and if there be no fulness, then is the continent greater than the content: so of knowledge itself, and the mind of man, whereto the senses are but reporters, he defineth likewise in these words, placed after that Kalendar or Ephemerides which he maketh of the diversities of times and seasons for all actions and purposes; and concludeth thus: *God hath made all things beautiful, or decent, in the true return of their seasons: Also he hath placed the world in man's heart, yet cannot man find out the work which God worketh from the beginning to the end:* declaring not obscurely, that God hath framed the mind of man as a mirror or glass, capable of the image of the universal world, and joyful to receive the impression thereof, as the eye joyeth to receive light; and not only delighted in beholding the variety of things and vicissitude of times, but raised also to find out and discern the ordinances and decrees, which throughout all those changes are infallibly observed. And although he doth insinuate that the supreme or summary law of nature, which he calleth *The work which God worketh from the beginning to the end*, is not possible to be found out by man; yet that doth not derogate from the capacity of the mind, but may be referred to the impediments, as of shortness of life, ill conjunction of labours, ill tradition of knowledge over from hand to hand, and many other inconveniences, whereunto the condition of man is subject. For that nothing parcel of the world is denied to man's inquiry and invention, he doth in another place rule over, when he *saith, The spirit of man is as the lamp of God, wherewith he searcheth the inwardness of all secrets.* It then such be the capacity and receipt of the mind of man, it is manifest that there is no danger at all in the proportion or quantity of knowledge, how large soever, lest it should make it swell or out-compass itself; no, but it is merely the quality of knowledge, which, be it in quantity more or less, if it be taken without the true corrective thereof, hath in it some nature of venom or malignity, and some effects of that venom, which is ventosity or swelling. This corrective spice, the mixture whereof maketh knowledge so sovereign, is charity, which the Apostle immediately addeth to the former clause: for so he saith, *Knowledge bloweth up, but charity buildeth up;* not unlike unto that which he delivereth in another place: *If I spake,* saith he, *with the tongues of men and angels, and had not charity, it were but as a tinkling cymbal;* not but that it is an excellent thing to speak with the tongues of men and angels, but because, if it be severed from charity, and not referred to the good of men and mankind, it hath rather a sounding and unworthy glory, than a meriting and substantial virtue. And as for that censure of Salomon, concerning the excess of writing and reading books, and the anxiety of spirit which redoundeth from knowledge; and that admonition of Saint Paul, *That we be not seduced by vain philosophy;* let those places be rightly understood, and they do indeed excellently set forth the true bounds and limitations, whereby human knowledge is confined and circumscribed; and yet without any such contracting or coarctation, but that it may comprehend all the universal nature of things; for these limitations are three: the first, *That we do not so place our felicity in knowledge, as we forget our mortality:* the second, *That we make application of our knowledge, to give ourselves repose and contentment, and not distaste or repining:* the third, *That we do not presume by the contemplation of nature to attain to the mysteries of God.* . . .

And therefore it was most aptly said by one of Plato's school, *That the sense of man carrieth a* resemblance with the sun, which (as we see) openeth and revealeth all the terrestrial globe; but then again it obscureth and concealeth the stars and celestial globe: so doth the sense discover natural things, but it darkeneth and shutteth up divine. And hence it is true that it hath proceeded, that divers great learned men have been heretical, whilst they have sought to fly up to the secrets of the Deity by the waxen wings of the senses. And as for the conceit that too much knowledge should incline a man to atheism, and that the ignorance of second causes should make a more devout dependence upon God, which is the first cause; first, it is good to ask the question which Job asked of his friends: *Will you lie for God, as one man will do for another, to gratify him?* For certain it is that God worketh nothing in nature but by second causes: and if they would have it otherwise believed, it is mere imposture, as it were in favour towards God; and nothing else but to offer to the author of truth the unclean sacrifice of a lie. But further, it is an assured truth, and a conclusion of experience, that a little or superficial knowledge of philosophy may incline the mind of man to atheism, but a further proceeding therein doth bring the mind back again to religion. For in the entrance of philosophy, when the second causes, which are next unto the senses, do offer themselves to the mind of man, if it dwell and stay there it may induce some oblivion of the highest cause; but when a man passeth on further, and seeth the dependence of causes, and the works of Providence, then, according to the allegory of the poets, he will easily believe that the highest link of nature's chain must needs be tied to the foot of Jupiter's chair. To conclude therefore, let no man upon a weak conceit of sobriety or an ill-applied moderation think or maintain, that a man can search too far, or be too well studied in the book of God's word, or in the book of God's works, divinity or philosophy; but rather let men endeavour an endless progress or proficience in both; only let men beware that they apply both to charity, and not to swelling; to use, and not to ostentation; and again, that they do not unwisely mingle or confound these learnings together.

II

1. And as for the disgraces which learning receiveth from politiques, they be of this nature; that learning doth soften men's minds, and makes them more unapt for the honour and exercise of arms; that it doth mar and pervert men's dispositions for matter of government and policy, in making them too curious and irresolute by variety of reading, or too peremptory or positive by strictness of rules and axioms, or too immoderate and overweening by reason of the greatness of examples, or too incompatible and differing from the times by reason of the dissimilitude of examples; or at least, that it doth divert men's travails from action and business, and bringeth them to a love of leisure and privateness; and that it doth bring into states a relaxation of discipline, whilst every man is more ready to argue than to obey and execute. Out of this conceit, Cato, surnamed the Censor, one of the wisest men indeed that ever lived, when Carneades the philosopher came in embassage to Rome, and that the young men of Rome began to flock about him, being allured with the sweetness and majesty of his eloquence and learning, gave counsel in open senate that they should give him his dispatch with all speed, lest he should infect and enchant the minds and affections of the youth, and at unawares bring in an alteration of the manners and customs of the state....

2. But these and the like imputations have rather a countenance of gravity than any ground of justice: for experience doth warrant, that both in persons and in times there hath been a meeting and concurrence in learning and arms, flourishing and excelling in the same men and

the same ages. For as for men, there cannot be a better nor the like instance, as of that pair, Alexander the Great and Julius Caesar the Dictator; whereof the one was Aristotle's scholar in philosophy, and the other was Cicero's rival in eloquence. . . .

Neither can it otherwise be: for as in man the ripeness of strength of the body and mind cometh much about an age, save that the strength of the body cometh somewhat the more early, so in states, arms and learning, whereof the one correspondeth to the body, the other to the soul of man, have a concurrence or near sequence in times.

3. And for matter of policy and government, that learning should rather hurt, than enable thereunto, is a thing very improbable: we see it is accounted an error to commit a natural body to empiric physicians, which commonly have a few pleasing receipts whereupon they are confident and adventurous, but know neither the causes of diseases, nor the complexions of patients, nor peril of accidents, nor the true method of cures: we see it is a like error to rely upon advocates or lawyers, which are only men of practice and not grounded in their books, who are many times easily surprised when matter falleth out besides their experience, to the prejudice of the causes they handle: so by like reason it cannot be but a matter of doubtful consequence if states be managed by empiric statesmen, not well mingled with men grounded in learning. But contrariwise, it is almost without instance contradictory that ever any government was disastrous that was in the hands of learned governors. . . .

4. And as for those particular seducements or indispositions of the mind for policy and government, which learning is pretended to insinuate; if it be granted that any such thing be, it must be remembered withal, that learning ministereth in every of them greater strength of medicine or remedy than it offereth cause of indisposition or infirmity. For if by a secret operation it make men perplexed and irresolute, on the other side by plain percept it teacheth them when and upon what ground to resolve; yea, and how to carry things in suspense without prejudice, till they resolve. If it make men positive and regular, it teacheth them what things are in their nature demonstrative, and what are conjectural, and as well the use of distinctions and exceptions, as the latitude of principles and rules. If it mislead by disproportion or dissimilitude of examples, it teacheth men the force of circumstances, the errors of comparisons, and all the cautions of application; so that in all these it doth rectify more effectually than it can pervert. And these medicines it conveyeth into men's minds much more forcibly by the quickness and penetration of examples. For let a man look into the errors of Clement the seventh, so lively described by Guicciardine, who served under him, or into the errors of Cicero, painted out by his own pencil in his Epistles to Atticus, and he will fly apace from being irresolute.

5. And for the conceit that learning should dispose men to leisure and privateness, and make men slothful; it were a strange thing if that which accustometh the mind to a perpetual motion and agitation should induce slothfulness: whereas contrariwise it may be truly affirmed, that no kind of men love business for itself but those that are learned; for other persons love it for profit, as an hireling, that loves the work for the wages; or for honour, as because it beareth them up in the eyes of men, and refresheth their reputation, which otherwise would wear; or because it putteth them in mind of their fortune, and giveth them occasion to pleasure and displeasure; or because it exerciseth some faculty wherein they take pride, and so entertaineth them in good humour and pleasing conceits toward themselves; or because it advanceth any other their ends. So that as it is said of untrue valours, that some men's valours are in the eyes of them that look on; so such men's industries are in the eyes of others, or at least in regard of

their own designments: only learned men love business as an action according to nature, as agreeable to health of mind as exercise is to health of body, taking pleasure in the action itself, and not in the purchase: so that of all men they are the most indefatigable, if it be towards any business which can hold or detain their mind.

6. And if any man be laborious in reading and study and yet idle in business and action, if groweth from some weakness of body or softness of spirit; such as Seneca speaketh of: *Quidam tam sunt umbratiles, ut putent in turbido esse quicquid in luce est;* and not of learning: well may it be that such a point of a man's nature may make him give himself to learning, but it is not learning that breedeth any such point in his nature.

7. And that learning should take up too much time or leisure; I answer, the most active or busy man that hath been or can be, hath (no question) many vacant times of leisure, while he expecteth the tides and returns of business (except he be either tedious and of no dispatch, or lightly and unworthily ambitious to meddle in things that may be better done by others), and then the question is but how those spaces and times of leisure shall be filled and spent; whether in pleasures or in studies.

So as no man need doubt that learning will expulse business, but rather it will keep and defend the possession of the mind against idleness and pleasure, which otherwise at unawares may enter to the prejudice of both.

8. Again, for that other conceit that learning should undermine the reverence of laws and government, it is assuredly a mere depravation and calumny, without all shadow of truth. For to say that a blind custom of obedience should be a surer obligation than duty taught and understood, it is to affirm, that a blind may may tread surer by a guide than a seeing man can by a light....

Let this therefore serve for answer to politiques, which in their humorous severity, or in their feigned gravity, have presumed to throw imputations upon learning; which redargution nevertheless (save that we know not whether our labours may extend to other ages) were not needful for the present, in regard of the love and reverence towards learning, which the example and countenance of two so learned princes, Queen Elizabeth and your Majesty, being as Castor and Pollux, *lucida sidera*, stars of excellent light and most benign influence, hath wrought in all men of place and authority in our nation.

III

1. Now therefore we come to that third sort of discredit or diminution of credit that groweth unto learning from learned men themselves, which commonly cleaveth fastest: it is either from their fortune, or from their manners, or from the nature of their studies. For the first, it is not in their power; and the second is accidental; the third only is proper to be handled: but because we are not in hand with true measure, but with popular estimation and conceit, it is not amiss to speak somewhat of the two former. The derogations therefore which grow to learning from the fortune or condition of learned men, are either in respect of scarcity of means, or in respect of privateness of life and meanness of employments.

2. Concerning want, and that it is the case of learned men usually to begin with little, and not to grow rich so fast as other men, by reason they convert not their labours chiefly to lucre and increase, it were good to leave the common place in commendation of poverty to some friar to handle, to whom much was attributed by Machiavel in this point; when he said, *That the*

kingdom of the clergy had been long before at an end, if the reputation and reverence towards the poverty of friars had *not borne out the scandal of the superfluilies and excesses of bishops and prelates.* So a man might say that the felicity and delicacy of princes and great persons had long since turned to rudeness and barbarism, if the poverty of learning had not kept up civility and honour of life....

3. And for meanness of employment, that which is most traduced to contempt is that the government of youth is commonly allotted to them; which age, because it is the age of least authority, it is transferred to the disesteeming of those employments wherein youth is conversant, and which are conversant about youth. But how unjust this traducement is (if you will reduce things from popularity of opinion to measure of reason) may appear in that we see men are more curious what they put into a new vessel than into a vessel seasoned; and what mould they lay about a young plant than about a plant corroborate; so as the weakest terms and times of all things use to have the best applications and helps. And will you hearken to the Hebrew rabbins? *Your young men shall see visions, and your old men shall dream dreams;* say they youth is the worthier age, for that visions are nearer apparitions of God than dreams? ...

4. As touching the manners of learned men, it is a thing personal and individual: and no doubt there be amongst them, as in other professions, of all temperatures: but yet so as it is not without truth which is said, that *Abeunt sludia in mores*, studies have an influence and operation upon the manners of those that are conversant in them.

5. But upon an attentive and indifferent review, I for my part cannot find any disgrace to learning can proceed from the manners of learned men; not inherent to them as they are learned; except it be a fault (which was the supposed fault of Demosthenes, Cicero, Cato the second, Seneca, and many more) that because the times they read of are commonly better than the times they live in, and the duties taught better than the duties practised, they contend sometimes too far to bring things to perfection, and to reduce the corruption of manners to honesty of precepts or examples of too great height. And yet hereof they have caveats enough in their own walks. For Solon, when he was asked whether he had given his citizens the best laws, answered wisely, *Yea of such as they would receive....*

6. Another fault likewise much of this kind hath been incident to learned men; which is, that they have esteemed the preservation, good, and honour of their countries or masters before their own fortunes or safeties. For so saith Demosthenes unto the Athenians; *If it please you to note it, my counsels unto you are not such whereby I should grow great amongst you, and you become little amongst the Grecians; but they be of that nature, as they are sometimes not good for me to give, but are always good for you to follow....* But for this point of tender sense and fast obligation of duty which learning doth endue the mind withal, howsoever fortune may tax it, and many in the depth of their corrupt principles may despise it, yet it will receive an open allowance, and therefore needs the less disproof or excusation.

7. Another fault incident commonly to learned men, which may be more probably defended than truly denied, is, that they fail sometimes in applying themselves to particular persons: which want of exact application ariseth from two causes; the one, because the largeness of their mind can hardly confine itself to dwell in the exquisite observation or examination of the nature and customs of one person.... But there is a second cause, which is no inability, but a rejection upon choice and judgement. For the honest and just bounds of observation by one person upon another, extend no further but to understand him sufficiently, whereby not to give him offence, or whereby to be able to give him faithful counsel, or whereby to stand upon reasonable guard and caution in respect of a man's self. But to be speculative into another man to

the end to know how to work him, or wind him, or govern him, proceedth from a heart that is double and cloven and not entire and ingenuous; which as in friendship it is want of integrity, so towards princes or superiors is want of duty.

8. There is yet another fault (with which I will conclude this part) which is often noted in learned men, that they do many times fail to observe decency and discretion in their behaviour and carriage, and commit errors in small and ordinary points of action, so as the vulgar in small and ordinary points of action, so as the vulgar sort of capacities do make a judgement of them in greater matters by that which they find wanting in them in smaller.... I refer them also to that which Plato said of his master Socrates, whom he compared to the gallipots of apothecaries, which on the outside had apes and owls and antiques but contained within sovereign and precious liquors and confections; acknowledging that to an external report he was not without superficial levities and deformities, but was inwardly replenished with excellent virtues and powers. And so much touching the point of manners of learned men.

9. But in the mean time I have no purpose to give allowance to some conditions and courses base and unworthy, wherein divers professors of learning have wronged themselves and gone too far; such as were those trencher philosphers which in the later age of the Roman state were usually in the houses of great persons, being little better than solemn parasites....

Neither is the modern dedication of books and writings, as to patrons, to be commended: for that books (such as are worthy the name of books) ought to have no patrons but truth and reason. And the ancient custom was to dedicate them only to private and equal friends, or to entitle the books with their names: or if to kings and great persons, it was to some such as the argument of the book was fit and proper for: but these and the like courses may deserve rather reprehension than defence.

IV

1. Now I proceed to those errors and vanities which have intervened amongst the studies themselves of the learned, which is that which is principal and proper to the present argument; wherein my purpose is not to make a justification of the errors, but by a censure and separation of the errors to make a justification of that which is good and sound, and to deliver that from the aspersion of the other.

2. There be therefore chiefly three vanities in studies, whereby learning hath been most traduced. For those things we do esteem vain, which are either false or frivolous, those which either have no truth or no use: and those persons we esteem vain, which are either credulous or curious; and curiosity is either in matter or words: so that in reason as well as in experience there fall out to be these three distempers (as I may term them) of learning: the first, fantastical learning; the second, contentious learning; and the last, delicate learning; vain imaginations, vain altercations, and vain affectations; and with the last I will begin. Martin Luther, conducted (no doubt) by an higher providence, but in discourse of reason, finding what a province he had undertaken against the bishop of Rome and the degenerate traditions of the church, and finding his own solitude, being no ways aided by the opinions of his own time, was enforced to awake all antiquity, and to call former times to his succours to make a party against the present time: so that the ancient authors, both in divinity and in humanity, which had long time slept in libraries, began generally to be read and revolved. This by consequence did draw on a necessity of a more exquisite travail in the languages original, wherein those authors did write, for the better understanding

of those authors, and the better advantage of pressing and applying their words. And thereof grew again a delight in their manner of style and phrase, and an admiration of that kind of writing. . . .

This grew speedily to an excess; for men began to hunt more after words than matter; more after the choiceness of the phrase, and the round and clean composition of the sentence, and the sweet falling of the clauses, and the varying and illustration of their works with tropes and figures, than after the weight of matter, worth of subject, soundness of argument, life of invention, or depth of judgement. . . .

3. Here therefore is the first distemper of learning, when men study words and not matter. . . .

5. The second which followeth is in nature worse than the former: for as substance of matter is better than beauty of words, so contrariwise vain matter is worse than vain words. . . . Surely, like as many substances in nature which are solid do putrify and corrupt into worms; so it is the property of good and sound knowledge to putrify and dissolve into a number of subtle, idle, unwholesome, and (as I may term them) vermiculate questions, which have indeed a kind of quickness and life of spirit, but no soundness of matter or goodness of quality. This kind of degenerate learning did chiefly reign amongst the schoolmen: who having sharp and strong wits, and abundance of leisure, and small variety of reading, but their wits being shut up in the cells of a few authors (chiefly Aristotle their dictator) as their persons were shut up in the cells of monasteries and colleges, and knowing little history, either of nature or time, did out of no great quantity of matter and infinite agitation of wit spin out unto us those laborious webs of learning which are extant in their books. For the wit and mind of man, if it work upon matter, which is the contemplation of the creatures of God, worketh according to the stuff and is limited thereby; but if it work upon itself, as the spider worketh his web, then it is endless, and brings forth indeed cobwebs of learning, admirable for the fineness of thread and work, but of no substance or profit.

6. This same unprofitable subtility or curiosity is of two sorts; either in the subject itself that they handle, when it is a fruitless speculation or controversy (whereof there are no small number both in divinity and philosophy), or in the manner or method of handling of a knowledge. . . . For were it not better for a man in a fair room to set up one great light, or branching candlestick of lights, than to go about with a small watch candle into every corner? And such is their method, that rests not so much upon evidence of truth proved by arguments, authorities, similitudes, examples, as upon particular confutations and solutions of every scruple, cavillation, and objection; breeding for the most part one question as fast as it solveth another; even as in the former resemblance, when you carry the light into one corner, you darken the rest. . . .

7. Notwithstanding, certain it is that if those schoolmen to their great thirst of truth and unwearied travail of wit had joined variety and universality of reading and contemplation, they had proved excellent lights, to the great advancement of all learning and knowledge; but as they are, they are great undertakers indeed, and fierce with dark keeping. But as in the inquiry of the divine truth, their pride inclined to leave the oracle of God's word, and to vanish in the mixture of their own inventions; so in the inquisition of nature, they ever left the oracle of God's works, and adored the deceiving and deformed images which the unequal mirror of their own minds, or a few received authors or principles, did represent unto them. And thus much for the second disease of learning.

8. For the third vice or disease of learning, which concerneth deceit or untruth, it is of all the rest the foulest; as that which doth destroy the essential form of knowledge, which is noth-

ing but a representation of truth: for the truth of being and the truth of knowing are one, differing no more than the direct beam and the beam reflected. . . .

9. This facility of credit and accepting or admitting things weakly authorized or warranted, is of two kinds according to the subject: for it is either a belief of history, or, as the lawyers speak, matter of fact; or else of matter of art and opinion. As to the former, we see the experience and inconvenience of this error in ecclesiastical history; which hath too easily received and registered reports and narrations of miracles wrought by martyrs, hermits, or monks of the desert, and other holy men, and their relics, shrines, chapels, and images: which though they had a passage for a time by the ignorance of the people, the superstitious simplicity of some, and the politic toleration of others, holding them but as divine poesies; yet after a period of time, when the mist began to clear up, they grew to be esteemed but as old wives' fables, impostures of the clergy, illusions of spirits, and badges of Antichrist, to the great scandal and detriment of religion. . . .

11. And as for the facility of credit which is yielded to arts and opinions, it is likewise of two kinds; either when too much belief is attributed to the arts themselves, or to certain authors in any art. The sciences themselves, which have had better intelligence and confederacy with the imagination of man than with his reason, are three in number; astrology, natural magic, and alchemy: of which sciences, nevertheless, the ends or pretences are noble. For astrology pretendeth to discover that correspondence or concatenation which is between the superior globe and the inferior: natural magic pretendeth to call and reduce natural philosophy from variety of speculations to the magnitude of works: and alchemy pretendeth to make separation of all the unlike parts of bodies which in mixtures of nature are incorporate. But the derivations and prosecutions to these ends, both in the theories and in the practices, are full of error and vanity. . . .

12. And as for the overmuch credit that hath been given unto authors in sciences, in making them dictators, that their words should stand, and not consuls to give advice; the damage is infinite that sciences have received thereby, as the principal cause that hath kept them low at a stay without growth or advancement. For hence it hath comen, that in arts mechanical the first deviser comes shortest, and time addeth and perfecteth; but in sciences the first author goeth furthest, and time leeseth and corrupteth. So we see, artillery, sailing, printing, and the like, were grossly managed at the first, and by time accommodated and refined: but contrariwise, the philosophies and sciences of Aristotle, Plato, Democritus, Hippocrates, Euclides, Archimedes, of most vigour at the first and by time degenerate and imbased. . .

For as water will not ascend higher than the level of the first springhead from whence it descendeth, so knowledge derived from Aristotle, and exempted from liberty of examination, will not rise again higher than the knowledge of Aristotle. . . .

Thus have I gone over these three diseases of learning; besides the which there are some other rather peccant humours than formed diseases, which nevertheless are not so secret and intrinsic but that they fall under a popular observation and traducement and therefore are not to be passed over.

V

1. The first of these is the extreme affecting of two extremities: the one antiquity, the other novelty; wherein it seemeth the children of time do take after the nature and malice of the father. . . .

8. Another error is an impatience of doubt, and haste to assertion without due and mature suspension of judgement. For the two ways of contemplation are not unlike the two ways of action commonly spoken of by the ancients: the one plain and smooth in the beginning, and in the end impassable; the other rough and troublesome in the entrance, but after a while fair and even: so it is in contemplation; if a man will begin with certainties, he shall end in doubts; but if he will be content to begin with doubts, he shall end in certainties. . . .

11. But the greatest error of all the rest is the mistaking or misplacing of the last or furthest end of knowledge. For men have entered into a desire of learning and knowledge, sometimes upon a natural curiosity and inquisitive appetite; sometimes to entertain their minds with variety and delight; sometimes for ornament and reputation; and sometimes to enable them to victory of wit and contradiction; and most times for lucre and profession; and seldom sincerely to give a true account of their gift of reason, to the benefit and use of men: as if there were sought in knowledge a couch whereupon to rest a searching and restless spirit; or a terrace for a wandering and variable mind to walk up and down with a fair prospect; or a tower of state for a proud mind to raise itself upon; or a fort or commanding ground for strife and contention; or a shop for profit or sale; and not a rich storehouse for the glory of the Creator and the relief of man's estate. . . . But as both heaven and earth do conspire and contribute to the use and benefit of man; so the end ought to be, from both philosophies to separate and reject vain speculations, and whatsoever is empty and void, and to preserve and augment whatsoever is solid and fruitful: that knowledge may not be as a courtesan, for pleasure and vanity only, or as a bond-woman, to acquire and gain to her master's use; but as a spouse, for generation, fruit, and comfort.

René Descartes

René Descartes (1596–1650) is often called the founder of modern epistemology due to his enunciation of the powers of the human mind in *Discourse on Method* (1637). His most well-known maxim, *cogito ergo sum* (I think, therefore I am), is the core of the French philosophical current known as Cartesianism. Cartesianism describes any metaphysical system that is predicated on the human mind's capacity to access reality, and has only been contested in the twentieth century.

Descartes was not a philosopher in our modern sense of the term. Trained in a Jesuit school where emphasis was placed upon the *method* through which scholars studied the classical, primarily theological, curriculum, Descartes applied this method to medicine and chemistry. He eventually abandoned the methods of the humanities in favor of mathematics, which he found to be less biased and more capable of delineating truth and reason. Descartes' interest in mathematics, especially coordinate or analytic geometry, led him to formulate a metaphysical theory based upon mathematical exactitude. Descartes was so certain of the primacy of mathematics to the representation of reality that he described the tree of knowledge in this manner: the roots of the tree were metaphysics, its trunk was physics, and its branches were the other sciences including medicine and ethics.

In applying the geometric method to philosophy, Descartes attempted to prove the rationalism of human cognition. This certainty was interpreted as arrogance by many of his contemporaries. Although influenced by the skeptical current of his age, Descartes could not remain doubtful of one ultimate certainty, that of his own existence.

RENÉ DESCARTES
(1637)

Discourse

on Method

PART I

Good sense is, of all things among men, the most equally distributed; for every one thinks himself so abundantly provided with it, that those even who are the most difficult to satisfy in everything else, do not usually desire a larger measure of this quality than they already possess. And in this it is not likely that all are mistaken: the conviction is rather to be held as testifying that the power of judging aright and of distinguishing truth from error, which is properly what is called good sense or reason, is by nature equal in all men; and that the diversity of our opinions, consequently, does not arise from some being endowed with a larger share of reason than others, but solely from this, that we conduct our thoughts along different ways, and do not fix our attention on the same objects. For to be possessed of a vigorous mind is not enough; the prime requisite is rightly to apply it. The greatest minds, as they are capable of the highest excellences, are open likewise to the greatest aberrations; and those who travel very slowly may yet make far greater progress, provided they keep always to the straight road, than those who, while they run, forsake it. . . .

And besides these, I know of no other qualities that contribute to the perfection of the mind; for as to the reason or sense, inasmuch as it is that alone which constitutes us as men, and distinguishes us from the brutes, I am disposed to believe that it is to be found complete in each individual; and on this point to adopt the common opinion of philosophers, who say that

Trans. by John Veitch (New York, E.P. Dutton & Co., 1912), pp. 3–9, 13–18, 26–28.

the difference of greater and less holds only among the *accidents*, and not among the *forms or natures of individuals* of the same *species*.

I will not hesitate, however, to avow my belief that it has been my singular good fortune to have very early in life fallen in with certain tracks which have conducted me to considerations and maxims, of which I have formed a method that gives me the means, as I think, of gradually augmenting my knowledge, and of raising it by little and little to the highest point which the mediocrity of my talents and the brief duration of my life will permit me to reach. For I have already reaped from it such fruits that, although I have been accustomed to think lowly enough of myself, and although when I look with the eye of a philosopher at the varied courses and pursuits of mankind at large, I find scarcely one which does not appear vain and useless, I nevertheless derive the highest satisfaction from the progress I conceive myself to have already made in the search after truth, and cannot help entertaining such expectations of the future as to believe that if, among the occupations of men as men, there is any one really excellent and important, it is that which I have chosen. . . .

My present design, then, is not to teach the method which each ought to follow for the right conduct of his reason, but solely to describe the way in which I have endeavoured to conduct my own. . . .

From my childhood, I have been familiar with letters; and as I was given to believe that by their help a clear and certain knowledge of all that is useful in life might be acquired, I was ardently desirous of instruction. But as soon as I had finished the entire course of study, at the close of which it is customary to be admitted into the order of the learned, I completely changed my opinion. For I found myself involved in so many doubts and errors, that I was convinced I had advanced no farther in all my attempts at learning, than the discovery at every turn of my own ignorance. And yet I was studying in one of the most celebrated schools in Europe, in which I thought there must be learned men, if such were anywhere to be found. I had been taught all that others learned there; and not contented with the sciences actually taught us, I had, in addition, read all the books that had fallen into my hands, treating of such branches as are esteemed the most curious and rare. I knew the judgment which others had formed of me; and I did not find that I was considered inferior to my fellows, although there were among them some who were already marked out to fill the places of our instructors. And, in fine, our age appeared to me as flourishing, and as fertile in powerful minds as any preceding one. I was thus led to take the liberty of judging of all other men by myself, and of concluding that there was no science in existence that was of such a nature as I had previously been given to believe.

I still continued, however, to hold in esteem the studies of the schools. I was aware that the languages taught in them are necessary to the understanding of the writings of the ancients; that the grace of fable stirs the mind; that the memorable deeds of history elevate it; and, if read with discretion, aid in forming the judgment; that the perusal of all excellent books is, as it were, to interview with the noblest men of past ages, who have written them, and even a studied interview, in which are discovered to us only their choicest thoughts; that eloquence has incomparable force and beauty; that poesy has its ravishing graces and delights; that in the mathematics there are many refined discoveries eminently suited to gratify the inquisitive, as well as further all the arts and lessen the labour of man; that numerous highly useful precepts and exhortations to virtue are contained in treatises on morals; that theology points out the path to heaven; that philosophy affords the means of discoursing with an appearance of truth on all matters, and commands the admiration of the more simple; that jurisprudence, medicine, and the other sciences, secure for their cultivators honours and riches; and, in fine, that it is useful to bestow some attention upon all, even upon those abounding the most in superstition and error that we may be in a position to determine their real value and guard against being deceived.

But I believed that I had already given sufficient time to languages, and likewise to the reading of the writings of the ancients, to their histories and fables. For to hold converse with those of other ages and to travel, are almost the same thing. It is useful to know something of the manners of different nations, that we may be enabled to form a more correct judgment regarding our own, and be prevented from thinking that everything contrary to our customs is ridiculous and irrational,—a conclusion usually come to by those whose experience has been limited to their own country. On the other hand, when too much time is occupied in travelling, we become strangers to our native country; and the over curious in the customs of the past are generally ignorant of those of the present. Besides, fictitious narratives lead us to imagine the possibility of many events that are impossible; and even the most faithful histories, if they do not wholly misrepresent matters, or exaggerate their importance to render the account of them more worthy of perusal, omit, at least, almost always the meanest and least striking of the attendant circumstances; hence it happens that the remainder does not represent the truth, and that such as regulate their conduct by examples drawn from this source, are apt to fall into the extravagances of the knight-errants of romance, and to entertain projects that exceed their powers.

I esteemed eloquence highly, and was in raptures with poesy; but I thought that both were gifts of nature rather than fruits of study. Those in whom the faculty of reason is predominant, and who most skillfully dispose their thoughts with a view to render them clear and intelligible, are always the best able to persuade others of the truth of what they lay down, though they should speak only in the language of Lower Brittany, and be wholly ignorant of the rules of rhetoric; and those whose minds are stored with the most agreeable fancies, and who can give expression to them with the greatest embellishment and harmony, are still the best poets, though unacquainted with the art of poetry.

I was especially delighted with the mathematics, on account of the certitude and evidence of their reasonings; but I had not as yet a precise knowledge of their true use; and thinking that they but contributed to the advancement of the mechanical arts, I was astonished that foundations, so strong and solid, should have had no loftier superstructure reared on them. On the other hand, I compared the disquisitions of the ancient moralists to very towering and magnificent palaces with no better foundation than sand and mud: they laud the virtues very highly, and exhibit them as estimable far above anything on earth; but they give us no adequate criterion of virtue, and frequently that which they designate with so fine a name is but apathy, or pride, or despair, or parricide.

I revered our theology, and aspired as much as any one to reach heaven: but being given assuredly to understand that the way is not less open to the most ignorant than to the most learned, and that the revealed truths which lead to heaven are above our comprehension, I did not presume to subject them to the impotency of my reason; and I thought that in order competently to undertake their examination, there was need of some special help from heaven, and of being more than man.

Of philosophy I will say nothing, except that when I saw that it had been cultivated for many ages by the most distinguished men, and that yet there is not a single matter within its sphere which is not still in dispute, and nothing, therefore, which is above doubt, I did not presume to anticipate that my success would be greater in it than that of others; and further, when I considered the number of conflicting opinions touching a single matter that may be upheld by learned men; while there can be but one true, I reckoned as well-nigh false all that was only probable.

As to the other sciences, inasmuch as these borrow their principles from philosophy, I judged that no solid superstructures could be reared on foundations so infirm; and neither the honour nor the gain held out by them was sufficient to determine me to their cultivation: for I was not, thank Heaven, in a condition which compelled me to make merchandise of science for the bettering of my fortune; and though I might not profess to scorn glory as a cynic, I yet made very slight account of that honour which I hoped to acquire only through fictitious titles. And, in fine, of false sciences I thought I knew the worth sufficiently to escape being deceived by the professions of an alchemist, the predictions of an astrologer, the impostures of a magician, or by the artifices and boasting of any of those who profess to know things of which they are ignorant.

For these reasons, as soon as my age permitted me to pass from under the control of my instructors, I entirely abandoned the study of letters, and resolved no longer to seek any other science than the knowledge of myself, or of the great book of the world. I spent the remainder of my youth in travelling, in visiting courts and armies, in holding intercourse with men of different dispositions and ranks, in collecting varied experience, in providing myself in the different situations into which fortune threw me, and, above all, in making such reflection on the matter of my experience as to secure my improvement. For it occurred to me that I should find much more truth in the reasonings of each individual with reference to the affairs in which he is personally interested, and the issue of which must presently punish him if he has judged amiss, than in those conducted by a man of letters in his study, regarding speculative matters that are of no practical moment, and followed by no consequences to himself, farther, perhaps, than that they foster his vanity the better the more remote they are from common sense; requiring, as they must in this case, the exercise of greater ingenuity and art to render them probable. In addition, I had always a most earnest desire to know how to distinguish the true from the false, in order that I might be able clearly to discriminate the right path in life, and proceed in it with confidence.

It is true that, while busied only in considering the manners of other men, I found here, too, scarce any ground for settled conviction, and remarked hardly less contradiction among them than in the opinions of the philosophers. So that the greatest advantage I derived from the study consisted in this, that, observing many things which, however extravagant and ridiculous to our apprehension, are yet by common consent received and approved by other great nations, I learned to entertain too decided a belief in regard to nothing of the truth of which I had been persuaded merely by example and custom; and thus I gradually extricated myself from many errors powerful enough to darken our natural intelligence, and incapacitate us in great measure from listening to reason. But after I had been occupied several years in thus studying the book of the world, and in essaying to gather some experience, I at length resolved to make myself an object of study, and to employ all the powers of my mind in choosing the paths I ought to follow, an undertaking which was accompanied with greater success than it would have been had I never quitted my country or my books. . . .

I had become aware, even so early as during my college life, that no opinion, however absurd and incredible, can be imagined, which has not been maintained by some one of the philosophers and afterwards in the course of my travels I remarked that all those whose opinions are decidedly repugnant to ours are not on that account barbarians and savages, but on the contrary that many of these nations make an equally good, if not a better, use of their reason than we do. I took into account also the very different character which a person brought up from infancy in France or Germany exhibits, from that which, with the same mind originally, this individual would have possessed had he lived always among the Chinese or with savage, and the circumstance that in dress itself the fashion which pleased us ten years ago, and which may again, perhaps, be received into favour before ten years have gone, appears to us at this moment extravagant and ridiculous. I was thus led to infer that the ground of our opinions is far more custom and example than any certain knowledge. And, finally, although such be the ground of our opinions. I remarked that a plurality of suffrages is no guarantee of truth where it is at all of difficult discovery, as in such cases it is much more likely that it will be found by one than by many. I could, however, select from the crowd no one whose opinions seemed worthy of preference, and thus I found myself constrained, as it were, to use my own reason in the conduct of my life.

But like one walking alone and in the dark, I resolved to proceed so slowly and with such circumspection, that if I did not advance far, I would at least guard against falling. I did not even choose to dismiss summarily any of the opinions that had crept into my belief without having been introduced by reason, but first of all took sufficient time carefully to satisfy myself of the general nature of the task I was setting myself, and ascertain the true method by which to arrive at the knowledge of whatever lay within the compass of my powers.

Among the branches of philosophy, I had, at an earlier period, given some attention to logic, and among those of the mathematics to geometrical analysis and algebra,—three arts or sciences which ought, as I conceived, to contribute something to my design. But, on examination, I found that, as for logic, its syllogisms and the majority of its other percepts are of avail rather in the communication of what we already know, or even as the art of Lully, in speaking without judgment of things of which we are ignorant, than in the investigation of the unknown; and although this science contains indeed a number of correct and very excellent percepts, there are, nevertheless, so many others, and these either injurious or superfluous, mingled with the former, that it is almost quite as difficult to effect a severance of the true from the false as it is to extract a Diana or a Minerva from a rough block of marble. Then as to the analysis of the ancients and the algebra of the moderns, besides that they embrace only matters highly abstract, and, to appearance, of no use, the former is so exclusively restricted to the consideration of figures, that it can exercise the understanding only on condition of greatly fatiguing the imagination; and, in the latter, there is so complete a subjection to certain rules and formulas, that there results an art full of confusion and obscurity calculated to embarrass, instead of a science fitted to cultivate the mind. By these considerations I was induced to seek some other method which would comprise the advantages of the three and be exempt from their defects. And as a multitude of laws often only hampers justice, so that a state is best governed when, with few laws, these are rigidly administered; in like manner, instead of the great number of percepts of which logic is composed, I believed that the four following would prove perfectly sufficient for me, provided I took the firm and unwavering resolution never in a single instance to fail in observing them.

The *first* was never to accept anything for true which I did not clearly know to be such; that is to say, carefully to avoid precipitancy and prejudice, and to comprise nothing more in my judgment than what was presented to my mind so clearly and distinctly as to exclude all ground of doubt.

The *second*, to divide each of the difficulties under examination into as many parts as possible, and as might be necessary for its adequate solution.

The *third*, to conduct my thoughts in such order that by commencing with objects the simplest and easiest to know, I might ascend by little and little, and as it were, step by step, to the knowledge of the more complex assigning in thought a certain order even to those objects which in their own nature do not stand in a relation of antecedence and sequence.

And the *last*, in every case to make enumerations so complete, and reviews so general, that I might be assured that nothing was omitted.

The long chains of simple and easy reasoning by means of which geometers are accustomed to reach the conclusions of their most difficult demonstrations, had led me to imagine that all things, to the knowledge of which man is competent, are mutually connected in the same way, and that there is nothing so far removed from us as to be beyond our reach, or so hidden that we cannot discover it, provided only we abstain from accepting the false for the true, and always preserve in our thoughts the order necessary for the deduction of one truth from another. And I had little difficulty in determining the objects with which it was necessary to commence, for I was already persuaded that it must be with the simplest and easiest to know, and, considering that of all those who have hitherto sought truth in the sciences, the mathematicians alone have been able to find any demonstrations, that is, any certain and evident reasons, I did not doubt that such must have been the rule of their investigations. I resolved to commence, therefore, with the examination of the simplest objects, not anticipating, however, from this any other advantage than that to be found in accustoming my mind to the love and nourishment of truth, and to a distaste for all such reasonings as were unsound. But I had no intention on that account of attempting to master all the particular sciences commonly denominated mathematics: but observing that however different their objects, they all agree in considering only the various relations or proportions subsisting among those objects, I thought it best for my purpose to consider these proportions in the most general form possible, without referring them to any objects in particular, except such as would most facilitate the knowledge of them, and without by any means restricting them to these, that afterwards I might thus be the better able to apply them to every other class of objects to which they are legitimately applicable. Perceiving further, that in order to understand these relations I should sometimes have to consider them one by one, and sometimes only to bear them in mind, or embrace them in the aggregate, I thought that, in order the better to consider them individually, I should view them as subsisting between straight lines, than which I could find no objects more simple, or capable of being more distinctly represented to my imagination and senses; and on the other hand, that in order to retain them in the memory, or embrace an aggregate of many, I should express them by certain characters the briefest possible. In this way I believed that I could borrow all that was best both in geometrical analysis and in algebra, and correct all the defects of the one by help of the other.

And, in point of fact, the accurate observance of these few percepts gave me, I take the liberty of saying, such ease in unravelling all the questions embraced in these two sciences, that in the two or three months I devoted to their examination, not only did I reach solutions of questions I had formerly deemed exceedingly difficult, but even as regards questions of the solution of which I continued ignorant, I was enabled, as it appeared to me, to determine the means whereby, and the extent to which, a solution was possible; results attributable to the circumstance that I commenced with the simplest and most general truths, and that thus each truth discovered was a rule available in the discovery of subsequent ones. Nor in this perhaps shall I appear too vain, if it be considered that, as the truth on any particular point is one, whoever apprehends the truth, knows all that on that point can be known. The child, for example, who has been instructed in the elements of arithmetic, and has made a particular addition, according to rule, may be assured that he has found, with respect to the sum of the numbers before him, all that in this instance is within the reach of human genius. Now, in conclusion, the method which teaches adherence to the true order, and an exact enumeration of all the conditions of the thing sought includes all that gives certitude to the rules of arithmetic.

But the chief ground of my satisfaction with this method, was the assurance I had of thereby exercising my reason in all matters, if not with absolute perfection, at least with the greatest attainable by me: besides, I was conscious that by its use my mind was becoming gradually habituated to clearer and more distinct conceptions of its objects; and I hoped also, from not having restricted this method to any particular matter, to apply it to the difficulties of the other sciences, with not less success than to those of algebra. I should not, however, on this account have ventured at once on the examination of all the difficulties of the sciences which presented themselves to me, for this would have been contrary to the order prescribed in the method, but observing that the knowledge of such is dependent on principles borrowed from philosophy, in which I found nothing certain, I thought it necessary first of all to endeavour to establish its principles. And because I observed, besides, that an inquiry of this kind was of all others the greatest moment, and one in which precipitancy and anticipation in judgment were most to be dreaded, I thought that I ought not to approach it till I had reached a more mature age (being at that time but twenty-three), and had first of all employed much of my time in preparation for the work, as well by eradicating from my mind all the erroneous opinions I had up to that moment accepted, as by amassing variety of experience to afford materials for my reasonings, and by continually exercising myself in my chosen method with a view to increased skill in its application.

PART IV

I am in doubt as to the propriety of making my first meditations in the place above mentioned matter of discourse; for these are so metaphysical, and so uncommon, as not, perhaps, to be acceptable to every one. And yet, that it may be determined whether the foundations that I have laid are sufficiently secure, I find myself in a measure constrained to advert to them. I had long before remarked that, in relation to practice, it is sometimes necessary to adopt, as if above doubt, opinions which we discern to be highly uncertain, as has been already said; but as I then desired to give my attention solely to the search after truth, I thought that a procedure exactly the opposite was called for, and that I ought to reject as absolutely false all opinions in regard to which I could suppose the least ground for doubt, in order to ascertain whether after that there remained aught in my belief that was wholly indubitable. Accordingly, seeing that our senses sometimes deceive us, I was willing to suppose that there existed nothing really such as they presented to us; and because some men err in reasoning, and fall into paralogisms, even on the simplest matters of geometry, I, convinced that I was as open to error as any other, rejected as false all the reasonings I had hitherto taken for demonstrations; and finally, when I considered that the very same thoughts (presentations) which we experience when awake may also be experienced when we are asleep, while there is at that time not one of them true, I supposed that all the objects (presentations) that had ever entered into my mind when awake, had in them no more truth than the illusions of my dreams. But immediately upon this I observed that, whilst I thus wished to think that all was false, it was absolutely necessary that I, who thus thought, should be somewhat; and as I observed that this truth, *I think [therefore] I am* [*cogito ergo sum*], was so certain and of such evidence, that no ground of doubt, however extravagant, could be alleged by the sceptics capable of shaking it, I concluded that I might, without scruple, accept it as the first principle of the philosophy of which I was in search.

In the next place, I attentively examined what I was, and as I observed that I could suppose that I had no body, and that there was no world nor any place in which I might be; but that I could not therefore suppose that I was not; and that, on the contrary, from the very circumstance that I thought to doubt of the truth of other things, it most clearly and certainly followed that I was; while, on the other hand, if I had only ceased to think, although all the other objects which I had ever imagined had been in reality existent, I would have had no reason to believe that I existed; I thence concluded that I was a substance whose whole essence or nature consists only in thinking, and which, that it may exist, has need of no place, nor is dependent on any material thing; so that "I," that is to say, the mind by which I am what I am, is wholly distinct from the body, and is even more easily known than the latter, and is such, that although the latter were not, it would still continue to be all that it is.

After this I inquired in general into what is essential to the truth and certainty of a proposition; for since I had discovered one which I knew to be true, I thought that I must likewise be able to discover the ground of this certitude. And as I observed that in the words *I think, hence I am*, there is nothing at all which gives me assurance of their truth beyond this, that I see very clearly that in order to think it is necessary to exist, I concluded that I might take, as a general rule, the principle, that all the things which we very clearly and distinctly conceive are true, only observing, however, that there is some difficulty in rightly determining the objects which we distinctly conceive.

In the next place, from reflecting on the circumstance that I doubted, and that consequently my being was not wholly perfect (for I clearly saw that it was a greater perfection to know than to doubt), I was led to inquire whence I had learned to think of something more perfect than myself; and I clearly recognised that I must hold this notion from some nature which in reality was more perfect. As for the thoughts of many other objects external to me, as of the sky, the earth, light, heat, and a thousand more, I was less at a loss to know whence these came; for since I remarked in them nothing which seemed to render them superior to myself, I could believe that, if these were true, they were dependencies on my own nature, in so far as it possessed a certain perfection, and, if they were false, that I held them from nothing, that is to say, that they were in me because of a certain imperfection of my nature. But this could not be the case with the idea of a nature more perfect than myself; for to receive it from nothing was a thing manifestly impossible; and, because it is not less repugnant that the more perfect should be an effect of, and dependence on the less perfect, than that something should proceed from nothing, it was equally impossible that I could hold it from myself: accordingly, it but remained that it had been placed in me by a nature which was in reality more perfect than mine, and which even possessed within itself all the perfections of which I could form any idea; that is to say, in a single word, which was God. . . .

John Locke

In the opinion of Thomas Jefferson, three men—Francis Bacon, Isaac Newton, and John Locke—were the greatest of the great men who had ever lived. This, of course, reflected Jefferson's commitment to the Enlightenment values that they did so much to further. The reputation of Locke (1632-1704) rested on two great books, his *Second Treatise of Government* and his *Essay Concerning Human Understanding*, which is excerpted here. Locke spent seventeen years pondering what questions the human understanding was capable of addressing. His great epistemological answer laid the foundation of the Anglo-American empirical tradition with its assertion that all babies are born with blank minds which their senses then fill up. In his *Second Treatise*, Locke argued that all men were endowed with natural rights that reason prompted them to secure with a mutual contract establishing government. In his *Essay*, he demonstrated philosophically the impact of the environment, a lesson that soon became linked to the idea of progress. Both masterpieces, these works shared the unusual fate of pushing political thought and philosophy in radical directions that were hardly imaginable before their time.

JOHN LOCKE
(1690)

Essay

Concerning

Human Understanding

BOOK I:

ON INNATE NOTIONS
Chapter I: Introduction

Sect. 1. *An inquiry into the understanding, pleasant and useful.*—Since it is the understanding that sets man above the rest of sensible beings, and gives him all the advantage and dominion which he has over them; it is certainly a subject, even from its nobleness, worth our labour to inquire into. The understanding, like the eye, whilst it makes us see and perceive all other things, takes no notice of itself; and it requires art and pains to set it at a distance, and make it its own object. But whatever be the difficulties that lie in the way of this inquiry, whatever it be that keeps us so much in the dark to ourselves, sure I am, that all the light we can let in upon our own minds, all the acquaintance we can make with our own understandings, will not only be very pleasant, but bring great advantages, in directing our thoughts in the search of other things.

Sect. 2. *Design*—This, therefore, being my purpose, to inquire into the original, certainty, and extent of human knowledge, together with the grounds and degrees of belief, opinion, and assent; I shall not at present meddle with the physical consideration of the mind, or trouble myself to examine wherein its essence consists, or by what motions of our spirits, or alterations of our bodies, we come to have any sensation by our organs, or any ideas in our understandings; and whether those ideas do, in their formation, any, or all of them, depend on matter or no: these are speculations, which, however curious and entertaining, I shall decline, as lying,

Hayes and Zell, Philadelphia, 1860, I: pp. 1–3; IV: pp. 411–36.

out of my way, in the design I am now upon. It shall suffice to my present purpose, to consider the discerning faculties of a man, as they are employed about the objects which they have to do with: and I shall imagine I have not wholly misemployed myself in the thoughts I shall have on this occasion, if, in this historical, plain method, I can give any account of the ways whereby our understandings come to attain those notions of things we have, and can set down any measures of the certainty of our knowledge, or the grounds of those persuasions, which are to be found amongst men, so various, different, and wholly contradictory; and yet asserted somewhere or other with such assurance and confidence, that he that shall take a view of the opinions of mankind, observe their opposition, and at the same time consider the fondness and devotion wherewith they are embraced, the resolution and eagerness wherewith they are maintained, may perhaps have reason to suspect, that either there is no such thing as truth at all, or that mankind hath no sufficient means to attain a certain knowledge of it.

Sect. 3. *Method*—It is, therefore, worth while to search out the bounds between opinion and knowledge; and examine by what measures, in things, whereof we have no certain knowledge, we ought to regulate our assent, and moderate our persuasions. In order whereunto, I shall pursue this following method.

First, I shall inquire into the original of those ideas, notions, or whatever else you please to call them, which a man observes, and is conscious to himself he has in his mind; and the ways whereby the understanding comes to be furnished with them.

Secondly, I shall endeavour to show what knowledge the understanding hath by those ideas; and the certainty, evidence, and extent of it.

Thirdly, I shall make some inquiry into the nature and grounds of faith or opinion; whereby I mean that assent which we give to any proposition as true, of whose truth yet we have no certain knowledge: and here we shall have occasion to examine the reasons and degrees of assent.

Sect. 4. *Useful to know the extent of our comprehension*—If, by this inquiry into the nature of the understanding, I can discover the powers thereof, how far they reach, to what things they are in any degree proportionate, and where they fail us; I suppose it may be of use to prevail with the busy mind of man to be more cautious in meddling with things exceeding its comprehension; to stop when it is at the utmost extent of its tether; and to sit down in a quiet ignorance of those things, which, upon examination, are found to be beyond the reach of our capacities. We should not then, perhaps, be so forward, out of an affectation of a universal knowledge, to raise questions, and perplex ourselves and others with disputes about things to which our understandings are not suited, and of which we cannot frame in our minds any clear or distinct perceptions, or whereof (as it has, perhaps, too often happened) we have not any notions at all. If we can find out how far the understanding can extend its views, how far it has faculties to attain certainty, and in what cases it can only judge and guess, we may learn to content ourselves with what is attainable by us in this state.

Sect. 5. *Our capacity suited to our state and concerns*—For, though the comprehension of our understandings comes exceeding short of the vast extent of things, yet we shall have cause enough to magnify the bountiful Author of our being, for that proportion and degree of knowledge he has bestowed on us, so far above all the rest of the inhabitants of this our mansion. Men have reason to be well satisfied with what God hath thought fit for them, since he has given them (as St. Peter says) . . . whatsoever is necessary for the conveniences of life, and information of virtue, and has put within the reach of their discovery the comfortable provision for this life, and the way that leads to a better. How short soever their knowledge may come of an universal or perfect comprehension of whatsoever is, it yet secures their great concernments, that they have light enough to lead them to the knowledge of their Maker, and the sight of their own duties. Men may find matter sufficient to busy their heads, and employ their hands with variety, delight, and satisfaction, if they will not boldly quarrel with their own constitution, and throw away the blessings their hands are filled with, because they are not big enough to grasp every thing. We shall not have much reason to complain of the narrowness of our minds, if we will but employ them about what may be of use to us; for of that they are very capable; and it will be an unpardonable, as well as childish peevishness, if we undervalue the advantages of our knowledge, and neglect to improve it to the ends for which it was given us, because there are some things that are set out of the reach of it. It will be no excuse to an idle and untoward servant, who would not attend his business by candlelight, to plead that he had not broad sunshine. The candle that is set up in us, shines bright enough for all our purposes. The discoveries we can make with this, ought to satisfy us, and we shall then use our understanding right, when we entertain all objects in that way and proportion that they are suited to our faculties, and upon those grounds they are capable of being proposed to us; and not peremptorily or intemperately require demonstration, and demand certainty, where probability only is to be had, and which is sufficient to govern all our concernments. If we will disbelieve every thing, because we cannot certainly know all things, we shall do much-what as wisely as he, who would not use his legs, but sit still and perish, because he had no wings to fly.

Sect. 6. *Knowledge of our capacity a cure of scepticism and idleness.*—When we know our own strength, we shall the better know what to undertake with hopes of success; and when we have well surveyed the powers of our own minds, and made some estimate what we may expect from them, we shall not be inclined either to sit still, and not set our thoughts on work at all, in despair of knowing any thing; or, on the other side, question every thing, and disclaim all knowledge, because some things are not to be understood. It is of great use to the sailor to know the length of his line, though he cannot with it fathom all the depths of the ocean. It is well he knows that it is long enough to reach the bottom, at such places as are necessary to direct his voyage, and caution him against running upon shoals that may ruin him. Our business here is not to know all things, but those which concern our conduct. If we can find out those measures where by a rational creature, put in that state in which man is in, in this world, may and ought to govern his opinions, and actions depending thereon, we need not to be troubled that some other things escape our knowledge.

Sect. 7. *Occasion of this essay.*—This was that which gave the first rise to this essay concerning the understanding. For I thought that the first step towards satisfying several inquiries the mind of man was very apt to run into, was to take a survey of our own understanding, examine our own powers, and see to what things they were adapted. Till that was done, I suspected we began at the wrong end, and in vain sought for satisfaction in a quiet and sure possession of truths that most concerned us, whilst we let loose our thoughts into the vast ocean of being; as if all that boundless extent were the natural and unbounded possession of our understandings, wherein there was nothing exempt from its decisions, or that escaped its comprehension. Thus men, extending their inquiries beyond their capacities, and letting their thoughts wander into those depths where they can find no sure footing, it is no wonder that they raise questions, and multiply disputes, which, never coming to any clear resolution, are proper only to continue and increase their doubts and to confirm them at last in perfect scepticism. Whereas, were the capacities of our understandings well considered, the extent of our knowledge discovered, and the horizon found, which sets the bounds between the enlightened and dark parts of things, between what is and what is not comprehensible by us; men would, perhaps, with less scruple acquiesce in the avowed ignorance of the one, and employ their thoughts and discourse with more advantage and satisfaction in the other. . . .

BOOK IV

OF KNOWLEDGE AND OPINION
Chapter XII: Of the Improvement of Our Knowledge

Sect. 1. *Knowledge is not from maxims.*—It having been the common received opinion among men of letters, that maxims were the foundation of all knowledge; and that the sciences were each of them built upon certain *praecognita*, from whence the understanding was to take its rise, and by which it was to conduct itself, in its inquiries into the matters belonging to that science; the beaten road of the schools has been, to lay down in the beginning one or more general propositions, as foundations whereon to build the knowledge that was to be had of that subject. These doctrines, thus laid down for foundations of any science, were called principles, as the beginnings from which we must set out, and look no farther backwards in our inquiries, as we have already observed.

Sect. 2. *(The occasion of that opinion).*—One thing which might probably give an occasion in this way of proceeding in other sciences, was (as I suppose) the good success it seemed to have in mathematics, wherein men being observed to attain a great certainty of knowledge, these sciences came by pre-eminence to be called . . . learning, or things learned, thoroughly learned, as having of all others the greatest certainty, clearness, and evidence in them.

Sect. 3. *But from the comparing clear and distinct ideas.*—But if any one will consider, he will (I guess) find, that the great advancement and certainty of real knowledge, which men arrived to in these sciences, was not owing to the influence of these principles, nor derived from any peculiar advantage they received from two or three general maxims, laid down in the beginning; but from the clear, distinct, complete ideas their thoughts were employed about, and the relation of equality and excess so clear between some of them, that they had an intuitive knowledge, and by that a way to discover it in others, and this without the help of those maxims. For I ask is it not possible for a young lad to know, that his whole body is bigger than his little finger, but by virtue of this axiom, that the whole is bigger than a part; nor be assured of it, till he has learned that maxim? Or cannot a country wench know, that having received a shilling from one that owes her three, and a shilling also from another that owes her three, the remaining debts in each of their hands are equal? Cannot she know this, I say, unless she fetch the certainty of it from this maxim, that if you take equals from equals, the remainder will be equals, a maxim which possibly she never heard or thought of? I desire any one to consider, from what has been elsewhere said, which is known first and clearest by most people, the particular instance, or the general rule; and which it is that gives life and birth to the other. These general rules are but the comparing our more general and abstract ideas, which are the workmanship of the mind made, and names given to them, for the easier despatch in its reasonings, and drawing into comprehensive terms, and short rules, its various and multiplied observations. But knowledge began in the mind, and was founded on particulars; though afterward, perhaps no notice be taken thereof: it being natural for the mind (forward still to enlarge its knowledge) most attentively to lay up those general notions, and make the proper use of them, which is to disburden the memo of the cumbersome load of particulars....

Sect. 4. *Dangerous to build upon precarious principles.*—That which I have here to do, is to inquire, whether if it be the readiest way to knowledge to begin with general maxims, and build upon them, it be yet a safe way to take the principles which are laid down in any other science as unquestionable truths; and so receive them without examination, and adhere to them, without suffering them to be doubted of, because mathematicians have been so happy of the fair, to use none but self-evident and undeniable. If this be so, I know not what may not pass for truth in morality, what may not be introduced and proved in natural philosophy.

Let that principle of some of the philosophers, that all is matter, and that there is nothing else, be received for certain and indubitable, and it will be easy to be seen, by the writings of some that have revived it again in our days, what consequences it will lead us into. Let any one, with Polemo, take the world; or with the stoics, the aether, or the sun; or with Anaximenes, the air, to be God; and what a divinity, religion, and worship must we needs have! Nothing can be so dangerous as principles thus taken up without questioning or examination; especially if they be such as concern morality, which influence men's lives, and give a bias to all their actions. Who might not justly expect another kind of life in Aristippus, who placed happiness in bodily pleasure; and in Antistheases, who made virtue sufficient to felicity? And he who, with Plato, shall place beatitude in the knowledge of God, will have his thoughts raised to other contemplations than those who look not beyond this spot of earth, and those perishing things which are to be had in it. He that, with Archelaus, shall lay it down as a principle, that right and wrong, honest and dishonest, are defined only by laws, and not by nature, will have other measures of moral rectitude and pravity than those who take it for granted, that we are under obligations antecedent to all human constitutions.

Sect. 5. *This is no certain way to truth.*—If therefore those that pass for principles are not certain (which we must have some way to know, that we may be able to distinguish them from those that are doubtful) but are only made so to us by our blind assent, we are liable to be misled by them; and instead of being guided into truth, we shall, by principles, be only confirmed in mistake and error.

Sect. 6. *But to compare clear complete ideas under steady names.*—But since the knowledge of the certainty of principles, as well as of all other truths, depends only upon the perception we have of the agreement or disagreement of our ideas, the way to improve our knowledge is not, I am sure, blindly, and with an implicit faith, to receive and swallow principles; but is, I think, to get and fix in our minds clear, distinct, and complete ideas, as far as they are to be had, and annex to them proper and constant names. And thus, perhaps, without any other principles but barely considering those ideas, and by comparing them one with another, finding their agreement and disagreement, and their several relations and habitudes; we shall get more true and clear knowledge, by the conduct of this one rule, than by taking up principles, and thereby putting our minds into the disposal of others.

Sect. 7. *The true method of advancing in knowledge is by considering our abstract ideas.*—We must, therefore, if we will proceed as reason advises, adapt our methods of inquiry to the nature of the ideas we examine, and the truth we search after. General and certain truths are only founded in the habitudes and relations of abstract ideas. A sagacious and methodical application of our thoughts, for the finding out these relations, is the only way to discover all that can be put with truth and certainty concerning them into general propositions. By what steps we are to proceed in these is to be learned in the schools of the mathematicians, who from very plain and easy beginnings, by gentle degrees, and a continued chain of reasonings, proceed to the discovery and demonstration of truths, that appear at first sight beyond human capacity. The art of finding proofs, and the admirable methods they have invented for the singling out, and laying in order, those intermediate ideas that demonstratively show the equality or inequality of inapplicable quantities, is that which has carried them so far, and produced such wonderful and unexpected discoveries: but whether something like this, in respect of other ideas, as well as those of magnitude, may not in time be found out, I will not determine. This, I think, I may say, that if other ideas, that are the real as well as nominal essences of their species were pursued in the way familiar to mathematicians, they would carry our, thoughts farther, and with greater evidence and clearness, than possibly we are apt to imagine.

Sect. 8. *By which morality also may be made clearer.*—This gave me the confidence to advance that conjecture ... that morality is capable of demonstration as well as mathematics. For the ideas that ethics are conversant about being all real essences, and such as I imagine have a discoverable connexion and agreement one with another: so far as we can find their habitudes and relations, so far we shall be possessed of certain real and general truths; and I doubt not, but, if a right method were taken, a great part of morality might be made out with that clearness, that could leave, to a considering man, no more reason to doubt, than he could have to doubt of the truth of propositions in mathematics, which have been demonstrated to him.

Sect. 9. *But knowledge of bodies is to be improved only by experience.*—In our search after the knowledge of substances, our want of ideas, that are suitable to such a way of proceeding, obliges us to a quite different method. We advance not here, as in the other (where our abstract ideas are real as well as nominal essences) by contemplating our ideas, and considering their relations and correspondences; that helps us very little, for the reasons that, in another place, we have at large set down. By which I think it is evident, that substances afford matter of very little general knowledge; and the bare contemplation of their abstract ideas will carry us but a very little way in the search of truth and certainty. What then are we to do for the improvement of our knowledge in substantial beings? Here we are to take quite a contrary course; the want of ideas of their real essences sends us from our own thoughts to the things themselves as they exist. Experience here must teach me what reason cannot: and it is by trying alone that I can certainly know what other qualities coexist with those of my complex idea. ...

Sect. 10. *This may procure us convenience, not science.*—I deny not but a man, accustomed to rational and regular experiments, shall be able to see farther into the nature of bodies, and guess righter at their yet unknown properties, than one that is a stranger to them: but yet, as I have said, this is but judgment and opinion, not knowledge and certainty. This way of getting and improving our knowledge in substances only by experience and history, which is all that the weakness of our faculties in this state of mediocrity we are in in this world can attain to, makes me suspect that natural philosophy is not capable of being made a science. We are able, I imagine, to reach very little general knowledge concerning the species of bodies, and their several properties. Experiments and historical observations we may have, from which we may draw advantages of case and health, and thereby increase our stock of conveniences for this life; but beyond this, I fear, our talents reach not, nor are our faculties, as I guess, able to advance.

Sect. 11. *We are fitted for moral knowledge and natural improvements.*—From whence it is obvious to conclude that since our faculties are not fitted to penetrate into the internal fabric and real essences of bodies; but yet plainly discover to us the being of a God, and the knowledge of ourselves, enough to lead us into a full and clear discovery of our duty and great concernment; it will become us, as rational creatures, to employ those faculties we have about what they are adapted to, and follow the direction of nature, where it seems to point us out the way. For it is rational to conclude that our employment lies in those inquiries, and in that sort of knowledge, which is most suited to our natural capacities, and carries in it our greatest interest, *i.e.* the condition of our eternal estate. Hence I think I may conclude, that morality is the proper science and business of mankind in general (who are both concerned and fitted to search out their *summum bonum*), as several arts, conversant about several parts of nature, are the lot and private talent of particular men, for the common use of human life, and their own particular subsistence in this world. Of what consequence the discovery of one natural body, and its properties, may be to human life, the whole great continent of America is a convincing instance; whose ignorance in useful arts, and want of the greatest part of the conveniences of life, in a country that abounded with all sorts of natural plenty, I think may be attributed to their ignorance of what was to be found in a very ordinary despicable stone, I mean the mineral of iron. And whatever we think of our parts or improvements in this part of the world, where knowledge and plenty seem to vie with each other; yet to any one that will seriously reflect on it, I suppose it will appear past doubt, that were the use of iron lost among us, we should in a few ages be unavoidably reduced to the wants and ignorance of the ancient saving Americans, whose natural endowments and provisions come no way short of those of the most flourishing and polite nations. So that he who first made known the use of that one contemptible mineral may be truly styled the father of arts, and author of plenty.

Sect. 12. *But must beware of hypothesis and wrong principles.*—I would not therefore be thought to disesteem or dissuade the study of nature. I readily agree the contemplation of his works gives us occasion to admire, revere, and glorify their Author: and, if rightly directed may be of greater benefit to mankind than the monuments of exemplary charity, that have at so great charge been raised by the founders of hospitals and almshouses. He that first invented printing, discovered the use of the compass, or made public the virtue and right use of kin kina, did more for the propagation of knowledge, for the supply and increase of useful commodities, and saved more from the grave, than those who built colleges, workhouses, and hospitals. All that I would say is, that we should not be too forwardly possessed with the opinion or expectation of knowledge, where it is not to be had, or by ways that will not attain to it; that we should not take doubtful systems for complete sciences, nor unintelligible notions for scientifical demonstrations. In the knowledge of bodies, we must be content to glean what we can from particular experiments; since we cannot, from a discovery of their real essences, grasp at a time whole sheaves, and in bundles comprehend the nature and properties of whole species together. . . .

Sect. 13. *The true use of hypotheses.*—Not that we may not, to explain any phenomena of nature, make use of any probable hypothesis whatsoever: hypotheses, if they are well made, are at least great helps to the memory, and often direct us to new discoveries. But my meaning is, that we should not take up any one too hastily (which the mind that would always penetrate into the causes of things, and have principles to rest on, is very apt to do til we have very well examined particulars, and made several experiments in that thing which we would explain by our hypothesis, and see whether it will agree to them all; whether our principles will carry us quite through, and not be as inconsistent with one phenomenon of nature as they seem to accommodate and explain another. And at least that we take care, that the name of principles deceive us not, nor impose on us, by making us receive that for an unquestionable truth which is really at best but a very doubtful conjecture, such as are most (I had almost said all) of the hypotheses in natural philosophy....

Chapter XVI: Of the Degrees of Assent

Sect. 4. *The right use of it, is mutual charity and forbearance.*—Since therefore it is unavoidable to the greatest part of men, if not all, to have several opinions without certain and indubitable proofs of their truth, and it carries too great an imputation of ignorance, lightness, or folly, for men to quit and renounce their former tenets presently upon the offer of an argument which they cannot immediately answer, and show the insufficiency of; it would methinks become all men to maintain peace, and the common offices of humanity and friendship, in the diversity of opinions; since we cannot reasonably expect that any one should readily and obsequiously quit his own opinion, and embrace ours with a blind resignation to an authority which the understanding of man acknowledges not. For however it may often mistake, it can own no other guide but reason, nor blindly submit to the will and dictates of another. If he, you would bring over to your sentiments, be one that examines before he assents, you must give him leave at his leisure to go over the account again, and, recalling what is out of his mind, examine all the particulars, to see on which side the advantage lies: and if he will not think our arguments of weight enough to engage him anew in so much pains, it is but what we often do ourselves in the like case; and we should take it amiss if others should prescribe to us what points we should study. And if he be one who takes his opinions upon trust, how can we imagine that he should renounce those tenets which time and custom have so settled in his mind, that he thinks them self-evident, and of an unquestionable certainty; or which he takes to be impressions he has received from God himself, or from men sent by him? How can we expect, I say, that opinions thus settled should be given up to the arguments or authority of a stranger or adversary; especially if there be any suspicion of interest or design, as there never fails to be where men find themselves ill treated? We should do well to commiserate our mutual ignorance, and endeavour to remove it in all the gentle and fair ways of information; and not instantly treat others ill, as obstinate and perverse, because they will not renounce their own, and receive our opinions; or at least those we would force upon them, when it is more than probable that we are no less obstinate in not embracing some of theirs. For where is the man that has incontestable evidence of the truth of all that he holds, or of the falsehood of all he condemns; or can say, that he has examined to the bottom of his own or other men's opinions? The necessity of believing without knowledge, may, often upon very slight grounds, in this fleeting state of action and blindness we are in, should make us more busy and careful to inform ourselves than constrain others. At least those who have not thoroughly examined to the bottom all their own tenets, must confess they are unfit to prescribe to others; and are unreasonable in imposing that as truth on other men's belief which they themselves have not searched into, nor weighted the arguments of probability on which they should receive or reject it. Those who have fairly and truly examined, and are thereby got past doubt in all the doctrines they profess and govern themselves by, would have a juster pretence to require others to follow them; but these are so few in number, and find so little reason to be magisterial in their opinions, that nothing insolent and imperious is to be expected from them; and there is reason to think that, if men were better instructed themselves, they would be less imposing on others. . . .

Sect. 9. *Experiences and testimonies clashing infinitely vary the degrees of probability.* . . . The difficulty is, when testimonies contradict common experience, and the reports of history and witnesses clash with the ordinary course of nature, or with one another; there it is where diligence, attention, and exactness are required, to form a right judgment, and to proportion, the assent to the different evidence and probability of the thing; which rises and falls according as those two foundations of credibility, viz., common observation in like cases, and particular, testimonies in that particular instance, favour or contradict it. These are liable to so great a variety of contrary observations, circumstances, report, different qualifications, tempers, designs, oversights, &c. of the reporters, that it is impossible to reduce to precise rules the various degrees wherein men give their assent. This only may be said in general, that as the arguments and proofs *pro* and *con.*, upon due examination, nicely weighing every particular circumstance, shall to any one appear upon the whole matter, in a greater or less degree to preponderate on either side: so they are fitted to produce in the mind such different entertainment as we call belief, conjecture, guess, doubt, wavering, distrust, disbelief, &c.

Sect. 10. *Traditional testimonies, the farther removed, the less their proofs.*—This is what concerns assent in matters wherein testimony is made use of: concerning which, I think, it may not, be amiss to take notice of a rule observed in the law of England; which is, that though the attested copy of a record be good proof, yet the copy of a copy, ever so well attested, and by ever so credible witnesses, will not be admitted as a proof in judicature. This is so generally approved as reasonable, and suited to the wisdom and caution to be used in our inquiry after material truths, that I never yet heard of any one that blamed it. This practice, if it be allowable in the decisions of right and wrong, carries this observation along with it, viz. that any testimony, the farther off it is from the original truth, the less force and proof it was. The being and existence of the thing itself is what I call the original truth. A credible man vouching his knowledge of it is a good proof: but if another equally credible do witness it from his report, the testimony is weaker; and a third that attests the hearsay of an hearsay, is yet less considerable. So that, in traditional truths, each remove weakens the force of the proof: and the more hands the tradition has successively passed through, the less strength and evidence does it receive from. This I thought necessary to be taken notice of, because I find among some men the quite contrary commonly practised, who look on opinions to gain force by growing older; and what a thousand years since would not, to a rational man, contemporary with the first voucher, have appeared at all probable, is now urged as certain beyond all question, only because several have since, from him, said it one after another. Upon this ground, propositions, evidently false, or doubtful enough in their first beginning, come by an inverted rule of probability, to pass for authentic truths; and those which found or deserved little credit from the months of their first authors, are thought to grow venerable by age, and are urged as undeniable.

Sect. 11. *Yet history is of great use.*—I would not be thought here to lessen the credit and use of history; it is all the light we have in many cases, and we receive from it a great part of the useful truths we have, with a convincing evidence. I think nothing more valuable than the records of antiquity; I wish we had more of them, and more uncorrupted. But this truth itself forces me to say, that no probability can arise higher than its first original. What has no other evidence than the single testimony of one only witness, must stand or fall by his only testimony, whether good, bad, or indifferent; and though cited afterward by hundreds of others, one after another, is so far from receiving any strength thereby, that it is only the weaker. Passion, interest, inadvertent, mistake of his meaning, and a thousand odd reasons, or capricios, men's minds are acted by (impossible to be discovered) may make one man quote another man's words or meaning wrong. He that has but ever so little examined the citations of writers cannot doubt how little credit the quotations deserve, where the originals are wanting; and consequently how much less quotations of quotations can be relied on. This is certain, that what in one age was affirmed upon slight grounds, can never after come to be more valid in future ages by being often repeated. But the farther still it is from the original, the less valid it is, and has always less force in the mouth or writing of him that last made use of it, than in his from whom he received it. . . .

Sect. 18. *Men not in so many errors as imagined.*—But notwithstanding the great noise made in the world about errors and opinions, I must do mankind that right as to say there are not so many men in errors and wrong opinions as is commonly supposed. Not that I think they embrace the truth; but, indeed, because concerning those doctrines they keep such a stir about, they have no thought, no opinion at all. For if any one should a little catechise the greatest part of the partizans of most of the sects in the world, he would not find, concerning those matters they are so zealous for, that they have any opinions of their own: much less would he have reason to think, that they took them upon the examination of arguments, and appearance of probability. They are resolved to stick to a party, that education or interest has engaged them in; and there, like the common soldiers of an army, show their courage and warmth as their leaders direct, without ever examining, or so much as knowing the cause they contend for. If a man's life shows that he has no serious regard for religion, for what reason should we think that he beats his head about the opinions of his church, and troubles himself to examine the grounds of this or that doctrine? It is enough for him to obey his leaders, to have his hand and his tongue ready for the support of the common cause, and thereby approve himself to those who can give him credit, preferment, or protection in that society. Thus men become professors of, and combatants for, those opinions they were never convinced of, nor proselytes to; no, nor ever had so much as floating in their heads; and though one cannot say, there are fewer improbable or erroneous opinions in the world than there are; yet it is certain, there are fewer that actually assent to them, and mistake them for truth, than is imagined.

Adam Smith

A professor of moral philosophy at the University of Glasgow, Adam Smith (1723–1790) wrote the first comprehensive account of the operation of the new market economy. His work displayed a system of thought that formulated general principles and identified a means to predict and understand collective human behavior. Smith's interpretation identifies the functioning of a constant, universal human nature operating at the level of the individual and links it to a larger aggregate effect. Human beings inherently disposed to trade and barter sought their self-interest in market bargains. Their profit-maximizing efforts were regulated not by well-crafted laws or the wisdom of magistrates, but rather through the competition of other profit-maximizing market participants. As Smith commented, it was not through the benevolence of the butcher and the baker that we got our good, cheap meat and bread, but rather through their own self-interested drive to secure as much trade for themselves as possible. In an equally indirect manner, Smith saw that it was the accumulation of savings that enabled ambitious manufacturers to reap the advantages of the division of labor. Though not restricted to mere profit motives and avarice, the general drive for self-improvement leads individuals to invest in ways that promote the highest, most efficient use of resources and the optimal functioning of the economy as a whole. Building on the example of the division of labor in a pin factory, and tying the significance of this division to the widening of the market and the cost advantages produced by competition, *The Wealth of Nations* (1776) applied reason and natural process in ways that made sense to the new, entrepreneurial classes in the industrializing Britain of Smith's time.

In this sense, *The Wealth of Nations* moved beyond both a study of the natural world and an emphasis on the individual to consider questions of government and human relations. Beneath the chaotic variation of human affairs, Smith found a larger sense of order in invisible social forces and unintended consequences. Smith's model for optimal economics does not eliminate poverty. Yet, despite the persistence of social inequality, the division of labor raises the standard of living for even the lowest classes. Unequal and unvirtuous, Smith's system nevertheless provided its own answer to the question of justice and invited governments to make laws that function in harmony with its principles. For Smith, knowledge, derived from an understanding of nature, invites men to accept the profound responsibility of shaping society accordingly.

ADAM SMITH
(1796)

An Inquiry
Into the Nature
and Causes of the
Wealth of Nations

INTRODUCTION AND PLAN OF THE WORK

The annual labour of every nation is the fund which originally supplies it with all the necessaries and conveniences of life which it annually consumes, and which consist always either in the immediate produce of that labour, or in what is purchased with that produce from other nations.

According therefore, as this produce, or what is purchased with it, bears a greater or smaller proportion to the number of those who are to consume it, the nation will be better or worse supplied with all the necessaries and conveniencies for which it has occasion.

But this proportion must in every nation be regulated by two different circumstances; first, by the skill, dexterity, and judgment with which its labour is generally applied; and, secondly, by the proportion between the number of those who are employed in useful labour, and that of those who are not so employed. Whatever be the soil, climate, or extent of territory of any particular nation, the abundance or scantiness of its annual supply must, in that particular situation, depend upon those two circumstances. . . .

Whatever be the actual state of the skill, dexterity, and judgment with which labour is applied in any nation, the abundance or scantiness of its annual supply must depend, during the continuance of that state, upon the proportion between the number of those who are annually employed in useful labour, and that of those who are not so employed. The number of useful and productive labourers, it will hereafter appear, is every where in proportion to the quantity

Wealth of Nations (London, A. Strahan and T. Cachell, 1796), Book I, pp. 5–17; Book II, pp. 1–30.

of capital stock which is employed in getting them to work, and to the particular way in which it is so employed.

OF THE DIVISION OF LABOR

The greatest improvement in the productive powers of labour, and the greater part of the skill, dexterity, and judgment with which it is any where directed, or applied, seem to have been the effects of the division of labour.

The effects of the division of labour, in the general business of society, will be more easily understood, by considering in what manner it operates in some particular manufactures. . . .

To take an example, therefore, from a very trifling manufacture; but one in which the division of labour has been very often taken notice of, the trade of the pin-maker; a workman not educated to this business (which the division of labour has rendered a distinct trade), nor acquainted with the use of the machinery employed in it (to the invention of which the same division of labour has probably given occasion), could scarce, perhaps, with his utmost industry, make one pin in a day, and certainly could not make twenty. But in the way in which this business is now carried on, not only the whole work is a peculiar trade, but it is divided into a number of branches, of which the greater part are likewise peculiar trades. One man draws out the wire, another straights it, a third cuts it, a fourth points it, a fifth grinds it at the top for receiving the head; to make the head requires two or three distinct operations; to put it on, is a peculiar business, to whiten the pins is another; it is even a trade by itself to put them into the paper; and the important business of making a pin is, in this manner, divided into about eighteen distinct operations, which, in some manufactories, are all performed by distinct hands, though in others the same man will sometimes perform two or three of them. I have seen a small manufactory of this kind where ten men only were employed, and where some of them consequently performed two or three distinct operations. But though they were very poor, and therefore but indifferently accommodated with the necessary machinery, they could, when they exerted themselves, make among them about twelve pounds of pins in a day. There are in a pound upwards of four thousand pins of a middling size. Those ten persons, therefore, could make among them upwards of forty-eight thousand pins in a day. Each person, therefore, making a tenth part of forty-eight thousand pins, might be considered as making four thousand eight hundred pins in a day. But if they had all wrought separately and independently, and without any of them having been educated to this peculiar business, they certainly could not each of them have made twenty, perhaps not one pin in a day; that is, certainly, not the two hundred and fortieth, perhaps not the four thousand eight hundredth part of what they are at present capable of performing, in consequence of a proper division and combination of their different operations.

In every other art and manufacture, the effects of the division of labour are similar to what they are in this very trifling one; though, in many of them, the labour can neither be so much subdivided, nor reduced to so great a simplicity of operation. The division of labour, however, so far as it can be introduced, occasions, in every art, a proportionable increase of the productive powers of labour. The separation of different trades and employments from one another, seems to have taken place, in consequence of this advantage. This separation too is generally carried furthest in those countries which enjoy the highest degree of industry and improvement; what is the work of one man in a rude state of society, being generally that of several in an improved one. In every improved society, the farmer is generally nothing but a farmer; the manufacturer, nothing but a manufacturer. The labour too which is necessary to produce any one complete manufacture, is almost always divided among a great number of hands. How many different trades are employed in each branch of the linen and woollen manufactures, from the growers of the flax and the wool, to the bleachers and smoothers of the linen, or to the dyers and dressers of the cloth! The nature of agriculture, indeed, does not admit of so many subdivisions of labour, nor of so complete a separation of one business from another, as manufactures. . . .

This great increase of the quantity of work, which, in consequence of the division of labour, the same number of people are capable of performing, is owing to three different circumstances; first, to the increase of dexterity in every particular workman; secondly, to the saving of the time which is commonly lost in passing from one species of work to another; and lastly, to the invention of a great number of machines which facilitate and abridge labour, and enable one man to do the work of many.

First, the improvement of the dexterity of the workman necessarily increases the quantity of the work he can perform; and the division of labour, by reducing every man's business to some one simple operation, and by making this operation the sole employment of his life, necessarily increases very much the dexterity of the workman. A common smith, who, though accustomed to handle the hammer, has never been used to make nails, if upon some particular occasion he is obliged to attempt it, will scarce, I am assured, be able to make above two or three hundred nails in a day, and those too very bad ones. A smith who has been accustomed to make nails, but whose sole or principal business has not been that of a nailer, can seldom with his utmost diligence make more than eight hundred or a thousand nails in a day. I have seen several boys under twenty years of age who had never exercised any other trade but that of making nails, and who, when they exerted themselves, could make, each of them, upwards of two thousand three hundred nails in a day. The making of a nail, however, is by no means one of the simplest operations. The same person blows the bellows, stirs or mends the fire as there is occasion, heats the iron, and forges every part of the nail: In forging the head too he is obliged to change his tools. The different operations into which the making of a pin, or of a metal button, is subdivided, are all of them much more simple, and the dexterity of the person, of whose life it has been the sole business to perform them, is usually much greater. The rapidity with which some of the operations of those manufactures are performed, exceeds what the human hand could, by those who had never seen them, be supposed capable of acquiring.

Secondly, the advantage which is gained by saving the time commonly lost in passing from one sort of work to another, is much greater than we should at first view be apt to imagine it. It is impossible to pass very quickly from one kind of work to another, that is carried on in a different place, and with quite different tools. A country weaver, who cultivates a small farm, must lose a good deal of time in passing from his loom to the field, and from the field to his loom. When the two trades can be carried on in the same workhouse, the loss of time is no doubt much less. It is even in this case, however, very considerable. A man commonly saunters a little in turning his hand from one sort of employment to another. When he first begins the new work he is seldom very keen and hearty; his mind, as they say, does not go to it, and for some time he rather trifles than applies to good purpose. The habit of sauntering and of indolent careless application, which is naturally, or rather necessarily acquired by every country workman who is obliged to change his work and his tools every half hour, and to apply his hand in twenty different ways almost every day of his life; renders him almost always slothful and lazy, and incapable of any vigorous application even on the most pressing occasions. Independent, therefore, of his deficiency in point of dexterity, this cause alone must always reduce considerably the quantity of work which he is capable of performing.

Thirdly, and lastly, every body must be sensible how much labour is facilitated and abridged by the application of proper machinery. It is unnecessary to give any example. I shall only observe, therefore, that the invention of all those machines by which labour is so much facilitated and abridged, seems to have been originally owing to the division of labour. Men are much more likely to discover easier and readier methods of attaining any object, when the whole attention of their minds is directed towards that single object, than when it is dissipated among a great variety of things. But in consequence of the division of labour, the whole of every man's attention comes naturally to be directed towards some one very simple object. It is naturally to be expected, therefore, that some one or other of those who are employed in each particular branch of labour should soon find out easier and readier methods of performing their own particular work, wherever the nature of it admits of such improvement. A great part of the machines made use of in those manufactures in which labour is most subdivided, were originally the inventions of common workmen, who, being each of them employed in some very simple operation, naturally turned their thoughts towards finding out earlier and readier methods of performing it. Whoever has been much accustomed to visit such manufactures, must frequently have been shewn very pretty machines, which were the inventions of such workmen, in order to facilitate and quicken their own particular part of the work. In the first fire-engines, a boy was constantly employed to open and shut alternately the communication between the boiler and the cylinder, according as the piston either ascended or descended. One of those boys, who loved to play with his companions, observed that, by tying a string from the handle of the valve which opened this communication to another part of the machine, the valve would open and shut without his assistance, and leave him at liberty to divert himself with his play-fellows. One of the greatest improvements that has been made upon this machine, since it was first invented, was in this manner the discovery of a boy who wanted to save his own labour.

All the improvements in machinery, however, have by no means been the inventions of those who had occasion to use the machines. Many improvements have been made by the ingenuity of the makers of the machines, when to make them became the business of a peculiar trade; and some by that of those who are called philosophers or men of speculation, whose trade it is not to do any thing, but to observe every thing; and who, upon that account, are often capable of combining together the powers of the most distant and dissimilar objects. In the progress of society, philosophy or speculation becomes, like every other employment, the principal or sole trade and occupation of a particular class of citizens. Like every other employment too, it is subdivided into a great number of different branches, each of which affords occupation to a peculiar tribe or class of philosophers; and this subdivision of employment in philosophy, as well as in every other business, improves dexterity, and saves time. Each individual becomes more expert in his own peculiar branch, more work is done upon the whole, and the quantity of science is considerably increased by it.

It is the great multiplication of the productions of all the different arts, in consequence of the division of labour, which occasions, in a well-governed society, that universal opulence which extends itself to the lowest ranks of the people. Every workman has a great quantity of his own work to dispose of beyond what he himself has occasion for; and every other workman being exactly in the same situation, he is enabled to exchange a great quantity of his own goods for a great quantity, or, what comes to the same thing, for the price of a great quantity of theirs. He supplies them abundantly with what they have occasion for, and they accommodate him as amply with what he has occasion for, and a general plenty diffuses itself through all the different ranks of the society.

Observe the accommodation of the most common artificer or day-labourer in a civilized and thriving country, and you will perceive that the number of people of whose industry a part, though but a small part, has been employed in procuring him this accommodation, exceeds all computation. The woollen coat, for example, which covers the day-labourer, as coarse and rough as it may appear, is the produce of the joint labour of a great multitude of workmen. The shepherd, the sorter of the wool, the wool-comber or carder, the dyer, the scribbler, the spinner, the weaver, the fuller, the dresser, with many others, must all join their different arts in order to complete even this homely production. How many merchants and carriers, besides, must have been employed in transporting the materials from some of those workmen to others who often live in a very distant part of the country! how much commerce and navigation in particular, how many ship-builders, sailors, sail-makers, rope-makers, must have been employed in order to bring together the different drugs made use of by the dyer, which often come from the remotest corners of the world! What a variety of labour too is necessary in order to produce the tools of the meanest of those workmen! To say nothing of such complicated machines.

BOOK II
Of the Accumulation of Capital, or of Productive and Unproductive Labour

There is one sort of labour which adds to the value of the subject upon which it is bestowed: there is another which has no such effect. The former, as it produces a value, may be called productive; the latter, unproductive labour. Thus the labour of a manufacturer adds, generally, to the value of the materials which he works upon, that of his own maintenance, and of his master's profit. The labour of a menial servant, on the contrary, adds to the value of nothing. Though the manufacturer has his wages advanced to him by his master, he, in reality, costs him no expence, the value of those wages being generally restored, together with a profit, in the improved value of the subject upon which his labour is bestowed. But the maintenance of a menial servant never is restored. A man grows rich by employing a multitude of manufacturers; he grows poor, by maintaining a multitude of menial servants. The labour of the latter, however, has its value, and deserves its reward as well as that of the former. But the labour of the manufacturer fixes and realizes itself in some particular subject or vendible commodity, which lasts for some time at least after that labour is past. It is, as it were, a certain quantity of labour stocked and stored up to be employed, if necessary, upon some other occasion. That subject, or what is the same thing, the price of that subject, can afterwards, if necessary, put into motion a quantity of labour equal to that which had originally produced it. The labour of the menial servant, on the contrary, does not fix or realize itself in any particular subject or vendible commodity. His services generally perish in the very instant of their performance, and seldom leave any trace or value behind them, for which an equal quantity of service could afterwards be procured.

The labour of some of the most respectable orders in the society is, like that of menial servants, unproductive of any value, and does not fix or realize itself in any permanent subject, or vendible commodity, which endures after that labour is past, and for which an equal quantity of labour could afterwards be procured. The sovereign, for example, with all the officers both of justice and war who serve under him, the whole army and navy, are unproductive labourers. They are the servants of the public, and are maintained by a part of the annual produce of the industry of other people. Their service, how honourable, how useful, or how necessary soever, produces nothing for which an equal quantity of service can afterwards be procured. The protection, security, and defence of the commonwealth, the effect of their labour this year, will not purchase its protection, security, and defence for the year to come. In the same class must be ranked, some both of the gravest and most important, and some of the most frivolous professions: churchmen, lawyers, physicians, men of letters of all kinds; players, buffoons, musicians, opera-singers, opera-dancers, &c. The labour of the meanest of these has a certain value, regulated by the very same principles which regulate that of every other sort of labour; and that of the noblest and most useful, produces nothing which could afterwards purchase or procure an equal quantity of labour. Like the declamation of the actor, the harangue of the orator, or the tune of the musician, the work of all of them perishes in the very instant of its production.

Both productive and unproductive labourers, and those who do not labour at all, are all equally maintained by the annual produce of the land and labour of the country. This produce, how great soever, can never be infinite, but must have certain limits. According, therefore, as a smaller or greater proportion of it is in any one year employed in maintaining unproductive hands, the more in the one case and the less in the other will remain for the productive, and the next year's produce will be greater or smaller accordingly; the whole annual produce, if we expect the spontaneous productions of the earth, being the effect of productive labour.

Though the whole annual produce of the land and labour of every country, is, no doubt, ultimately destined for supplying the consumption of its inhabitants, and for procuring a revenue to them; yet when it first comes either from the ground, or from the hands of the productive labourers, it naturally divides itself into two parts. One of them, and frequently the largest, is, in the first place, destined for replacing a capital, or for renewing the provisions, materials, and finished work, which had been withdrawn from a capital; the other for constituting a revenue either to the owner of this capital, as the profit of his stock; or to some other person, as the rent of his land. Thus, of the produce of land, one part replaces the capital of the farmer; the other pays his profit and the rent of the landlord; and thus constitutes a revenue both to the owner of this capital, as the profits of his stock; and to some other person, as the rent of his land. Of the produce of a great manufactory, in the same manner, one part, and that always the largest, replaces the capital of the undertaker of the work; the other pays his profit, and thus constitutes a revenue to the owner of this capital.

That part of the annual produce of the land and labour of any country which replaces a capital, never is immediately employed to maintain any but productive hands. It pays the wages of productive labour only. That which is immediately destined for constituting a revenue either as profit or as rent, may maintain indifferently either productive or unproductive hands.

Whatever part of his stock a man employs as a capital, he always expects is to be replaced to him with a profit. He employs it, therefore, in maintaining productive hands only; and after having served in the function of a capital to him, it constitutes a revenue to them. Whenever he employs any part of it in maintaining unproductive hands of any kind, that part is, from that moment, withdrawn from his capital, and placed in his stock reserved for immediate consumption.

Unproductive labourers, and those who do not labour at all, are all maintained by revenue; either, first, by that part of the annual produce which is originally destined for constituting a revenue to some particular persons, either as the rent of land or as the profits of stock; or, secondly, by that part which, though originally destined for replacing a capital and for maintaining productive labourers only, yet when it comes into their hands, whatever part of it is over and above their necessary subsistence, may be employed in maintaining indifferently either productive or unproductive hands.

Thus, not only the great landlord or the rich merchant, but even the common workman, if his wages are considerable, may maintain a menial servant; or he may sometimes go to a play or a puppet-show, and so contribute his share towards maintaining one set of unproductive labourers; or he may pay some taxes, and thus help to maintain another set, more honourable and useful, indeed, but equally unproductive. No part of the annual produce, however, which had been originally destined to replace a capital, is ever directed towards maintaining unproductive hands, till after it has put into motion its full complement of productive labour, or all that it could put into motion in the way in which it was employed. The workman must have earned his wages by work done, before he can employ any part of them in this manner. That part too is generally but a small one. It is his spare revenue only, of which productive labourers have seldom a great deal. They generally have some, however; and in the payment of taxes the greatness of their number may compensate, in some measure, the smallness of their contribution. The rent of land and the profits of stock are every-where, therefore, the principal sources from which unproductive hands derive their subsistence. These are the two sorts of revenue of which the owners have generally most to spare. They might both maintain indifferently either productive or unproductive hands. They seem, however, to have some predilection for the latter. The expence of a great lord feeds generally more idle than industrious people. The rich merchant, though with his capital he maintains industrious people only, yet by his expence, that is, by the employment of his revenue, he feeds commonly the very same sort as the great lord.

The proportion, therefore, between the productive and unproductive hands, depends very much in every country upon the proportion between that part of the annual produce, which, as soon as it comes either from the ground or from the hands of the productive labourers, is destined for replacing a capital, and that which is destined for constituting a revenue, either as rent, or as profit. This proportion is very different in rich from what it is in poor countries. . . .

That part of the annual produce, therefore, which, as soon as it comes either from the ground, or from the hands of the productive labourers, is destined for replacing a capital, is not only much greater in rich than in poor countries, but bears a much greater proportion to that which is immediately destined for constituting a revenue either as rent or as profit. The funds destined for the maintenance of productive labour, are not only much greater in the former than in the latter, but bear a much greater proportion to those which, though they may be employed to maintain either productive or unproductive hands, have generally a predilection for the latter.

The proportion between those different funds necessarily determines in every country the general character of the inhabitants as to industry or idleness. We are more industrious than our forefathers; because in the present times the funds destined for the maintenance of industry, are much greater in proportion to those which are likely to be employed in the maintenance of idleness, than they were two or three centuries ago. Our ancestors were idle for want of a sufficient encouragement to industry. It is better, says the proverb, to play for nothing, than to work for nothing. In mercantile and manufacturing towns, where the inferior ranks of people are chiefly maintained by the employment of capital, they are in general industrious, sober, and thriving; as in many English, and in most Dutch towns....

The proportion between capital and revenue, therefore, seems everywhere to regulate the proportion between industry and idleness. Wherever capital predominates, industry prevails; wherever revenue, idleness. Every increase or diminution of capital, therefore, naturally tends to increase or diminish the real quantity of industry, the number of productive hands, and consequently the exchangeable value of the annual produce of the land and labour of the country, the real wealth and revenue of all its inhabitants.

Capitals are increased by parsimony, and diminished by prodigality and misconduct.

Whatever a person saves from his revenue he adds to his capital, and either employs it himself in maintaining an additional number of productive hands, or enables some other person to do so, by lending it to him for an interest, that is, for a share of the profits. As the capital of an individual can be increased only by what he saves from his annual revenue or his annual gains, so the capital of a society, which is the same with that of all the individuals who compose it, can be increased only in the same manner.

Parsimony, and not industry, is the immediate cause of the increase of capital. Industry, indeed, provides the subject which parsimony accumulates. But whatever industry might acquire, if parsimony did not save and store up, the capital would never be the greater.

Parsimony, by increasing the fund which is destined for the maintenance of productive hands, tends to increase the number of those hands whose labour adds to the value of the subject upon which it is bestowed. It tends therefore to increase the exchangeable value of the annual produce of the land and labour of the country. It puts into motion an additional quantity of industry, which gives an additional value to the annual produce.

What is annually saved is as regularly consumed as what is annually spent, and nearly in the same time too; but it is consumed by a different set of people. That portion of his revenue which a rich man annually spends, is in most cases consumed by idle guests, and menial servants, who leave nothing behind them in return for their consumption. That portion which he annually saves, as for the sake of the profit it is immediately employed as a capital, is consumed in the same manner, and nearly in the same time too, but by a different set of people, by labourers, manufacturers, and artificers, who re-produce with a profit the value of their annual consumption. His revenue, we shall suppose, is paid him in money. Had he spent the whole, the food, clothing, and lodging, which the whole could have purchased, would have been distributed among the former set of people. By saving a part of it, as that part is for the sake of the profit immediately employed as a capital either by himself or by some other person, the food, clothing, and lodging, which may be purchased with it, are necessarily reserved for the latter. The consumption is the same, but the consumers are different.

By what a frugal man annually saves, he not only affords maintenance to an additional number of productive hands, for that or the ensuing year, but, like the founder of a public workhouse, he establishes as it were a perpetual fund for the maintenance of an equal number in all times to come. The perpetual allotment and destination of this fund, indeed, is not always guarded by an positive law, by any trust-right or deed of mortmain. It is always guarded, however, by a very powerful principle, the plain and evident interest of every individual to whom any share of it shall ever belong. No part of it can ever afterwards be employed to maintain any but productive hands, without an evident loss to the person who thus perverts it from its proper destination. . . .

The same quantity of money, besides, cannot long remain in any country in which the value of the annual produce diminishes. The sole use of money is to circulate consumable goods. By means of it, provisions, materials, and finished work, are bought and sold, and distributed to their proper consumers. The quantity of money, therefore, which can be annually employed in any country, must be determined by the value of the consumable goods annually circulated within it. These must consist either in the immediate produce of the land and labour of the country itself, or in something which had been purchased with some part of the produce. Their value, therefore, must diminish as the value of that produce diminution and along with it the quantity of money which can be employed in circulating them. But the money which by this annual diminution of produce is annually thrown out of domestic circulation, will not be allowed to lie idle. The interest of whoever possesses it, requires that it should be employed. But having no employment at home, it will, in spite of all laws and prohibitions, be sent abroad, and employed in purchasing consumable goods which may be of some use at home. Its annual exportation will in this manner continue for some time to add something to the annual consumption of the country beyond the value of its own annual produce. What in the days of its prosperity had been saved from that annual produce, and employed in purchasing gold and silver, will contribute for some little time to support its consumption in adversity. The exportation of gold and silver is, in this case, not the cause, but the effect of its declension, and may even, for some little time, alleviate the misery of that declension.

The quantity of money, on the contrary, must in every country naturally increase as the value of the annual produce increases. The value of the consumable goods annually circulated within the society being greater, will require a greater quantity of money to circulate them. A part of the increased produce, therefore, will naturally be employed in purchasing, wherever it is to be had, the additional quantity of gold and silver necessary for circulating the rest. The increase of those metals will in this case be the effect, not the cause, of the public prosperity. Gold and silver are purchased every-where in the same manner. The food, clothing, and lodging, the revenue and maintenance of all those whose labour or stock is employed in bringing them from the mine to the market, is the price paid for them in Peru as well as in England. The country which has this price to pay, will never be long without the quantity of those metals which it has occasion for; and no country will ever long retain a quantity which it has no occasion for.

Whatever, therefore, we may imagine the real wealth and revenue of a country to consist in, whether in the value of the annual produce of its land and labour, as plain reason seems to dictate; or in the quantity of the precious metals which circulate within it, as vulgar prejudices suppose; in either view of the matter, every prodigal appears to be a public enemy, and every frugal man a public benefactor.

The effects of misconduct are often the same as those of prodigality. Every injudicious and unsuccessful project in agriculture, mines, fisheries, trade, or manufactures, tends in the same manner to diminish the funds destined for the maintenance of productive labour. In every such project, though the capital is consumed by productive hands only, yet, as by the injudicious manner in which they are employed, they do not reproduce the full value of their consumption, there must always be some diminution in what would otherwise have been the productive funds of the society.

It can seldom happen, indeed, that the circumstances of a great nation can be much affected either by the prodigality or misconduct of individuals; the profusion or imprudence of some, being always more than compensated by the frugality and good conduct of others.

With regard to profusion, the principle which prompts to expence, is the passion for present enjoyment; which, though sometimes violent and very difficult to be restrained, is in general only momentary and occasional. But the principle which prompts to save, is the desire of bettering our condition, a desire which, though generally calm and dispassionate, comes with us from the womb, and never leaves us till we go into the grave. In the whole interval which separates those two moments, there is scarce perhaps a single instant in which any man is so perfectly and completely satisfied with his situation, as to be without any wish of alteration or improvement of any kind. An augmentation of fortune is the means by which the greater part of men propose and wish to better their condition. It is the means the most vulgar and the most obvious; and the most likely way of augmenting their fortune, is to save and accumulate some part of what they acquire, either regularly and annually, or upon some extraordinary occasions. Though the principle of expence, therefore, prevails in almost all men upon some occasions, and in some men upon almost all occasions, yet in the greater part of men, taking the whole course of their life at an average, the principle of frugality seems not only to predominate, but to predominate very greatly.

With regard to misconduct, the number of prudent and successful undertakings is every-where much greater than that of injudicious and unsuccessful ones. After all our complaints of the frequency of bankrupticies, the unhappy men who fall into this misfortune make but a very small part of the whole number engaged in trade, and all other sorts of business; not much more perhaps than one in a thousand. Bankruptcy is perhaps the greatest and most humiliating calamity which can befal an innocent man. The greater part of men, therefore, are sufficiently careful to avoid it. Some, indeed, do not avoid it; as some do not avoid the gallows.

Great nations are never impoverished by private, though they sometimes are by public prodigality and misconduct. The whole, or almost the whole public revenue, is in most countries employed in maintaining unproductive hands. Such are the people who compose a numerous and splendid court, a great ecclesiastical establishment, great fleets and armies, who in time of peace produce nothing, and in time of war acquire nothing which can compensate the expence of maintaining them, even while the war lasts. Such people, as they themselves produce nothing, are all maintained by the produce of other men's labour. When multiplied, therefore, to an unnecessary number, they may in a particular year consume so great a share of this produce, as not to leave a sufficiency for maintaining the productive labourers, who should reproduce it next year. The next year's produce, therefore, will be less than that of the foregoing, and if the same disorder should continue, that of the third year will be still less than that of the second. Those unproductive hands, who should be maintained by a part only of the spare revenue of the people, may consume so great a share of their whole revenue, and therefore oblige so great a number to encroach upon their captials, upon the funds destined for the maintenance of productive labour, that all the frugality and good conduct of individuals may not be able to compensate the waste and degradation of produce occasioned by this violent and forced encroachment.

This frugality and good conduct, however, is upon most occasions, it appears from experience, sufficient to compensate, not only the private prodigality and misconduct of individuals, but the public extravagance of government. The uniform, constant, and uninterrupted effort of every man to better his condition, the principle from which public and national, as well as private opulence is originally derived, is frequently powerful enough to maintain the natural progress of things toward improvement, in spite both of the extravagance of government, and of the greatest errors of administration. Like the unknown principle of animal it frequently restores health and vigour to the constitution, in spite, not only of the disease, but of the absurd prescriptions of the doctor....

But though the profusion of government must, undoubtedly have retraded the natural progress of England towards wealth and improvement, it has not been able to stop it. The annual product of its land and labour is, undoubtedly, much greater at present than it was either at the restoration or at the revolution. The capital therefore, annually employed in cultivating this land, and in maintaining this labour, must likewise be much greater. In the midst of all the exactions of government, this capital has been silently and gradually accumulated by the private frugality and good conduct of individuals, by their universal, continual, and uninterrupted effort to better their own condition. It is this effort, protected by law and allowed by liberty to exert itself in the manner that is most advantageous, which has maintained the progress of England towards opulence and improvement in almost all former times, and which, it is to be hoped, will do so in all future times. England, however, as it has never been blessed with a very parismonious government, so parsimony has at no time been the characteristical virtue of its inhabitants. It is the highest impertinence and presumption, therefore, in kings and ministers, to pretend to watch over the economy of private people, and to restrain their expence, either by sumptuary laws, or by prohibiting the importation of foreign luxuries. They are themselves always, and without any exception, the greatest spendthrifts in the society. Let them look well after their own expence, and they may safely trust private people with theirs. If their own extravagance does not ruin the state, that of their subjects never will.

David Hume

Newton's principal achievements in the realm of astronomical reckoning, when generalized to the level of assumptions about the orderliness of the natural world based on a modest experimental philosophy, were readily exportable and enthusiastically transported into other fields of inquiry, among them the philosophical writings of David Hume (1711–1776). That "all would be light" following Newton, however, was perhaps more a testament to the optimism of the Enlightenment than a true gauge of the immediate effects on fields other than astrophysics. Much work remained to be done at the opening of the eighteenth century, and not all of it seemed certain. How, for example, to explain in Newtonian terms the growth of a plant, or the existence of laws based on private property? When taken up in relation to these subjects, few of Newton's ideas remained other than his general insistence upon a systematic empiricism. This was enough, however, to fuel certain Enlightenment philosophies of the social world with revolutionary potential for criticizing an older order of society. Yet how the Newtonian revolution would transform the study of the thought itself, the traditional domain of philosophy, was uncertain.

This is the central problem carried forward into the work of David Hume: a tension between the confident application of reason to the real world, and an uncertainty about the nature of that same external reality. Hume's work in philosophy, like that of his acquaintances—Adam Smith in economics and Jean-Jacques Rousseau in political philosophy—was fundamental to the development of Enlightenment thought. He sought to push the empirical philosophy implicit in Newton's methods to its logical conclusion, and in doing so came to doubt the very possibility of scientific knowledge itself. In this he continued the Enlightenment tradition of strict avoidance of comforting metaphysical assertions, but unlike some earlier zealots, he found a useful, even necessary place in social life of the seemingly irrational world of custom and tradition. Along the way, he managed to give substance to the principle of natural law in his writings on morals and politics. Reason, for Hume, was a powerful thing, and when judiciously managed, its products—orderly government and a rational understanding of basic social institutions—could be great. If left to itself as sole authority, however, reason could quickly undo all that it had accomplished elsewhere, perhaps even the Newtonian world-picture with its presumed regularity of cause and effect.

DAVID HUME
(1752)

That Politics

May Be Reduced

to a Science

It is a question with several, whether there be any essential difference between one form of government and another? and, whether every form may not become good or bad, according as it is well or ill administered? Were it once admitted, that all governments are alike, and that the only difference consists in the character and conduct of the governors, most political disputes would be at an end, and all *Zeal* for one constitution above another must be esteemed mere bigotry and folly. But, though a friend to moderation, I cannot forbear condemning this sentiment, and should be sorry to think, that human affairs admit of no greater stability, than what they receive from the casual humors and characters of particular men.

It is true, those who maintain that the goodness of all government consists in the goodness of the administration, may cite many particular instances in history, where the very same government, in different hands, has varied suddenly into the two opposite extremes of good and bad. Compare the French government under Henry III and under Henry IV. Oppression, levity, artifice on the part of the rulers; faction, sedition, treachery, rebellion, disloyalty on the part of the subjects: These compose the character of the former miserable era. But when the patriot and heroic prince, who succeeded, was once firmly seated on the throne, the government, the people, every thing, seemed to be totally changed; and all from the difference of the temper and conduct of these two sovereigns. Instances of this kind may be multiplied, almost without number, from ancient as well as modern history, foreign as well as domestic.

But here it may be proper to make a distinction. All absolute governments must very much depend on the administration; and this is one of the great inconveniences attending that form

---

of government. But a republican and free government would be an obvious absurdity, if the particular checks and controls, provided by the constitution, had really no influence, and made it not the interest, even of bad men, to act for the public good. Such is the intention of these forms of government, and such is their real effect, where they are wisely constituted: As, on the other hand, they are the source of all disorder, and of the blackest crimes, where either skill or honesty has been wanting in their original frame and institution.

So great is the force of laws, and of particular forms of government, and so little dependence have they on the humours and tempers of men, that consequences almost as general and certain may sometimes be deduced from them, as any which the mathematical science afford us.

The constitution of the Roman republic gave the whole legislative power to the people, without allowing a negative voice either to the nobility or consuls. The unbounded power they possessed in a collective, not a representative body. The consequences were: when the people, by success and conquest, had become very numerous, and had spread themselves to a great distance from the capital, the city tribes, though the most contemptible, carried almost every vote: They were therefore, most cajoled by every one that affected popularity: They were supported in idleness by the general distribution of corn, and by particular bribes which they received from almost every candidate: By this means, they became every day more licentious, and the Campus Martius was a perpetual scene of tumult and sedition: Armed slaves were introduced among these rascally citizens, so that the whole government fell into anarchy; and the greatest happiness which the Romans could look for, was the despotic power of the Caesars. Such are the effects of democracy without a representative.

A Nobility may possess the whole, or any part of the legislative power of a state, in two different ways. Either every nobleman shares the power as a part of the whole body; or the whole body enjoys the power as composed of parts, which have each a distinct power and authority. The Venetian aristocracy is an instance of the first kind of government; the Polish, of the second. In the Venetian government the whole body of nobility possesses the whole power, and no nobleman has any authority which he receives not from the whole. In the Polish government every nobleman, by means of his fiefs, has a distinct hereditary authority over his vassals, and the whole body has no authority but what it receives from the concurrence of its parts. The different operations and tendencies of these two species of government might be made apparent even *a priori*. A Venetian nobility is preferable to a Polish, let the humours and education of men be ever so much varied. A nobility, who possess their power in common, will preserve peace and order, both among themselves, and their subjects; and no member can have authority enough to control the laws for a moment. The nobles will preserve their authority over the people, but without any grievous tyranny, or any breach of private property; because such a tyrannical government promotes not the interests of the whole body, however it may that of some individuals. There will be a distinction of rank between the nobility and people, but this will be the only distinction in the state. The whole nobility will form one body, and the whole people another, without any of those private feuds and animosities, which spread ruin and desolation every where. It is easy to see the disadvantages of a Polish nobility in every one of these particulars.

It is possible so to constitute a free government, as that a single person, call him a doge, prince, or king, shall possess a large share of power, and shall form a proper balance or counterpoise to the other parts of the legislature. This chief magistrate may be either *elective* or *hered-*

itary; and though the former institution may, to a superficial view, appear the most advantageous; yet a more accurate inspection will discover in it greater inconveniences than in the latter, and such as are founded on causes and principles eternal and immutable. The filling of the throne, in such a government, is a point of too great and too general interest not to divide the whole people into factions: Whence a civil war, the greatest of ills, may be apprehended almost with certainty, upon every vacancy. The principle elected must be either a *Foreigner* or a *Native*: The former will be ignorant of the people whom he is to govern; suspicious of his new subjects, and suspected by them; giving his confidence entirely to strangers who will have no other care but of enriching themselves in the quickest manner, while their master's favour and authority are able to support them. A native will carry into the throne all his private animosities and friendships, and will never be viewed in his elevation without exciting the sentiment of envy in those who formerly considered him as their equal. Not to mention that a crown is too high a reward ever to be given to merit alone, and will always induce the candidates to employ force, or money, or intrigue, to procure the votes of the electors: So that such an election will give no better chance for superior merit in the prince, than if the state had trusted to birth alone for determining the sovereign.

It may, therefore, be pronounced as an universal axiom in politics, *That an hereditary prince, a nobility without vassals, and a people voting by their representatives, form the best* monarchy, aristocracy and democracy. But in order to prove more fully, that politics admit of general truths, which are invariable by the humour or education either of subject or sovereign, it may not be amiss to observe some other principles of this science, which may seem to deserve that character. . . .

Legislators, therefore, ought not to trust the future government of a state entirely to chance, but ought to provide a system of laws to regulate the administration of public affairs to the latest posterity. Effects will always correspond to causes; and wise regulations, in any commonwealth, are the most valuable legacy that can be left to future ages. In the smallest court or office, the stated forms and methods by which business must be conducted, are found to be a considerable check on the natural depravity of mankind. Why should not the case be the same in public affairs? Can we ascribe the stability and wisdom of the Venetian government, through so many ages, to any thing but the form of government? And is it not easy to point out those defects in the original constitution, which produced the tumultuous governments of Athens and Rome, and ended at last in the ruin of these two famous republics? And so little dependence has this affair on the humours and education of particular men, that one part of the same republic may be wisely conducted, and another weakly, by the very same men, merely on account of the differences of the forms and institutions by which these parts are regulated. Historians inform us that this was actually the case with Genoa. For while the state was always full of sedition, and tumult, and disorder, the bank of St. George, which had become a considerable part of the people, was conducted, for several ages, with the utmost integrity and wisdom.

The ages of greatest public spirit are not always most eminent for private virtue. Good laws may beget order and moderation in the government, where the manners and customs have instilled little humanity or justice into the tempers of men. The most illustrious period of the Roman history, considered in a political view, is that between the beginning of the first and end of the last Punic war; the due balance between the nobility and people being then fixed by the contests of the tribunes, and not being yet lost by the extent of conquests. Yet at this very time, the horrid practice of poisoning was so common, that, during part of the season, a Practor punished capitally for this crime above three thousand persons in a part of Italy; and found informations of this nature still multiplying upon him. There is a similar, or rather a worse instance, in the more early times of the commonwealth; so depraved in private life were that people, whom in their histories we so much admire. I doubt not but they were really more virtuous during the time of the two *Triumvirates*; when they were tearing their common country to pieces, and spreading slaughter and desolation over the face of the earth, merely for the choice of tyrants.

Here, then, is a sufficient inducement to maintain, with the utmost zeal, in every free state, those forms and institutions by which liberty is secured, the public good consulted, and the avarice or ambition of particular men restrained and punished. Nothing does more honour to human nature, than to see it susceptible of so noble a passion; as nothing can be a greater indication of meanness of heart in any man than to see him destitute of it. A man who loves only himself, without regard to friendship and desert, merits the severest blame; and a man, who is only susceptible of friendship, without public spirit, or a regard to the community, is deficient in the most material part of virtue.

But this is a subject which needs not be longer insisted on at present. There are enough zealots on both sides, who kindle up the passions of their partisans, and, under pretence of public good, pursue the interests and ends of their particular faction. For my part, I shall always be more fond of promoting moderation than zeal; though perhaps the surest way of producing moderation in every party is to increase our zeal for the public. Let us therefore try, if it be possible, from the foregoing doctrine, to draw a lesson of moderation with regard to the parties into which our country is at present divided; at the same time, that we allow not this moderation to abate the industry and passion, with which every individual is bound to pursue the good of his country. . . .

DAVID HUME
(1752)

Of the Origin
of Justice and
Property

We now proceed to examine two questions, viz. concerning the manner, in which the rules of justice are establish'd by the artifice of men; and concerning the reasons, which determine us to attribute to the observance or neglect of these rules a moral beauty and deformity. These questions will appear afterwards to be distinct. We shall begin with the former.

Of all the animals, with which this globe is peopled, there is none towards whom nature seems, at first sight, to have exercis'd more cruelty than towards man, in the numberless wants and necessities, with which she has loaded him, and in the slender means, which she affords to the relieving these necessities. In other creatures these two particulars generally compensate each other. If we consider the lion as a voracious and carnivorous animal, we shall easily discover him to be very necessitous; but if we turn our eye to his make and temper, his agility, his courage, his arms, and his force, we shall find, that his advantages hold proportion with his wants. The sheep and ox are depriv'd of all these advantages; but their appetites are moderate, and their food is of easy purchase. In man alone, this unnatural conjunction of infirmity, and of necessity, may be observ'd in its greatest perfection. Not only the food, which is requir'd for his sustenance, flies his search and approach, or at least requires his labour to be produc'd, but he must be possess'd of cloaths and lodging, to defend him against the injuries of the weather; tho' to consider him only in himself, he is provided neither with arms, nor force, nor other natural abilities, which are in any degree answerable to so many necessities.

'Tis by society alone he is able to supply his defects, and raise himself up to an equality with his fellow-creatures, and even acquire a superiority above them. By society all his infirmities are compensated; and tho' in that situation his wants multiply every moment upon him, yet his abilities are still more augmented, and leave him in every respect more satisfied and happy, than 'tis possible for him, in his savage and solitary condition, ever to become. When every individual person labours a-part, and only for himself, his force is too small to execute any considerable work; his labour being employ'd in supplying all his different necessities, he never attains a perfection in any particular art; and as his force and success are not at all times equal, the least failure in either of these particulars must be attended with inevitable ruin and misery. Society provides a remedy for these *three* inconveniences. By the conjunction of forces, our power is augmented: By the partition of employments, our ability increases: And by mutual succour we are less expos'd to fortune and accidents. 'Tis by this additional *force, ability*, and *security*, that society become advantageous.

But in order to form society, 'tis requisite not only that it be advantageous, but also that men be sensible of these advantages; and 'tis impossible, in their wild uncultivated state, that by study and reflexion alone, they should ever be able to attain this knowledge. Most fortunately, therefore, there is conjoin'd to those necessities, whose remedies are remote and obscure, another necessity, which having a present and more obvious remedy, may justly be regarded as the first and original principle of human society. This necessity is no other than that natural appetite betwixt the sexes, which unites them together, and preserves their union, till a new tye takes place in their concern for their common offspring. This new concern becomes also a principle of union betwixt the parents and offspring, and forms a more numerous society; where the parents govern by the advantage of their superior strength and wisdom, and at the same time are restrain'd in the exercise of their authority by that natural affection, which they bear their children. In a little time, custom and habit operating on the tender minds of the children, makes them sensible of the advantages, which they may reap from society, as well as fashions them by degrees for it, by rubbing off those rough corners and untoward affections, which prevent their coalition.

For it must be confest, that however the circumstances of human nature may render an union necessary, and however those passions of lust and natural affection may seem to render it unavoidable; yet there are other particulars in our *natural temper*, and in our *outward circumstances*, which are very incommodious, and are even contrary to the requisite conjunction. Among the former, we may justly esteem our *selfishness* to be the most considerable. I am sensible, that, generally speaking, the representations of this quality have been carried much too far; and that the descriptions, which certain philosophers delight so much to form of mankind in this particular, are as wide of nature as any accounts of monsters, which we meet with in fables and romances. So far from thinking, that men have no affection for any thing beyond themselves, I am of opinion, that tho' it be rare to meet with one, who loves any single person better than himself; yet 'tis as rare to meet with one, in whom all the kind affections, taken together, do not over-balance all the selfish. Consult common experience: Do you not see that tho' the whole expence of the family be generally under the direction of the master of it, yet there are few that do not bestow the largest part of their fortunes on the pleasures of their wives, and the education of their children, reserving the smallest portion for their own proper use and entertainment. This is what we may observe concerning such as have those endearing ties; and may presume, that the case would be the same with others, were they plac'd in a like situation.

But tho' this generosity must be acknowledg'd to the honour of human nature, we may at the same time remark, that so noble an affection, instead of fitting men for large societies, is almost as contrary to them, as the most narrow selfishness. For while each person loves himself better than any other single person, and in his love to others bears the greatest affection to his relations and acquaintance, this must necessarily produce an opposition of passions, and a consequent opposition of actions; which cannot but be dangerous to the new-establish'd union.

'Tis however worth while to remark, that this contrariety of passions wou'd be attended with but small danger, did it not concur with a peculiarity in our *outward circumstances*, which affords it an opportunity of exerting itself. There are three different species of goods, which we are possess'd of; the internal satisfaction of our minds, the external advantages of our body, and the enjoyment of such possessions as we have acquir'd by our industry and good fortune. We are perfectly secure in the enjoyment of the first. The second may be ravish'd from us, but can be of no advantage to him who deprives us of them. The last only are both expos'd to the violence of others, and may be transferr'd without suffering any loss or alteration; while at the same time, there is not a sufficient quantity of them to supply every one's desires and necessities. As the improvement, therefore, of these goods is the chief advantage of society, so the *instability* of their possession, along with their *scarcity*, is the chief impediment.

In vain shou'd we expect to find, in *uncultivated nature*, a remedy to this inconvenience; or hope for any inartificial principle of the human mind, which might controul those partial affections, and make us overcome the temptations arising from our circumstances. The idea of justice can never serve to this purpose, or be taken for a natural principle, capable of inspiring men with an equitable conduct towards each other. That virtue, as it is now understood, wou'd never have been dream'd of among rude and savage men. For the notion of injury or injustice implies an immorality or vice committed against some other person: And as every immorality is deriv'd from some defect or unsoundness of the passions, and as this defect must be judg'd of, in a great measure, from the ordinary course of nature in the constitution of the mind; 'twill be easy to know, whether we be guilty of any immorality, with regard to others, by considering the natural, and usual force of those several affections, which are directed towards them. Now it appears, that in the original frame of our mind, our strongest attention is confin'd to ourselves; our next is extended to our relations and acquaintance; and 'tis only the weakest which reaches to strangers and indifferent persons. This partiality, then, and unequal affection, must not only have an influence on our behaviour and conduct in society, but even on our ideas of vice and virtue; so as to make us regard any remarkable transgression of such a degree of partiality, either by too great an enlargement, or contraction of the affections, as vicious and immoral. This we may observe in our common judgments concerning actions, where we blame a person, who either centers all his affections in his family, or is so regardless of them, as, in any opposition of interest, to give the preference to a stranger, or mere chance acquaintance. From all which it follows, that our natural uncultivated ideas of morality, instead of providing a remedy for the partiality of our affections, do rather conform themselves to that partiality, and give it an additional force and influence.

The remedy, then, is not deriv'd from nature, but from *artifice*; or more properly speaking, nature provides a remedy in the judgment and understanding, for what is irregular and incommodious in the affections. For when men, from their early education in society, have become sensible of the infinite advantages that result from it, and have besides acquir'd a new affection to company and conversation; and when they have observ'd, that the principal disturbance in society arises from those goods, which we call external, and from their looseness and easy transition from one person to another; they must seek for a remedy, by putting these goods, as far as possible, on the same footing with the fix'd and constant advantages of the mind and body. This can be done after no other manner, than by a convention enter'd into by all the members of the society to bestow stability on the possession of those external goods, and leave every one in the peaceable enjoyment of what he may acquire by his fortune and industry. By this means, every one knows what he may safely possess; and the passions are restrain'd in their partial and contradictory motions. Nor is such a restraint contrary to these passions; for if so, it cou'd never be enter'd into, nor maintain'd; but it is only contrary to their heedless and impetuous movement. Instead of departing from our own interest, or from that of our nearest friends, by abstaining from the possessions of others, we cannot better consult both these interests, than by such a convention; because it is by that means we maintain society, which is so necessary to their well-being and subsistence, as well as to our own.

This convention is not of the nature of a *promise*: For even promises themselves, as we shall see afterwards, arise from human conventions. It is only a general sense of common interest; which sense all the members of the society express to one another, and which induces them to regulate their conduct by certain rules. I observe, that it will be for my interest to leave another in the possession of his goods, *provided* he will act in the same manner with regard to me. He is sensible of a like interest in the regulation of his conduct. When this common sense of interest is mutually express'd, and is known to both, it produces a suitable resolution and behaviour. And this may properly enough be call'd a convention or agreement betwixt us, tho' without the interposition of a promise; since the actions of each of us have a reference to those of the other, and are perform'd upon the supposition, that something is to be perform'd on the other part. Two men, who pull the oars of a boat, do it by an agreement or convention, tho' they have never given promises to each other. Nor is the rule concerning the stability of possession the less deriv'd from human conventions, that it arises gradually, and acquires force by a slow progression, and by our repeated experience of the inconveniences of transgressing it. On the contrary, this experience assures us still more, that the sense of interest has become common to all our fellows, and gives us a confidence of the future regularity of their conduct: And 'tis only on the expectation of this, that our moderation and abstinence are founded. In like manner are languages gradually establish'd by human conventions without any promise. In like manner do gold and silver become the common measures of exchange, and are esteem'd sufficient payment for what is of a hundred times their value.

After this convention, concerning abstinence from the possessions of others, is enter'd into, and every one has acquir'd a stability in his possessions, there immediately arise the ideas of justice and injustice; as also those of *properly*, *right*, and *obligation*. The latter are altogether unintelligible without first understanding the former. Our property is nothing but those goods, whose constant possession is establish'd by the laws of society; that is, by the laws of justice. Those, therefore, who make use of the words *property*, or *right*, or *obligation*, before they have explain'd the origin of justice, or even make use of them in that explication, are guilty of a very gross fallacy, and can never reason upon any solid foundation. A man's property is some object related to him. This relation is not natural, but moral, and founded on justice. 'Tis very preposterous, therefore, to imagine, that we can have any idea of property, without fully comprehending the nature of justice, and shewing its origin in the artifice and contrivance of men. The origin of justice explains that of property. The same artifice gives rise to both. As our first and most natural sentiment of morals is founded on the nature of our passions, and gives the preference to ourselves and friends, above strangers; 'tis impossible there can be naturally any such thing as a fix'd right or property, while the opposite passions of men impel them in contrary directions, and are not restrain'd by any convention or agreement.…

'Tis certain, that no affection of the human mind has both a sufficient force, and a proper direction to counter-balance the love of gain, and render men fit members of society, by making them abstain from the possessions of others. Benevolence to strangers is too weak for this purpose; and as to the other passions, they rather inflame this avidity, when we observe, that the larger our possessions are, the more ability we have of gratifying all our appetites. There is no passion, therefore, capable of controlling the interested affection, but the very affection itself, by an alteration of its direction. Now this alteration must necessarily take place upon the least reflection, since 'tis evident, that the passion is much better satisfy'd by its restraint, than by its liberty, and that in preserving society, we make much greater advances in the acquiring possessions, than in the solitary and forlorn condition, which must follow upon violence and an universal licence. The question, therefore, concerning the wickedness or goodness of human nature, enters not in the least into that other question concerning the origin of society; nor is there any thing to be consider'd but the degrees of men's sagacity or folly. For whether the passion of self-interest be esteemed vicious or virtuous, 'tis all a case; since itself alone restrains it: So that if it be virtuous, men become social by their virtue; if vicious, their vice has the same effect.…

I have already observ'd, that justice takes its rise from human conventions; and that these are intended as a remedy to some inconveniences, which proceed from the concurrence of certain *qualities* of the human mind with the *situation* of external objects. The qualities of the mind are *selfishness* and *limited generosity*: And the situation of external objects is their *easy change*, join'd to their *scarcity* in comparison of the wants and desires of men. But however philosophers may have been bewilder'd in those speculations, poets have been guided more infallibly, by a certain taste or common instinct, which in most kinds of reasoning goes farther than any of that art and philosophy, with which we have been yet acquainted. They easily perceiv'd, if every man had a tender regard for another, or if nature supplied abundantly all our wants and desires, that the jealously of interest, which justice supposes, could no longer have place; nor would there be any occasion for those distinctions and limits of property and possession, which at present are in use among mankind. Increase to a sufficient degree the benevolence of men, or the bounty of nature, and you render justice useless, by supplying its place with much nobler virtues, and more valuable blessings. The selfishness of men is animated by the few possessions we have, in proportion to our wants; and 'tis to restrain this selfishness, that men have been oblig'd to separate themselves from the community, and to distinguish betwixt their own goods and those of others.

Nor need we have recourse to the fictions of poets to learn this; but beside the reason of the thing, may discover the same truth by common experience and observation. 'Tis easy to remark, that a cordial affection renders all things common among friends; and that married people in particular mutually lose their property, and are unacquainted with the *mine* and *thine*, which are so necessary, and yet cause such disturbance in human society. The same effect arises from any alteration in the circumstances of mankind; as when there is such a plenty of any thing as satisfies all the desires of men: In which case the distinction of property is entirely lost, and every thing remains in common. This we may observe with regard to air and water, tho' the most valuable of all external objects; and may easily conclude, that if men were supplied with every thing in the same abundance, or if *every one* had the same affection and tender regard for *every one* as for himself; justice and injustice would be equally unknown among mankind.

Here then is a proposition, which, I think, may be regarded as certain, *that 'tis only from the selfishness and confin'd generosity of men, along with the scanty provision nature has made for his wants, that justice derives its origin.* If we look backward we shall find, that this proposition bestows an additional force on some of those observations, which we have alredy made on this subject.

First, we may conclude from it, that a regard to public interest, or a strong extensive benevolence, is not our first and original motive for the observation of the rules of justice; since 'tis allow'd, that if men were endow'd with such a benevolence, these rules would never have been dreamt of.

Secondly, we may conclude from the same principle, that the sense of justice is not founded on reason, or on the discovery of certain connexions and relations of ideas, which are eternal, immutable, and universally obligatory. For since it is confest, that such an alteration as that above-mention'd, in the temper and circumstances of mankind, wou'd entirely alter our duties and obligations, 'tis necessary upon the common system, *that the sense of virtue is deriv'd from reason,* to shew the change which this must produce in the relations and ideas. But 'tis evident, that the only cause, why the extensive generosity of man, and the perfect abundance of every thing, wou'd destroy the very idea of justice, is because they render it useless; and that, on the other hand, his confin'd benevolence, and his necessitous condition, give rise to that virtue, only by making it requisite to the publick interest, and to that of every individual. 'Twas therefore a concern for our own, and the publick interest, which made us establish the laws of justice; and nothing can be more certain, than that it is not any relation of ideas, which gives us this concern, but our impressions and sentiments, without which every thing in nature is perfectly indifferent to us, and can never in the least affect us. The sense of justice, therefore, is not founded on our ideas, but on our impressions.

Thirdly, we may farther confirm the foregoing proposition, *that those impressions, which give rise to this sense of justice, are not natural to the mind of man, but arise from artifice and human conventions.* For since any considerable alteration of temper and circumstances destroys equally justice and injustice; and since such an alteration has an effect only by changing our own and the publick interest; it follows, that the first establishment of the rules of justice depends on these different interests. But if men pursu'd the publick interest naturally, and with a hearty affection, they wou'd never have dream'd of restraining each other by these rules; and if they pursu'd their own interest, without any precaution, they wou'd run head-long into every kind of injustice and violence. These rules, therefore, are artificial, and seek their end in an oblique and indirect manner; nor is the interest, which gives rise to them, of a kind that cou'd be pursu'd by the natural and inartificial passions of men.

To make this more evident, consider, that tho' the rules of justice are establish'd merely by interest, their connexion with interest is somewhat singular, and is different from what may be observ'd on other occasions. A single act of justice is frequently contrary to *public interest;* and were it to stand alone, without being follow'd by other acts, may, in itself, be very prejudicial to society. When a man of merit, of a beneficent disposition, restores a great fortune to a miser, or a seditious bigot, he has acted justly and laudably, but the public is a real sufferer. Nor is every single act of justice, consider'd apart, more conducive to private interest, than to public; and 'tis easily conceiv'd how a man may impoverish himself by a signal instance of integrity, and have reason to wish, that with regard to that single act, the laws of justice were for a moment suspended in the universe. But however single acts of justice may be contrary, either to public or private interest, 'tis certain, that the whole plan or scheme is highly conducive, or indeed absolutely requisite, both to the support of society, and the well-being of every individual. 'Tis impossible to separate the good from the ill. Property must be stable, and must be fix'd by general rules. Tho' in one instance the public be a sufferer, this momentary ill is amply compensated by the steady prosecution of the rule, and by the peace and order, which it establishes in society. And even every individual person must find himself a gainer, on ballancing the account; since, without justice, society must immediately dissolve, and everyone must fall into that savage and solitary condition, which is infinitely worse than the worst situation that can possibly be suppos'd in society. When therefore men have had experience enough to observe, that whatever may be the consequence of any single act of justice, perform'd by a single person, yet the whole system of actions, concurr'd in by the whole society, is infinitely advantageous to the whole, and to every part; it is not long before justice and property take place. Every member of society is sensible of this interest: Every one expresses this sense to his fellows, along with the resolution he has taken of squaring his actions by it, on condition that others will do the same. No more is requisite to induce any one of them to perform an act of justice, who has the first opportunity. This becomes an example to others. And thus justice establishes itself by a kind of convention or agreement; that is, by a sense of interest, suppos'd to be common to all, and where every single act is perform'd in expectation that others are to perform the like. Without such a convention, no one wou'd ever have dream'd, that there was such a virtue as justice, or have been induc'd to conform his actions to it. Taking any single act, my justice may be pernicious in every respect; and 'tis only upon the supposition, that others are to imitate my example, that I can be induc'd to embrace that virtue; since nothing but this combination can render justice advantageous, or afford me any motives to conform my self to its rules.

We come now to the *second* question we propos'd, *viz. Why we annex the idea of virtue to justice, and of vice to injustice.* This question will not detain us long after the principles, which we have already establish'd. All we can say of it at present will be dispatch'd in a few words: And for farther satisfaction, the reader must wait till we come to the *third* part of this book. The *natural* obligation to justice, *viz.* interest, has been fully explain'd; but as to the *moral* obligation, or the sentiment of right and wrong, 'twill first be requisite to examine the natural virtues, before we can give a full and satisfactory account of it.

After men have found by experience, that their selfishness and confin'd generosity, acting at their liberty, totally incapacitate them for society; and at the same time have observ'd, that society is necessary to the satisfaction of those very passions, they are naturally induc'd to lay themselves under the restraint of such rules, as may render their commerce more safe and commodious. To the imposition then, and observance of these rules, both in general, and in every particular instance, they are at first induc'd only by a regard to interest; and this motive, on the first formation of society, is sufficiently strong and forcible. But when society has become numerous, and has encreas'd to a tribe or nation, this interest is more remote; nor do men so readily perceive, that disorder and confusion follow upon every breach of these rules, as in a more narrow and contracted society. But tho' in our own actions we may frequently lose sight of that interest, which we have in maintaining order, and may follow a lesser and more present interest, we never fail to observe the prejudice we receive, either mediately or immediately, from the injustice of others; as not being in that case either blinded by passion, or bypass'd by any contrary temptation. Nay when the injustice is so distant from us, as no way to affect our interest, it still displeases us; because we consider it as prejudicial to human society, and pernicious to every one that approaches the person guilty of it. We partake of their uneasiness by *sympathy*; and as every thing, which gives uneasiness in human actions, upon the general survey, is call'd Vice, and whatever produces satisfaction, in the same manner, is denominated Virtue; this is the reason why the sense of moral good and evil follows upon justice and injustice. And tho' this sense, in the present case, be deriv'd only from contemplating the actions of others, yet we fail not to extend it even to our own actions. The *general rule* reaches beyond those instances, from which it arose; while at the same time we naturally *sympathize* with others in the sentiments they entertain of us. *Thus self-interest is the original motive to the establishment of justice: but a sympathy with public interest is the source of the moral approbation, which attends that virtue.* . . .

DAVID HUME
(1739)

Of Scepticism
with Regard to
Reason

In all demonstrative sciences the rules are certain and infallible; but when we apply them, our fallible and uncertain faculties are very apt to depart from them, and fall into error. We must, therefore, in every reasoning form a new judgment, as a check or controul on our first judgment or belief; and must enlarge our view to comprehend a kind of history of all the instances, wherein our understanding has deceiv'd us, compar'd with those, wherein its testimony was just and true. Our reason must be consider'd as a kind of cause, of which truth is the natural effect; but such-a-one as by the irruption of other causes, and by the inconstancy of our mental powers, may frequently be prevented. By this means all knowledge degenerates into probability; and this probability is greater or less, according to our experience of the veracity or deceitfulness of our understanding, and according to the simplicity or intricacy of the question.

There is no Algebraist nor Mathematician so expert in his science, as to place entire confidence in any truth immediately upon his discovery of it, or regard it as any thing, but a mere probability. Every time he runs over his proofs, his confidence encreases; but still more by the approbation of his friends; and is rais'd to its utmost perfection by the universal assent and applauses of the learned world. Now 'tis evident, that this gradual encrease of assurance is nothing but the addition of new probabilities, and is deriv'd from the constant union of causes and effects, according to past experience and observation.

In accompts of any length or importance, Merchants seldom trust to the infallible certainty of numbers for their security; but by the artificial structure of the accompts, produce

From David Hume, *A Treatise of Human Nature* (Oxford: Clarendon Press, 1896), pp. 180–87, 484–500, 263–71.

a probability beyond what is deriv'd from the skill and experience of the accomptant. For that is plainly of itself some degree of probability; tho' uncertain and variable, according to the degrees of his experience and length of the a long numeration exceeds probability, I may safely affirm, that there scarce is any proposition concerning numbers, of which we can have a fuller security. For 'tis easily possible, by gradually diminishing the numbers, to reduce the longest series of addition to the most simple question, which can be form'd, to an addition of two single numbers; and upon this supposition we shall find it impracticable to shew the precise limits of knowledge and of probability, or discover that particular number, at which the one ends and the other begins. But knowledge and probability are of such contrary and disagreeing natures, that they cannot well run insensibly into each other, and that because they will not divide, but must be either entirely present, or entirely absent. Besides, if any single addition were certain, every one wou'd be so, and consequently the whole or total sum; unless the whole can be different from all its parts. I had almost said, that this was certain; but I reflect, that it must reduce *itself*, as well as every other reasoning, and from knowledge degenerate into probability.

Since therefore all knowledge resolves itself into probability, and becomes at last of the same nature with that evidence, which we employ in common life, we must now examine this latter species of reasoning, and see on what foundation it stands.

In every judgment, which we can form concerning probability, as well as concerning knowledge, we ought always to correct the first judgment, deriv'd from the nature of the object, by another judgment, deriv'd from the nature of the understanding. 'Tis certain a man of solid sense and long experience ought to have, and usually has, a greater assurance in his opinions, than one that is foolish and ignorant, and that our sentiments have different degrees of authority, even with ourselves, in proportion to the degrees of our reason and experience. In the man of the best sense and longest experience, this authority is never entire; since even such-a-one must be conscious of many errors in the past, and must still dread the like for the future. Here then arises a new species of probability to correct and regulate the first, and fix its just standard and proportion. As demonstration is subject to the controul of probability, so is probability liable to a new correction by a reflex act of the mind, wherein the nature of our understanding, and our reasoning from the first probability become our objects.

Having thus found in every probability, beside the original uncertainty inherent in the subject, a new uncertainty deriv'd from the weakness of that faculty, which judges, and having adjusted these two together, we are oblig'd by our reason to add a new doubt deriv'd from the possibility of error in the estimation we make of the truth and fidelity of our faculties. This is a doubt, which immediately occurs to us, and of which, if we wou'd closely pursue our reason, we cannot avoid giving a decision. But this decision, tho' it shou'd be favourable to our preceeding judgment, being founded only on probability, must weaken still further our first evidence, and must itself be weaken'd by a fourth doubt of the same kind, and so on *in infinitum*; till at last there remain nothing of the original probability, however great we may suppose it to have been, and however small the diminution by every new uncertainty. No finite object can subsist under a decrease repeated *in infinitum*; and even the vastest quantity, which can enter into human imagination must in this manner be reduc'd to nothing. Let our first belief be never so strong, it must infallibly perish by passing thro' so many new examinations, of which each diminishes somewhat of its force and vigour. When I reflect on the natural fallibility of my judgment, I have less confidence in my opinions, than when I only consider the objects concerning which I reason; and when I proceed still farther, to turn the scrutiny against every successive estimation I make of my faculties, all the rules of logic require a continual diminution, and at last a total extinction of belief and evidence.

Shou'd it here be ask'd me, whether I sincerely assent to this argument, which I seem to take such pains to inculcate, and whether I be really one of those sceptics, who hold that all is uncertain, and that our judgment is not in *any* thing possest of *any* measures of truth and falshood; I shou'd reply, that this question is entirely superfluous, and that neither I, nor any other person was ever sincerely and constantly of that opinion. Nature, by an absolute and uncontroulable necessity has determin'd us to judge as well as to breathe and feel; nor can we any more forbear viewing certain objects in a stronger and fuller light, upon account of their customary connexion with a present impression, than we can hinder ourselves from thinking as long as we are awake, or seeing the surrounding bodies, when we turn our eyes towards them in broad sunshine. Whoever has taken the pains to refute the cavils of this *total* scepticism, has really disputed without an antagonist, and endeavour'd by arguments to establish a faculty, which nature has antecedently implanted in the mind, and render'd unavoidable.

My intention then in displaying so carefully the arguments of that fantastic sect, is only to make the reader sensible of the truth of my hypothesis, *that all our reasonings concerning causes and effects are deriv'd from nothing but custom; and that belief is more properly an act of the sensitive, than of the cogitative part of our natures.* I have here prov'd, that the very same principles, which make us form a decision upon any subject, and correct that decision by the consideration of our genius and capacity, and of the situation of our mind, when we examin'd that subject; I say, I have prov'd, that these same principles, when carry'd farther, and apply'd to every new reflex judgment, must, by continually diminishing the original evidence, at last reduce it to nothing, and utterly subvert all belief and opinion. If belief, therefore, were a simple act of the thought, without any peculiar manner of conception, or the addition of a force and vivacity, it must infallibly destroy itself, and in every case terminate in a total suspense of judgment. But as experience will sufficiently convince any one, who thinks it worth while to try, that tho' he can find no error in the foregoing arguments, yet he still continues to believe, and think, and reason as usual, he may safely conclude, that his reasoning and belief is some sensation or peculiar manner of conception, which 'tis impossible for mere ideas and reflections to destroy.

But here, perhaps, it may be demanded, how it happens, even upon my hypothesis, that these arguments above-explain'd produce not a total suspense of judgment, and after what manner the mind ever retains a degree of assurance in any subject? For as these new probabilities, which by their repetition perpetually diminish the original evidence, are founded on the very same principles, whether of thought or sensation, as the primary judgment, it may seem unavoidable, that in either case they must equally subvert it, and by the opposition, either of contrary thoughts or sensations, reduce the mind to a total uncertainty. I suppose, there is some question propos'd to me, and that after revolving over the impressions of my memory and senses, and carrying my thoughts from them to such objects, as are commonly conjoin'd with them, I feel a stronger and more forcible conception on the one side, than on the other. This strong conception forms my first decision. I suppose, that afterwards I examine my judgment itself, and observing from experience, that 'tis sometimes just and sometimes erroneous, I consider it as regulated by contrary principles or causes, of which some lead to truth, and some to error; and in ballancing these contrary causes, I diminish by a new probability the assurance of my first decision. This new probability is liable to the same diminution as the foregoing, and so on, *in infinitum*. 'Tis therefore demanded, *how it happens, that even after all we retain a degree of belief, which is sufficient for our purpose, either in philosophy or common life.*

I answer, that after the first and second decision; as the action of the mind becomes forc'd and unnatural, and the ideas faint and obscure; tho' the principles of judgment, and the ballancing of opposite causes be the same as at the very beginning; yet their influence on the imagination, and the vigour they add to, or diminish from the thought, is by no means equal. Where the mind reaches not its objects with easiness and facility, the same principles have not the same effect as in a more natural conception of the ideas; nor does the imagination feel a sensation, which holds any proportion with that which arises from its common judgments and opinions. The attention is on the stretch: The posture of the mind is uneasy; and the spirits being diverted from their natural course, are not govern'd in their movements by the same laws, at least not to the same degree, as when they flow in their usual channel.

If we desire similar instances, 'twill not be very difficult to find them. The present subject of metaphysics will supply us abundantly. The same argument, which wou'd have been esteem'd convincing in a reasoning concerning history or politics, has little or no influence in these abstruser subjects, even tho' it be perfectly comprehended; and that because there is requir'd a study and an effort of thought, in order to its being comprehended: And this effort of thought disturbs the operation of our sentiments, on which the belief depends. The case is the same in other subjects. The straining of the imagination always hinders the regular flowing of the passions and sentiments. A tragic poet, that wou'd represent his heroes as very ingenious and witty in their misfortunes, wou'd never touch the passions. As the emotions of the soul prevent any subtile reasoning and reflection, so these latter actions of the mind are equally prejudicial to the former. The mind, as well as the body, seems to be endow'd with a certain precise degree of force and activity, which it never employs in one action, but at the expence of all the rest. This is more evidently true, where the actions are of quite different natures; since in that case the force of the mind is not only diverted, but even the disposition chang'd, so as to render us incapable of a sudden transition from one action to the other, and still more of performing both at once. No wonder, then, the conviction, which arises from a subtile reasoning, diminishes in proportion to the efforts, which the imagination makes to enter into the reasoning, and to conceive it in all its parts. Belief, being a lively conception, can never be entire, where it is not founded on something natural and easy.

This I take to be the true state of the question, and cannot approve of that expeditious way, which some take with the sceptics, to reject at once all their arguments without enquiry or examination. If the sceptical reasonings be strong, say they, 'tis a proof, that reason may have some force and authority: if weak, they can never be sufficient to invalidate all the conclusions of our understanding. This argument is not just; because the sceptical reasonings, were it possible for them to exist, and were they not destroy'd by their subtility, wou'd be successively both strong and weak, according to the successive dispositions of the mind. Reason first appears in possession of the throne, prescribing laws, and imposing maxims, with an absolute sway and authority. Her enemy, therefore, is oblig'd to take shelter under her protection, and by making use of rational arguments to prove the fallaciousness and imbecility of reason, produces, in a manner, a patent under her hand and seal. This patent has at first an authority, proportion'd to the present and immediate authority of reason, from which it is deriv'd. But as it is suppos'd to be contradictory to reason, it gradually diminishes the force of that governing power, and its own at the same time; till at last they both vanish away into nothing, by a regular and just diminution. The sceptical and dogmatical reasons are of the same kind, tho' contrary in their operation and tendency; so that where the latter is strong, it has an enemy of equal force in the former to encounter; and as their forces were at first equal, they still continue so, as long as either of them subsists; nor does one of them lose any force in the contest, without taking as much from its antagonist. 'Tis happy, therefore, that nature breaks the force of all sceptical arguments in time, and keeps them from having any considerable influence on the understanding. Were we to trust entirely to their self-destruction, that can never take place, 'till they have first subverted all conviction, and have totally destroy'd human reason.

CONCLUSION OF THIS BOOK

But before I launch out into those immense depths of philosophy, which lie before me, I find myself inclin'd to stop a moment in my present station, and to ponder that voyage, which I have undertaken, and which undoubtedly requires the utmost art and industry to be brought to a happy conclusion. Methinks I am like a man, who having struck on many shoals, and having narrowly escap'd ship-wreck in passing a small frith, has yet the temerity to put out to sea in the same leaky weather-beaten vessel, and even carries his ambition so far as to think of compassing the globe under these disadvantageous circumstances. My memory of past errors and perplexities, makes me diffident for the future. The wretched condition, weakness, and disorder of the faculties, I must employ in my enquiries, encrease my apprehensions. And the impossibility of amending or correcting these faculties, reduces me almost to despair, and makes me resolve to perish on the barren rock, on which I am at present, rather than venture myself upon that boundless ocean, which runs out into immensity. This sudden view of my danger strikes me with melancholy; and as 'tis usual for that passion, above all others, to indulge itself; I cannot forbear feeding my despair, with all those desponding reflections, which the present subject furnishes me with in such abundance.

I am first affrighted and confounded with that forelorn solitude, in which I am plac'd in my philosophy, and fancy myself some strange uncouth monster, who not being able to mingle and unite in society, has been expell'd all human commerce, and left utterly abandon'd and disconsolate. Fain wou'd I run into the crowd for shelter and warmth; but cannot prevail with myself to mix with such deformity. I call upon others to join me, in order to make a company apart; but no one will hearken to me. Every one keeps at a distance, and dreads that storm, which beats upon me from every side. I have expos'd myself to the enmity of all metaphysicians, logicians, mathematicians, and even theologians; and can I wonder at the insults I must suffer? I have declar'd my dis-approbation of their systems; and can I be surpriz'd, if they shou'd express a hatred of mine and of my person? When I look abroad, I foresee on every side, dispute, contradiction, anger, calumny and detraction. When I turn my eye inward, I find nothing but doubt and ignorance. All the world conspires to oppose and contradict me; tho' such is my weakness, that I feel all my opinions loosen and fall of themselves, when unsupported by the approbation of others. Every step I take is with hesitation, and every new reflection makes me dread an error and absurdity in my reasoning.

For with what confidence can I venture upon such bold enterprizes, when beside those numberless infirmities peculiar to myself, I find so many which are common to human nature? Can I be sure, that in leaving all establish'd opinions I am following truth; and by what criterion shall I distinguish her, even if fortune shou'd at last guide me on her foot-steps? After the most accurate and exact of my reasonings, I can give no reason why I shou'd assent to it; and feel nothing but a *strong* propensity to consider objects *strongly* in that view, under which they appear to me. Experience is a principle, which instructs me in the several conjunctions of objects for the past. Habit is another principle, which determines me to expect the same for the future; and both of them conspiring to operate upon the imagination, make me form certain ideas in a more intense and lively manner, than others, which are not attended with the same advantages. Without this quality, by which the mind enlivens some ideas beyond others (which seemingly is so trivial, and so little founded on reason) we cou'd never assent to any argument, nor carry our view beyond those few objects, which are present to our senses. Nay, even to these objects we cou'd never attribute any existence, but what was dependent on the senses; and must comprehend them entirely in that succession of perceptions, which constitutes our self or person. Nay farther, even with relation to that succession, we cou'd only admit of those perceptions, which are immediately present to our consciousness, nor cou'd those lively images, with which the memory presents us, be ever receiv'd as true pictures of past perceptions. The memory, senses, and understanding are, therefore, all of them founded on the imagination, or the vivacity of our ideas. . . .

This deficiency in our ideas is not, indeed, perceiv'd in common life, nor are we sensible, that in the most usual conjunctions of cause and effect we are as ignorant of the ultimate principle, which binds them together, as in the most unusual and extraordinary. But this proceeds merely from an illusion of the imagination; and the question is, how far we ought to yield to these illusions. This question is very difficult, and reduces us to a very dangerous dilemma, whichever way we answer it. For if we assent to every trivial suggestion of the fancy; beside that these suggestions are often contrary to each other; they lead us into such errors, absurdities, and obscurities, that we must at last become asham'd of our credulity. Nothing is more dangerous to reason than the flights of the imagination, and nothing has been the occasion of more mistakes among philosophers. Men of bright fancies may in this respect be compar'd to those angels, whom the scripture represents as covering their eyes with their wings. This has already appear'd in so many instances, that we may spare ourselves the trouble of enlarging upon it any farther.

But on the other hand, if the consideration of these instances makes us take a resolution to reject all the trivial suggestions of the fancy, and adhere to the understanding, that is, to the general and more establish'd properties of the imagination; even this resolution, if steadily executed, wou'd be dangerous, and attended with the most fatal consequences. For I have already shewn, that the understanding, when it acts alone, and according to its most general principles, entirely subverts itself, and leaves not the lowest degree of evidence in any proposition, either in philosophy or common life. We save ourselves from this total scepticism only by means of that singular and seemingly trivial property of the fancy, by which we enter with difficulty into remote views of things, and are not able to accompany them with so sensible an impression, as we do those, which are more easy and natural . . .

But what have I here said, that reflections very refin'd and metaphysical have little or no influence upon us? This opinion I can scarce forbear retracting, and condemning from my present feeling and experience. The *intense* view of these manifold contradictions and imperfections in human reason has so wrought upon me, and heated my brain, that I am ready to reject all belief and reasoning, and can look upon no opinion even as more probable or likely than another. Where am I, or what? From what causes do I derive my existence, and to what condition shall I return? Whose favour shall I court, and whose anger must I dread? What beings surround me? and on whom have I any influence, or who have any influence on me? I am confounded with all these questions, and begin to fancy myself in the most deplorable condition imaginable, inviron'd with the deepest darkness, and utterly depriv'd of the use of every member and faculty.

Most fortunately it happens, that since reason is incapable of dispelling these clouds, nature herself suffices to that purpose, and cures me of this philosophical melancholy and delirium, either by relaxing this bent of mind, or by some avocation, and lively impression of my senses, which obliterate all these chimeras. I dine, I play a game of back-gammon, I converse, and am merry with my friends; and when after three or four hours' amusement, I wou'd return to these speculations, they appear so cold, and strain'd, and ridiculous, that I cannot find in my heart to enter into them any farther.

Here then I find myself absolutely and necessarily determin'd to live, and talk, and act like other people in the common affairs of life. But notwithstanding that my natural propensity, and the course of my animal spirits and passions reduce me to this indolent belief in the general maxims of the world, I still feel such remains of my former disposition, that I am ready to throw all my books and papers into the fire, and resolve never more to renounce the pleasures of life for the sake of reasoning and philosophy. For those are my sentiments in that splenetic humour, which governs me at present. I may, nay I must yield to the current of nature, in submitting to my senses and understanding; and in this blind submission I shew most perfectly my sceptical disposition and principles. But does follow, that I must strive against the current of nature, which leads me to indolence and pleasure; that I must seclude myself, in some measure, from the commerce and society of men, which is so agreeable; and that I must torture my brain with subtilities and sophistries, at the very time that I cannot satisfy myself concerning the reasonableness of so painful an application, nor have any tolerable prospect of arriving by its means at truth and certainty. Under what obligation do I lie of making such an abuse of time? And to what end can it serve either for the service of mankind, or for my own private interest? No: If I must be a fool, as all those who reason or believe any thing *certainly* are, my follies shall at least be natural and agreeable. Where I strive against my inclination, I shall have a good reason for my resistance; and will no more be led a wandering into such dreary solitudes, and rough passages, as I have hitherto met with.

These are the sentiments of my spleen and indolence; and indeed I must confess, that philosophy has nothing to oppose to them, and expects a victory more from the returns of a serious good-humour'd disposition, than from the force of reason and conviction. In all the incidents of life we ought still to preserve our scepticism. If we believe, that fire warms, or water refreshes, 'tis only because it costs us too much pains to think otherwise. Nay if we are philosophers, it ought only to be upon sceptical principles, and from an inclination, which we feel to the employing ourselves after that manner. Where reason is lively, and mixes itself with some propensity, it ought to be assented to. Where it does not, it never can have any title to operate upon us. . . .

Gordon S. Wood

A professor of history at Brown University and an authority on the American Revolution, Gordon S. Wood focuses this article on the question of how Enlightenment thinkers conceived of causality. Attributing political and social events to the actions of individuals, many living in the eighteenth century found meaning in concepts of conspiracy. By the end of that century, however, ideas of complex social processes and unintended consequences began to fill the intellectual gap formerly occupied by understandings of specific, personal responsibility. As writers like Adam Smith produced new models of causality, new ways of interpreting reality emerged. That attempt to understand society in terms of larger principles and processes rather than individuals would gain even more significance through the intellectual and popular understandings produced by nineteenth-century thinkers like Marx and Tocqueville.

GORDON S. WOOD
(1982)

Conspiracy and the Paranoid Style:

Causality and Deceit in the

Eighteenth Century

... More than any other period of English history, the century or so that followed the
Restoration was the great era of conspiratorial fears and imaginary intrigues.... Everywhere
people sensed designs within designs, cabals within cabals; there were court conspiracies,
backstairs conspiracies, ministerial conspiracies, factional conspiracies, aristocratic conspiracies, and by the last half of the eighteenth century even conspiracies of gigantic secret societies
that cut across national boundaries and spanned the Atlantic....

Such conspiratorial thinking, moreover, was not confined to the English-speaking world.
Some of the most grandiose and elaborate plots of the century were imagined by Frenchmen of
various social ranks. Like the American Revolution, the French Revolution was born in an
atmosphere of conspiratorial fears. There were plots by the ministers, by the queen, by the
aristocracy, by the clergy; everywhere there were secret managers behind the scenes pulling
the strings of the great events of the Revolution. The entire Revolution was even seen by some
as the planned consequence of a huge Masonic conspiracy. The paranoid style, it seems, was a
mode of expression common to the age....

To understand how "reasonable people" could believe in the prevalence of plots, we should
begin by taking their view of events at face value and examine what it rationally implied. It was
obviously a form of causal explanation, a "tendency of many causes to one event," said Samuel
Johnson. To us this is a crude and peculiar sort of causal explanation because it rests entirely on
individual intentions or motives. It is, as Hofstadter pointed out, a "rationalistic" and "personal"
explanation: "decisive events are not taken as part of the stream of history, but as the consequences

Reprinted from the *William and Mary Quarterly* 39 (1982) by permission of Gordon S. Wood.

of someone's will." To those who think in conspiratorial terms, things do not "just happen", they are "brought about, step by step, by will and intention." Concatenations of events are the products not, as we sophisticated historians might say, of "social forces" or "the stream of history" but of the concerted designs of individuals.

The paranoid style, in other words, is a mode of causal attribution based on particular assumptions about the nature of social reality and the necessity of moral responsibility in human affairs. It presumes a world of autonomous, freely acting individuals who are capable of directly and deliberately bringing about events through their decisions and actions, and who thereby can be held morally responsible for what happens. We are the heirs of this conception of cause, and its assumptions still permeate our culture, although, as our system of criminal punishment shows, in increasingly archaic and contradictory ways. Most of the eighteenth-century world of thought remains our world, so much so, indeed, that we have trouble perceiving how different we really are. We may still talk about causes and effects, but, as Hofstadter's invocation of "the stream of history" suggests, we often do so in ways the eighteenth century would not have understood. If we are to make sense of that period's predilection for conspiratorial thinking, we must suspend our modern understanding about how events ought to be explained and open ourselves to that different world.

There had, of course, been many conspiratorial interpretations of political affairs before the eighteenth century. Such interpretations rested on modes of apprehending reality that went back to classical antiquity. For centuries men had relied on "the spirit of classic ethical psychology, upon an *analyse du coeur humain*, not upon discovery or premonitions of historical forces" in explaining public events. There was nothing new in seeing intrigue, deceit, and cabals in politics. From Sallust's description of Cataline through Machiavelli's lengthy discussion in his *Discourses* conspiracy was a common feature of political theory. But classical and Renaissance accounts of plots differed from most of the conspiratorial interpretations of the eighteenth century. They usually described actions by which ambitious politicians gained control of governments: conspiracy was taken for granted as a normal means by which rulers were deposed. Machiavelli detailed dozens of such plots. Indeed, he wrote, "many more princes have lost their lives and their positions through them than through open war." Such conspiracies occurred within the small ruling circles of a few great men in limited political worlds where everyone knew everyone else. The classical and Renaissance discussions of conspiracies have a matter-of-fact quality. They were not imagined or guessed at; they happened. Cataline actually plotted to take over Rome; Brutus and Cassius really did conspire against Caesar.

During the early modern era conspiracy continued to be a common term of politics. Seventeenth-century England was filled with talk and fears of conspiracies of all kinds. There were French plots, Irish plots, Popish plots, Whig plots, Tory plots, Jacobite plots; there was even "the Meal Tub Plot." Yet by this period many of the conspiracies had become very different from those depicted in earlier centuries of Western history. To be sure, some of them, like the Gunpowder Plot of 1605 to blow up Parliament or the "Rye House Plot" of 1683 to seize the king, were of the traditional sort described by Machiavelli, designed to subvert the existing government. But other references to conspiracy took a new and different form. The term was still pejorative and charged with suspicion, but now it became used more vaguely and broadly to refer to any combination of persons, including even members of the government itself, united for a presumed common end. The word acquired a more general and indeterminate meaning in political discourse. Its usage suggested confusion rather than certainty. Conspiracies like those of Charles II's Cabal became less matters of fact and more matters of inference. Accounts of plots by court or government were no longer descriptions of actual events but interpretations of otherwise puzzling concatenations of events. By the eighteenth century conspiracy was not simply a means of explaining how rulers were deposed; it had become a common means of explaining how rulers and others directing political events really operated. It was a term used not so much by those intimate with the sources of political events as by those removed from the events and, like Farquhar's Scrub, bewildered by them.

Unlike the schemes of antiquity and the Renaissance, which flowed from the simplicity and limitedness of politics, the conspiratorial interpretations of the Augustan Age flowed from the expansion and increasing complexity of the political world. Unprecedented demographic and economic developments in early modern Europe were massively altering the nature of society and politics. There were more people more distanced from one another and from the apparent centers of political decision making. The conceptual worlds of many individuals were being broadened and transformed. The more people became strangers to one another and the less they knew of one another's hearts, the more suspicious and mistrustful they became, ready as never before in Western history to see deceit and deception at work. Relationships between superiors and subordinates, rulers and ruled, formerly taken for granted, now became disturbingly problematical, and people became uncertain of who was who and who was doing what. Growing proportions of the population were more politically conscious and more concerned with what seemed to be the abused power and privileges of ruling elites. Impassioned efforts were made everywhere to arouse "the vigilance of the public eye" against those few men "who cannot exist without a scheme in their heads," those "turbulent, scheming, maliciously cunning, plotters of mischief." The warnings against rulers grew more anxious and fearful, the expressions of suspicion more frenzied and strident, because assumptions about how public affairs operated became more and more separated from reality. It was easy for a fifteenth-century nobleman, describing political events, to say that "it will be sufficient to speak of the high-ranking people, for it is through them that God's power and justice are made known." But by the eighteenth century this tracing of all events back to the ambitions and actions of only the high-ranking leaders was being stretched to the breaking point. Society was composed not simply of great men and their retainers but of numerous groups, interests, and "classes" whose actions could not be easily deciphered. Human affairs were more complicated, more interdependent, and more impersonal than they had ever been in Western history.

Yet at this very moment when the world was outrunning man's capacity to explain it in personal terms, in terms of the passions and schemes of individuals, the most enlightened of the age were priding themselves on their ability to do just that. The widespread resort to conspiratorial interpretations grew out of this contradiction.

Conspiratorial interpretations—attributing events to the concerned designs of willful individuals—became a major means by which educated men in the early modern period ordered and gave meaning to their political world. Far from being symptomatic of irrationality, this conspiratorial mode of explanation represented an enlightened stage in Western man's long struggle to comprehend his social reality. It flowed from the scientific promise of the Enlightenment and represented an effort, perhaps in retrospect a last desperate effort, to hold men personally and morally responsible for their actions.

Personalistic explanations had, of course, long been characteristic of premodern European society and are still characteristic of primitive peoples. Premodern men lacked our modern repertory of explanations and could not rely on those impersonal forces such as industrialization, modernization, or the "stream of history" that we so blithely invoke to account for complicated combinations of events. They were unable, as we say, to "rise to the conception of movements." For that different, distant world the question asked of an event was not "how did it happen?" but "who did it?"

Yet despite this stress on persons rather than processes, premodern men always realized that much of what happened was beyond human agency and understanding. Even those classical and Renaissance writers who stressed that events were due to "the wisdoms and follies, the virtues and vices of individuals who made decisions" built their histories and tragic dramas around the extent to which such heroic individuals could prevail against unknown fortune. Ultimately the world seemed uncontrollable and unpredictable, ruled by mysterious forces of fate or chance, shadowed in inscrutability.

At the opening of the modern era Protestant reformers invoked divine providence and the omnipotence of God in order to stamp out the traditional popular reliance on luck and magic and to renew a sense of design and moral purpose in the world. Life, they held, was not a lottery but the working out of God's purpose and judgements, or "special providences." Men were morally responsible for events; even natural catastrophes like earthquakes and floods were seen as divine punishments for human misbehavior. Still, it remained evident that life was uncertain and precarious and that God moved in very mysterious ways. As the Puritan Increase Mather observed as late as 1684, "*things many times come to pass contrary to humane probabilities and the rational Conjectures and expectations of men.*" Nature itself was not always consistent, for things sometimes acted "*otherwise than according to their natures and proper inclinations.*" Humans might glimpse those parts of God's design that he chose to reveal, but ultimately they could never "be able fully to understand by what Rules the Holy and Wise God ordereth all events Prosperous and adverse which come to pass in the world." If there was comfort in knowing that what seemed chaotic, fortuitous, or accidental was in reality directed by God, it nonetheless remained true that the "ways of Providence are unsearchable."

At the very time that Mather was writing, however, God was preparing to "let Newton be": the treatise that was to be enlarged into the first book of the *Principia* was completed in 1684. Of course the scientific revolution of the seventeenth century—or, more accurately, the new Western consciousness of which that revolution was the most important expression—did not make all immediately light. Yet many people now had less fear of chaos and contingency and greater confidence in their ability to understand events, so much so that sophisticates like George Savile, marquis of Halifax, could even warn against "that common error of applying God's judgments upon particular occasions." The world lost some of its mystery and became more manipulatable. Although the new science tended to remove man from the center of the physical universe, at the same time it brought him to the center of human affairs in ways that even classical and Renaissance thinkers had scarcely conceived of. It promised him the capacity to predict and control not only nature but his own society, and it proceeded to make him directly and consciously responsible for the course of human events. Ultimately the implications of this momentous shift created the cultural matrix out of which eighteenth-century conspiratorial interpretations developed.

The new science assumed a world of mechanistic cause and effect in which what happens does so only because something else happened before. Philosophers since Aristotle had talked of causes but never before in terms of such machine-like regularity, such chains of consequences. "When the world became a machine," writes Jacob Bronowski, "[cause] became the god within the machine." Mechanistic causality became the paradigm in which the enlightened analysis of all behavior and events now had to take place. Cause was something that produced an effect; every effect had a cause; the cause and its effect were integrally related. Such thinking created a new world of laws, measurements, predictions, and constancies or regularities of behavior—all dependent on the same causes producing the same effects. "The knowledge of particular phenomena may gratify a barren curiosity," Samuel Stanhope Smith told a generation of Princeton students, "but they are of little real use, except, as they tend to establish some general law, which will enable the accurate observer to predict similar effects in all time to come, in similar circumstances, and to depend upon the result. Such general laws alone deserve the name of science."

The change in consciousness came slowly, confusedly, and reluctantly. Few were immediately willing to abandon belief in the directing providence of God. Newton himself endeavored to preserve God's autonomy. "A God without dominion, providence, and final causes," he said, "is nothing but Fate and Nature." In fact, the Christian belief that nature was ordered by God's will was an essential presupposition of early modern science. Yet despite the continued stress by Newton's followers on God's control over the workings of nature, many eighteenth-century philosophers gradually came to picture the deity as a clockmaker, and some even went so far as to deny that God had anything at all to do with the physical movement of the universe. The logic of the new science implied a world that ran itself.

To posit the independence of the natural world was exciting enough; to conceive of a human world without God's judgements and providences was simply breathtaking: it was in fact what centrally defined the Enlightenment. The work of John Locke and other philosophers opened reflective minds to the startling supposition that society, though no doubt ordained in principle by God, was man's own creation—formed and sustained, and thus alterable, by human beings acting autonomously and purposefully. It came to seem that if men could understand the natural order that God had made, then perhaps they could eventually understand the social order that they themselves had made. From the successes of natural science, or what the eighteenth century termed natural philosophy, grew the conviction that moral laws—the chains of cause and effect in human behavior—could be discovered that would match those of the physical world. Thus was generated eighteenth-century moral philosophy—the search for the uniformities and regularities of man's behavior that has proliferated into the various social sciences of our own time.

Finding the laws of behavior became the consuming passion of the Enlightenment. In such a liberal and learned world there could no longer be any place for miracles or the random happenings of chance. Chance, it was now said, was "only a name to cover our ignorance of the cause of any event." God may have remained the primary cause of things, but in the minds of the enlightened he had left men to work out the causes and effects of their lives free from his special interventions. All that happened in society was to be reduced to the strictly human level of men's motivations and goals. "Humanity," said William Warburton in 1727, "is the only cause of human vicissitudes." The source of man's calamities, wrote Constantin François de Chasseboeuf, comte de Volney in 1791, lay not in "the distant heavens. . . . it resides in man himself, he carries it with him in the inward recesses of his own heart." Such beliefs worked their way through every variety of intellectual endeavor in the age. They produced not only a new genre of literature—the novel with its authorial control and design—but also a new kind of man-centered causal history, one based on the same assumptions as the age's conspiratorial interpretations.

English history since the Revolution of 1688, as Henry St. John, Viscount Bolingbroke saw it from the vantage point of the 1730s, was "not the effect of ignorance, mistakes, or what we call chance, but of design and scheme in those who had the sway at that time." This could be proved by seeing "events that stand recorded in history . . . as they followed one another, or as they produced one another, causes or effects, immediate or remote." "History supplies the defects of our own experience" and demonstrates that there are really no such things as accidents; "it shows us causes as in fact they were laid, with their immediate effects: and it enables us to guess at future events." "History," said Edward Gibbon simply, "is the science of causes and effects."

Extending this concept from the realm of natural phenomena into the moral world of human affairs was not an easy matter. Natural philosophers like Newton had sought to stave off the numbing necessitarianism implied in a starkly mechanistic conception of cause and effect by positing various God-inspired "active principles" as the causal agents of motion, gravity, heat, and the like. Even those later eighteenth-century scientists who saw nature as self-contained and requiring no divine intervention whatsoever still presumed various energizing powers in matter itself. The need for some sort of active principle in human affairs was felt even more acutely, for the new mechanistic philosophy posed a threat to what Arthur O. Lovejoy has called the "intense ethical inwardness" of Western Christendom. The belief "that whatever moves and acts does so mechanically and necessarily" was ultimately incompatible with personalistic thinking and cast doubt on man's moral responsibility for his actions. If human affairs were really the consequence of one thing repeatedly and predictably following upon another, the social world would become as determined as the physical world seemed to be. Theologians like Jonathan Edwards welcomed this logic and subtly used the new cause-and-effect philosophy to justify God's sovereignty. But other moral philosophers had no desire to create a secular version of divine providence or to destroy the voluntarism of either God or man, and thus sought to find a place for free will in the operations of the machine. They did so not by repudiating the paradigm of cause and effect but by trying to identify causes in human affairs with the motives, mind, or will of individuals. Just as natural scientists like Cadwallader Colden, believing that in a mechanistic physical world "there must be some power or force, or principle of Action," groped toward a modern concept of energy, so too did moral philosophers seek to discover the powers or principles of action that lay behind the sequences of human affairs—in effect, looking within the minds and hearts of men for the moral counterpart of Colden's physical energy.

Such efforts to reconcile the search for laws of human behavior with the commitment to moral capability lay behind the numerous controversies over free will that bedeviled the eighteenth century. To be enlightened, it seemed, was to try one's hand at writing an essay on what David Hume called "the most contentious question of metaphysics"—the question of liberty and necessity. Despite all the bitter polemics between the libertarians and the necessitarians, however, both sides were caught up in the new thinking about causality. Both assumed, as Hume pointed out, that "the conjunction between motives and voluntary actions is as regular and uniform, as that between the cause and effect in any part of nature." Men's motives or will thus became the starting point in the sequential chain of causes and effects in human affairs. All human actions and events could now be seen scientifically as the products of men's intentions. If they were not, if men "are not necessarily determined by motives," then, said the Scottish moralist Thomas Reid, "all their actions must be capricious." Only by identifying causes with motives was any sort of human science and predictability possible, and only then could morality be preserved in the new, mechanistic causal world.

Since it was "granted on all hands, that moral good and evil lie in the state of mind, or prevailing internal disposition of the agent," searching out the causes of social events meant discovering in these agents the motives, the "voluntary choice and design," that led them to act—the energizing principle, the inner springs of their behavior. "Every moral event must have an answerable cause. . . . Every such event must then have a *moral* cause." Moral deeds implied moral doers; when things happen in society, individuals with particular intentions, often called "designs," must be at the bottom of them. All social processes could be reduced to specific individual passions and interests. "Ambition and avarice," wrote the Revolutionary historian Mercy Otis Warren, "are *the leading springs* which generally actuate the restless mind. From these *primary sources of corruption* have arisen all the rapine and confusion, the depredation and ruin, that have spread distress over the face of the earth from the days of Nimrod to Cesar, and from Cesar to an arbitrary prince of the house of Brunswick." This widespread belief that explanations of social phenomena must be sought in the moral nature of man himself ultimately reduced all eighteenth-century moral philosophy—its history and its social analysis—to what would come to be called psychology.

Once men's designs were identified as the causes of human events, the new paradigm of causality worked to intensify and give a scientific gloss to the classic concern with the human heart and the ethical inwardness of Christian culture. Indeed, never before or since in Western history has man been held so directly and morally responsible for the events of his world. Because the new idea of causality presumed a homogeneous identity, an "indissoluble connection," between causes and effects, it became difficult to think of social effects, however remote in time, that were not morally linked to particular causes, that is, to particular human designs. There could be no more in the effects than existed in the causes. "Outward actions being determined by the will," they partook "of the nature of moral good or evil only with reference to their cause, viz. internal volition."

It could now be taken for granted that the cause and the effect were so intimately related that they necessarily shared the same moral qualities. Whatever the particular moral character of the cause, that is, the motive or inclination of the actor, "the effect appears to be of the same kind." Good intentions and beliefs would therefore result in good actions; evil motives caused evil actions. Of course, mistakes might happen, and occasionally actions "proceeded not from design." But continued or regular moral actions could follow only from similar moral intentions. Only by assuming this close relationship between causes and effects—"this *inference* from motives to voluntary actions; from characters to conduct," said Hume—was the eighteenth-century science of human behavior made possible.

This presumed moral identity between cause and effect, between motive and deed, accounts for the excited reaction of moralists to Bernard Mandeville's satiric paradox of "private vices, publick benefits." Mandeville was unusual for his time in grasping the complexity of public events and the ways in which political effects could outrun and differ from their causes. "We ought," he wrote, "to forebear judging rashly of ministers and their actions, especially when we are unacquainted with every circumstance of an affair. Measures may be rightly concerted, and such causalties intervene, as may make the best design miscarry. . . . Humane understanding is too shallow to foresee the result of what is subject to many variations." Such skepticism could not be easily tolerated by that enlightened and moral age. Mandeville and all those who would ignore private intentions in favor of public results threatened to unhinge both man's moral responsibility for his actions and the homogeneous relation that presumably existed between cause and effect. To break the necessary moral connection between cause and effect, to make evil the author of good and vice versa, would be, it was said, "to confound all differences of character, to destroy all distinction between right and wrong, and to make the most malicious and the most benevolent being of precisely the same temper and disposition."

Mandeville clearly perceived that much of human activity had become an "incomprehensible Chain of Causes." But he, like others of his time, had no better way of describing the multitude of complicated and crisscrossing causal chains he saw than to invoke the traditional Protestant concept of "providence." For those who would be enlightened and scientific, this resort to the mysterious hand of God was no explanation of human affairs at all but rather a step backward into darkness. Things happened, as John Adams noted, by human volition, either "by Accident or Design." Some confusing event or effect might be passed off as an accident—the result of somebody's mistaken intention—but a series of events that seemed to form a pattern could be no accident. Having only the alternative of "providence" as an impersonal abstraction to describe systematic linkages of human actions, the most enlightened of the age could only conclude that regular patterns of behavior were the consequences of concerted human intentions—that is, the result of a number of people coming together to promote a collective design or conspiracy. The human mind, it seemed to Jonathan Edwards, had a natural disposition, "when it sees a thing begin to be," not only "to conclude certainly, that there is a *Cause* of it," but also, "if it sees a thing to be in a very orderly, regular and exact, manner to conclude that some Design regulated and disposed it." Although Edwards was arguing here for God's "exact regulation of a very great multitude of particulars," a similar leap from a particular cause to a general design was made by eighteenth-century theorists who sought to account for the regularity of human actions by the coincident purposes, not of God, but of human beings.

Many enlightened thinkers of the eighteenth century could therefore no more accept the seeming chaos and contingency of events than the Puritans had. Like the Puritans, they presumed the existence of an ordering power lying beneath the apparently confused surface of events—not God's concealed will, of course, but natural causes embodied in the hidden intentions and wills of men. Those who saw only random chance in events simply did not know enough about these hidden human wills. Just as devout Puritans believed that nothing occurred without God's providence, so the liberal-minded believed that nothing occurred without some person willing it. Earlier, men had sought to decipher the concealed or partially revealed will of God; now they sought to understand the concealed or partially exposed wills of human beings. That, in a nutshell, was what being enlightened was all about.

Some might continue to suggest that "the ways of Heaven are inscrutable; and frequently, the most unlooked-for events have arisen from seemingly the most inadequate causes," and of course others continued to believe that motives and actions did not always coincide, trusting with Dr. Johnson in the old English proverb that "Hell is paved with good intentions." But for those who knew how cause and effect really worked, deception and conspiracy were more morally coherent and intellectually satisfying explanations of the apparent difference between professions and deeds. When effects "cannot be accounted for by any visible cause," it was rational to conclude that "there must be, therefore, some men behind the curtain" who were secretly bringing them about. This commonplace image of figures operating "behind the curtain" was the consequence of a political world that was expanding and changing faster than its available rational modes of explanation could handle. . . .

Well before the close of the eighteenth century, even while conspiratorial interpretations were flourishing under the aegis of enlightened science, alternative ways of explaining events were taking form, prompted by dynamic social changes that were stretching and contorting any simple linkage between human intentions and actions, causes and effects. The expanding, interdependent economic order obviously relied on the activity of thousands upon thousands of insignificant producers and traders whose various and conflicting motives could hardly be deciphered, let alone judged. The growing number of persons and interests participating in politics made causal evaluations ever more difficult. Causes seemed farther and farther removed from their consequences, sometimes disappearing altogether into a distant murkiness. As a result, the inferences of plots and deceptions used to close the widening gap between events and the presumed designs of particular individuals became even more elaborate and contrived. Many were still sure that every social effect, every political event, had to have a purposive human agent as a cause. But men now distinguished more frequently between "remote" and "proximate" causes and between "immediate" and "permanent" effects. Although many continued to assume that the relationship between causes and their effects was intrinsic and morally homogeneous, some moralists noted bewilderingly and sometimes cynically how personal vices like self-love and self-interest could have contrary, indeed beneficial, consequences for society. Men everywhere wrestled with the demands the changing social reality was placing on their thought. Some suggested that self-love might even be a virtue; others complained of "a kind of *mandevillian* chymistry" that converted avarice into benevolence; still others questioned the presumed identity between private motives and public consequences.

Little of this was followed out in any systematic way in the Anglo-American world until the appearance in the latter half of the eighteenth century of that remarkable group of Scottish intellectuals who worked out, in an extraordinary series of writings, a new understanding of the relationship between individuals and events. These Scottish "social scientists" did not and could not by themselves create a new way of conceiving of human affairs, but their writings were an especially clear crystallization of the changes gradually taking place in Western consciousness during the last third of the eighteenth century. Adam Ferguson, Adam Smith, and John Millar sought to undermine what Duncan Forbes has called "a dominant characteristic of the historical thought of the age"—the "tendency to explain events in terms of conscious action by individuals." These Scottish moral philosophers had come to realize more clearly than most eighteenth-century thinkers that men pursuing their own particular aims were led by an "invisible hand" into promoting an end that was no part of their intentions. Traditional historians, complained Ferguson in his *History of Civil Society*, had seen all events as the "effect of design. An author and a work, like cause and effect, are perpetually coupled together." But reality was not so simple. Men, "in striving to remove inconveniences, or to gain apparent and contiguous advantages, arrive at ends which even their imagination could not anticipate, . . . and nations stumble upon establishments, which are indeed the result of human action, but not the execution of any human design."

Such momentous insights would in time help to transform all social and historical thinking in the Western world. But it took more than the writings of philosophers—it took the experiencing of tumultuous events—to shake most European intellectuals out of their accustomed ways of thinking. The French Revolution, more than any other single event, changed the consciousness of Europe. The Revolution was simply too convulsive and too sprawling, involving the participation of too many masses of people, to be easily confined within conventional personalistic and rationalistic modes of explanation. For the most sensitive European intellectuals the Revolution became the cataclysm that shattered once and for all the traditional moral affinity between cause and effect, motives and behavior. That the actions of liberal, enlightened, and well-intentioned men could produce such horror, terror, and chaos, that so much promise could result in so much tragedy, became, said Shelley, "the master theme of the epoch in which we live." What the French Revolution revealed, wrote Wordsworth, speaking for a generation of disillusioned intellectuals, was "this awful truth" that "sin and crime are apt to start from their very opposite qualities." Many European thinkers continued, of course, to describe what happened as the deliberate consequence of the desires and ambitions of individuals. But the scale and complexity of the Revolution now required conspiratorial interpretations of an unprecedented sort. No small group of particular plotters could account for its tumult and mass movements; only elaborately organized secret societies, like the Illuminati or the Freemasons, involving thousands of individuals linked by sinister designs, could be behind the Europe-wide upheaval.

Although such conspiratorial interpretations of the Revolution were everywhere, the best minds—Hegel's in particular—now knew that the jumble of events that made up the Revolution were so complex and overwhelming that they could no longer be explained simply as the products of personal intention. For these thinkers, history could no longer be a combination of individual events managed by particular persons, but had to become a complicated flow or process, a "stream," that swept men along. . . .

The story of this vast transformation in the way men explain events is central to the history of modern Western thought. Indeed, so huge and complicated is it that our easy generalizations are apt to miss its confused and agonized significance for individuals and to neglect the piecemeal ways in which it was worked out in the minds of people—not great philosophers like Hegel or Adam Smith, but more ordinary people, workaday clergymen, writers, and politicians caught up in the problems and polemics of the moment. . . .

Although this concept of the social process transcending the desires of particular individuals presaged a new social order, it was in some respects merely a throwback to a premodern Protestant understanding of divine sovereignty. Many Americans, even nonevangelicals like George Washington, had always been able to "trace the finger of Providence through those dark and mysterious events." Now this traditional notion of providence took on a new importance and even among secular-minded thinkers became identified with "progress" and with the natural principles of society created by multiplicities of people following their natural desires free from artificial restraints, particularly those imposed by laws and government. Providence no longer meant, as it often had in the past, the special interpositions of God in the events of the world but was now increasingly identified almost wholly with the natural pattern these events seemed to form. With such a conception, the virtuous or vicious character of individual beliefs and intentions in the movement of events no longer seemed to matter. Even the "pursuit of gold" could have beneficial results, for "by some interesting filiation, 'there's a Divinity, that shapes our ends'."

As nineteenth-century society became more interdependent and complicated, however, sensitive and reflective observers increasingly saw the efficient causes of events becoming detached from particular self-acting individuals and receding from view. "Small but growing numbers of people," writes historian Thomas L. Haskell in the most perceptive account we have of this development, "found it implausible or unproductive to attribute genuine causal power to those elements of society with which they were intimately and concretely familiar." As these ideas evolved, laying the basis for the emergence of modern social science, attributing events to the conscious design of particular individuals became more and more simplistic. Conspiratorial interpretations of events still thrived, but now they seemed increasingly primitive and quaint.

By our own time, dominated as it is by professional social science, conspiratorial interpretations have become so out of place that, as we have seen, they can be accounted for only as mental aberrations, as a paranoid style symptomatic of psychological disturbance. In our post-industrial, scientifically saturated society, those who continue to attribute combinations of events to deliberate human design may well be peculiar sorts of persons—marginal people, perhaps, removed from the centers of power, unable to grasp the conceptions of complicated causal linkages offered by sophisticated social scientists, and unwilling to abandon the desire to make simple and clear moral judgments of events. But people with such conspiratorial beliefs have not always been either marginal or irrational. Living in this complicated modern world, where the very notion of causality is in doubt, should not prevent us from seeing that at another time and in another culture most enlightened people accounted for events in just this particular way.

Immanuel Kant

Immanuel Kant (1724–1804) led the quiet life of a scholar as a professor of logic and meta-physics in Konigsberg, Prussia. Kant is known as the founder of critical philosophy. Surveying the new scientific truths of his time Kant embarked upon a voyage to obtain certain evidence of the human ability to know, his goal being the transcendence of the philosophical currents of his era, namely rationalism and empiricism. To this extent, Kant delineated the function of reason within the synthesis of sensory data. Yet Kant's work was far more theoretically com-plex than a simplistic assertion of human rationalism. In distinct contrast to René Descartes, he was convinced that the thought process (understanding) and perception (sense) are dis-tinct cognitive capacities. Departing from this dualistic perspective, Kant attempted to assert the authority of science, while simultaneously guarding the autonomy and viability of ethical judgments in his magnum opus, the *Critique of Pure Reason* (1781). Moving beyond strictly empirical assertions concerning human reason, Kant "recognized that aesthetic judgement had to be construed as distinct from practical reason (moral judgement) and understanding (scientific knowledge), and that it formed a necessary though problematic bridge between the two."[1]

The following excerpt belies the difficult nature of such an aim. The journal article "What is Enlightenment?" (1784), written for the Enlightened monarch Frederick the Great, displays an untempered optimism towards the possibilities of education and human volition. If man had still not succeeded in releasing himself from the shackles of ignorance, Kant viewed this form of progress as a distinct possibility. More importantly within the text, Kant espoused the concepts of free thought and reason within the public sphere. Kant articulated the ideal of the bourgeois public sphere, in which practical use of reason was thought to enable and institutionalize public forms of discourse. These public forums for argument, rather than the archaic "might makes right" justification of political power, would enable rational political consensus. While Kant rendered a simplistic or succinct analysis of reason problematic, he remained convinced of its emancipatory potential.

[1]   David Harvey, *The Condition of Postmodernity*, p. 19.

IMMANUEL KANT
(1784)

What Is

Enlightenment?

Enlightenment is man's release from his self-incurred tutelage. Tutelage is man's inability to make use of his understanding without direction from another. Self-incurred is this tutelage when it cause lies not in lack of reason but in lack of resolution and courage to use it without direction from another. *Sapere aude!* "Have courage to use your own reason!"—that is the motto of enlightenment.

Laziness and cowardice are the reasons why so great a portion of mankind, after nature has long since discharged them from external direction (*naturaliter maiorennes*), nevertheless remains under lifelong tutelage, and why it is so easy for others to set themselves up as their guardians. It is so easy not to be of age. If I have a book which understands for me, a pastor who has a conscience for me, a physician who decides my diet, and so forth, I need not trouble myself. I need not think, if I can only pay—others will readily undertake the irksome work for me.

That the step to competence is held to be very dangerous by the far greater portion of mankind (and by the entire fair sex)—quite apart from its being arduous—is seen to by those guardians who have so kindly assumed superintendence over them. After the guardians have first made their domestic cattle dumb and have made sure that these placid creatures will not dare take a single step without the harness of the cart to which they are tethered, the guardians then show them the danger which threatens if they try to go alone. Actually, however, this danger is not so great, for by falling a few times they would finally learn to walk alone. But an example of this failure makes them timid and ordinarily frightens them away from all further trials.

"What Is Enlightenment?" was originally written in 1784. This translation comes from *Kant's Political Writings*, Hans Reiss, ed.; H.B. Nisbet, trans. (Cambridge: Cambridge University Press, 1971), pp. 85–92. ©Cambridge University Press, 1971. Reprinted by permission.

For any single individual to work himself out of the life under tutelage which has become almost his nature is very difficult. He has come to be fond of this state, and he is for the present really incapable of making use of his reason, for no one has ever let him try it out. Statutes and formulas, those mechanical tools of the rational employment or rather misemployment of his natural gifts, are the fetters of an everlasting tutelage. Whoever throws them off makes only an uncertain leap over the narrowest ditch because he is not accustomed to that kind of free motion. Therefore, there are few who have succeeded by their own exercise of mind both in freeing themselves from incompetence and in achieving a steady pace.

But that the public should enlighten itself is more possible; indeed, if only freedom is granted, enlightenment is almost sure to follow. For there will always be some independent thinkers, even among the established guardians of the great masses, who, after throwing off the yoke of tutelage from their own shoulders, will disseminate the spirit of the rational appreciation of both their own worth and every man's vocation for thinking for himself. But be it noted that the public, which has first been brought under this yoke by their guardians, forces the guardians themselves to remain bound when it is incited to do so by some of the guardians who are themselves capable of some enlightenment—so harmful is it to implant prejudices, for they later take vengeance on their cultivators or on their descendants. Thus the public can only slowly attain enlightenment. Perhaps a fall of personal despotism or of avaricious or tyrannical oppression may be accomplished by revolution, but never a true reform in ways of thinking. Rather, new prejudices will serve as well as old ones to harness the great unthinking masses.

For this enlightenment, however, nothing is required but freedom, and indeed the most harmless among all the things to which this term can properly be applied. It is the freedom to make public use of one's reason at every point. But I hear on all sides, "Do not argue!" The officer says: "Do not argue but drill!" The tax collector: "Do not argue but pay!" The cleric: "Do not argue but believe!" Only one prince in the world says, "Argue as much as you will, and about what you will, but obey!" Everywhere there is restriction on freedom.

Which restriction is an obstacle to enlightenment, and which is not an obstacle but a promoter of it? I answer: The public use of one's reason must always be free, and it alone can bring about enlightenment among men. The private use of reason, on the other hand, may often be very narrowly restricted without particularly hindering the progress of enlightenment By the public use of one's reason I understand the use which a person makes of it as a scholar before the reading public. Private use I call that which one may make of it in a particular civil post or office which is entrusted to him. Many affairs which are conducted in the interest of the community require a certain mechanism through which some members of the community must passively conduct themselves with an artificial unanimity, so that the government may direct them to public ends, or at least prevent them from destroying those ends. Here argument is certainly not allowed—one must obey. But so far as a part of the mechanism regards himself at the same time as a member of the whole community or of a society of world citizens, and thus in the role of a scholar who addresses the public (in the proper sense of the word) through his writings, he certainly can argue without hurting the affairs for which he is in part responsible as a passive member. Thus it would be ruinous for an officer in service to debate about the suitability or utility of a command given to him by his superior; he must obey. But the right to make remarks on errors in the military service and to lay them before the public for judgment cannot equitably be refused him as a scholar. The citizen cannot refuse to pay the taxes imposed on him; indeed, an impudent complaint at those levied on him can be punished as a scandal (as it could occasion general refractoriness). But the same person nevertheless does not act contrary to his duty as a citizen when, as a scholar, he publicly expresses his thoughts on the inappropriateness or even the injustice of these levies. Similarly a clergyman is obligated to make his sermon to his pupils in catechism and his congregation conform to the symbol of the church which he serves, for he has been accepted on this condition. But as a scholar he has complete freedom, even the calling, to communicate to the public all his carefully tested and well-meaning thoughts on that which is erroneous in the symbol and to make suggestions for the better organization of the religious body and church. In doing this there is nothing that could be laid as a burden on his conscience. For what he teaches as a consequence of his office as a representative of the church, this he considers something about which he has no freedom to teach according to his own lights; it is something which he is appointed to propound at the dictation of and in the name of another. He will say, "Our church teaches this or that; those are the proofs which it adduces." He thus extracts all practical uses for his congregation from statutes to which he himself would not subscribe with full conviction but to the enunciation of which he can very well pledge himself because it is not impossible that truth lies hidden in them, and, in any case, there is at least nothing in them contradictory to inner religion. For if he believed he had found such in them, he could not conscientiously discharge the duties of his office; he would have to give it up. The use, therefore, which an appointed teacher makes of his reason before his congregation, is merely private, because this congregation is only a domestic one (even if it be a large gathering); with respect to it, as a priest, he is not free, nor can he be free, because he carries out the orders of another. But as a scholar, whose writings speak to his public, the world, the clergyman in the public use of his reason enjoys an unlimited freedom to use his own reason and to speak in his own person. An age cannot bind itself and ordain to put the succeeding one into such a condition that it cannot extend its (at best very occasional) knowledge, purify itself of errors, and progress in general enlightenment. That would be a crime against human nature, the proper destination of which lies precisely in this progress; and the descendants would be fully justified in rejecting those decrees as having been made in an unwarranted and malicious manner.

The touchstone of everything that can be concluded as a law for a people lies in the question whether the people could have imposed such a law on itself. Now such a religious compact might be possible for a short and definitely limited time, as it were, in expectation of a better. One might let every citizen, and especially the clergyman, in the role of scholar, make his comments freely and publicly, i.e., through writing, on the erroneous aspects of the present institution. The newly introduced order might last until insight into the nature of these things had become so general and widely approved that through uniting their voices (even if not unanimously) they could bring a proposal to the throne to take those congregations under protection which had united into a changed religious organization according to their better ideas, without however, hindering others who wish to remain in the order. But to unite in a permanent religious institution which is not to be subject to doubt before the public even in the lifetime of one man, and thereby to make a period of time fruitless in the progress of mankind toward improvement, thus working to the disadvantage of posterity—that is absolutely forbidden. For himself (and only for a short time) a man may postpone enlightenment in what he ought to know, but to renounce it for himself and even more to renounce it for posterity is to injure and trample on the rights of mankind.

If we are asked, "Do we now live in an *enlightened age?*" the answer is, "No," but we do live in an *age of enlightenment*. As things now stand, much is lacking which prevents men from being, or easily becoming, capable of correctly using their own reason in religious matters with assurance and free from outside direction. But, on the other hand, we have clear indications that the field has now been opened wherein men may freely deal with these things and that the obstacles to general enlightenment or the release from self-imposed tutelage are gradually being reduced. In this respect, this is the age of enlightenment, or the century of Frederick.

A prince who does not find it unworthy of himself to say that he holds it to be his duty to prescribe nothing to men in religious matters but to give them complete freedom while renouncing the haughty name of *tolerance*, is himself enlightened and deserves to be esteemed by the greatful world and posterity as the first, at least from the side of government, who divested the human race of its tutelage and left each man free to make use of his reason in matters of conscience. Under him venerable ecclesiastics are allowed, in the role of scholars, and without infringing on their official duties, freely to submit for public testing their judgments and views which here and there diverge from the established symbol. And an even greater freedom is enjoyed by those who are restricted by no official duties. This spirit of freedom spreads beyond this land, even to those in which it must struggle with external obstacles erected by a government which misunderstands its own interest. For an example gives evidence to such a government that in freedom there is not the least cause for concern about public peace and the stability of the community. Men work themselves gradually out of barbarity if only intentional artifices are not made to hold them in it.

I have placed the main point of enlightenment—the escape of men from their self-incurred tutelage—chiefly in matters of religion because our rulers have no interest in playing the guardian with respect to the arts and sciences and also because religious incompetence is not only the most harmful but also the most degrading of all. But the manner of thinking of the head of a state who favors religious enlightenment goes further, and he sees that there is no danger to his lawgiving in allowing his subjects to make public use of their reason and to publish their thoughts on a better formulation of his legislation and even their open-minded criticisms of the laws already made. Of this we have a shining example wherein no monarch is superior to him whom we honor.

But only one who is himself enlightened, is not afraid of shadows, and has a numerous and well-disciplined army to assure public peace, can say: "Argue as much as you will, and about what you will, only obey!" A republic could not dare say such a thing. Here is shown a strange and unexpected trend in human affairs in which almost everything, looked at in the large, is paradoxical. A greater degree of civil freedom appears advantageous to the freedom of mind of the people, and yet it places inescapable limitations upon it; a lower degree of civil freedom, on the contrary, provides the mind with room for each man to extend himself to his full capacity. As nature has uncovered from under this hard shell the seed for which she most tenderly cares—the propensity and vocation to free thinking—this gradually works back upon the character of the people, who thereby gradually become capable of managing freedom; finally, it affects the principles of government, which finds it to its advantage to treat men, who are now more than machines, in accordance with their dignity.

Marquis de Condorcet

To identify the Enlightenment squarely with the popular connotations of "progress" would be an over-simplification; to identify such progress squarely with the Marquis de Condorcet (1743–1794), however, would be entirely proper. Condorcet's most famous work, the *Sketch of the Progress of the Human Mind* (1796), is characterized by an enthusiastic, unrestrained optimism regarding humankind's potential for material, intellectual, and social improvement. Such confidence, in the breadth of human aspirations which it includes, and in their particular combinations, did not easily suit earlier Enlightenment thinkers. The leading French man of letters, Voltaire, was never able to convince himself that clear-thinking and commonsense reason could significantly alter the balance of good and evil in the world; philosopher David Hume agreed with Voltaire that humanity stood as great a chance of regressing to barbarism as of attaining political, religious, or moral stability, let alone indefinite progress. Neither Voltaire nor Hume was deterred, however, from offering concrete suggestions for the rearrangement of social institutions along more rational lines; yet their confidence was moderated by an estimation of human nature as influenced as much by non-rational as by rational forces. In the final writings of Condorcet represented in this selection, this hesitation is overcome, and the progress of humankind is made a direct function of the rational faculties of the race. This vision, often seen as a culmination of the Enlightenment, was to be tremendously influential in the following century.

Condorcet was a mathematician by training, and his confidence in the progressive potential of a "social calculus" may have its roots in his own attempt to use the mathematical study of probability to determine the proper number of jurors necessary for a true decision in judicial practice. Mathematics could be used as a concrete basis for the solution of political and administrative problems, whether they took the form of the trial jury or the inequality of wealth, which Condorcet proposed to correct through the implementation of a program of social insurance for the elderly, widowed, or unfortunate. The principle of equality, fundamental to mathematics, as Condorcet hoped these examples would show, could and must be the organizing principle of a rationally ordered society. Neither Voltaire nor Hume had made this assertion, but neither of them, nor any of the several thinkers so far treated in this volume, had been presented with a revolution in France, one that would demand such visions of confidence and provide the opportunity to test them in the act of founding a new society. Condorcet welcomed and participated in the revolution, which he hoped would embrace not only France but the world, and which eventually resulted in his own imprisonment in 1794.

Condorcet's confidence that he could speak of the nature and mechanics of social progress with scientific certainty allowed him to view the expansion of Enlightenment culture to non-European peoples as an unqualified benefit. Savage nations and those suffering despotic governments were to be shown their rights as guaranteed by natural law; reason alone would win their adherence to Enlightenment politics and ethics. The global role of Europe was one of peaceful education. A spokesman for the abolition of slavery, for religious toleration, and the education of all, Condorcet was nonetheless viewed by some revolutionaries as insufficiently egalitarian, and was executed on this account.

MARQUIS DE CONDORCET
(1796)

Sketch

of the Progress

of the Human Mind

TENTH EPOCH
Future Progress of Mankind

If man can predict, almost with certainty, those appearances of which he understands the laws; if, even when the laws are unknown to him, experience or the past enables him to foresee, with considerable probability, future appearances; why should we suppose it a chimerical undertaking to delineate, with some degree of truth, the picture of the future destiny of mankind from the results of its history? The only foundation of faith in the natural sciences is the principle, that the general laws, known or unknown, which regulate the phenomena of the universe, are regular and constant; and why should this principle, applicable to the other operations of nature, be less true when applied to the development of the intellectual and moral faculties of man? In short, as opinions formed from experience, relative to the same class of objects, are the only rule by which men of soundest understanding are governed in their conduct, why should the philosopher be proscribed from supporting his conjectures upon a similar basis, provided he attribute to them no greater certainty than the number, the consistency, and the accuracy of actual observations shall authorise?

Our hopes, as to the future condition of the human species, may be reduced to three points: the destruction of inequality between different nations; the progress of equality in one and the same nation; and lastly, the real improvement of man.

Will not every nation one day arrive at the state of civilization attained by those people

---

From *Outline of an Historical Sketch of the Progress of the Human Mind* (Philadelphia: Lang & Ustick, 1796), pp. 250–61, 226–69, 271–81, 284–93.

who are most enlightened, most free, most exempt from prejudices, as the French, for instance, and the Anglo-Americans? Will not the slavery of countries subjected to kings, the barbarity of African tribes, and the ignorance of savages gradually vanish? Is there upon the face of the globe a single spot the inhabitants of which are condemned by nature never to enjoy liberty, never to exercise their reason?

Does the difference of knowledge, of means, and of wealth, observable hitherto in all civilized nations, between the classes into which the people constituting those nations are divided; does that inequality, which the earliest progress of society has augmented, or, to speak more properly, produced, belong to civilization itself, or to the imperfections of the social order? ...

In a word, will not men be continually verging towards that state, in which all will possess the requisite knowledge for conducting themselves in the common affairs of life by their own reason, and of maintaining that reason uncontaminated by prejudices; in which they will understand their rights, and exercise them according to their opinion and their conscience; in which all will be able, by the development of their faculties, to procure the certain means of providing for their wants; lastly, in which folly and wretchedness will be accidents, happening only now and then, and not the habitual lot of a considerable portion of society? ...

In examining the ... questions we have enumerated, we shall find the strongest reasons to believe, from past experience, from observation of the progress which the sciences and civilization have hitherto made, and from the analysis of the march of the human understanding, and the development of its faculties, that nature has fixed no limits to our hopes.

If we take a survey of the existing state of the globe, we shall perceive, in the first place, that in Europe the principles of the French constitution are those of every enlightened mind. We shall perceive that they are too widely disseminated, and too openly professed, for the efforts of tyrants and priests to prevent them from penetrating by degrees into the miserable cottages of their slaves, where they will soon revive those embers of good sense, and rouse that silent indignation which the habit of suffering and terror have failed totally to extinguish in the minds of the oppressed.

If we next look at the different nations, we shall observe in each, particular obstacles opposing, or certain dispositions favouring this revolution. We shall distinguish some in which it will be effected, perhaps slowly, by the wisdom of the respective governments; and others in which, rendered violent by resistance, the governments themselves will necessarily be involved in its terrible and rapid motions.

Can it be supposed that either the wisdom or the senseless feuds of European nations, co-operating with the slow but certain effects of the progress of their colonies, will not shortly produce the independence of the entire new world; and that then, European population, lending its aid, will fail to civilize or cause to disappear, even without conquest, those savage nations still occupying there immense tracts of country?

Run through the history of our projects and establishments in Africa or in Asia, and you will see our monopolies, our treachery, our sanguinary contempt for men of a different complexion or different creed, and the proselyting fury or the intrigues of our priests, destroying that sentiment of respect and benevolence which the superiority of our information and the advantages of our commerce had at first obtained.

But the period is doubtless approaching, when, no longer exhibiting to the view of these people corrupters only or tyrants, we shall become to them instruments of benefit, and the generous champions of their redemption from bondage.

The cultivation of the sugar cane, which is now establishing itself in Africa, will put an end to the shameful robbery by which, for two centuries, that country has been depopulated and depraved.

Already, in Great Britain, some friends of humanity have set the example; and if its Machiavelian government, forced to respect public reason, has not dared to oppose this measure, what may we not expect from the same spirit, when, after the reform of an object and venal constitution, it shall become worthy of a humane and generous people? Will not France be eager to imitate enterprises which the philanthropy and the true interest of Europe will equally have dictated? Spices are already introduced into the French islands, Guiana, and some English settlements; and we shall soon witness the fall of that monopoly which the Dutch have supported by such a complication of perfidy, of oppression, and of crimes. The people of Europe will learn in time that exclusive and chartered companies are but a tax upon the respective nation, granted for the purpose of placing a new instrument in the hands of its government for the maintenance of tyranny.

Then will the inhabitants of the European quarter of the world, satisfied with an unreflected commerce, too enlightened as to their own rights to sport with the rights of others, respect that independence which they have hitherto violated with such audacity. Then will their establishments, instead of being filled by the creatures of power, who, availing themselves of a place or a privilege, hasten, by rapine and perfidy, to amass wealth, in order to purchase, on their return, honours and titles, be peopled with industrious men, seeking in those happy climates that ease and comfort which in their native country eluded their pursuit. There will they be retained by liberty, ambition having soft its allurements; and those settlements of robbers will then become colonies of citizens, by whom will be planted in Africa and Asia the principles and example of the freedom, reason, and illumination of Europe. To those monks also, who inculcate on the natives of the countries in question the most shameful superstitions only, and who excite disgust by menacing them with a new tyranny, will succeed men of integrity and benevolence, anxious to spread among these people truths useful to their happiness, and to enlighten them upon their interests as well as their rights: for the love of truth is also a passion; and when it shall have at home no gross prejudices to combat, no degrading errors to dissipate, it will naturally extend its regards, and convey its efforts to remote and foreign climes.

These immense countries will afford ample scope for the gratification of this passion. In one place will be found a numerous people, who, to arrive at civilization, appear only to wait till we shall furnish them with the means; and, who, treated as brothers by Europeans, would instantly become their friends and disciples. In another will be seen nations crouching under the yoke of sacred despots or stupid conquerors, and who, for so many ages, have looked for some friendly hand to deliver them: while a third will exhibit either tribes nearly savage, excluded from the benefits of superior civilization by the severity of their climate, which deters those who might otherwise be disposed to communicate these benefits from making the attempt; or else conquering hordes, knowing no law but force, no trade but robbery. The advances of these two last classes will be more slow, and accompanied with more frequent storms; it may even happen that, reduced in numbers in proportion as they see themselves repelled by civilized nations, they will in the end wholly disappear, or their scanty remains become blended with their neighbours.

We might shew that these events will be the inevitable consequence not only of the progress of Europe, but of that freedom which the republic of France, as well as of America, have it in their power, and feel it to be their interest, to restore to the commerce of Africa and Asia: and that they must also necessarily result alike, whether from the new policy of European nations, or their obstinate adherence to mercantile prejudices. . . .

The march of these people will be less slow and more sure than ours has been, because they will derive from us that light which we have been obliged to discover, and because for them to acquire the simple truths and infallible methods which we have obtained after long wandering in the mazes of error, it will be sufficient to seize upon their developments and proofs in our discourses and publications. . . .

Then will arrive the moment in which the sun will observe in its course free nations only, acknowledging no other matter than their reason; in which tyrants and slaves, priests and their stupid or hypocritical instruments, will no longer exist but in history and upon the stage; in which our only concern will be to lament their past victims and dupes, and, by the recollection of their horrid enormities, to exercise a vigilant circumspection, that we may be able instantly to recognise and effectually to stifle by the force of reason, the feeds of superstition and tyranny, should they ever presume again to make their appearance upon the earth.

In tracing the history of societies we have had occasion to remark, that there frequently exists a considerable distinction between the rights which the law acknowledges in the citizens of a state, and those which they really enjoy; between the equality established by political institutions, and that which takes place between the individual members; and that to this disproportion was chiefly owing the destruction of liberty in the ancient republics, the storms which they had to encounter, and the weakness that surrendered them into the power of foreign tyrants.

Three principal causes may be assigned for these distinctions: inequality of wealth, inequality of condition between him whose resources of subsistence are secured to himself and descendable to his family, and him whose resources are annihilated with the termination of his life, or rather of that part of his life in which he is capable of labour; and lastly, inequality of instruction.

It will therefore behave us to shew, that these three kinds of real inequality must continually diminish; but without becoming absolutely extinct, since they have natural and necessary causes, which it would be absurd as well as dangerous to think of destroying; nor can we attempt even to destroy entirely their effects, without opening at the same time more fruitful sources of inequality, and giving to the rights of man a more direct and more fatal blow.

It is easy to prove that fortunes naturally tend to equality, and that their extreme disproportion either could not exist, or would quickly cease, if positive law had not introduced factitious means of amassing and perpetuating them; if an entire freedom of commerce and industry were brought forward to supersede the advantages which prohibitory laws and fiscal rights necessarily give to the rich over the poor; if duties upon every sort of transfer and convention, if prohibitions to certain kinds, and the tedious and expensive formalities prescribed to other kinds; if the uncertainty and expence attending their execution had not palsied the efforts of the poor, and swallowed up their little accumulations; if political institutions had not laid certain prolific sources of opulence open to a few, and shut them against the many; if avarice, and the other prejudices incident to an advanced age, did not preside over marriages; in fine, if the simplicity of our manners and the wisdom of our institutions were calculated to prevent riches from operating as the means of gratifying vanity or ambition, at the same time that an ill-judged austerity, by forbidding us to render them a means of costly pleasures, should not force us to preserve the wealth that had once been accumulated.

Let us compare, in the enlightened nations of Europe, the actual population with the extent of territory; let us observe, amidst the spectacle of their culture and their industry, the way in which labour and the means of subsistence are distributed, and we shall see that it will be impossible to maintain these means in the same extent, and of consequence to maintain the same mass of population, if any considerable number of individuals cease to have, as now, nothing but their industry, and the pittance necessary to set it at work, or to render its profit equal to the supplying their own wants and those of their family. But neither this industry, not the scanty reserve we have mentioned, can be perpetuated, except so long as the life and health of each head of a family is perpetuated. Their little fortune therefore is at best an annuity, but in reality with features of precariousness that an annuity wants: and from hence results a most important difference between this class of society and the class of men whose resources consist either of a landed income, or the interest of a capital, which depends little upon personal industry, and is therefore not subject to familiar risks.

There exists then a necessary cause of inequality of dependence, and even of penury, which menaces without ceasing the most numerous and active class of our societies.

This inequality, however, may be in great measure destroyed, by setting chance against chance.... If instruction become more equal, industry thence acquires greater equality, and from industry the effect is communicated to fortunes; and equality of fortunes necessarily contributes to that of instruction, while equality of nations, like that established between individuals, have also a mutual operation upon each other.

In fine, instruction, properly directed, corrects the natural inequality of the faculties, instead of strengthening it, in like manner as good laws remedy the natural inequality of the means of subsistence, or as, in societies whose institutions shall have effected this equality, liberty, though subjected to a regular government, will be more extensive, more complete, than in the independence of savage life. Then has the social art accomplished its end, that of securing and extending for all the enjoyment of the common rights which impartial nature has bequeathed to all.

The advantages that must result from the state of improvement, of which I have proved we may almost entertain the certain hope, can have no limit but the absolute perfection of the human species, since, in proportion as different kinds of equality shall be established as to the various means of providing for our wants, as to a more universal instruction, and a more entire liberty, the more real will be this equality, and the nearer will it approach towards embracing every thing truly important to the happiness of mankind.

It is then by examining the progression and the laws of this perfection, that we can alone arrive at the knowledge of the extent or boundary of our hopes.

It has never yet been supported, that all the facts of nature, and all the means of acquiring precision in the computation and analysis of those facts, and all the connections of objects with each other, and all the possible combinations of ideas, can be exhausted by the human mind. The mere relations of magnitude, the combinations, quantity and extent of this idea alone, form already a system too immense for the mind of man ever to grasp the whole of it; a portion, more vast than that which he may have penetrated, will always remain unknown to him. It has, however, been imagined, that, as man can know a part only of the subjects which the nature of his intelligence permits him to investigate, he must at length reach the point at which, the numbers and complication of those he already knows having absorbed all his powers, farther progress will become absolutely impossible.

But, in proportion as facts are multiplied, man learns to class them, and reduce them to more general facts, at the same time that the instruments and methods for observing them, and registering them with exactness, acquire a new precision: in proportion as relations more multifarious between a greater number of objects are discovered, man continues to reduce them to relations of a wider denomination, to express them with greater simplicity, and to present them in a way which may enable a given strength of mind, with a given quantity of attention, to take in a greater number than before: in proportion as the understanding embraces more complicated combinations, a simple mode of announcing these combinations renders them more easy to be treated. Hence it follows that truths, the discovery of which was accompanied with the most laborious efforts, and which at first could not be comprehended but by men of the severest attention, will after a time be unfolded and proved in methods that are not above the efforts of an ordinary capacity. And thus should the methods that led to new combinations be exhausted, should their applications to questions, still unresolved, demand exertions greater than the time or the powers of the learned can bestow, more general methods, means more simple would soon come to their aid, and open a farther career to genius. The energy, the real extent of the human intellect may remain the same; but the instruments which it can employ will be multiplied and improved; but the language which fixes and determines the ideas will acquire more precision and compass; and it will not be here, as in the science of mechanics, where, to increase the force, we must diminish the velocity; on the contrary, the methods by which genius will arrive at the discovery of new truths, augment at once both the force and the rapidity of its operations. . . .

If we pass to the progress of the arts, those arts particularly the theory of which depends on these very same sciences, we shall find that it can have no inferior limits; that their processes are susceptible of the same improvement, the same simplifications, as the scientific methods; that instruments, machines, looms, will add every day to the capabilities and skill of man—will augment at once the excellence and precision of his works, while they will diminish the time and labour necessary for executing them; and that then will disappear the obstacles that still oppose themselves to the progress in question, accidents which will be foreseen and prevented; and lastly, the unhealthiness at present attendant upon certain operations, habits and climates.

A smaller portion of ground will then be made to produce a proportion of provisions of higher value or greater utility; a greater quantity of enjoyment will be procured at a smaller expence of consumption; the same manufactured or artificial commodity will be produced at a smaller expense of raw materials, or will be stronger and more durable; every foil will be appropriated to productions which will satisfy a greater number of wants with the least labour, and taken in the smallest quantities.

It may, however, be demanded, whether, amidst this improvement in industry and happiness, where the wants and faculties of men will continually become better proportioned, each successive generation possess more various stores, and of consequence in each generation the number of individuals be greatly increased; it may, I say, be demanded, whether these principles of improvement and increase may not, by their continual operation, ultimately lead to degeneracy and destruction? Whether the number of inhabitants in the universe at length exceeding the means of existence, there will not result a continual decay of happiness and population, and a progress towards barbarism, or at least a sort of oscillation between good and evil? Will not this oscillation, in societies arrived at this epoch, be a perennial source of peri-odical calamity and distress? In a word, do not these confederations point out the limit at which all farther improvement will become impossible, and consequently the perfectibility of man arrive at a period which in the immensity of ages it may attain, but which it can never pass?. . .

But supposing the affirmative, supposing it actually to take place, there would result from it nothing alarming, either to the happiness of the human race, or its indefinite perfectibility; if we consider, that prior to this period the progress of reason will have walked hand in hand with that of the sciences; that the absurd prejudices of superstition will have ceased to infuse into morality a harshness that corrupts and degrades, instead of purifying and exalting it; that men will then know, that the duties they may be under relative to propagation will consist not in the question of giving *existence* to a greater number of beings, but *happiness*; will have for their object, the general welfare of the human species; of the society in which they live; of the family to which they are attached; and not the puerile idea of encumbering the earth with useless and wretched mortals. Accordingly, there might then be a limit to the possible mass of provision, and of consequence to the greatest possible population, without that premature destruction, so contrary to nature and to social prosperity, of a portion of the beings who may have received life, being the result of those limits.

But it requires little penetration to perceive how imperfect is still the development of the intellectual and moral faculties of man; how much farther the sphere of his duties, including therein the influence of his actions upon the welfare of his fellow creatures and of the society to which he belongs, may be extended by a more fixed, a more profound and more accurate observation of that influence; how many questions still remain to be solved, how many social ties to be examined, before we can ascertain the precise catalogue of the individual rights of man, as well as of the rights which the social state confers upon the whole community with regard to each member. Have we even ascertained with any precision the limits of these rights, whether as they exist between different societies, or in any single society, over its members, in cases of division and hostility; or, in fine, the rights of individuals, their spontaneous unions in the case of a primitive formation, or their separations when separation becomes necessary?

The application of the arithmetic of combinations and probabilities to these sciences, promises an improvement by so much the more considerable, as it is the only means of giving to their results an almost mathematical precision, and of appreciating their degree of certainty or probability. The facts upon which these results are built may, indeed, without calculation, and by a glance only, lead to some general truths; teach us whether the effects produced by such a cause have been favourable or the reverse: but if these facts have neither been counted nor estimated; if these effects have not been the object of an exact admeasurment, we cannot judge of the quantity of good or evil they contain: if the good or evil nearly balance each other, nay, if the difference be not considerable, we cannot pronounce with certainty to which side the balance inclines. Without the application of this arithmetic, it would be almost impossible to choose, with sound reason, between two combinations proposing to themselves the same end, when their advantages are not distinguishable by any considerable difference. In fine, without this alliance, these sciences would remain forever gross and narrow, for want of instru-ments of sufficient polish to lay hold of the futility of truth—for want of machines sufficiently accurate to found the bottom of the well where it conceals its wealth.

There is another species of progress, appertaining to the sciences in question, equally important; I mean, the improvement of their language, at present so vague and so obscure. To this improvement must they owe the advantage of becoming popular, even in their first elements. Genius can triumph over these inaccuracies, as over other obstacles; it can recognise the features of truth, in spite of the mask that conceals or disfigures them. But how is the man who can devote but a few leisure moments to instruction to do this? how is he to acquire and retain the most simple truths, if they be disguised by an inaccurate language? The fewer ideas he is able to collect and combine, the more requisite it is that they be just and precise. He has no fund of truths stored up in his mind, by which to guard himself against error; nor is his understanding so strengthened and refined by long exercise, that he can catch those feeble rays of light which escape under the obscure and ambiguous dress of an imperfect and vicious phraseology.

In manner as the mathematical and physical sciences tend to improve the arts that are employed for our most simple wants, so is it not equally in the necessary order of nature that the moral and political sciences should exercise a similar influence upon the motives that direct our sentiments and our actions?

What is the object of the improvement of laws and public institutions, consequent upon the progress of these sciences, but to reconcile, to approximate, to blend and unite into one mass the common interest of each individual with the common interest of all? What is the end of the social art, but to destroy the opposition between these two apparently jarring sentiments?

What vicious habit can be mentioned, what practice contrary to good faith, what crime even, the origin and first cause of which may not be traced in the legislation, institutions, and prejudices of the country in which we observe such habit, such practice, or such crime to be committed?

In short, does not the well-being, the prosperity, resulting from the progress that will be made by the useful arts, in consequence of their being founded upon a found theory, resulting, also, from an improved legislation, built upon the truths of the political sciences, naturally dispose men to humanity, to benevolence, and to justice? Do not all the observations, in fine, which we proposed to develop in this work prove, that the moral goodness of man, the necessary consequence of his organization, is, like all his other faculties, susceptible of an indefinite improvement? and that nature has connected, by a chain which cannot be broken, truth, happiness, and virtue?

Among those causes of human improvement that are of most importance to the general welfare, must be included, the total annihilation of the prejudices which have established between the sexes an inequality of rights, fatal even to the party which it favours. In vain might we search for motives by which to justify this principle, in difference of physical organization, of intellect, or of moral sensibility. It had at first no other origin but abuse of strength, and all the attempts which have since been made to support it are idle sophisms. . . .

Would not this homage, so long in paying, to the divinities of equity and good sense, put an end to a too fertile principle of injustice, cruelty, and crime, by superseding the opposition hitherto maintained between that natural propensity, which is, of all others the most imperious, and the most difficult to subdue, and the interests of man, or the duties of society? Would it not produce, what has hitherto been a mere chimera, national manners of a nature mild and pure, formed, not by imperious privations, by hypocritical appearances, by reserves imposed by the fear of shame or religious terrors, but by habits freely contracted, inspired by nature and avowed by reason?

The people being more enlightened, and having resumed the right of disposing for themselves of their blood and their treasure, will learn by degrees to regard war as the most dreadful
of all calamities, the most terrible of all crimes. The first wars that will be superseded, will be
those into which the usurpers of sovereignty have hitherto drawn their subjects for the maintenance of rights pretendedly hereditary.

Nations will know, that they cannot become conquerors without losing their freedom;
that perpetual confederations are the only means of maintaining their independence; that their
object should be security, and not power. By degrees commercial prejudices will die away; a
false mercantile interest will lose the terrible power of imbuing the earth with blood, and of
ruining nations under the idea of enriching them. As the people of different countries will at
last be drawn into closer intimacy, by the principles of politics and morality, as each, for its
own advantage, will invite foreigners to an equal participation of the benefits which it may
have derived either from nature or its own industry, all the causes which produce, envenom,
and perpetuate national animosities, will one by one disappear, and will no more furnish to
war-like insanity either fuel or pretext. . . .

The progress of the sciences secures the progress of the art of instruction, which again
accelerates in its turn that of the sciences; and this reciprocal influence, the action of which is
incessantly increased, must be ranked in the number of the most prolific and powerful causes of
the improvement of the human race. At present, a young man, upon finishing his studies and
quitting our schools, may know more of the principles of mathematics than Newton acquired
by profound study, or discovered by the force of his genius, and may exercise the instrument of
calculation with a readiness which at that period was unknown. The same observation, with
certain restrictions, may be applied to all the sciences. In proportion as each shall advance, the
means of compressing, within a smaller circle, the proofs of a greater number of truths, and of
facilitating their comprehension, will equally advance. Thus, notwithstanding future degrees of
progress, not only will men of equal genius find themselves, at the same period of life, upon a
level with the actual state of science, but, respecting every generation, what may be acquired in
a given space of time, by the same strength of intellect and the same degree of attention, will
necessarily increase, and the elementary part of each science, that part which every man may
attain, becoming more and more extended, will include, in a manner more complete, the
knowledge necessary for the direction of every man in the common occurrences of life, and for
the free and independent exercise of his reason. . . .

We have still two other means of general application to consider, and which must influence at once both the improvement of the art of instruction and that of the sciences. One is a
more extensive and more perfect adoption of what may be called technical methods; the other,
the institution of an universal language.

By technical methods I understand, the art of uniting a great number of objects in an
arranged and systematic order by which we may be enabled to perceive at a glance their bearings and connections, seize in an instant their combinations, and form from them the more
readily new combinations.

Let us develope the principles, let us examine the utility of this art, as yet in its infancy, and
we shall find that, when improved and perfected, we might derive from it, either the advantage
of possessing within the narrow compass of a picture, what it would be often difficult, for
volumes to explain to us so readily and so well; or the means, still more valuable, of presenting
isolated facts in a disposition and view best calculated to give us their general results. We shall

perceive how, by means of a small number of these pictures or tables, the use of which may be easily learned, men who have not been able to appropriate such useful details and elementary knowledge as may apply to the purposes of common life, may turn to them at the shortest notice; and how elementary knowledge itself, in all those sciences where this knowledge is founded either upon a regular code of truths or a series of observations and experiments, may hereby be facilitated.

An universal language is that which expresses by signs, either the direct objects, or those well-defined collections constituted of simple and general ideas, which are to be found or may be introduced equally in the understandings of all mankind; or lastly, the general relations of these ideas, the operations of the human mind, the operations peculiar to any science, and the mode of process in the arts. Thus, such persons as shall have become masters of these signs, the method of combining and the rules for constructing them, will understand what is written in this language, and will read it with similar facility in the language of their own country, whatever it may happen to be. . . .

A language like this has not the inconvenience of a scientific idiom, different from the vernacular tongue. We have before observed, that the use of such an idiom necessarily divides societies into two extremely unequal classes; the one composed of men, understanding the language, and, therefore, in possession of the key to the sciences; the other of those who, incapable of learning it, find themselves reduced almost to an absolute impossibility of acquiring knowledge. On the contrary, the universal language we are supporting, might be learned, like the language of algebra, with the science itself; the sign might be known at the same instant with the object, the idea, or the operation which it expresses. He who, having attained the elements of a science, should wish to prosecute farther his enquiries, would find in books, not only truths that he could understand, by means of those signs, of which he already knows the value, but the explanation of the new signs of which he has need in order to ascend to higher truths. . . .

It might be shown that this language, improving every day, acquiring incessantly greater extent, would be the means of giving to every object that comes within the reach of human intelligence, a rigour, and precision, that would facilitate the knowledge of truth, and render error almost impossible. Then would the march of every science be as infallible as that of the mathematics, and the propositions of every system acquire, as far as nature will admit, geometrical demonstration and certainty. . . .

The organic perfectibility or deterioration of the classes of the vegetable, or species of the animal kingdom, may be regarded as one of the general laws of nature.

This law extends itself to the human race; and it cannot be doubted that the progress of the sanative art, that the use of more wholesome food and more comfortable habitations, that a mode of life which shall develope the physical powers by exercise, without at the same time impairing them by excess; in fine, that the destruction of the two most active causes of deterioration, penury and wretchedness on the one hand, and enormous wealth on the other, must necessarily tend to prolong the common duration of man's existence, and secure him a more constant health and a more robust constitution. It is manifest that the improvement of the practice of medicine, become more efficacious in consequence of the progress of reason and the social order, must in the end put a period to transmissible or contagious disorders, as well to those general maladies resulting from climate, aliments, and the nature of certain occupations. Nor would it be difficult to prove that this hope might be extended to almost every other malady, of which it is probable we shall hereafter discover the most remote causes. Would it even be absurd to suppose this quality of melioration in the human species as susceptible of an indefinate advancement; to suppose that a period must one day arrive when death will be nothing more than the effect either of extraordinary accidents, or of the flow and gradual decay of the vital powers; and that the duration of the middle space, of the interval between the birth of man and this decay, will itself have no assignable limit? Certainly man will not become immortal; but may not the distance between the moment in which he draws his first breath, and the common term when, in the course of nature, without malady or accident, he finds it impossible any longer to exist, be necessarily protracted? As we are now speaking of a progress that is capable of being represented with precision, by numerical quantities or by lines, we shall embrace the opportunity of explaining the two meanings that may be affixed to the word *indefinite*. . . .

Lastly, may we not include in the same circle the intellectual and moral faculties? May not our parents, who transmit to us the advantages or defects of their conformation, and from whom we receive our features and shape, as well as our propensities to certain physical affections, transmit to us also that part of organization upon which intellect, strength of understanding, energy of foul or moral sensibility depend? Is it not probable that education, by improving these qualities, will at the same time have an influence upon, will modify and improve this organization itself? Analogy, an investigation of the human faculties, and even some facts, appear to authorize these conjectures, and thereby to enlarge the boundary of our hopes.

Such are the questions with which we shall terminate the last division of our work. And how admirably calculated is this view of the human race, emancipated from its chains, released alike from the dominion of chance, as well as from that of the enemies of its progress, and advancing with a firm and indeviate step in the paths of truth, to console the philosopher lamenting the errors, the flagrant acts of injustice, the crimes with which the earth is still polluted? It is the contemplation of this prospect that rewards him for all his efforts to assist the progress of reason and the establishment of liberty. He dares to regard these efforts as a part of the eternal chain of the definite of mankind; and in this persuasion he finds the true delight of virtue, the pleasure of having performed a durable service, which no vicissitude will ever destroy in a fatal operation calculated to restore the reign of prejudice and slavery. This sentiment is the asylum into which he retires, and to which the memory of his persecutors cannot follow him: he unites himself in imagination with man restored to his rights, delivered from oppression, and proceeding with rapid strides in the path of happiness; he forgets his own misfortunes while his thoughts are thus employed; he lives no longer to adversity, calumny and malice, but becomes the associate of these wiser and more fortunate beings whose enviable condition he so earnestly contributed to produce.

Ernst Cassirer

A German historian who came to the United States before World War II, Ernst Cassirer was known for his studies in the philosophy and history of science. Cassirer emphasized the ways in which the scientific study of nature during the seventeenth and eighteenth centuries shaped new understandings of how the mind produces knowledge. According to Cassirer, understandings of the power of the thinking subject to fully investigate and analyze the natural object encouraged Enlightenment philosophers and scientists to view human reason as a tool with which to formulate laws in the process of understanding the infinite universe itself. Experimentation allowed for the advanced study of the world, and as Cassirer explains it, thinkers like Galileo found truth not in God's word but in the proof of their own works.

ERNST CASSIRER
(1951)

Nature and
Natural Science

The modern concept of nature, as its shape becomes increasingly articulate from the Renaissance on and as it seeks philosophical foundation and justification in the great systems of the seventeenth century—in Descartes, Spinoza, and Leibniz—is characterized above all by the new relationship which develops between sensibility and intellect, between experience and thought, between the sensible world and the intelligible world.

The requirement is now, not merely to sense dimly the law of activity in nature, but to know this law precisely and to express it in clear concepts. Neither feeling nor sense perception nor imagination can satisfy this requirement; it can be fulfilled only if the connection between the individual and the whole, between "appearance" and "idea," is looked for in a hitherto untried manner. Sense observation must be combined with exact measurement, and the new theory of nature must grow out of these two factors. This theory too, as established in the works of Kepler and Galileo, is still imbued with a strong religious impulse which acts as a driving force. Its constant aim is to find signs of the divinity of nature in natural law. But precisely because of its underlying religious tendency this theory of nature inevitably comes into conflict with traditional forms of belief. Looked at from this viewpoint, the fight which the Church carried on against the advance of the modern spirit of mathematical science now becomes quite understandable. The Church was not assailing individual accomplishments of scientific investigation. Reconciliation would have been possible between these and church doctrine. Galileo himself for a long time believed in such a reconciliation and honestly strove for it. But the tragic misunder-

Ernst Cassirer, *The Philosophy of Enlightenment.* Trans by Fritz C. A. Koelln and James P. Pettegrove. Copyright © 1951 Princeton University Press. Reprinted by permission of Princeton University Press.

standing which was his eventual downfall was the fact that he looked in the wrong place for the opposition he was endeavoring to reconcile, and that he himself underestimated the radical innovation in methodological attitude which had taken place within him. Hence he did not approach the conflict at its real foundation but merely tried to adjust and balance results derived from his basic standpoint. In reality it was not the new cosmology which church authorities so vehemently opposed; for as a mere mathematical "hypothesis" they could just as well accept the Copernican as the Ptolemaic system. But what was not to be tolerated, what threatened the very foundations of the Church, was the new concept of truth proclaimed by Galileo. Alongside of the truth of revelation comes now an independent and original truth of nature.

This truth is revealed not in God's word but in his work; it is not based on the testimony of Scripture or tradition but is visible to us at all times. But it is understandable only to those who know nature's handwriting and can decipher her text. The truth of nature cannot be expressed in mere words; the only suitable expression lies in mathematical constructions, figures and numbers. And in these symbols nature presents itself in perfect form and clarity. Revelation by means of the sacred word can never achieve such brightness and transparency, such precision, for words as such are always varicolored and ambiguous admitting a variety of interpretations. Their meaning must always be given them by man and must therefore be fragmentary. In nature, on the other hand, the whole plan of the universe lies before us in its undivided and inviolable unity, evidently waiting for the human mind to recognize and express it.

And according to the judgment of the eighteenth century such a mind had meantime appeared. What Galileo had called for became reality in Newton; the problem posed by the Renaissance seemed to have been solved in a surprisingly short time. Galileo and Kepler had grasped the idea of natural law in all its breadth and depth, and in its fundamental methodological meaning; but they had only been able to illustrate the application of this law in individual cases, in the phenomena of freely falling bodies and of planetary motion. Room for doubt remained; for proof was still lacking that the strict law, which had been shown to govern the parts, was also valid for the whole, and that the universe as such could be approached and adequately understood by way of the exact concepts of mathematical knowledge. Newton's work offered such proof. Here it was no longer a matter of a particular natural phenomenon, it was not merely the reduction of a limited field of phenomena to rule and order; on the contrary, in Newton it was a question of establishing and clearly expressing a—rather the—cosmic law. This law seemed assured in Newton's theory of gravitation. Thus was the victory of human knowledge decided and an elemental power of knowledge had been discovered which seemed equal to the elemental power of nature. In this sense the whole eighteenth century understood and esteemed Newton's achievement. In Newton it honored the great empirical scientist; it does not, however, stop here, but more and more emphatically points out that Newton not only gave hard and fast rules to nature but to philosophy as well. Not less important than the results of Newton's investigations are his so-called rules of philosophy (regulae philosophandi) which he found valid in natural science and established forever in this field of knowledge. The unreserved admiration and veneration of the eighteenth century for Newton is derived from this conception of his achievement. By virtue of its results and its aim alone this achievement appears great and incomparable but, in the light of the method by which its aim had been accomplished, it seems even greater. Newton first showed science the way leading from arbitrary and phantastic assumptions to the clarity of the concept, from darkness to light:

"Nature and Nature's laws lay hid in night,
God said: 'Let Newton be,' and all was light."

These verses from Pope express most effectively the kind of veneration which Newton
enjoys in the thinking of the Enlightenment. Thanks to Newton, it believed it stood finally on
firm ground which could never again be shaken by any future revolution of natural science. The
correlation between nature and human knowledge has now been established once and for all
and the bond between them is henceforth inseverable. Both members of the correlation are
quite independent but by virtue of their independence they are, nevertheless, in complete
harmony. Nature in man, as it were, meets nature in the cosmos half way and finds its own
essence there. Whoever finds the one is sure to find the other. The philosophy of nature of the
Renaissance understood by "nature" the law which springs from the essence of things and with
which they are originally endowed, not the law they receive from without. "Nature is nothing
but a force implanted in things and the law by which all entities proceed along their proper
paths." To find this law we must not project our own ideas and subjective imaginings into nature;
we must rather follow nature's own course and determine it by observation and experiment, by
measurement and calculation. But our basic standards for measurement are not to be derived
from sense data alone. They originate in those universal functions of comparing and counting,
of combining and differentiating, which constitute the nature of the intellect. Thus the autonomy of the intellect corresponds to the pure autonomy of nature. In one and the same intellectual process of emancipation the philosophy of the Enlightenment attempts to show the
self-sufficiency of both nature and intellect. Both are now to be recognized as elemental and to
be firmly connected with one another. Thus any mediation between the two which is based on a
transcendent power or a transcendent being becomes superfluous. Such mediation cannot
further strengthen the bond between nature and mind. On the contrary, the intervention of a
transcendent being, by the mere approach to the problem which it involves and by the questioning to which it subjects nature and mind, loosens this bond and must in the long run sever it
completely. And indeed the metaphysics of "occasionalism" in modern times had taken just this
step; it had sacrificed the autonomous action of nature and the autonomous form of the mind to
the omnipotence of the divine First Cause. Against this relapse into transcendence the philosophy of the Enlightenment proclaims the pure principle of immanence both for nature and for
knowledge. Both must be understood in terms of their own essence, and this is no dark, mysterious "something," impenetrable to intellect; this essence consists rather in principles which are
perfectly accessible to the mind since the mind is able to educe them from itself and to enunci-
ate them systematically.

By this basic conception is to be explained the almost unlimited power which scientific
knowledge gains over all the thought of the Enlightenment. D'Alembert called the eighteenth
century the philosophical century but with equal justification and pride this era often labeled
itself the century of natural science. The organization of natural science had already made great
progress in the seventeenth century, and even then it had reached a certain inner completion. In
England, the founding of the Royal Society in 1660 created a fixed center for all scientific
pursuits. It had functioned even earlier as a free organization of individual scientists; and so,
even before the royal decree of foundation gave it official sanction and an official constitution, it
had been active as an "invisible college." And even then it represented a certain methodological
viewpoint; it emphasized time and again that no concept in physics was admissible which had

not first passed the empirical test and proved itself by experiment. The movement which starts here soon reaches France, where it finds its first support in the Academie des Sciences founded by Colbert in 1666. But not until the eighteenth century does the movement achieve its full breadth and effectiveness in all fields of intellectual life. It now goes beyond the sphere of the academies and learned societies. From a mere matter of scholarly interest it now becomes the concern of all civilization. It is no longer merely the empirical scientists, the mathematicians and physicists, who participate in this movement but also those thinkers who are seeking a new orientation of all the intellectual sciences. A renewal of these sciences, deeper insight into the spirit of laws, of society, of politics, and even of poetry, seems impossible unless it is pursued in the light of the great model of the natural sciences. Again it is d'Alembert who not only person-ally brought about this alliance between the natural and the intellectual sciences but who also in his *Elements of Philosophy* expressed with the greatest clarity the principle on which the alliance rests: "Natural science from day to day accumulates new riches. Geometry, by extending its limits, has borne its torch into the regions of physical science which lay nearest at hand. The true system of the world has been recognized. . . . In short, from the earth to Saturn, from the history of the heavens to that of insects, natural philosophy has been revolutionized; and nearly all other fields of knowledge have assumed new forms . . . the discovery and application of a new method of philosophizing, the kind of enthusiasm which accompanies discoveries, a certain exaltation of ideas which the spectacle of the universe produces in us; all these causes have brought about a lively fermentation of minds.

Spreading throughout nature in all directions, this fermentation has swept with a sort of violence everything before it which stood in its way, like a river which has burst its dams. . . . Thus, from the principles of the secular sciences to the foundations of religious revelation, from metaphysics to matters of taste, from music to morals, from the scholastic disputes of theolo-gians to matters of commerce, from natural law to the arbitrary laws of nations . . . everything has been discussed, analyzed, or at least mentioned. The fruit or sequel of this general efferves-cence of minds has been to cast new light on some matters and new shadows on others, just as the effect of the ebb and flow of the tides leaves some things on the shore and washes others away." No reputable thinker of the eighteenth century entirely escaped the influence of this basic tendency.

In his *Conversations on the Plurality of Worlds* Fontenelle tries to explain Cartesian cosmology by comparing the events of nature with those of a large stage. The spectator in the orchestra sees a series of events which come and go in varied sequence. He is absorbed in the contemplation of these events and delighted with the profusion of pictures which pass before him, without wondering how they are produced. But if perchance there is a mechanic among the audience, he will not be satisfied with merely beholding these pictures. He will not rest until he has discov-ered the causes of these phenomena, until he has penetrated the mechanism behind all these changing scenes. The behavior of the philosopher is like that of the mechanic. But here the difficulty is increased by the circumstance that nature, in the spectacle it constantly presents, has so carefully hidden its mechanism that it has taken us centuries to come upon its mysterious springs of action. Not until modern times was man permitted to look behind the scenes; science sees not only phenomena themselves, but also the clockworks which bring them about. Far from diminishing the charm of the drama, such insight materially enhances its value. Many people erroneously hold the opinion that knowledge of the mechanics according to which the universe behaves detracts from its dignity because such knowledge reduces the universe to a clockwork.

"I esteem the universe all the more," writes Fontenelle, "since I have known that it is like a watch. It is surprising that nature, admirable as it is, is based on such simple things."

The comparison which Fontenelle draws here is no mere play of wit; it involves an idea of decisive importance for the entire structure of natural science in the seventeenth century. Descartes' philosophy of nature had given this idea its form and universal application. Nature cannot be understood if it is taken merely as a sum total of phenomena, if one considers only the extension of its events in space or their temporal sequence. One must trace the phenomena back to their principles, and the principles are nowhere else to be found than in the laws of motion. Once these laws have been discovered and reduced to exact mathematical expression, the path of all future knowledge is marked out. We only have to develop completely what is implicitly contained in these laws in order to have a synopsis of all nature and to understand the universe in its innermost structure. Descartes' treatise on the system of the world was intended as the execution of this basic theoretical plan. Its motto was: "Give me matter and I will build you a world." Thought no longer wants to accept the world simply as empirically given; it sets itself the task of analyzing the structure of the universe, in fact, of producing this structure with its own resources. Beginning with its own clear and distinct ideas, it finds in them the model for all reality. Mathematical principles and axioms of thought lead it safely through the entire realm of nature. For there is a definite path, a single uninterrupted chain of deduction, which stretches from the highest and most general causes of natural events down to the special laws of nature and even to every individual effect, no matter how complex. There is no barrier between the realm of clear and distinct concepts and the realm of facts, between geometry and physics. Since the substance of physical body consists in pure extension, knowledge of this extension, that is, geometry, is master of physics. Geometry expresses the nature of the corporeal world and its general fundamental properties in exact definitions and proceeds from these by an uninterrupted chain of thought to the determination of the particular and the factual.

But this ambitious project of Cartesian physics had not passed the empirical test. The further Descartes proceeded along this path and the more closely he approached the special phenomena of nature, the greater were the difficulties which he encountered. He met these difficulties only because he constantly resorted to new and more complicated mechanisms and entangled himself in a network of hypotheses. This finely spun texture is torn to pieces by Newton. He too seeks universal mathematical principles in nature but he no longer believes it possible to reduce physics to geometry. He advocates rather the independent function and the unique character of physical investigation, and this character is founded in the method of experimentation and the method of inductive reasoning. The path of physical investigation does not lead from top to bottom, from axioms and principles to facts, but rather from the latter to the former. We cannot begin with general assumptions about the nature of things and then derive from them a knowledge of particular events; we must rather begin with this knowledge, as given us in direct observation, and in a gradual ascent try to get back to the first causes and to the simple elements of natural processes. The ideal of deduction is now confronted with the ideal of analysis. And analysis is by nature unending; it cannot be limited to a definite, verifiable chain of thought which could be anticipated *a priori*. It must rather be taken up anew at every stage of empirical science. Analysis knows no absolute end but only relative and provisional stopping points. Newton also looked upon his fundamental doctrine, the general theory of gravitation, only as such a provisional point of rest. For he is satisfied to show that gravity is a universal phenomenon of nature without inquiring after its ultimate causes. Newton expressly rejects a mechanical theory of gravitation because experience does not offer sufficient evidence for such a theory. Nor does he claim any metaphysical foundation for gravity, for this too for the physicist would mean an unjustifiable transgression of boundaries. He is concerned solely with the phenomena of gravity; and he tries to express these phenomena not in a mere concept, in an abstract definition, but in a comprehensive mathematical formula which implicitly contains them as concrete individual cases and completely describes them. Physical theory neither pretends to, nor should, venture beyond pure description of natural phenomena. Seen from this standpoint gravity is of course a general property of matter but it does not have to be regarded as one of its essential properties. Natural philosophy that undertakes to construct the world in pure thought, out of mere concepts, is according to Newton always exposed to a double temptation and danger. Wherever it finds any general, universally recurring quality of things, it must either hypostatize this quality, that is, make it an absolutely real, original quality of being; or it must resolve and reduce it to a derivative of general antecedent causes. But to genuine empiricism the one procedure is as foreign as the other. Empiricism is satisfied with establishing the phenomena; but it knows, on the other hand, that no phenomenon is absolutely final and incapable of further analysis. This analysis must not, however, take place prematurely in thought; it must rather be awaited in the course of experimental progress. In this sense Newton insists that gravity is for the time being a "last" element of nature, a provisionally irreducible quality which cannot be sufficiently explained on the basis of any known mechanism; but this does not exclude the possibility that on the basis of future observations this quality too may become reducible to simpler natural phenomena. The assumption of some kind of occult qualities, to which scholastic physics appealed, is of course arbitrary and meaningless. On the other hand, it would mark an important advance for scientific insight if we were to succeed in reducing the wealth of natural phenomena to a few fundamental properties of matter and to definite principles of motion, even if the causes of these properties and principles should meantime remain unknown.

In these classical dicta, as they appear, for instance, at the end of his *Optics,* Newton clearly outlined the program for all natural science in the eighteenth century. The crucial point in the natural science of this time is that at which it consciously and energetically advances from Descartes to Newton. The ideal of a purely mechanical philosophy of nature, such as Fontenelle in the statements quoted above had proclaimed, was gradually superseded until it was finally abandoned entirely by the epistemologists of modern physics. Condillac in his *Treatise on Systems* which appeared in 1759 vigorously urges that the "spirit of systems" which had produced the great metaphysical edifices of the seventeenth century be banished from physics. Instead of any general, but arbitrary, explanation based on the apparent "nature of things," there must appear simple observation of phenomena and clear designation of their empirical connection. The physicist must finally give up trying to explain the mechanism of the universe; he has done enough if he succeeds in establishing definite general relations in nature. . . .

The task of freeing natural science from the domination of theology appeared as a relatively simple matter to Enlightenment thought. To accomplish this task it was merely necessary to utilize the heritage of preceding centuries; the separation which had already taken place in fact, had now to be realized conceptually. Thus everything that is achieved in this direction is rather a conclusion than a really new intellectual beginning; it is merely the clarification of a methodological development which could be looked upon as established by the progress of science in the seventeenth and eighteenth centuries. When, however, this same science is asked to justify itself, a new and more radical problem arises. What is the use of freeing natural science from all theologico-metaphysical content and of limiting it to purely empirical statements, if we do not, on the other hand, succeed in eliminating metaphysical elements from its structure? And does not every statement which goes beyond the simple affirmation of an immediate object of sense perception contain just such an element? Is the systematic structure of nature, the absolute homogeneity of experience, itself a result of experience? Is it deducible from, and demonstrable by, experience? Or does it not rather constitute a premise of experience? And is not this premise, this logical *a priori*, just as questionable as any metaphysical or theological *a priori* could be? One should not only eliminate all individual concepts and judgments from the realm of empirical science; one should finally have the courage to pursue this tendency to its logical conclusion: one should even withdraw from the concept of nature the support of the concept of God. What will then become of the apparent necessity of nature, of its general, eternal, and inviolable laws? Is this necessity based upon an intuitive certainty, or upon any other rigorous deductive proof? Or must we forego all such proofs and make up our minds to take the last step, namely, to acknowledge that the world of facts can only support itself and that we seek in vain for any other firmer foundation, for a rational ground, for this world?

In all these questions we have anticipated the development from the phenomenalism of mathematical natural science to the skepticism of Hume. This is not merely a question of an intellectual construction, but of a concrete historical process which can be traced step by step in eighteenth century thought and elucidated in all its relations and ramifications. Hitherto historians of thought have failed on this point, and hence have missed the real source of Hume's skepticism. Hume's point of departure does not appear if, as has consistently been the case, we are satisfied with placing his teachings in the light of English empiricism and developing and deriving them historically from the presuppositions of empiricism. Hume's doctrine is not to be understood as an end but as a new beginning; it is more than a mere link in that chain of thought which leads from Bacon to Hobbes, from Hobbes to Locke, and from Locke to Berkeley. From all these thinkers Hume has, to be sure, adopted certain tools of thought, namely, the conceptual and systematic apparatus of empiricism and sensationalism. But his characteristic and specific question derives from another source, namely, from the continuity and linear progression of scientific thought in the seventeenth and eighteenth centuries. An important link in this chain is the contribution of the Newtonian school, especially the systematic treatment which Newton's fundamental conceptions received at the hands of Dutch philosophers and scientists. These conceptions were developed with remarkable consistency and constancy; the Dutch scholars attempted to base on them a logic of the experimental sciences. In seventeenth century Holland the trend toward exact observation of facts and the development of a strictly experimental method were combined in exemplary fashion with a critical mode of thinking whose objective was a clear determination of the meaning and value of scientific hypotheses. The great Dutch scientist, Christian Huygens, is the classic example of such a combination. In his *Treatise on Light (Traite de la lumiere,* 1690) Huygens formulates principles of the relation of experience and thought, of theory and observation, which far surpass Descartes in their clarity and precision. He emphasizes that one cannot attain the same clarity in physics as is possible in mathematical demonstrations and inferences, and that there can be no intuitive certainty of the fundamental truths of physics. Physics requires simply a "moral certainty," which, however, can be raised to such a high degree of probability that for all practical purposes it is as good as a rigorous proof.

For if the conclusions reached under the assumption of a certain hypothesis are completely veri-fied by experience, and especially if on the basis of these conclusions one can predict new observations which are verifiable by experiment, then that kind of truth has been attained to which alone physics may lay claim. The Dutch physicists of the eighteenth century build on these foundations in the belief that in the Newtonian theory they have the highest and final confirmation of their viewpoint. For no other hypothetical elements are supposed to have been introduced in this theory than those which can be put to the test of immediate experience. S'Gravesande, when in the year 1717 he is called to a professorship of mathematics and astron-omy at the University of Leyden, attempts in his inaugural address to develop and elucidate in detail the Newtonian theory. But in so doing he encountered a strange and difficult problem. When as a result of certain observations we anticipate other cases which we have not directly observed, our prediction is based on the axiom of the uniformity of nature. Without this axiom, without this assumption that the laws which pertain in nature today will continue to be valid, there would obviously be no foundation for conclusions about the future which are based on past experience. But how can this axiom itself be proved? S'Gravesande replies: This is not a strictly logical, but a pragmatic, axiom; its validity does not lie in the necessity of thought, but in that of action. For all action, all practical relationships with things, would be impossible, if we could not assume that the lessons of former experience will be valid in the future. Scientific prediction does not then involve the syllogistically necessary conclusions of formal logic; it is, nevertheless, a valid and indispensable conclusion by analogy. But we must and can be content with such a conclusion, for that must indeed be true whose denial would imply the negation of all man's empirical existence and of all his social life.

Thus quite suddenly things have taken a strange turn; the certainty of physics is no longer based on purely logical presuppositions but on a biological and sociological presupposition. S'Gravesande himself tries to belittle the novelty and radicalism of this idea by taking refuge once more in a metaphysical interpretation and explanation. "The author of nature," he declares, "has made it necessary for us to reason by analogy, which consequently can be a legitimate basis for our reasoning." In this conclusion s'Gravesande's transition to another kind of reasoning becomes distinctly noticeable. For does the psychological and biological necessity of an infer-ence by analogy predicate anything with respect to the logical necessity or the objective truth of the inference? Mathematical empiricism here stands on the threshold of skeptical empiricism, and the step from Newton to Hume is henceforth inevitable. The two viewpoints are now sepa-rated only by a wall so thin a mere breath could blow it down. In order to lay the keystone of his doctrine of the certainty of knowledge, Descartes had to appeal to the "truthfulness of God." To deny the absolute validity of the concepts and principles of pure mathematics which we grasp with the greatest clarity would be tantamount to doubting this truthfulness. Now, however, in order to make sure of the truth of the highest physical principles—in other words, of the truth of experience—we must indeed have recourse to God, but to his goodness rather than his truth-fulness. For it follows from God's goodness that a conviction which is vital and necessary to man must have some objective foundation in the nature of things. If we consider the goodness of the creator, we can rely on conclusions by analogy, says s'Gravesande: "For the certainty of analogy is based on the invariability of those laws which could not be subject to change without the human race feeling it and perishing in a short time." But the fundamental problem of physical method now becomes a problem of theodicy. If one eliminates the question of theodicy or answers it in the negative, then the question of the certainty of physical induction appears in an entirely new light. And it is just this transformation that takes place in Hume. Mathematical empiricism had reached the point where the uniformity of nature rested only on a sort of belief. Hume accepts this conclusion, but he robs the belief of its metaphysical disguise and removes all its transcendent elements. It is no longer based on religious, but on purely psychological grounds; it springs from a purely immanent necessity of human nature. In this sense Hume's doctrine of belief is a continuation and an ironic resolution of lines of thought which had attempted to give a religious foundation to the science of experience. This resolution consists in an exchange of roles in the relation between science and religion. Now it is not religion which, thanks to its higher, "absolute" truth, can provide a solid foundation for science; it is rather the relativity of scientific knowledge which draws religion also into its magic circle. Religion, like science, is incapable of a rational, strictly objective justification; we must be satisfied with deriving them both from their subjective sources, and if not with justifying them, at least with understanding them, as manifestations of certain fundamental and original instincts of human nature.

And the same conclusion, toward which we are driven on the one hand by the problem of causality, is urged upon us on the other hand by the problem of substance. Here, too, mathematical empiricism had anticipated a decisive development. It had disputed the idea that among the various fundamental qualities of matter which we encounter in experience there exists no definite relationship of sequence and consubstantiality, and that any one quality could be deduced from any other according to the rules of formal logic. Such a deduction was the ideal which Descartes had set up for physics. Beginning with the purely geometrical qualities, Descartes tries to show how these contain all other properties which we ordinarily attribute to the corporeal world. All qualities of matter, including its impenetrability and weight, can be reduced to mere extension. Extension is thus the truth, the essence, the substance of the corporeal world, while all other qualities are reduced to the status of mere accidents, that is, of contingent qualities. But Newton and his school oppose to Descartes' deductive ideal a purely inductive ideal. They insist that, as long as we follow experience closely, we never arrive at anything but the regular co-existence of properties, and we do not succeed in deriving one property from the other. For the development of this problem, too, it is especially instructive to observe the teachings of the Dutch physicists. Both s'Gravesande and his pupil and successor, Musschenbroek, repeatedly stress the fact that it is meaningless to distinguish between essential and non-essential properties of matter. For we can never know whether or not some natural law which is universally confirmed by experience and hence acknowledged as a general law of nature—for instance, the law of inertia—will reveal to us some essential and necessary property of physical bodies. "We simply do not know whether they are to be derived merely from certain fundamental properties with which God has endowed physical bodies, but which are in no sense essential and necessary; or, finally, whether the effects we see are produced by external causes." We can regard extension and shape, motion and rest, weight and inertia with empirical certainty as fundamental properties of matter; but there is nothing to prevent the existence, along with these qualities which are known to us, of other qualities which we shall perhaps discover in the future, and which we shall have equal or greater reason to look upon as elementary and original. Thus, with respect also to any ultimate distinctions among the properties of physical bodies, we must realize once and for all that there can be no final decision. Instead of distinguishing between essence and appearance and of deriving the latter from the former, we must operate entirely within the phenomenal world; instead of trying to explain one property in terms of another, we must rest content with the empirical coexistence of the various characteristics exhibited by experience. In terms of actual knowledge we shall lose nothing by rejecting all transcendent qualities of physical bodies; we shall only rid ourselves of an ideal which again and again has been an obstacle to the progress of empirical science. Obviously, then, it is only a step from this view to the complete abandonment of the concept of substance, to the assumption that the idea of a thing is simply the idea of a mere sum or aggregate of qualities. The transition takes place gradually and unnoticed. The attempt to eliminate all metaphysical elements from empirical philosophy finally gains so much ground that it casts doubt upon the logical foundations of this philosophy as well. . . .

Nineteenth-Century

Social Theory

Introduction

The nineteenth century was alternately driven by an idea of progress nurtured during the Enlightenment and haunted by the attempt to make that notion a reality in the practical form of revolution. The landmarks offered by the ideal of the one and the memory of the other only slowly receded from the historical horizon in the years after Napoleon's downfall of 1815, never entirely ceasing to provide the new century with its cardinal points of historical orientation. Whether viewed as shoals dangerously encroaching upon the course of nations, or as headlands beckoning a brighter future, these landmarks of history and philosophy were soon to find themselves the subjects of the scientific discussion they had helped to popularize during the Enlightenment. Successions of thinkers set out to devise a social theory that would either affirm or delegitimate by rational means what history had so abruptly accomplished during the transformations of the late eighteenth century.

In 1776 the coastal Atlantic colonies of North America had revolted against their master, the British Empire; soon afterward, in 1789, France underwent a revolution that rid the country of an ancient monarchy and engulfed Europe, as well as the colonial world, in the longest period of sustained warfare in modern European history. Both of these revolutions had been prefigured in the earlier English Civil War and Revolution of the seventeenth century. Yet both upheavals, particularly the French one, were remarkable for the mythology they bore along with them, a mythology that asserted the possibility of wiping clean the slate of past history, with all of its errors and abuses, in order to build society anew. Revolution had cleared the way for this new society in the eighteenth century; the nineteenth century would build it with the blueprint of Reason.

For many of the inheritors of these revolutionary struggles, the new rational society that was to replace the older, less sound, and less just order was to model itself after what is known as the "liberal" ideal of social organization. "Liberalism," as it came to be known, was the grand vision that was passed on from the Enlightenment to reformers and increasingly powerful middle classes of the nineteenth century, acknowledged by friends and foes alike as a significant new force on the historical scene. Liberals felt that society should be organized on the basis of freedom of the individual from institutional interference in the everyday conduct of one's professional and private life. To further this vision, liberals drew upon the great political theorists of the Enlightenment to make their case that representative and parliamentary democracies were the forms of government most capable of guaranteeing such freedom.

Liberalism, however, as the compass by which the progress of nations was to be directed, was not a political philosophy ensured of immediate, unqualified success. Even by the end of the century, liberalism was by no means unconditionally victorious. Although the French had done away with one monarchy, they were soon to replace it with another, and near the close of our period most European nations had crafted some sort of political compromise between older, monarchical traditions and the newer ideals of democratic representation. As for the United States, it was to develop its own particular variety of democratic conservatism, which, since the beginning, has been wary of the modern changes embraced by advocates of liberalism.

In spite of the many obstacles facing liberalism, supporters of liberalism as a form of political and moral culture managed, over the course of the nineteenth century, to forge a consensus on both sides of the Atlantic that humankind had emerged from the tyranny of past ages into the light of reason and benevolent interaction. Trade, not war, would guarantee peace between nations, while science and technology would assure the eradication of all those ills (poverty, sickness, ignorance) that earlier times had accepted as the "will of God," or the necessary consequences of social stability. The nineteenth century witnessed the powerful alliance of science, liberal politics, and market economics in the name of a crusade against the shadows of obscurantism, the ravage of nature, and the imperfect nature of man himself. It was the great age of Progress. In all cases, on any side of the political spectrum, political positions depended for their conviction upon some relation of appraisal, whether critical or positive, towards revolutionary history and the place of modern science in the world. Historical progress in history and the reason of natural science became ideologically inseparable.

Yet just as there are those today who dispute the notion of the "progress" of this general alliance of science, liberalism, and capitalism, so it was during the nineteenth century. The very power of the liberal vision may be said to have provoked some of the greatest minds of the nineteenth century to provide detailed and elaborate accounts of the unforeseen and often undesirable social changes taking place, in order to better express their reservations and cautions. In order to understand the classic texts of nineteenth-century thought, we must have some sense of the complexity of the society that welded together the liberal vision and defended it from its critics while at the same time allowing alternative visions to grow in the shadows. Supporters and critics of modernity did not live in two different worlds; they were both of their time.

The French and American revolutions defined the major social and political tensions that would persist throughout the nineteenth century. They may be followed along three lines: (1) the rise of liberal democracy and the problem of suffrage; (2) the expansion of the market economy and the development of proletarian classes, utopian movements, and conservative groupings in opposition to capitalism; and (3) an increasingly confident culture of science, and the challenges this posed to faith and belief in free will. While all of the writers in this unit are European, much of what they say and the context that helped them say it may be extended to the American context.

The republican ideals expressed in the inaugural documents of the American and French

Revolutions—the Declaration of Independence and the Declaration of the Rights of Man, respectively, both attesting to universally valid rights ordained by nature to all men—lived on in the nineteenth century as radical, somewhat dangerous, propositions. While on the one hand it was unclear for the first half of the century whether or not liberalism, based on the above ideals, was a viable form of political life (a criticism leveled by aristocrats and more conservative members of the middle classes), on the other it was a matter of contention just who should receive representation once it was in fact established. Propertyless men, women, and slaves in the United States were all excluded from this realm of political involvement well into the nineteenth century. In Europe, especially, after the execution of the French King Louis XVI in 1793 along with thousands of aristocrats and citizens, republican ideals were suspect in the eyes of many, and carried with them powerful associations of the revolutionary excess that had accompanied their initiation.

Fear of revolt, of the sort that brought about and sustained the French Revolution, began as an aristocratic specialty. For a generation of conservative aristocrats, Napoleon Bonaparte's return from exile to rally his troops at Waterloo in 1815 was an emblem of the invidious nature of the new political order announced by the Enlightenment, bent on introducing havoc into time-honored political traditions. The most determined efforts to maintain the status quo of the old regime in the face of increasing industrialization and cries for political reform were, however, repeatedly counterbalanced by popular revolts that branded the minds of both the middle classes and aristocracies. On two occasions, in 1830 and 1848, revolutions of one form or another swept across Europe and directly threatened autocratic or oligarchical regimes and the restricted voting block of elites. In the United States, the differentiation of the northern and southern societies and economies led to ideological confrontation on the subject of the place of slaves in the republican schema.

As this pressure contributed to the expansion of suffrage in various countries (England dramatically expanded the vote in the Reform Bill of 1832; France established universal male suffrage in 1848), and as the new industrial relations of capitalism demanded greater numbers of workers uprooted from traditional agriculture-based communities and concentrated in urban centers, fear of revolt was passed along to the bourgeois and middle classes which had gained political authority after the revolution of 1830. Restoration of aristocratic and monarchical power in Western Europe was unlikely after 1830. With middle classes more firmly in control, especially after 1848, revolution ceased to be a cause and became instead a threat.

As for the growing numbers of peasants and working people excluded from liberal politics (especially in the German-speaking lands of Eastern Europe), they did not feel drawn to the aspirations of liberalism, and increasingly began to conceive of their place in society along class lines. Nonetheless, based on the general compromises and consolidations of power achieved within these limitations by, roughly, 1830, the nineteenth century is often thought of as the triumphal century of the bourgeois class. There are many competing definitions of what makes an individual a member of the bourgeoisie, but we take the term to designate those whose investments fueled the capitalist economy, along with bureaucrats and professionals, whose services supported the commercial system.

As such, members of the bourgeoisie held very great power over those who were not themselves involved in industry or trade, but who instead had to sell their labor for wages. This was certainly nothing new; the political and economic conditions of the nineteenth century were the culmination of several centuries of social transformation. Yet the pace of this industrial development reached an unprecedented momentum; and it was the bourgeoisie that sought to control and direct it. If ever the bourgeoisie as a class made up the ruling elite, it was in Europe after 1870. Their culture, politics, and mores are those that today most readily characterize the nineteenth century.

The political visions of the bourgeois or middle classes had taken shape in the conflicts of the French Revolution. The struggle between absolute monarchies and the Rights of Man, however, was an opposition that had not been designed to accommodate the voice of a group increasingly vocal and visible throughout the nineteenth century, that of the working class. This new split between worker and bourgeois did not fit easily into older, pre-Revolutionary political thought (especially its French variety—Rousseau, Montesquieu, and Voltaire), which did not account for wealth generated by the labor of unrepresented people.

Social theory evolved along the lines of these political and class conflicts over the course of the nineteenth century, but also varied according to national tradition. In predominantly commercial Britain, the revolutionary declarations of the French faith in natural law as an ordering principle of society had never been attractive. The sort of universal moral theory associated with the French Revolution emphasized the collective nature of social life, and the idea that legitimate government must, in its form and operations, take natural law as its basis. In Britain, which had managed to govern itself for centuries without an explicit rationalization of its judiciary or administration, French political ideals had to make room for the quite different philosophies of utility—approaches interested less in ordered laws than in practical effects.

Likewise, many nineteenth-century reform and utopian movements generally deplored the sort of ethical and economic individualism promoted by British thinkers. They ranged in their agendas from the modest goals of parliamentary representation as sought by British socialists, known as Chartists, to the communal organization of non-repetitive labor and sensual gratification advocated by Charles Fourier in France, to the stern revolutionary activity of Marx's proletariat directed against the owners of production. The French ideals of absolute human rights, most effectively embodied in the sovereignty of collectivities such as the "nation," can be seen in the logic that underlay the abolitionist movement in the United States that pitted the natural rights of all, even African-Americans, against the Southern apologists who sought to preserve their traditional ways of life. The above reformist groups were unsatisfied with any social theory based on mechanical, individualistic premises; they sought to expand upon communal ideals of the revolutionary period in the face of the strains of an industrial age.

The rapid social changes of the nineteenth century, especially between 1850–1900, stimulated deeper questioning of the founding ideals of the Enlightenment. The very success of liberal democracy in Europe by the later decades of the 1800s made the confrontation of certain irregularities unavoidable. Thus, the free will or conscious control of one's moral actions that was theoretically necessary for the operation of liberal politics seemed valid in the political sphere, but less valid in those realms not consciously ordered according to egalitarian principles, such as the marketplace. Criticism of the ideological exclusiveness that buttressed the inegalitarian nineteenth-century family, the art world, and the world of education and academe—and, later in the century, those non-European lands held under colonial domination—mounted as time wore on. As for science, it was especially uncertain after Darwin whether science would remain a faithful servant of liberal tenets. By the final decades of the century, then, certain of the most basic of Enlightenment assumptions were under considerable strain just, ironically, as they were considered by many to have prevailed.

From the point of view of the social and economic conflicts fundamental to nineteenth-century European history, modernity is understandable as a complex of tensions, rather than the story of one dominant tendency. The tensions that make up this complex are found holding between the ideal of the politically and morally free citizen and the aspirations of those who would determine society and the individual by scientific principles alone; and between the belief in individualism and progress as sponsored by the bourgeoisie, and the concern for the stabilizing effects of tradition regarded nostalgically by royalists and their sympathizers. Similarly, modernity prescribed strikingly different roles for men and women: the confinement of all that was considered feminine and irrational to cluttered Victorian interiors, and the public supremacy of the evolutionarily-perfected bourgeois male ego. In the workplace, the tension was between the owners of production and the large population that found it necessary to offer their labor for sale—we may term this complex "modernity."

The thinkers addressed in this section—French aristocrat Alexis de Tocqueville, and the Germans Karl Marx, Friedrich Nietzsche, and Max Weber—each offer their own formulations of these nineteenth-century social conflicts. These writings remain some of the most profound and consequential statements on the problems engendered by modernity. The questions they pose, the methods and models they use, and the issues they investigate have all echoed down to our own times. Five themes orient these writings to the contexts in which they were produced: (1) society as a human invention; (2) history and historicism; (3) the "critique" as a philosophical attitude and practice; (4) the distinction between the subject and object and the consequences of this dichotomy for "objective knowledge"; and (5) the notion of a "synthesis," or a theoretical reconciliation between subject and object, ideal and material, and the role of scientific objectivity in this process. Each of the authors included here treats one or more of these problems.

History as we know it was an invention of the nineteenth century, and of German scholars in particular. By *history* is meant a concern with verification of sources and evidence by a competent, trained community of scholars. Though different forms of historical writing had existed long before, the sort of history that emerged in the middle of the nineteenth century was a species apart. Historicism sought to portray a period in its own terms by entering into its own peculiar way of being and thinking. The most extreme forms of this type of scholarship argue for a discontinuity between various periods, claiming that each period had its own essential spirit, apart from which it could not be understood. Thus, the historical approach to knowledge emphasized the particular in contrast to the universal, using such phrases as "the genius of the nation" or "the spirit of the times" to describe the essence of an epoch or a people.

This way of thinking has its roots in Romanticism, a cultural movement that grew up in reaction to the aggressive rationalism of the Enlightenment. Romantic thinkers and artists argued for the equal if not superior value of art and spirituality, aspects of human experience which they felt were underappreciated in Enlightenment philosophy. History as it was practiced in the nineteenth century had definite associations with the artistic goals of Romanticism; and the use of art, rather than formal reason, as a model for writing about human society and life was common among nineteenth-century thinkers. History, however, was not entirely bound by the standards of artistic creation, or the "aesthetic," and many historians balanced the aesthetic aspects of historical interpretations with an insistence on scientific rigor in analysis of documents and judgement of sources.

Although historicism asserted discontinuity, faith in history as an objective process allowed scholars to claim the ground of reason for their interpretations, and claim that reason enabled them to decipher otherwise incomprehensible cultures and time periods. The German historian Leopold von Ranke (1795–1886), in his efforts to increase the rigor of history through meticulous attention to detail and his belief that the acts of people in all periods may be understood only through comprehension of the single great idea of the time, exemplifies this sort of practice. He, like other historians of his time, felt that earlier historical writings had neither been "objective" nor "scientific," nor had they attempted to tell a full story on the basis of their evidence. Ranke led the German "Historical School," which greatly influenced later generations of historians worldwide.

Another intellectual practice, the "critique," also took form at this time. Following up on the German philosopher Immanuel Kant's attempts to reconcile reason and morality under the rubric of a critique, and given form in the political upheaval of the French Revolution and its absolute rejection of the past, the critique came to play an increasingly important role among artists and thinkers of the time, and animated some of the most volatile utopian movements. It was based on the idea that some one particular human activity, be it intellectual, artistic, or political, could offer the rest of humanity the critical vision necessary to help it move forward on the road to progress and reason. The notion of critique was taken up by many who acted or claimed to be "modern."

Artists adopting the motto "art for art's sake" felt that art could serve the purpose of criticizing the shallowness of bourgeois society; painters such as Jean François Millet (1814–1875) and Gustave Courbet (1819–1877) thought that realistic paintings of the life of peasants would jar bourgeois spectators into contemplating the brutality of physical labor. A long line of German philosophers after Kant, such as Fichte, Hegel, and Marx, thought that critical history could be used to sift what was best from the past into a philosophy of history that would project the results of its study onto an ideal future. Kant himself, in his *Critique of Pure Reason* (1781), sought to establish the means by which reason could be made to support the advance of moral freedom. History of this variety, of course, is often at odds with the sort of Rankean history described above.

Like historicism, the critique demanded a foundation of rationally justifiable, and hence universally valid, propositions from which to operate. The person eager to make a critique had first to construct the grounds upon which he may do so, and establish that these grounds were true for all times and places. Paradoxically, the artistic and philosophical critiques crafted in the nineteenth century were often based on Enlightenment ideals that society at large seemed to dismiss; the role of the philosophical or artistic "critic" was thus often left to the articulation of a new social class, that of the intellectuals. In taking up the project of the "critique," intellectuals and artists often based their social criticisms on Enlightenment conceptions of equality and freedom, even when it was the Enlightenment itself that they sought to attack.

According to the Enlightenment notions of scientific knowledge and rational politics, that which was subjective was individual and particular; that which was "objective" and rational was universal, common to all. Such a split between the objective and the subjective had been a fundamental of Western philosophy since Descartes, and a likeness of it is discernible in Platonic thought. The power available to those employing a critique was itself derived from this dichotomy—English utilitarianism carried it to one possible extreme by declaring that what was Good in the absolute sense was what was good for the greatest number.

"Objectivity" itself took on this mantle of the universal as a means of reinforcing consensus in a society animated more by individual competition than traditional allegiances. This effort to remove the "subject" from knowledge claims had certain consequences; in the human and natural sciences, great power went to those who could define what was "subject" to scientific investigation—that which could be questioned, and that which was to do the questioning.

The subject-object split penetrated one's very physical being as well, introducing a disjuncture between those aspects of one's mental and physical life considered irrational and subjective, and those practices and behaviors, such as conscious thought or money-making (but not sex or religion), considered rational and, for all intents and purposes, natural, or given in the order of things. The boundaries enforced within individual psyches between what was "natural" and "normal" and what was "deviant" or "degenerate" redirected vague energies into strange forms of behavior that comprise what is referred to as the dark side of modernity. The nineteenth century was the great age of, among other things, clinical neuroses and "hysterical" women. This was the ground upon which psychotherapy developed, asserting that human emotional and sexual drives were channeled into ever-more-removed forms of expression when confronted with the restraints of civilized society.

As science claimed more and more of nature's province for itself, it seemed that those elements of the human experience that were not bound up explicitly in material processes amenable to scientific observation would be denied any validity as contemporary meaningful phenomena. This stance, often described as materialist, was frequently espoused by those republican-minded individuals who looked to science as a gauge by which to orient and measure progress. Thus, many Frenchmen from the middle of the century onward responded to the philosophy of August Comte (1797–1857) as a secular faith that would explain everything in terms of the ever-increasing social proficiency and moral-practical benefit of science. Marx proudly named his revolutionary philosophy "materialist." Conservatives across Europe, allied with the Catholic Church in the name of higher spiritual values, deplored the secularization of civilization trumpeted by materialists and positivists (with whom they were associated). Positivists felt that allegiance to a man-made state would automatically follow from the discovery of the social laws which held society together. Comte's doctrines, labeled together as "positivism," were to have a pan-European impact on notions of the nature and proper practice of science, and the ends to which science should be put.

The philosophical standpoint of "idealism" was felt to be the opposite of positivism. Idealist philosophies usually argued for the role of a disembodied "mind" or "judgement" superior to empirical observation and capable of synthesizing the latter in terms of abstract laws. "Idealist" ways of thinking about the world were often voiced among German-speaking peoples. German idealism, disposed as it was to those aspects of the human experience that defied material embodiment and scientific explanation and examination (such as history, some forms of psychology, and art) was deeply influenced by the search among historians for the spirit of past epochs, the immaterial essence that gave life to particular civilizations. As early as Kant, the strain introduced by overemphasizing the material or the spiritual aspects of reality was felt to be disconcerting, and philosophical predilections swung back and forth between the two extremes.

Two of the most significant thinkers whose writings appear in the following pages, Karl Marx and Max Weber, were concerned with precisely this dilemma: discontinuity between two forms of experience. These two forms could be viewed as the material and the ideal worlds, or as the objective and the subjective. The drive for synthesis that motivated Sigmund Freud, for example, led him to search out the biological aspects and natural logic of those seemingly intangible and supremely illogical of experiences—dreams. Freud argued that an individual's sex life and the subduing of biological instincts were represented in, and subsequently affected by, a person's subconscious. With this argument, Freud managed to fashion a form of synthesis between ideal and material spheres, achieving a theoretical balance of the sort that typifies the preoccupations of some of the greatest minds of the nineteenth century.

Finally, the notion that "society" existed independent of nature, God, or individual men, on its own terms entirely, engaged nineteenth-century imaginations. Whether societies should adapt themselves to the laws of nature, as was suggested by Adam Smith, or to their historical traditions, as described in the writings of the French thinker Montesquieu (1689–1755) and the German philosopher Herder (1744–1803), were questions that depended on a conception of God's place in social life as far removed. Comte provided yet another alternative in advocating the establishment of society on the basis of reason. In all of these writings, the social became a more and more distinct realm. Society was composed of individuals, rather than the sum of all individuals. Though it was claimed that society, too, was regulated by laws, they were not necessarily those of the natural world, and they might be uncomfortably contradictory to accepted morality. The notions of society and of social structure itself are some of the most problematic yet useful ideas to have appeared in full bloom in the nineteenth century.

Armed with the above thumbnail sketch of nineteenth-century political and intellectual history, the reader will perhaps better understand what is at stake when Alexis de Tocqueville asks himself whether the French Revolution really did break with the heavy weight of tradition to forge a new era, or whether history inevitably imposes its continuity despite the most fervent efforts to prevent it from doing so. Was the democratic experiment as Tocqueville knew it in the United States of the 1830s a recipe for despotism, or truly the road to the fulfillment of liberty, equality, fraternity, and a veritable emancipation from history? Likewise, it is especially important to view Karl Marx's writings in the context in which they appeared, rather than via the reductions of his thought that have been prevalent since the Cold War. Was Marx really an economic determinist, or did he succeed in the drive for synthesis that animated Immanuel Kant and Max Weber? In the case of Nietzsche, contemporary readers are likely to see much that is now culturally pervasive, along with much that is morally repellent, although in his time, his readers' attitudes may well have been just the reverse of our own. Such diverse expressions and reactions have all been labeled aspects of modernity at one time or another. Though each of them characterizes a particular aspect of modernity as it developed in the nineteenth century, they were all fundamentally related to the underlying social, political, and intellectual structures that arose, not without conflict and never without opposition, from the exalted ambitions of the Enlightenment.

Alexis de Tocqueville

Tocqueville (1805–1859), a man of noble birth destined for a career in law and politics, was one of the greatest nineteenth-century analysts of the French Revolution and the role of democracy in Europe and the United States. The revolution was a living memory in Tocqueville's day as it was not for later historians. It was impossible to live in Tocqueville's period and not be conscious of being related to the great events of the last decades of the preceding century. In the years after 1789, the French had busied themselves with coming to know the newly constituted French "nation" by surveying its lands, peoples, and resources in order to better administer and control them. This enterprise was closely linked with the legal-istic culture emerging from the Revolution, in which the primacy of constitutional law entailed historical investigation of the forms such laws had taken in the past. It is clear that Tocqueville bore this legalistic spirit in both his interpretations of political life in the United States and in his reconstruction of the slow evolution of conflict between moral and political institutions in pre-Revolutionary France. Like the law, the structures Tocqueville saw running through society were based on more-or-less conscious, formal relations between groups of people and the rights and obligations they had towards one another. On top of this legal framework rose a more abstract notion of a certain vital "spirit" that belonged to each group as long as that group fulfilled its appropriate function. Many of the issues Tocqueville raised sound quite contemporary: discussion of the growth of centralized power and the threats this posed to individual liberties; the breakdown of the age-old traditions that resulted in the moral dissolution of collective bonds; and an uncanny consciousness of historical distance and change. In *The Old Regime and the French Revolution*, Tocqueville more than once stressed the historical distance between his time and that of his grandfathers; the twilight of the monarchy and bustling decades of economic expansion in mid-century Europe were worlds apart, even though, as Tocqueville tells us, individuals who had lived through the Revolutionary period still walked the streets of Paris. For modern man, such as Tocqueville, the past was nearly irretrievably alien, and retrieving it required the faculty of *Verstehen*, as the German historians put it, or the means by which a past no longer embodied in living values or traditions is reconstructed. For an aristocrat eager to revisit his ancestors, method must invent tradition.

ALEXIS DE TOCQUEVILLE

(1835)

Democracy

in America

INTRODUCTION

Among the novel objects that attracted my attention during my stay in the United States, nothing struck me more forcibly than the general equality of conditions. I readily discovered the prodigious influence which this primary fact exercises on the whole course of society, by giving a certain direction to public opinion, and a certain tenor to the laws; by imparting new maxims to the governing powers, and peculiar habits to the governed.

I speedily perceived that the influence of this fact extends far beyond the political character and the laws of the country, and that it has no less empire over civil society than over the government; it creates opinions, engenders sentiments, suggests the ordinary practices of life, and modifies whatever it does not produce.

The more I advanced in the study of American society, the more I perceived that the equality of conditions is the fundamental fact from which all others seem to be derived, and the central point at which all my observations constantly terminated.

I then turned my thoughts to our own hemisphere, where I imagined that I discerned something analogous to the spectacle which the New World presented to me. I observed that the equality of conditions is daily advancing toward those extreme limits which it seems to have reached in the United States; and that the democracy which governs the American communities, appears to be rapidly rising into power in Europe.

I hence conceived the idea of the book which is now before the reader.

Published as *The Republic of the United States of America* (A. S. Barnes and Co., New York, 1863), I: pp. 1, 13, 257–61, 270–72, 275–77, 280–87, II: pp. 1–3, 34–35, 99–103, 352–55.

It is evident to all alike that a great democratic revolution is going on among us; but there are two opinions as to its nature and consequences. To some it appears to be a novel accident, which as such may still be checked; to others it seems irresistible, because it is the most uniform, the most ancient, and the most permanent tendency which is to be found in history....

In perusing the pages of our history, we shall scarcely meet with a single great event, in the lapse of seven hundred years, which has not turned to the advantage of equality....

Whithersoever we turn our eyes, we shall discover the same continual revolution throughout the whole of Christendom.

The various occurrences of national existence have everywhere turned to the advantage of democracy; all men have aided it by their exertions: those who have intentionally laboured in its cause, and those who have served it unwittingly—those who have fought for it, and those who have declared themselves its opponents—have all been driven along in the same track, have all laboured to one end, some ignorantly, and some unwillingly; all have been blind instruments in the hands of God.

The gradual development of the equality of conditions is, therefore, a providential fact, and it possesses all the characteristics of a divine decree: it is universal, it is durable, it constantly eludes all human interference, and all events as well as all men contribute to its progress.

Would it, then, be wise to imagine that a social impulse which dates from so far back, can be checked by the efforts of a generation? Is it credible that the democracy which has annihilated the feudal system, and vanquished kings, will respect the citizen and the capitalist? Will it stop now that it has grown so strong and its adversaries so weak?

None can say which way we are going, for all terms of comparison are wanting: the equality of conditions is more complete in the Christian countries of the present day, than it has been at any time, or in any part of the world; so that the extent of what already exists prevents us from foreseeing what may be yet to come.

The whole book which is here offered to the public, has been written under the impression of a kind of religious dread, produced in the author's mind by the contemplation of so irresistible a revolution, which has advanced for centuries in spite of such amazing obstacles, and which is still proceeding in the midst of the ruins it has made.

It is not necessary that God himself should speak in order to disclose to us the unquestionable signs of his will; we can discern them in the habitual course of nature, and in the invariable tendency of events; I know, without a special revelation, that the planets move in the orbits traced by the Creator's finger.

If the men of our time were led by attentive observation and by sincere reflection, to acknowledge that the gradual and progressive development of social equality is at once the past and future of their history, this solitary truth would confer the sacred character of a divine decree upon the change. To attempt to check democracy would be in that case to resist the will of God, and the nations would then be constrained to make the best of the social lot awarded to them by Providence.

The Christian nations of our age seem to me to present a most alarming spectacle; the impulse which is bearing them along is so strong that it cannot be stopped, but it is not yet so rapid that it cannot be guided: their fate is in their hands; yet a little while and it may be so no longer.

The first duty which is at this time imposed upon those who direct our affairs is to educate the democracy; to warm its faith, if that be possible; to purify its morals; to direct its energies; to substitute a knowledge of business for its inexperience, and an acquaintance with its true interests for its blind propensities; to adapt its government to time and place; and to modify it in compliance with the occurrences and the actors of the age.

A new science of politics is indispensable to a new world....

On one side were wealth, strength, and leisure, accompanied by the refinement of luxury, the elegance of taste, the pleasures of wit, and the religion of art. On the other were labor, and a rude ignorance; but in the midst of this coarse and ignorant multitude, it was not uncommon to meet with energetic passions, generous sentiments, profound religious convictions, and independent virtues.

The body of a state thus organized, might boast of its stability, its power, and above all, of its glory.

But the scene is now changed, and gradually the two ranks mingle; the divisions which once severed mankind, are lowered; property is divided, power is held in common, the light of intelligence spreads, and the capacities of all classes are equally cultivated; the state becomes democratic, and the empire of democracy is slowly and peaceably introduced into the institutions and manners of the nation.

I can conceive a society in which all men would profess an equal attachment and respect for the laws of which they are the common authors; in which the authority of the state would be respected as necessary, though not as divine; and the loyalty of the subject to the chief magistrate would not be a passion, but a quiet and rational persuasion. Every individual being in the possession of rights which he is sure to retain, a kind of manly reliance and reciprocal courtesy would arise between all classes, alike removed from pride and meanness.

The people, well acquainted with its true interests, would allow, that in order to profit by the advantages of society, it is necessary to satisfy its demands. In this state of things, the voluntary association of the citizens might supply the individual exertions of the nobles, and the community would be alike protected from anarchy and from oppression.

I admit that in a democratic state thus constituted, society will not be stationary; but the impulses of the social body may be regulated and directed forward; if there be less splendour than in the halls of an aristocracy, the contrast of misery will be less frequent also; the pleasures of enjoyment may be less excessive, but those of comfort will be more general; the sciences may be less perfectly cultivated, but ignorance will be less common; the impetuosity of the feelings will be repressed, and the habits of the nation softened; there will be more vices and fewer crimes.

In the absence of enthusiasm and of an ardent faith, great sacrifices may be obtained from the members of a commonwealth by an appeal to their understandings and their experience: each individual will feel the same necessity for uniting with his fellow-citizens to protect his own weakness; and as he knows that if they are to assist he must co-operate, he will readily perceive that his personal interest is identified with the interest of the community.

The nation, taken as a whole, will be less brilliant, less glorious, and perhaps less strong; but the majority of the citizens will enjoy a greater degree of prosperity, and the people will remain quiet, not because it despairs of melioration, but because it is conscious of the advantages of its condition.

If all the consequences of this state of things were not good or useful, society would at least have appropriated all such as were useful and good; and having once and for ever renounced the social advantages of aristocracy, mankind would enter into possession of all the benefits which democracy can afford.

But here it may be asked what we have adopted in the place of those institutions, those ideas, and those customs of our forefathers which we have abandoned.

The spell of royalty is broken, but it has not been succeeded by the majesty of the laws; the people have learned to despise all authority. But fear now extorts a larger tribute of obedience than that which was formerly paid by reverence and by love.

I perceive that we have destroyed those independent beings which were able to cope with tyranny single-handed; but it is the government that has inherited the privileges of which families, corporations, and individuals, have been deprived; the weakness of the whole community has, therefore, succeeded to that influence of a small body of citizens, which, if it was sometimes oppressive, was often conservative.

The division of property has lessened the distance which separated the rich from the poor; but it would seem that the nearer they draw to each other, the greater is their mutual hatred, and the more vehement the envy and the dread with which they resist each other's claims to power; the notion of right is alike insensible to both classes, and force affords to both the only argument for the present, and the only guarantee for the future.

The poor man retains the prejudices of his forefathers without their faith, and their ignorance without their virtues; he has adopted the doctrine of self-interest as the rule of his actions, without understanding the science which controls it, and his egotism is no less blind than his devotedness was formerly.

If society is tranquil, it is not because it relies upon its strength and its well-being, but because it knows its weakness and its infirmities: a single effort may cost it its life; everybody feels the evil, but no one has courage or energy enough to seek the cure; the desires, the regret, the sorrows, and the joys of the time, produce nothing that is visible or permanent, like the passions of old men which terminate in impotence.

We have, then, abandoned whatever advantages the old state of things afforded, without receiving any compensation from our present condition; having destroyed an aristocracy, we seem inclined to survey its ruins with complacency, and to fix our abode in the midst of them. . . .

Where are we then? . . .

Has such been the fate of the centuries which have preceded our own? and has man always inhabited a world, like the present, where nothing is linked together, where virtue is without genius, and genius without honour; where the love of order is confounded with a taste for oppression, and the holy rites of freedom with a contempt of law; where the light thrown by conscience on human actions is dim, and where nothing seems to be any longer forbidden or allowed, honorable or shameful, false or true?

I cannot, however, believe that the Creator made man to leave him in an endless struggle with the intellectual miseries which surround us: God destines a calmer and a more certain future to the communities of Europe; I am unacquainted with his designs, but I shall not cease to believe in them because I cannot fathom them, and I had rather mistrust my own capacity than his justice.

There is a country in the world where the great revolution which I am speaking of seems nearly to have reached its natural limits; it has been effected with ease and simplicity, say rather that this country has attained the consequences of the democratic revolution which we are undergoing, without having experienced the revolution itself.

The emigrants who fixed themselves on the shores of America in the beginning of the seventeenth century, severed the democratic principle from all the principles which repressed it in the old communities of Europe, and transplanted it unalloyed to the New World. It has there been allowed to spread in perfect freedom, and to put forth its consequences in the laws by influencing the manners of the country.

It appears to me beyond a doubt, that sooner or later we shall arrive, like the Americans, at an almost complete equality of conditions. But I do not conclude from this, that we shall ever be necessarily led to draw the same political consequences which the Americans have derived from a similar social organization. I am far from supposing that they have chosen the only form of government which a democracy may adopt; but the identity of the efficient cause of laws and manners in the two countries is sufficient to account for the immense interest we have in becoming acquainted with its effects in each of them.

It is not, then, merely to satisfy a legitimate curiosity that I have examined America; my wish has been to find instruction by which we may ourselves profit. Whoever should imagine that I have intended to write a panegyric would be strangely mistaken, and on reading this book, he will perceive that such was not my design: nor has it been my object to advocate any form of government in particular, for I am of opinion that absolute excellence is rarely to be found in any legislation; I have not even affected to discuss whether the social revolution, which I believe to be irresistible, is advantageous or prejudicial to mankind; I have acknowledged this revolution as a fact already accomplished or on the eve of its accomplishment; and I have selected the nation, from among those which have undergone it, in which its development has been the most peaceful and the most complete, in order to discern its natural consequences, and, if it be possible, to distinguish the means by which it may be rendered profitable. I confess that in America I saw more than America; I sought the image of democracy itself, with its inclinations, its character, its prejudices, and its passions, in order to learn what we have to fear or to hope from its progress.

What the Real Advantages are Which American Society
Derives from the Government of the Democracy
General Tendency of the Laws Under the Rule of the American Democracy,
and Habits of Those Who Apply Them

The defects and the weaknesses of a democratic government may very readily be discovered; they are demonstrated by the most flagrant instances, while its beneficial influence is less perceptibly exercised. A single glance suffices to detect its evil consequences. But its good qualities can only be discerned by long observation. The laws of the American democracy are frequently defective or incomplete; they sometimes attack vested rights, or give a sanction to others which are dangerous to the community; but even if they were good, the frequent changes which they undergo would be an evil. How comes it, then, that the American republics prosper, and maintain their position?. . .

Democratic laws generally tend to promote the welfare of the greatest possible number; for they emanate from a majority of the citizens, who are subject to error, but who cannot have an interest opposed to their own advantage. The laws of an aristocracy tend, on the contrary, to concentrate wealth and power in the hands of the minority, because an aristocracy, by its very nature, constitutes a minority. It may therefore be asserted, as a general proposition, that the purpose of a democracy, in the conduct of its legislation, is useful to a greater number of citizens than that of an aristocracy. This is, however, the sum total of its advantages.

Aristocracies are infinitely more expert in the science of legislation than democracies ever can be. They are possessed of a self-control which protects them from the errors of a temporary excitement; and they form lasting designs which they mature with the assistance of favourable opportunities. Aristocratic government proceeds with the dexterity of art; it understands how to make the collective force of all its laws converge at the same time to a given point. Such is not the case with democracies, whose laws are almost always ineffective or inopportune. The means of democracy are therefore more imperfect than those of aristocracy, and the measures which it unwittingly adopts are frequently opposed to its own case; but the object it has in view is more useful.

Let us now imagine a community so organized by nature, or by its constitution, that it can support the transitory action of bad laws, and that it can await, without destruction, the general tendency of the legislation: we shall then be able to conceive that a democratic government, notwithstanding its defects, will be most fitted to conduce to the prosperity of this community. This is precisely what has occurred in the United States; and I repeat, what I have before remarked, that the great advantage of the Americans consists in their being able to commit faults which they may afterward repair.

An analogous observation may be made respecting public officers. It is easy to perceive that the American democracy frequently errs in the choice of the individuals to whom it intrusts the power of the administration; but it is more difficult to say why the state prospers under their rule. In the first place it is to be remarked that if in a democratic state the governors have less honesty and less capacity than elsewhere, the governed on the other hand are more enlightened and more attentive to their interests. As the people in democracies is more incessantly vigilant in its affairs, and more jealous of its rights, it prevents its representatives from abandoning that general line of conduct which its own interest prescribes. In the second place, it must be remembered that if the democratic magistrate is more apt to misuse his power, he possesses it for a shorter period of time. But there is yet another reason which is still more general and conclusive. It is no doubt of importance to the welfare of nations that they should be governed by men of talents and virtue; but it is perhaps still more important that the interests of those men should not differ from the interests of the community at large; for if such were the case, virtues of a high order might become useless, and talents might be turned to a bad account.

I say that it is important that the interests of the persons in authority should not conflict with or oppose the interests of the community at large; but I do not insist upon their having the same interests as the *whole* population, because I am not aware that such a state of things ever existed in any country.

No political form has hitherto been discovered, which is equally favourable to the prosperity and the development of all the classes into which society is divided. These classes continue to form, as it were, a certain number of distinct nations in the same nation; and experience has shown that it is no less dangerous to place the fate of these classes exclusively in the hands of any one of them, than it is to make one people the arbiter of the destiny of another. When the rich alone govern, the interest of the poor is always endangered; and when the poor make the laws, that of the rich incurs very serious risks. The advantage of democracy does not consist, therefore, as has sometimes been asserted, in favouring the prosperity of all, but simply in contributing to the well-being of the greatest possible number.

The men who are mistrusted with the direction of public affairs in the United States, are frequently inferior, both in point of capacity and of morality, to those whom aristocratic institutions would raise to power. But their interest is identified and confounded with that of the majority of their fellow-citizens. They may frequently be faithless, and frequently mistake; but they will never systematically adopt a line of conduct opposed to the will of the majority; and it is impossible that they should give a dangerous or an exclusive tendency to the government.

The mal-administration of a democratic magistrate is a mere isolated fact, which only occurs during the short period for which he is elected. Corruption and incapacity do not act as common interests, which may connect men permanently with one another. A corrupt or an incapable magistrate will not concert his measures with another magistrate, simply because that individual is as corrupt and as incapable as himself; and these two men will never unite their endeavors to promote the corruption and inaptitude of their remote posterity. The ambition and the manoeuvers of the one will serve, on the contrary, to unmask the other. The vices of a magistrate, in democratic states, are usually peculiar to his own person.

But under aristocratic governments public men are swayed by the interest of their order, which, if it is sometimes confounded with the interests of the majority, is very frequently distinct from them. This interest is the common and lasting bond which unites them together; it induces them to coalesce, and to combine their efforts in order to attain an end which does not always ensure the greatest happiness of the greatest number; and it serves not only to connect the persons in authority, but to unite them to a considerable portion of the community, since a numerous body of citizens belongs to the aristocracy, without being invested with official functions. The aristocratic magistrate is therefore constantly supported by a portion of the community, as well as by the government of which he is a member.

The common purpose which connects the interest of the magistrates in aristocracies, with that of a portion of their contemporaries, identifies it with that of future generations; their influence belongs to the future as much as to the present. The aristocratic magistrate is urged at the same time toward the same point, by the passions of the community, by his own, and I may almost add, by those of his posterity. Is it, then, wonderful that he does not resist such repeated impulses? And, indeed, aristocracies are often carried away by the spirit of their order without being corrupted by it; and they unconsciously fashion society to their own ends, and prepare it for their own descendants. . . .

Activity Which Pervades All the Branches of the Body Politic in the United States; Influence Which It Exercises Upon Society

On passing from a country in which free institutions are established to one where they do not exist, the traveller is struck by the change; in the former all is bustle and activity, in the latter everything is calm and motionless. In the one, melioration and progress are the general topics of inquiry; in the other, it seems as if the community only aspired to repose in the enjoyment of the advantages which it has acquired. Nevertheless, the country which exerts itself so strenuously to promote its welfare is generally more wealthy and more prosperous than that which appears to be so contented with its lot; and when we compare them together, we can scarcely conceive how so many new wants are daily felt in the former, while so few seem to occur in the latter.

If this remark is applicable to those free countries in which monarchical and aristocratic institutions subsist, it is still more striking with regard to democratic republics. In these states it is not only a portion of the people which is busied with the melioration of its social condition, but the whole community is engaged in the task; and it is not the exigencies and the convenience of a single class for which a provision is to be made, but the exigencies and the convenience of all ranks of life.

It is not impossible to conceive the surpassing liberty which the Americans enjoy; some idea may likewise be formed of the extreme equality which subsists among them; but the politics, activity which pervades the United States must be seen in order to be understood. No sooner do you set foot upon the American soil than you are stunned by a kind of tumult; a confused clamour is heard on every side; and a thousand simultaneous voices demand the immediate satisfaction of their social wants. Everything is in motion around you; here, the people of one quarter of a town are met to decide upon the building of a church; there, the election of a representative is going on; a little farther, the delegates of a district are posting to the town in order to consult upon some local improvements; or in another place the labourers of a village quit their ploughs to deliberate upon the project of a road or a public school. Meetings are called for the sole purpose of declaring their disapprobation of the line of conduct pursued by the government; while in other assemblies the citizens salute the authorities of the day as the fathers of their country.

This ceaseless agitation which democratic government has introduced into the political world, influences all social intercourse.

Unlimited Power of the Majority in the United States, and the Consequences

The very essence of democratic government consists in the absolute sovereignty of the majority: for there is nothing in democratic states which is capable of resisting it. Most of the American constitutions have sought to increase this natural strength of the majority by artificial means.

The legislature is, of all political institutions, the one which is most easily swayed by the wishes of the majority. The Americans determined that the members of the legislature should be elected by the people immediately, and for a very brief term, in order to subject them, not only to the general convictions, but even to the daily passions of their constituents. The members of both houses are taken from the same class in society, and are nominated in the same manner; so that the modifications of the legislative bodies are almost as rapid and quite as irresistible as those of a single assembly. It is to a legislature thus constituted, that almost all the authority of the government has been intrusted.

But while the law increased the strength of those authorities which of themselves were strong, it enfeebled more and more those which were naturally weak. It deprived the representatives of the executive of all stability and independence; and by subjecting them completely to the caprices of the legislature, it robbed them completely of the slender influence which the nature of a democratic government might have allowed them to retain. In several states the judicial power was also submitted to the elective discretion of the majority; and in all them its existence was made to depend on the pleasure of the legislative authority, since the representatives were empowered annually to regulate the stipend of the judges.

Custom, however, has done even more than law. A proceeding which will in the end set all the guarantees of representative government at naught, is becoming more and more general in the United States: it frequently happens that the electors, who choose a delegate, point out a certain line of conduct to him, and impose upon him a certain number of positive obligations which he is pledged to fulfill. With the exception of the tumult, this comes to the same thing as if the majority of the populace held its deliberations in the market-place.

Several other circumstances concur in rendering the power of the majority in America, not only preponderant, but irresistible. The moral authority of the majority is partly based upon the notion, that there is more intelligence and more wisdom in a great number of men collected together than in a single individual, and that the quantity of legislators is more important than their quality. The theory of equality is in fact applied to the intellect of man; and human pride is thus assailed in its last retreat, by a doctrine which the minority hesitate to admit, and in which they very slowly concur. Like all other powers, and perhaps more than all other powers, the authority of the many requires the sanction of time; at first it enforces obedience by constraint; but its laws are not respected until they have long been maintained.

The right of governing society, which the majority supposes itself to derive from its superior intelligence, was introduced into the United States by the first settlers; and this idea, which would be sufficient of itself to create a free nation, has now been amalgamated with the manners of the people, and the minor incidents of social intercourse.

The French, under the old monarchy, held it for a maxim (which is still a fundamental principle of the English constitution), that the king could do no wrong; and if he did wrong, the blame was imputed to his advisers. This notion was highly favorable to habits of obedience; and it enabled the subject to complain of the law, without ceasing to love and honor the lawgiver. The Americans entertain the same opinion with respect to the majority.

The moral power of the majority is founded upon yet another principle, which is, that the interests of the many are to be preferred to those of the few. It will readily be perceived that the respect here professed for the rights of the majority must naturally increase or diminish according to the state of parties. When a nation is divided into several irreconcilable factions, the privilege of the majority is often overlooked, because it is intolerable to comply with its demands.

If there existed in America a class of citizens whom the legislating majority sought to deprive of exclusive privileges, which they had possessed for ages, and to bring down from an elevated station to the level of the ranks of the multitude, it is probable that the minority would be less ready to comply with its laws. But as the United States were colonized by men holding an equal rank among themselves, there is as yet no natural or permanent source of dissension between the interests of its different inhabitants.

There are certain communities in which the persons who constitute the minority can never hope to draw over the majority to their side, because they must then give up the very point which is at issue between them. Thus, an aristocracy can never become a majority while it retains its exclusive privileges, and it cannot cede its privileges without ceasing to be an aristocracy.

In the United States, political questions cannot be taken up in so general and absolute a manner; and all parties are willing to recognise the rights of the majority, because they all hope to turn those rights to their own advantage at some future time. The majority therefore in that country exercises a prodigious actual authority, and a moral influence which is scarcely less preponderant; no obstacles exist which can impede, or so much as retard its progress, or which can induce it to heed the complaints of those whom it crushes upon its path. This state of things is fatal in itself and dangerous for the future.

Tyranny of the Majority

I hold it to be an impious and an execrable maxim that, politically speaking, a people has a right to do whatsoever it pleases; and yet I have asserted that all authority originates in the will of the majority. Am I, then, in contradiction with myself?

A general law—which bears the name of justice—has been made and sanctioned, not only by a majority of this or that people, but by a majority of mankind. The rights of every people are consequently confined within the limits of what is just. A nation may be considered in the light of a jury which is empowered to represent society at large, and to apply the great and general law of justice. Ought such a jury, which represents society, to have more power than the society in which the laws it applies originate?

When I refuse to obey an unjust law, I do not contest the right which the majority has of commanding, but I simply appeal from the sovereignty of the people to the sovereignty of mankind. It has been asserted that a people can never entirely outstep the boundaries of justice and of reason in those affairs which are more peculiarly its own; and that consequently full power may fearlessly be given to the majority by which it is represented. But this language is that of a slave.

A majority taken collectively may be regarded as a being whose opinions, and most frequently whose interests, are opposed to those of another being, which is styled a minority. If it be admitted that a man, possessing absolute power, may misuse that power by wronging his adversaries, why should a majority not be liable to the same reproach? Men are not apt to change their characters by agglomeration; nor does their patience in the presence of obstacles increase with the consciousness of their strength. And for these reasons I can never willingly invest any number of my fellow-creatures with that unlimited authority which I should refuse to any one of them.

I do not think that it is possible to combine several principles in the same government, so as at the same time to maintain freedom, and really to oppose them to one another. The form of government which is usually termed *mixed* has always appeared to me to be a mere chimera. Accurately speaking, there is no such thing as a mixed government (with the meaning usually given to that word), because in all communities some one principle of action may be discovered, which preponderates over the others. England in the last century, which has been more especially cited as an example of this form of government, was in point of fact an essentially aristocratic state, although it comprised very powerful elements of democracy: for the laws and customs of the country were such, that the aristocracy could not but preponderate in the end, and subject the direction of public affairs to its own will. The error arose from too much attention being paid to the actual struggle which was going on between the nobles and the people, without considering the probable issue of the contest, which was in reality the important point. When a community really has a mixed government, that is to say, when it is equally divided between two adverse principles, it must either pass through a revolution, or fall into complete dissolution.

I am therefore of opinion that some one social power must always be made to predominate over the others; but I think that liberty is endangered when this power is checked by no obstacles which may retard its course, and force it to moderate its own vehemence.

Unlimited power is in itself a bad and dangerous thing; human beings are not competent to exercise it with discretion; and God alone can be omnipotent, because his wisdom and his justice are always equal to his power. But no power upon earth is so worthy of honor for itself, or of reverential obedience to the rights which it represents, that I would consent to admit its uncontrolled and all-predominant authority. When I see that *the* right and the means of absolute command are conferred on a people or upon a king, upon an aristocracy or a democracy, a monarchy or a republic, I recognise the germe of tyranny, and I journey onward to a land of more hopeful institutions.

In my opinion the main evil of the present democratic institutions of the United States does not arise, as is often asserted in Europe, from their weakness, but from their overpowering strength; and I am not so much alarmed at the excessive liberty which reigns in that country, as at the very inadequate securities which exist against tyranny.

When an individual or a party is wronged in the United States, to whom can he apply for redress? If to public opinion, public opinion constitutes the majority; if to the legislature, it represents the majority, and implicitly obeys its instructions; if to the executive power, it is appointed by the majority and is a passive tool in its hands; the public troops consist of the majority under arms; the jury is the majority invested with the right of hearing judicial cases; and in certain states even the judges are elected by the majority. However iniquitous or absurd the evil of which you complain may be, you must submit to it as well as you can. . . .

If, on the other hand, a legislative power could be so constituted as to represent the majority without necessarily being the slave of its passions; an executive, so as to retain a certain degree of uncontrolled authority; and a judiciary, so as to remain independent of the two other powers; a government would be formed which would still be democratic, without incurring any risk of tyrannical abuse.

I do not say that tyrannical abuses frequently occur in America at the present day; but I maintain that no sure barrier is established against them, and that the causes which mitigate the government are to be found in the circumstances and the manners of the country more than in its laws. . . .

Power Exercised by the Majority in America Upon Opinion

It is in the examination of the display of public opinion in the United States, that we clearly perceive how far the power of the majority surpasses all the powers with which we are acquainted in Europe. Intellectual principles exercise an influence which is so invisible and often so inappreciable, that they baffle the toils of oppression. At the present time the most absolute monarchs in Europe are unable to prevent certain notions, which are opposed to their authority, from circulating in secret throughout their dominions, and even in their courts. Such is not the case in America; so long as the majority is still undecided, discussion is carried on; but as soon as its decision is irrevocably pronounced, a submissive silence is observed; and the friends, as well as the opponents of the measure, unite in assenting to its propriety. The reason of this is perfectly clear: no monarch is so absolute as to combine all the powers of society in his own hands, and to conquer all opposition, with the energy of a majority, which is invested with the right of making and of executing the laws.

The authority of a king is purely physical, and it controls the actions of the subject without subduing his private will; but the majority possesses a power which is physical and moral at the same time; it acts upon the will as well as upon the actions of men, and it represses not only all contest, but all controversy.

I know no country in which there is so little true independence of mind and freedom of discussion as in America. In any constitutional state in Europe every sort of religious and political theory may be advocated and propagated abroad; for there is no country in Europe so subdued by any single authority, as not to contain citizens who are ready to protect the man who raises his voice in the cause of truth, from the consequences of his hardihood. If he is unfortunate enough to live under an absolute government, the people is upon his side; if he inhibits a free country, he may find a shelter behind the authority of the throne, if he require one. The aristocratic part of society supports him in some countries, and the democracy in others. But in a nation where democratic institutions exist, organized like those of the United States, there is but one sole authority, one single element of strength and of success, with nothing beyond it.

In America, the majority raises very formidable barriers to the liberty of opinion: within these barriers an author may write whatever he pleases, but he will repent it if he ever step beyond them. Not that he is exposed to the terrors of an auto-da-fé, but he is tormented by the slights and persecutions of daily obloquy. His political career is closed for ever, since he has offended the only authority which is able to promote his success. Every sort of compensation, even that of celebrity, is refused to him. Before he published his opinions, he imagined that he held them in common with many others; but no sooner has he declared them openly, than he is loudly censured by his overbearing opponents, while those who think, without having the courage to speak, like him, abandon him in silence. He yields at length, oppressed by the daily efforts he has been making, and he subsides into silence as if he was tormented by remorse for having spoken the truth.

Fetters and headsmen were the coarse instruments which tyranny formerly employed; but the civilization of our age has refined the arts of despotism, which seemed however to have been sufficiently perfected before. The excesses of monarchical power had devised a variety of physical means of oppression; the democratic republics of the present day have rendered it as entirely an affair of the mind, as that will which it is intended to coerce. Under the absolute sway of an individual despot, the body was attacked in order to subdue the soul; and the soul escaped the blows which were directed against it, and rose superior to the attempt; but such is not the course adopted by tyranny in democratic republics; there the body is left free, and the soul is enslaved. The sovereign can no longer say, "You shall think as I do on pain of death;" but he says, "You are free to think differently from me, and to retain your life, your property, and all that you possess; but if such be your determination, you are henceforth an alien among your people. You may retain your civil rights, but they will be useless to you, for you will never be chosen by your fellow-citizens, if you solicit their suffrages; and they will affect to scorn you, if you solicit their esteem. You will remain among men, but you will be deprived of the rights of mankind. Your fellow-creatures will shun you like an impure being; and those who are most persuaded of your innocence will abandon you too, lest they should be shunned in their turn. Go in peace! I have given you your life, but it is an existence incomparably worse than death."

Absolute monarchies have thrown an odium upon despotism; let us beware lest democratic republics should restore oppression, and should render it less odious and less degrading in the eyes of the many, by making it still more onerous to the few.

Works have been published in the proudest nations of the Old World, expressly intended to censure the vices and deride the follies of the time; Labruyère inhabited the palace of Louis XIV, when he composed his chapter upon the Great, and Molière criticised the courtiers in the very pieces which were acted before the court. But the ruling power in the United States is not to be made game of; the smallest reproach irritates its sensibility, and the slightest joke which has any foundation in truth renders it indignant; from the style of its language to the more solid virtues of its character, everything must be made the subject of encomium. No writer, whatever be his eminence, can escape from this tribute of adulation to his fellow-citizens. The majority lives in the perpetual exercise of self-applause; and there are certain truths which the Americans can only learn from strangers or from experience.

If great writers have not at present existed in America, the reason is very simply given in these facts; there can be no literary genius without freedom of opinion, and freedom of opinion does not exist in America. The inquisition has never been able to prevent a vast number of anti-religious books from circulating in Spain. The empire of the majority succeeds much better in the United States, since it actually removes the wish of publishing them. Unbelievers are to be met with in America, but, to say the truth, there is no public organ of infidelity. Attempts have been made by some governments to protect the morality of nations by prohibiting licentious books. In the United States no one is punished for this sort of works, but no one is induced to write them; not because all the citizens are immaculate in their manners, but because the majority of the community is decent and orderly.

In these cases the advantages derived from the exercise of this power are unquestionable; and I am simply discussing the nature of the power itself. This irresistible authority is a constant fact, and its beneficent exercise is an accidental occurrence....

Influence of Democracy on the Progress of Opinion in the United States.
Philosophical Method Among the Americans

I think that in no country in the civilized world is less attention paid to philosophy than in the United States. The Americans have no philosophical school of their own; and they care but little for all the schools into which Europe is divided, the very names of which are scarcely known to them.

Nevertheless it is easy to perceive that almost all the inhabitants of the United States conduct their understanding in the same manner, and govern it by the same rules; that is to say, that without ever having taken the trouble to define the rules of a philosophical method, they are in possession of one, common to the whole people.

To evade the bondage of system and habit, of family-maxims, class-opinions, and, in some degree, of national prejudices; to accept tradition only as a means of information, and existing facts only as a lesson used in doing otherwise and doing better; to seek the reason of things for oneself, and in oneself alone; to tend to results without being bound to means, and to aim at the substance through the form; —such are the principal characteristics of what I shall call the philosophical method of the Americans.

But if I go further, and if I seek among these characteristics that which predominates over and includes almost all the rest, I discover, that in most of the operations of the mind, each

American appeals to the individual exercise of his own understanding alone.

America is therefore one of the countries in the world where philosophy is least studied, and where the precepts of Descartes are best applied. Nor is this surprising. The Americans do not read the works of Descartes, because their social condition deters them from speculative studies; but they follow his maxims, because this very social condition naturally disposes their understanding to adopt them.

In the midst of the continual movement which agitates a democratic community, the tie which unites one generation to another is relaxed or broken; every man readily loses the trace of the ideas of his forefathers or takes no care about them.

Nor can men living in this state of society derive their belief from the opinions of the class to which they belong; for, so to speak, there are no longer any classes, or those which still exist are composed of such mobile elements, that their body can never exercise a real control over its members.

As to the influence which the intelligence of one man has on that of another, it must necessarily be very limited in a country where the citizens, placed on the footing of a general similitude, are all closely seen by each other; and where, as no signs of incontestable greatness or superiority are perceived in any one of them, they are constantly brought back to their own reason as the most obvious and proximate source of truth. It is not only confidence in this or that man which is then destroyed, but the taste for trusting the *ipse dixit* of any man whatsoever. Every one shuts himself up in his own breast, and affects from that point to judge the world.

The practice which obtains among the Americans of fixing the standard of their judgment in themselves alone, leads them to other habits of mind. As they perceive that they succeed in resolving without assistance all the little difficulties which their practical life presents, they readily conclude that every thing in the world may be explained, and that nothing in it transcends the limits of the understanding. Thus they fall to denying what they cannot comprehend; which leaves them but little faith for whatever is extraordinary, and an almost insurmountable distaste for whatever is supernatural. As it is on their own testimony that they are accustomed to rely, they like to discern the object which engages their attention with extreme clearness; they therefore strip off as much as possible all that covers it, they rid themselves of whatever separates them from it, they remove whatever conceals it from sight, in order to view it more closely and in the broad light of day. This disposition of the mind soon leads them to contemn forms, which they regard as useless and inconvenient veils placed between them and the truth.

The Americans then have not required to extract their philosophical method from books; they have found it in themselves. . . .

The Principle of Equality Suggests to the Americans the Idea of the Indefinite Perfectibility of Man

Equality suggests to the human mind several ideas which would not have originated from any other source, and it modifies almost all those previously entertained. I take as an example the idea of human perfectibility, because it is one of the principal notions that the intellect can conceive, and because it constitutes of itself a great philosophical theory, which is every instant to be traced by its consequences in the practice of human affairs.

Although man has many points of resemblance with the brute creation, one characteristic is peculiar to himself—he improves; they are incapable of improvement. Mankind could not fail to discover this difference from its earliest period. The idea of perfectibility is therefore as old as the world: equality did not give birth to it, although it has imparted to it a novel character.

When the citizens of a community are classed according to their rank, their profession or their birth, and when all men are constrained to follow the career which happens to open before them, every one thinks that the utmost limits of human power are to be discerned in proximity to himself, and none seeks any longer to resist the inevitable law of his destiny. . . .

In proportion as castes disappear and the classes of society approximate—as manners, customs and laws vary, from the tumultuous intercourse of men—as new facts arise—as new truths are brought to light—as ancient opinions are dissipated and others take their place—the image of an ideal perfection, for ever on the wing, presents itself to the human mind. Continual changes are then every instant occurring under the observation of every man: the position of some is rendered worse; and he learns but too well, that no people and no individual, how enlightened soever they may be, can lay claim to infallibility;—the condition of others is improved; whence he infers that man is endowed with an indefinite faculty of improvement. His reverses teach him that none may hope to have discovered absolute good—his success stimulates him to the neverending pursuit of it. Thus, for ever seeking—for ever falling, to rise again—often disappointed, but not discouraged—he tends unceasingly toward that unmeasured greatness so indistinctly visible at the end of the long track which humanity has yet to tread.

It can hardly be believed how many facts naturally flow from the philosophical theory of the indefinite perfectibility of man, or how strong an influence it exercises even on men who, living entirely for the purposes of action and not of thought, seem to conform their actions to it, without knowing anything about it. . . .

Influence of Democracy on the Feelings of the Americans

Why Democratic Nations Show a More Ardent and Enduring Love of Equality than of Liberty

The first and most intense passion which is engendered by the equality of conditions is, I need hardly say, the love of that same equality. My readers will therefore not be surprised that I speak of it before all others. . . .

Upon close inspection, it will be seen that there is in every age some peculiar and preponderating fact with which all others are connected; this fact almost always gives birth to some pregnant idea or some ruling passion, which attracts to itself, and bears away in its course, all the feelings and opinions of the time: it is like a great stream, toward which each of the surrounding rivulets seem to flow. . . .

I think that democratic communities have a natural taste for freedom: left to themselves, they will seek it, cherish it, and view any privation of it with regret. But for equality, their passion is ardent, insatiable, incessant, invincible: they call for equality in freedom; if they cannot obtain that, they still call for equality in slavery. They will endure poverty, servitude, barbarism—but they will not endure aristocracy.

This is true at all times, and especially true in our own. All men and all powers seeking to cope with this irresistible passion, will be overthrown and destroyed by it. In our age, freedom cannot be established without it, and despotism itself cannot reign without its support. . . .

General Survey of the Subject

Before I close for ever the theme that has detained me so long, I would fain take a parting survey of all the various characteristics of modern society, and appreciate at last the general influence to be exercised by the principle of equality upon the fate of mankind; but I am stopped by the difficulty of the task, and in presence of so great an object my sight is troubled, and my reason fails.

The society of the modern world which I have sought to delineate, and which I seek to judge, has but just come into existence. Time has not yet shaped it into perfect form: the great revolution by which it has been created is not yet over; and amid the occurrences of our time, it is almost impossible to discern what will pass away with the revolution itself, and what will survive its close. The world which is rising into existence is still half encumbered by the remains of the world which is waning into decay; and amid the vast perplexity of human affairs, none can say how much of ancient institutions and former manners will remain, or how much will completely disappear.

Although the revolution which is taking place in the social condition, the laws, the opinions and the feelings of men, is still very far from being terminated, yet its results already admit of no comparison with anything that the world has ever before witnessed. I go back from age to age up to the remotest antiquity: but I find no parallel to what is occurring before my eyes: as the past has ceased to throw its light upon the future, the mind of man wanders in obscurity.

Nevertheless, in the midst of a prospect so wide, so novel, and so confused, some of the more prominent characteristics may already be discerned and pointed out. The good things and the evils of life are more equally distributed in the world: great wealth tends to disappear, the number of small fortunes to increase; desires and gratifications are multiplied, but extraordinary prosperity and irremediable penury are alike unknown. The sentiment of ambition is universal, but the scope of ambition is seldom vast. Each individual stands apart in solitary weakness; but society at large is active, provident, and powerful: the performances of private persons are insignificant, those of the State immense.

There is little energy of character; but manners are mild, and laws humane. If there be few instances of exalted heroism or of virtues of the highest, brightest, and purest temper, men's habits are regular, violence is rare, and cruelty almost unknown. Human existence becomes longer, and property more secure: life is not adorned with brilliant trophies, but it is extremely easy and tranquil. Few pleasures are either very refined or very coarse; and highly polished manners are as uncommon as great brutality of tastes. Neither men of great learning, nor extremely ignorant communities, are to be met with; genius becomes more rare, information more diffused. The human mind is impelled by the small efforts of all mankind combined together, not by the strenuous activity of certain men. There is less perfection, but more abundance, in all the productions of the arts. The ties of race, of rank, and of country are relaxed; the great bond of humanity is strengthened.

If I endeavour to find out the most general and the most prominent of all these different characteristics, I shall have occasion to perceive, that what is taking place in men's fortunes manifests itself under a thousand other forms. Almost all extremes are softened or blunted: all that was most prominent is superseded by some mean term, at once less lofty and less low, less brilliant and less obscure, than what before existed in the world.

When I survey this countless multitude of beings, shaped in each other's likeness, amidst whom nothing rises and nothing falls, the sight of such universal uniformity saddens and chills me, and I am tempted to regret that state of society which has ceased to be. When the world was full of men of great importance and extreme insignificance, of great wealth and extreme poverty, of great learning and extreme ignorance, I turned aside from the latter to fix my observation on the former alone, who gratified my sympathies. But I admit that this gratification arose from my own weakness: it is because I am unable to see at once all that is around me, that I am allowed thus to select and separate the objects of my predilection from among so many others. Such is not the case with that Almighty and Eternal Being, whose gaze necessarily includes the whole of created things, and who surveys distinctly, though at once, mankind and man.

We may naturally believe that it is not the singular prosperity of the few, but the greater well-being of all, which is most pleasing in the sight of the Creator and Preserver of men. What appears to me to be man's decline, is to His eye advancement; what afflicts me is acceptable to Him. A state of equality is perhaps less elevated, but it is more just; and its justice constitutes its greatness and its beauty. I would strive then to raise myself to this point of the Divine contemplation, and thence to view and to judge the concerns of men.

No man, upon the earth, can as yet affirm absolutely and generally, that the new state of the world is better than its former one; but it is already easy to perceive that this state is different. Some vices and some virtues were so inherent in the constitution of an aristocratic nation, and are so opposite to the character of a modern people, that they can never be infused into it; some good tendencies and some bad propensities which were unknown to the former, are natural to the latter; some ideas suggest themselves spontaneously to the imagination of the one, which are utterly repugnant to the mind of the other. They are like two distinct orders of human beings, each of which has its own merits and defects, its own advantages and its own evils. Care must therefore be taken not to judge the state of society, which is now coming into existence by notions derived from a state of society which no longer exists; for as these states of society are exceedingly different in their structure, they cannot be submitted to a just or fair comparison.

It would be scarcely more reasonable to require of our own contemporaries the peculiar virtues which originated in the social condition of their forefathers, since that social condition is itself fallen, and has drawn into one promiscuous ruin the good and evil which belonged to it.

But as yet these things are imperfectly understood. I find that a great number of my contemporaries undertake to make a certain selection from among the institutions, the opinions, and the ideas which originated in the aristocratic constitution of society as it was: a portion of these elements they would willingly relinquish, but they would keep the remainder and transplant them into their new world. I apprehend that such men are wasting their time and their strength in virtuous but unprofitable efforts.

The object is not to retain the peculiar advantages which the inequality of conditions bestows upon mankind, but to secure the new benefits which equality may supply. We have not to seek to make ourselves like our progenitors, but to strive to work out that species of greatness and happiness which is our own.

For myself, who now look back from this extreme limit of my task, and discover from afar, but at once, the various objects which have attracted my more attentive investigation upon my way, I am full of apprehensions and of hopes. I perceive mighty dangers which it is possible to ward off—mighty evils which may be avoided or alleviated; and I cling with a firmer hold to the belief, that for democratic nations to be virtuous and prosperous they require but to will it.

I am aware that many of my contemporaries maintain that nations are never their own masters here below, and that they necessarily obey some insurmountable and unintelligent power, arising from anterior events, from their race, or from the soil and climate of their country. Such principles are false and cowardly; such principles can never produce aught but feeble men and pusillanimous nations. Providence has not created mankind entirely independent or entirely free. It is true that around every man a fatal circle is traced, beyond which he cannot pass; but within the wide verge of that circle he is powerful and free: as it is with man, so with communities. The nations of our time cannot prevent the conditions of men from becoming equal: but it depends upon themselves whether the principle of equality is to lead them to servitude or freedom, to knowledge or barbarism, to prosperity or to wretchedness.

Karl Marx

The texts presented in this section cover what may be thought of as two distinct periods in the intellectual development of Karl Marx (1818–1883): the preceding and following periods of the European-wide popular revolts of 1848. The early Marx, from the start a zealous advocate of a sort of secular Judeo-Christian morality that critiqued the inequalities of his day, was chiefly philosophical. It was during this period that he developed his notion of alienation that he would carry into his later analysis of surplus value and the exploitation of the proletariat. The alienation of the individual described a state of affairs in which, for one reason or another, all of one's essence was not fully possessed. The tradition of alienation goes back most directly to the German philosopher Hegel (1770–1831), who argued that one could perceive one's true relation to the world, and thereby advance history. This is the dynamic taken up by Marx in his early work. When he took up economic analysis in a more concrete fashion, he transposed the notion of alienation into the social relations of the shop-floor, a place in which workers gave their labor for wages. He argued that this alienation was surplus value, or the profit of the capitalist—something that was rightfully the possession of the worker.

The "springtime of peoples," as the year of the revolution and nationalist aspiration, 1848, had come to be known, turned into a bitter disappointment for many. Although numerous liberal political reforms were achieved, many more radical thinkers were disappointed that the revolution had not gone further, and had been quelled across Europe. After the post-1848 conservative backlash quashed all signs of rebelliousness, Marx took up the task of laying the groundwork for the scientific basis of a successful revolution. If the working classes had failed in their dream-like efforts to overthrow oppressive regimes, then once they had been adequately armed with a science that would counter that of the ruling classes, their success would only be a matter of time. To this end, Marx directed his work in the second half of the nineteenth century, culminating in the three volumes of *Capital*, which was published after extended observation of the economy of Great Britain, the most advanced market economy of the day. In these works, Marx's previous philosophical background takes the implicit role of a method based on such concepts as the dialectic, praxis, production, materialism, and idealism. His notion of alienation offers the moral guidance for his detailed analysis of the functioning of industrial capitalism.

KARL MARX

(1859)

Preface to

A Contribution to the

Critique of Political Economy

I am omitting a general introduction which I had jotted down because on closer reflection any anticipation of results still to be proved appears to me to be disturbing, and the reader who on the whole desires to follow me must be resolved to ascend from the particular to the general. A few indications concerning the course of my own politico-economic studies may, on the other hand, appear in place here.

I was taking up law, which discipline, however, I only pursued as a subordinate subject along with philosophy and history. In the year 1842-44, as editor of the *Rheinische Zeitung*, I experienced for the first time the embarrassment of having to take part in discussions on so-called material interests. The proceedings of the Rhenish Landtag on thefts of wood and parcelling of landed property, the official polemic which Herr von Schaper, then *Oberpräsident* of the Rhine Province, opened against the *Rheinische Zeitung* on the conditions of the Moselle peasantry, and finally debates on free trade and protective tariffs provided the first occasions for occupying myself with economic questions. On the other hand, at that time when the good will "to go further" greatly outweighed knowledge of the subject, a philosophically weakly tinged echo of French socialism and communism made itself audible in the *Rheinische Zeitung*. I declared myself against this amateurism, but frankly confessed at the same time in a controversy with the *Allgemeine Augsburger Zeitung* that my previous studies did not permit me even to venture any judgment on the content of the French tendencies. Instead, I eagerly seized on the illusion of the managers of the *Rheinische Zeitung*, who thought that by a weaker attitude on

Reprinted from *The Marx-Engels Reader*, Second Edition, ed. Robert C. Tucker, pp. 3–6, 70–80, 149–75. By permission of W. W. Norton & Company, Inc. © 1978, 1972 by W.W. Norton & Company, Inc.

the part of the paper they could secure a remission of the death sentence passed upon it, to withdraw from the public stage into the study.

The first work which I undertook for a solution of the doubts which assailed me was a critical review of the Hegelian philosophy of right, a work the introduction to which appeared in 1844 in the *Deutsch-Französische Jahrbücher*, published in Paris. My investigation led to the result that legal relations as well as forms of state are to be grasped neither from themselves nor from the so-called general development of the human mind, but rather have their roots in the material conditions of life, the sum total of which Hegel, following the example of the Englishmen and Frenchmen of the eighteenth century, combines under the name of "civil society," that, however, the anatomy of civil society is to be sought in political economy. The investigation of the latter, which I began in Paris, I continued in Brussels, whither I had emigrated in consequence of an expulsion order of M. Guizot. The general result at which I arrived and which, once won, served as a guiding thread for my studies, can be briefly formulated as follows: In the social production of their life, men enter into definite relations that are indispensable and independent of their will, relations of production which correspond to a definite stage of development of their material productive forces. The sum total of these relations of production constitutes the economic structure of society, the real foundation, on which rises a legal and political superstructure and to which correspond definite forms of social consciousness. The mode of production of material life conditions the social, political and intellectual life process in general. It is not the consciousness of men that determines their being, but, on the contrary, their social being that determines their consciousness. At a certain stage of their development, the material productive forces of society come in conflict with the existing relations of production, or—what is but a legal expression for the same thing—with the property relations within which they have been at work hitherto. From forms of development of the productive forces these relations turn into their fetters. Then begins an epoch of social revolution. With the change of the economic foundation the entire immense superstructure is more or less rapidly transformed. In considering such transformations a distinction should always be made between the material transformation of the economic conditions of production, which can be determined with the precision of natural science, and the legal, political, religious, aesthetic or philosophic—in short, ideological forms in whch men become conscious of this conflict and fight it out. Just as our opinion of an individual is not based on what he thinks of himself, so can we not judge of such a period of transformation by its own consciousness; on the contrary, this consciousness must be explained rather from the contradictions of material life, from the existing conflict between the social productive forces and the relations of production. No social order ever perishes before all the productive forces for which there is room in it have developed; and new, higher relations of production never appear before the material conditions of their existence have matured in the womb of the old society itself. Therefore mankind always sets itself only such tasks as it can solve; since, looking at the matter more closely, it will always be found that the task itself arises only when the material conditions for its solution already exist or are at least in the process of formation. In broad outlines Asiatic, ancient, feudal, and modern bourgeois modes of production can be designated as progressive epochs in the economic formation of society. The bourgeois relations of production are the last antagonistic form of the social process of production—antagonistic not in the sense of individual antagonism, but of one arising from the social conditions of life of the individuals; at the same time the productive forces developing in the womb of bourgeois society create the material conditions for the solution of that antagonism. This social formation brings, therefore, the prehistory of human society to a close.

Frederick Engels, with whom, since the appearance of his brilliant sketch on the criticism of the economic categories (in the *Deutsch-Französische Jahrbücher*), I maintained a constant exchange of ideas by correspondence, had by another road (compare his *The Condition of the Working Class in England in 1844*) arrived at the same result as I, and when in the spring of 1845 he also settled in Brussels, we resolved to work out in common the opposition of our view to the ideological view of German philosophy, in fact, to settle accounts with our erstwhile philosophical conscience. The resolve was carried out in the form of a criticism of post-Hegelian philosophy. The manuscript, two large octavo volumes, had long reached its place of publication in Westphalia when we received the news that altered circumstances did not allow of its being printed. We abandoned the manuscript to the gnawing criticism of the mice all the more willingly as we had achieved our main purpose—self-clarification. Of the scattered works in which we put our views before the public at that time, now from one aspect, now from another, I will mention only the *Manifesto of the Communist Party*, jointly written by Engels and myself, and *Discours sur le libre échange* published by me. The decisive points of our view were first scientifically, although only polemically, indicated in my work published in 1847 and directed against Proudhon: *Misère de la Philosophie*, etc. A dissertation written in German on *Wage Labour*, in which I put together my lectures on this subject delivered in the Brussels German Workers' Society, was interrupted, while being printed, by the February Revolution and my consequent forcible removal from Belgium.

The editing of the *Neue Rheinische Zeitung* in 1848 and 1849, and the subsequent events, interrupted my economic studies which could only be resumed in the year 1850 in London. The enormous material for the history of political economy which is accumulated in the British Museum, the favourable vantage point afforded by London for the observation of bourgeois society, and finally the new stage of development upon which the latter appeared to have entered with the discovery of gold in California and Australia, determined me to begin afresh from the very beginning and to work through the new material critically. These studies led partly of themselves into apparently quite remote subjects on which I had to dwell for a shorter or longer period. Especially, however, was the time at my disposal curtailed by the imperative necessity of earning my living. My contributions, during eight years now, to the first English-American newspaper, the *New York Tribune*, compelled an extraordinary scattering of my studies, since I occupy myself with newspaper correspondence proper only in exceptional cases. However, articles on striking economic events in England and on the Continent constituted so considerable a part of my contributions that I was compelled to make myself familiar with practical details which lie outside the sphere of the actual science of political economy.

This sketch of the course of my studies in the sphere of political economy is intended only to show that my views, however they may be judged and however little they coincide with the interested prejudices of the ruling classes, are the results of conscientious investigation lasting many years. But at the entrance to science, as at the entrance to hell, the demand must be posted:

Qui si convien lasciare ogni sospetto;
Ogni viltà convien che qui sia morta.

KARL MARX
(1844)

The

Philosophical

Manuscripts of 1844

ESTRANGED LABOUR

We have proceeded from the premises of political economy. We have accepted its language and its laws. We presupposed private property, the separation of labour, capital and land, and of wages, profit of capital and rent of land—likewise division of labour, competition, the concept of exchange-value, etc. On the basis of political economy itself, in its own words, we have shown that the worker sinks to the level of a commodity and becomes indeed the most wretched of commodities; that the wretchedness of the worker is in inverse proportion to the power and magnitude of his production; that the necessary result of competition is the accumulation of capital in a few hands, and thus the restoration of monopoly in a more terrible form; that finally the distinction between capitalist and land-rentier, like that between the tiller of the soil and the factory-worker, disappears and that the whole of society must fall apart into the two classes—the property-*owners* and the propertyless *workers*.

Political economy proceeds from the fact of private property, but it does not explain it to us. It expresses in general, abstract formulae the *material* process through which private property actually passes, and these formulae it then takes for *laws*. It does not *comprehend* these laws—i.e., it does not demonstrate how they arise from the very nature of private property. Political economy does not disclose the source of the division between labour and capital, and between capital and land. When, for example, it defines the relationship of wages of profit, it takes the interest of the capitalists to be the ultimate cause; i.e., it takes for granted what it is supposed to evolve. Similarly, competition comes in everywhere. It is explained from external circumstances.

Reprinted from *The Marx–Engels Reader*, Second Edition, ed. Robert C. Tucker. By permission of W. W. Norton & Company, Inc. © 1978, 1972 by W.W. Norton & Company, Inc.

As to how far these external and apparently fortuitous circumstances are but the expression of a necessary course of development, political economy teaches us nothing. We have seen how, to it, exchange itself appears to be a fortuitous fact. The only wheels which political economy sets in motion are *avarice* and the *war amongst the avaricious—competition*.

Precisely because political economy does not grasp the connections within the movement, it was possible to counterpose, for instance, the doctrine of competition to the doctrine of monopoly, the doctrine of craft-liberty to the doctrine of the corporation, the doctrine of the division of landed property to the doctrine of the big estate—for competition, craft-liberty and the division of landed property were explained and comprehended only as fortuitous, premediated and violent consequences of monopoly, the corporation, and feudal property, not as their necessary, inevitable and natural consequences.

Now, therefore, we have to grasp the essential connection between private property, avarice, and the separation of labour, capital and landed property; between exchange and competition, value and the devaluation of men, monopoly and competition, etc.; the connection between this whole estrangement and the *money*-system.

Do not let us go back to a fictitious primordial condition as the political economist does, when he tries to explain. Such a primordial condition explains nothing. He merely pushes the question away into a grey nebulous distance. He assumes in the form of fact, of an event, what he is supposed to deduce—namely, the necessary relationship between two things—between, for example, division of labour and exchange. Theology in the same way explains the origin of evil by the fall of man: that is, it assumes as a fact, in historical form, what has to be explained.

We proceed from an *actual* economic fact.

The worker becomes all the poorer the more wealth he produces, the more his production increases in power and range. The worker becomes an ever cheaper commodity the more commodities he creates. With the *increasing value* of the world of things proceeds in direct proportion the *devaluation* of the world of men. Labour produces not only commodities; it produces itself and the worker as a *commodity*—and does so in the proportion in which it produces commodities generally.

This fact expresses merely that the object which labour produces—labour's product—confronts it as *something alien*, as a *power independent* of the producer. The product of labour is labour which has been congealed in an object, which has become material: it is the *objectification* of labour. Labour's realization is its objectification. In the conditions dealt with by political economy this realization of labour appears as *loss of reality* for the workers; objectification as *loss of the object* and *object-bondage*; appropriation as *estrangement*, as *alienation*.

So much does labour's realization appear as loss of reality that the worker loses reality to the point of starving to death. So much does objectification appear as loss of the object that the worker is robbed of the objects most necessary not only for his life but for his work. Indeed, labour itself becomes an object which he can get hold of only with the greatest effort and with the most irregular interruptions. So much does the appropriation of the object appear as estrangement that the more objects the worker produces the fewer can he possess and the more he falls under the dominion of his product, capital.

All these consequences are contained in the definition that the worker is related to the *product of his labour* as to an *alien* object. For on this premise it is clear that the more the worker spends himself, the more powerful the alien objective world becomes which he creates over-against himself, the poorer he himself—his inner world—becomes, the less belongs to him as his own. It is the same in religion. The more man puts into God, the less he retains in himself. The worker puts his life into the object; but now his life no longer belongs to him but to the object. Hence, the greater this activity, the greater is the worker's lack of objects. Whatever the product of his labour is, he is not. Therefore the greater this product, the less is he himself. The *alienation* of the worker in his product means not only that his labour becomes an object, an *external* existence, but that it exists *outside him*, independently, as something alien to him, and that it becomes a power of its own confronting him; it means that the life which he has conferred on the object confronts him as something hostile and alien.

Let us now look more closely at the *objectification*, at the production of the worker; and therein at the *estrangement*, the *loss* of the object, his product.

The worker can create nothing without *nature*, without the *sensuous external world*. It is the material on which his labor is manifested, in which it is active, from which and by means of which it produces.

But just as nature provides labor with the *means of life* in the sense that labour cannot *live* without objects on which to operate, on the other hand, it also provides the *means of life* in the more restricted sense—i.e., the means for the physical subsistence of the *worker* himself.

Thus the more the worker by his labour *appropriates* the external world, sensuous nature, the more he deprives himself of *means of life* in the double respect: first, that the sensuous external world more and more ceases to be an object belonging to his labour—to be his labour's *means of life*; and secondly, that it more and more ceases to be *means of life* in the immediate sense, means for the physical subsistence of the worker.

Thus in this double respect the worker becomes a slave of his object, first, in that he receives an *object of labour*, i.e., in that he receives *work*; and secondly, in that he receives *means of subsistence*. Therefore, it enables him to exist, first, as a *worker*; and, second, as a *physical subject*. The extremity of this bondage is that it is only as a *worker* that he continues to maintain himself as a *physical subject*, and that it is only as a *physical subject* that he is a *worker*.

(The laws of political economy express the estrangement of the worker in his object thus: the more the worker produces, the less he has to consume; the more values he creates, the more valueless, the more unworthy he becomes; the better formed his product, the more deformed becomes the worker; the more civilized his object, the more barbarous becomes the worker; the mightier labour becomes, the more powerless becomes the worker; the more ingenious labour becomes, the duller becomes the worker and the more he becomes nature's bondsman.)

Political economy conceals the estrangement inherent in the nature of labour by not considering the direct relationship between the worker (labour) *and production.* It is true that labour produces for the rich wonderful things—but for the worker it produces privation. It produces palaces—but for the worker, hovels. It produces beauty—but for the worker, deformity. It replaces labour by machines—but some of the workers it throws back to a barbarous type of labour, and the other workers it turns into machines. It produces intelligence—but for the worker idiocy, cretinism.

The direct relationship of labour to its produce is the relationship of the worker to the objects of his production. The relationship of the man of means to the objects of production and to production itself is only a *consequence* of this first relationship—and confirms it. We shall consider this other aspect later.

When we ask, then, what is the essential relationship of labour we are asking about the relationship of the *worker* to production.

Till now we have been considering the estrangement, the alienation of the worker only in one of its aspects, i.e., the worker's *relationship to the products of his labour.* But the estrangement is manifested not only in the result but in the *act of production*—within the *producing activity* itself. How would the worker come to face the product of his activity as a stranger, were it not that in the very act of production he was estranging himself from himself? The product is after all but the summary of the activity of production. If then the product of labour is alienation, production itself must be active alienation, the alienation of activity, the activity of alienation. In the estrangement of the object of labour is merely summarized the estrangement, the alienation, in the activity of labour itself.

What, then, constitutes the alienation of labour?

First, the fact that labour is *external* to the worker, i.e., it does not belong to his essential being; that in his work, therefore, he does not affirm himself but denies himself, does not feel content but unhappy, does not develop freely his physical and mental energy but mortifies his body and ruins his mind. The worker therefore only feels himself outside his work, and in his work feels outside himself. He is at home when he is not working, and when he is working he is not at home. His labour is therefore not voluntary, but coerced; it is *forced labour.* It is therefore not the satisfaction of a need; it is merely a *means* to satisfy needs external to it. Its alien character emerges clearly in the fact that as soon as no physical or other compulsion exists, labour is shunned like the plague. External labour, labour in which man alienates himself, is a labour of self-sacrifice, of mortification. Lastly, the external character of labour for the worker appears in the fact that it is not his own, but someone else's, that it does not belong to him, that in it he belongs, not to himself, but to another. Just as in religion the spontaneous activity of the human imagination, of the human brain and the human heart, operates independently of the individual—that is, operates on him as an alien, divine or diabolical activity—in the same way the worker's activity is not his spontaneous activity. It belongs to another; it is the loss of his self.

As a result, therefore, man (the worker) no longer feels himself to be freely active in any but his animal functions—eating, drinking, procreating, or at most in his dwelling and in dressing-up, etc.; and in his human functions he no longer feels himself to be anything but an animal. What is animal becomes human and what is human becomes animal.

Certainly eating, drinking, procreating, etc., are also genuinely human functions. But in the abstraction which separates them from the sphere of all other human activity and turns them into sole and ultimate ends, they are animal.

We have considered the act of estranging practical human activity, labour, in two of its aspects. (1) The relation of the worker to the *product of labour* as an alien object exercising power over him. This relation is at the same time the relation to the sensuous external world, to the objects of nature as an alien world antagonistically opposed to him. (2) The relation of labour to the *act of production* within the *labour* process. This relation is the relation of the worker to his own activity as an alien activity not belonging to him; it is activity as suffering, strength as weakness, begetting as emasculating, the worker's *own* physical and mental energy, his personal life or what is life other than activity—as an activity which is turned against him, neither depends on nor belongs to him. Here we have *self-estrangement,* as we had previously the estrangement of the *thing.*

We have yet a third aspect of *estranged labour* to deduce from the two already considered.

Man is a species being, not only because in practice and in theory he adopts the species as his object (his own as well as those of other things), but—and this is only another way of expressing it—but also because he treats himself as the actual, living species; because he treats himself as a *universal* and therefore a free being.

The life of the species, both in man and in animals, consists physically in the fact that man (like the animal) lives on inorganic nature; and the more universal man is compared with an animal, the more universal is the sphere of inorganic nature on which he lives. Just as plants, animals, stones, the air, light, etc., constitute a part of human consciousness in the realm of theory, partly as objects of natural science, partly as objects of art—his spiritual inorganic nature, spiritual nourishment which he must first prepare to make it palatable and digestible—so too in the realm of practice they constitute a part of human life and human activity. Physically man lives only on these products of nature, whether they appear in the form of food, heating, clothes, a dwelling, or whatever it may be. The universality of man is in practice manifested precisely in the universality which makes all nature his *inorganic* body—both inasmuch as nature is (1) his direct means of life, and (2) the material, the object, and the instrument of his life-activity. Nature is man's *inorganic body*—nature, that is, in so far as it is not itself the human body. Man *lives* on nature—means that nature is his *body*, with which he must remain in continuous intercourse if he is not to die. That man's physical and spiritual life is linked to nature means simply that nature is linked to itself, for man is a part of nature.

In estranging from man (1) nature, and (2) himself, his own active functions, his life-activity, estranged labour estranges the *species* from man. It turns for him the *life of the species* into a means of individual life. First it estranges the life of the species and individual life, and secondly it makes individual life in its abstract form the purpose of the life of the species, likewise in its abstract and estranged form.

For in the first place labour, *life-activity, productive life* itself, appears to man merely as a *means* of satisfying a need—the need to maintain the physical existence. Yet the productive life is the life of the species. It is life-engendering life. The whole character of a species—its species character—is contained in the character of its life-activity; and free, conscious activity is man's species character. Life itself appears only as *a means to life*.

The animal is immediately identical with its life-activity. It does not distinguish itself from it. It is *its life-activity*. Man makes his life-activity itself the object of his will and of his consciousness. He has conscious life-activity. It is not a determination with which he directly merges. Conscious life-activity directly distinguishes man from animal life-activity. It is just because of this that he is a species being. Or it is only because he is a species being that he is a Conscious Being, i.e., that his own life is an object for him. Only because of that is his activity free activity. Estranged labour reverses this relationship, so that it is just because man is a conscious being that he makes his life-activity, his *essential* being, a mere means to his *existence*.

In creating an *objective world* by his practical activity, in *working-up* inorganic nature, man proves himself a conscious species being, i.e., as a being that treats the species as its own essential being, or that treats itself as a species being. Admittedly animals also produce. They build themselves nests, dwellings, like the bees, beavers, ants, etc. But an animal only produces what it immediately needs for itself or its young. It produces one-sidedly, whilst man produces universally. It produces only under the dominion of immediate physical need, whilst man produces even when he is free from physical need and only truly produces in freedom therefrom. An animal produces only itself, whilst man reproduces the whole of nature. An animal's product belongs immediately to its physical body, whilst man freely confronts his product. An animal forms things in accordance with the standard and the need of the species to which it belongs, whilst man knows how to produce in accordance with the standard of every species, and knows how to apply everywhere the inherent standard to the object. Man therefore also forms things in accordance with the laws of beauty.

It is just in the working-up of the objective world, therefore, that man first really proves himself to be a *species being*. This production is his active species life. Through and because of this production, nature appears as *his* work and his reality. The object of labour is, therefore, the *objectification of man's species life*: for he duplicates himself not only, as in consciousness, intellectually, but also actively, in reality, and therefore he contemplates himself in a world that he has created. In tearing away from man the object of his production, therefore, estranged labour tears from him his *species life*, his real species objectivity, and transforms his advantage over animals into the disadvantage that his inorganic body, nature, is taken from him.

Similarly, in degrading spontaneous activity, free activity, to a means, estranged labour makes man's species life a means to his physical existence.

The consciousness which man has of his species is thus transformed by estrangement in such a way that the species life becomes for him a means.

Estranged labour turns thus:

(3) *Man's species being*, both nature and his spiritual species property, into a being *alien* to him, into a *means* to his *individual existence*. It estranges man's own body from him, as it does external nature and his spiritual essence, his *human* being.

(4) An immediate consequence of the fact that man is estranged from the product of his labour, from his life-activity, from his species being is the *estrangement of man* from *man*. If a man is confronted by himself, he is confronted by the *other* man. What applies to a man's relation to his work, to the product of his labour and to himself, also holds of a man's relation to the other man, and to the other man's labour and object of labour.

In fact, the proposition that man's species nature is estranged from him means that one man is estranged from the other, as each of them is from man's essential nature.[5]

The estrangement of man, and in fact every relationship in which man stands to himself, is first realized and expressed in the relationship in which a man stands to other men.

Hence within the relationship of estranged labour each man views the other in accordance with the standard and the position in which he finds himself as a worker.

We took our departure from a fact of political economy—the estrangement of the worker and his production. We have formulated the concept of this fact—*estranged, alienated* labour. We have analysed this concept—hence analysing merely a fact of political economy.

Let us now see, further, how in real life the concept of estranged, alienated labour must express and present itself.

If the product of labour is alien to me, if it confronts me as an alien power, to whom, then, does it belong?

If my own activity does not belong to me, if it is an alien, a coerced activity, to whom, then, does it belong?

To a being *other* than me.

Through *estranged, alienated labour*, then, the worker produces the relationship to this labour of a man alien to labour and standing outside it. The relationship of the worker to labour engenders the relation to it of the capitalist, or whatever one chooses to call the master of labour. *Private property* is thus the product, the result, the necessary consequence, of *alienated labour*, of the external relation of the worker to nature and to himself.

Private property thus results by analysis from the concept of *alienated labour*—i.e., of *alienated man*, of estranged labour, of estranged life, of *estranged* man.

True, it is as a result of the *movement of private property* that we have obtained the concept of *alienated labour (of alienated life)* from political economy. But on analysis of this concept it becomes clear that though private property appears to be the source, the cause of alienated labour, it is really its consequence, just as the gods *in the beginning* are not the cause but the effect of man's intellectual confusion. Later this relationship becomes reciprocal.

Only at the very culmination of the development of private property does this, its secret, re-emerge, namely, that on the one hand it is the *product* of alienated labour, and that secondly it is the *means* by which labour alienates itself, the *realization of this alienation*.

This exposition immediately sheds light on various hitherto unsolved conflicts.

(1)Political economy starts from labour as the real soul of production; yet to labour it gives nothing, and to private property everything. From this contradiction Proudhon has concluded in favour of labour and against private property. We understand, however, that this apparent contradiction is the contradiction of *estranged labour* with itself, and that political economy has merely formulated the laws of estranged labour.

We also understand, therefore, that *wages* and *private property* are identical: where the product, the object of labour pays for labour itself, the wage is but a necessary consequence of labour's estrangement, for after all in the wage of labour, labour does not appear as an end in itself but as the servant of the wage. We shall develop this point later, and meanwhile will only deduce some conclusions.

A *forcing-up of wages* (disregarding all other difficulties, including the fact that it would only be by force, too, that the higher wages, being an anomaly, could be maintained) would therefore be nothing but *better payment for the slave*, and would not conquer either for the worker or for labour their human status and dignity.

Indeed, even the *equality of wages* demanded by Proudhon only transforms the relationship of the present-day worker to his labour into the relationship of all men to labour. Society is then conceived as an abstract capitalist.

Wages are a direct consequence of estranged labour, and estranged labour is the direct cause of private property. The downfall of the one aspect must therefore mean the downfall of the other.

(2)From the relationship of estranged labour to private property it further follows that the emancipation of society from private property, etc., from servitude, is expressed in the *political* form of the *emancipation of the workers;* not that *their* emancipation alone was at stake but because the emancipation of the workers contains universal human emancipation—and it contains this, because the whole of human servitude is involved in the relation of the worker to production, and every relation of servitude is but a modification and consequence of this relation.

Just as we have found the concept of *private property* from the concept of *estranged, alienated labour by analysis,* in the same way every *category* of political economy can be evolved with the help of these two factors; and we shall find again in each category, e.g., trade, competition, capital, money, only a *definite* and *developed expression* of the first foundations....

KARL MARX
(1847)

The

Communist

Manifesto

A spectre is haunting Europe—the spectre of communism. All the powers of old Europe have entered into a holy alliance to exorcise this spectre: Pope and Czar, Metternich and Guizot, French Radicals and German police-spies.

. . .

The history of all hitherto existing society is the history of class struggles.

Freeman and slave, patrician and plebeian, lord and serf, guild-master and journeyman, in a word, oppressor and oppressed, stood in constant opposition to one another, carried on an uninterrupted, now hidden, now open fight, a fight that each time ended, either in a revolutionary reconstitution of society at large, or in the common ruin of the contending classes.

In the earlier epochs of history, we find almost everywhere a complicated arrangement of society into various orders, a manifold gradation of social rank. In ancient Rome we have patricians, knights, plebeians, slaves; in the Middle Ages, feudal lords, vassals, guild-masters, journeymen, apprentices, serfs; in almost all of these classes, again, subordinate gradations.

The modern bourgeois society that has sprouted from the ruins of feudal society, has not done away with class antagonisms. It has but established new classes, new conditions of oppression, new forms of struggle in place of the old ones.

Our epoch, the epoch of the bourgeoisie, possesses, however, this distinctive feature: It has simplified the class antagonisms. Society as a whole is more and more splitting up into two great hostile camps, into two great classes directly facing each other—bourgeoisie and proletariat.

From the serfs of the Middle Ages sprang the chattered burghers of the earliest towns. From these burgesses the first elements of the bourgeoisie were developed.

The discovery of America, the rounding of the Cape, opened up fresh ground for the rising bourgeoisie. The East Indian and Chinese markets, the colonization of America, trade with the colonies, the increase in the means of exchange and in commodities generally, gave to commerce, to navigation, to industry, an impulse never before known, and thereby, to the revolutionary element in the tottering feudal society, a rapid development.

The feudal system of industry, in which industrial production was monopolized by closed guilds, now no longer sufficed for the growing wants of the new markets. The manufacturing system took its place. The guild-masters were pushed aside by the manufacturing middle class; division of labor between the different corporate guilds vanished in the face of division of labor in each single workshop.

Meantime the markets kept ever growing, the demand ever rising. Even manufacture no longer sufficed. Thereupon, steam and machinery revolutionized industrial production. The place of manufacture was taken by the giant, modern industry, the place of the industrial middle class, by industrial millionaires—the leaders of whole industrial armies, the modern bourgeois.

Modern industry has established the world market, for which the discovery of America paved the way. This market has given an immense development to commerce, to navigation, to communication by land. This development has, in its turn, reacted on the extension of industry; and in proportion as industry, commerce, navigation, railways extended, in the same proportion the bourgeoisie developed, increased its capital, and pushed into the background every class handed down from the Middle Ages.

We see, therefore, how the modern bourgeoisie is itself the product of a long course of development, of a series of revolutions in the modes of production and of exchange.

Each step in the development of the bourgeoisie was accompanied by a corresponding political advance of that class. An oppressed class under the sway of the feudal nobility, it became an armed and self-governing association in the medieval commune; here independent urban republic (as in Italy and Germany), there taxable "third estate" of the monarchy (as in France); afterwards, in the period of manufacture proper, serving either the semi-feudal or the absolute monarchy as a counterpoise against the nobility, and, in fact, cornerstone of the great monarchies in general—the bourgeoisie has at last, since the establishment of modern industry and of the world market, conquered for itself, in the modern representative state, exclusive political sway. The executive of the modern state is but a committee for managing the common affairs of the whole bourgeoisie.

The bourgeoisie has played a most revolutionary role in history.

The bourgeoisie, wherever it has got the upper hand, has put an end to all feudal, patriarchal, idyllic relations. It has pitilessly torn asunder the motley feudal ties that bound man to his "natural superiors," and has left no other bond between man and man than naked self-interest, than callous "cash payment." It has drowned the most heavenly ecstasies of religious fervor, of chivalrous enthusiasm, of philistine sentimentalism, in the icy water of egotistical calculation. It has resolved personal worth into exchange value, and in place of the numberless indefeasible chartered freedoms, has set up that single, unconscionable freedom—Free Trade. In one word, for exploitation, veiled by religious and political illusions, it has substituted naked, shameless, direct, brutal exploitation.

The bourgeoisie has stripped of its halo every occupation hitherto honored and looked up to with reverent awe. It has converted the physician, the lawyer, the priest, the poet, the man of science, into its paid wage-laborers.

The bourgeoisie has torn away from the family its sentimental veil, and has reduced the family relation to a mere money relation.

The bourgeoisie has disclosed how it came to pass that the brutal display of vigor in the Middle Ages, which reactionaries so much admire, found its fitting complement in the most slothful indolence. It has been the first to show what man's activity can bring about. It has accomplished wonders for surpassing Egyptian pyramids, Roman aqueducts, and Gothic cathedrals; it has conducted expeditions that put in the shade all former migrations of nations and crusades.

The bourgeoisie cannot exist without constantly revolutionizing the instruments of production, and thereby the relations of production, and with them the whole relations of society. Conservation of the old modes of production in unaltered form, was, on the contrary, the first condition of existence for all earlier industrial classes. Constant revolutionizing of production, uninterrupted disturbance of all social conditions, everlasting uncertainty and agitation distinguish the bourgeois epoch from all earlier ones. All fixed, fast-frozen relations, with their train of ancient and venerable prejudices and opinions, are swept away, all new-formed ones become antiquated before they can ossify. All that is solid melts into air, all that is holy is profaned, and man is at last compelled to face with sober senses his real conditions of life and his relations with his kind.

The need of a constantly expanding market for its products chases the bourgeoisie over the whole surface of the globe. It must nestle everywhere, settle everywhere, establish connections everywhere.

The bourgeoisie has through its exploitation of the world market given a cosmopolitan character to production and consumption in every country. To the great chargin of reactionaries, it has drawn from under the feet of industry the national ground on which it stood. All old-established national industries have been destroyed or are daily being destroyed. They are dislodged by new industries, whose introduction becomes a life and death question for all civilized nations, by industries that no longer work up indigenous raw material, but raw material drawn from the remotest zones; industries whose products are consumed, not only at home, but in every quarter of the globe. In place of the old wants, satisfied by the production of the country, we find new wants, requiring for their satisfaction the products of distant lands and climes. In place of the old local and national seclusion and self-sufficiency, we have intercourse in every direction, universal inter-dependence of nations. And as in material, so also in intellectual production. The intellectual creations of individual nations become common property. National one-sidedness and narrow-mindedness become more and more impossible, and from the numerous national and local literatures there arises a world literature.

The bourgeoisie, by the rapid improvement of all instruments of production, by the immensely facilitated means of communication, draws all nations, even the most barbarian, into civilization. The cheap prices of its commodities are the heavy artillery with which it batters down all Chinese walls, with which it forces the barbarians' intensely obstinate hatred of foreigners to capitulate. It compels all nations, on pain of extinction, to adopt the bourgeois mode of production; it compels them to introduce what it calls civilization into their midst, i.e., to become bourgeois themselves. In a word, it creates a world after its own image.

The bourgeoisie has subjected the country to the rule of the towns. It has created enormous cities, has greatly increased the urban population as compared with the rural, and has thus rescued a considerable part of the population from the idiocy of rural life. Just as it has made the country dependent on the towns, so it has made barbarian and semi-barbarian countries dependent on the civilized ones, nations of peasants on nations of bourgeois, the East on the West.

More and more the bourgeoisie keeps doing away with the scattered state of the population, of the means of production, and of property. It has agglomerated population, centralized means of production, and has concentrated property in a few hands. The necessary consequence of this was political centralization. Independent, or but loosely connected provinces, with separate interests, laws, governments, and systems of taxation, became lumped together into one nation, with one government, one code of laws, one national class interest, one frontier, and one customs tariff.

The bourgeoisie, during its rule of scarce one hundred years has created more massive and more colossal productive forces than have all preceding generations together. Subjection of nature's forces to man, machinery, application of chemistry to industry and agriculture, steam-navigation, railways, electric telegraphs, clearing of whole continents for cultivation, canalisation of rivers, whole populations conjured out of the ground—what earlier century had even a presentiment that such productive forces slumbered in the lap of social labour?

We see then that the means of production and of exchange, which served as the foundation for the growth of the bourgeoisie, were generated in feudal society. At a certain stage in the development of these means of production and of exchange, the conditions under which feudal society produced and exchanged, the feudal organisation of agriculture and manufacturing industry, in a word, the feudal relations of property became no longer compatible with the already developed productive forces; they became so many fetters. They had to be burst asunder; they were burst asunder.

Into their place stepped free competition, accompanied by a social and political constitution adapted to it, and by the economic and political sway of the bourgeois class.

A similar movement is going on before our own eyes. Modern bourgeois society with its relations of production, of exchange and of property, a society that has conjured up such gigantic means of production and of exchange, is like the sorcerer who is no longer able to control the powers of the nether world whom he has called up by his spells. For many a decade past the history of industry and commerce is but the history of the revolt of modern productive forces against modern conditions of production, against the property relations that are the conditions for the existence of the bourgeoisie and of its rule. It is enough to mention the commercial crises that by their periodical return put the existence of the entire bourgeois society on trial, each time more threateningly. In these crises a great part not only of the existing products, but also of the previously created productive forces, are periodically destroyed. In these crises there breaks out an epidemic that, in all earlier epochs, would have seemed an absurdity—the epidemic of over-production. Society suddenly finds itself put back into a state of momentary barbarism; it appears as if a famine, a universal war of devastation had cut off the supply of every means of subsistence; industry and commerce seem to be destroyed. And why? Because there is too much civilization, too much means of subsistence, too much industry, too much commerce. The productive forces at the disposal of society no longer tend to further the development of the conditions of bourgeois property; on the contrary, they have become too powerful for these conditions, by which they are fettered, and no sooner do they overcome these fetters than they bring disorder into the whole of bourgeois society, endanger the existence of bourgeois property. The conditions of bourgeois society are too narrow to comprise the wealth created by them. And how does the bourgeoisie get over these crises? On the one hand, by enforced destruction of a mass of productive forces; on the other, by the conquest of new markets, and by the more thorough exploitation of the old ones. That is to say, by paving the way for more extensive and more destructive crises, and by diminishing the means whereby crises are prevented.

The weapons with which the bourgeoisie felled feudalism to the ground are now turned against the bourgeoisie itself.

But not only has the bourgeoisie forged the weapons that bring death to itself; it has also called into existence the men who are to wield those weapons—the modern working class—the proletarians.

Hitherto, every form of society has been based, as we have already seen, on the antagonism of oppressing and oppressed classes. But in order to oppress a class, certain conditions must be assured to it under which it can, at least, continue its lavish existence. The serf, in the period of serfdom, raised himself to membership in the commune, just as the petty bourgeois, under the yoke of feudal absolutism, managed to develop into a bourgeois. The modern laborer, on the contrary, instead of rising with the progress of industry, sinks deeper and deeper below the conditions of existence of his own class. He becomes a pauper, and pauperism develops more rapidly than population and wealth. And here it becomes evident, that the bourgeoisie is unfit any longer to be the ruling class in society, and to impose its conditions of existence upon society as an overriding law. It is unfit to rule because it is incompetent to assure an existence to its slave within his slavery, because it cannot help letting him sink into such a state, that it has to feed him, instead of being fed by him. Society can no longer live under this bourgeoisie, in other words, its existence is no longer compatible with society.

The essential condition for the existence and sway of the bourgeois class, is the formation and augmentation of capital; the condition for capital is wage-labor. Wage-labor rests exclusively on competition between the laborers. The advance of industry, whose involuntary promoter is the bourgeoisie, replaces the isolation of the laborers, due to competition, by their revolutionary combination, due to association. The development of modern industry, therefore, cuts from under its feet the very foundation on which the bourgeoisie produces and appropriates products. What the bourgeoisie therefore produces, above all, are its own grave-diggers. Its fall and the victory of the proletariat are equally inevitable.

. . .

The Communists disdain to conceal their views and aims. They openly declare that their ends can be attained only by the forcible overthrow of all existing social conditions. Let the ruling classes tremble at a Communistic revolution. The proletarians have nothing to lose but their chains. They have a world to win. WORKING MEN OF ALL COUNTRIES, UNITE.

KARL MARX
(1847)

The

German

Ideology

A. Ideology in General, German Ideology in Particular

The premises from which we begin are not arbitrary ones, not dogmas, but real premises from which abstraction can only be made in the imagination. They are the real individuals, their activity and the material conditions under which they live, both those which they find already existing and those produced by their activity. These premises can thus be verified in a purely empirical way.

The first premise of all human history is, of course, the existence of living human individuals. Thus the first fact to be established is the physical organisation of these individuals and their consequent relation to the rest of nature. Of course, we cannot here go either into the actual physical nature of man, or into the natural conditions in which man finds himself—geological, orohydrographical, climatic and so on. The writing of history must always set out from these natural bases and their modification in the course of history through the action of men.

Men can be distinguished from animals by consciousness, by religion or anything else you like. They themselves begin to distinguish themselves from animals as soon as they begin to *produce* their means of subsistence, a step which is conditioned by their physical organisation. By producing their means of subsistence men are indirectly producing their actual material life.

The way in which men produce their means of subsistence depends first of all on the

Reprinted from *The Marx–Engels Reader*, Second Edition, ed. Robert C. Tucker, pp. 3–6, 70–80, 149–75, by permission of W.W. Norton & Company, Inc. © 1978, 1972 by W. W. Norton & Company, Inc.

nature of the actual means of subsistence they find in existence and have to reproduce. This mode of production must not be considered simply as being the reproduction of the physical existence of the individuals. Rather it is a definite form of activity of these individuals, a definite form of expressing their life, a definite *mode of life* on their part. As individuals express their life, so they are. What they are, therefore, coincides with their production, both with *what* they produce and with *how* they produce. The nature of individuals thus depends on the material conditions determining their production.

This production only makes its appearance with the *increase of population*. In its turn this presupposes the *intercourse* [*Verkehr*] of individuals with one another. The form of this intercourse is again determined by production. . . .

1. History

Since we are dealing with the Germans, who are devoid of premises, we must begin by stating the first premise of all human existence and, therefore, of all history, the premise, namely, that men must be in a position to live in order to be able to "make history." But life involves before everything else eating and drinking, a habitation, clothing and many other things. The first historical act is thus the production of the means to satisfy these needs, the production of material life itself. And indeed this is an historical act, a fundamental condition of all history, which today, as thousands of years ago, must daily and hourly be fulfilled merely in order to sustain human life. Even when the sensuous world is reduced to a minimum, to a stick as with Saint Bruno, it presupposes the action of producing the stick. Therefore in any interpretation of history one has first of all to observe this fundamental fact in all its significance and all its implications and to accord it its due importance. It is well known that the Germans have never done this, and they have never, therefore, had an *earthly* basis for history and consequently never a historian. The French and the English, even if they have conceived the relation of this fact with so-called history only in an extremely one-sided fashion, particularly as long as they remained in the toils of political ideology, have nevertheless made the first attempts to give the writing of history a materialistic basis by being the first to write histories of civil society, of commerce and industry.

The second point is that the satisfaction of the first need (the action of satisfying, and the instrument of satisfaction which has been acquired) leads to new needs; and this production of new needs is the first historical act. Here we recognise immediately the spiritual ancestry of the great historical wisdom of the Germans who, when they run out of positive material and when they can serve up neither theological nor political nor literary rubbish, assert that this is not history at all, but the "prehistoric era." They do not, however, enlighten us as to how we proceed from this nonsensical "prehistory" to history proper; although, on the other hand, in their historical speculation they seize upon this "prehistory" with especial eagerness because they imagine themselves safe there from interference on the part of "crude facts," and, at the same time, because there they can give full rein to their speculative impulse and set up and knock down hypotheses by the thousand.

The third circumstance which, from the very outset, enters into historical development, is that men, who daily remake their own life, begin to make other men, to propagate their kind: the relation between man and woman, parents and children, the *family*. The family, which to begin with is the only social relationship, becomes later, when increased needs create new social relations and the increased population new needs, a subordinate one (except in Germany), and must then be treated and analysed according to the existing empirical data, not according to "the concept of the family," as is the custom in Germany. These three aspects of social activity are not of course to be taken as three different stages, but just as three aspects or, to make it clear to the Germans, three "moments," which have existed simultaneously since the dawn of history and the first men, and which still assert themselves in history today.

The production of life, both of one's own in labour and of fresh life in procreation, now appears as a double relationship: on the one hand as a natural, on the other as a social relationship. By social we understand the co-operation of several individuals, no matter under what conditions, in what manner and to what end. It follows from this that a certain mode of production, or industrial stage, is always combined with a certain mode of co-operation, or social stage, and this mode of co-operation is itself a "productive force." Further, that the multitude of productive forces accessible to men determines the nature of society, hence, that the "history of humanity" must always be studied and treated in relation to the history of industry and exchange. But it is also clear how in Germany it is impossible to write this sort of history, because the Germans lack not only the necessary power of comprehension and the material but also the "evidence of their senses," for across the Rhine you cannot have any experience of these things since history has stopped happening. Thus it is quite obvious from the start that there exists a materialistic connection of men with one another, which is determined by their needs and their mode of production, and which is as old as men themselves. This connection is ever taking on new forms, and thus presents a "history" independently of the existence of any political or religious nonsense which would especially hold men together.

Only now, after having considered four moments, four aspects of the primary historical relationships, do we find that men also possess "consciousness"; but, even so, not inherent, not "pure" consciousness. From the start the "spirit" is afflicted with the curse of being "burdened" with matter, which here makes its appearance in the form of agitated layers of air, sounds, in short, of language. Language is as old as consciousness, language is practical consciousness that exists also for other men, and for that reason alone it really exists for me personally as well; language, like consciousness, only arises from the need, the necessity, of intercourse with other men. Where there exists a relationship, it exists for me: the animal does not enter into "*relations*" with anything, it does not enter into any relation at all. For the animal, its relation to others does not exist as a relation. Consciousness is, therefore, from the very beginning a social product, and remains so as long as men exist at all. Consciousness is at first, of course, merely consciousness concerning the *immediate* sensuous environment and consciousness of the limited connection with other persons and things outside the individual who is growing self-conscious. At the same time it is consciousness of nature, which first appears to men as a completely alien, all-powerful and unassailable force, with which men's relations are purely animal and by which they are overawed like beasts; it is thus a purely animal consciousness of nature (natural religion).

We see here immediately: this natural religion or this particular relation of men to nature is determined by the form of society and vice versa. Here, as everywhere, the identity of nature and man appears in such a way that the restricted relation of men to nature determines their restricted relation to one another, and their restricted relation to one another determines men's restricted relation to nature, just because nature is as yet hardly modified historically; and, on the other hand, man's consciousness of the necessity of associating with the individuals around him is the beginning of the consciousness that he is living in society at all. This beginning is as animal as social life itself at this stage. It is mere herd-consciousness, and at this point man is only distinguished from sheep by the fact that with him consciousness takes the place of instinct or that his instinct is a conscious one. This sheep-like or tribal consciousness receives its further development and extension through increased productivity, the increase of needs, and, what is fundamental to both of these, the increase of population. With these there develops the division of labour, which was originally nothing but the division of labour in the sexual act, then that division of labour which develops spontaneously or "naturally" by virtue of natural predisposition (e.g., physical strength), needs, accidents, etc., etc. Division of labour only becomes truly such from the moment when a division of material and mental labour appears. From this moment onwards consciousness *can* really flatter itself that it is something other than consciousness of existing practice, that it *really* represents something without representing something real; from now on consciousness is in a position to emancipate itself from the world and to proceed to the formation of "pure" theory, theology, philosophy, ethics, etc. But even if this theory, theology, philosophy, ethics, etc., comes into contradiction with the existing relations, this can only occur because existing social relations have come into contradiction with existing forces of production; this, moreover, can also occur in a particular national sphere of relations through the appearance of the contradiction, not within the national orbit, but between this national consciousness and the practice of other nations, i.e., between the national and the general consciousness of a nation (as we see it now in Germany).

Moreover, it is quite immaterial what consciousness starts to do on its own: out of all such muck we get only the one inference that these three moments, the forces of production, the state of society, and consciousness, can and must come into contradiction with one another, because the *division of labour* implies the possibility, nay the fact that intellectual and material activity—enjoyment and labour, production and consumption—devolve on different individuals, and that the only possibility of their not coming into contradiction lies in the negation in its turn of the division of labour. It is self-evident, moreover, that "spectres," "bonds," "the higher being," "concept," "scruple," are merely the idealistic, spiritual expression, the conception apparently of the isolated individual, the image of very empirical fetters and limitations, within which the mode of production of life and the form of intercourse coupled with it move.

With the division of labour, in which all these contradictions are implicit, and which in its turn is based on the natural division of labour in the family and the separation of society into individual families opposed to one another, is given simultaneously the *distribution*, and indeed the *unequal* distribution, both quantitative and qualitative, of labour and its products, hence property: the nucleus, the first form, of which lies in the family, where wife and children are the slaves of the husband. This latent slavery in the family, though still very crude, is the first property, but even at this early stage it corresponds perfectly to the definition of modern economists who call it the power of disposing of the labour-power of others. Division of labour and private property are, moreover, identical expressions: in the one the same thing is affirmed with reference to activity as is affirmed in the other with reference to the product of the activity.

Further, the division of labour implies the contradiction between the interest of the separate individual or the individual family and the communal interest of all individuals who have intercourse with one another. And indeed, this communal interest does not exist merely in the imagination, as the "general interest," but first of all in reality, as the mutual interdependence of the individuals among whom the labour is divided. And finally, the division of labour offers us the first example of how, as long as man remains in natural society, that is, as long as a cleavage exists between the particular and the common interest, as long, therefore, as activity is not voluntarily, but naturally, divided, man's own deed becomes an alien power opposed to him, which enslaves him instead of being controlled by him. For as soon as the distribution of labour comes into being, each man has a particular, exclusive sphere of activity, which is forced upon him and from which he cannot escape. He is a hunter, a fisherman, a shepherd, or a critical critic, and must remain so if he does not want to lose his means of livelihood; while in communist society, where nobody has one exclusive sphere of activity but each can become accomplished in any branch he wishes, society regulates the general production and thus makes it possible for me to do one thing today and another tomorrow, to hunt in the morning, fish in the afternoon, rear cattle in the evening, criticise after dinner, just as I have a mind, without ever becoming hunter, fisherman, shepherd or critic. This fixation of social activity, this consolidation of what we ourselves produce into an objective power above us, growing out of our control, thwarting our expectations, bringing to naught our calculations, is one of the chief factors in historical development up till now.

And out of this very contradiction between the interest of the individual and that of the community the latter takes an independent form as the *State*, divorced from the real interests of individual and community, and at the same time as an illusory communal life, always based, however, on the real ties existing in every family and tribal conglomeration—such as flesh and blood, language, division of labour on a larger scale, and other interests—and especially, as we shall enlarge upon later, on the classes, already determined by the division of labour, which in every such mass of men separate out, and of which one dominates all the others. It follows from this that all struggles within the State, the struggle between democracy, aristocracy, and monarchy, the struggle for the franchise, etc., etc., are merely the illusory forms in which the real struggles of the different classes are fought out among one another (of this the German theoreticians have not the faintest inkling, although they have received a sufficient introduction to the subject in the *Deutsch-Französische Jahrbücher* and *Die heilige Familie*). Further, it follows that every class which is struggling for mastery, even when its domination, as is the case with the proletariat, postulates the abolition of the old form of society in its entirety and of domination itself, must first conquer for itself political power in order to represent its interest in turn as the general interest, which in the first moment it is forced to do. Just because individuals seek *only* their particular interest, which for them does not coincide with their communal interest (in fact the general is the illusory form of communal life), the latter will be imposed on them as an interest "alien" to them, and "independent" of them, as in its turn a particular, peculiar "general" interest; or they themselves must remain within this discord, as in democracy. On the other hand, too, the *practical* struggle of these particular interests, which constantly *really* run counter to the communal and illusory communal interests, makes *practical* intervention and control necessary through the illusory "general" interest in the form of the State. The social power, i.e., the multiplied productive force, which arises through the co-operation of different individuals as it is determined by the division of labour, appears to these individuals, since their co-operation is not voluntary but has come about naturally, not as their own united power, but as an alien force existing outside them, of the origin and goal of which they are ignorant, which they thus cannot control, which on the contrary passes through a peculiar series of phases and stages independent of the will and the action of man, nay even being the prime governor of these. . . .

Civil society embraces the whole material intercourse of individuals within a definite stage of the development of productive forces. It embraces the whole commercial and industrial life of a given stage and, insofar, transcends the State and the nation, though, on the other hand again, it must assert itself in its foreign relations as nationality, and inwardly must organise itself as State. The term "civil society" [*bürgerliche Gesellschaft*] emerged in the eighteenth century, when property relationships had already extricated themselves from the ancient and medieval communal society. Civil society as such only develops with the bourgeoisie; the social organisation evolving directly out of production and commerce, which in all ages forms the basis of the State and of the rest of the idealistic superstructure, has, however, always been designated by the same name.

2. *Concerning the Production of Consciousness*

In the whole conception of history up to the present this real basis of history has either been totally neglected or else considered as a minor matter quite irrelevant to the course of history. History must, therefore, always be written according to an extraneous standard; the real production of life seems to be primeval history, while the truly historical appears to be separated from ordinary life, something extra-superterrestrial. With this the relation of man to nature is excluded from history and hence the antithesis of nature and history is created. The exponents of this conception of history have consequently only been able to see in history the political actions of princes and States, religious and all sorts of theoretical struggles, and in particular in each historical epoch have had to *share the illusion of that epoch.* . . .

History is nothing but the succession of the separate generations, each of which exploits the materials, the capital funds, the productive forces handed down to it by all preceding generations, and thus, on the one hand, continues the traditional activity in completely changed circumstances and, on the other, modifies the old circumstances with a completely changed activity. This can be speculatively distorted so that later history is made the goal of earlier history, e.g., the goal ascribed to the discovery of America is to further the eruption of the French Revolution. Thereby history receives its own special aims and becomes "a person ranking with other persons" (to wit: "Self-Consciousness, Criticism, the Unique," etc.), while what is designated with the words "destiny," "goal," "germ," or "ideal" of earlier history is nothing more than an abstraction formed from later history, from the active influence which earlier history exercises on later history.

The further the separate spheres, which act on one another, extend in the course of this development, the more the original isolation of the separate nationalities is destroyed by the developed mode of production and intercourse and the division of labour between various nations naturally brought forth by these, the more history becomes world history. Thus, for instance, if in England a machine is invented, which deprives countless workers of bread in India and China, and overturns the whole form of existence of these empires, this invention becomes a world-historical fact. Or again, take the case of sugar and coffee which have proved their world-historical importance in the nineteenth century by the fact that the lack of these products, occasioned by the Napoleonic Continental System, caused the Germans to rise against Napoleon, and thus became the real basis of the glorious Wars of Liberation of 1813. From this it follows that this transformation of history into world history is not indeed a mere abstract act on the part of the "self-consciousness," the world spirit, or of any other metaphysical spectre, but a quite material, empirically verifiable act, an act the proof of which every individual furnishes as he comes and goes, eats, drinks and clothes himself.

The ideas of the ruling class are in every epoch the ruling ideas: i.e., the class which is the ruling *material* force of society, is at the same time its ruling *intellectual* force. The class which has the means of material production at its disposal, has control at the same time over the means of mental production, so that thereby, generally speaking, the ideas of those who lack the means of mental production are subject to it. The ruling ideas are nothing more than the ideal expression of the dominant material relationships, the dominant material relationships grasped as ideas; hence of the relationships which make the one class the ruling one, therefore, the ideas of its dominance. The individuals composing the ruling class possess among other things consciousness, and therefore think. Insofar, therefore, as they rule as a class and determine the extent and compass of an epoch, it is self-evident that they do this in its whole range, hence among other things rule also as thinkers, as producers of ideas, and regulate the production and distribution of the ideas of their age: thus their ideas are the ruling ideas of the epoch. For instance, in an age and in a country where royal power, aristocracy and bourgeoisie are contending for mastery and where, therefore, mastery is shared, the doctrine of the separation of powers proves to be the dominant idea and is expressed as an "eternal law."

The division of labour, which we have already seen above as one of the chief forces of history up till now, manifests itself also in the ruling class as the division of mental and material labour, so that inside this class one part appears as the thinkers of the class (its active, conceptive ideologists, who make the perfecting of the illusion of the class about itself their chief source of livelihood), while the others' attitude to these ideas and illusions is more passive and receptive, because they are in reality the active members of this class and have less time to make up illusions and ideas about themselves. Within this class this cleavage can even develop into a certain opposition and hostility between the two parts, which, however, in the case of a practical collision, in which the class itself is endangered, automatically comes to nothing, in which case there also vanishes the semblance that the ruling ideas were not the ideas of the ruling class and had a power distinct from the power of this class. The existence of revolutionary ideas in a particular period presupposes the existence of a revolutionary class; about the premises for the latter sufficient has already been said above.

If now in considering the course of history we detach the ideas of the ruling class from the ruling class itself and attribute to them an independent existence, if we confine ourselves to saying that these or those ideas were dominant at a given time, without bothering ourselves about the conditions of production and the producers of these ideas, if we thus ignore the individuals and world conditions which are the source of the ideas, we can say, for instance, that during the time that the aristocracy was dominant, the concepts honour, loyalty, etc., were dominant, during the dominance of the bourgeoisie the concepts freedom, equality, etc. The ruling class itself on the whole imagines this to be so. This conception of history, which is common to all historians, particularly since the eighteenth century, will necessarily come up against the phenomenon that increasingly abstract ideas hold sway, i.e., ideas which increasingly take on the form of universality. For each new class which puts itself in the place of one ruling before it, is compelled, merely in order to carry through its aim, to represent its interest as the common interest of all the members of society, that is, expressed in ideal form: it has to give its ideas the form of universality, and represent them as the only rational, universally valid ones. The class making a revolution appears from the very start, if only because it is opposed to a *class*, not as a class but as the representative of the whole of society; it appears as the whole mass of society confronting the one ruling class. It can do this because, to start with, its interest really is more connected with the common interest of all other non-ruling classes, because under the pressure of hitherto existing conditions its interest has not yet been able to develop as the particular interest of a particular class. Its victory, therefore, benefits also many individuals of the other classes which are not winning a dominant position, but only insofar as it now puts these individuals in a position to raise themselves into the ruling class. When the French bourgeoisie overthrew the power of the aristocracy, it thereby made it possible for many proletarians to raise themselves above the proletariat, but only insofar as they became bourgeois. Every new class, therefore, achieves its hegemony only on a broader basis than that of the class ruling previously, whereas the opposition of the non-ruling class against the new ruling class later develops all the more sharply and profoundly. Both these things determine the fact that the struggle to be waged against this new ruling class, in its turn, aims at a more decided and radical negation of the previous conditions of society than could all previous classes which sought to rule.

This whole semblance, that the rule of a certain class is only the rule of certain ideas, comes to a natural end, of course, as soon as class rule in general ceases to be the form in which society is organised, that is to say, as soon as it is no longer necessary to represent a particular interest as general or the "general interest" as ruling.

Once the ruling ideas have been separated from the ruling individuals and, above all, from the relationships which result from a given stage of the mode of production, and in this way the conclusion has been reached that history is always under the sway of ideas, it is very easy to abstract from these various ideas "*the* idea," the notion, etc., as the dominant force in history, and thus to understand all these separate ideas and concepts as "forms of self-determination" on the part of *the* concept developing in history. It follows then naturally, too, that all the relationships of men can be derived from the concept of man, man as concieved, the essence of man, *Man*. This has been done by the speculative philosophers. Hegel himself confesses at the end of the *Geschichtsphilosophie* that he "has considered the progress of the *concept* only" and has represented in history the "true *theodicy*." Now one can go back again to the producers of the "concept," to the theorists, ideologists and philosophers, and one comes then to the conclusion that the philosophers, the thinkers as such, have at all times been dominant in history: a conclusion, as we see, already expressed by Hegel. The whole trick of proving the hegemony of the spirit in history (hierarchy Stirner calls it) is thus confined to the following three efforts.

No. 1. One must separate the ideas of those ruling for empirical reasons, under empirical conditions and as empirical individuals, from these actual rulers, and thus recognise the rule of ideas or illusions in history.

No. 2. One must bring an order into this rule of ideas, prove a mystical connection among the successive ruling ideas, which is managed by understanding them as "acts of self-determination on the part of the concept" (this is possible because by virtue of their empirical basis these ideas are really connected with one another and because, conceived as *mere* ideas, they become self-distinctions, distinctions made by thought).

No. 3. To remove the mystical appearance of this "self-determining concept" it is changed into a person—"Self-Consciousness"—or, to appear thoroughly materialistic, into a series of persons, who represent the "concept" in history, into the "thinkers," the "philosophers," the ideologists, who again are understood as the manufacturers of history, as the "council of guardians," as the rulers. Thus the whole body of materialistic elements has been removed from history and now full rein can be given to the speculative steed.

Whilst in ordinary life every shopkeeper is very well able to distinguish between what somebody professes to be and what he really is, our historians have not yet won even this trivial insight. They take every epoch at its word and believe that everything it says and imagines about itself is true.

This historical method which reigned in Germany and especially the reason why, must be understood from its connection with the illusion of ideologists in general, e.g., the illusions of the jurists, politicians (of the practical statesmen among them, too), from the dogmatic dreamings and distortions of these fellows; this is explained perfectly easily from their practical position in life, their job, and the division of labour.

Friedrich Nietzsche

If Marx argued for a conception of society as a social totality in which historically constructed social relations shaped consciousness, Nietzsche (1844–1900), German philologist and philosopher, stood in diametrical opposition to him. Nietzsche criticized such notions of totality and the scientific pretensions that supported them. For Nietzsche, there was no value in ideas of totality. The obsession with Truth based on stable meaning was a function of the displacement of traditional Christian virtue by the more recent substitutes offered by science, all of which was attributable to the general cultural mediocrity accompanying the rise of mass industrial society. Nietzsche would have nothing to do with the totality of this society.

In this respect, Nietzsche acted on many of the same impulses that prompted conservative, sociologically oriented writers such as Tocqueville. Europe in earlier centuries had certainly known of "the people," "the vulgar," and "the rude" but with the rapid demographic transformation of European populations over the course of the nineteenth century, "the masses" came to represent a reality that incorporated these previous meanings in a new, more strictly biological sense. Conceived less in terms of the older oppositions between the "natural" and the "artificial" urban society presented, to Nietzsche and others, a spectacle of a vast arena of competition and adaptation according to the pressure for survival.

It is no coincidence that much of Nietzsche's writing refers to society as composed of "populations," and of those who are "fit" for this or "unfit" for that. The use of Darwinian metaphors (though not necessarily Darwinian evolution per se) in relation to society was an increasingly popular intellectual recourse in an age during which it was felt that a society based on individualistic principles must at the same time have some means of recognizing inequalities of talent and ability. The anonymity of the crowd, lack of distinction brought about by democratic conformity, and routinization of daily behavior at the expense of creative vitality were all functions of the late-nineteenth-century urban environment that Nietzsche found repulsive.

How could one make room for true individuals in the midst of masses of mediocrity? Nietzsche's answer: by rejecting the universalistic pretensions of modern science, and by accepting the possibility that not only our knowledge of reality, but reality itself, may be much less certain than nineteenth-century science would have us believe. Modern science encouraged absolute Truth as a shield against real virtue, which does not need the reassurance of absolutes. If a few scientific laws regulated everything, then all was safely subordinate to a higher authority (science in one case, God in the other). Nietzsche, along with many artists of his period, felt that this overtly-rationalistic form of culture diluted something very special in the human spirit, and that the only way to respect the creative, self-forming drive in the individual was to live one's life according to one's own rules. Each life is a work of art, to be judged by its own standards of virtue. This highly relativistic argument is of a sort seen by many postmodernists as liberating; at the same time, modernists view it as exceptionally dangerous.

FRIEDRICH NIETZSCHE
(1882)

Selected

Aphorisms from

The Gay Science

Long live physics!—How many people know how to observe something? Of the few who do, how many observe themselves? "Everybody is farthest away—from himself"; all who try the reins know this to their chagrin, and the maxim "know thyself!" addressed to human beings by a god, is almost malicious. That the case of self-observation is indeed as desperate as that is attested best of all by the manner in which *almost everybody* talks about the essence of moral actions—this quick, eager, convinced, and garrulous manner with its expression, its smile, and its obliging ardor! One seems to have the wish to say to you: "But my dear friend, precisely this is my specialty. You have directed your question to the one person who is entitled to answer you. As it happens, there is nothing about which I am as wise as about this. To come to the point: when a human being judges 'this is right' and then infers 'therefore it must be done,' and then proceeds to *do* what he has thus recognized as right and designated as necessary—then the essence of his action is *moral*."

But my friend, you are speaking of three actions instead of one. When you judge "this is right," that is an action, too. Might it not be possible that one could judge in a moral and in an immoral manner? *Why* do you consider this, precisely this, right?

"Because this is what my conscience tells me; and the voice of conscience is never immoral, for it alone determines what is to be moral."

But why do you *listen* to the voice of your conscience? And what gives you the right to consider such a judgment true and infallible? For this *faith*—is there no conscience for that? Have you never heard of an intellectual conscience? A conscience behind your "conscience"?

Your judgment "this is right" has a pre-history in your instincts, likes, dislikes, experiences, and lack of experiences. "*How* did it originate there?" you must ask, and then also: "What is it that impels me to listen to it?" You can listen to its commands like a good soldier who hears his officer's command. Or like a woman who loves the man who commands. Or like a flatterer and coward who is afraid of the commander. Or like a dunderhead who obeys because no objection occurs to him. In short, there are a hundred ways in which you can listen to your conscience. But that you take this or that judgment for the voice of conscience—in other words, that you feel something to be right—may be due to the fact that you have never thought much about yourself and simply have accepted blindly that what you had been *told* ever since your childhood was right; or it may be due to the fact that what you call your duty has up to this point brought you sustenance and honors—and you consider it "right" because it appears to you as your own "condition of existence" (and that you have a *right* to existence seems irrefutable to you).

For all that, the *firmness* of your moral judgment could be evidence of your personal abjectness, of impersonality; your "moral strength" might have its source in your stubbornness—or in your inability to envisage new ideals. And, briefly, if you had thought more subtly, observed better, and learned more, you certainly would not go on calling this "duty" of yours and this "conscience" of yours duty and conscience. Your understanding *of the manner in which moral judgments have originated* would spoil these grand words for you, just as other grand words, like "sin" and "salvation of the soul" and "redemption" have been spoiled for you.—And now don't cite the categorical imperative, my friend! This term tickles my ear and makes me laugh despite your serious presence. It makes me think of the old Kant who had obtained the "thing in itself" *by stealth*—another very ridiculous thing!—and was punished for this when the "categorical imperative" crept stealthily into his heart and led him *astray—back* to "God," "soul," "freedom," and "immortality," like a fox who loses his way and goes astray back into his cage. Yet it had been *his* strength and cleverness that had *broken open* the cage!

What? You admire the categorical imperative within you? This "firmness" of your so-called moral judgment? This "unconditional" feeling that "here everyone must judge as I do"? Rather admire your *selfishness* at this point. And the blindness, pettiness, and frugality of your selfishness. For it is selfish to experience one's own judgment as a universal law; and this selfishness is blind, petty, and frugal because it betrays that you have not yet discovered yourself nor created for yourself an ideal of your own, your very own—for that could never be somebody else's and much less that of all, all!

Anyone who still judges "in this case everybody would have to act like this" has not yet taken five steps toward self-knowledge. Otherwise he would know that there neither are nor can be actions that are the same; that every action that has ever been done was done in an altogether unique and irretrievable way, and that this will be equally true of every future action; that all regulations about actions relate only to their coarse exterior (even the most inward and subtle regulations of all moralities so far); that these regulations may lead to some semblance of sameness, *but really only to some semblance*; that as one contemplates or looks back upon *any* action at all, it is and remains impenetrable; that our opinions about "good" and "noble" and "great" can never be *proved true* by our actions because every action is unknowable; that our opinions, valuations, and tables of what is good certainly belong among the most powerful levers in the involved mechanism of our actions, but that in any particular case the law of their mechanism is indemonstrable.

Let us therefore *limit* ourselves to the purification of our opinions and valuations and to the *creation of our own new tables of what is good*, and let us stop brooding about the "moral value of our actions"! Yes, my friends, regarding all the moral chatter of some about others it is time to feel nauseous. Sitting in moral judgment should offend our taste. Let us leave such chatter and such bad taste to those who have nothing else to do but drag the past a few steps further through time and who never live in the present—which is to say the many, the great majority. We, however, *want to become those we are* human beings who are new, unique, incomparable, who give themselves laws, who create themselves. To that end we must become the best learners and discoverers of everything that is lawful and necessary in the world: we must become *physicists* in order to be able to be *creators* in this sense—while hitherto all valuations and ideals have been based on *ignorance* of physics or were constructed so as to *contradict* it. Therefore: long live physics! And even more so that which *compels* us to turn to physics—our honesty!

The "humaneness" of the future.—When I contemplate the present age with the eyes of some remote age, I can find nothing more remarkable in present-day humanity than its distinctive virtue and disease which goes by the name of "the historical sense." This is the beginning of something altogether new and strange in history: If this seed should be given a few centuries and more, it might ultimately become a marvelous growth with an equally marvelous scent that might make our old earth more agreeable to live on. We of the present day are only just beginning to form the chain of a very powerful future feeling, link for link—we hardly know what we are doing. It almost seems to us as if it were not a matter of a new feeling but rather a decrease in all old feelings; the historical sense is still so poor and cold, and many people are attacked by it as by a frost and made still poorer and colder. To others it appears as a sign of stealthily approaching old age, and they see our planet as a melancholy invalid who wants to forget his present condition and therefore writes the history of his youth. This is actually one color of this new feeling: Anyone who manages to experience the history of humanity as a whole as *his own history* will feel in an enormously generalized way all the grief of an invalid who thinks of health, of an old man who thinks of the dreams of his youth, of a lover deprived of his beloved, of the martyr whose ideal is perishing, of the hero on the evening after a battle that has decided nothing but brought him wounds and the loss of his friend. But if one endured, if one *could* endure this immense sum of grief of all kinds while yet being the hero who, as the second day of battle breaks, welcomes the dawn and his fortune, being a person whose horizon encompasses thousands of years past and future, being the heir of all the nobility of all past spirit—an heir with a sense of obligation, the most aristocratic of old nobles and at the same time the first of a new nobility—the like of which no age has yet seen or dreamed of; if one could burden one's soul with all of this—the oldest, the newest, losses, hopes, conquests, and the victories of humanity; if one could finally contain all this in one soul and crowd it into a single feeling—this would surely have to result in a happiness that humanity has not known so far: the happiness of a god full of power and love, full of tears and laughter, a happiness that, like the sun in the evening, continually bestows its inexhaustible riches, pouring them into the sea, feeling richest, as the sun does, only when even the poorest fisherman is still rowing with golden oars! This godlike feeling would then be called—humaneness.

The meaning of our cheerfulness. The greatest recent event—that "God is dead," that the belief in the Christian god has become unbelievable—is already beginning to cast its first shadows over

Europe. For the few at least, whose eyes—the *suspicion* in whose eyes is strong and subtle enough for this spectacle, some sun seems to have set and some ancient and profound trust has been turned into doubt; to them our old world must appear daily more like evening, more mistrustful, stranger, "older." But in the main one may say: The event itself is far too great, too distant, too remote from the multitude's capacity for comprehension even for the tidings of it to be thought of as having *arrived* as yet. Much less may one suppose that many people know as yet *what* this event really means—and how much must collapse now that this faith has been undermined because it was built upon this faith, propped up by it, grown into it; for example, the whole of our European morality. This long plenitude and sequence of breakdown, destruction, ruin, and cataclysm that is now impending—who could guess enough of it today to be compelled to play the teacher and advance proclaimer of this monstrous logic of terror, the prophet of a gloom and an eclipse of the sun whose like has probably never yet occurred on earth?

Even we born guessers of riddles who are, as it were, waiting on the mountains, posted between today and tomorrow, stretched in the contradiction between today and tomorrow, we firstlings and premature births of the coming century, to whom the shadows that must soon envelop Europe really *should* have appeared by now—why is it that even we look forward to the approaching gloom without any real sense of involvement and above all without any worry and fear for *ourselves*? Are we perhaps still too much under the impression of the *initial consequences* of this event—and these initial consequences, the consequences for *ourselves*, are quite the opposite of what one might perhaps expect: They are not at all sad and gloomy but rather like a new and scarcely describable kind of light, happiness, relief, exhilaration, encouragement, dawn.

Indeed, we philosophers and "free spirits" feel, when we hear the news that "the old god is dead," as if a new dawn shone on us; our heart overflows with gratitude, amazement, premonitions, expectation. At long last the horizon appears free to us again, even if it should not be bright; at long last our ships may venture out again, venture out to face any danger; all the daring of the lover of knowledge is permitted again; the sea, *our* sea, lies open again; perhaps there has never yet been such an "open sea."

How we, too, are still pious.—In science convictions have no rights of citizenship, as one says with good reason. Only when they decide to descend to the modesty of hypotheses, of a provisional experimental point of view, of a regulative fiction, they may be granted admission and even a certain value in the realm of knowledge—though always with the restriction that they remain under police supervision, under the police of mistrust. —But does this not mean, if you consider it more precisely, that a conviction may obtain admission to science only when it *ceases* to be a conviction? Would it not be the first step in the discipline of the scientific spirit that one would not permit oneself any more convictions?

Probably this is so; only we still have to ask: *To make it possible for this discipline to begin,* must there not be some prior conviction—even one that is so commanding and unconditional that it sacrifices all other convictions to itself? We see that science also rests on a faith; there simply is no science "without presuppositions." The question whether *truth* is needed must not only have been affirmed in advance, but affirmed to such a degree that the principle, the faith, the conviction finds expression: "*Nothing* is needed *more* than truth, and in relation to it everything else has only second-rate value."

This unconditional will to truth—what is it? Is it the will *not to allow oneself to be deceived?* Or is it the will *not to deceive?* For the will to truth could be interpreted in the second way, too—if only the special case "I do not want to deceive myself" is subsumed under the generalization "I do not want to deceive." But why not deceive? But why not allow oneself to be deceived?

Note that the reasons for the former principle belong to an altogether different realm from those for the second. One does not want to allow oneself to be deceived because one assumes that it is harmful, dangerous, calamitous to be deceived. In this sense, science would be a long-range prudence, a caution, a utility; but one could object in all fairness: How is that? Is wanting not to allow oneself to be deceived really less harmful, less dangerous, less calamitous? What do you know in advance of the character of existence to be able to decide whether the greater advantage is on the side of the unconditionally mistrustful or of the unconditionally trusting? But if both should be required, much trust *as well as* much mistrust, from where would science then be permitted to take its unconditional faith or conviction on which it rests, that truth is more important than any other thing, including every other conviction? Precisely this conviction could never have come into being if both truth and untruth constantly proved to be useful, which is the case. Thus—the faith in science, which after all exists undeniably, cannot owe its origin to such a calculus of utility; it must have originated *in spite of* the fact that the disutility and dangerousness of "the will to truth," of "truth at any price" is proved to it constantly. "At any price": how well we understand these words once we have offered and slaughtered one faith after another on this altar!

Consequently, "will to truth" does *not* mean "I will not allow myself to be deceived" but—there is no alternative—"I will not deceive, not even myself"; *and with that we stand on moral ground.* For you only have to ask yourself carefully, "Why do you not want to deceive?" especially if it should seem—and it does seem!—as if life aimed at semblance, meaning error, deception, simulation, delusion, self-delusion, and when the great sweep of life has actually always shown itself to be on the side of the most unscrupulous *polytropoi.* Charitably interpreted, such a resolve might perhaps be a quixotism, a minor slightly mad enthusiasm; but it might also be something more serious, namely, a principle that is hostile to life and destructive.—"Will to truth"—that might be a concealed will to death.

Thus the question "Why science?" leads back to the moral problem: *Why have morality at all* when life, nature, and history are "not moral"? No doubt, those who are truthful in that audacious and ultimate sense that is presupposed by the faith in science *thus affirm another world* than the world of life, nature, and history; and insofar as they affirm this "other world"—look, must they not by the same token negate its counterpart, this world, *our* world?—But you will have gathered what I am driving at, namely, that it is still a *metaphysical faith* upon which our faith in science rests—that even we seekers after knowledge today, we godless anti-metaphysicians still take our fire, too, from the flame lit by a faith that is thousands of years old, that Christian faith which was also the faith of Plato, that God is the truth, that truth is divine.—But what if this should become more and more incredible, if nothing should prove to be divine any more unless it were error, blindness, the lie—if God himself should prove to be our most enduring lie?

Believers and their need to believe.— How much one needs a *faith* in order to flourish, how much that is "firm" and that one does not wish to be shaken because one *clings* to it, that is a measure of the degree of one's strength (or, to put the point more clearly, of one's weakness). Christianity, it seems to me, is still needed by most people in old Europe even today; therefore it still finds believers. For this is how man is: An article of faith could be refuted before him a thousand times—if he needed it, he would consider it "true" again and again, in accordance with that famous "proof of strength" of which the Bible speaks.

Metaphysics is still needed by some; but so is that impetuous *demand for certainty* that today discharges itself among large numbers of people in a scientific-positivistic form. The demand that one *wants* by all means that something should be firm (while on account of the ardor of this demand one is easier and more negligent about the demonstration of this certainty)—this, too, is still the demand for a support, a prop, in short, that *instinct of weakness* which, to be sure, does not create religious, metaphysical systems, and convictions of all kinds but—conserves them.

Actually, what is steaming around all of these positivistic systems is the vapor of a certain pessimistic gloom, something that smells of weariness, fatalism, disappointment, and fear of new disappointments—or else ostentatious wrath, a bad mood, the anarchism of indignation, and whatever other symptoms and masquerades of the feeling of weakness there may be. Even the vehemence with which our most intelligent contemporaries lose themselves in wretched nooks and crannies, for example, into patriotism (I mean what the French call *chauvinisme* and the Germans "German") or into petty aesthetic creeds after the manner of French *naturalisme* (which drags up and bares only that part of nature which inspires nausea and simultaneous amazement—today people like to call this part *la vérité vraie* or into nihilism à la Petersburg (meaning the *belief in unbelief* even to the point of martyrdom always manifests above all the *need* for a faith, a support, backbone, something to fall back on.

Faith is always coveted most and needed most urgently where will is lacking; for will, as the affect of command, is the decisive sign of sovereignty and strength. In other words, the less one knows how to command, the more urgently one covets someone who commands, who commands severely—a god, prince, class, physician, father confessor, dogma, or party conscience. From this one might perhaps gather that the two world religions, Buddhism and Christianity, may have owed their origin and above all their sudden spread to a tremendous collapse and *disease of the will*. And that is what actually happened: both religions encountered a situation in which the will had become diseased, giving rise to a demand that had become utterly desperate for some "thou shalt." Both religions taught fanaticism in ages in which the will had become exhausted, and thus they offered innumerable people some support, a new possibility of willing, some delight in willing. For fanaticism is the only "strength of the will" that even the weak and insecure can be brought to attain, being a sort of hypnotism of the whole system of the senses and the intellect for the benefit of an excessive nourishment (hypertrophy) of a single point of view and feeling that henceforth becomes dominant—which the Christian calls his *faith*. Once a human being reaches the fundamental conviction that he *must* be commanded, he becomes "a believer." Conversely, one could conceive of such a pleasure and power of self-determination, such a *freedom* of the will that the spirit would take leave of all faith and every wish for certainty, being practiced in maintaining himself on insubstantial ropes and possibilities and dancing even near abysses. Such a spirit would be the *free spirit* par excellence.

On the "genius of the species." The problem of consciousness (more precisely, of becoming conscious of something) confronts us only when we begin to comprehend how we could dispense with it; and now physiology and the history of animals place us at the beginning of such comprehension (it took them two centuries to catch up with *Leibniz's* suspicion which soared ahead). For we could think, feel, will, and remember, and we could also "act" in every sense of that word, and yet none of all this would have to "enter our consciousness" (as one says metaphorically). The whole of life would be possible without, as it were, seeing itself in a mirror. Even now, for that matter, by far the greatest portion of our life actually takes place without this mirror effect; and this is true even of our thinking, feeling, and willing life, however offensive this may sound to older philosophers. For *what purpose*, then, any consciousness at all when it is in the main *superfluous?*

Now, if you are willing to listen to my answer and the perhaps extravagant surmise that it involves, it seems to me as if the subtlety and strength of consciousness always were proportionate to a man's (or animal's) *capacity for communication*, and as if this capacity in turn were proportionate to the *need for communication*. But this last point is not to be understood as if the individual human being who happens to be a master in communicating and making understandable his needs must also be most dependent on others in his needs. But it does seem to me as if it were that way when we consider whole races and chains of generations: Where need and distress have forced men for a long time to communicate and to understand each other quickly and subtly, the ultimate result is an excess of this strength and art of communication— as it were, a capacity that has gradually been accumulated and now waits for an heir who might squander it. (Those who are called artists are these heirs; so are orators, preachers, writers—all of them people who always come at the end of a long chain, "late born" every one of them in the best sense of that word and, as I have said, by their nature squanderers.)

Supposing that this observation is correct, I may now proceed to the surmise that *consciousness has developed only under the pressure of the need for communication;* that from the start it was needed and useful only between human beings (particularly between those who commanded and those who obeyed); and that it also developed only in proportion to the degree of this utility. Consciousness is really only a net of communication between human beings; it is only as such that it had to develop; a solitary human being who lived like a beast of prey would not have needed it. That our actions, thoughts, feelings, and movements enter our own consciousness— at least a part of them—that is the result of a "must" that for a terribly long time lorded it over man. As the most endangered animal, he *needed* help and protection, he needed his peers, he had to learn to express his distress and to make himself understood; and for all of this he needed "consciousness" first of all, he needed to "know" himself what distressed him, he needed to "know" how he felt, he needed to "know" what he thought. For, to say it once more: Man, like every living being, thinks continually without knowing it; the thinking that rises to *consciousness* is only the smallest part of all this—the most superficial and worst part—for only this conscious thinking *takes the form of words, which is to say signs of communication*, and this fact uncovers the origin of consciousness.

In brief, the development of language and the development of consciousness (*not* of reason but merely of the way reason enters consciousness) go hand in hand. Add to this that not only language serves as a bridge between human beings but also a mien, a pressure, a gesture. The emergence of our sense impressions into our own consciousness, the ability to fix them and, as it were, exhibit them externally, increased proportionately with the need to communicate them to *others* by means of signs. The human being inventing signs is at the same time the human being who becomes ever more keenly conscious of himself. It was only as a social animal that man acquired self-consciousness—which he is still in the process of doing, more and more.

My idea is, as you see, that consciousness does not really belong to man's individual existence but rather to his social or herd nature; that, as follows from this, it has developed subtley only insofar as this is required by social or herd utility. Consequently, given the best will in the world to understand ourselves as individually as possible, "to know ourselves," each of us will always succeed in becoming conscious only of what is not individual but "average." Our thoughts themselves are continually governed by the character of consciousness—by the "genius of the species" that commands it—and translated back into the perspective of the herd. Fundamentally, all our actions are altogether incomparably personal, unique, and infinitely individual; there is no doubt of that. But as soon as we translate them into consciousness *they no longer seem to be.*

This is the essence of phenomenalism and perspectivism as I understand them: Owing to the nature of *animal consciousness*, the world of which we can become conscious is only a surface-and-sign world, a world that is made common and meaner; whatever becomes conscious *becomes* by the same token shallow, thin, relatively stupid, general, sign, herd signal; all becoming conscious involves a great and thorough corruption, falsification, reduction to superficialities, and generalization. Ultimately, the growth of consciousness becomes a danger; and anyone who lives among the most conscious Europeans even knows that it is a disease.

You will guess that it is not the opposition of subject and object that concerns me here: This distinction I leave to the epistemologists who have become entangled in the snares of grammar (the metaphysics of the people). It is even less the opposition of "thing-in-itself" and appearance; for we do not "know" nearly enough to be entitled to any such distinction. We simply lack any organ for knowledge, for "truth": we "know" (or believe or imagine) just as much as may be *useful* in the interests of the human herd, the species; and even what is here called "utility" is ultimately also a mere belief, something imaginary, and perhaps precisely that most calamitous stupidity of which we shall perish some day.

The origin of our concept of "knowledge."—I take this explanation from the street. I heard one of the common people say, "he knew me right away." Then I asked myself: What is it that the common people take for knowledge? What do they want when they want "knowledge"? Nothing more than this: Something strange is to be reduced to something *familiar.* And we philosophers—have we really meant *more* than this when we have spoken of knowledge? What is familiar means what we are used to so that we no longer marvel at it, our everyday, some rule in which we are stuck, anything at all in which we feel at home. Look, isn't our need for knowledge precisely this need for the familiar, the will to uncover under everything strange, unusual, and questionable something that no longer disturbs us? Is it not the *instinct of fear* that bids us to know? And is the jubilation of those who attain knowledge not the jubilation over the restoration of a sense of security?

Here is a philosopher who fancied that the world was "known" when he had reduced it to the "idea." Was it not because the "idea" was so familiar to him and he was so well used to it—because he hardly was afraid of the "idea" any more?

How easily these men of knowledge are satisfied! Just have a look at their principles and their solutions of the world riddle with this in mind! When they find something in things—under them, or behind them—that is unfortunately quite familiar to us, such as our multiplication tables or our logic, or our willing and desiring—how happy they are right away! For "what is familiar is known" on this they are agreed. Even the most cautious among them suppose that what is familiar is at least *more easily knowable* than what is strange, and that, for example, sound method demands that we start from the "inner world," from the "facts of consciousness," because this world is *more familiar to us.* Error of errors! What is familiar is what we are used to; and what we are used to is most difficult to "know"—that is, to see as a problem; that is, to see as strange, as distant, as "outside us."

The great certainty of the natural sciences in comparison with psychology and the critique of the elements of consciousness—one might almost say, with the *unnatural* sciences—is due precisely to the fact that they choose for their object what is *strange*, while it is almost contradictory and absurd to even *try* to choose for an object what is not-strange.

"Science" as a prejudice.—It follows from the laws of the order of rank that scholars, insofar as they belong to the spiritual middle class, can never catch sight of the really great problems and question marks; moreover, their courage and their eyes simply do not reach that far—and above all, their needs which led them to become scholars in the first place, their inmost assumptions and desires that things might be such and such, their fears and hopes all come to rest and are satisfied too soon. Take, for example, that pedantic Englishman, Herbert Spencer. What makes him "enthuse" in his way and then leads him to draw a line of hope, a horizon of desirability—that eventual reconciliation of "egoism and altruism" about which he raves—almost nauseates the likes of us; a human race that adopted such Spencerian perspectives as its ultimate perspectives would seem to us worthy of contempt, of annihilation!

But the mere fact that he had to experience as his highest hope something that to others appears and may appear only as a disgusting possibility poses a question mark that Spencer would have been incapable of foreseeing.

It is no different with the faith with which so many materialistic natural scientists rest content nowadays, the faith in a world that is supposed to have its equivalent and its measure in human thought and human valuations—a "world of truth" that can be mastered completely and forever with the aid of our square little reason. What? Do we really want to permit existence to be degraded for us like this—reduced to a mere exercise for a calculator and an indoor diversion for mathematicians? Above all, one should not wish to divest existence of its *rich ambiguity* that is a dictate of good taste, gentlemen, the taste of reverence for everything that lies beyond your horizon. That the only justifiable interpretation of the world should be one in which *you* are justified because one can continue to work and do research scientifically in *your* sense (you really mean, mechanistically?)—an interpretation that permits counting, calculating, weighting, seeing, and touching, and nothing more—that is a crudity and naivete, assuming that it is not a mental illness, an idiocy.

Would it not be rather probable that, conversely, precisely the most superficial and external aspect of existence—what is most apparent, its skin and sensualization—would be grasped first—and might even be the only thing that allowed itself to be grasped? A "scientific" interpretation of the world, as you understand it, might therefore still be one of the *most stupid* of all possible interpretations of the world, meaning that it would be one of the poorest in meaning. This thought is intended for the ears and consciences of our mechanists who nowadays like to pass as philosophers and insist that mechanics is the doctrine of the first and last laws on which all existence must be based as on a ground floor. But an essentially mechanical world would be an essentially *meaningless* world. Assuming that one estimated the *value* of a piece of music according to how much of it could be counted, calculated, and expressed in formulas: how absurd would such a "scientific" estimation of music be! What would one have comprehended, understood, grasped of it? Nothing, really nothing of what is "music" in it!

Our new "infinite."—How far the perspective character of existence extends or indeed whether existence has any other character than this; whether existence without interpretation, without "sense," does not become "nonsense"; whether, on the other hand, all existence is not essentially actively engaged in *interpretation*—that cannot be decided even by the most industrious and most scrupulously conscientious analysis and self-examination of the intellect; for in the course of this analysis the human intellect cannot avoid seeing itself in its own perspectives, and *only* in these. We cannot look around our own corner: it is a hopeless curiosity that wants to know what other kinds of intellects and perspectives there *might* be; for example, whether some beings might be able to experience time backward, or alternately forward and backward (which would involve another direction of life and another concept of cause and effect). But I should think that today we are at least far from the ridiculous immodesty that would be involved in decreeing from our corner that perspectives are permitted only from this corner. Rather has the world become "infinite" for us all over again, inasmuch as we cannot reject the possibility that *it may include infinite interpretations*. Once more we are seized by a great shudder; but who would feel inclined immediately to deify again after the old manner this monster of an unknown world? And to worship the unknown henceforth as "the Unknown One"? Alas, too many *ungodly* possibilities of interpretation are included in the unknown, too much devilry, stupidity, and foolishness of interpretation—even our own human, all too human folly, which we know.

FRIEDRICH NIETZSCHE
(1886)

Selected Aphorisms from

Beyond Good and Evil:

Prelude to a

Philosophy of the Future

Physiologists should think before putting down the instinct of self-preservation as the cardinal instinct of an organic being. A living thing seeks above all to *discharge* its strength—life itself is *will to power;* self-preservation is only one of the indirect and most frequent *results*.

In short, here as everywhere else, let us beware of *superfluous* teleological principles—one of which is the instinct of self-preservation (we owe it to Spinoza's inconsistency). Thus method, which must be essentially economy of principles, demands it.

It is perhaps just dawning on five or six minds that physics, too, is only an interpretation and exegesis of the world (to suit us, if I may say so!) and *not* a world-explanation; but insofar as it is on belief in the senses, it is regarded as more, and for a long time to come must be regarded as more—namely, as an explanation. Eyes and fingers speak in its favor, visual evidence and palpableness do, too: this strikes an age with fundamentally plebeian tastes as fascinating, persuasive, and *convincing*—after all, it follows instinctively the canon of truth of eternally popular sensualism. What is clear, what is "explained"? Only what can be seen and felt—every problem has to be pursued to that point. Conversely, the charm of the Platonic way of thinking, which was a *noble* way of thinking, consisted precisely in *resistance* to obvious sense-evidence—perhaps among men who enjoyed even stronger and more demanding senses than our contemporaries, but who knew how to find a higher triumph in remaining masters of their senses—and this by means of pale, cold, gray concept nets which they threw over the motley whirl of the senses—

the mob of the senses, as Plato said. In this overcoming of the world, and interpreting of the world in the manner of Plato, there was an *enjoyment* different from that which the physicists of today offer us—and also the Darwinists and anti-teleologists among the workers in physiology, with their principle of the "smallest possible force" and the greatest possible stupidity. "Where man cannot find anything to see or to grasp, he has no further business"—that is certainly an imperative different from the Platonic one, but it may be the right imperative for a tough, industrious race of machinists and bridge-builders of the future, who have nothing but *rough* work to do.

There are still harmless self-observers who believe that there are "immediate certainties"; for example, "I think," or as the superstition of Schopenhauer put it, "I will"; as though knowledge here got hold of its object purely and nakedly as "the thing in itself," without any falsification on the part of either the subject or the object. But that "immediate certainty," as well as "absolute knowledge" and the "thing in itself," involve a *contradictio in adjecto*, I shall repeat a hundred times; we really ought to free ourselves from the seduction of words!

Let the people suppose that knowledge means knowing things entirely; the philosopher must say to himself: When I analyze the process that is expressed in the sentence, "I think," I find a whole series of daring assertions that would be difficult, perhaps impossible, to prove; for example, that it is *I* who think, that there must necessarily be something that thinks, that thinking is an activity and operation on the part of a being who is thought of as a cause, that there is an "ego," and, finally, that it is already determined what is to be designated by thinking—that I *know* what thinking is. For if I had not already decided within myself what it is, by what standard could I determine whether that which is just happening is not perhaps "willing" or "feeling"? In short, the assertion "I think" assumes that I *compare* my state at the present moment with other states of myself which I know, in order to determine what it is; on account of this retrospective connection with further "knowledge," it has, at any rate, no immediate certainty for me.

In place of the "immediate certainty" in which the people may believe in the case at hand, the philosopher thus finds a series of metaphysical questions presented to him, truly searching questions of the intellect; to wit: "From where do I get the concept of thinking? Why do I believe in cause and effect? What gives me the right to speak of an ego, and even of an ego as cause, and finally of an ego as the cause of thought?" Whoever ventures to answer these metaphysical questions at once by an appeal to a sort of *intuitive* perception, like the person who says, "I think, and know that this, at least, is true, actual, and certain"—will encounter a smile and two question marks from a philosopher nowadays. "Sir," the philosopher will perhaps give him to understand, "it is improbable that you are not mistaken; but why insist on the truth?"

With regard to the superstitions of logicians, I shall never tire of emphasizing a small terse fact, which these superstitious minds hate to concede—namely, that a thought comes when "it" wishes, and not when "I" wish, so that it is a falsification of the facts of the case to say that the subject "I" is the condition of the predicate "think." *It* thinks; but that this "it" is precisely the famous old "ego" is, to put it mildly, only a supposition, an assertion, and assuredly not an "immediate certainty." After all, one has even gone too far with this "it thinks"—even the "it" contains an *interpretation* of the process, and does not belong to the process itself. One infers here according to the grammatical habit: "Thinking is an activity; every activity requires an agent; consequently—"

It was pretty much according to the same schema that the older atomism sought, besides the operating "power," that lump of matter in which it resides and out of which it operates— the atom. More rigorous minds, however, learned at last to get along without this "earth-residuum," and perhaps some day we shall accustom ourselves, including the logicians, to get along without the little "it" (which is all that is left of the honest little old ego).

It is certainly not the least charm of a theory that it is refutable; it is precisely thereby that it attracts subtler minds. It seems that the hundred-times-refuted theory of a "free will" owes its persistence to this charm alone; again and again someone comes along who feels he is strong enough to refute it.

Philosophers are accustomed to speak of the will as if it were the best-known thing in the world; indeed, Schopenhauer has given us to understand that the will alone is really known to us, absolutely and completely known, without subtraction or addition. But again and again it seems to me that in this case, too, Schopenhauer only did what philosophers are in the habit of doing—he adopted a *popular prejudice* and exaggerated it. Willing seems to me to be above all something *complicated*, something that is a unit only as a word—and it is precisely in this one word that the popular prejudice lurks, which has defeated the always inadequate caution of philosophers. So let us for once be more cautious, let us be "unphilosophical": let us say that in all willing there is, first, a plurality of sensations, namely, the sensation of the state *"away from which,"* the sensation of the state *"towards which,"* the sensations of this *"from"* and *"towards"* themselves, and then also an accompanying muscular sensation, which, even without our putting into motion "arms and legs," begins its action by force of habit as soon as we "will" anything.

Therefore, just as sensations (and indeed many kinds of sensations) are to be recognized as ingredients of the will, so, secondly, should thinking also: in every act of the will there is a ruling thought—let us not imagine it possible to sever this thought from the "willing," as if any will would then remain over!

Third, the will is not only a complex of sensation and thinking, but it is above all an *affect*, and specifically the affect of the command. That which is termed "freedom of the will" is essentially the affect of superiority in relation to him who must obey: "I am free, 'he' must obey"— this consciousness is inherent in every will; and equally so the straining of the attention, the straight look that fixes itself exclusively on one aim, the unconditional evaluation that "this and nothing else is necessary now," the inward certainly that obedience will be rendered—and whatever else belongs to the position of the commander. A man who *wills* commands something within himself that renders obedience, or that he believes renders obedience.

But now let us notice what is strangest about the will—this manifold thing for which the people have only one word: inasmuch as in the given circumstances we are at the same time the commanding *and* the obeying parties, and as the obeying party we know the sensations of constraint, impulsion, pressure, resistance, and motion, which usually begin immediately after the act of will; inasmuch as, on the other hand, we are accustomed to disregard this duality, and to deceive ourselves about it by means of the synthetic concept "I," a whole series of erroneous conclusions, and consequently of false evaluations of the will itself, has become attached to the act of willing—to such a degree that he who wills believes sincerely that willing *suffices* for action. Since in the great majority of cases there has been exercise of will only when the effect of the command—that is, obedience; that is, the action—was to be *expected*, the *appearance* has translated itself into the feeling, as if there were a *necessity of effect*. In short, he who wills believes with a fair amount of certainty that will and action are somehow one; he ascribes the success, the carrying out of the willing, to the will itself, and thereby enjoys an increase of the sensation of power which accompanies all success.

"Freedom of the will"—that is the expression for the complex state of delight of the person exercising volition, who commands and at the same time identifies himself with the executor of the order—who, as such, enjoys also the triumph over obstacles, but thinks within himself that it was really his will itself that overcame them. In this way the person exercising volition adds the feelings of delight of his successful executive instruments, the useful "underwills" or under-souls—indeed, our body is but a social structure composed of many souls—to his feelings of delight as commander. *L'effet c'est moi*: what happens here is what happens in every well-constructed and happy commonwealth; namely, the governing class identifies itself with the successes of the commonwealth. In all willing it is absolutely a question of commanding and obeying, on the basis, as already said, of a social structure composed of many "souls." Hence a philosopher should claim the right to include willing as such within the sphere of morals—morals being understood as the doctrine of the relations of supremacy under which the phenomenon of "life" comes to be.

That individual philosophical concepts are not anything capricious or autonomously evolving, but grow up in connection and relationship with each other; that, however suddenly and arbitrarily they seem to appear in the history of thought, they nevertheless belong just as much to a system as all the members of the fauna of a continent—is betrayed in the end also by the fact that the most diverse philosophers keep filling in a definite fundamental scheme of possible philosophies. Under an invisible spell, they always revolve once more in the same orbit; however independent of each other they may feel themselves with their critical or systematic wills, something within them leads them, something impels them in a definite order, one after the other—to wit, the innate systematic structure and relationship of their concepts. Their thinking is, in fact, far less a discovery than a recognition, a remembering, a return and a home-coming to a remote, primordial, and inclusive household of the soul, out of which those concepts grew originally: philosophizing is to this extent a kind of atavism of the highest order. The strange family resemblance of all Indian, Greek, and German philosophizing is explained easily enough. Where there is affinity of languages, it cannot fail, owing to the common philosophy of grammar—I mean, owing to the unconscious domination and guidance by similar grammatical functions—that everything is prepared at the outset for a similar development and sequence of philosophical systems; just as the way seems barred against certain other possibilities of world-interpretation. It is highly probable that philosophers within the domain of the Ural-Altaic languages (where the concept of the subject is least developed) look otherwise "into the world," and will be found on paths of thought different from those of the Indo-Germanic peoples and the Muslims: the spell of certain grammatical functions is ultimately also the spell of *physiological* valuations and racial conditions.

So much by way of rejecting Locke's superficiality regarding the origin of ideas.

The *causa sui* is the best self-contradiction that has been conceived so far, it is a sort of rape and perversion of logic; but the extravagant pride of man has managed to entangle itself profoundly and frightfully with just this nonsense. The desire for "freedom of the will" in the superlative metaphysical sense, which still holds sway, unfortunately, in the minds of the half-educated; the desire to bear the entire and ultimate responsibility for one's actions oneself, and to absolve God, the world, ancestors, chance, and society involves nothing less than to be precisely this *causa sui* and, with more than Münchhausen's audacity, to pull oneself up into existence by the hair, out of the swamps of nothingness. Suppose someone were thus to see through the boorish simplicity of this celebrated concept of "free will" and put it out of his head altogether, I beg of him to carry his "enlightenment" a step further, and also put out of his head the contrary of this monstrous conception of "free will": I mean "unfree will," which amounts to a misuse of cause and effect. One should not wrongly reify "cause" and "effect," as the natural scientists do (and whoever, like them, now "naturalizes" in his thinking), according to the prevailing mechanical doltishness which makes the cause press and push until it "effects" its end; one should use "cause" and "effect" only as pure concepts, that is to say, as conventional fictions for the purpose of designation and communication—*not* for explanation. In the "in itself" there is nothing of "causal connections," of "necessity," or of "psychological non-freedom"; there the effect does *not* follow the cause, there is no rule of "law." It is *we* alone who have devised cause, sequence, for-each-other, relativity, constraint, number, law, freedom, motive, and purpose; and when we project and mix this symbol world into things as if it existed "in itself," we act once more as we have always acted—*mythologically*. The "unfree will" is mythology; in real life it is only a matter of *strong* and *weak* wills.

It is almost always a symptom of what is lacking in himself when a thinker senses in every "causal connection" and "psychological necessity" something of constraint, need, compulsion to obey, pressure, and unfreedom; it is suspicious to have such feelings—the person betrays himself. And in general, if I have observed correctly, the "unfreedom of the will" is regarded as a problem from two entirely opposite standpoints, but always in a profoundly *personal* manner: some will not give up their "responsibility", their belief in *themselves*, the personal right to *their* merits at any price (the vain races belong to this class). Others, on the contrary, do not wish to be answerable for anything, or blamed for anything, and owing to an inward self-contempt, seek to *lay the blame for themselves somewhere else*. The latter, when they write books, are in the habit today of taking the side of criminals; a sort of socialist pity is their most attractive disguise. And as a matter of fact, the fatalism of the weak-willed embellishes itself surprisingly when it can pose as *"la religion de la souffrance humaine"*; that is its "good taste."

Forgive me as an old philologist who cannot desist from the malice of putting his finger on bad modes of interpretation: but "nature's conformity to law," of which you physicists talk so proudly, as though—why, it exists only owing to your interpretation and bad "philology." It is no matter of fact, no "text," but rather only a naïvely humanitarian emendation and perversion of meaning, with which you make abundant concessions to the democratic instincts of the modern soul! "Everywhere equality before the law; nature is no different in that respect, no better off than we are"—a fine instance of ulterior motivation, in which the plebeian antagonism to everything privileged and autocratic as well as a second and more refined atheism are disguised once more. "Ni Dieu, ni maitre"—that is what you, too, want; and therefore "cheers for the law of nature!"—is it not so? But as said above, that is interpretation, not text; and somebody might come along who, with opposite intentions and modes of interpretation, could read out of the same "nature," and with regard to the same phenomena, rather the tyrannically inconsiderate and relentless enforcement of claims of power—an interpreter who would picture the unexceptional and unconditional aspects of all "will to power" so vividly that almost every word, even the word "tyranny" itself, would eventually seem unsuitable, or a weakening and attenuating metaphor—being too human—but he might, nevertheless, end by asserting the same about this world as you do, namely, that it has a "necessary" and "calculable" course, not because laws obtain in it, but because they are absolutely lacking, and every power draws its ultimate consequences at every moment. Supposing that this also is only interpretation—and you will be eager enough to make this objection?—well, so much the better.

O sancta simplicitas! In what strange simplification and falsification man lives! One can never cease wondering once one has acquired eyes for this marvel! How we have made everything around us clear and free and easy and simple! how we have been able to give our senses a passport to everything superficial, our thoughts a divine desire for wanton leaps and wrong inferences! how from the beginning we have contrived to retain our ignorance in order to enjoy an almost inconceivable freedom, lack of scruple and caution, heartiness, and gaiety of life—in order to enjoy life! And only on this now solid, granite foundation of ignorance could knowledge rise so far—the will to knowledge on the foundation of a far more powerful will: the will to ignorance, to the uncertain, to the untrue! Not as its opposite, but—as its refinement!

Even if language, here as elsewhere, will not get over its awkwardness, and will continue to talk of opposites where there are only degrees and many subtleties of gradation; even if the inveterate Tartuffery of morals, which now belongs to our unconquerable "flesh and blood," infects the words even of those of us who know better—here and there we understand it and laugh at the way in which precisely science at its best seeks most to keep us in this simplified, thoroughly artificial, suitably constructed and suitably falsified world—at the way in which, willy-nilly, it loves error, because, being alive, it loves life.

Independence is for the very few; it is a privilege of the strong. And whoever attempts it even with the best right but without inner constraint proves that he is probably not only strong, but also daring to the point of recklessness. He enters into a labyrinth, he multiplies a thousandfold the dangers which life brings with it in any case, not the least of which is that no one can see how and where he loses his way, becomes lonely, and is torn piecemeal by some minotaur of conscience. Supposing one like that comes to grief, this happens so far from the comprehension of men that they neither feel it nor sympathize. And he cannot go back any longer. Nor can he go back to the pity of men.

When one is young, one venerates and despises without that art of nuances which constitutes the best gain of life, and it is only fair that one has to pay dearly for having assaulted men and things in this manner with Yes and No. Everything is arranged so that the worst of tastes, the taste for the unconditional, should be cruelly fooled and abused until a man learns to put a little art into his feelings and rather to risk trying even what is artificial—as the real artists of life do.

The wrathful and reverent attitudes characteristic of youth do not seem to permit themselves any rest until they have forged men and things in such a way that these attitudes may be vented on them—after all, youth in itself has something of forgery and deception. Later, when the young soul, tortured by all kinds of disappointments, finally turns suspiciously against itself, still hot and wild, even in its suspicion and pangs of conscience—how wroth it is with itself now! how it tears itself to pieces, impatiently! how it takes revenge for its long self-delusion, just as if it had been a deliberate blindness! In this transition one punishes oneself with mistrust against one's own feelings; one tortures one's own enthusiasm with doubts; indeed, one experiences even a good conscience as a danger, as if it were a way of wrapping oneself in veils and the exhaustion of subtler honesty—and above all one takes sides, takes sides on principle, *against* "youth"—Ten years later one comprehends that all this, too—was still youth.

During the longest part of human history—so-called prehistorical times—the value or disvalue of an action was derived from its consequences. The action itself was considered as little as its origin. It was rather the way a distinction or disgrace still reaches back today from a child to its parents, in China: it was the retroactive force of success or failure that led men to think well or ill of an action. Let us call this period the *pre-moral* period of mankind: the imperative "know thyself!" was as yet unknown.

In the last ten thousand years, however, one has reached the point, step by step, in a few large regions on the earth, where it is no longer the consequences but the origin of an action that one allows to decide its value. On the whole this is a great event which involves a considerable refinement of vision and standards; it is the unconscious aftereffect of the rule of aristocratic values and the faith in "descent"—the sign of a period that one may call *moral* in the narrower sense. It involves the first attempt at self-knowledge. Instead of the consequences, the origin: indeed a reversal of perspective! Surely, a reversal achieved only after long struggles and vacillations. To be sure, a calamitous new superstition, an odd narrowness of interpretation, thus become dominant: the origin of an action was interpreted in the most definite sense as origin in an *intention*; one came to agree that the value of an action lay in the value of the intention. The intention as the whole origin and prehistory of an action—almost to the present day this prejudice dominated moral praise, blame, judgment, and philosophy on earth.

But today—shouldn't we have reached the necessity of once more resolving on a reversal and fundamental shift in values, owing to another self-examination of man, another growth in profundity? Don't we stand at the threshold of a period which should be designated negatively, to begin with, as *extra-moral*? After all, today at least we immoralists have the suspicion that the decisive value of an action lies precisely in what is *unintentional* in it, while everything about it that is intentional, everything about it that can be seen, known, "conscious," still belongs to its surface and skin—which, like every skin, betrays something but *conceals* even more. In short, we believe that the intention is merely a sign and symptom that still requires interpretation—moreover, a sign that means too much and therefore, taken by itself alone, almost nothing. We believe that morality in the traditional sense, the morality of intentions, was a prejudice, precipitate and perhaps provisional—something on the order of astrology and alchemy—but in any case something that must be overcome. The overcoming of morality, in a certain sense even the self-overcoming of morality—let this be the name for that long secret work which has been saved up for the finest and most honest, also the most malicious, consciences of today, as living touchstones of the soul.

There is no other way: the feelings of devotion, self-sacrifice for one's neighbor, the whole morality of self-denial must be questioned mercilessly and taken to court—no less than the aesthetics of "contemplation devoid of all interest" which is used today as a seductive guise for the emasculation of art, to give it a good conscience. There is too much charm and sugar in these feelings of "for others," "*not* for myself," for us not to need to become doubly suspicious at this point and to ask: "are these not perhaps—*seductions?*"

That they *please*—those who have them and those who enjoy their fruits, and also the mere spectator—this does not yet constitute an argument in their *favor* but rather invites caution. So let us be cautious.

Whatever philosophical standpoint one may adopt today, from every point of view the *erroneousness* of the world in which we think we live is the surest and firmest fact that we can lay eyes on: we find reasons upon reasons for it which would like to lure us to hypotheses concerning a deceptive principle in "the essence of things." But whoever holds our thinking itself, "the spirit," in other words, responsible for the falseness of the world—an honorable way out which is chosen by every conscious or unconscious *advocatus dei*—whoever takes this world, along with space, time, form, movement, to be falsely *inferred*—anyone like that would at least have ample reason to learn to be suspicious at long last of all thinking. Wouldn't thinking have put over on us the biggest hoax yet? And what warrant would there be that it would not continue to do what it has always done?

In all seriousness: the innocence of our thinkers is somehow touching and evokes reverence, when today they still step before consciousness with the request that it should please give them *honest* answers; for example, whether it is "real," and why it so resolutely keeps the external world at a distance, and other questions of that kind. The faith in "immediate certainties" is a *moral* naïveté that reflects honor on us philosophers; but—after all we should not be "*merely* moral" men. Apart from morality, this faith is a stupidity that reflects little honor on us. In bourgeois life ever-present suspicion may be considered a sign of "bad character" and hence belong among things imprudent; here, among us, beyond the bourgeois world and its Yes and No—what should prevent us from being imprudent and saying: a philosopher has nothing less than a *right* to "bad character," as the being who has so far always been fooled best on earth; he has a *duty* to suspicion today, to squint maliciously out of every abyss of suspicion.

Forgive me the joke of this gloomy grimace and trope; for I myself have learned long ago to think differently, to estimate differently with regard to deceiving and being deceived, and I keep in reserve at least a couple of jostles for the blind rage with which the philosophers resist being deceived. Why *not*? It is no more than a moral prejudice that truth is worth more than mere appearance; it is even the worst proved assumption there is in the world. Let at least this much be admitted: there would be no life at all if not on the basis of perspective estimates and appearances; and if, with the virtuous enthusiasm and clumsiness of some philosophers, one wanted to abolish the "apparent world" altogether—well, supposing *you* could do that, at least nothing would be left of your "truth" either. Indeed, what forces us at all to suppose that there is an essential opposition of "true" and "false"? Is it not sufficient to assume degrees of apparentness and, as it were, lighter and darker shadows and shades of appearance—different "values," to use the language of painters? Why couldn't the world *that concerns us*—be a fiction? And if somebody asked, "but to a fiction there surely belongs an author?"—couldn't one answer simply: *why*? Doesn't this "belongs" perhaps belong to the fiction, too? Is it not permitted to be a bit ironical about the subject no less than the predicate and object? Shouldn't philosophers be permitted to rise above faith in grammar? All due respect for governesses—but hasn't the time come for philosophy to renounce the faith of governesses?

O Voltaire! O humaneness! O nonsense! There is something about "truth," about the *search* for truth; and when a human being is too human about it—"*il ne cherche le vrai que pour faire le bien*"—I bet he finds nothing.

Suppose nothing else were "given" as real except our world of desires and passions, and we could not get down, or up, to any other "reality" besides the reality of our drives—for thinking is merely a relation of these drives to each other: is it not permitted to make the experiment and to ask the question whether this "given" would not be *sufficient* for also understanding on the basis of this kind of thing the so-called mechanistic (or "material") world? I mean, not as a deception, as "mere appearance," an "idea" (in the sense of Berkeley and Schopenhauer) but as holding the same rank of reality as our affect—as a more primitive form of the world of affects in which everything still lies contained in a powerful unity before it undergoes ramifications and developments in the organic process (and, as is only fair, also becomes tenderer and weaker)—as a kind of instinctive life in which all organic functions are still synthetically intertwined along with self-regulation, assimilation, nourishment, excretion, and metabolism—as a *pre-form* of life.

In the end not only is it permitted to make this experiment; the conscience of *method* demands it. Not to assume several kinds of causality until the experiment of making do with a single one has been pushed to its utmost limit (to the point of nonsense, if I may say so)—that is a moral of method which one may not shirk today—it follows "from its definition," as a mathematician would say. The question is in the end whether we really recognize the will as *efficient*, whether we believe in the causality of the will: if we do—and at bottom our faith in this is nothing less than our faith in causality itself—then we have to make the experiment of positing the causality of the will hypothetically as the only one. "Will," of course, can affect only "will"—and not "matter" (not "nerves," for example). In short, one has to risk the hypothesis whether will does not affect will wherever "effects" are recognized—and whether all mechanical occurrences are not, insofar as a force is active in them, will force, effects of will.

Suppose, finally, we succeeded in explaining our entire instinctive life as the development and ramification of *one* basic form of the will—namely, of the will to power, as *my* proposition has it; suppose all organic functions could be traced back to this will to power and one could also find in it the solution of the problem of procreation and nourishment—it is *one* problem—then one would have gained the right to determine *all* efficient force univocally as—*will to power*. The world viewed from inside, the world defined and determined according to its "intelligible character"—it would be "will to power" and nothing else.

What happened most recently in the broad daylight of modern times in the case of the French Revolution—that gruesome farce which, considered closely, was quite superfluous, though noble and enthusiastic spectators from all over Europe contemplated it from a distance and interpreted it according to their own indignations and enthusiasms for so long, and so passionately, that *the text finally disappeared under the interpretation*—could happen once more as a noble posterity might misunderstand the whole past and in that way alone make it tolerable to look at.

Or rather: isn't this what has happened even now? haven't we ourselves been this "noble posterity"? And isn't now precisely the moment when, insofar as we comprehend this, it is all over?

Nobody is very likely to consider a doctrine true merely because it makes people happy or virtuous—except perhaps the lovely "idealists" who become effusive about the good, the true, and the beautiful and allow all kinds of motley, clumsy, and benevolent desiderata to swim around in utter confusion in their pond. Happiness and virtue are no arguments. But people like to forget—even sober spirits—that making unhappy and evil are no counter-arguments. Something might be true while being harmful and dangerous in the highest degree. Indeed, it might be a basic characteristic of existence that those who would know it completely would perish, in which case the strength of a spirit should be measured according to how much of the "truth" one could still barely endure—or to put it more clearly, to what degree one would *require* it to be thinned down, shrouded, sweetened, blunted, falsified.

But there is no doubt at all that the evil and unhappy are more favored when it comes to the discovery of certain *parts* of truth, and that the probability of their success here is greater—not to speak of the evil who are happy, a species the moralists bury in silence. Perhaps hardness and cunning furnish more favorable conditions for the origin of the strong, independent spirit and philosopher than that gentle, fine, conciliatory good-naturedness and art of taking things lightly which people prize, and prize rightly, in a scholar. Assuming first of all that the concept "philosopher" is not restricted to the philosopher who writes books—or makes books of *his* philosophy.

The ancient theological problem of "faith" and "knowledge" —or, more clearly, of instinct and reason—in other words, the question whether regarding the valuation of things instinct deserves more authority than rationality, which wants us to evaluate and act in accordance with reasons, with a "why?"—in other words, in accordance with expedience and utility—this is still the ancient moral problem that first emerged in the person of Socrates and divided thinking people long before Christianity. Socrates himself, to be sure, with the taste of his talent—that of a superior dialectician—had initially sided with reason; and in fact, what did he do his life long but laugh at the awkward incapacity of noble Athenians who, like all noble men, were men of instinct and never could give sufficient information about the reasons for their actions? In the end, however, privately and secretly, he laughed at himself, too: in himself he found, before his subtle conscience and self-examination, the same difficulty and incapacity. But is that any reason, he encouraged himself, for giving up the instincts? One has to see to it that they as well as reason receive their due—one must follow the instincts but persuade reason to assist them with good reasons. This was the real *falseness* of that great ironic, so rich in secrets; he got his conscience to be satisfied with a kind of self-trickery: at bottom, he had seen through the irrational element in moral judgments.

Plato, more innocent in such matters and lacking the craftiness of the plebeian, wanted to employ all his strength—the greatest strength any philosopher so far has had at his disposal—to prove to himself that reason and instinct of themselves tend toward one goal, the good, "God." And since Plato, all theologians and philosophers are on the same track—that is, in moral matters it has so far been instinct, or what the Christians call "faith," or "the herd," as I put it, that has triumphed. Perhaps Descartes should be excepted, as the father of rationalism (and hence the grandfather of the Revolution) who conceded authority to reason alone: but reason is merely an instrument, and Descartes was superficial.

Whoever has traced the history of an individual science finds a clue in its development for understanding the most ancient and common processes of all "knowledge and cognition." There as here it is the rash hypotheses, the fictions, the good dumb will to "believe," the lack of mistrust and patience that are developed first; our senses learn only late, and never learn entirely, to be subtle, faithful, and cautious organs of cognition. Our eye finds it more comfortable to respond to a given stimulus by reproducing once more an image that it has produced many times before, instead of registering what is different and new in an impression. The latter would require more strength, more "morality." Hearing something new is embarrassing and difficult for the ear; foreign music we do not hear well. When we hear another language we try involuntarily to form the sounds we hear into words that sound more familiar and more like home to us: thus the German, for example, transformed *arcubalista*, when he heard that, into *Armbrust*. What is new finds our senses, too, hostile and reluctant; and even in the "simplest" processes of sensation the affects dominate, such as fear, love, hatred, including the passive affects of laziness.

Just as little as a reader today reads all of the individual words (let alone syllables) on a page—rather he picks about five words at random out of twenty and "guesses" at the meaning that probably belongs to these five words—just as little do we see a tree exactly and completely with reference to leaves, twigs, color, and form; it is so very much easier for us simply to improvise some approximation of a tree. Even in the midst of the strangest experiences we still do the same: we make up the major part of the experience and can scarcely be forced *not* to contemplate some event as its "inventors." All this means: basically and from time immemorial we are—*accustomed to lying*. Or to put it more virtuously and hypocritically, in short, more pleasantly: one is much more of an artist than one knows.

In an animated conversation I often see the face of the person with whom I am talking so clearly and so subtly determined in accordance with the thought he expresses, or that I believe has been produced in him, that this degree of clarity far surpasses my powers of vision: so the subtle shades of the play of the muscles and the expression of the eyes *must* have been made up by me. Probably the person made an altogether different face, or none at all.

What, in the end, is common?
Words are acoustical signs for concepts; concepts, however, are more or less definite image signs for often recurring and associated sensations, for groups of sensations. To understand one another, it is not enough that one use the same words; one also has to use the same words for the same species of inner experiences; in the end one has to have one's experience in *common*.

Therefore the human beings of *one* people understand one another better than those belonging to different peoples even if they employ the same language; or rather when human beings have long lived together under similar conditions (of climate, soil, danger, needs, and work), what *results* from this is people who "understand one another"—a people. In all souls an equal number of often recurring experiences has come to be predominant over experiences that come more rarely: on the basis of the former one understands the other, quickly and ever more quickly—the history of language is the history of a process of abbreviation—and on the basis of such quick understanding one associates, ever more closely.

The greater the danger is, the greater is the need to reach agreement quickly and easily about what must be done; not misunderstanding one another in times of danger is what human beings simply cannot do without in their relations. In every friendship or love affair one still makes this test: nothing of that sort can endure once one discovers that one's partner associates different feelings, intentions, nuances, desires, and fears with the same words. (Fear of the "eternal misunderstanding"—that is the benevolent genius which so often keeps persons of different sex from rash attachments to which their senses and hearts prompt them—this and *not* some Schopenhauerian "genius of the species"!)

Which group of sensations is aroused, expresses itself, and issues commands in a soul most quickly, is decisive for the whole order of rank of its values and ultimately determines its table of goods. The values of a human being betray something of the *structure* of his soul and where it finds its conditions of life, its true need.

Assuming next that need has ever brought close to one another only such human beings as could suggest with similar signs similar requirements and experiences, it would follow on the whole that easy communicability of need—which in the last analysis means the experience of merely average and *common* experiences—must have been the most powerful of all powers at whose disposal man has been so far. The human beings who are more similar, more ordinary, have had, and always have, an advantage; those more select, subtle, strange, and difficult to understand, easily remain alone, succumb to accidents, being isolated, and rarely propagate. One must invoke tremendous counter-forces in order to cross this natural, all too natural *progressus in simile*, the continual development of man toward the similar, ordinary, average, herd-like—*common!*

Max Weber

The authors in this volume have all, so far, taken a fairly critical stance towards what we call "modernity." This is not to say that there was lack of significantly self-confident articulations or positivistic spirit driving liberal democracy in the nineteenth century. Yet it does suggest that in an age of increasing materialism and religious crisis, those who felt that certain dimensions of the human experience were being de-emphasized, denuded, if not coerced into silence, felt themselves more and more relegated to positions of social marginality. In this circumstance, they were given to harsher evaluations of their social environment. In some sense, German thought may be said to have taken on this role with regard to the thought of Western Europe, chiefly that of Britain and France.

Max Weber (1864–1920) was a professional academic who reached his maturity in the decades following the unification of the German nation in 1870. He was well situated within the established institutions of the time. Yet he, like other Germans raised in close contact with idealist traditions, felt that the overdetermined rationalism of French positivism and British political economy left little room for proper understanding of historical context. History, as opposed to logic, was where more spiritual manifestations of human experience were to be found. Weber's concern for the role of context in history may be viewed as his response to the threat posed to German cultural identity by the dominance of materialism among the British and French.

Weber was in no sense marginalized as an individual, although his voice may be read as characteristic of liberal disillusionment in Germany around the turn of the century. His life and work, like those of so many great writers, gave expression to a spiritual conflict shared by many of his artistic and intellectual contemporaries. His most well-known work, *The Protestant Ethic and the Spirit of Capitalism* (1904–1905), bears this out strikingly. In a move that seeks to recuperate—from vulgar Marxists as well as conventional economic historians—some sense of the role of intangible, spiritual concerns in the history of mankind, Weber takes great care to isolate the probable effect that strong Calvinist convictions had on certain practices that would have by themselves greatly facilitated what we now consider "capitalist" behavior. Capitalism proceeded by virtue of the expansion of a mentality based on calculation and standardization, an ethos which Weber argued was similar to that of some early Protestant sects. Weber tried to show that while this spiritual boost played an important role in early capitalist development, the modern age was experiencing the relentless encroachment of the rationalizing spirit into social realms regulated according to different patterns. The very need for maintaining and directing such a rationalization for extensive administrative organizations, such as ministries, bureaus, and corporate hierarchies, suggests the problem.

A great triumph in execution for the place of "culture" in historical analysis (for Weber, culture was all that which could not be reduced to economic or material bases), it also served as a tragic commentary on the very processes threatening those nontangible aspects of civilization that give life meaning. For though religion had helped to frame the ethical basis for capitalism, the materialism as advocated by nineteenth-century positivists was becoming less and less a choice and more and more of a necessity.

Towards the end of his life, Weber expressed little hope that the processes of rationalization inherent in the capitalist enterprise, and the corresponding explosion of bureaucracy that accompanied the functions of the modern state, would leave much room for either the sort of faith that had allowed capitalism to flourish in the first place, or the liberties that had motivated so many to challenge the authority of monarchical government in the name of freedom for all.

It is indeed, in Weber's view, by two cruel twists that modernity turns back upon itself: the material necessities of maintaining a growing economy themselves turn against absolute faith, and the machinery of government required to manage and serve masses of free and equal individuals itself works towards the diminishment of those individual freedoms it was established to guarantee. The situation in which capitalist countries found themselves was one of being trapped in what Weber called an "iron cage," in which the demands of the capitalist system had become so overwhelming that individuals could no longer have any choice as to whether or not they would accept its rationalizing ethos.

MAX WEBER
(1904–05)

The Protestant Ethic
and the Spirit of Capitalism

AUTHOR'S INTRODUCTION

A product of modern European civilization, studying any problem of universal history, is
bound to ask himself to what combination of circumstances the fact should be attributed that
in Western civilization, and in Western civilization only, cultural phenomena have appeared
which (as we like to think) lie in a line of development having *universal* significance and value.

Only in the West does science exist at a stage of development which we recognize to-day
as valid. Empirical knowledge, reflection on problems of the cosmos and of life, philosophical
and theological wisdom of the most profound sort, are not confined to it, though in the case of
the last the full development of a systematic theology must be credited to Christianity under
the influence of Hellenism, since there were only fragments in Islam and in a few Indian sects.
In short, knowledge and observation of great refinement have existed elsewhere, above all in
India, China, Babylonia, Egypt. But in Babylonia and elsewhere astronomy lacked—which
makes its development all the more astounding—the mathematical foundation which it first
received from the Greeks. The Indian geometry had no rational proof; that was another product of the Greek intellect, also the creator of mechanics and physics. The Indian natural
sciences, though well developed in observation, lacked the method of experiment, which was,
apart from beginnings in antiquity, essentially a product of the Renaissance, as was the modern
laboratory. Hence medicine, especially in India, though highly developed in empirical tech-

Reprint of pp. 13–77, 153–83, trans. by Talcott Parsons (New York: Charles Scribner's Sons, 1958),
by permission of Routledge, Inc.

nique, lacked a biological and particularly a biochemical foundation. A rational chemistry has been absent from all areas of culture except the West.

The highly developed historical scholarship of China did not have the method of Thucydides. Machiavelli, it is true, had predecessors in India; but all Indian political thought was lacking in a systematic method comparable to that of Aristotle, and, indeed, in the possession of rational concepts. Not all the anticipations in India (School of Mimamsa), nor the extensive codification especially in the Near East, nor all the Indian and other books of law, had the strictly systematic forms of thought, so essential to a rational jurisprudence, of the Roman law and of the Western law under its influence. A structure like the canon law is known only to the West.

A similar statement is true of art. The musical ear of other peoples has probably been even more sensitively developed than our own, certainly not less so. Polyphonic music of various kinds has been widely distributed over the earth. The co-operation of a number of instruments and also the singing of parts have existed elsewhere. All our rational tone intervals have been known and calculated. But rational harmonious music, both counterpoint and harmony, formation of the tone material on the basis of three triads with the harmonic third; our chromatics and enharmonics, not interpreted in terms of space, but, since the Renaissance, of harmony; our orchestra, with its string quartet as a nucleus, and the organization of ensembles of wind instruments; our bass accompaniment; our system of notation, which has made possible the composition and production of modern musical works, and thus their very survival; our sonatas, symphonies, operas; and finally, as means to all these, our fundamental instruments, the organ, piano, violin, etc.; all these things are known only in the Occident, although programme music, tone poetry, alteration of tones and chromatics, have existed in various musical traditions as means of expression.

In architecture, pointed arches have been used elsewhere as a means of decoration, in antiquity and in Asia; presumably the combination of pointed arch and cross-arched vault was not unknown in the Orient. But the rational use of the Gothic vault as a means of distributing pressure and of roofing spaces of all forms, and above all as the constructive principle of great monumental buildings and the foundation of a *style* extending to sculpture and painting, such as that created by our Middle Ages, does not occur elsewhere. The technical basis of our architecture came from the Orient. But the Orient lacked that solution of the problem of the dome and that type of classic rationalization of all art—in painting by the rational utilization of lines and spatial perspective—which the Renaissance created for us. There was printing in China. But a printed literature, designed *only* for print and only possible through it, and, above all, the Press and periodicals, have appeared only in the Occident. Institutions of higher education of all possible types, even some superficially similar to our universities, or at least academies, have existed (China, Islam). But a rational, systematic, and specialized pursuit of science, with trained and specialized personnel, has only existed in the West in a sense at all approaching its present dominant place in our culture. Above all is this true of the trained official, the pillar of both the modern State and of the economic life of the West. He forms a type of which there have heretofore only been suggestions, which have never remotely approached its present importance for the social order. Of course the official, even the specialized official, is a very old constituent of the most various societies. But no country and no age has ever experienced, in the same sense as the modern Occident, the absolute and complete dependence of its whole existence, of the political, technical, and economic conditions of its life, on a specially trained *organization* of officials. The most important functions of the everyday life of society have come to be in the hands of technically, commercially, and above all legally trained government officials.

Organization of political and social groups in feudal classes has been common. But even the feudal state of *rex et regnum* in the Western sense has only been known to our culture. Even more are parliaments of periodically elected representatives, with government by demagogues and party leaders as ministers responsible to the parliaments, peculiar to us, although there have, of course, been parties, in the sense of organizations for exerting influence and gaining control of political power, all over the world. In fact, the State itself, in the sense of a political association with a rational, written constitution, rationally ordained law, and an administration bound to rational rules or laws, administered by trained officials, is known, in this combination of characteristics, only in the Occident, despite all other approaches to it.

And the same is true of the most fateful force in our modern life, capitalism. The impulse to acquisition, pursuit of gain, of money, of the greatest possible amount of money, has in itself nothing to do with capitalism. This impulse exists and has existed among waiters, physicians, coachmen, artists, prostitutes, dishonest officials, soldiers, nobles, crusaders, gamblers, and beggars. One may say that it has been common to all sorts and conditions of men at all times and in all countries of the earth, wherever the objective possibility of it is or has been given. It should be taught in the kindergarten of cultural history that this naive idea of capitalism must be given up once and for all. Unlimited greed for gain is not in the least identical with capitalism, and is still less its spirit. Capitalism *may* even be identical with the restraint, or at least a rotational tempering, of this irrational impulse. But capitalism is identical with the pursuit of profit, and forever *renewed* profit, by means of continuous, rational, capitalistic enterprise. For it must be so: in a wholly capitalistic order of society, an individual capitalistic enterprise which did not take advantage of its opportunities for profit-making would be doomed to extinction.

Let us now define our terms somewhat more carefully than is generally done. We will define a capitalistic economic action as one which rests on the expectation of profit by the utilization of opportunities for exchange, that is on (formally) peaceful chances of profit. Acquisition by force (formally and actually) follows its own particular laws, and it is not expedient, however little one can forbid this, to place it in the same category with action which is, in the last analysis, oriented to profits from exchange. Where capitalistic acquisition is rationally pursued, the corresponding action is adjusted to calculations in terms of capital. This means that the action is adapted to a systematic utilization of goods or personal services as means of acquisition in such a way that, at the close of a business period, the balance of the enterprise in money assets (or, in the case of a continuous enterprise, the periodically estimated money value of assets) exceeds the capital, i.e., the estimated value of the material means of production used for acquisition in exchange. It makes no difference whether it involves a quantity of goods entrusted *in natura* to a travelling merchant, the proceeds of which may consist in other goods *in natura* acquired by trade, or whether it involves a manufacturing enterprise, the assets of which consist of buildings, machinery, cash, raw materials, partly and wholly manufactured goods, which are balanced against liabilities. The important fact is always that a calculation of capital in terms of money is made, whether by modern book-keeping methods or in any other way, however primitive and crude. Everything is done in terms of balances: at the beginning of the enterprise an initial balance, before every individual decision a calculation to ascertain its probable profitableness, and at the end a final balance to ascertain how much profit has been made. For instance, the initial balance of a *commenda* transaction would determine an agreed money value of the assets put into it (so far as they were not in money form already), and a final balance would form the estimate on which to base the distribution of profit and loss at the end. So far as the transactions are rational, calculation underlies every single action of the partners. That a really accurate calculation or estimate may not exist, that the procedure is pure guess-work, or simply traditional and conventional, happens even to-day in every form of capitalistic enterprise where the circumstances do not demand strict accuracy. But these are points affecting only the *degree* of rationality of capitalistic acquisition.

For the purpose of this conception all that matters is that an actual adaptation of economic action to a comparison of money income with money expenses takes place, no matter how primitive the form. Now in this sense capitalism and capitalistic enterprises, even with a considerable rationalization of capitalistic calculation, have existed in all civilized countries of the earth, so far as economic documents permit us to judge. In China, India, Babylon, Egypt, Mediterranean antiquity, and the Middle Ages, as well as in modern times. These were not merely isolated ventures, but economic enterprises which were entirely dependent on the continual renewal of capitalistic undertakings, and even continuous operations. However, trade especially was for a long time not continuous like our own, but consisted essentially in a series of individual undertakings. Only gradually did the activities of even the large merchants acquire an inner cohesion (with branch organizations, etc.). In any case, the capitalistic enterprise and the capitalistic entrepreneur, not only as occasional but as regular entrepreneurs, are very old and were very widespread.

Now, however, the Occident has developed capitalism both to a quantitative extent, and (carrying this quantitative development) in types, forms, and directions which have never existed elsewhere. All over the world there have been merchants, wholesale and retail, local and engaged in foreign trade. Loans of all kinds have been made, and there have been banks with the most various functions, at least comparable to ours of, say, the sixteenth century. . . . Whenever money finances of public bodies have existed, money-lenders have appeared, as in Babylon, Hellas, India, China, Rome. They have financed wars and piracy, contracts and building operations of all sorts. In overseas policy they have functioned as colonial entrepreneurs, as planters with slaves, or directly or indirectly forced labour, and have farmed domains, offices, and, above all, taxes. They have financed party leaders in elections and *condottieri* in civil wars. And, finally, they have been speculators in chances for pecuniary gain of all kinds. This kind of entrepreneur, the capitalistic adventurer, has existed everywhere. With the exception of trade and credit and banking transactions, their activities were predominantly of an irrational and speculative character, or directed to acquisition by force, above all the acquisition of booty, whether directly in war or in the form of continuous fiscal booty by exploitation of subjects.

The capitalism of promoters, large-scale speculators, concession hunters, and much modern financial capitalism even in peace time, but, above all, the capitalism especially concerned with exploiting wars, bears this stamp even in modern Western countries, and some, but only some, parts of large-scale international trade are closely related to it, to-day as always.

But in modern times the Occident has developed, in addition to this, a very different form of capitalism which has appeared nowhere else: the rational capitalistic organization of (formally) free labour. Only suggestions of it are found elsewhere. Even the organization of unfree labour reached a considerable degree of rationality only on plantations and to a very limited extent in the *Ergasteria* of antiquity. In the manors, manorial workshops, and domestic industries on estates with serf labour it was probably somewhat less developed. Even real domestic industries with free labour have definitely been proved to have existed in only a few isolated cases outside the Occident. The frequent use of day labourers led in a very few cases—especially State monopolies, which are, however, very different from modern industrial organization—to manufacturing organizations, but never to a rational organization of apprenticeship in the handicrafts like that of our Middle Ages.

Rational industrial organization, attuned to a regular market, and neither to political nor irrationally speculative opportunities for profit, is not, however, the only peculiarity of Western capitalism. The modern rational organization of the capitalistic enterprise would not have been possible without two other important factors in its development: the separation of business from the household, which completely dominates modern economic life, and closely connected with it, rational book-keeping. A spatial separation of places of work from those of residence exists elsewhere, as in the Oriental bazaar and in the *ergasteria* of other cultures. The development of capitalistic associations with their own accounts is also found in the Far East, the Near East, and in antiquity. But compared to the modern independence of business enterprises, those are only small beginnings. The reason for this was particularly that the indispensable requisites for this independence, our rational business book-keeping and our legal separation of corporate from personal property, were entirely lacking, or had only begun to develop. The tendency everywhere else was for acquisitive enterprises to arise as parts of a royal or manorial *household* (of the *oikos*), which is, as Rodbertus has perceived, with all its superficial similarity, a fundamentally different, even opposite, development.

However, all these peculiarities of Western capitalism have derived their significance in the last analysis only from their association with the capitalistic organization of labour. Even what is generally called commercialization, the development of negotiable securities and the rationalization of speculation, the exchanges, etc., is connected with it. For without the rational capitalistic organization of labour, all this, so far as it was possible at all, would have nothing like the same significance, above all for the social structure and all the specific problems of the modern Occident connected with it. Exact calculation—the basis of everything else—is only possible on a basis of free labour.

And just as, or rather because, the world has known no rational organization of labour outside the modern Occident, it has known no rational socialism. Of course, there has been civic economy, a civic food-supply policy, mercantilism and welfare policies of princes, rationing, regulation of economic life, protectionism, and *laissez-faire* theories (as in China). The world has also known socialistic and communistic experiments of various sorts: family, religious, or military communism, State socialism (in Egypt), monopolistic cartels, and consumers' organizations. But although there have everywhere been civic market privileges, companies, guilds, and all sorts of legal differences between town and country, the concept of the citizen has not existed outside the Occident, and that of the bourgeoisie outside the modern Occident. Similarly, the proletariat as a class could not exist, because there was no rational organization of free labour under regular discipline. Class struggles between creditor and debtor classes; landowners and the landless, serfs, or tenants; trading interests and consumers or landlords, have existed everywhere in various combinations. But even the Western mediaeval struggles between putters-out and their workers exist elsewhere only in beginnings. The modern conflict of the large-scale industrial entrepreneur and free-wage labourers was entirely lacking. And thus there could be no such problems as those of socialism.

Hence in a universal history of culture the central problem for us is not, in the last analysis, even from a purely economic view-point, the development of capitalistic activity as such, differing in different cultures only in form: the adventurer type, or capitalism in trade, war, politics, or administration as sources of gain. It is rather the origin of this sober bourgeois capitalism with its rational organization of free labour. Or in terms of cultural history, the problem is that of the origin of the Western bourgeois class and of its peculiarities, a problem which is certainly closely connected with that of the origin of the capitalistic organization of labour, but is not quite the same thing. For the bourgeois as a class existed prior to the development of the peculiar modern form of capitalism, though, it is true, only in the Western hemisphere.

Now the peculiar modern Western form of capitalism has been, at first sight, strongly influenced by the development of technical possibilities. Its rationality is to-day essentially dependent on the calculability of the most important technical factors. But this means fundamentally that it is dependent on the peculiarities of modern science, especially the natural sciences based on mathematics and exact and rational experiment. On the other hand, the development of these sciences and of the technique resting upon them now receives important stimulation from these capitalistic interests in its practical economic application. It is true that the origin of Western science cannot be attributed to such interests. Calculation, even with decimals, and algebra have been carried on in India, where the decimal system was invented. But it was only made use of by developing capitalism in the West, while in India it led to no modern arithmetic or book-keeping. Neither was the origin of mathematics and mechanics determined by capitalistic interests. But the *technical* utilization of scientific knowledge, so important for the living conditions of the mass of people, was certainly encouraged by economic considerations, which were extremely favourable to it in the Occident. But this encouragement was derived from the peculiarities of the social structure of the Occident. We must hence ask, from *what* parts of that structure was it derived, since not all of them have been of equal importance?

Among those of undoubted importance are the rational structures of law and of administration. For modern rational capitalism has need, not only of the technical means of production, but of a calculable legal system and of administration in terms of formal rules. Without it adventurous and speculative trading capitalism and all sorts of politically determined capitalisms are possible, but no rational enterprise under individual initiative, with fixed capital and certainty of calculations. Such a legal system and such administration have been available for economic activity in a comparative state of legal and formalistic perfection only in the Occident. We must hence inquire where that law came from. Among other circumstances, capitalistic interests have in turn undoubtedly also helped, but by no means alone nor even principally, to prepare the way for the predominance in law and administration of a class of jurists specially trained in rational law. But these interests did not themselves create that law. Quite different forces were at work in this development. And why did not the capitalistic interests do the same in China or India? Why did not the scientific, the artistic, the political, or the economic development there enter upon that path of rationalization which is peculiar to the Occident?

For in all the above cases it is a question of the specific and peculiar rationalism of Western culture. Now by this term very different things may be understood, as the following discussion will repeatedly show. There is, for example, rationalization of mystical contemplation, that is of an attitude which, viewed from other departments of life, is specifically irrational, just as much as there are rationalizations of economic life, of technique, of scientific research, of military training, of law and administration. Furthermore, each one of these fields may be rationalized in terms of very different ultimate values and ends, and what is rational from one point of view may well be irrational from another. Hence rationalizations of the most varied character have existed in various departments of life and in all areas of culture. To characterize their differences from the view-point of cultural history it is necessary to know what departments are rationalized, and in what direction. It is hence our first concern to work out and to explain genetically the special peculiarity of Occidental rationalism, and within this field that of the modern Occidental form. Every such attempt at explanation must, recognizing the fundamental importance of the economic factor, above all take account of the economic conditions. But at the same time the opposite correlation must not be left out of consideration. For though the development of economic rationalism is partly dependent on rational technique and law, it is at the same time determined by the ability and disposition of men to adopt certain types of practical rational conduct. When these types have been obstructed by spiritual obstacles, the development of rational economic conduct has also met serious inner resistance. The magical and religious forces, and the ethical ideas of duty based upon them, have in the past always been among the most important formative influences on conduct. In the studies collected here we shall be concerned with these forces.

Two older essays have been placed at the beginning which attempt, at one important point, to approach the side of the problem which is generally most difficult to grasp: the influence of certain religious ideas on the development of an economic spirit, or the *ethos* of an economic system. In this case we are dealing with the connection of the spirit of modern economic life with the rational ethics of ascetic Protestantism. Thus we treat here only one side of the causal chain. The later studies on the Economic Ethics of the World Religions attempt, in the form of a survey of the relations of the most important religions to economic life and to the social stratification of their environment, to follow out both causal relationships, so far as it is necessary in order to find points of comparison with the Occidental development. For only in this way is it possible to attempt a causal evaluation of those elements of the economic ethics of the Western religions which differentiate them from others, with a hope of attaining even a tolerable degree of approximation. Hence these studies do not claim to be complete analyses of cultures, however brief. On the contrary, in every culture they quite deliberately emphasize the elements in which it differs from Western civilization. They are, hence, definitely oriented to the problems which seem important for the understanding of Western culture from *this* view-point. With our object in view, any other procedure did not seem possible. But to avoid misunderstanding we must here lay special emphasis on the limitation of our purpose.

In another respect the uninitiated at least must be warned against exaggerating the importance of these investigations. The Sinologist, the Indologist, the Semitist, or the Egyptologist, will of course find no facts unknown to him. We only hope that he will find nothing definitely wrong in points that are essential. How far it has been possible to come as near this ideal as a non-specialist is able to do, the author cannot know. It is quite evident that anyone who is forced to rely on translations, and furthermore on the use and evaluation of monumental, documentary, or literary sources, has to rely himself on a specialist literature which is often highly controversial, and the merits of which he is unable to judge accurately. Such a writer must make modest claims for the value of his work. All the more so since the number of available translations of real sources (that is, inscriptions and documents) is, especially for China, still very small in comparison with what exists and is important. From all this follows the definitely provisional character of these studies, and especially of the parts dealing with Asia. Only the specialist is entitled to a final judgment. And, naturally, it is only because expert studies with this special purpose and from this particular view-point have not hitherto been made, that the present ones have been written at all. They are destined to be superseded in a much more important sense than this can be said, as it can be, of all scientific work. But however objectionable it may be, such trespassing on other special fields cannot be avoided in comparative work. But one must take the consequences by resigning oneself to considerable doubts regarding the degree of one's success.

Fashion and the zeal of the *literati* would have us think that the specialist can to-day be spared, or degraded to a position subordinate to that of the seer. Almost all sciences owe something to dilettantes, often very valuable view-points. But dilettantism as a leading principle would be the end of science. He who yearns for seeing should go to the cinema, though it will be offered to him copiously to-day in literary form in the present field of investigation also. Nothing is farther from the intent of these thoroughly serious studies than such an attitude. And, I might add, whoever wants a sermon should go to a conventicle. The question of the relative value of the cultures which are compared here will not receive a single word. It is true that the path of human destiny cannot but appall him who surveys a section of it. But he will do well to keep his small personal commentaries to himself, as one does at the sight of the sea or of majestic mountains, unless he knows himself to be called and gifted to give them expression in artistic or prophetic form. In most other cases the voluminous talk about intuition does nothing but conceal a lack of perspective toward the object, which merits the same judgment as a similar lack of perspective toward men.

Some justification is needed for the fact that ethnographical material has not been utilized to anything like the extent which the value of its contributions naturally demands in any really thorough investigation, especially of Asiatic religions. This limitation has not only been imposed because human powers of work are restricted. This omission has also seemed to be permissible because we are here necessarily dealing with the religious ethics of the classes which were the culture-bearers of their respective countries. We are concerned with the influence which *their* conduct has had. Now it is quite true that this can only be completely known in all its details when the facts from ethnography and folk-lore have been compared with it. Hence we must expressly admit and emphasize that this is a gap to which the ethnographer will legitimately object. I hope to contribute something to the closing of this gap in a systematic study of the Sociology of Religion. But such an undertaking would have transcended the limits of this investigation with its closely circumscribed purpose. It has been necessary to be content with bringing out the points of comparison with our Occidental religions as well as possible.

Finally, we may make a reference to the *anthropological* side of the problem. When we find again and again that, even in departments of life apparently mutually independent, certain types of rationalization have developed in the Occident, and only there, it would be natural to suspect that the most important reason lay in differences of heredity. The author admits that he is inclined to think the importance of biological heredity very great. But in spite of the notable achievements of anthropological research, I see up to the present no way of exactly or even approximately measuring either the extent or, above all, the form of its influence on the development investigated here. It must be one of the tasks of sociological and historical investigation first to analyse all the influences and causal relationships which can satisfactorily be explained in terms of reactions to environmental conditions. Only then, and when comparative racial neurology and psychology shall have progressed beyond their present and in many ways very promising beginnings, can we hope for even the probability of a satisfactory answer to that problem. In the meantime that condition seems to me not to exist, and an appeal to heredity would therefore involve a premature renunciation of the possibility of knowledge attainable now, and would shift the problem to factors (at present) still unknown.

CHAPTER I
Religious Affiliation and Social Stratification

A glance at the occupational statistics of any country of mixed religious composition brings to light with remarkable frequency a situation which has several times provoked discussion in the Catholic press and literature, and in Catholic congresses in Germany, namely, the fact that business leaders and owners of capital, as well as the higher grades of skilled labour, and even more the higher technically and commercially trained personnel of modern enterprises, are overwhelmingly Protestant. This is true not only in cases where the difference in religion coincides with one of nationality, and thus of cultural development, as in Eastern Germany between Germans and Poles. The same thing is shown in the figures of religious affiliation almost wherever capitalism, at the time of its great expansion, has had a free hand to alter the social distribution of the population in accordance with its needs, and to determine its occupational structure. The more freedom it has had, the more clearly is the effect shown. It is true that the greater relative participation of Protestants in the ownership of capital, in management, and the upper ranks of labour in great modern industrial and commercial enterprises, may in part be explained in terms of historical circumstances which extend far back into the past, and in which religious affiliation is not a cause of the economic conditions, but to a certain extent appears to be a result of them. Participation in the above economic functions usually involves some previous ownership of capital, and generally an expensive education; often both. These are to-day largely dependent on the possession of inherited wealth, or at least on a certain degree of material well-being. A number of those sections of the old Empire which were most highly developed economically and most favoured by natural resources and situation, in particular a majority of the wealthy towns, went over to Protestantism in the sixteenth century. The results of that circumstance favour the Protestants even to-day in their struggle for economic existence. There arises thus the historical question: why were the districts of highest economic development at the same time particularly favourable to a revolution in the Church? The answer is by no means so simple as one might think.

The emancipation from economic traditionalism appears, no doubt, to be a factor which would greatly strengthen the tendency to doubt the sanctity of the religious tradition, as of all traditional authorities. But it is necessary to note, what has often been forgotten, that the Reformation meant not the elimination of the Church's control over everyday life, but rather the substitution of a new form of control for the previous one. It meant the repudiation of a control which was very lax, at that time scarcely perceptible in practice, and hardly more than formal, in favour of a regulation of the whole of conduct which, penetrating to all departments of private and public life, was infinitely burdensome and earnestly enforced. The rule of the Catholic Church, "punishing the heretic, but indulgent to the sinner", as it was in the past even more than to-day, is now tolerated by peoples of thoroughly modern economic character, and was borne by the richest and economically most advanced peoples on earth at about the turn of the fifteenth century. The rule of Calvinism, on the other hand, as it was enforced in the sixteenth century in Geneva and in Scotland, at the turn of the sixteenth and seventeenth centuries in large parts of the Netherlands, in the seventeenth in New England, and for a time in England itself, would be for us the most absolutely unbearable form of ecclesiastical control of the individual which could possibly exist. That was exactly what large numbers of the old commercial aristocracy of those times, in Geneva as well as in Holland and England, felt about it. And what the reformers complained of in those areas of high economic development was not too much supervision of life on the part of the Church, but too little. Now how does it happen that at that time those countries which were most advanced economically, and within them the rising bourgeois middle classes, not only failed to resist this unexampled tyranny of Puritanism, but even developed a heroism in its defence? For bourgeois classes as such have seldom before and never since displayed heroism. It was "the last of our heroisms", as Carlyle, not without reason, has said.

But further, and especially important: it may be, as has been claimed, that the greater participation of Protestants in the positions of ownership and management in modern economic life may to-day be understood, in part at least, simply as a result of the greater material wealth they have inherited. But there are certain other phenomena which cannot be explained in the same way. Thus, to mention only a few facts: there is a great difference discoverable in Baden, in Bavaria, in Hungary, in the type of higher education which Catholic parents, as opposed to Protestant, give their children. That the percentage of Catholics among the students and graduates of higher educational institutions in general lags behind their proportion of the total population, may, to be sure, be largely explicable in terms of inherited differences of wealth. But among the Catholic graduates themselves the percentage of those graduating from the institutions preparing, in particular, for technical studies and industrial and commercial occupations, but in general from those preparing for middle-class business life, lags still farther behind the percentage of Protestants. On the other hand, Catholics prefer the sort of training which the humanistic Gymnasium affords. That is a circumstance to which the above explanation does not apply, but which, on the contrary, is one reason why so few Catholics are engaged in capitalistic enterprise.

Even more striking is a fact which partly explains the smaller proportion of Catholics among the skilled labourers of modern industry. It is well known that the factory has taken its skilled labour to a large extent from young men in the handicrafts; but this is much more true of Protestant than of Catholic journeymen. Among journeymen, in other words, the Catholics show a stronger propensity to remain in their crafts, that is they more often become master craftsmen, whereas the Protestants are attracted to a larger extent into the factories in order to fill the upper ranks of skilled labour and administrative positions. The explanation of these cases is undoubtedly that the mental and spiritual peculiarities acquired from the environment, here the type of education favoured by the religious atmosphere of the home community and the parental home, have determined the choice of occupation, and through it the professional career.

The smaller participation of Catholics in the modern business life of Germany is all the more striking because it runs counter to a tendency which has been observed at all times including the present. National or religious minorities which are in a position of subordination to a group of rulers are likely, through their voluntary or involuntary exclusion from positions of political influence, to be driven with peculiar force into economic activity. Their ablest members seek to satisfy the desire for recognition of their abilities in this field, since there is no opportunity in the service of the State. This has undoubtedly been true of the Poles in Russia and Eastern Prussia, who have without question been undergoing a more rapid economic advance than in Galicia, where they have been in the ascendant. It has in earlier times been true of the Huguenots in France under Louis XIV, the Nonconformists and Quakers in England, and, last but not least, the Jew for two thousand years. But the Catholics in Germany have shown no striking evidence of such a result of their position. In the past they have, unlike the Protestants, undergone no particularly prominent economic development in the times when they were persecuted or only tolerated, either in Holland or in England. On the other hand, it is a fact that the Protestants (especially certain branches of the movement to be fully discussed later) both as ruling classes and as ruled, both as majority and as minority, have shown a special tendency to develop economic rationalism which cannot be observed to the same extent among Catholics either in the one situation or in the other. Thus the principal explanation of this difference must be sought in the permanent intrinsic character of their religious beliefs, and not only in their temporary external historico-political situations.

It will be our task to investigate these religions with a view to finding out what peculiarities they have or have had which might have resulted in the behaviour we have described. On superficial analysis, and on the basis of certain current impressions, one might be tempted to express the difference by saying that the greater other-worldliness of Catholicism, the ascetic character of its highest ideals, must have brought up its adherents to a greater indifference toward the good things of this world. Such as explanation fits the popular tendency in the judgment of both religions. On the Protestant side it is used as a basis of criticism of those (real or imagined) ascetic ideals of the Catholic way of life, while the Catholics answer with the accusation that materialism results from the secularization of all ideals through Protestantism. One recent writer has attempted to formulate the difference of their attitudes toward economic life in the following manner: "The Catholic is quieter, having less of the acquisitive impulse; he prefers a life of the greatest possible security, even with a smaller income, to a life of risk and excitement, even though it may bring the chance of gaining honour and riches. The proverb says jokingly, 'either eat well or sleep well'. In the present case the Protestant prefers to eat well, the Catholic to sleep undisturbed."

In fact, this desire to eat well may be a correct though incomplete characterization of the motives of many nominal Protestants in Germany at the present time. But things were very different in the past: the English, Dutch, and American Puritans were characterized by the exact opposite of the joy of living, a fact which is indeed, as we shall see, most important for our present study. Moreover, the French Protestants, among others, long retained, and retain to a certain extent up to the present, the characteristics which were impressed upon the Calvinistic Churches everywhere, especially under the cross in the time of the religious strug-gles. Nevertheless (or was it, perhaps, as we shall ask later, precisely on that account?) it is well known that these characteristics were one of the most important factors in the industrial and capitalistic development of France, and on the small scale permitted them by their persecution remained so. If we may call this seriousness and the strong predominance of religious interests in the whole conduct of life otherworldliness, then the French Calvinists were and still are at least as otherworldly as, for instance, the North German Catholics, to whom their Catholicism is undoubtedly as vital a matter as religion is to any other people in the world. Both differ from the predominant religious trends in their respective countries in much the same way. The Catholics of France are, in their lower ranks, greatly interested in the enjoyment of life, in the upper directly hostile to religion. Similarly, the Protestants of Germany are to-day absorbed in worldly economic life, and their upper ranks are most indifferent to religion. Hardly anything shows so clearly as this parallel that, with such vague ideas as that of the alleged otherworldliness of Catholicism, and the alleged materialistic joy of living of Protestantism, and others like them, nothing can be accomplished for our purpose. In such general terms the distinction does not even adequately fit the facts of to-day, and certainly not of the past. If, however, one wishes to make use of it at all, several other observations present themselves at once which, combined with the above remarks, suggest that the supposed conflict between other-worldliness, asceticism, and ecclesiastical piety on the one side, and participation in capitalistic acquisition on the other, might actually turn out to be an intimate relationship.

As a matter of fact it is surely remarkable, to begin with quite a superficial observation, how large is the number of representatives of the most spiritual forms of Christian piety who have sprung from commercial circles. In particular, very many of the most zealous adherents of Pietism are of this origin. It might be explained as a sort of reaction against mammonism on the part of sensitive natures not adapted to commercial life, and, as in the case of Francis of Assisi, many Pietists have themselves interpreted the process of their conversion in these terms. Similarly, the remarkable circumstance that so many of the greatest capitalistic entrepreneurs—down to Cecil Rhodes—have come from clergymen's families might be explained as a reaction against their ascetic upbringing. But this form of explanation fails where an extraordinary capitalistic business sense is combined in the same persons and groups with the most intensive forms of a piety which penetrates and dominates their whole lives. Such cases are not isolated, but these traits are characteristic of many of the most important Churches and sects in the history of Protestantism. Especially Calvinism, wherever it has appeared, has shown this combination. However little, in the time of the expansion of the Reformation, it (or any other Protestant belief) was bound up with any particular social class, it is characteristic and in a certain sense typical that in French Huguenot Churches monks and business men (merchants, craftsmen) were particularly numerous among the proselytes, especially at the time of the persecution. Even the Spaniards knew that heresy (i.e., the Calvinism of the Dutch) promoted trade, and this coincides with the opinions which Sir William Petty expressed in his discussion of the reasons for the capitalistic development of the Netherlands. Gothein rightly calls the Calvinistic diaspora the seed-bed of capitalistic economy. Even in this case one might consider the decisive factor to be the superiority of the French and Dutch economic cultures from which these communities sprang, or perhaps the immense influence of exile in the breakdown of traditional relationships. But in France the situation was, as we know from Colbert's struggles, the same even in the seventeenth century. Even Austria, not to speak of other countries, directly imported Protestant craftsmen.

But not all the Protestant denominations seem to have had an equally strong influence in this direction.

That of Calvinism, even in Germany, was among the strongest, it seems, and the reformed faith more than the others seems to have promoted the development of the spirit of capitalism, in the Wupperthal as well as elsewhere. Much more so than Lutheranism, as comparison both in general and in particular instances, especially in the Wupperthal, seems to prove. Even more striking, as it is only necessary to mention, is the connection of a religious way of life with the most intensive development of business acumen among those sects whose otherworldliness is as proverbial as their wealth, especially the Quakers and the Mennonites. The part which the former have played in England and North America fell to the latter in Germany and the Netherlands. That in East Prussia Frederick William I tolerated the Mennonites as indispensable to industry, in spite of their absolute refusal to perform military service, is only one of the numerous well-known cases which illustrates the fact, though, considering the character of that monarch, it is one of the most striking. Finally, that this combination of intense piety with just as strong a development of business acumen, was also characteristic of the Pietists, is common knowledge.

In this purely introductory discussion it is unnecessary to pile up more examples. For these few already all show one thing: that the spirit of hard work, of progress, or whatever else it may be called, the awakening of which one is inclined to ascribe to Protestantism, must not be understood, as there is a tendency to do, as joy of living nor in any other sense as connected with the Enlightenment. The old Protestantism of Luther, Calvin, Knox, Voet, had precious little to do with what to-day is called progress. To whole aspects of modern life which the most extreme religionist would not wish to suppress to-day, it was directly hostile. If any inner relationship between certain expressions of the old Protestant spirit and modern capitalistic culture is to be found, we must attempt to find it, for better or worse, not in it its alleged more or less materialistic or at least anti-ascetic joy of living, but in its purely religious characteristics. Montesquieu says of the English that they "had progressed the farthest of all peoples of the world in three important things: in piety, in commerce, and in freedom". Is it not possible that their commercial superiority and their adaptation to free political institutions are connected in some way with that record of piety which Montesquieu ascribes to them?...

CHAPTER II
The Spirit of Capitalism

In the title of this study is used the somewhat pretentious phrase, the *spirit* of capitalism. What is to be understood by it? The attempt to give anything like a definition of it brings out certain difficulties which are in the very nature of this type of investigation.

If any object can be found to which this term can be applied with any understandable meaning, it can only be an historical individual, i.e. a complex of elements associated in historical reality which we unite into a conceptual whole from the standpoint of their cultural significance.

Such an historical concept, however, since it refers in its content to a phenomenon significant for its unique individuality, cannot be defined according to the formula *genus proximum, differentia specifica*, but it must be gradually put together out of the individual parts which are taken from historical reality to make it up. Thus the final and definitive concept cannot stand at the beginning of the investigation, but must come at the end. We must, in other words, work out in the course of the discussion, as its most important result, the best conceptual formulation of what we here understand by the spirit of capitalism, that is the best from the point of view which interests us here. This point of view (the one of which we shall speak later) is, further, by no means the only possible one from which the historical phenomena we are investigating can be analysed. Other standpoints would, for this as for every historical phenomenon, yield other characteristics as the essential ones. The result is that it is by no means necessary to understand by the spirit of capitalism only what it will come to mean to *us* for the purposes of our analysis. This is a necessary result of the nature of historical concepts which attempt for their methodological purposes not to grasp historical reality in abstract general formulae, but in concrete genetic sets of relations which are inevitably of a specifically unique and individual character.

Thus, if we try to determine the object, the analysis and historical explanation of which we are attempting, it cannot be in the form of a conceptual definition, but at least in the beginning only a provisional description of what is here meant by the spirit of capitalism. Such a description is, however, indispensable in order clearly to understand the object of the investigation. For this purpose we turn to a document of that spirit which contains what we are looking for in almost classical purity, and at the same time has the advantage of being free from all direct relationship to religion, being thus, for our purposes, free of preconceptions.

"Remember, that *time* is money. He that can earn ten shillings a day by his labour, and goes abroad, or sits idle, one half of that day, though he spends but sixpence during his diversion or idleness, ought not to reckon *that* the only expense; he has really spent, or rather thrown away, five shillings besides.

"Remember, that *credit* is money. If a man lets his money lie in my hands after it is due, he gives me the interest, or so much as I can make of it during that time. This amounts to a considerable sum where a man has good and large credit, and makes good use of it.

"Remember, that money is of the prolific, generating nature. Money can beget money, and its offspring can beget more, and so on. Five shillings turned is six, turned again it is seven and threepence, and so on, till it becomes a hundred pounds. The more there is of it, the more it produces every turning, so that the profits rise quicker and quicker. He that kills a breeding-sow, destroys all her offspring to the thousandth generation. He that murders a crown, destroys all that it might have produced, even scores of pounds."

"Remember this saying, *The good paymaster is lord of another man's purse*. He that is known to pay punctually and exactly to the time he promises, may at any time, and on any occasion, raise all the money his friends can spare. This is sometimes of great use. After industry and frugality, nothing contributes more to the raising of a young man in the world than punctuality and justice in all his dealings; therefore never keep borrowed money an hour beyond the time you promised, lest a disappointment shut up your friend's purse for ever.

"The most trifling actions that affect a man's credit are to be regarded. The sound of your hammer at five in the morning, or eight at night, heard by a creditor, makes him easy six months longer; but if he sees you at a billiard-table, or hears your voice at a tavern, when you should be at work, he sends for his money the next day; demands it, before he can receive it, in a lump.

"It shows, besides, that you are mindful of what you owe; it makes you appear a careful as well as an honest man, and that still increases your credit.

"Beware of thinking all your own that you possess, and of living accordingly. It is a mistake that many people who have credit fall into. To prevent this, keep an exact account for some time both of your expenses and your income. If you take the pains at first to mention particulars, it will have this good effect: you will discover how wonderfully small, trifling expenses mount up to large sums, and will discern what might have been, and may for the future be saved, without occasioning any great inconvenience."

"For six pounds a year you may have the use of one hundred pounds, provided you are a man of known prudence and honesty.

"He that spends a groat a day idly, spends idly above six pounds a year, which is the price for the use of one hundred pounds.

"He that wastes idly a groat's worth of his time per day, one day with another, wastes the privilege of using one hundred pounds each day.

"He that idly loses five shillings' worth of time, loses five shillings, and might as prudently throw five shillings into the sea.

"He that loses five shillings, not only loses that sum, but all the advantage that might be made by turning it in dealing, which by the time that a young man becomes old, will amount to a considerable sum of money."

It is Benjamin Franklin who preaches to us in these sentences. . . . That it is the spirit of capitalism which here speaks in characteristic fashion, no one will doubt, however little we may wish to claim that everything which could be understood as pertaining to that spirit is contained in it. . . . Truly what is here preached is not simply a means of making one's way in the world, but a peculiar ethic. The infraction of its rules is treated not as foolishness but as forgetfulness of duty. That is the essence of the matter. It is not mere business astuteness, that sort of thing is common enough, it is an ethos. *This* is the quality which interests us.

When Jacob Fugger, in speaking to a business associate who had retired and who wanted to persuade him to do the same, since he had made enough money and should let others have a chance, rejected that as pusillanimity and answered that "he (Fugger) thought otherwise, he wanted to make money as long as he could", the spirit of his statement is evidently quite different from that of Franklin. What in the former case was an expression of commercial daring and a personal inclination morally neutral, in the latter takes on the character of an ethically coloured maxim for the conduct of life. The concept spirit of capitalism is here used in this specific sense, it is the spirit of modern capitalism. For that we are here dealing only with Western European and American capitalism is obvious from the way in which the problem was stated. Capitalism existed in China, India, Babylon, in the classic world, and in the Middle Ages. But in all these cases, as we shall see, this particular ethos was lacking.

Now, all Franklin's moral attitudes are coloured with utilitarianism. Honesty is useful, because it assures credit; so are punctuality, industry, frugality, and that is the reason they are virtues. A logical deduction from this would be that where, for instance, the appearance of honesty serves the same purpose, that would suffice, and an unnecessary surplus of this virtue would evidently appear to Franklin's eyes as unproductive waste. And as a matter of fact, the story in his autobiography of his conversion to those virtues, or the discussion of the value of a strict maintenance of the appearance of modesty, the assiduous belittlement of one's own deserts in order to gain general recognition later, confirms this impression. According to Franklin, those virtues, like all others, are only in so far virtues as they are actually useful to the individual, and the surrogate of mere appearance is always sufficient when it accomplishes the end in view. It is a conclusion which is inevitable for strict utilitarianism. The impression of many Germans that the virtues professed by Americanism are pure hypocrisy seems to have been confirmed by this striking case. But in fact the matter is not by any means so simple. Benjamin Franklin's own character, as it appears in the really unusual candidness of his autobiography, belies that suspicion. The circumstance that he ascribes his recognition of the utility of virtue to a divine revelation which was intended to lead him in the path of righteousness, shows that something more than mere garnishing for purely egocentric motives is involved.

In fact, the *summum bonum* of this ethic, the earning of more and more money, combined with the strict avoidance of all spontaneous enjoyment of life, is above all completely devoid of any eudaemonistic, not to say hedonistic, admixture. It is thought of so purely as an end in itself, that from the point of view of the happiness of, or utility to, the single individual, it appears entirely transcendental and absolutely irrational. Man is dominated by the making of money, by acquisition as the ultimate purpose of his life. Economic acquisition is no longer subordinated to man as the means for the satisfaction of his material needs. This reversal of what we should call the natural relationship, so irrational from a naive point of view, is evidently as definitely a leading principle of capitalism as it is foreign to all peoples not under capitalistic influence. At the same time it expresses a type of feeling which is closely connected with certain religious ideas. If we thus ask, *why* should "money be made out of men", Benjamin Franklin himself, although he was a colourless deist, answers in his autobiography with a quotation from the Bible, which his strict Calvinistic father drummed into him again and again in his youth: "Seest thou a man diligent in his business? He shall stand before kings". The earning of money within the modern economic order is, so long as it is done legally, the result and the expression of virtue and proficiency in a calling; and this virtue and proficiency are, as it is now not difficult to see, the real Alpha and Omega of Franklin's ethic, as expressed in the passages we have quoted, as well as in all his works without exception.

And in truth this peculiar idea, so familiar to us to-day, but in reality so little a matter of course, of one's duty in a calling, is what is most characteristic of the social ethic of capitalistic culture, and is in a sense the fundamental basis of it. It is an obligation which the individual is supposed to feel and does feel towards the content of his professional activity, no matter in what it consists, in particular no matter whether it appears on the surface as a utilization of his personal powers, or only of his material possessions (as capital)....

But the origin and history of such ideas is much more complex than the theorists of the superstructure suppose. The spirit of capitalism, in the sense in which we are using the term, had to fight its way to supremacy against a whole world of hostile forces. A state of mind such as that expressed in the passages we have quoted from Franklin, and which called forth the applause of a whole people, would both in ancient times and in the Middle Ages have been proscribed as the lowest sort of avarice and as an attitude entirely lacking in self-respect. It is, in fact, still regularly thus looked upon by all those social groups which are least involved in or adapted to modern capitalistic conditions. This is not wholly because the instinct of acquisition was in those times unknown or undeveloped, as has often been said... The difference between the capitalistic and pre-capitalistic spirits is not to be found at this point...

The difference does not lie in the degree of development of any impulse to make money. *The auri sacra fames is as* old as the history of man. But we shall see that those who submitted to it without reserve as an uncontrolled impulse, such as the Dutch sea-captain who "would go through hell for gain, even though he scorched his sails", were by no means the representatives of that attitude of mind from which the specifically modern capitalistic spirit as a mass phenomenon is derived, and that is what matters. At all periods of history, wherever it was possible, there has been ruthles acquisition, bound to no ethical norms whatever. Like war and piracy, trade has often been unrestrained in its relations with foreigners and those outside the group. The double ethic has permitted here what was forbidden in dealings among brothers.

Capitalistic acquisition as an adventure has been at home in all types of economic society which have known trade with the use of money and which have offered it opportunities, through *commenda*, farming of taxes, State loans, financing of wars, ducal courts and office-holders. Likewise the inner attitude of the adventurer, which laughs at all ethical limitations, has been universal. Absolute and conscious ruthlessness in acquisition has often stood in the closest connection with the strictest conformity to tradition. Moreover, with the breakdown of tradition and the more or less complete extension of free economic enterprise, even to within the social group, the new thing has not generally been ethically justified and encouraged, but only tolerated as a fact. And this fact has been treated either as ethically indifferent or as reprehensible, but unfortunately unavoidable. This has not only been the normal attitude of all ethical teachings, but, what is more important, also that expressed in the practical action of the average man of pre-capitalistic times, pre-capitalistic in the sense that the rational utilization of capital in a permanent enterprise and the rational capitalistic organization of labour had not yet become dominant forces in the determination of economic activity. Now just this attitude was one of the strongest inner obstacles which the adaptation of men to the conditions of an ordered bourgeois-capitalistic economy has encountered everywhere.

The most important opponent with which the spirit of capitalism, in the sense of a definite standard of life claiming ethical sanction, has had to struggle, was that type of attitude and reaction to new situations which we may designate as traditionalism. . . .

One of the technical means which the modern employer uses in order to secure the greatest possible amount of work from his men is the device of piece-rates. In agriculture, for instance, the gathering of the harvest is a case where the greatest possible intensity of labour is called for, since, the weather being uncertain, the difference between high profit and heavy loss may depend on the speed with which the harvesting can be done. Hence a system of piece-rates is almost universal in this case. And since the interest of the employer in a speeding up of harvesting increases with the increase of the results and the intensity of the work, the attempt has again and again been made, by increasing the piece-rates of the workmen, thereby giving them an opportunity to earn what is for them a very high wage, to interest them in increasing their own efficiency. But a peculiar difficulty has been met with surprising frequency: raising the piece-rates has often had the result that not more but less has been accomplished in the same time, because the worker reacted to the increase not by increasing but by decreasing the amount of his work. A man, for instance, who at the rate of 1 mark per acre mowed 2 1/2 acres per day and earned 2 1/2 marks, when the rate was raised to 1.25 marks per acre mowed, not 3 acres, as he might easily have done, thus earning 3.75 marks, but only 2 acres, so that he could still earn the 2 1/2 marks to which he was accustomed. The opportunity of earning more was less attractive than that of working less. He did not ask: how much can I earn in a day if I do as much work as possible? but: how much must I work in order to earn the wage, 2 1/2 marks, which I earned before and which takes care of my traditional needs? This is an example of what is here meant by traditionalism. A man does not "by nature" wish to earn more and more money, but simply to live as he is accustomed to live and to earn as much as is necessary for that purpose. Wherever modern capitalism has begun its work of increasing the productivity of human labour by increasing its intensity, it has encountered the immensely stubborn resistance of this leading trait of pre-capitalistic labour. . . .

Labour must, on the contrary, be performed as if it were an absolute end in itself, a calling. But such an attitude is by no means a product of nature. It cannot be evoked by low wages or high ones alone, but can only be the product of a long and arduous process of education. Today, capitalism, once in the saddle, can recruit its labouring force in all industrial countries with comparative ease. In the past this was in every case an extremely difficult problem. . . .

We provisionally use the expression spirit of (modern) capitalism to describe that attitude which seeks profit rationally and systematically in the manner which we have illustrated by the example of Benjamin Franklin. This, however, is justified by the historical fact that that attitude of mind has on the one hand found its most suitable expression in capitalistic enterprise, while on the other the enterprise has derived its most suitable motive force from the spirit of capitalism. . . .

The management, for instance, of a bank, a wholesale export business, a large retail establishment, or of a large putting-out enterprise dealing with goods produced in homes, is certainly only possible in the form of a capitalistic enterprise. Nevertheless, they may all be carried on in a traditionalistic spirit. In fact, the business of a large bank of issue cannot be carried on in any other way. The foreign trade of whole epochs has rested on the basis of monopolies and legal privileges of strictly traditional character. In retail trade—and we are not here talking of the small men without capital who are continually crying out for Government aid—the revolution which is making an end of the old traditionalism is still in full swing. It is the same development which broke up the old putting-out system, to which modern domestic labour is related only in form. How this revolution takes place and what is its significance may, in spite of the fact these things are so familiar, be again brought out by a concrete example.

Until about the middle of the past century the life of a putter-out was, at least in many of the branches of the Continental textile industry, what we should to-day consider very comfortable. We may imagine its routine somewhat as follows: The peasants came with their cloth, often (in the case of linen) principally or entirely made from raw material which the peasant himself had produced, to the town in which the putter-out lived, and after a careful, often official, appraisal of the quality, received the customary price for it. The putter-out's customers, for markets any appreciable distance away, were middlemen, who also came to him, generally not yet following samples, but seeking traditional qualities, and bought from his warehouse, or, long before delivery, placed orders which were probably in turn passed on to the peasants. Personal canvassing of customers took place, if at all, only at long intervals. Otherwise correspondence sufficed, though the sending of samples slowly gained ground. The number of business hours was very moderate, perhaps five to six a day, sometimes considerably less; in the rush season, where there was one, more. Earnings were moderate; enough to lead a respectable life and in good times to put away a little. On the whole, relations among competitors were relatively good, with a large degree of agreement on the fundamentals of business. A long daily visit to the tavern, with often plenty to drink, and a congenial circle of friends, made life comfortable and leisurely.

The form of organization was in every respect capitalistic; the entrepreneur's activity was of a purely business character; the use of capital, turned over in the business, was indispensable; and finally, the objective aspect of the economic process, the book-keeping, was rational. But it was traditionalistic business, if one considers the spirit which animated the entrepreneur: the traditional manner of life, the traditional rate of profit, the traditional amount of work, the traditional manner of regulating the relationships with labour, and the essentially traditional circle of customers and the manner of attracting new ones. All these dominated the conduct of the business, were at the basis, one may say, of the *ethos* of this group of business men.

Now at some time this leisureliness was suddenly destroyed, and often entirely without any essential change in the form of organization, such as the transition to a unified factory, to mechanical weaving, etc. What happened was, on the contrary, often no more than this: some young man from one of the putting-out families went out into the country, carefully chose weavers for his employ, greatly increased the rigour of his supervision of their work, and thus turned them from peasants into labourers. On the other hand, he would begin to change his marketing methods by so far as possible going directly to the final consumer, would take the details into his own hands, would personally solicit customers, visiting them every year, and above all would adapt the quality of the product directly to their needs and wishes. At the same time he began to introduce the principle of low prices and large turnover. There was repeated what everywhere and always is the result of such a process of rationalization: those who would not follow suit had to go out of business. The idyllic state collapsed under the pressure of a bitter competitive struggle, respectable fortunes were made, and not lent out at interest, but always reinvested in the business. The old leisurely and comfortable attitude toward life gave way to a hard frugality in which some participated and came to the top, because they did not wish to consume but to earn, while others who wished to keep on with the old ways were forced to curtail their consumption.

And, what is most important in this connection, it was not generally in such cases a stream of new money invested in the industry which brought about this revolution—in several cases known to me the whole revolutionary process was set in motion with a few thousands of capital borrowed from relations—but the new spirit, the spirit of modern capitalism, had set to work. The question of the motive forces in the expansion of modern capitalism is not in the first instance a question of the origin of the capital sums which were available for capitalistic uses, but, above all, of the development of the spirit of capitalism. . . .

And, as a rule, it has been neither dare-devil and unscrupulous speculators, economic adventurers such as we meet at all periods of economic history, nor simply great financiers who have carried through this change, outwardly so inconspicuous, but nevertheless so decisive for the penetration of economic life with the new spirit. On the contrary, they were men who had grown up in the hard school of life, calculating and daring at the same time, above all temperate and reliable, shrewd and completely devoted to their business, with strictly bourgeois opinions and principles.

One is tempted to think that these personal moral qualities have not the slightest relation to any ethical maxims, to say nothing of religious ideas, but that the essential relation between them is negative. The ability to free oneself from the common tradition, a sort of liberal enlightenment, seems likely to be the most suitable basis for such a business man's success. And to-day that is generally precisely the case. Any relationship between religious beliefs and conduct is generally absent, and where any exists, at least in Germany, it tends to be of the negative sort. The people filled with the spirit of capitalism to-day tend to be indifferent, if not hostile, to the Church. The thought of the pious boredom of paradise has little attraction for their active natures; religion appears to them as a means of drawing people away from labour in this world. If you ask them what is the meaning of their restless activity, why they are never satisfied with what they have, thus appearing so sensless to any purely worldly view of life, they would perhaps give the answer, if they known any at all: "to provide for my children and grand-children". But more often and, since that motive is not peculiar to them, but was just as effective for the traditionalist, more correctly, simply: that business with its continuous work has become a necessary part of their lives. That is in fact the only possible motivation, but it at the same time expresses what is, seen from the view-point of personal happiness, so irrational about this sort of life, where a man exists for the sake of his business, instead of the reverse.

Of course, the desire for the power and recognition which the mere fact of wealth brings plays its part. When the imagination of a whole people has once been turned toward purely quantitative bigness, as in the United States, this romanticism of numbers exercises an irresistible appeal to the poets among business men. Otherwise it is in general not the real leaders, and especially not the premanently successful entreprenuers, who are taken in by it. In particular, the resort to entailed estates and the nobility, with sons whose conduct at the university and in the officers' corps tries to cover up their social origin, as has been the typical history of German capitalistic parvenu families, is a product of later decadence. The ideal type of the capitalistic entreprenuer, as it has been represented even in Germany by occasional outstanding examples, has no relation to such more or less refined climbers. He avoids ostentation and uncessary expenditure, as well as conscious enjoyment of his power, and is embarassed by the outward signs of the social recognition which he receives. His manner of life is, in other words, often, and we shall have to investigate the historical significance of just this important fact, distinguished by a certain ascetic tendency, as appears clearly enough in the sermon of Franklin which we have quoted. It is, namely, by no means exceptional, but rather the rule, for him to have a sort of modesty which is essentially more honest than the reserve which Franklin so shrewdly recommends. He gets nothing out of his wealth for himself, except the irrational sense of having done his job well.

But it is just that which seems to the pre-capitalistic man so incomprehensible and mysterious, so unworthy and contemptible. That anyone should be able to make it the sole purpose of his life-work, to sink into the grave weighed down with a great material load of money and goods, seems to him explicable only as the product of a perverse instinct, the *auri sacra fames*.

At present under our individualistic political, legal, and economic institutions, with the forms of organization and general structure which are peculiar to our economic order, this spirit of capitalism might be understandable, as has been said, purely as a result of adaptation. The capitalistic system so needs this devotion to the calling of making money, it is an attitude toward material goods which is so well suited to that system, so intimately bound up with the conditions of survival in the economic struggle for existence, that there can to-day no longer be any question of a necessary connection of that acquisitive manner of life with any single *Weltanschauung*. In fact, it no longer needs the support of any religious forces, and feels the attempts of religion to influence economic life, in so far as they can still be felt at all, to be as much an unjustified interference as its regulation by the State. . . .

Some moralists of that time, especially of the nominalistic school, accepted developed capitalistic business forms as inevitable, and attempted to justify them, especially commerce, as necessary. The *industria* developed in it they were able to regard, though not without contradictions, as a legitimate source of profit, and hence ethically unobjectionable. But the dominant doctrine rejected the spirit of capitalistic acquisition as *turpitudo*, or at least could not give it a positive ethical sanction. An ethical attitude like that of Benjamin Franklin would have been simply unthinkable. . . .

Now, how could activity, which was at best ethically tolerated, turn into a calling in the sense of Benjamin Franklin? The fact to be explained historically is that in the most highly capitalistic centre of that time, in Florence of the fourteenth and fifteenth centuries, the money and capital market of all the great political Powers, this attitude was considered ethically unjustifiable, or at best to be tolerated. But in the backwoods small bourgeois circumstances of Pennsylvania in the eighteenth century, where business threatened for simple lack of money to fall back into barter, where there was hardly a sign of large enterprise, where only the earliest beginnings of banking were to be found, the same thing was considered the essence of moral conduct, even commanded in the name of duty. To speak here of a reflection of material conditions in the ideal superstructure would be patent nonsense. What was the background of ideas which could account for the sort of activity apparently directed toward profit alone as a calling toward which the individual feels himself to have an ethical obligation? For it was this idea which gave the way of life of the new entrepreneur its ethical foundation and justification. . . .

CHAPTER V
Asceticism and the Spirit of Capitalism

In order to understand the connection between the fundamental religious ideas of ascetic Protestantism and its maxims for everyday economic conduct, it is necessary to examine with especial care such writings as have evidently been derived from ministerial practice. For in a time in which the beyond meant everything, when the social position of the Christian depended upon his admission to the communion, the clergyman, through his ministry, Church discipline, and preaching, exercised an influence (as a glance at collections of *consilia, casus conscientiae,* etc., shows) which we modern men are entirely unable to picture. In such a time the religious forces which express themselves through such channels are the decisive influences in the formation of national character.

For the purposes of this chapter, though by no means for all purposes, we can treat ascetic Protestantism as a single whole. But since that side of English Puritanism which was derived from Calvinism gives the most consistent religious basis for the idea of the calling, we shall, following our previous method, place one of its representatives at the centre of the discussion. Richard Baxter stands out above many other writers on Puritan ethics, both because of his eminently practical and realistic attitude, and, at the same time, because of the universal recognition accorded to his works, which have gone through many new editions and translations. . . .

Now, in glancing at Baxter's *Saints' Everlasting Rest,* or his *Christian Directory,* or similar works of others, one is struck at first glance by the emphasis placed, in the discussion of wealth and its acquisition, on the ebionitic elements of the New Testament. Wealth as such is a great danger; its temptations never end, and its pursuit is not only senseless as compared with the dominating importance of the Kingdom of God, but it is morally suspect. Here asceticism seems to have turned much more sharply against the acquisition of earthly goods than it did in Calvin, who saw no hindrance to the effectivenes of the clergy in their wealth, but rather a thoroughly desirable enhancement of their prestige. Hence he permitted them to employ their means profitably. Examples of the condemnation of the pursuit of money and goods may be gathered without end from Puritan writings, and may be contrasted with the late mediaeval ethical literature, which was much more open-minded on this point.

Moreover, these doubts were meant with perfect seriousness; only it is necessary to examine them somewhat more closely in order to understand their true ethical significance and implications. The real moral objection is to relaxation in the security of possession, the enjoyment of wealth with the consequence of idleness and the temptations of the flesh, above all of distraction from the pursuit of a righteous life. In fact, it is only because possession involves this danger of relaxation that it is objectionable at all. For the saints' everlasting rest is in the next world; on earth man must, to be certain of his state of grace, "do the works of him who sent him, as long as it is yet day." Not leisure and enjoyment, but only activity serves to increase the glory of God, according to the definite manifestations of His will.

Waste of time is thus the first and in principle the deadliest of sins. The span of human life is infinitely short and precious to make sure of one's own election. Loss of time through sociability, idle talk, luxury, even more sleep than is necessary for health, six to at most eight hours, is worthy of absolute moral condemnation. It does not yet hold, with Franklin, that time is money, but the proposition is true in a certain spiritual sense. It is infinitely valuable because every hour lost is lost to labour for the glory of God. Thus inactive contemplation is also valueless, or even directly reprehensible if it is at the expense of one's daily work. For it is less pleasing to God than the active performance of His will in a calling. Besides, Sunday is provided for that, and, according to Baxter, it is always those who are not diligent in their callings who have no time for God when the occasion demands it.

Accordingly, Baxter's principal work is dominated by the continually repeated, often almost passionate preaching of hard, continuous bodily or mental labour. It is due to a combination of two different motives. Labour is, on the one hand, an approved ascetic technique, as it always has been in the Western Church, in sharp contrast not only to the Orient but to almost all monastic rules the world over. It is in particular the specific defence against all those temptations which Puritanism united under the name of the unclean life, whose role for it was by no means small. The sexual asceticism of Puritanism differs only in degree, not in fundamental principle, from that of monasticism; and on account of the Puritan conception of marriage, its practical influence is more far-reaching than that of the latter. For sexual intercourse is permitted, even within marriage, only as the means willed by God for the increase of His glory according to the commandment, "Be fruitful and multiply." Along with a moderate vegetable diet and cold baths, the same prescription is given for all sexual temptations as is used against religious doubts and a sense of moral unworthiness: "Work hard in your calling." But the most important thing was that even beyond that labour came to be considered in itself the end of life, ordained as such by God. St. Paul's "He who will not work shall not eat" holds unconditionally for everyone. Unwillingness to work is symptomatic of the lack of grace.

Here the difference from the mediaeval view-point becomes quite evident. Thomas Aquinas also gave an interpretation of that statement of St. Paul. But for him labour is only necessary *naturali ratione* for the maintenance of individual and community. Where this end is achieved, the precept ceases to have any meaning. Moreover, it holds only for the race, not for every individual. It does not apply to anyone who can live without labour on his possessions, and of course contemplation, as a spiritual form of action in the Kingdom of God, takes precedence over the commandment in its literal sense. Moreover, for the popular theology of the time, the highest form of monastic productivity lay in the increase of the *Thesaurus ecclesiae* through prayer and chant.

Now only do these exceptions to the duty to labour naturally no longer hold for Baxter, but he holds most emphatically that wealth does not exempt anyone from the unconditional command. Even the wealthy shall not eat without working, for even though they do not need to labour to support their own needs, there is God's commandment which they, like the poor, must obey. For everyone without exception God's Providence has prepared a calling, which he should profess and in which he should labour. And this calling is not, as it was for the Lutheran, a fate to which he must submit and which he must make the best of, but God's commandment to the individual to work for the divine glory. . . .

It is true that the usefulness of a calling, and thus its favour in the sight of God, is measured primarily in moral terms, and thus in terms of the importance of the goods produced in it for the community. But a further, and, above all, in practice the most important, criterion is found in private profitableness. For if that God, whose hand the Puritan sees in all the occurrences of life, shows one of His elect a chance of profit, he must do it with a purpose. Hence the faithful Christian must follow the call by taking advantage of the opportunity. "If God show you a way in which you may lawfully get more than in another way (without wrong to your soul or to any other), if you refuse this, and choose the less gainful way, you cross one of the ends of your calling, and you refuse to be God's steward, and to accept His gifts and use them for Him when He requireth it: you may labour to be rich for God, though not for the flesh and sin."

Wealth is thus bad ethically only in so far as it is a temptation to idleness and sinful enjoyment of life, and its acquisition is bad only when it is with the purpose of later living merrily and without care. But as a performance of duty in a calling it is not only morally permissible, but actually enjoined. The parable of the servant who was rejected because he did not increase the talent which was entrusted to him seemed to say so directly. To wish to be poor was, it was often argued, the same as wishing to be unhealthy; it is objectionable as a glorification of works and derogatory to the glory of God. Especially begging, on the part of one able to work, is not only the sin of slothfulness, but a violation of the duty of brotherly love according to the Apostle's own word. . . .

Let us now try to clarify the points in which the Puritan idea of the calling and the premium it placed upon ascetic conduct was bound directly to influence the development of a capitalistic way of life. As we have seen, this asceticism turned with all its force against one thing: the spontaneous enjoyment of life and all it had to offer. This is perhaps most characteristically brought out in the struggle over the *Book of Sports* which James I and Charles I made into law expressly as a means of counteracting Puritanism, and which the latter ordered to be read from all the pulpits. The fanatical opposition of the Puritans to the ordinances of the King, permitting certain popular amusements on Sunday outside of Church hours by law, was not only explained by the disturbance of the Sabbath rest, but also by resentment against the intentional diversion from the ordered life of the saint, which it caused. And, on his side, the King's threats of severe punishment for every attack on the legality of those sports were motivated by his purpose of breaking the anti-authoritarian ascetic tendency of Puritanism, which was so dangerous to the State. The feudal and monarchical forces protected the pleasure seekers against the rising middle-class morality and the anti-authoritarian ascetic conventicles, just as to-day capitalistic society tends to protect those willing to work against the class morality of the proletariat and the anti-authoritarian trade union.

As against this the Puritans upheld their decisive characteristic, the principle of ascetic conduct. For otherwise the Puritan aversion to sport, even for the Quakers, was by no means simply one of principle. Sport was accepted if it served a rational purpose, that of recreation necessary for physical efficiency. But as a means for the spontaneous expression of undisciplined impulses, it was under suspicion; and in so far as it became purely a means of enjoyment, or awakened pride, raw instincts or the irrational gambling instinct, it was of course strictly condemned. Impulsive enjoyment of life, which leads away both from work in a calling and from religion, was as such the enemy of rational asceticism, whether in the form of seigneurial sports, or the enjoyment of the dance-hall or the public-house of the common man. . . . That powerful tendency toward uniformity of life, which to-day so immensely aids the capitalistic interest in the standardization of production, had its ideal foundations in the repudiation of all idolatry of the flesh. . . .

Although we cannot here enter upon a discussion of the influence of Puritanism in all these directions, we should call attention to the fact that the toleration of pleasure in cultural goods, which contributed to purely aesthetic or athletic enjoyment, certainly always ran up against one characteristic limitation: they must not cost anything. Man is only a trustee of the goods which have come to him through God's grace. He must, like the servant in the parable, give an account of every penny entrusted to him, and it is at least hazardous to spend any of it for a purpose which does not serve the glory of God but only one's own enjoyment. What person, who keeps his eyes open, has not met representatives of this view-point even in the present? The idea of a man's duty to his possessions, to which he subordinates himself as an obedient steward, or even as an acquisitive machine, bears with chilling weight on his life. The greater the possessions the heavier, if the ascetic attitude toward life stands the test, the feeling of responsibility for them, for holding them undiminished for the glory of God and increasing them by restless effort. The origin of this type of life also extends in certain roots, like so many aspects of the spirit of capitalism, back into the Middle Ages. But it was in the ethic of ascetic Protestantism that it first found a consistent ethical foundation. Its significance for the development of capitalism is obvious.

This worldly Protestant asceticism, as we may recapitulate up to this point, acted powerfully against the spontaneous enjoyment of possessions; it restricted consumption, especially of luxuries. On the other hand, it had the psychological effect of freeing the acquisition of goods from the inhibitions of traditionalistic ethics. It broke the bonds of the impulse of acquisition in that it not only legalized it, but (in the sense discussed) looked upon it as directly willed by God. The campaign against the temptations of the flesh, and the dependence on external things, was, not a struggle against the rational acquisition, but against the irrational use of wealth. . . .

On the side of the production of private wealth, asceticism condemned both dishonesty and impulsive avarice. What was condemned as covetousness, the pursuit of riches for their own sake. For wealth in itself was a temptation. But here asceticism was the power "which ever seeks the good but ever creates evil"; what was evil in its sense was possession and its temptations. For, in conformity with the Old Testament and in analogy to the ethical valuation of good works, asceticism looked upon the pursuit of wealth as an end in itself as highly reprehensible; but the attainment of it as a fruit of labour in a calling was a sign of God's blessing. And even more important: the religious valuation of restless, continuous, systematic work in a worldly calling, as the highest means to asceticism, and at the same time the surest and most evident proof of rebirth and genuine faith, must have been the most powerful conceivable lever for the expansion of that attitude toward life which we have here called the spirit of capitalism.

When the limitation of consumption is combined with this release of acquisitive activity, the inevitable practical result is obvious: accumulation of capital through ascetic compulsion to save. The restraints which were imposed upon the consumption of wealth naturally served to increase it by making possible the productive investment of capital. . . .

As far as the influence of the Puritan outlook extended, under all circumstances—and this is, of course, much more important than the mere encouragement of capital accumulation—it favoured the development of a rational bourgeois economic life; it was the most important, and above all the only consistent influence in the development of that life. It stood at the cradle of the modern economic man. . . .

A specifically bourgeois economic ethic had grown up. With the consciousness of standing in the fullness of God's grace and being visibly blessed by Him, the bourgeois business man, as long as he remained within the bounds of formal correctness, as long as his moral conduct was spotless and the use to which he put his wealth was not objectionable, could follow his pecuniary interests as he would and feel that he was fulfilling a duty in doing so. The power of religious asceticism provided him in addition with sober, conscientious, and unusually industrious workmen, who clung to their work as to a life purpose willed by God.

Finally, it gave him the comforting assurance that the unequal distribution of the goods of this world was a special dispensation of Divine Providence, which in these differences, as in particular grace, pursued secret ends unknown to men. . . .

One of the fundamental elements of the spirit of modern capitalism, and not only of that but of all modern culture: rational conduct on the basis of the idea of the calling, was born—that is what this discussion has sought to demonstrate—from the spirit of Christian asceticism. One has only to re-read the passage from Franklin, quoted at the beginning of this essay, in order to see that the essential elements of the attitude which was there called the spirit of capitalism are the same as what we have just shown to be the content of the Puritan worldly asceticism, only without the religious basis, which by Franklin's time had died away. The idea that modern labour has an ascetic character is of course not new. Limitation to specialized work, with a renunciation of the Faustian universality of man which it involves, is a condition of any valuable work in the modern world; hence deeds and renunciation inevitably condition each other today. This fundamentally ascetic trait of middle-class life, if it attempts to be a way of life at all, and not simply the absence of any, was what Goethe wanted to teach, at the height of his wisdom, in the *Wanderjahren*, and in the end which he gave to the life of his *Faust*. For him the realization meant a renunciation, a departure from an age of full and beautiful humanity, which can no more be repeated in the course of our cultural development than can the flower of the Athenian culture of antiquity.

The Puritan wanted to work in a calling; we are forced to do so. For when ascerticism was carried out of monastic cells into everyday life, and began to dominate worldly mortality, it did its part in building the tremendous cosmos of the modern economic order. This order is now bound to the technical and economic conditions of machine production which to-day determine the lives of all the individuals who are born into this mechanism, not only those directly concerned with economic acquisition, with irresistible force. Perhaps it will so determine them until the last ton of fossilized coal is burnt. In Baxter's view the care for external goods should only lie on the shoulders of the "saint like a light cloak, which can be thrown aside at any moment". But fate decreed that the cloak should become an iron cage.

Since asceticism undertook to remodel the world and to work out its ideals in the world, material goods have gained an increasing and finally an inexorable power over the lives of men as at no previous period in history. To-day the spirit of religious asceticism—whether finally, who knows?—has escaped from the cage. But victorious capitalism, since it rests on mechanical foundations, needs its support no longer. The rosy blush of its laughing heir, the Enlightenment, seems also to be irretrievably fading, and the idea of duty in one's calling prowls about in our lives like the ghost of dead religious beliefs. Where the fulfilment of the calling cannot directly be related to the highest spiritual and cultural values, or when, on the other hand, it need not be felt simply as economic compulsion, the individual generally abandons the attempt to justify it at all. In the field of its highest development, in the United States, the pursuit of wealth, stripped of its religious and ethical meaning, tends to become associated with purely mundane passions, which often actually give it the character of sport.

No one knows who will live in this cage in the future, or whether at the end of this tremendous development entirely new prophets will arise, or there will be a great rebirth of old ideas and ideals, or, if neither, mechanized petrification, embellished with a sort of convulsive self-importance. For of the last stage of this cultural development, it might well be truly said: "Specialists without spirit, sensualists without heart; this nullity imagines that it has attained a level of civilization never before achieved."

But this brings us to the world of judgments of value and of faith, with which this purely historical discussion need not be burdened. The next task would be rather to show the significance of ascetic rationalism, which has only been touched in the foregoing sketch, for the content of practical social ethics, thus for the types of organization and the functions of social groups from the conventicle to the State. Then its relations to humanistic rationalism, its ideals of life and cultural influence; further to the development of philosophical and scientific empiricism, to technical development and to spiritual ideals would have to be analysed. Then its historical development from the mediaeval beginnings of worldly asceticism to its dissolution into pure utilitarianism would have to be traced out through all the areas of ascetic religion. Only then could the quantitative cultural significance of ascetic Protestantism in its relation to the other plastic elements of modern culture be estimated.

Here we have only attempted to trace the fact and the direction of its influence to their motives in one, though a very important point. But it would also further be necessary to investigate how Protestant Asceticism was in turn influenced in its development and its character by the totality of social conditions, especially economic. The modern man is in general, even with the best will, unable to give religious ideas a significance for culture and national character which they deserve. But it is, of course, not my aim to substitute for a one-sided materialistic an equally one-sided spiritualistic causal interpretation of culture and of history. Each is equally possible, but each, if it does not serve as the preparation, but as the conclusion of an investigation, accomplishes equally little in the interest of historical truth.

MAX WEBER
(1904–05)

"Objectivity" in
Social Science and
Science Policy

We have designated as "cultural sciences" those disciplines which analyze the phenomena of life in terms of their cultural significance. The *significance* of a configuration of cultural phenomena and the basis of this significance cannot however be derived and rendered intelligible by a system of analytical laws (Gesetzesbegriffen), however perfect it may be, since the significance of cultural events presupposes a *value-orientation* towards these events. The concept of culture is a *value-concept*. Empirical reality becomes "cultures" to us because and insofar as we relate it to value ideas. It includes those segments and only those segments of reality which have become significant to us because of this value-relevance. Only a small portion of existing concrete reality is colored by our value-conditioned interest and it alone is significant to us. It is significant because it reveals relationships which are important to use due to their connection with our values. Only because and to the extent that this is the case is it worthwhile for us to know it in its individual features. We cannot discover, however, what is meaningful to us by means of a "presuppositionless" investigation of empirical data. Rather perception of its meaningfulness to us is the presupposition of its becoming an *object* of investigation. Meaningfulness naturally does not coincide with laws as such, and the more general the law the less the coincidence. . . . The *goal* of our investigation is reached through the exposition of those laws and concepts, precise as it may be. The question as to what should be the object of universal conceptualization cannot be decided "presuppositionlessly" but only with reference to the *significance* which certain segments of that infinite multiplicity which we call "commerce" have for culture. We seek knowledge of an historical phenomenon, meaning by historical: significant in its individuality (*Eigenart*). And the decisive element in this is that only through the presupposition that a finite part alone of the infinite variety of phenomena is significant, does the knowledge of an individual phenomenon become logically meaningful. Even with the widest imaginable knowledge of "laws," we are helpless in the face of the question: how is the *causal explanation* of an *individual* fact possible—since a *description* of even the smallest slice of reality can never be exhaustive? The number and type of causes which have influenced any given event are always infinite and there is nothing in the things themselves to set some of them apart as alone meriting attention. A chaos of "existential judgments" about countless individual events would be the only result of a serious attempt to analyze reality "without presuppositions." And even this result is only seemingly possible, since every single perception discloses on closer examination an infinite number of constituent perceptions which can never be exhaustively expressed in a judgement. Order is brought into this chaos only on the condition that in every case only a *part* of concrete reality is interesting and *significant* to us, because only it is related to the *cultural values* with which we approach reality. Only certain sides of the infinitely complex concrete phenomenon, namely those to which we attribute a general *cultural significance*—are therefore worthwhile knowing. They alone are objects of causal explanation. And even this causal explanation evinces the same character; an *exhaustive* causal investigation of any concrete phenomena in its full reality is not only practically impossible—it is simply nonsense. We select only those causes to which are to be imputed in the individual case, the "essential" feature of an event. Where the *individuality* of a phenomenon is concerned, the question of causality is not a question of *laws* but of concrete causal *relationships*; it is not a question of the subsumption of the event under some general rubric as a representative case but of its imputation as a consequence of some constellation. It is in brief a *question of imputation*. Wherever the causal explanation of a "cultural phenomenon—an "historical individual" is under consideration, the knowledge of causal *laws* is not the *end* of the investigation but only a *means*. It facilitates and renders possible the causal imputation to their concrete causes of those components of a phenomenon the individuality of which is culturally significant. So far and only so far as it achieves this, is it valuable for our knowledge of concrete relationships. And the more "general," i.e., the more abstract the laws, the less they can contribute to the causal imputation of *individual* phenomena and, more indirectly, to the understanding of the significance of cultural events.

What is the consequence of all this?

Naturally, it does not imply that the knowledge of *universal* propositions, the construction of abstract concepts, the knowledge of regularities and the attempt to formulate "*laws*" have no scientific justification in the cultural sciences. Quite the contrary, if the causal knowledge of the historians consists of the imputation of concrete effects to concrete causes, a *valid* imputation of any individual effect without the application of "*nomological*" *knowledge*—i.e., the knowledge of recurrent causal sequences—would in general be impossible. Whether a single individual component of a relationship is, in a concrete case, to be assigned causal responsibility for an effect, the causal explanation of which is at issue, can in doubtful cases be determined only by estimating the effects which we *generally* expect from it and from the other components of the same complex which are relevant to the explanation. In other words, the "*adequate*" effects of the causal elements involved must be considered in arriving at any such conclusion. The extent to which the historian (in the widest sense of the word) can perform this imputation in a reasonably certain manner with his imagination sharpened by personal experience and trained in analytic methods and the extent to which he must have recourse to the aid of special disciplines which make if possible, varies with the individual case. Everywhere, however, and hence also in the sphere of complicated economic processes, the more certain and the more comprehensive our general knowledge the greater is the *certainty* of imputation. This proposition is not in the least affected by the fact that even in the case of all so-called "economic laws" without exception, we are concerned here not with "laws" in the narrower exact natural science sense, but with *adequate* causal relationships expressed in rules and with the application of the category of "objective possibility." The establishment of such regularities is not the *end* but rather the *means* of knowledge. It is entirely a question of expediency, to be settled separately for each individual case, whether a regularly recurrent causal relationship of everyday experience should be formulated into a "law." Laws are important and valuable in the exact natural sciences, in the measure that those sciences are *universally valid*. For the knowledge of historical phenomena in their concreteness, the most general laws, because they are most devoid of content are also the least valuable. The more comprehensive the validity—or scope—of a term, the more it leads us away from the richness of reality since in order to include the common elements of the largest possible number of phenomena, it must necessarily be as abstract as possible and hence *devoid* of content. In the cultural sciences, the knowledge of the universal or general is never valuable in itself.

The conclusion which follows from the above is that an "objective" analysis of cultural events, which proceeds according to the thesis that the ideal of science is the reduction of empirical reality of "laws," is meaningless. It is not meaningless, as is often maintained, because cultural or psychic events for instance are "objectively" less governed by laws. It is meaningless for a number of other reasons. Firstly, because the knowledge of social laws is not knowledge of social reality but is rather one of the various aids used by our minds for attaining this end; secondly, because knowledge of *cultural* events is inconceivable except on a basis of the *significance* which the concrete constellations of reality have for us in certain *individual* concrete situations. In *which* sense and in *which* situations this is the case is not revealed to us by any law; it is decided according to the *value-ideas* in the light of which we view "culture" in each individual case. "Culture" is a finite segment of the meaningless infinity of the world process, a segment on which *human beings* confer meaning and significance. This is true even for the human being who views a *particular* culture as a mortal enemy and who seeks to "return to nature." He can attain this point of view only after viewing the culture in which he lives from the standpoint of his values, and finding it "too soft." This is the purely logical-formal fact which is involved when we speak of the logically necessary rootedness of all historical entities (*historische Individuen*) in "evaluative ideas." The transcendental presupposition of every *cultural science* lies not in our finding a certain culture or any "culture" in general to be *valuable* but rather in the fact that we are *cultural beings*, endowed with the capacity and the will to take a deliberate attitude towards the world and to lend it *significance*. Whatever this significance may be, it will lead us to judge certain phenomena of human existence in its light and to respond to them as being (positively or negatively) meaningful. Whatever may be the content of this attitude—these phenomena have cultural significance for us and on this significance alone rests its scientific interest. Thus when we speak here of the conditioning of cultural knowledge through *evaluative* ideas (*Wertideen*) (following the terminology of modern logic), it is done in the hope that we will not be subject to crude misunderstandings such as the opinion that cultural significance should be attributed only to *valuable* phenomena. Prostitution is a *cultural* phenomenon just as much as religion or money. All three are cultural phenomena *only* because and *only* insofar as their existence and the form which they historically assume touch directly or indirectly on our cultural *interests* and arouse our striving for knowledge concerning problems brought into focus by the evaluative ideas which give *significance* to the fragment of reality analyzed by those concepts.

All knowledge of cultural reality, as may be seen, is always knowledge from *particular points of view*. When we require from the historian and social research worker as an elementary presupposition that they distinguish the important from the trivial and that he should have the necessary "point of view" for this distinction, we mean that they must understand how to relate the events of the real world consciously or unconsciously to universal "cultural values" and to select out those relationships which are significant for us. If the notion that those standpoints can be derived from the "facts themselves" continually recurs, it is due to the naive self-deception of the specialist who is unaware that it is due to the evaluative ideas with which he unconsciously approaches his subject matter, that he has selected from an absolute infinity a tiny portion with the study of which he *concerns* himself. In connection with this selection of individual special "aspects of the event which always and everywhere occurs, consciously or unconsciously, there also occurs that element of cultural-scientific work which is referred to by the often-heard assertion that the "personal" element of a scientific work is what is really valuable in it, and that personality must be expressed in every work if it existence is to be justified. To be sure, without the investigator's evaluative ideas, there would be no principle of selection of subject-matter and no meaningful knowledge of the concrete reality. Just as without the investigator's conviction regarding the significance of particular cultural facts, every attempt to analyze concrete reality is absolutely meaningless, so the direction of his personal belief, the refraction of values in the prism of his mind, gives direction to his work. And the values to which the scientific genius relates the object of his inquiry may determine, i.e., decide the "conception" of a whole epoch, not only concerning what is regarded as "valuable" but also concerning what is significant or insignificant, "important" or "unimportant" in the phenomena. . . .

However, there emerges from this the meaninglessness of the idea which prevails occasionally even among historians, namely, that the goal of the cultural sciences, however far it may be from realization, is to construct a closed system of concepts, in which reality is synthesized in some sort of *permanently* and *universally* valid classification and from which it can again be deduced. The stream of immeasurable events flows unendingly towards eternity. The cultural problems which move men form themselves ever anew and in different colors, and the boundaries of that area in the infinite stream of concrete events which acquires meaning and significance for us, i.e., which becomes an "historical individual," are constantly subject to change. The intellectual contexts from which it is viewed and scientifically analyzed shift. The points of departure of the cultural sciences remain changeable throughout the limitless future as long as a Chinese ossification of intellectual life does not render mankind incapable of setting new questions to the eternally inexhaustible flow of life. A systematic science of culture, even only in the sense of a definitive, objectively valid, systematic fixation of the problems which it should treat, would be senseless in itself. Such an attempt could only produce a collection of numerous, specifically particularized, heterogeneous and disparate viewpoints in the light of which reality becomes "culture" through being significant in its unique character.

Norman Birnbaum

Alexis de Tocqueville was not the only scholar to have set the United States apart from the history and culture of European nations; such a distinction has been commonplace of cultural, political, and intellectual expression since the first European visited the New World. Tocqueville had argued that the future of democratic modernity in both the United States and Europe was headed down two distinctly different paths. The sentiment has persisted into the twentieth century. Norman Birnbaum, himself an American-born sociologist, has spent much of his career attempting to bring the power of European social theory to bear on the substance of an American experience that he feels has progressed without the tools equal to its understanding. To this end he served as a co-founding editor of the *New Left Review* in 1957, seeking to draw European traditions of critically engaged philosophy and sociology into an American intellectual environment whose focus on consensus was felt to have restricted its capacity for fundamental criticisms of the status quo.

Having been led to European social theory out of dissatisfaction with the North American conceptual climate, Birnbaum's exposure to the dogmatic Marxism of Stalinist Russia and the satellite nations of Eastern Europe imposed upon him the necessity of a more subtle, multifaceted appreciation of Marx's work. "I have found it difficult," he wrote in 1977, "to think of Marxism exclusively as an attempt to construct a rigorous theory of history" (*Towards a Reflexive Sociology*). His interest in the relations between Marxism and religion stem from this experience of the contrast between the dogmatism of the East and the complacency of the West, and the suspicion that Marxism had itself become a secular religion.

The confrontation of Marxism with Weber's thesis on the role of Protestantism in the emergence of a capitalist economy in Europe represents Birnbaum's effort to retain a sense of total social structure provided by Marx, while recognizing the manifest presence of religious motivations in the early history of capitalism. For Birnbaum, Weber and Marx must be brought into conversation with one another for a sociological understanding of modern society to proceed—to borrow the title of a book he edited—*Beyond the Classics*.

NORMAN BIRNBAUM
(1953)

Conflicting Interpretations

of the Rise of Capitalism:

Marx and Weber

The Post-War years have witnessed a considerable growth of interest in Max Weber among sociologists in England and the U.S. This paper is an attempt to recall some of the polemical origins of a major theme in Weber's work: the function of ideology as an independent variable in social development. Weber struck upon this theme in the course of inquiry into the emergence of capitalism in western society—an inquiry that focused on England. A comparison of Weber's explanation of this phenomenon with that of Marx, whose historical materialism it so drastically challenged, is at once a venture in sociological analysis, and a study in intellectual history.

Less than half a century separated Weber from Marx. Perhaps the fullest presentation of the latter's views on the genesis of capitalism in the west appeared in the famous twenty-fourth chapter of *Capital*, published in 1867. Weber's views crystallized as early as 1904, when he first published *The Protestant Ethic and the Spirit of Capitalism*. This was the first of a series of studies Weber undertook on the relationship of religious ideology to social development, studies published in the *Religionssoziologie* and later summarized, in a very general way, in the final chapter of the *General Economic History*, which is actually a transcription of Weber's last course of lectures.

Both Marx and Weber were deeply influenced by the historicist tendency of German social thought. This tendency, which found full early expression in the writings of Hegel, held that social existence is process, that each historical epoch and social structure is unique, to be

This article originally appeared in *The British Journal of Sociology* 4 (1953). Reprinted by permission of Routledge, Inc.

understood by laws referable only to itself. Marx and Weber, each in his way, broke with these postulates. Marx rejected historicism's predominantly idealistic interpretation of the content of social process, asserting that the decisive events were in the realm of social relationships, not in the sphere of the evolution of ideas. And in fashioning a theory which insisted on underlying regularities in social change, Marx also rejected the notion of the total uniqueness of historical epochs and social structures. Yet Marx retained historicism's sense of process and transformation. Weber, especially in the posthumously published *Wirtschaft und Gesellschaft*, attempted to formulate some general categories that would apply to all historical epochs: this too constituted a break with historicism. . . .

Both thinkers, moreover, laboured on problems that had some special immediacy for Germans. Germany had, up to the large-scale introduction of capitalism in the nineteenth century, a curious amalgam of rational-legal and traditionalist political organization (in terms employed by Weber in his typology of authority). We can anticipate a bit at this point: Weber strongly implied these terms are descriptive not alone of authority structures but of the total organization of society. Industrial capitalism, with its intrinsically dynamic qualities, had severely disruptive effects on German society. This rendered capitalism a particular problem to German social thinkers, by contrast with England where a more gradual development allowed figures like Adam Smith and David Ricardo to treat the capitalist economic processes as more "natural". It is against this background that we can understand the concern of both Marx and Weber with capitalism not as a limited, economic system, but with its effects on society as a whole—on familial structure, political authority, personality organization and on cultural phenomena like science and art. . . .

The phenomenon both Marx and Weber wished to explain was the development, unique in world historical perspective, of an economic system in western Europe in which the following attributes were combined. The means of production were concentrated in the hands of a relatively small segment of the population. Labour was performed by a mass of formally free workers selling their services on a market. New social values called for a maximization of efficiency in the means of production through a relentless application of canons of rationality, and prescribed unlimited gain as an end of economic behaviour.

This development was all the more remarkable against the feudal background, with its fixed and unfree social relationships, the irrational and spendthrift way of life of the feudal ruling classes, and the magical character of medieval European culture. Both thinkers agreed on the uniqueness of the new economic structure, and both agreed that it could not be treated simply as such, that it entailed a new type of society. They also agreed on the enormous productivity of this new society, in cultural as well as material terms: sections of the *Communist Manifesto*, paradoxically, eulogize the bourgeoisie.

Marx and Weber held that the new social values embodied in capitalist economic activity were not "natural"—they were precipitates of historical development. Marx delighted to jibe at bourgeois economists for mistaking attitudes and behaviour specific to capitalism for functions of some generic human nature. Weber insisted that the means and ends of action under capitalism were not simply expressions of some universal economic impulse but constituted a definite, socially-sanctioned form taken by the more general human demand for want satisfaction.

Weber emphasized the distinction between traditional and rational social values in depicting the sharp contrast between feudalism and capitalism. Traditionalism in economic behaviour, for Weber, meant fixation on an immutable standard of concrete preferences. Rationality, on the other hand, entailed a continual weighing of preferences in terms of the relative cost of attaining each. And the injunction to unlimited gain was much more abstract, much more devoid of specific concrete content, than the typically fixed goals of traditionalist economics. Traditionalism also included the transmission of sancrosanct ways of attaining its fixed preferences. Rationality, however, prescribed a perpetual critique of economic means: these were no longer sancrosanct, but subject to the criteria of technical efficiency. Every hitherto fixed way of doing things was now to be examined and, if necessary, replaced. The point Weber made, and in which Marx concurred, was that the canons of rationality no less than the *dicta* of traditionalism were arbitrary in the sense that both were concrete sets of values, guiding action that took historically variable form. Thus Weber asserted: "A man does not by nature wish to earn more and more money, but simply to live as he is accustomed and to earn as much as is necessary for that purpose."

The application of the canon of rationality unloosed an intrinsically dynamic force in economic behaviour. A given producer was no longer obliged to confine his activities to a limited sphere, if he could maximize gain in another one. The effects of this continuous calculation of means-ends relationships were experienced in all other aspects of capitalist society as well: rationality, so destructive of precedent, could hardly be confined to economic life. It gave a decisive cast to the entire modern cultural *ethos*. (Weber argued that a rational-legal state was the only political structure that allowed this calculability in economic activity: traditionalist states were much too bound by specific precedent and arbitrary administrative decision. Weber went so far as to make this rational-legal, or bureaucratic, state a precondition for the emergence of capitalism.) Although rationality is a key point in Weber's analysis of the distinctive characteristics of capitalism, Marx was also well aware of it. Witness this passage from the *Communist Manifesto*:

> The bourgeoisie cannot exist without constantly revolutionizing the instruments of production . . . conservation of the old modes of production was, on the contrary, the first condition of existence for all earlier industrial classes. Constant revolutionizing of production, uninterrupted disturbance of all social conditions, everlasting uncertainty and agitation distinguish the bourgeois epoch from all earlier ones. All fixed, fast-frozen relations, with their train of ancient and venerable prejudices and opinions, are swept away, all new formed ones become antiquated before they can ossify. All that is solid melts into air, all that is holy is profaned. . . .

To recapitulate, Marx and Weber agreed on the cultural characteristics of capitalist society. Like all other societies, its economic goals are arbitrary in the sense that they are standards of value (in the capitalist case, the injunction to unlimited gain)—between any two sets of which choice is a matter of arbitrary preference. The value of unlimited gain was not one found in traditionalist systems, with their injunctions to limited economic gains. Further, capitalism represented a break with traditionalism in economic means as well as economic ends. This does not mean that capitalism was undisciplined, by contrast with sanctified traditional procedures. But it does mean that the specific capitalist economic discipline was that of the maximization of technical efficiency. Marx and Weber both agreed that this had wide consequences for non-economic activity. Weber argued that this canon is fundamentally incompatible with a magical or sacramental view of the world. Marx, too, recognized the connection between the emergence of capitalism and the banishment of magic from the west: "At the date when, in England, people gave up the practise of burning witches, they began to hang the forgers of banknotes." As we shall see, Marx and Weber differed on the explanation of this connection, but hardly on its existence. . . .

Late in his life, Marx was credited with the observation: "Je ne suis pas Marxiste." He expressed, in this way, his repudiation of the over-mechanical utilization of this theory by his followers, their lack of specification of the variables he had introduced into sociological analysis. We should be relatively unenlightened as to what Marx meant, were we to-day to discuss him as an economic determinist or as a historical materialist without defining the meaning of these terms. Marx was *not* an economic determinist in the sense that he thought economic motives the decisive ones in the social action of individuals. It is, indeed, crucial to our contrast of Marx and Weber that Marx left motivation relatively unanalysed. It is precisely in the unanalysed parts of a generally well-elaborated theory (the questions to which it gives offhand answers) that we may find its flaws. Marx knew that he had to account for motivation, but did so in terms that are, by contrast with other aspects of his work, strikingly undeveloped. . . .

Every society, according to the sociology of Marx, has a set of economic institutions, a social relationship system allocating roles in the production, distribution and utilization of goods. This system is organized around a society's production technology, and is acutely responsive to changes in technological complexity and efficiency. (Property relations, under this view, are aspects of this social relationship system, and aspects of a highly variable kind, when viewed in historical perspective.) Roles in the economic system determine roles in the status system: broad strata of the population group together in terms of economic similarities. Taken together, these two systems constitute a class system, and the members of a given class share common interests, values and a style of life. The allocations dictated by the economic system determine not only differences in status, for they include differences in political power as well. Thus the way to understand the functioning of a total society is to treat its economic institutions as the key variable.

The notion that economic institutions constitute the critical variable in the organization of society is, of course, especially emphasized in the historical aspects of the theory of historical materialism. All societies are in a continual process of change. Changes in material factors determine the direction of historical change for the society as a whole. Indeed, major processes of historical change are inconceivable without a material basis in the sense of a change in economic institutions.

The Marxist theory of motivation developed within this framework has two components. The first emphasizes the role of purely external pressures on individuals: force, fraud and compulsion. The second begins with a concept of class interests, and involves a theory of ideology: this component is central to the present discussion. For Marx, despite his emphasis on the varieties of coercion, was aware of the fact of consensus in society—that agreement on basic values among all its members, or substantial sections of them, such that individuals want to do what they have to do, and voluntarily, even eagerly, perform their social roles. How, then, did he explain it?

Position in a class endows an individual with a set of interests, a stake in certain present aspects of the society, or a potential for gain should the society undergo changes of a determinate sort. These interests are intuitively or rationally understood by the members of a class or their political leaders. Class interests not infrequently directly dictate social action. But, in perhaps the more common case, class interests determine action indirectly, and are effective through the medium of an ideology, an elaborated rationalization of a set of class interests. This ideology, in Marxist terms, comprises values as well as belief-systems, imperatives as well as world-images. We can see that for both sorts of action, that based directly on class interests or that following the imperatives of ideology, Marx inserted the economically determining factor well back in the process, in the genesis of class position. Economic motives were not, for him, the decisive motives in action. Thus the familiar dictum, "Religion is the opiate of the masses", clearly states that action would take a different course, were the opiate removed.

Although this theory may account for uniformities in the motivation of members of a single class, it had yet to account for consensual phenomena of an inter-class sort. To meet this difficulty, Marx advanced the proposition that the class which controlled the means of production could and did impose its ideology on the rest of society. The failure of the members, leaders or ideologists of a class to comprehend their real interests leads them to accept the ideology of another, opposed, stratum and so underlies this imposition. At this point Engels introduced the notion of "false consciousness"—a process by which men incorrectly assess the sources of their beliefs, attributing these to the history of thought, for instance, rather than to their real roots in the system of production. It is in this context that Marxist theory could explain how patriotism and religion unified societies.

What may we say about all of this? Marx recognized the social function of common values and developed his theory of ideology, partially to explain it. But Marx did not explain how class position, effective through class interests, generates ideology. He seemed to assume that this was done mechanically and automatically. But unless one specifies the relationships accounting for observed correlations of social facts, one may overlook more useful explanations for the observed correlations. It was precisely of this *lacuna* in Marxism that Weber was to make so much.

Marx's failure to specify the mechanisms by which common values are produced left quite implicit another function of such values, and the general ideological systems from which they derive. For such systems have uses other than their functions for society as a whole: they have definite psychological functions for individuals. These systems assure individuals a coherent world-image and are an indispensable factor in maintaining psychological stability.

Marx left these functions quite implicit: he seemed to assume an infinite sort of plasticity to human nature, such that these functions could be met by *any* ideology and its associated values. Thus Marx did not even pose a problem Weber was to find so important: what values led to given patterns of social behaviour?

Again, we may say that if social relationship systems (for example, a class system) determine the behaviour of individuals, they may do so through processes not inferable from a narrow description of the system itself. These processes, overlooked, may account for behaviour one had mistakenly attributed to the system as narrowly defined. The psychological processes we have just mentioned may play precisely such a role, as may the other mechanisms that translate class position into action—all unspecified by Marx. It was at these points that Weber was to mount his attack on historical materialism ... implications pointing beyond a concern with government or its equivalent. The characterization of various authority structures as charismatic, rational-legal or traditional refers to the bases of legitimacy: the values enjoining acceptance of the authority. Weber's analysis made clear, however, that political values can only be separated from the other values of a society with great artificiality. Weber's typology of authority was really a typology of the more general value-system endowing a society with consensus.

For Weber assumed that social behaviour is of a piece: a society traditionalist in economic relationships usually does not possess a rational-legal authority structure. The value-system of a society limits the possibilities for institutional variation within it: too much of a shift in the bases of legitimation and the structure of behaviour it allows, from one segment of a society to another, can produce severe disruptions in institutional function. We may recall, at this point, Weber's insistence on the connection between rational political administration in Europe and the rise of rationalized economic activity.

Weber, however, by no means saw societies as emanations of values. In the final phrases of *The Protestant Ethic*, he specifically renounced the intention of substituting what he termed a one-sided spiritualistic interpretation of history for an equally one-sided materialistic interpretation. But in his analyses of stratification and the phenomena associated with it, Weber held that economic institutions were not the only relevant critical variables. Differential prestige distribution, for instance, and variations in style of life might counter-balance the effects of economic factors in the genesis and functioning of a stratification system. Within the context of this view of the bases of stratification, however, Weber was not unaware of the effects of class systems on ideology and values. In his later years he discussed the class basis of religion in the following terms. Religion of privileged, ruling strata emphasize this-worldly values. Members of such strata feel intrinsically worthy because of their present social positions, and their religious beliefs justify the social system that allowed them such elevation. Members of underprivileged and oppressed strata, far from feeling worthy in terms of what they *are*, emphasize the importance of what they will *become*. They emphasize other-worldly values, and their religions depict a future salvation entailing a radical transformation of society's present relationships.

Clearly, religion interpreted in these terms is religion treated as a class ideology. But Weber made explicit what Marx left implicit. He asserted that religion answered the needs of men for some coherent account of their life situation. . . .

Salvation religion and ethical religiosity has a source other than the social situation of the negatively privileged and that bourgeois rationality which is conditioned by the practical life situation—the intellect considered of itself, especially the metaphysical needs of the human spirit, which is compelled to struggle with ethical and religious questions not by material compulsion alone, but through its own inner necessity to comprehend the world as a meaningful cosmos and to know what attitude to take before it.

If, as Weber asserted, religious systems and their associated values meet the individual's general psychological needs, the relationship between these needs and the individual's social position becomes problematical. The connection between the two does exist; but it is not a mechanical one and the sociological analysis of ideology cannot overlook it. The relationship was crucial to Weber's analysis.

Weber, again, cannot be understood as a one-sided ideological determinist. He did emphasize the relatively independent development of systems of ideas. He denied that ideas are simply "reflections" of a class position, or that class interests may be understood apart from a class's conception of these interests, its ideology and its values. And he did insist, as we shall see in discussing his substantive analysis of western capitalism, that ideas (taken in conjunction with other factors) can exercise some independent influence on the course of historical development.

We have said that the failure to analyse the properties of the relationship between class position and ideology might lead to faulty interpretation of the observed facts. We have also said that Marx left these properties unanalysed, and assumed that class position automatically produced an appropriate ideology. Having postulated "the metaphysical needs of the human spirit" Weber could demonstrate that it was precisely this psychological property of the relationship that Marx left unanalysed. This opened the way for his assertion that this property of the relationship might affect historical development in its own way, and not simply as a derivative of a more basic factor, economic institutions. Thus Weber's interpretation of the observed correlations between class position and ideology took cognizance of the initial facts Marx had noted, but refined and so amended the analysis.

Weber held that ideology had independent effects on behaviour, but insisted that these effects could be just as unanticipated as those resulting from material factors. Thus Weber warned: "If one wishes to study at all the influence of a religion on life, one must distinguish between its official teachings and the sort of actual procedure upon which, in reality, perhaps against its own will, it placed a premium, in this world or the next." In the same way, he was to say of the Reformation that its cultural consequences "were predominantly unforeseen and even unwished for results of the labors of the Reformers".

We have criticized Marx's theory of ideology for assuming what it had to demonstrate: that ideas are simply reflections of social position and exercise no independent effects on historical development. How did Weber demonstrate his thesis? If Marx intersected the historical process arbitrarily, was not Weber's intersection of it, albeit at a different point, no less arbitrary? Weber solved this difficulty by going outside the process of western history—by undertaking a series of studies we can understand as sociological equivalents to experimentation.

Experimental method has this advantage: if the scientist wishes to test the effects of a single variable, he can hold all other variables constant while altering the one under examination. The reconstruction of a single historical process allows no such control of experimental conditions, although it may be a necessary preliminary to such control. In this sense, we can charge Marx with failure to explore the possibility that, under different conditions, the material factors he saw as decisive in the west might have had results other than the ones he attributed to them.

But Weber took advantage of the fact that history has left us with the record of its own sociological experiments. Several large-scale civilizations have developed in relative isolation from each other: the west, China and India, among others. By tracing out economic developments in each, Weber attempted to hold constant the material preconditions for western-style capitalism. This enabled him to focus on religious ideology, in each society, to see if it had independent effects. Comparative method, then, may be called a sociological equivalent of experimentation. What Weber did, moreover, was to analyse comparative materials with a very specific hypothesis in mind—a hypothesis derived from his encounter with Marxist theory....

Marx treated capitalism as a product of the feudal social system. Wars exhausted the feudal ruling class while its irrational and spendthrift way of life (itself a factor in causing these wars) emphasized consumption and not production. This emphasis gave rise to a wealthy merchant class, and financial powers developed in the medieval cities to assist in these mercantile transactions. Late in medieval times money became the decisive power of feudal Europe. Only in this way could the rural lords convert their desires into commodities. The rise in the price of English wool, a result of the development of a market for it in the Flemish woollen industry, provoked the money-hungry feudal lords to enclosures. These enclosures restricted their lands to sheep-pasturage, and either drove the peasants away or severely altered their social position. These changes had, according to Marx, an economic basis. But on this, developed a new super-structure: "With the coming of money rent the traditional and customary relations between the landlord and the subject tillers of the soil, who possessed a part of the land, is turned into a pure money relation, fixed by the rules of positive law."...

Marx's system had a relentless consistency, but its worth seems to lie in its assertion of the existence of historical connections rather than the explication of their full structure. The ratio-nalization of economic life that Marx attributed to the "immanent laws of capitalist develop-ment" is precisely what Weber sought to explain in the light of a broader sociological perspective, conscious that what Marx regarded as inextricably forged together could, on other historic anvils, be shaped another way.

Comparative method allowed Weber to make an estimate of the relative effects of material and ideological factors in the rise of capitalism, not only in the west as contrasted with other societies, but also among Catholic, Lutheran and Calvinist segments of western society. Population growth and the influx of precious metals were dismissed as the sole inciting causes of the rise of western capitalism by Weber in view of their effects in India and China, from which capitalism hardly issued. (Capitalism meant something very specific to Weber: the orga-nization of formally free labour in methodical, rational and disciplined work.) Weber argued that the two factors mentioned above were effective in the west only insofar as the labour rela-tions system allowed. This was a material argument; but we may recall that Weber did not wish to promulgate a one-sided interpretation. And Weber emphasized, as we shall see, some of the ideological and psychological dynamics of that labour relations system.

Weber's freedom from the notion of progressive direction in history enabled him to study India and China without treating these societies as "arrested" or "preliminary" variants of capi-talism. Marx and his followers, on the contrary, tend to do the latter—and precluded compar-ative correction of their analyses of the west. The Indian and Chinese studies strengthened Weber's emphasis on the economic consequences of religious belief....

Medieval Catholicism provided its believers with an escape mechanism, as it were, from their guilt in the confessional. The sacramental power of the priest was a residue of magical belief. Medieval Catholicism thus allowed relief and prevented rationalization. The Catholic lived morally, in Weber's words, from "hand to mouth"—his life was a succession of acts, each judged by its intention, not a systematized whole. Only a special group, the monks, had an incentive to rationalize their lives. For the layman, this system dispensed grace in a magical way. The absence of harshness and rationalization for the common man produced a genial and benign acceptance of life. And since the world and its institutions were viewed as lower sections of the supernatural order, traditional standards were created and received a religious sanctification.

Luther, the first heroic figure of the Reformation, rejected the notion that the church possessed magical powers. But his doctrine of *solafideism*, that men could be saved by faith alone, rested on an indwelling notion of grace. Men were vessels of the divine, and since the divine was incarnate on earth, God had decreed the current social order. This, in its own way, sancti-fied traditionalism in economics and authoritarianism in politics. Luther did, however, intro-duce the notion of the calling as applying to all, not only monks: God's injunction to the individual to work in his allotted sphere. We shall see how Calvinism transformed this notion.

Calvin posed an absolutely transcendental God, decreeing salvation or damnation at will.

This created a terrible inner isolation for the believer, an intolerable burden of anxiety to know whether he was one of the elect. This anxiety forced the development of Calvinism (after Calvin) in a Puritan direction. One could know one was saved by works, which could not, however, ensure one's salvation. Deprived of the relief of the confessional, deprived of the inward conception of grace possessed by Lutheranism (Calvinism distrusted the feelings as chimerical), Puritanism turned outward. . . .

The bearers of this Christian asceticism were the new middle classes of England and Holland. The Puritans, under the notion of the calling, were enjoined to make the most of their opportunities in the world, provided they did not relapse into the state of the natural man. One could pile up wealth, for not to do so would be to deny one's duty in one's calling. But one could not use wealth for pleasure. "The idea of a man's duty to his possessions, to which he subordinates himself as an obedient steward, or even as an acquisitive machine, bears with chilling weight on his life." (Marx speaks of the "fetishism of commodities"; here Weber gave this conception a definite ideological source.) The notion of the transcendence of God and the impersonality of the world led the Puritans to reject traditionalism; they thus had a religious sanctification for the destruction of traditionalist restrictions. Meanwhile, "the emphasis on the ascetic importance of a fixed calling provided an ethical justification of the modern specialized division of labor. In a similar way, the providential interpretation of profit-making justified the activities of the business man." Thus the Puritans had religious incentives of the strongest sort to utilize the opportunities attendant upon the disruption of the feudal system. They could not utilize their wealth for spendthrift consumption in the manner of the former ruling classes, for to do so would be to repudiate the ascetic standards they honoured. Perforce, they re-invested. . . .

Rejection of the possibility of the intervention of a church body or a state in the individual's path to salvation led to a political anti-authoritarianism that Weber contrasted with the social quietism of Lutheranism. He cited the political institutions of Puritan England and America as cases in point, in contrast with those of Lutheran Germany. The Puritan injunction against idolatry of the flesh, Weber adds, has also resulted in an anti-Caesarist tendency in the political life of Puritan countries.

What Weber was saying in all of this was that the institutions of capitalism were no outgrowth of the feudal system in any mechanistic sense. They demanded a specific set of values, and specific psychological qualities, for maximum utilization of their potential. The social history of England and the economic role of the Puritans in British sixteenth- and seventeenth-century society provides European evidence for the role of religious ideas in historical development. Weber also cited as evidence the absence of rationalization in Lutheran Germany and in the Catholic countries, the importation of Calvinists by European rulers desirous of encouraging industry, even early twentieth-century occupational differentiation statistics comparing Catholics and Protestants—well after the secularized development of capitalism had made Puritans of all the children of the west.

Weber really made two points in reference to Calvinism. Its values were such that it sanctified capitalist activity, providing an ideology that set the Puritans onto the restless pursuit of gain. But along with the values the Puritans possessed, they were also organized as personalities to function in this methodical, ruthless way. It was this inner ruthlessness and conviction that led them to break traditionalism, that sustained them against church and state. The inner development of religious thought to the point of Calvinism and the production of hard Puritan characters had to take place before economic activity could be rationalized in a way that Marx saw as an automatic consequence of the opportunities provided by the inner disruption of the medieval social system. By inserting an ideological and a psychological variable (the latter, to be sure, more implicitly) in historical analysis, Weber showed that the explication of variables relatively implicit in Marxist analysis may alter the conclusions that analysis reached, without essentially altering the facts it considered.

Weber's concern with the independent effects of ideology on social development, then, originated in his polemical encounter with Marxism. This led him to develop at least an implicit general theory to oppose to that of his great nineteenth-century predecessor. The immediate occasion for this development, however, was Weber's concern with the facts of Marx's central empirical case: the rise of capitalism. In analysing these facts, Weber fairly may be said to have built on Marx's work.

Marx, who treated ideology as a dependent variable in the process of social transformation, formulated this problem more precisely than had his predecessors in the history of social thought. Weber in his turn utilized Marx, not by accepting his hypotheses but by testing them and amending them. He eschewed the assumption of a mechanical production of values (and of ideology, generally) and made explicit what Marx had left implicit: the psychological functions of belief systems. This explication allowed him to point out that ideology did not derive automatically from social position but was, rather, a means of interpreting that position: a possible function of ideology, under this viewpoint, was to give direction to social change. . . .

Challenges to

Nineteenth-Century Theory

The Emergence

of the Culture Concept

and the Sociology of Science

Introduction

During the first half of the twentieth century many individuals began to question seriously the assumptions about human nature that had underlain the Enlightenment project and to explore the disjuncture between the modern faith in progress and the reality of modern life. The work of Ruth Benedict, Clifford Geertz, Claude Lévi-Strauss, and Thomas Kuhn, among others, challenged the modern supposition that the accumulation of knowledge through scientific practice necessarily bettered the human condition. In contrast to the grand theorists of the nineteenth century like Alexis de Tocqueville and Karl Marx, twentieth-century social scientists tended to sound less confident about the future and less secure in the capacity of the West to bring "light" to the farthest reaches of the globe. The twentieth-century critique of modernity emerged as part of a general recognition of some of the contradictions and inconsistencies central to the modern impulse.

The imperialist projects undertaken by both Europeans and Americans during the late nineteenth and early twentieth centuries exemplifies some of the inconsistencies inherent to modern thought and practice. Although European nations began colonizing the Americas in the early sixteenth century when the Spaniard Hernando Cortés conquered Mexico in 1519, the imperialism of the late nineteenth century took place on an unprecedented scale. In the years between 1880 and 1900 Western nations divided most of the globe among themselves. During this period Britain had colonial possessions in Africa, India, the Middle East, and the Caribbean; France had colonies in Africa and South East Asia. In 1898 the United States annexed Hawaii and in 1899, after defeating Spain in the Spanish-American war, took possession of the Philippines, Puerto Rico, and Guam.

To many observers, Western imperial expansion represented the triumph of Enlightenment values. Imperial domination of subjected peoples was legitimized by the notion that Westerners were serving the interests of the "less civilized" by wiping out superstition, magic, and false religion and substituting in their place justice, reason, and truth. This sense of responsibility for bringing civilization to "savages" was called the "White Man's Burden."

Yet colonialism flouted the liberal principles which enlightened governments had affirmed since the democratic revolutions of the eighteenth century. In the era of colonialism, nations assumed control over foreign people without their consent and without bringing them into the political community, undermining the liberal principle that a just government derived its legitimacy from the consent of the governed. Through colonization, Westerners created an "other" which collectively was thought to be incapable of self-government and in the process challenged the Enlightenment conception of a universal human nature. During the height of Western expansion, Darwinian observations about the animal kingdom were applied to human beings, and a notion of a hierarchy of races was developed which located Western civilization at the apex. This evolutionary biology served to legitimate colonialism as a political system in much the same way that Smith's science of the market and the Enlightenment conception of man as inherently rational justified the establishment of liberal democratic capitalism. Westerners repeatedly looked to science for ideas about society.

While there were myriad events which contributed to the onset of World War I (1914–1918), colonialism was certainly an important factor. It was in the process of building and protecting their empires that Western nations created the large armies and navies which fought and killed each other with such tremendous success during the course of the war. It has been estimated that over ten million men were killed in the fighting. The high casualty rate was in part due to the advances made in weaponry which included the development of the machine gun, poison gas, tanks, and the submarine. The irony that the very technology championed since the Enlightenment was responsible for unprecedented destruction put into question the modern faith in technology as a vehicle for progress.

In the wake of World War I, thoughtful people began to question the extent to which Western culture could be viewed as synonymous with progress and civilization. How could the West claim that its civilization was founded on reason and rationality when the war revealed the extent of the West's capacity for brutality? Were Westerners really any more civilized than those peoples whom they had conquered in the name of civilization? Americans, who had often exhibited some unease about their European heritage, began to see Europe as enormously corrupt. This idea was so pervasive at the popular level it contributed to the refusal of the United States to join the League of Nations at the close of the war.

The attempt to answer some of the questions raised by the war was partly responsible for the formation of the modern discipline of anthropology and the development of the scientific concept of culture which stressed the importance of society over nature in shaping personality. Introduced into social scientific thinking by the German anthropologist, Franz Boas, the culture concept began to undermine the naturalistic Darwinian model of human behavior that had long reinforced racist and sexist thinking.

In the last quarter of the nineteenth century, Darwin's theory of evolution in the animal world was appropriated by scholars trying to make the study of society more rigorously scientific. British thinkers such as the Herbert Spencer and William Graham Sumner talked about social life as a "struggle for existence" in which the best "competitor" survived. Social Darwinism often served to legitimate overt racism, imperialism, and the ill effects of industrialization by rationalizing the status quo as natural and inevitable.

Use of the culture concept by Boas and his students Ruth Benedict and Margaret Mead in a series of comparative analyses of different societies provided a scientific refutation of social Darwinism. Benedict presented the case for culture forcefully in her 1934 book *Patterns of*

Culture, in which she advocated the principle of cultural relativism and dismissed an evolutionary understanding of social development. In a similar fashion, women social scientists like Helen Bradford Thompson at the University of Chicago used a less developed concept of culture to begin chipping away at notions of inherited sexual difference upon which the nineteenth-century ideology of separate spheres for men and women was based.

The contemporary anthropologist Clifford Geertz has suggested that the discipline of anthropology originated in the need to overturn that Enlightenment conception which stressed human nature as "regularly organized, as thoroughly invariant, and as marvelously simple as Newton's universe."[1] The anthropologist's move to complicate the Enlightenment view of human nature by emphasizing man's adaptability, plasticity, and complexity opened new areas of uncertainty even as scholars sought to close the door on social Darwinism and biological determinism. If social organization could take a multiplicity of different forms, if mankind was endlessly creative in the development of social institutions, how could one decide that the social organization of Western nations was inherently superior? The idea of cultural relativism, which modern anthropological work inspired, became a defining feature of twentieth-century modernism.

Although cultural relativism as a theory in the social sciences was not completely analogous to relativity as a theory in the physical sciences, both served to undermine the Western faith in absolutes. The theory of relativity, developed by Swiss physicist Albert Einstein in 1905, was considered revolutionary precisely because it was premised on the belief that neither time nor space were fixed or distinct entities as Aristotle and Newton had assumed. In relativity theory the experience of time and space depended upon the position of the observer in relationship to the observed phenomena. In this view observers might watch the same event, disagree about the time in which it took place, and all be correct, depending upon the speed at which they were moving when the event took place. Truth thus became highly dependent upon perspective, a notion that further undermined the modern faith in absolutes.

In 1926, the German scientist Werner Heisenberg developed what has come to be known as the "uncertainty principle" and forever undermined the possibility of a completely deterministic model of the universe. Heisenberg's uncertainty principle specified that whenever a person attempted to observe a particle of matter, the observer had an effect upon that particle; thus, one could never determine the state of things as they existed outside observation. Prediction, then, becomes impossible. Heisenberg's principle was incorporated into the theory of quantum mechanics, which offered a series of possibilities instead of a prediction of any one outcome. Even as the notion of moral and physical absolutes was increasingly called into question, the idea of an irrational, chaotic, and unpredictable world remained an anathema. For instance, Einstein, who died in 1955, was always resistant to the theory of quantum mechanics even though his own work contributed to its formulation: he dismissed the new concept by declaring that "God does not play dice."[2]

For many individuals who lived through the middle decades of the twentieth century, however, it seemed as though God did in fact play dice. In 1929, when the New York stock market crashed, the lives of millions of people were disrupted. The Great Depression was international in scope, spreading from New York out towards Europe as American investors sold their foreign securities and pulled the rug out from under the postwar revival of European economies. By 1931 the German economy was at a standstill, as was the British credit system. In 1933, over one third of the American labor force was unemployed. It is estimated that between 1929 and 1932, world production declined by over 38 percent. The economic nationalism that countries practiced in order to protect their own domestic markets contributed to a climate of increasing hostility. In Germany, nationalist sentiment and economic depression provided a fertile ground for the growth of the Nazi party.

Hostility to Jews had been pervasive throughout Europe since the Middle Ages, yet anti-Semitic sentiment prior to the nineteenth century was based primarily on religious prejudice, as opposed to the nationalism that fueled European anti-Semitic thought through the nineteenth and early twentieth centuries. Anti-Semitism reached new heights in Germany during the 1930s with the rise of the Nazi party under the leadership of Adolf Hitler. Although the instability of many European nations during the 1930s contributed to the power vacuum that made Hitler's aggression possible, it was Nazi Germany that was ultimately responsible for the outbreak of World War II (1939–1945) and for the Holocaust, in which approximately six million Jews were exterminated in Nazi concentration camps.

The atrocities committed during World War II were not committed by the Germans alone. In the course of the war the United States and Britain killed over fifty thousand civilians in the firebombing of Dresden. The United States dropped two atomic bombs on the Japanese cities of Hiroshima and Nagasaki killing at least 200,000 people. Statistics compiled after the war ended estimated the total number of casualties for all parties at around 45 million men, women, and children.

Perhaps one of the most important legacies of World War II, but by no means the only one, was the onset of the Cold War. The climate of anxiety and fear produced by the nuclear arms race between the Soviet Union and the United States was an ever-present reality that defined the parameters of political, social, and artistic freedom in the post-war world, and gave the so-called Cold War its chilling realities. The possibility of nuclear destruction brought the awareness of the destructive capacity of science to new heights. At the same time the industrial production which the war effort required, and the military-industrial complex created in its aftermath, ushered in a new age of prosperity for the industrial democracies of the West. The paradox of the mid-twentieth century was that postwar growth in Europe and America was rooted in huge investments in defense spending and the stockpiling of nuclear missiles.

If at the outset of the twentieth century a sense of crisis led to new approaches within the social sciences, the sense of uncertainty engendered by the Cold War began to affect the way individuals felt about the modern project of science itself. Science could no longer be viewed as a value-neutral inductive process that stood apart from politics. On the one hand science was seen as responsible for the economic growth and high standard of living which Westerners enjoyed. Similarly, many viewed nuclear technology as the sole guarantee that liberal democracy would prevail in the face of perceived Soviet expansionism. It was during this time that the link between science and politics was solidified through the growth of the military-industrial complex which linked the university research and private industry under the umbrella of national defense priorities.

The link between technology and prosperity was analyzed from many different angles. During the 1950s, one of the most positive ways of thinking about the two was modernization theory. Modernization theory posited a scheme of social development loosely modeled on evolutionary thinking. Reminiscent of the Scots' conjectural history, modernization theorists believed that all societies passed through specific stages of economic growth. Western industrial democracies represented the most advanced stage of development, but the disbursal of technology to other countries would allow them to accelerate their own development along the same linear path. For modernization theorists, questions of cultural relativism were ignored in the interest of extending the blessings of material prosperity. Modernization theory depended on structural-functionalism—ideas of society as a system or systems in which change in one part would trigger change in the other. For modernization theorists, the United States' "benign presence" in the world, through such institutions as the Peace Corps, might serve as a model of successful development for other nations to emulate.

Although the 1950s was a decade of prosperity for most of the Western world, these years were not quite as placid or tranquil as artifacts of popular culture from the period suggest. Many social critics at the time argued that prosperity brought with it its own corrupting tendencies as affluence made individuals weak and complacent. Paul Goodman's *Growing Up Absurd* (1956) laments the rise of a bureaucratic, organized, and stagnant culture "disastrous to the growth of excellence and manliness." For historian Daniel Bell the culture of the 1950s was homogenizing and politically narrow, a fact he blamed on prosperity and the consequent loss of purpose and focus. It was during the 1950s that the modern Civil Rights movement began in the United States when blacks, in part inspired by inflated Cold War rhetoric that lauded the United States as the beacon of freedom and democracy, protested their own unequal treatment within the polity.

In 1962, in the midst of the Cold War, historian and philosopher of science Thomas Kuhn wrote a work destined to forever change our thinking about disciplinary knowledge. *The Structure of Scientific Revolutions*, also included in this book, opened a Pandora's box of questions that remain with us to this day. At its most basic level, Kuhn's work, which sold over one million copies worldwide, was a sociology of scientific practice which historicized scientific truth. Kuhn suggested that in the course of practicing what he termed "normal" science, scientists worked within paradigms that set the parameters of basic research. These paradigms could never be absolutely verified through rigorous empirical testing and were adopted or rejected by scientific communities in terms of how well they satisfied the specific needs of that community of practitioners at the time.

Kuhn's work provided insights for those interested in the nature of the relationship between politics and scientific practice. Others found more radical claims in his work which added up to a dismissal of the long-standing notion that science is a cumulative enterprise which can establish the fundamental laws of the universe. The importance of Kuhn's work to scholars in all sorts of disciplines during the late 1960s and early 70s suggests that modern individuals would never again see science as a completely objective endeavor.

Kuhn's suggestion that science was not an objective system of inquiry echoed a similar claim made with respect to language by the Swiss linguist Ferdinand Saussure in the early years of the twentieth century. Saussure argued against the belief that language was a system of objective designations to implement descriptions of the outside world. Instead, Saussure investigated language as a socially created system of signs which corresponded with material reality only indirectly. The implications of Saussure's work for scholars in a host of disciplines was a shift away from inductive efforts to know reality and accumulate knowledge, in favor of a search for meaning. Kuhn's work opened the door for similar critiques of science.

Despite the many criticisms leveled against science, progress, and moral absolutism, it is important to remember that none of the authors whose work is included here accept the extreme relativist or historicist position. The writings of Benedict, Geertz, and Kuhn combine to redefine radically our understanding of men and women and the practice of inquiry, moving us away from the search for knowledge toward an analysis of meaning. And while the analysis of meaning may problematize our ability to find causal links and make predictions, this meaning is firmly grounded in an external reality that we can perceive, however imperfectly.

NOTES

1   Clifford Geertz, "The Impact of the Concept of Culture on the Concept of Man," in *The Interpretation of Cultures* (New York: Basic Books, 1973), p. 34.
2   Stephen Hawking, *A Brief History of Time* (New York: Bantam Books, 1988), pp. 53–57.

John Dewey

The American philosopher John Dewey is well known for his many contributions to the development of American social science (particularly the disciplines of education and psychology), his voluminous writings on art and politics, and his commitment to the social reform
efforts that swept American cities during the early decades of the twentieth century. Dewey
served on the faculty of the University of Chicago from 1894 through 1904, directing work in
education, philosophy, and psychology. During this time he also directed the university's
Laboratory School and served as a trustee for Chicago's famous social settlement, Hull
House. Dewey moved from Chicago to New York in 1904 where he became a professor of
philosophy at Columbia University.

While Dewey's writing addressed a host of different questions, issues, and contemporary social problems, he is perhaps best known for his contributions to the pragmatist tradition in philosophical thinking. Pragmatism is a particularly American school of philosophical
inquiry founded by Charles Sanders Peirce at the turn of the century and popularized by
Dewey and William James. Pragmatist philosophy is generally interested in questions of epistemology as opposed to questions of metaphysics; asking how we know what we know as
opposed to working out ultimate, final, or fundamental truths about reality. In Dewey's
thought, knowledge is contextual, the endpoint of sustained inquiry into a specific problem.

Later theorists in the pragmatist tradition, like the late twentieth-century American
philosopher Richard Rorty, view Dewey's work as crucial to a developing conception of knowledge as nothing more than "what we are justified in believing." Many scholars see a similar
conception of knowledge in the work of Thomas Kuhn, whose writings are also included in
this volume. While Dewey's work may lend support to historicist and relativist conceptions
of truth, he remained committed to a belief in the progressive nature of inquiry and the
emancipatory possibilities of science.

JOHN DEWEY
(1938)

Common Sense
and Scientific Inquiry

Upon the biological level, organisms have to respond to conditions about them in ways that modify those conditions and the relations of organisms to them so as to restore the reciprocal adaptation that is required for the maintenance of life-functions. Human organisms are involved in the same sort of predicament. Because of the effect of cultural conditions, the problems involved not only have different contents but are capable of statement *as* problems so that inquiry can enter as a factor in their resolution. For in a cultural environment, physical conditions are modified by the complex of customs, traditions, occupations, interests and purposes which envelops them. Modes of response are correspondingly transformed. They avail themselves of the significance which things have acquired, and of the *meanings* provided by language. Obviously, rocks as minerals signify something more in a group that has learned to work iron than is signified either to sheep and tigers or to a pastoral or agricultural group. The meanings of related symbols, which form the language of a group, also, introduce a new type of attitudes and hence of modes of response. I shall designate the environment in which human beings are *directly* involved the common sense environment or "world," and inquiries that take place in making the required adjustments in behavior common sense inquiries.

As is brought out later, the problems that arise in such situations of interaction may be reduced to problems of the use and enjoyment of the objects, activities and products, material and ideological, (or "ideal") of the world in which individuals live. Such inquiries are, accordingly, different from those which have knowledge as their goal. The attainment of knowledge

Reprinted from Jo Ann Boydston, ed., *Logic: The Theory of Inquiry* (1938), in *John Dewey: The Later Works, 1925–53,* (Carbondale and Edwardsville, Ill.: Southern Illinois University Press, 1986), vol. 12, pp. 66–85, with permission of the press.

of some things is necessarily involved in common sense inquiries, but it occurs for the sake of settlement of some issue of use and enjoyment, and not, as in scientific inquiry, for its own sake. In the latter, there is no *direct* involvement of human beings in the *immediate* environment— a fact which carries with it the ground of distinguishing the theoretical from the practical.

The use of the term *common sense* is somewhat arbitrary from a linguistic point of view. But the existence of the kinds of situations referred to and of the kind of inquiries that deal with the difficulties and predicaments they present cannot be doubted. They are those which continuously arise in the conduct of life and the ordering of day-by-day behavior. They are such as constantly arise in the development of the young as they learn to make their way in the physical and social environments in which they live; they occur and recur in the life-activity of every adult, whether farmer, artisan, professional man, law-maker or administrator; citizen of a state, husband, wife, or parent. On their very face they need to be discriminated from inquiries that are distinctively scientific, or that aim at attaining confirmed facts, "laws" and theories.

They need, accordingly, to be designated by some distinctive word, and *common sense* is used for that purpose. Moreover, the term is not wholly arbitrary even from the standpoint of linguistic usage. In the *Oxford Dictionary*, for example, is found the following definition of common sense: "Good sound practical sense; combined tact and readiness in dealing with the ordinary affairs of life." Common sense in this signification applies to behavior in its connection with the *significance* of things.

There is, clearly, a distinctively intellectual content involved; *good sense* is, in ordinary language, good *judgment*. Sagacity is power to discriminate the factors that are relevant and important in significance in given situations; it is power of discernment; in a proverbial phrase, ability to tell a hawk from a hernshaw, chalk from cheese, and to bring the discriminations made to bear upon what is to be done and what is to be abstained from, in the "ordinary affairs of life." That which, in the opening paragraphs, was called the mode of inquiry dealing with situations of use and enjoyment, is, after all, but a formal way of saying what the dictionary states in its definition of common sense.

There is, however, another dictionary definition: "The general sense, feeling, judgement of mankind or a community." It is in this sense that we speak of the *deliverances* of common sense as if they were a body of settled truths. It applies not to things in their significance but to *meanings* accepted. When the Scottish school of Reid and Stewart erected "common sense" into an ultimate authority and arbiter of philosophic questions, they were carrying this signification to its limit. The reference to practical sagacity in dealing with problems of response and adaptation in use and enjoyment has now gone into the background. "Common" now means "*general*." It designates the conceptions and beliefs that are currently accepted without question by a given group or by mankind in general. They are *common* in the sense of being widely, if not universally, accepted. They are *sense*, in the way in which we speak of the "sense of a meeting" and in which we say things do or do not "make sense." They have something of the same ultimacy and immediacy for a group that "sensation" and "feeling" have for an individual in his contact with surrounding objects. It is a commonplace that every cultural group possesses a set of meanings which are so deeply embedded in its customs, occupations, traditions and ways of interpreting its physical environment and group-life, that they form the basic categories of the language-system by which details are interpreted. Hence they are regulative and "normative" of specific beliefs and judgments.

There is a genuine difference between the two meanings of common sense. But from the standpoint of a given group there is a definite deposit of agreement. They are both of them connected with the conduct of life in relation to an existing environment: one of them in judging the significance of things and events with reference to what should be done; the other, in the ideas that are used to direct and justify activities and judgments. Tabus are, first, customary ways of activities. To us they are mistaken rather than sagacious ways of action. But the system of meanings embodied in the language that carries tradition gives them authority in such highly practical matters as the eating of food and the behavior that is proper in the presence of chieftains and members of the family configuration, so that they control the relations of males and females and persons of various kinship degrees. To us, such conceptions and beliefs are highly impractical; to those who held them they were matters of higher practical importance than were special modes of behavior in dealing with particular objects. For they set the standards for judging the latter and acting in reference to them. It is possible today, along with our knowledge of the enormous differences that characterize various cultures, to find some unified deposit of activities and of meanings in the "common sense and feeling of *mankind*," especially in matters of basic social cohesion.

In any case, the difference between the two meanings may be reduced, without doing violence to the facts, to the difference between phases and aspects of special practical situations that are looked into, questioned and examined with reference to what may or should be done at a particular time and place and the rules and precepts that are taken for granted in reaching all conclusions and in all socially correct behavior. Both are concerned, one directly and the other indirectly, with "the ordinary affairs of life," in the broad sense of life.

I do not suppose that a generalization of the inquiries and conclusions of this type under the caption of "use and enjoyment" needs much exposition for its support. Use and enjoyment are the ways in which human beings are directly connected with the world about them. Questions of food, shelter, protection, defense, etc., are questions of the use to be made of materials of the environment and of the attitudes to be taken practically towards members of the same group and to other groups taken as wholes. Use, in turn, is for the sake of some consummation or enjoyment. Some things that are far beyond the scope of direct use, like stars and dead ancestors, are objects of magical use, and of enjoyment in rites and legends. If we include the correlative negative ideas of disuse, of abstinence from use, and toleration and suffering, problems of use and enjoyment may be safely said to exhaust the domain of common sense inquiry.

There is direct connection between this fact and the concern of common sense with the *qualitative*. It is by discernment of qualities that the fitness and capacity of things and events for use is decided; that proper foodstuffs, for example, are told or discriminated from those that are unfit, poisonous or tabued. That enjoyment-suffering is qualitative through and through and is concerned with situations in their pervasive qualitative character, is almost too obvious for mention. Furthermore, the operations and responses that are engaged in use and enjoyment of situations are qualitatively marked off. Tanning skins is a process qualitatively different from that of weaving baskets or shaping clay into jars; the rites that are responsive to death are qualitatively different from those appropriate to birth and weddings. Inferiors, superiors and equals are treated in modes of greeting and approach that are qualitatively unlike.

The reason for calling attention to these commonplace facts is that they bring out the basic difference between the subject-matters characteristic of common sense and of scientific inquiries; and they also indicate the differences between the problems and procedures of inquiry that are characteristic of common sense in different stages of culture. I shall first consider the latter point. Common sense in respect to both its content of ideas and beliefs, and its methods of procedure, is anything but a constant. Both its content and its methods alter from time to time not merely in detail but in general pattern. Every invention of a new tool and utensil, every improvement in technique, makes some difference in what is used and enjoyed and in the inquiries that arise with reference to use and enjoyment, with respect to both significance and meaning. Changes in the regulative scheme of relations within a group, family, clan or nation, react even more intensively into some older system of uses and enjoyments.

One has only to note the enormous differences in the contents and methods of common sense in modes of life that are respectively dominantly nomadic, agricultural and industrial. Much that was once taken without question as a matter of common sense is forgotten or actively condemned. Other old conceptions and convictions continue to receive theoretical assent and strong emotional attachment because of their prestige. But they have little hold and application in the ordinary affairs of life. For example, ideas and practices which, in primitive tribes, were interwoven with practically every concern of ordinary affairs, are later relegated to a separate domain, religious or esthetic.

The business of one age becomes the sport and amusement of another age. Even scientific theories and interpretations continue to be affected by conceptions that have ceased to be determinative in the actual practice of inquiry. The special bearing of the fact that "common sense" is anything but a constant upon logical formulations, will concern us in the sequel. Here it is enough to call attention to a point which will later receive detailed examination: namely, the very fitness of the Aristotelian logical organon in respect to the culture and common sense of a certain group in the period in which it was formulated unfits it to be a logical formulation of not only the science but even of the common sense of the present cultural epoch.

I recur now to the bearing of the fact that common sense inquiries are concerned with qualitative matter and operations upon their distinction from scientific inquiries. Fundamentally, the distinction is ... that between significances and meanings that are determined in reference to pretty direct existential application and those that are determined on the ground of their systematic relations of coherence and consistency with one another. All that the present mode of statement adds is that, in the first case, "existential application" means application in *qualitative* use and enjoyment of the environment. On the other hand, both the history of science and the present state of science prove that the goal of the systematic relationship of facts and conceptions to one another is dependent upon *elimination* of the qualitative as such and upon reduction to non-qualitative formulation.

The problem of the relation of the domain of common sense to that of science has notoriously taken the form of opposition of the qualitative to the non-qualitative; largely, but not exclusively, the quantitative. The difference has often been formulated as the difference between perceptual material and a system of conceptual constructions. In this form it has constituted, in recent centuries, the chief theme of epistemology and metaphysics. From the standpoint that controls the present discussion, the problem is not epistemological (save as that word means the *logical*) nor is it metaphysical or ontological. In saying that it is logical, it is affirmed that the question at issue is that of the relation to each other of different kinds of *problems*, since difference in the type of problem demands different emphases in inquiry. It is because of this fact that different logical forms accrue to common sense and scientific objects. From this point of view, the question, summarily stated, is that of the relation to each other of the subject-matters of practical uses and concrete enjoyments and of scientific conclusions; not the subject matters of two different domains whether epistemological or ontological.

The conclusion to be later reached is here anticipated to serve as a guide in following the further discussion. (1) Scientific subject-matter and procedures grow out of the direct problems and methods of common sense, of practical uses and enjoyments, and (2) react into the latter in a way that enormously refines, expands and liberates the contents and the agencies at the disposal of common sense. The separation and opposition of scientific subject-matter to that of common sense, when it is taken to be final, generates those controversial problems of epistemology and metaphysics that still dog the course of philosophy. When scientific subject-matter is seen to bear genetic and functional relation to the subject-matter of common sense, these problems disappear. Scientific subject-matter is intermediate, not final and complete in itself.

I begin the discussion by introducing and explaining the denotative force of the word *situation*. Its import may perhaps be most readily indicated by means of a preliminary negative statement. What is designated by the word "situation" is *not* a single object or event or set of objects and events. For we never experience nor form judgments about objects and events in isolation, but only in connection with a contextual whole. This latter is what is called a "situation." I have mentioned the extent in which modern philosophy had been concerned with the problem of existence as perceptually and conceptually determined. The confusions and fallacies that attend the discussion of this problem have a direct and close connection with the difference between an object and a situation. Psychology has paid much attention to the question of the *process* of perception, and has for its purpose described the perceived object in terms of the results of analysis of the process.

I pass over the fact that, no matter how legitimate the virtual identification of process and product may be for the special purpose of *psychological* theory, the identification is thoroughly dubious as a generalized ground of philosophical discussion and theory. I do so in order to call attention to the fact that by the very nature of the case the psychological treatment takes a *singular* object or event for the subject-matter of its analysis. In actual experience, there is never any such isolated singular object or event; *an* object or event is always a special part, phase, or aspect, of an environing experienced world—a situation. The singular object stands out conspicuously because of its especially focal and crucial position at a given time in determination of some problem of use or enjoyment which the *total* complex environment presents. There is always a *field* in which observation of *this* or *that* object or event occurs. Observation of the latter is made for the sake of finding out what that *field* is with reference to some active adaptive response to be made in carrying forward a *course* of behavior. One has only to recur to animal perception, occurring by means of sense organs, to note that isolation of what is perceived from the course of life-behavior would be not only futile, but obstructive, in many cases fatally so.

A further conclusion follows. When the act and object of perception are isolated from their place and function in promoting and directing a successful course of activities in behalf of use-enjoyment, they are taken to be exclusively *cognitive*. The perceived object, orange, rock, piece of gold, or whatever, is taken to be an object of *knowledge per se*. In the sense of being discriminatingly noticed, it *is* an object of knowledge, but not of knowledge as ultimate and self-sufficient. It is noted or "known" only so far as guidance is thereby given to direction of behavior; so that the situation in which it is found can be appropriately enjoyed or some of its conditions be so used that enjoyment will result or suffering be obviated. It is only when an object of focal observation is regarded as an object of knowledge in isolation that there arises the notion that there are two kinds of knowledge, and two kinds of objects of knowledge, so opposed to each other that philosophy must either choose which is "real" or find some way of reconciling their respective "realities." When it is seen that in common sense inquiry there is no attempt made to know the object or event *as such* but only to determine what it signifies with respect to the way in which the entire situation should be dealt with, the opposition and conflict do not arise. The object or event in question is perceived as part of the environing world, not in and by itself; it is rightly (validly) perceived if and when it acts as clew and guide in use-enjoyment. We live and act in connection with the existing environment, not in connection with isolated objects, even though a singular thing may be crucially significant in deciding how to respond to total environment.

Recurring to the main topic, it is to be remarked that a situation is a whole in virtue of its immediately pervasive quality. When we describe it from the psychological side, we have to say that the situation as a qualitative whole is sensed or *felt*. Such an expression is, however, valuable only as it is taken negatively to indicate that it is *not*, as such, an object in *discourse*. Stating that it is *felt* is wholly misleading if it gives the impression that the situation *is* a feeling or an emotion or anything mentalistic. On the contrary, feeling, sensation and emotion have themselves to be identified and described in terms of the immediate presence of a total qualitative situation.

The pervasively qualitative is not only that which binds all constituents into a whole but it is also unique; it constitutes in each situation an *individual* situation, indivisible and unduplicable. Distinctions and relations are instituted *within* a situation; *they* are recurrent and repeatable in different situations. Discourse that is not controlled by reference to a situation is not discourse, but a meaningless jumble, just as a mass of pied type is not a font much less a sentence. A universe of experience is the precondition of a universe of discourse. Without its controlling presence, there is no way to determine the relevancy, weight or coherence of any designated distinction or relation. The universe of experience surrounds and regulates the universe of discourse but never appears as such within the latter. It may be objected that what was previously said contradicts this statement. For we have been discoursing about universes of experience and situations, so that the latter have been brought within the domain of symbols. The objection, when examined, serves to elicit an important consideration. It is a commonplace that a universe of discourse cannot be a term or element within itself. One universe of discourse may, however, be a term of discourse within *another* universe. The same principle applies in the case of universes of experience.

The reader, whether he agrees or not with what has been said, whether he understands it or not, *has*, as he reads the above passages, a uniquely qualified experienced situation, and his reflective understanding of what is said is controlled by the nature of that immediate situation. One cannot decline to *have* a situation for that is equivalent to having no experience, not even one of disagreement. The most that can be refused or declined is the having of that *specific* situation in which there is reflective recognition (discourse) of the presence of former situations of the kind stated. This very declination is, nevertheless, identical with initiation of another encompassing qualitative experience as a unique whole.

In other words, it *would* be a contradiction if I attempted to demonstrate by means of discourse, the existence of universes of experience. It is not a contradiction by means of discourse to *invite* the reader to have for himself that kind of an immediately experienced situation in which the presence of a situation as a universe of experience is seen to be the encompassing and regulating condition of all discourse.

There is another difficulty in grasping the meaning of what has been said. It concerns the use of the word "quality." The word is usually associated with something specific, like *red, hard, sweet;* that is, with distinctions made within a total experience. The intended contrasting meaning may be suggested, although not adequately exemplified, by considering such qualities as are designated by the terms distressing, perplexing, cheerful, disconsolate. For these words do not designate specific qualities in the way in which *hard,* say, designates a particular quality of a rock. For such qualities permeate and color *all* the objects and events that are involved in an experience. The phrase "tertiary qualities," happily introduced by Santayana, does not refer to a third quality like in kind to the "primary" and "secondary" qualities of Locke and merely happening to differ in content. For a tertiary quality qualifies *all* the constituents to which it applies in thoroughgoing fashion.

Probably the meaning of *quality*, in the sense in which quality is said to pervade all elements and relations that are or can be instituted in discourse and thereby to constitute them an individual whole, can be most readily apprehended by referring to the esthetic use of the word. A painting is said to have quality, or a particular painting to have a Titian or Rembrandt quality. The word thus used most certainly does not refer to any particular line, color or part of the painting. It is something that affects and modifies all the constituents of the picture and all of their relations. It is not anything that can be expressed in words for it is something that must be *had*. Discourse may, however, point out the qualities, lines and relations by means of which pervasive and unifying quality is achieved. But so far as this discourse is separated from *having* the immediate total experience, a reflective object takes the place of an esthetic one. Esthetic experience, in its emphatic sense, is mentioned as a way of calling attention to situations and universes of experience. The intended force of the illustration would be lost if esthetic experience as such were supposed to exhaust the scope and significance of a "situation." As has been said, a qualitative and qualifying situation is present as the background and the control of *every* experience. It was for a similar reason that it was earlier stated that reference to tertiary qualities was not adequately exemplary. For such qualities as are designated by "distressing," "cheerful," etc., are *general*, while the quality of distress and cheer that marks an existent situation is not general but is unique and inexpressible in words.

I give one further illustration from a different angle of approach. It is more or less a commonplace that it is possible to carry on observations that amass facts tirelessly and yet the observed "facts" lead nowhere. On the other hand, it is possible to have the work of observation so controlled by a conceptual framework fixed in advance that the very things which are genuinely decisive in the problem in hand and its solution, are completely overlooked. Everything is forced into the predetermined conceptual and theoretical scheme. The way, and the only way, to escape these two evils, is sensitivity to the quality of a situation as a whole. In ordinary language, a problem must be felt before it can be stated. If the unique quality of the situation is *had* immediately, then there is something that regulates the selection and the weighing of observed facts and their conceptual ordering.

The discussion has reached the point where the basic problem of the relation of common sense material and methods to that of scientific subject-material and method, can be explicitly discussed. In the first place, science takes its departure of necessity from the qualitative objects, processes, and instruments of the common sense world of use and concrete enjoyments and sufferings. The scientific theory of colors and light is extremely abstract and technical. But it is *about* the colors and light involved in everyday affairs. Upon the common sense level, light and colors are not experienced or inquired into as things in isolation nor yet as qualities of objects viewed in isolation. They are experienced, weighed and judged in reference to their place in the occupations and arts (including social ceremonial arts as well as fine arts) the group carries on. Light is a dominant factor in the daily routine of rising from sleep and going about one's business. Differences in the duration of the light of sun and moon interpenetrate almost every tribal custom. Colors are signs of what can be done and of how it should be done in some inclusive situation—such as, judging the prospects of the morrow's weather; selection of appropriate clothing for various occasions; dyeing, making rugs, baskets and jars; and so on in diverse ways too obvious and tedious to enumerate. They play their part either in practical decisions and activities or in enjoyed celebrations, dances, wakes, feasts, etc. What holds of light and color applies to all objects, events and qualities that enter into everyday common sense affairs.

Gradually and by processes that are more or less torturous and originally unplanned, definite technical processes and instrumentalities are formed and transmitted. Information about things, their properties and behaviors, is amassed, independently of any particular immediate application. It becomes increasingly remote from the situations of use and enjoyment in which it originated. There is then a background of materials and operations available for the development of what we term science, although there is still no sharp dividing line between common sense and science. For purposes of illustration, it may be supposed that primitive astronomy and primitive methods of keeping track of time (closely connected with astronomical observations) grew out of the practical necessities of groups with herds in care of animals with respect to mating and reproduction, and of agricultural groups with reference to sowing, tilling and reaping. Observation of the change of position of constellations and stars, of the relation of the length of daylight to the sun's place in relation to the constellations along the line of the equinox provided the required information. Instrumental devices were developed in order that the observations might be made; definite techniques for using the instruments followed.

Measurement of angles of inclination and declination was a practical part of meeting a practical need. The illustration is, from a historical point of view, more or less speculative. But something of this general kind certainly effected the transition from what we call common sense to what we call science. If we were to take the practical needs of medicine in healing the sick and dealing with wounds, in their relation to the growth of physiological and anatomical knowledge, the case would be even clearer. In the early history of Greek reflective thought, art, or *techne*, and science, were synonymous.

But this is not the whole of the story. Oriental cultures, especially the Assyrian, Babylonian and Egyptian, developed a division between "lower" and "higher" techniques and kinds of knowledge. The lower, roughly speaking, was in possession of those who did the daily practical work; carpentering, dyeing, weaving, making pottery, trading, etc. The higher came to be the possession of a special class, priests and the successors of primitive medicine men. Their knowledge and techniques were "higher" because they were concerned with what were supposed to be matters of ultimate concern; the welfare of the people and especially its rulers—and this welfare involved transactions with the powers that ruled the universe. *Their* kind of practical activity was so different from that of artisans and traders, the objects involved were so different, the social status of the persons engaged in carrying on the activities in question was so enormously different, that the activity of the guardians and administrators of the higher knowledge and techniques was not "practical" in the sense of practical that applied to the ordinary useful worker. These facts contained dualism in embryo, indeed in more or less mature form. This, when it was reflectively formulated, became the dualism of the empirical and rational, of theory and practice, and, in our own day, of common sense and science.

The Greeks were much less subject to ecclesiastic and autocratic political control than were the peoples mentioned. The Greeks are pointed to with considerable justice as those who freed thought and knowledge from external control. But in one fundamentally important way they fixed, for subsequent intellectual history, the division just mentioned—although changing its direction and interpretation. Science and philosophy (which were still one) constituted the higher form of knowledge and activity. It alone was "rational" and alone deserved the names of knowledge and of activity that was "pure" because liberated from the constraints of practice. Experimental knowledge was confined to the artisan and trader, and their activity was "practical" because it was concerned with satisfaction of needs and desires—most of the latter, as in the case of the trader, being base and unworthy anyway.

The free citizen was not supposed to engage in any of these pursuits but to devote himself to politics and the defense of the city-state. Although the scientist-philosopher was compelled by constraint of the body to give some time and thought to satisfaction of wants, *as* a scientist-philosopher he was engaged in exercising his reason upon rational objects, thereby attaining the only possible complete freedom and perfect enjoyment. The definitely socio-practical division between workers and non-citizens who were servile, and the members of the leisure class who were free citizens, was converted by philosophic formulation into a division between practice and theory, experience and reason. Strictly scientific-philosophic knowledge and activity were finally conceived to be supra-social as well as supra-empirical. They connected those who pursued them with the divine and cut them off from their fellows.

I have engaged in what seems to be a historical excursus not for the sake of giving historical information but in order to indicate the origin of the distinction between empirical knowledge and practice on one hand and rational knowledge and pure activity on the other; between knowledge and practice that are admittedly of social origin and intent and the insight and activity that were supposed to have no social and practical bearings. This origin is itself social-cultural. Such is the irony of the situation. Relatively free as were the minds of Greek thinkers, momentous as were their accomplishments in certain directions, after Greek culture ceased to be a living thing and its products were carried over into different cultures, the inheritance from the Greeks became an incubus upon the progress of experience and of science, save in mathematics. Even in the latter field it kept mathematics for a long time subservient to strictly geometrical formulation.

The later revival of genuine science undoubtedly drew stimulus and inspiration from the products of Greek thought. But these products were reanimated by contact and interaction with just the things of ordinary experience and the instruments of use in practical arts which in classic Greek thought were supposed to contaminate the purity of science. There was a return to the conditions and factors mentioned earlier: qualitative materials, processes and instruments. Phenomena of heat, light and electricity became matters to be experienced under controlled conditions instead of matters to receive rational formulation through pure intellect. The lens and compass and a multitude of the tools and processes of the practical arts were borrowed and adapted to the needs of scientific inquiry. The ordinary processes that had long been at home in the arts, weakening and intensifying, combining and separating, dissolving and evaporating, precipitating and infusing, heating and cooling, etc., etc., were no longer scorned. They were adopted as means of finding out something about nature, instead of being employed only for the sake of accomplishing objects of use and enjoyment.

Symbolic instrumentalities, especially, underwent tremendous reconstruction; they were refined as well as expanded. On one hand they were constructed and related together on the basis of their applicability, through operations, to existence, and they were freed, on the other hand, from reference to direct application in use and enjoyment. The physical problems that emerged in pursuit of experiential knowledge of nature thus required and evoked new symbolic means of registration and manipulation. Analytic geometry and calculus became primary modes of conceptual response as quantity, change and motion were found to be not irrational accidents but the keys with which to solve the mysteries of natural existence. Language was, nonetheless, an old and familiar qualitative achievement. The most exact comprehensive mathematical language hardly compares as an achievement with the creation of intelligible speech by primitive peoples. Finally, the test of the validity of conceptions formulated and developed in rational discourse was found to reside in their applicability to existential qualitative material. They were no longer taken to be "true" as constituents of rational discourse in isolation but valid in the degree in which they were capable of organizing the qualitative materials of common sense and of instituting control over them. Those semantic-conceptual constructions that indicate with the greatest degree of definiteness the way in which they are to be applied are, even as conceptions, the most truly rational ones. At every point in the practice of scientific inquiry, the old separation between experience and reason, between theory and doing, was destroyed.

In consequence, the contents and techniques of common sense underwent a revolutionary change. It was noted earlier that common sense is not a constant. But the most revolutionary change it has ever undergone is that effected by the infiltration and incorporation of scientific conclusions and methods into itself. Even the procedures and materials that are connected with elementary environmental conditions of life, such things as food, clothing, shelter and locomotion, have undergone tremendous transformation, while unprecedented needs and unprecedented powers of satisfying them have also emerged. The effect of the embodiment of science in the common sense world and the activities that deal with it in the domain of human relationships is as great as that which has taken place in relation to physical nature. It is only necessary to mention the social changes and problems that have arisen from the new technologies of production and distribution of goods and services. For these technologies are the direct product of the new science. To relate in detail the ways in which science has affected the area of common sense in respect to the relationships of person to person, group to group, people to people, would be to relate the story of social change in the last few centuries. Applications of science in revolutionizing the forces and conditions of production, distribution and communication have of necessity tremendously modified the conditions under which human beings live and act in connection with one another, whether the conditions be those of interchange and friendly association or of opposition and war.

It is not intimated that the incorporation of scientific conclusions and operations into the common sense attitudes, beliefs and intellectual methods of what is now taken for granted as matters of common sense is as yet complete or coherent. The opposite is the case. In the most important matters the effect of science upon the content and procedures of common sense has been disintegrative. This disintegrative influence is a social, not a logical, fact. But it is the chief reason why it seems so easy, so "natural," to make a sharp division between common sense inquiry and its logic and scientific inquiry and its logic.

Two aspects of the disintegration which creates the semblance of complete opposition and conflict will be noted. One of them is the fact, already noted, that common sense is concerned with a field that is dominantly qualitative, while science is compelled by its own problems and goals to state its subject-matter in terms of magnitude and other mathematical relations which are non-qualitative. The other fact is that since common sense is concerned, directly and indirectly, with problems of use and enjoyment, it is inherently teleological. Science, on the other hand, has progressed by elimination of "final causes" from every domain with which it is concerned, substituting measured correspondences of change. It operates, to use the old terminology, in terms of "efficient causation," irrespective of ends and values. Upon the basis of the position here taken, these differences are due to the fact that different types of problems demand different modes of inquiry for their solution, not to any ultimate division in existential subject-matter.

The subject-matter of science is stated in symbol-constellations that are radically unlike those familiar to common sense; in what, in effect, is a different language. Moreover, there is much highly technical material that has not been incorporated into common sense even by way of technological application in "material" affairs. In the region of highest importance to common sense, namely, that of moral, political, economic ideas and beliefs, and the methods of forming and confirming them, science has had even less effect. Conceptions and methods in the field of human relationships are in much the same state as were the beliefs and methods of common sense in relation to physical nature before the rise of experimental science. These considerations fix the meaning of the statement that the difference that now exists between common sense and science is a social, rather than a logical, matter. If the word "language" is used not just formally, but to include its content of substantial meanings, the difference is a difference of languages.

The problems of science demand a set of data and a system of meanings and symbols so differentiated that science cannot rightly be called "organized common sense." But it is a potential organ for *organizing* common sense in its dealing with its own subject-matter and problems and this potentiality is far from actualization. In the techniques which affect human use of the materials of physical nature in production, science has become a powerful agency of organization. As far as issues of enjoyment, of consumption, are concerned, it has taken little effect. Morals and the problems of social control are hardly touched. Beliefs, conceptions, customs and institutions, whose rise antedated the modern period, still have possession of the field. The union of this fact with the highly technical and remote language of science creates and maintains the feeling and idea of a complete gap. The paths of communication between common sense and science are as yet largely one-way lanes. Science takes its departure from common sense, but the return road into common sense is devious and blocked by existing social conditions.

In the things of greatest import there is little intercommunication. Pre-scientific ideas and beliefs in morals and politics are, moreover, so deeply ingrained in tradition and habit and institutions, that the impact of scientific method is feared as something profoundly hostile to mankind's dearest and deepest interests and values. On the side of philosophical formulation, highly influential schools of thought are devoted to maintaining the domain of values, ideas and ideals as something wholly apart from any possibility of application of scientific methods. Earlier philosophic conceptions of the necessary separation between reason and experience, theory and practice, higher and lower activities, are used to justify the necessity of the division.

With respect to the second point, that of a seeming fundamental difference due to the fact that common sense is profoundly teleological in its controlling ideas and methods while science is deliberately indifferent to teleology, it must be noted that in spite of the theoretical difference, physical science has, in practical fact, liberated and vastly extended the range of ends open to common sense and has enormously increased the range and power of the means available for attaining them. In ancient thought, ends were fixed by nature; departure from those ends that were antecedently set and fixed by the very nature of things, was impossible; the attempt to institute ends of human devising was taken to be the sure road to confusion and chaos. In the moral field, this conception still exists and is even probably dominant. But in respect to "material" affairs, it has been completely abandoned. Inventions of new agencies and instruments create new ends; they create new consequences which stir men to form new purposes.

The original philosophical meaning of "ends" as fixed completions is almost forgotten. Instead of science eliminating ends and inquiries controlled by teleological considerations, it has, on the contrary, enormously freed and expanded activity and thought in telic matters. This effect is not a matter of opinion but of facts too obvious to be denied. The same sort of thing holds of the qualities with which common sense is inextricably concerned. Multitudes of new qualities have been brought into existence by the applications of physical science, and, what is even more important, our power to bring qualities within actual experience when we so desire, has been intensified almost beyond the possibility of estimate. Consider, as one instance alone, our powers with respect to qualities generated by light and electricity.

The foregoing survey is made for a double purpose. On the one hand the outstanding problem of our civilization is set by the fact that common sense in its content, its "world" and methods, is a house divided against itself. It consists in part, and that part the most vital, of regulative meanings and procedures that antedate the rise of experimental science in its conclusions and methods. In another part, it is what it is because of application of science. This cleavage marks every phase and aspect of modern life: religious, economic, political, legal, and even artistic.

The existence of this split is put in evidence by those who condemn the "modern" and who hold that the only solution of the chaos in civilization is to revert to the intellectual beliefs and methods that were authoritative in past ages, as well as by radicals and "revolutionaries." Between the two stand the multitude that is confused and insecure. It is for this reason that it is here affirmed that the basic problem of present culture and associated living is that of effecting integration where division now exists. The problem cannot be solved apart from a unified logical method of attack and procedure. The attainment of unified method means that the fundamental unity of the structure of inquiry in common sense and science be recognized, their difference being one in the problems with which they are directly concerned, not in their respective logics. It is not urged that attainment of a unified logic, a theory of inquiry, will resolve the split in our beliefs and procedures. But it is affirmed that it will not be resolved without it.

On the other hand, the problem of unification is one in and for logical theory itself. At the present time logics in vogue do not claim for the most part to be logics of inquiry. In the main, we are asked to take our choice between the traditional logic, which was formulated not only long before the rise of science but when also the content and methods of science were in radical opposition to those of present science, and the new purely "symbolistic logic" that recognizes only mathematics, and even at that is not so much concerned with methods of mathematics as with linguistic formulation of its results. The logic of science is not only separated from common sense, but the best that can be done is to speak of logic *and* scientific method as two different and independent matters. Logic in being "purified" from all experiential taint has become so formalistic that it applies only to itself . . . .

Ruth Benedict

Ruth Benedict first began her anthropological work as a student of Franz Boas at Columbia University in New York during the 1920s. Benedict is most renowned for her 1934 book *Patterns of Culture*. This work had a large impact outside the academic world. According to anthropologist Margaret Mead, a contemporary of Benedict who also studied under Boas, our familiarity with the term "culture" and our use of this word in daily conversation is due in large measure to the popularity of Benedict's work.

The emphasis that Benedict placed on culture in determining the behavior of individuals was a refutation of the biological determinism that had driven anthropological study since Darwin published *The Origin of Species* in 1859. Benedict's work rejected the social Darwinism so pervasive in late-nineteenth- and early-twentieth-century Western thought, and provided a scientific basis for opposition to those social movements premised on the application of Darwinian biology to human society in disciplines like eugenics.

Eugenics, from the Greek words meaning "well born," was a theory of heredity inspired by the work of Darwin's cousin Francis Galton. In the United States, eugenicists were an elite group of social reformers active in the early decades of the twentieth century who advocated social improvement through breeding. When Boas and his students Benedict and Mead argued for the primacy of culture over biology in human development, their work had explicitly political ramifications.

In her comparative analysis of the Zuni, Dobu, and Kwakiutl inhabitants of New Mexico, Melanesia, and the Pacific Northwest, respectively, Benedict built on Boas's work. Her discussion of cultural integration, based on the typologies—Apollonian, Dionysian, and Paranoid—reflected her interest in the discovery of certain basic principles around which an individual culture is organized. These terms have much the same aesthetic meaning in Benedict's discussion as they do in Nietzsche's, but here the ethical content is removed. The main premise of Benedict's comparative analysis of custom and social life is that the categories of normal and abnormal are social, as opposed to biological, constructs. As a woman scientist breaking down the barriers of the almost entirely male scientific profession, Benedict's concern with demonstrating that human capacity is plastic and varied across cultures had particular relevance to her own life.

While Benedict's conclusions lend themselves to an entirely relativist position, she herself never abandoned biology completely. Benedict was aware of the role of heredity in determining some of the parameters of human development even though her work refuted the eugenicist position. Although Benedict contributed to an anthropology that provided a place for the socially deviant individual and a foundation for the scientific opposition to racism, the notion of cultural determinism raised questions about individual free will and set the stage for Benedict's reconception of human beings, a conception that differed radically from those of her enlightened predecessors.

RUTH BENEDICT
(1934)

Patterns

of Culture

Anthropology is the study of human beings as creatures of society. It fastens its attention upon those physical characteristics and industrial techniques, those conventions and values, which distinguish one community from all others that belong to a different tradition.

The distinguishing mark of anthropology among the social sciences is that it includes for serious study other societies than our own. For its purposes any social regulation of mating and reproduction is as significant as our own, though it may be that of the Sea Dyaks, and have no possible historical relation to that of our civilization. To the anthropologist, our customs and those of a New Guinea tribe are two possible social schemes for dealing with a common problem, and in so far as he remains an anthropologist he is bound to avoid any weighting of one in favour of the other. He is interested in human behaviour, not as it is shaped by one tradition, our own, but as it has been shaped by any tradition whatsoever. He is interested in the great gamut of custom that is found in various cultures, and his object is to understand the way in which these cultures change and differentiate, the different forms through which they express themselves, and the manner in which the customs of any peoples function in the lives of the individuals who compose them.

Now custom has not been commonly regarded as a subject of any great moment. The inner workings of our own brains we feel to be uniquely worthy of investigation, but custom, we have a way of thinking, is behaviour at its most commonplace. As a matter of fact, it is the other way around. Traditional custom, taken the world over, is a mass of detailed behavior more astonishing than what any one person can ever evolve in individual actions no matter how aberrant. Yet that is a rather trivial aspect of the matter. The fact of first-rate importance is the predominant role that custom plays in experience and in belief, and the very great varieties it may manifest.

No man ever looks at the world with pristine eyes. He sees it edited by a definite set of customs and institutions and ways of thinking. Even in his philosophical probings he cannot go behind these stereotypes; his very concepts of the true and the false will still have reference to his particular traditional customs. John Dewey has said in all seriousness that the part played by custom in shaping the behaviour of the individual as over against any way in which he can affect traditional custom, is as the proportion of the total vocabulary of his mother tongue over against those words of his own baby talk that are taken up into the vernacular of his family. When one seriously studies social orders that have had the opportunity to develop autonomously, the figure becomes no more than an exact and matter-of-fact observation. The life-history of the individual is first and foremost an accommodation to the patterns and standards traditionally handed down in his community. From the moment of his birth the customs into which he is born shape his experience and behaviour. By the time he can talk, he is the little creature of his culture, and by the time he is grown and able to take part in its activities, its habits are his habits, its beliefs his beliefs, its impossibilities his impossibilities. Every child that is born into his group will share them with him, and no child born into one on the opposite side of the globe can ever achieve the thousandth part. There is no social problem it is more incumbent upon us to understand than this of the rôle of custom. Until we are intelligent as to its laws and varieties, the main complicating facts of human life must remain unintelligible.

The study of custom can be profitable only after certain preliminary propositions have been accepted, and some of these propositions have been violently opposed. In the first place any scientific study requires that there be no preferential weighting of one or another of the items in the series it selects for its consideration. In all the less controversial fields like the study of cacti or termites or the nature of nebulae, the necessary method of study is to group the relevant material and to take note of all possible variant forms and conditions. In this way we have learned all that we know of the laws of astronomy, or of the habits of the social insects, let us say. It is only in the study of man himself that the major social sciences have substituted the study of one local variation, that of Western civilization.

Anthropology was by definition impossible as long as these distinctions between ourselves and the primitive, ourselves and the barbarian, ourselves and the pagan, held sway over people's minds. It was necessary first to arrive at that degree of sophistication where we no longer set our own belief over against our neighbour's superstition. It was necessary to recognize that those institutions which are based on the same premises, let us say the supernatural, must be considered together, our own among the rest.

In the first half of the nineteenth century this elementary postulate of anthropology could not occur to the most enlightened person of Western civilization. Man, all down his history, has defended his uniqueness like a point of honour. In Copernicus' time this claim to supremacy was so inclusive that it took in even the earth on which we live, and the fourteenth century refused with passion to have this planet subordinated to a place in the solar scheme. By Darwin's time, having granted the solar system to the enemy, man fought with all the weapons at his command for the uniqueness of the soul, an unknowable attribute given by God to man in such a manner that it disproved man's ancestry in the animal kingdom. No lack of continuity in the argument, no doubts of the nature of this 'soul,' not even the fact that the nineteenth century did not care in the least to defend its brotherhood with any group of aliens—none of these facts counted against the first-rate excitement that raged on account of the indignity evolution proposed against the notion of man's uniqueness.

Both these battles we may fairly count as won—if not yet, then soon; but the fighting has only massed itself upon another front. We are quite willing to admit now that the revolution of the earth about the sun, or the animal ancestry of man, has next to nothing to do with the uniqueness of our human achievements. If we inhabit one chance planet out of a myriad of solar systems, so much the greater glory, and if all the ill-assorted human races are linked by evolution with the animal, the provable differences between ourselves and them are the more extreme and the uniqueness of our institutions the more remarkable. But *our* achievements, *our* institutions are unique; they are of a different order from those of lesser races and must be protected at all costs. So that today, whether it is a question of imperialism, or of race preju-dice, or of a comparison between Christianity and paganism, we are still preoccupied with the uniqueness, not of the human institutions of the world at large, which no one has ever cared about anyway, but of our own institutions and achievements, our own civilization.

Western civilization, because of fortuitous historical circumstances, has spread itself more widely than any other local group that has so far been known. It has standardized itself over most of the globe, and we have been led, therefore, to accept a belief in the uniformity of human behaviour that under other circumstances would not have arisen. Even very primitive peoples are sometimes far more conscious of the role of cultural traits than we are, and for good reason. They have had intimate experience of different cultures. They have seen their religion, their economic system, their marriage prohibitions, go down before the white man's. They have laid down the one and accepted the other, often uncomprehendingly enough, but they are quite clear that there are variant arrangements of human life. They will sometimes attribute dominant characteristics of the white man to his commercial competition, or to his institution of warfare, very much in the fashion of the anthropologist.

The white man has had a different experience. He has never seen an outsider, perhaps, unless the outsider has been already Europeanized. If he has travelled, he has very likely been around the world without ever staying outside a cosmopolitan hotel. He knows little of any ways of life but his own. The uniformity of custom, of outlook, that he sees spread about him seems convincing enough, and conceals from him the fact that it is after all an historical acci-dent. He accepts without more ado the equivalence of human nature and his own cultural stan-dards.

Yet the great spread of white civilization is not an isolated historical circumstance. The Polynesian group, in comparatively recent times, has spread itself from Ontong, Java, to Easter Island, from Hawaii to New Zealand, and the Bantu-speaking tribes spread from the Sahara to southern Africa. But in neither case do we regard these peoples as more than an overgrown local variation of the human species. Western civilization has had all its inventions in trans-portation and all its far-flung commercial arrangements to back up its great dispersion, and it is easy to understand historically how this came about.

The psychological consequences of this spread of white culture have been out of all proportion to the materialistic. This world-wide cultural diffusion has protected us as man had never been protected before from having to take seriously the civilizations of other peoples; it has given to our culture a massive universality that we have long ceased to account for histori-cally, and which we read off rather as necessary and inevitable. We interpret our dependence, in our civilization, upon economic competition, as proof that this is the prime motivation that human nature can rely upon, or we read off the behaviour of small children as it is moulded in our civilization and recorded in child clinics, as child psychology or the way in which the young human animal is bound to behave. It is the same whether it is a question of our ethics or of our family organization. It is the inevitability of each familiar motivation that we defend, attempting always to identify our own local ways of behaving with Behaviour, or our own socialized habits with Human Nature.

Now modern man has made this thesis one of the living issues in his thought and in his practical behaviour, but the sources of it go far back into what appears to be, from its universal distribution among primitive peoples, one of the earliest of human distinctions, the difference in kind between 'my own' closed group and the outsider. All primitive tribes agree in recognizing this category of the outsiders, those who are not only outside the provisions of the moral code which holds within the limits of one's own people, but who are summarily denied a place anywhere in the human scheme. A great number of the tribal names in common use, Zuñi, Déné, Kiowa, and the rest, are names by which primitive peoples know themselves, and are only their native terms for 'the human beings,' that is, themselves. Outside of the closed group there are no human beings. And this is in spite of the fact that from an objective point of view each tribe is surrounded by peoples sharing in its arts and material inventions, in elaborate practices that have grown up by a mutual give-and-take of behaviour from one people to another.

Primitive man never looked out over the world and saw 'mankind' as a group and felt his common cause with his species. From the beginning he was a provincial who raised the barriers high. Whether it was a question of choosing a wife or of taking a head, the first and important distinction was between his own human group and those beyond the pale. His own group, and all its ways of behaving, was unique.

So modern man, differentiating into Chosen People and dangerous aliens, groups within his own civilization genetically and culturally related to one another as any tribes in the Australian bush are among themselves, has the justification of a vast historical continuity behind his attitude. The Pygmies have made the same claims. We are not likely to clear ourselves easily of so fundamental a human trait, but we can at least learn to recognize its history and its hydra manifestations.

One of these manifestations, and one which is often spoken of as primary and motivated rather by religious emotions than by this more generalized provincialism, is the attitude that has universally held in Western civilizations so long as religion remained a living issue among them. The distinction between any closed group and outside peoples, becomes in terms of religion that between the true believers and the heathen. Between these two categories for thousands of years there were no common meeting-points. No ideas or institutions that held in the one were valid in the other. Rather all institutions were seen in opposing terms according as they belonged to one or the other of the very often slightly differentiated religions: on the one side it was a question of Divine Truth and the true believer, of revelation and of God; on the other it was a matter of mortal error, of fables, of the damned and of devils. There could be no question of equating the attitudes of the opposed groups and hence no question of understanding from objectively studied data the nature of this important human trait, religion.

We feel a justified superiority when we read a description such as this of the standard religious attitude. At least we have thrown off that particular absurdity, and we have accepted the study of comparative religion. But considering the scope a similar attitude has had in our civilization in the form of race prejudices, for example, we are justified in a little scepticism as to whether our sophistication in the matter of religion is due to the fact that we have outgrown naïve childishness, or simply to the fact that religion is no longer the area of life in which the important modern battles are staged. In the really live issues of our civilization we seem to be far from having gained the detachment that we have so largely achieved in the field of religion.

There is another circumstance that has made the serious study of custom a late and often a half-heartedly pursued discipline, and it is a difficulty harder to surmount than those of which we have just spoken. Custom did not challenge the attention of social theorists because it was the very stuff of their own thinking: it was the lens without which they could not see at all. Precisely in proportion as it was fundamental, it had its existence outside the field of conscious attention. There is nothing mystical about this blindness. When a student has assembled the vast data for a study of international credits, or of the process of learning, or of narcissism as a factor in psycho-neuroses, it is through and in this body of data that the economist or the psychologist or the psychiatrist operates. He does not reckon with the fact of other social arrangements where all the factors, it may be, are differently arranged. He does not reckon, that is, with cultural conditioning. He sees the trait he is studying as having known and inevitable manifestations, and he projects these as absolute because they are all the materials he has to think with. He identifies local attitudes of the 1930's with Human Nature, the description of them with Economics or Psychology.

Practically, it often does not matter. Our children must be educated in our pedagogical tradition, and the study of the process of learning in our schools is of paramount importance. There is the same kind of justification for the shrug of the shoulders with which we often greet a discussion of other economic systems. After all, we must live within the framework of mine and thine that our own culture institutionalizes.

That is true, and the fact that the varieties of culture can best be discussed as they exist in space gives colour to our nonchalance. But it is only limitation of historical material that prevents examples from being drawn rather from the succession of cultures in time. That succession we cannot escape if we would, and when we look back even a generation we realize the extent to which revision has taken place, sometimes in our most intimate behaviour. So far these revisions have been blind, the result of circumstances we can chart only in retrospect. Except for our unwillingness to face cultural change in intimate matters until it is forced upon us, it would not be impossible to take a more intelligent and directive attitude. The resistance is in large measure a result of our mis-understanding of cultural conventions, and especially an exaltation of those that happen to belong to our nation and decade. A very little acquaintance with other conventions, and a knowledge of how various these may be, would do much to promote a rational social order.

The study of different cultures has another important bearing upon present-day thought and behaviour. Modern existence has thrown many civilizations into close contact, and at the moment the overwhelming response to this situation is nationalism and racial snobbery. There has never been a time when civilization stood more in need of individuals who are genuinely culture-conscious, who can see objectively the socially conditioned behaviour of other peoples without fear and recrimination.

Contempt for the alien is not the only possible solution of our present contact of races and nationalities. It is not even as scientifically founded solution. Traditional Anglo-Saxon intolerance is a local and temporal culture-trait like any other. Even people as nearly of the same blood and culture as the Spanish have not had it, and race prejudice in the Spanish-settled countries is a thoroughly different thing from that in countries dominated by England and the United States. In this country it is obviously not an intolerance directed against the mixture of blood of biologically far-separated races, for upon occasion excitement mounts as high against the Irish Catholic in Boston, or the Italian in New England mill towns, as against the Oriental in California. It is the old distinction of the in-group and the out-group, and if we carry on the primitive tradition in this matter, we have far less excuse than savage tribes. We have travelled, we pride ourselves on our sophistication. But we have failed to understand the relativity of cultural habits, and we remain debarred from much profit and enjoyment in our human relations with peoples of different standards, and untrustworthy in our dealings with them.

The recognition of the cultural basis of race prejudice is a desperate need in present Western civilization. We have come to the point where we entertain race prejudice against our blood brothers the Irish, and where Norway and Sweden speak of their enmity as if they too represented different blood. The so-called race line, during a war in which France and Germany fight on opposite sides, is held to divide the people of Baden from those of Alsace, though in bodily form they alike belong to the Alpine sub-race.

In a day of footloose movements of people and of mixed marriages in the ancestry of the most desirable elements of the community, we preach unabashed the gospel of the pure race.

To this anthropology makes two answers. The first is as to the nature of culture and the second is as to the nature of inheritance. The answer as to the nature of culture takes us back to prehuman societies. There are societies where Nature perpetuates the slightest mode of behaviour by biological mechanisms, but these are societies not of men but of the social insects. The queen ant, removed to a solitary nest, will reproduce each trait of sex behaviour, each detail of the nest. The social insects represent Nature in a mood when she was taking no chances. The pattern of the entire social structure she committed to the ant's instinctive behaviour. There is no greater chance that the social classes of an ant society, or its patterns of agriculture, will be lost by an ant's isolation from its group than that the ant will fail to reproduce the shape of its antennae or the structure of its abdomen.

For better or for worse, man's solution lies at the opposite pole. Not one item of his tribal social organization, of his language, of his local religion, is carried in his germ-cell. In Europe, in other centuries, when children were occasionally found who had been abandoned and had maintained themselves in forests apart from other human beings, they were all so much alike that Linnaeus classified them as a distinct species, *Homo ferus*, and supposed that they were a kind of gnome that man seldom ran across. He could not conceive that these half-witted brutes were born human, these creatures with no interest in what went on about them, rocking themselves rhythmically back and forth like some wild animal in a zoo, with organs of speech and hearing that could hardly be trained to do service, who withstood freezing weather in rags and plucked potatoes out of boiling water without discomfort. There is no doubt, of course, that they were children abandoned in infancy, and what they had all of them lacked was association with their kind, through which alone man's faculties are sharpened and given form.

We do not come across wild children in our more humane civilization. But the point is made as clearly in any case of adoption of an infant into another race and culture. An Oriental child adopted by an Occidental family learns English, shows toward its foster parents the attitudes current among the children he plays with, and grows up to the same professions that they elect. He learns the entire set of the cultural traits of the adopted society, and the set of his real parents' group plays no part. The same process happens on a grand scale when entire peoples in a couple of generations shake off their traditional culture and put on the customs of an alien group. The culture of the American Negro in northern cities has come to approximate in detail that of the whites in the same cities. A few years ago, when a cultural survey was made of Harlem, one of the traits peculiar to the Negroes was their fashion of gambling on the last three unit figures of the next day's stock turnover. At least it cost less than the whites' corresponding predilection for gambling in the stocks themselves and was no less uncertain and exciting. It was a variation on the white pattern, though hardly a great departure. And most Harlem traits keep still closer to the forms that are current in white groups.

All over the world, since the beginning of human history, it can be shown that peoples have been able to adopt the culture of peoples of another blood. There is nothing in the biological structure of man that makes it even difficult. Man is not committed in detail by his biological constitution to any particular variety of behaviour. The great diversity of social solutions that man has worked out in different cultures in regard to mating, for example, or trade, are all equally possible on the basis of his original endowment. Culture is not a biologically transmitted complex.

What is lost in Nature's guaranty of safety is made up in the advantage of greater plasticity. The human animal does not, like the bear, grow himself a polar coat in order to adapt himself, after many generations, to the Arctic. He learns to sew himself a coat and put up a snow house. From all we can learn of the history of intelligence in pre-human as well as human societies, this plasticity has been the soil in which human progress began and in which it has maintained itself. In the ages of the mammoths, species after species without plasticity arose, overreached itself, and died out, undone by the development of the very traits it had biologically produced in order to cope with its environment. The beasts of prey and finally the higher apes came slowly to rely upon other than biological adaptations, and upon the consequent increased plasticity the foundations were laid, bit by bit, for the development of intelligence. Perhaps, as is often suggested, man will destroy himself by this very development of intelligence. But no one has suggested any means by which we can return to the biological mechanisms of the social insect, and we are left no alternative. The human cultural heritage, for better or for worse, is not biologically transmitted.

The corollary in modern politics is that there is no basis for the argument that we can trust our spiritual and cultural achievements to any selected hereditary germ-plasms. In our Western civilization, leadership has passed successively in different periods to the Semitic-speaking peoples, to the Hamitic, to the Mediterranean sub-group of the white race, and lately to the Nordic. There is no doubt about the cultural continuity of the civilization, no matter who its carriers were at the moment. We must accept all the implications of our human inheritance, one of the most important of which is the small scope of biologically transmitted behaviour, and the enormous role of the cultural process of the transmission of tradition.

The second answer anthropology makes to the argument of the racial purist concerns the nature of heredity. The racial purist is the victim of a mythology. For what is 'racial inheritance'? We know roughly what heredity is from father to son. Within a family line the importance of heredity is tremendous. But heredity is an affair of family lines. Beyond that it is mythology. In small and static communities like an isolated Eskimo village, 'racial' heredity and the heredity of child and parent are practically equivalent, and racial heredity therefore has meaning. But as a concept applied to groups distributed over a wide area, let us say, to Nordics, it has no basis in reality. In the first place, in all Nordic nations there are family lines which are represented also in Alpine or Mediterranean communities. Any analysis of the physical make-up of a European population shows overlapping: the dark-eyed, dark-haired Swede represents family lines that are more concentrated farther south, but he is to be understood in relation to what we know of these latter groups. His heredity, so far as it has any physical reality, is a matter of his family line, which is not confined to Sweden. We do not know how far physical types may vary without intermixture. We know that inbreeding brings about a local type. But this is a situation that in our cosmopolitan white civilization hardly exists, and when 'racial heredity' is invoked, as it usually is, to rally a group of persons of about the same economic status, graduating from much the same schools, and reading the same weeklies, such a category is merely another version of the in- and the out-group and does not refer to the actual biological homogeneity of the group.

What really binds men together is their culture,—the ideas and the standards they have in common. If instead of selecting a symbol like common blood heredity and making a slogan of it, the nation turned its attention rather to the culture that unites its people, emphasizing its major merits and recognizing the different values which may develop in a different culture, it would substitute realistic thinking for a kind of symbolism which is dangerous because it is misleading.

A knowledge of cultural forms is necessary in social thinking, and the present volume is concerned with this problem of culture. As we have just seen, bodily form, or race, is separable from culture, and can for our purposes be laid to one side except at certain points where for some special reason it becomes relevant. The chief requirement for a discussion of culture is that it should be based on a wide selection of possible cultural forms. It is only by means of such facts that we can possibly differentiate between those human adjustments that are culturally conditioned and those that are common and, so far as we can see, inevitable in mankind. We cannot discover by introspection or by observation of any one society what behaviour is 'instinctive,' that is, organically determined.

In order to class any behaviour as instinctive, much more is necessary than that it should be proved to be automatic. The conditioned response is as automatic as the organically determined, and culturally conditioned responses make up the greater part of our huge equipment of automatic behaviour.

Therefore the most illuminating material for a discussion of cultural forms and processes is that of societies historically as little related as possible to our own and to one another. With the vast network of historical contact which has spread the great civilizations over tremendous areas, primitive cultures are now the one source to which we can turn. They are a laboratory in which we may study the diversity of human institutions. With their comparative isolation, many primitive regions have had centuries in which to elaborate the cultural themes they have made their own. They provide ready to our hand the necessary information concerning the possible great variations in human adjustments, and a critical examination of them is essential for any understanding of cultural processes. It is the only laboratory of social forms that we have or shall have.

This laboratory has another advantage. The problems are set in simpler terms than in the great Western civilizations. With the inventions that make for ease of transportation, international cables and telephones and radio transmission, those that ensure permanence and widespread distribution to the printed page, the development of competing professional groups and cults and classes and their standardization over the world, modern civilization has grown too complex for adequate analysis except as it is broken up for the purpose into small artificial sections. And these partial analyses are inadequate because so many outside factors cannot be controlled. A survey of any one group involves individuals out of opposed heterogeneous groups, with different standards, social aims, home relations, and morality. The interrelation of these groups is too complicated to evaluate in the necessary detail. In primitive society, the cultural tradition is simple enough to be contained within the knowledge of individual adults, and the manners and morals of the group are moulded to one well-defined general pattern. It is possible to estimate the interrelation of traits in this simple environment in a way which is impossible in the cross-currents of our complex civilization.

Neither of these reasons for stressing the facts of primitive culture has anything to do with the use that has been classically made of this material. This use had to do with a reconstruction of origins. Early anthropologists tried to arrange all traits of different cultures in an evolutionary sequence from the earliest forms to their final development in Western civilization. But there is no reason to suppose that by discussing Australian religion rather than our own we are uncovering primordial religion, or that by discussing Iroquoian social organization we are returning to the mating habits of man's early ancestors.

Since we are forced to believe that the race of man is one species, it follows that man everywhere has an equally long history behind him. Some primitive tribes may have held relatively closer to primordial forms of behaviour than civilized man, but this can only be relative and our guesses are as likely to be wrong as right. There is no justification for identifying some one contemporary primitive custom with the original type of human behaviour. Methodologically there is only one means by which we may gain an approximate knowledge of these early beginnings. That is by a study of the distribution of those few traits that are universal or near-universal in human society. There are several that are well known. Of these everyone agrees upon animism, and the exogamous restrictions upon marriage. The conceptions, diverse as they prove to be, of the human soul, and of an after-life, raise more question. Beliefs as nearly universal as these we may justifiably regard as exceedingly old human inventions. This is not equivalent to regarding them as biologically determined, for they may have been very early inventions of the human race, 'cradle' traits which have become fundamental in all human thinking. In the last analysis they may be as socially conditioned as any local custom. But they have long since become automatic in human behaviour. They are old, and they are universal. All this, however, does not make the forms that can be observed today the original forms that arose in primordial times. Nor is there any way of reconstructing these origins from the study of their varieties. One may isolate the universal core of the belief and differentiate from this its local forms, but it is still possible that the trait took its rise in a pronounced local form and not in some original least common denominator of all observed traits.

For this reason the use of primitive customs to establish origins is speculative. It is possible to build up an argument for any origin that can be desired, origins that are mutually exclusive as well as those that are complementary. Of all the uses of anthropological material, this is the one in which speculation has followed speculation most rapidly, and where in the nature of the case no proof can be given.

Nor does the reason for using primitive societies for the discussion of social forms have necessary connection with a romantic return to the primitive. It is put forward in no spirit of poeticizing the simpler peoples. There are many ways in which the culture of one or another people appeals to us strongly in this era of heterogeneous standards and confused mechanical bustle. But it is not in a return to ideals preserved for us by primitive peoples that our society will heal itself of its maladies. The romantic Utopianism that reaches out toward the simpler primitive, attractive as it sometimes may be, is as often, in ethnological study, a hindrance as a help.

The careful study of primitive societies is important today rather, as we have said, because they provide case material for the study of cultural forms and processes. They help us to differentiate between those responses that are specific to local cultural types and those that are general to mankind. Beyond this, they help us to gauge and understand the immensely important role of culturally conditioned behaviour. Culture, with its processes and functions, is a subject upon which we need all the enlightenment we can achieve, and there is no direction in which we can seek with greater reward than in the facts of preliterate societies. . . .

The diversity of cultures can be endlessly documented. A field of human behaviour may be ignored in some societies until it barely exists; it may even be in some cases unimagined. Or it may almost monopolize the whole organized behaviour of the society, and the most alien situations be manipulated only in its terms. Traits having no intrinsic relation one with the other, and historically independent, merge and become inextricable, providing the occasion for behaviour that has no counterpart in regions that do not make these identifications. It is a corollary of this that standards, no matter in what aspect of behaviour, range in different cultures from the positive to the negative pole. We might suppose that in the matter of taking life all peoples would agree in condemnation. On the contrary, in a matter of homicide, it may be held that one is blameless if diplomatic relations have been severed between neighbouring countries, or that one kills by custom his first two children, or that a husband has right of life and death over his wife, or that it is the duty of the child to kill his parents before they are old. It may be that those are killed who steal a fowl, or who cut their upper teeth first, or who are born on a Wednesday. Among some peoples a person suffers torments at having caused an accidental death; among others it is a matter of no consequence. Suicide also may be a light matter, the recourse of anyone who has suffered some slight rebuff, an act that occurs constantly in a tribe. It may be the highest and noblest act a wise man can perform. The very tale of it, on the other hand, may be a matter for incredulous mirth, and the act itself impossible to conceive as a human possibility. Or it may be a crime punishable by law, or regarded as a sin against the gods.

The diversity of custom in the world is not, however, a matter which we can only helplessly chronicle. Self-torture here, head-hunting there, prenuptial chastity in one tribe and adolescent licence in another, are not a list of unrelated facts, each of them to be greeted with surprise wherever it is found or wherever it is absent. The tabus on killing oneself or another, similarly, though they relate to no absolute standard, are not therefore fortuitous. The significance of cultural behaviour is not exhausted when we have clearly understood that it is local and man-made and hugely variable. It tends also to be integrated. A culture, like an individual, is a more or less consistent pattern of thought and action. Within each culture there come into being characteristic purposes not necessarily shared by other types of society. In obedience to these purposes, each people further and further consolidates its experience, and in proportion to the urgency of these drives the heterogeneous items of behaviour take more and more congruous shape. Taken up by a well-integrated culture, the most ill-assorted acts become characteristic of its peculiar goals, often by the most unlikely metamorphoses. The form that these acts take we can understand only by understanding first the emotional and intellectual mainsprings of that society.

Such patterning of culture cannot be ignored as if it were an unimportant detail. The whole, as modern science is insisting in many fields, is not merely the sum of all its parts, but the result of a unique arrangement and interrelation of the parts that has brought about a new entity. Gunpowder is not merely the sum of sulphur and charcoal and saltpeter, and no amount of knowledge even of all three of its elements in all the forms they take in the natural world will demonstrate the nature of gunpowder. New potentialities have come into being in the resulting compound that were not present in its elements, and its mode of behaviour is indefinitely changed from that of any of its elements in other combinations.

Cultures, likewise, are more than the sum of their traits. We may know all about the distribution of a tribe's form of marriage, ritual dances, and puberty initiations, and yet understand nothing of the culture as a whole which has used these elements to its own purpose. This purpose selects from among the possible traits in the surrounding regions those which it can use, and discards those which it cannot. Other traits it recasts into conformity with its demands. The process of course need never be conscious during its whole course, but to overlook it in the study of the patternings of human behaviour is to renounce the possibility of intelligent interpretation.

This integration of cultures is not in the least mystical. It is the same process by which a style in art comes into being and persists. Gothic architecture, beginning in what was hardly more than a preference for altitude and light, became, by the operation of some canon of taste that developed within its technique, the unique and homogeneous art of the thirteenth century. It discarded elements that were incongruous, modified others to its purposes, and invented others that accorded with its taste.

When we describe the process historically, we inevitably use animistic forms of expression as if there were choice and purpose in the growth of this great art-form. But this is due to the difficulty in our language-forms. There was no conscious choice, and no purpose. What was at first no more than a slight bias in local forms and techniques expressed itself more and more forcibly, integrated itself in more and more definite standards, and eventuated in Gothic art.

What has happened in the great art-styles happens also in cultures as a whole. All the miscellaneous behaviour directed toward getting a living, mating, warring, and worshipping the gods, is made over into consistent patterns in accordance with unconscious canons of choice that develop within the culture. Some cultures, like some periods of art, fail of such integration, and about many others we know too little to understand the motives that actuate them. But cultures at every level of complexity, even the simplest, have achieved it. Such cultures are more or less successful attainments of integrated behaviour, and the marvel is that there can be so many of these possible configurations. . . .

If we are interested in cultural processes, the only way in which we can know the significance of the selected detail of behaviour is against the background of the motives and emotions and values that are institutionalized in that culture. The first essential, so it seems today, is to study the living culture, to know its habits of thought and the functions of its institutions, and such knowledge cannot come out of post-mortem dissections and reconstructions. . . .

The study of cultural behaviour, however, can no longer be handled by equating particular local arrangements with the generic primitive. Anthropologists are turning from the study of primitive culture to that of primitive cultures, and the implications of this change from the singular to the plural are only just beginning to be evident....

It is one of the philosophical justifications for the study of primitive peoples that the facts of simpler cultures may make clear social facts that are otherwise baffling and not open to demonstration. This is nowhere more true than in the matter of the fundamental and distinctive cultural configurations that pattern existence and condition the thoughts and emotions of the individuals who participate in those cultures. The whole problem of the formation of the individual's habit-patterns under the influence of traditional custom can best be understood at the present time through the study of simpler peoples. This does not mean that the facts and processes we can discover in this way are limited in their application to primitive civilizations. Cultural configurations are as compelling and as significant in the highest and most complex societies of which we have knowledge. But the material is too intricate and too close to our eyes for us to cope with it successfully....

We need all the enlightenment we can obtain from the study of thought and behaviour as it is organized in the less complicated groups....

Cultures are travelling along different roads in pursuit of different ends, and these ends and these means in one society cannot be judged in terms of those of another society, because essentially they are incommensurable.

All cultures, of course, have not shaped their thousand items of behaviour to a balanced and rhythmic pattern. Like certain individuals, certain social orders do not subordinate activities to a ruling motivation. They scatter. If at one moment they seem to be pursuing certain ends, at another they are off on some tangent apparently inconsistent with all that has gone before, which gives no clue to activity that will come after.

This lack of integration seems to be as characteristic of certain cultures as extreme integration is of others....

The relation of cultural integration to studies of Western civilization and hence to sociological theory is easily misunderstood. Our own society is often pictured as an extreme example of lack of integration. Its huge complexity and rapid changes from generation to generation make inevitable a lack of harmony between its elements that does not occur in simpler societies. The lack of integration is exaggerated and misinterpreted, however, in most studies because of a simple technical error. Primitive society is integrated in geographical units. Western civilization, however, is stratified, and different social groups of the same time and place live by quite different standards and are actuated by different motivations.

The effort to apply the anthropological culture area in modern sociology can only be fruitful to a very limited degree because different ways of living are today not primarily a matter of spatial distribution. There is a tendency among sociologists to waste time over the 'culture area concept.' There is properly no such 'concept.' When traits group themselves geographically, they must be handled geographically. When they do not, it is idle to make a principle out of what is at best a loose empirical category. In our civilization there is, in the anthropological sense, a uniform cosmopolitan culture that can be found in any part of the globe, but there is likewise unprecedented divergence between the labouring class and the Four Hundred, between those groups whose life centres in the church and those whose life centres on the race-track. The comparative freedom of choice in modern society makes possible important voluntary groups which stand for as different principles as the Rotary Clubs and Greenwich Village. The nature of the cultural processes is not changed with these modern conditions, but the unit in which they can be studied is no longer the local group....

There is no proper antagonism between the rôle of society and that of the individual. One of the most misleading misconceptions due to this nineteenth-century dualism was the idea that what was subtracted from society was added to the individual and what was subtracted from the individual was added to society. Philosophies of freedom, political creeds of *laissez faire*, revolutions that have unseated dynasties, have been built on this dualism. The quarrel in anthropological theory between the importance of the culture pattern and of the individual is only a small ripple from this fundamental conception of the nature of society.

In reality, society and the individual are not antagonists. His culture provides the raw material of which the individual makes his life. If it is meagre, the individual suffers; if it is rich, the individual has the chance to rise to his opportunity. Every private interest of every man and woman is served by the enrichment of the traditional stores of his civilization. The richest musical sensitivity can operate only within the equipment and standards of its tradition. It will add, perhaps importantly, to that tradition, but its achievement remains in proportion to the instruments and musical theory which the culture has provided. In the same fashion a talent for observation expends itself in some Melanesian tribe upon the negligible borders of the magico-religious field. For a realization of its potentialities it is dependent upon the development of scientific methodology, and it has no fruition unless the culture has elaborated the necessary concepts and tools.

The man in the street still thinks in terms of a necessary antagonism between society and the individual. In large measure this is because in our civilization the regulative activities of society are singled out, and we tend to identify society with the restrictions the law imposes upon us. The law lays down the number of miles per hour that I may drive an automobile. If it takes this restriction away, I am by that much the freer. This basis for a fundamental antagonism between society and the individual is naive indeed when it is extended as a basic philosophical and political notion. Society is only incidentally and in certain situations regulative, and law is not equivalent to the social order. In the simpler homogeneous cultures collective habit or custom may quite supersede the necessity for any development of formal legal authority. American Indians sometimes say: 'In the old days, there were no fights about hunting grounds or fishing territories. There was no law then, so everybody did what was right.' The phrasing makes it clear that in their old life they did not think of themselves as submitting to a social control imposed upon them from without. Even in our civilization the law is never more than a crude implement of society, and one it is often enough necessary to check in its arrogant career. It is never to be read off as if it were the equivalent of the social order.

Society in its full sense as we have discussed it in this volume is never an entity separable from the individuals who compose it. No individual can arrive even at the threshold of his potentialities without a culture in which he participates. Conversely, no civilization has in it any element which in the last analysis is not the contribution of an individual. Where else could any trait come from except from the behaviour of a man or a woman or a child?

It is largely because of the traditional acceptance of a conflict between society and the individual, that emphasis upon cultural behavior is so often interpreted as a denial of the autonomy of the individual.... Anthropology is often believed to be a counsel of despair which makes untenable a beneficent human illusion. But no anthropologist with a background of experience of other cultures has ever believed that individuals were automatons, mechanically carrying out the decrees of their civilization. No culture yet observed has been able to eradicate the differences in the temperaments of the persons who compose it. It is always a give-and-take. The problem of the individual is not clarified by stressing the antagonism between culture and the individual, but by stressing their mutual reinforcement. This rapport is so close that it is not possible to discuss patterns of culture without considering specifically their relation to individual psychology.

We have seen that any society selects some segment of the arc of possible human behaviour, and in so far as it achieves integration its institutions tend to further the expression of its selected segment and to inhibit opposite expressions. But these opposite expressions are the congenial responses, nevertheless, of a certain proportion of the carriers of that culture. We have already discussed the reasons for believing that this selection is primarily cultural and not biological. We cannot, therefore, even on theoretical grounds imagine that all the congenial responses of all its people will be equally served by the institutions of any culture. To understand the behaviour of the individual, it is not merely necessary to relate his personal life-history to his endowments, and to measure these against an arbitrarily selected normality. It is necessary also to relate his cogenial responses to the behaviour that is singled out in the institutions of his culture.

The vast proportion of all individuals who are born into any society always and whatever the idiosyncrasies of its institutions, assume, as we have seen, the behaviour dictated by that society. This fact is always interpreted by the carriers of that culture as being due to the fact that their particular institutions reflect an ultimate and universal sanity. The actual reason is quite different. Most people are shaped to the form of their culture because of the enormous malleability of their original endowment. They are plastic to the moulding force of the society into which they are born. It does not matter whether, with the Northwest Coast, it requires delusions of self-reference, or with our own civilization the amassing of possessions. In any case the great mass of individuals take quite readily the form that is presented to them. . . .

It is clear that culture may value and make socially available even highly unstable human types. If it chooses to treat their peculiarities as the most valued variants of human behaviour, the individuals in question will rise to the occasion and perform their social roles without reference to our usual ideas of the types who can make social adjustments and those who cannot. Those who function inadequately in any society are not those with certain fixed 'abnormal' traits, but may well be those whose responses have received no support in the institutions of their culture. The weakness of these aberrants is in great measure illusory. It springs, not from the fact that they are lacking in necessary vigour, but that they are individuals whose native responses are not reaffirmed by society. They are, as Sapir phrases it, 'alienated from an impossible world.' . . .

No society has yet attempted a self-conscious direction of the process by which its new normalities are created in the next generation. Dewey has pointed out how possible and yet how drastic such social engineering would be. For some traditional arrangements it is obvious that very high prices are paid, reckoned in terms of human suffering and frustration. If these arrangements presented themselves to us merely as arrangements and not as categorical imperatives, our reasonable course would be to adapt them by whatever means to rationally selected goals. What we do instead is to ridicule our Don Quixotes, the ludicrous embodiments of an outmoded tradition, and continue to regard our own as final and prescribed in the nature of things. . . .

Social thinking at the present time has no more important task before it than that of taking adequate account of cultural relativity. In the fields of both sociology and psychology the implications are fundamental, and modern thought about contacts of peoples and about our changing standards is greatly in need of sane and scientific direction. The sophisticated modern temper has made of social relativity, even in the small area which it has recognized, a doctrine of despair. It has pointed out its incongruity with the orthodox dreams of permanence and ideality and with the individual's illusions of autonomy. It has argued that if human experience must give up these, the nutshell of existence is empty. But to interpret our dilemma in these terms is to be guilty of an anachronism. It is only the inevitable cultural lag that makes us insist that the old must be discovered again in the new, that there is no solution but to find the old certainty and stability in the new plasticity. The recognition of cultural relativity carries with it its own values, which need not be those of the absolutist philosophies. It challenges customary opinions and causes those who have been bred to them acute discomfort. It rouses pessimism because it throws old formulas into confusion, not because it contains anything intrinsically difficult. As soon as the new opinion is embraced as customary belief, it will be another trusted bulwark of the good life. We shall arrive then at a more realistic social faith, accepting as grounds of hope and as new bases for tolerance the coexisting and equally valid patterns of life which mankind has created for itself from the raw materials of existence.

Claude Lévi-Strauss

French anthropologist Lévi-Strauss was widely held to have established ethnography as a proper science through the importation of the methods then current in linguistics during the late 1940s and early 1950s. Calling his field "structural anthropology" after the structural linguistics developed by specialists working in Czechoslovakia and the Soviet Union, Lévi-Strauss brought the study of meaning as it had evolved in the Saussurian tradition into the study of human culture, and of mythology in particular. Analysis of meaning in culture, as opposed to causality, came to be a defining feature of a broader, interdisciplinary "structuralism" that gained popularity in the 1960's, and which is often considered one of the first major steps in what is known as "the linguistic turn," or the increasing emphasis on the importance of language to the study of the social sciences and humanities.

Perhaps Lévi-Strauss's most influential work, *The Savage Mind* (1962), took as its subject that which had, from the seventeenth and eighteenth centuries onward, been thought of as un-modern, un-scientific, and therefore often simply irrational: the culture, civilization, and mentality of the "primitive" world. The academic reason frequently given for this disdain was that the customs, rituals, and beliefs of tribal societies simply did not make sense to European investigators. Lévi-Strauss, in *The Savage Mind* and elsewhere, set out to vindicate the world of savage thought by bringing order to it through the structural method. Just as Saussure had argued, on an elementary level, that words and the smaller component units of language only acquire meaning through relation and opposition to other such units, Lévi-Strauss argued that the key to understanding other cultures, and significant domains within our own, was to understand everything in context, or in its total relation to the cultural whole. This approach set itself against the earlier method of explaining cultural diversity in evolutionary terms, or the contemporary functionalist approach, which made its case for the practical, often economic, basis of all cultural practices.

Once this method was adopted, Western science, when thought of as the technical mastery of nature for the specific purpose of advancing material progress, could be shown to be a type of thought no more intricate, meticulous, or logically rigorous than the primitive systems of classification that Lévi-Strauss would make the focus of his book. What *were* essentially different were the ends towards which either mode of thought was directed. From the evolutionary, and often racist, intellectual hierarchy that placed rational science above primitive belief and practice, had emerged the relativistic notion of a savage mindset, just as furiously driven by the search for meaning as that of the scientist, which seeks to understand the world in a concrete rather than an abstract fashion, through an often highly complex system of classification of the natural world.

CLAUDE LÉVI-STRAUSS
(1962)

The

Savage

Mind

There still exists among ourselves an activity which on the technical plane gives us quite a good understanding of what a science we prefer to call 'prior' rather than 'primitive', could have been on the plane of speculation. This is what is commonly called 'bricolage' in French. In its old sense the verb 'bricoler' applied to ball games and billiards, to hunting, shooting and riding. It was however always used with reference to some extraneous movement: a ball rebounding, a dog straying or a horse swerving from its direct course to avoid an obstacle. And in our own time the 'bricoleur' is still someone who works with his hands and uses devious means compared to those of a craftsman.

The characteristic feature of mythical thought is that it expresses itself by means of a heterogeneous repertoire which, even if extensive, is nevertheless limited. It has to use this repertoire, however, whatever the task in hand because it has nothing else at its disposal. Mythical thought is therefore a kind of intellectual 'bricolage'—which explains the relation which can be perceived between the two.

Like 'bricolage' on the technical plane, mythical reflection can reach brilliant unforeseen results on the intellectual plane. Conversely, attention has often been drawn to the mytho-poetical nature of 'bricolage' on the plane of so-called 'raw' or 'naive' art, in architectural follies like the villa of Cheval the postman or the stage sets of Georges Méliès, or, again, in the case immortalized by Dickens in *Great Expectations* but no doubt originally inspired by observation, of Mr Wemmick's suburban 'castle' with its miniature drawbridge,

Reprinted from *The Savage Mind*, pp. 16–23, 36–43, 142–48, by Claude Lévi-Strauss, by permission of George Weidenfeld & Nicolson Limited and the University of Chicago Press.

its cannon firing at nine o'clock, its bed of salad and cucumbers, thanks to which its occupants could withstand a siege if necessary. . . .

The analogy is worth pursuing since it helps us to see the real relations between the two types of scientific knowledge we have distinguished. The 'bricoleur' is adept at performing a large number of diverse tasks; but, unlike the engineer, he does not subordinate each of them to the availability of raw materials and tools conceived and procured for the purpose of the project. His universe of instruments is closed and the rules of his game are always to make do with 'whatever is at hand', that is to say with a set of tools and materials which is always finite and is also heterogeneous because what it contains bears no relation to the current project, or indeed to any particular project, but is the contingent result of all the occasions there have been to renew or enrich the stock or to maintain it with the remains of previous constructions or destructions. The set of the 'bricoleur's' means cannot therefore be defined in terms of a project (which would presuppose besides, that, as in the case of the engineer, there were, at least in theory, as many sets of tools and materials or 'instrumental sets', as there are different kinds of projects). It is to be defined only by its potential use or, putting this another way and in the language of the 'bricoleur' himself, because the elements are collected or retained on the principle that 'they may always come in handy'. Such elements are specialized up to a point, sufficiently for the 'bricoleur' not to need the equipment and knowledge of all trades and professions, but not enough for each of them to have only one definite and determinate use. They each represent a set of actual and possible relations; they are 'operators' but they can be used for any operations of the same type.

The elements of mythical thought similarly lie half-way between percepts and concepts. It would be impossible to separate percepts from the concrete situations in which they appeared, while recourse to concepts would require that thought could, at least provisionally, put its projects (to use Husserl's expression) 'in brackets'. Now, there is an intermediary between images and concepts, namely signs. For signs can always be defined in the way introduced by Saussure in the case of the particular category of linguistic signs, that is, as a link between images and concepts. In the union thus brought about, images and concepts play the part of the signifying and signified respectively.

Signs resemble images in being concrete entities but they resemble concepts in their powers of reference. Neither concepts nor signs relate exclusively to themselves; either may be substituted for something else. Concepts, however, have an unlimited capacity in this respect, while signs have not. The example of the 'bricoleur' helps to bring out the differences and similarities. Consider him at work and excited by his project. His first practical step is retrospective. He has to turn back to an already existent set made up of tools and materials, to consider or reconsider what it contains and, finally and above all, to engage in a sort of dialogue with it and, before choosing between them, to index the possible answers which the whole set can offer to his problem. He interrogates all the heterogeneous objects of which his treasury is composed to discover what each of them could 'signify' and so contribute to the definition of a set which has yet to materialize but which will ultimately differ from the instrumental set only in the internal disposition of its parts. A particular cube of oak could be a wedge to make up for the inadequate length of a plank of pine or it could be a pedestal—which would allow the grain and polish of the old wood to show to advantage. In one case it will serve as extension, in the other as material. But the possibilities always remain limited by the particular history of each piece and by those of its features which are already determined by the use for which it was originally intended or the modifications it has undergone for other purposes. The elements which the 'bricoleur' collects and uses are 'pre-constrained' like the constitutive units of myth, the possible combinations of which are restricted by the fact that they are drawn from the language where they already possess a sense which sets a limit on their freedom of manoeuvre.... And the decision as to what to put in each place also depends on the possibility of putting a different element there instead, so that each choice which is made will involve a complete reorganization of the structure, which will never be the same as one vaguely imagined nor as some other which might have been preferred to it.

The engineer no doubt also cross-examines his resources. The existence of an 'interlocutor' is in his case due to the fact that his means, power and knowledge are never unlimited and that in this negative form he meets resistance with which he has to come to terms. It might be said that the engineer questions the universe, while the 'bricoleur' addresses himself to a collection of oddments left over from human endeavours, that is, only a sub-set of the culture. Again, Information Theory shows that it is possible, and often useful, to reduce the physicists' approaches to a sort of dialogue with nature. This would make the distinction we are trying to draw less clearcut. There remains however a difference even if one takes into account the fact that the scientist never carries on a dialogue with nature pure and simple but rather with a particular relationship between nature and culture definable in terms of his particular period and civilization and the material means at his disposal. He is no more able than the 'bricoleur' to do whatever he wishes when he is presented with a given task. He too has to begin by making a catalogue of a previously determined set consisting of theoretical and practical knowledge, of technical means, which restrict the possible solutions.

The difference is therefore less absolute than it might appear. It remains a real one, however, in that the engineer is always trying to make his way out of and go beyond the constraints imposed by a particular state of civilization while the 'bricoleur' by inclination or necessity always remains within them. This is another way of saying that the engineer works by means of concepts and the 'bricoleur' by means of signs. The sets which each employs are at different distances from the poles on the axis of opposition between nature and culture. One way indeed in which signs can be opposed to concepts is that whereas concepts aim to be wholly transparent with respect to reality, signs allow and even require the interposing and incorporation of a certain amount of human culture into reality. Signs, in Peirce's vigorous phrase 'address somebody'.

Both the scientist and 'bricoleur' might therefore be said to be constantly on the look out for 'messages'. Those which the 'bricoleur' collects are, however, ones which have to some extent been transmitted in advance—like the commercial codes which are summaries of the past experience of the trade and so allow any new situation to be met economically, provided that it belongs to the same class as some earlier one. The scientist, on the other hand, whether he is an engineer or a physicist, is always on the look out for *that other message* which might be wrested from an interlocutor in spite of his reticence in pronouncing on questions whose answers have not been rehearsed. Concepts thus appear like operators *opening up* the set being worked with and signification like the operator of its *reorganization*, which neither extends nor renews it and limits itself to obtaining the group of its transformations.

Images cannot be ideas but they can play the part of signs or, to be more precise, co-exist with ideas in signs and, if ideas are not yet present, they can keep their future place open for them and make its contours apparent negatively. Images are fixed, linked in a single way to the mental act which accompanies them. Signs, and images which have acquired significance, may still lack comprehension; unlike concepts, they do not yet possess simultaneous and theoretically unlimited relations with other entities of the same kind. They are however already *permutable*, that is, capable of standing in successive relations with other entities—although with only a limited number and, as we have seen, only on the condition that they always form a system in which an alteration which affects one element automatically affects all the others. On this plane logicians' 'extension' and 'intension' are not two distinct and complementary aspects but one and the same thing. One understands then how mythical thought can be capable of generalizing and so be scientific, even though it is still entangled in imagery. It too works by analogies and comparisons even though its creations, like those of the 'bricoleur', always really consist of a new arrangement of elements, the nature of which is unaffected by whether they figure in the instrumental set or in the final arrangement (these being the same, apart from the internal disposition of their parts): 'it would seem that mythological worlds have been built up, only to be shattered again, and that new worlds were built from the fragments' (Boas I, p. 18). Penetrating as this comment is, it nevertheless fails to take into account that in the continual reconstruction from the same materials, it is always earlier ends which are called upon to play the part of means: the signified changes into the signifying and vice versa.

This formula, which could serve as a definition of 'bricolage', explains how an implicit inventory or conception of the total means available must be made in the case of mythical thought also, so that a result can be defined which will always be a compromise between the structure of the instrumental set and that of the project. Once it materializes the project will therefore inevitably be at a remove from the initial aim (which was moreover a mere sketch), a phenomenon which the surrealists have felicitously called 'objective hazard'. Further, the 'bricoleur' also, and indeed principally, derives his poetry from the fact that he does not confine himself to accomplishment and execution: he 'speaks' not only *with* things, as we have already seen, but also through the medium of things: giving an account of his personality and life by the choices he makes between the limited possibilities. The 'bricoleur' may not ever complete his purpose but he always puts something of himself into it.

Mythical thought appears to be an intellectual form of 'bricolage' in this sense also. Science as a whole is based on the distinction between the contingent and the necessary, this being also what distinguishes event and structure. The qualities it claimed at its outset as peculiarly scientific were precisely those which formed no part of living experience and remained outside and, as it were, unrelated to events. This is the significance of the notion of primary qualities. Now, the characteristic feature of mythical thought, as of 'bricolage' on the practical plane, is that it builds up structured sets, not directly with other structured sets but by using the remains and debris of events: in French 'des bribes et des morceaux', or odds and ends in English, fossilized evidence of the history of an individual or a society. The relation between the diachronic and the synchronic is therefore in a sense reversed. Mythical thought, that 'bricoleur', builds up structures by fitting together events, or rather the remains of events, while science, 'in operation' simply by virtue of coming into being, creates its means and results in the form of events, thanks to the structures which it is constantly elaborating and which are its hypotheses and theories. But it is important not to make the mistake of thinking that these are two stages or phases in the evolution of knowledge. Both approaches are equally valid. Physics and chemistry are already striving to become qualitative again, that is, to account also for secondary qualities which when they have been explained will in their turn become means of explanation. And biology may perhaps be marking time waiting for this before it can itself explain life. Mythical thought for its part is imprisoned in the events and experiences which it never tires of ordering and re-ordering in its search to find them a meaning. But it also acts as a liberator by its protest against the idea that anything can be meaningless with which science at first resigned itself to a compromise....

This logic works rather like a kaleidoscope, an instrument which also contains bits and pieces by means of which structural patterns are realized. The fragments are products of a process of breaking up and destroying, in itself a contingent matter, but they have to be homologous in various respects, such as size, brightness of colouring, transparency. They can no longer be considered entities in their own right in relation to the manufactured objects of whose 'discourse' they have become the indefinable debris, but they must be so considered from a different point of view if they are to participate usefully in the formation of a new type of entity: one consisting of patterns in which, through the play of mirrors, reflections are equivalent to real objects, that is, in which signs assume the status of things signified. These patterns actualize possibilities whose number, though it may be very great, is not unlimited, for it is a function of the possible lay-out and balances which may be effected between bodies whose number itself is finite. Finally, and most important, these patterns produced by the conjunction of contingent events (the turning of the instrument by the person looking through it) and a law (namely that governing the construction of the kaleidescope, which corresponds to the invariant element of the constraints just mentioned) project models of intelligibility which are in a way provisional, since each pattern can be expressed in terms of strict relations between its part and since these relations have no content apart from the pattern itself, to which no object in the observer's experience corresponds—even though, by such a manoeuvre, particular objective structures, such as those of snow crystals or certain types of radiolaria and diatomaceae might be revealed while their empirical basis were yet unknown, to the observer who had not yet seen them.

One can conceive that such a concrete logic may be possible. It now remains to define its features and the way in which they can be observed in the course of ethnographic enquiry. Both an affective and an intellectual aspect become apparent.

The beings which native thought endows with significance are seen as exhibiting a certain affinity with man. The Ojibwa believe in a universe of supernatural beings:

Yet to call these beings supernatural slightly misinterprets the Indians' conception. They are a part of the natural order of the universe no less than man himself, whom they resemble in the possession of intelligence and emotions. Like man, too, they are male or female, and in some cases at least may even have families of their own. Some are tied down to definite localities, some move from place to place at will; some are friendly to Indians, others hostile....

Other observations emphasize that the feeling of indentification is stronger than the sense of difference:

A Hawaiian's oneness with the living aspect of native phenomena, that is, with spirit and God and with other persons as souls, is not correctly described by the word rapport, and certainly not by such words as sympathy, empathy, abnormal, supernormal or neurotic, mystical or magical. It is not 'extra-sensory', for it is partly of-the-sense and not-of-the-senses. It is just a part of natural consciousness for the normal Hawaiian....

The natives themselves are sometimes acutely aware of the 'concrete' nature of their science and contrast it sharply with that of the whites:

We know what the animals do, what are the needs of the beaver, the bear, the salmon, and other creatures, because long ago men married them and acquired this knowledge from their animal wives. Today the priests say we lie, but we know better. The white man has been only a short time in this country and knows very little about the animals; we have lived here thousands of years and were taught long ago by the animals themselves. The white man writes everything down in a book so that it will not be forgotten; but our ancestors married the animals, learned all their ways, and passed on the knowledge from one generation to another. . . .

This disinterested, attentive, fond and affectionate lore acquired and transmitted through the attachments of marriage and upbringing is here described with such noble simplicity that it seems superfluous to conjure up the bizarre hypotheses suggested to philosophers by too theoretical a view of the development of human knowledge. Nothing here calls for the intervention of a so-called 'principle of participation' or even for a mysticism embedded in metaphysics which we now perceive only through the distorting lens of the established religions.

The way in which this concrete knowledge works, its means and methods, the affective values with which it is imbued are to be found and can be observed very close to us, among those of our contemporaries whose tastes and profession put them in a situation in relation to animals which, *mutatis mutandis*, comes as close as our civilization allows to that which is usual among all hunting peoples, namely circus people and people working in zoos. Nothing is more instructive in this respect, after the native evidence just quoted, then the account given by the director of the Zürich zoo of his first tête-à-tête—if one may so call it—with a dolphin. He notes 'its exaggerated human eyes, its strange breathing hole, the torpedo shape and colour of its body, the completely smooth and waxy texture of its skin and not least its four impressive rows of equally sharp teeth in its beak-like mouth', but describes his feelings thus:

> Flippy was no fish, and when he looked at you with twinkling eyes from a distance of less than two feet, you had to stifle the question as to whether it was in fact an animal. So new, strange and extremely weird was this creature, that one was tempted to consider it as some kind of bewitched being. But the zoologist's brain kept on associating it with the cold fact, painful in this connection, that it was known to science by the dull name, *Tursiops truncatus*. . . .

Comment like this from the pen of a man of science is enough to show if indeed it is necessary, that theoretical knowledge is not incompatible with sentiment and that knowledge can be both objective and subjective at the same time. It also shows that the concrete relations between man and other living creatures sometimes, especially in civilizations in which science means 'natural science', colour the entire universe of scientific knowledge with their own emotional tone, which is itself the result of this primitive identification and, as Rousseau saw with his profound insight, responsible for all thought and society. But if a zoologist can combine taxonomy and the warmest affection, there is no reason to invoke distinct principles to explain the conjunction of these two attitudes in the thought of so-called primitive peoples.

Following Griaule, Dieterlen and Zahan have established the extensiveness and the systematic nature of native classification in the Sudan. The Dogon divide plants into twenty-two main families, some of which are further divided into eleven sub-groups. The twenty-two families, listed in the appropriate order, are divided into two series, one of which is composed of the families of odd numbers and the other of those of even ones. In the former, which symbolizes single births, the plants called male and female are associated with the rainy and the dry seasons respectively. In the latter, which symbolizes twin births, there is the same relation but in reverse. Each family is also allocated to one of three categories: tree, bush, grass; finally, each family corresponds to a part of the body, a technique, a social class and an institution. . . .

Facts of this kind caused surprise when they were first brought back from Africa. Very similar modes of classification had, however, been described considerably earlier in America, and it was these which inspired Durkheim's and Mauss's famous essay. The reader is referred to it, but it is worth adding a few further examples.

The Navaho Indians, who regard themselves as 'great classifiers', divide living creatures into two categories on the basis of whether they are or are not endowed with speech. The category of creatures without speech consists of animals and plants. Animals are divided into three groups, 'running', 'flying' and 'crawling'. Each of these groups is further divided in two ways: into 'travellers by land' and 'travellers by water' and into 'travellers by day' and 'travellers by night'. The division into species obtained by this means is not always the same as that of zoology. Thus birds grouped in pairs on the basis of a classification into male and female are in fact sometimes of the same sex but of different kinds. For the association is based on the one hand on their relative size and, on the other, on their place in the classification of colours and the function assigned to them in magic and ritual. . . . But native taxonomy is often precise and unambiguous enough to allow certain identifications, for instance, the one made only a few years ago of the 'Great Fly', mentioned in myths, with a tachinid *Hystricia pollinosa*.

Plants are named on the basis of three sorts of characteristics: their supposed sex, their medicinal properties and their visual or tactual appearance (prickly, sticky, etc.). Each of these three groups is subdivided into three further groups according to size (large, medium, small). The classification is of the same kind throughout the reserve of some twenty-five thousand square miles, in spite of the dispersion of its sixty thousand occupants over this rather extensive territory. . . .

Each animal or plant corresponds to a natural element, itself dependent on rites whose extreme complexity among the Navaho is well known. The following correspondences are found in the 'Flint-Chant': crane—sky; red songbird—sun; eagle—mountain; hawk—rock; bluebird—tree; hummingbird—plant; cornbeetle—earth; heron—water. . . .

The Hopi, like the Zuni who particularly engaged Durkheim's and Mauss's attention, classify living creatures and natural phenomena by means of a vast system of correspondences. The facing table is based on the information scattered in several authors. It is undoubtedly only a modest fragment of an entire system, many of whose elements are missing.

Similar correspondences are also known among people whose social structure is very much looser than that of the Pueblo: the Eskimo sculptor of salmon uses the wood whose colour is closet to that of their flesh for carving each species: 'All woods, they say, are salmon'. . . .

These are only a few of the examples which might be given. There would be even more examples than there are, had ethnologists not often been prevented from trying to find out about the complex and consistent conscious systems of societies they were studying by the assumptions they made about the simpleness and coarseness of 'primitives'. It did not occur to them that there could be such systems in societies of so low an economic and technical level since they made the unwarranted assumption that their intellectual level must be equally low. And it is only just beginning to be realized that the older accounts which we owe to the insight of such rare inquirers as Cushing do not describe exceptional cases but rather forms of science

	NORTH-WEST	SOUTH-WEST	SOUTH-EAST	NORTH-EAST	ZENITH	NADIR
COLOURS	yellow	blue, green	red	white	black	multicolored
ANIMALS	puma	bear	wild cat	wolf	vulture	snake
BIRDS	oriole	blue-bird (Sialia)	parrot	magpie	swallow	warbler
TREES	Douglas fir	white pine	red willow	aspen		
BUSHES	green rabbit-brush (chrysotham)	sage-brush (*Artemisia*)	cliff-rose (*Cowania stansburiana*)	grey rabbit brush (*Chrysothamnus*)		
FLOWERS	mariposa lily (*calochortus*)	larkspur (*delphinium*)	(*Castilleja*)	(*Anogra*)		
CORN	yellow	blue	red	white	purple	sweet
BEANS	French bean (*Phaseolus vulg.*)	butter-bean (*Phas. vulg.*)	dwarf bean	lima bean (*Phaseolus lunatus*)	various	

Beans were also divided into

light	light	white	white	blue
black	yellow	black	grey	red
red	brown	spotted	yellow	pink
			red	etc.
			black	

and thought which are extremely widespread in so-called primitive societies. We must therefore alter our traditional picture of this primitiveness. The 'savage' has certainly never borne any resemblance either to that creature barely emerged from an animal condition and still a prey to his needs and instincts who has so often been imagined nor to that consciousness governed by emotions and lost in a maze of confusion and participation. The examples given, and others which could be added, are evidence of thought which is experienced in all the exercises of speculation and resembles that of the naturalists and alchemists of antiquity and the middle ages: Galen, Pliny, Hermes Trismegistus, Albertus Magnus. . . . From this point of view 'totemic' classifications are probably closer than they look to the plant emblem systems of the Greeks and Romans, which were expressed by means of wreaths of olive, oak, laurel, wild celery, etc., or again to that practised by the medieval church where the choir was strewn with hay, rushes, ivy or sand according to the festival. . . .

The vast corpus of rites of the Osage, assembled and published by La Flesche, provides a wealth of illustrations, which are sometimes demonstrations, of the mutual convertibility of 'concrete classifiers': animals and plants, and 'abstract classifiers' such as numbers, directions, and the cardinal points. Thus, for example, bows and arrows figure in the list of clan names but it is not merely manufactured objects which are here in question. It is apparent from texts of prayers and invocations that one arrow is painted black and the other red and that this opposition of colours corresponds to that of day and night. The same symbolism recurs in the colours of the bow, red on the inside and black on the outside: shooting with the red and black bow, using alternatively a red and a black arrow, is an expression of Time, itself measured by the alternation of day and night. . . .

The concrete classifiers not only serve to convey ideas; they can also, in their sensory form, show that a logical problem has been solved or a contradiction surmounted. Among the Osage, when a pair of moccasins are made, their owner must perform a complex rite. This special attention accorded an article of clothing might seem surprising did the texts not reveal in the moccasin something other than its utilitarian function: the moccasin, a cultural object, is opposed to 'evil' grass which the walker tramples and crushes. It thus corresponds to a warrior who tramples his enemies underfoot. Now, in the sociocosmological scheme of the Osage, the martial function connotes the land moiety, to which grass also belongs. The particular symbolism of the moccasin is thus inconsistent with the general symbolism, since the moccasin is 'anti-land' in the former and congruent with land in the latter. The minutia of the ritual is clarified by the evidence of what one would like to call the logical instability of a manufactured article: an instability which a highly ritualized manufacturing technique precisely serves to palliate. . . .

In Osage thought, the most important opposition, which is also the simplest and has the greatest logical power, is that between the two moieties: *Tsi'-zhu*: sky, and *Hon'-ga*; subdivided into *Hon'-ga*, properly speaking: dry land, and Wa-zha'-zhe: water. Starting from here a complex grammar is developed by means of a system of correspondences with more concrete or more abstract domains but within which the original scheme, acting as a catalyst, initiates the crystallization of other schemes of two, three, four, or more variables. First the cardinal points, since, in the initiating hut, sky and land are opposed as north and south, and dry land and water as east and west respectively.

Secondly, the opposition of odd and even gives rise to a mystic numerology. The number six belongs to the sky moiety, the number seven to the land moiety, and their sum, thirteen, corresponds, on the cosmological plane, to the number of rays of the rising sun (which is a *demi-sun*) and, on the social plane, to the notable actions which may be counted to his credit by an accomplished warrior (who is a *demi-man*, since the function of war is the prerogative of one of the two moieties which together constitute the tribe).

Thus the quality and the unity of the two great divisions of the tribe might be symbolized as a man or an animal, but the Hon'-ga great division must always represent the right side of the man or animal and the Tsi'-zhu the great division of the left. This idea of the duality and unity of nature was not only reflected in the tribal organization but, in former times, instilled in the minds of the people by certain personal habits, as for instance members of the Hon'-ga great division when putting on their moccasins put the moccasin on the right foot first, while members of the Tsi'-zhu great division put the moccasin on the left foot first.

The number thirteen, as we have seen, is first of all the sum of the two social groups, right and left, north and south, winter and summer; thereafter it is specified concretely and developed logically. In the image of the rising sun, in which the beholder venerates the source of all life (thus facing east, which means that the south is on his right and the north on his left), the number thirteen can symbolize the union of two terms: six and seven, sky and land, etc. But when it relates to a star the solar symbolism is particularly attached to the sky moiety. Hence there come to be other concrete specifications of the number thirteen, in this case reserved to sub-groups of the other moiety: thirteen foot-prints of the black bear to represent the notable actions of the land clans and thirteen willow trees to represent those of the water clans. . .

Thirteen is thus the expression of a double human totality: collective, since the tribe is made up of two asymmetrical moieties (quantitatively: one is single, the other divided; and qualitatively: one in charge of peace, the other of war) and individual but equally asymmetrical (the right and the left). As a totality, this union of even and odd, of collective and individual, social and organic, is geared to the ternary cosmological scheme: there is a 'thirteen' of sky, a 'thirteen' of land, a 'thirteen' of water. Finally, added to this coding by elements, there is a coding by species where the two groups composed respectively of seven and six 'animals' are duplicated by the appearance of antagonists, thus (as might be foreseen) bringing the number of units of the system at the most concrete level to twenty-six. The seven animals and their antagonists are shown in the following table:

ANIMALS	ANTAGONISTS
lynx	young male deer, with curved horns
grey wolf	young male deer, with grey horns
male puma	full grown male deer, with dark horns
male black bear	hummock full of little bugs (insect?)
buffalo bull	high bank
elk	a plant whose blossoms always look up to the sun (*Silphium laciniatum*)
deer	no antagonist: his strength lies in flight

The system of six animals is less neat. It includes two varieties of owl, each opposed to a male raccoon, one young and one adult, the golden eagle opposed to the turkey, finally, apparently, the river mussel (the shell of which is used to make the mother of pearl pendants which symbolize the sun), buffalo hair (?), and a little pipe (?).

A logical structure—initially a simple opposition—thus fans out in two directions: one abstract, in the form of a numerology, and the other concrete, first of elements and then of species. On each level semantic short-circuits permit direct connections with the level furthest away. The level of species, which is also the most particularized of those we have considered, does not, however, constitute a sort of limit or stopping point of the system: the latter does not fall into inertia but continues to progress through new detotalizations and retotalizations which can take place on several planes.

Each clan possesses a 'symbol of life'—a totem or divinity—whose name it adopts: puma, black bear, golden eagle, young deer, etc. The clans are thus defined, in relation to each other, by means of differentiating features. Nevertheless, the ritual texts found each distinctive choice on a system of invariant characteristics, assumed to be common to all species: each affirms of itself what the puma, for instance, declares on its own account:

'Behold the soles of my feet, that are black in colour.
I have made the skin of the soles of my feet to be as my charcoal.
When the little ones [men] also make the skin of the soles of my feet to be as their charcoal,
They shall always have charcoal that will easily sink into their skin as they travel the path of life.
Behold the tip of my nose, that is black in color, etc.
Behold the tips of my ears, that are black in color, etc.
Behold the tip of my tail, that is black in color, etc.'

Each animal is thus decomposed into parts, according to a law of correspondence (muzzle = beak, etc.) and the equivalent parts are regrouped among themselves and then all together in terms of the same relevant characteristic: the presence of 'charcoaled' parts, on account of the protective role which the Osage attribute to fire and its product, charcoal, and finally, and by way of consequence, to the colour black. The 'black thing', charcoal, is the object of a special rite which warriors have to perform before going into battle. If they neglect to blacken their

CHARCOAL ANIMAL

		black	paws	black	muzzle	black	tail	etc.
N s	puma							
a p	bear							
t e	eagle							
u c	deer							
r i	swan							
a e								
l s	etc.							

faces, they will lose the right to recount their notable actions and to claim military honours. We therefore already have a system on two axes, one devoted to diversities and the other to similarities:

The analytic procedure which makes it possible to pass from categories to elements and from elements to species is thus extended by a sort of imaginary dismembering of each species, which progressively re-establishes the totality on another plane.

Clifford Geertz

The work of Clifford Geertz, an anthropologist at the Institute for Advanced Study at Princeton University, attacks the Enlightenment conception of human nature as entirely too simplistic and argues for a more dynamic view of culture in shaping individuals. Yet Geertz is similarly dissatisfied with the work of Benedict and other users of the "culture concept" because he sees their preoccupation with the search for universals as inherently reductive. In Geertz's view, the particularity of culture is essential to its meaning.

Geertz's understanding of culture is essentially a semiotic one. Viewing man "as an animal suspended in webs of significance he himself has spun, . . . culture as those webs, and the analysis of it to be therefore not experimental science in search of a law but an interpretive one in search of a meaning," Geertz opposes the categories of knowledge and meaning. In the process, Geertz reveals just how far away the critics of modernity have moved from the underlying premises that had grounded scientific practice in the past.

If science is no longer experimental, exactly how does a scientist proceed? In answer to this question Geertz offers us the methodology of "thick description." Using thick description, an ethnographer creates a text that is as faithful as possible to the particularities and details of the situation he seeks to explain. Geertz argues that the validity of an interpretation, its cogency, can be based on how well the anthropologist's text makes the foreign intelligible. In Geertz's paradigm, the difference between explanation and description becomes relatively small.

CLIFFORD GEERTZ
(1973)

Thick Description:
Toward an Interpretive
Theory of Culture

In her book *Philosophy in a New Key*, Susanne Langer remarks that certain ideas burst upon the intellectual landscape with a tremendous force. They resolve so many fundamental problems at once that they seem also to promise that they will resolve all fundamental problems, clarify all obscure issues. Everyone snaps them up as the open sesame of some new positive science, the conceptual center-point around which a comprehensive system of analysis can be built. The sudden vogue of such a *grande idée*, crowding out almost everything else for a while, is due, she says, "to the fact that all sensitive and active minds turn at once to exploiting it. We try it in every connection, for every purpose, experiment with possible stretches of its strict meaning, with generalizations and derivatives."

After we have become familiar with the new idea, however, after it has become part of our general stock of theoretical concepts, our expectations are brought more into balance with its actual uses, and its excessive popularity is ended. A few zealots persist in the old key-to-the-universe view of it; but less driven thinkers settle down after a while to the problems the idea has really generated. They try to apply it and extend it where it applies and where it is capable of extension; and they desist where it does not apply or cannot be extended. It becomes, if it was, in truth, a seminal idea in the first place, a permanent and enduring part of our intellectual armory. But it no longer has the grandiose, all-promising scope, the infinite versatility of apparent application, it once had. The second law of thermodynamics, or the principle of natural selection, or the notion of unconscious motivation, or the organization of the means of production does not explain everything, not even everything human, but it still explains something; and our attention shifts to isolating just what that something is, to disentangling ourselves from a lot of pseudoscience to which, in the first flush of its celebrity, it has also given rise.

Whether or not this is, in fact, the way all centrally important scientific concepts develop, I don't know. But certainly this pattern fits the concept of culture, around which the whole discipline of anthropology arose, and whose domination that discipline has been increasingly concerned to limit, specify, focus, and contain. It is to this cutting of the culture concept down to size, therefore actually insuring its continued importance rather than undermining it, that the essays below are all, in their several ways and from their several directions, dedicated. They all argue, sometimes explicitly, more often merely through the particular analysis they develop, for a narrowed, specialized, and, so I imagine, theoretically more powerful concept of culture to replace E. B. Tylor's famous "most complex whole," which, its originative power not denied, seems to me to have reached the point where it obscures a good deal more than it reveals.

The conceptual morass into which the Tylorean kind of *pot-au-feu* theorizing about culture can lead, is evident in what is still one of the better general introductions to anthropology, Clyde Kluckhohn's *Mirror for Man*. In some twenty-seven pages of his chapter on the concept, Kluckhohn managed to define culture in turn as: (1) "the total way of life of a people"; (2) "the social legacy the individual acquires from his group"; (3) "a way of thinking, feeling, and believing"; (4) "an abstraction from behavior"; (5) a theory on the part of the anthropologist about the way in which a group of people in fact behave; (6) a "storehouse of pooled learning"; (7) "a set of standardized orientations to recurrent problems"; (8) "learned behavior"; (9) a mechanism for the normative regulation of behavior; (10) "a set of techniques for adjusting both to the external environment and to other men"; (11) "a precipitate of history"; and turning, perhaps in desperation, to similes, as a map, as a sieve, and as a matrix. In the face of this sort of theoretical diffusion, even a somewhat constricted and not entirely standard concept of culture, which is at least internally coherent and, more important, which has a definable argument to make is (as, to be fair, Kluckhohn himself keenly realized) an improvement. Eclecticism is self-defeating not because there is only one direction in which it is useful to move, but because there are so many: it is necessary to choose.

The concept of culture I espouse, and whose utility the essays below attempt to demonstrate, is essentially a semiotic one. Believing, with Max Weber, that man is an animal suspended in webs of significance he himself has spun, I take culture to be those webs, and the analysis of it to be therefore not an experimental science in search of law but an interpretive one in search of meaning. It is explication I am after, construing social expressions on their surface enigmatical. But this pronouncement, a doctrine in a clause, demands itself some explication....

If you want to understand what a science is, you should look in the first instance not at its theories or its findings, and certainly not at what its apologists say about it; you should look at what the practitioners of it do.

In anthropology, or anyway social anthropology, what the practioners do is ethnography. And it is in understanding what ethnography is, or more exactly *what doing ethnography is*, that a start can be made toward grasping what anthropological analysis amounts to as a form of knowledge. This, it must immediately be said, is not a matter of methods. From one point of view, that of the textbook, doing ethnography is establishing rapport, selecting informants, transcribing texts, taking genealogies, mapping fields, keeping a diary, and so on. But it is not these things, techniques and received procedures, that define the enterprise. What defines it is the kind of intellectual effort it is: an elaborate venture in, to borrow a notion from Gilbert Ryle, "thick description."

Ryle's discussion of "thick description" appears in two recent essays of his (now reprinted in the second volume of his *Collected Papers*) addressed to the general question of what, as he puts it, *"Le Penseur"* is doing: "Thinking and Reflecting" and "The Thinking of Thoughts." Consider, he says, two boys rapidly contracting the eyelids of their right eyes. In one, this is an involuntary twitch; in the other, a conspiratorial signal to a friend. The two movements are, as movements, identical; from an I-am-a-camera, "phenomenalistic" observation of them alone, one could not tell which was twich and which was wink, or indeed whether both or either was twich or wink. Yet the difference, however unphotographable, between a twitch and a wink is vast; as anyone unfortunate enough to have had the first taken for the second knows. The winker is communicating, and indeed communicating in a quite precise and special way: (1) deliberately, (2) to someone in particular, (3) to impart a particular message, (4) according to a socially established code, and (5) without cognizance of the rest of the company. As Ryle points out, the winker has done two things, contracted his eyelids and winked, while the twitcher has done only one, contracted his eyelids. Contracting your eyelids on purpose when there exists a public code in which so doing counts as a conspiratorial signal *is* winking. That's all there is to it: a speck of behavior, a fleck of culture, and—*voilà!*—a gesture.

That, however, is just the beginning. Suppose, he continues, there is a third boy, who, "to give malicious amusement to his cronies," parodies the first boy's wink, as amateurish, clumsy, obvious, and so on. He, of course, does this in the same way the second boy winked and the first twitched: by contracting his right eyelids. Only this boy is neither winking nor twitching, he is parodying someone else's, as he takes it, laughable, attempt at winking. Here, too, a socially established code exists (he will "wink" laboriously, overobviously, perhaps adding a grimace—the usual artifices of the clown); and so also does a message. Only now it is not conspiracy but ridicule that is in the air. If the others think he is actually winking, his whole project misfires as completely, though with somewhat different results, as if they think he is twitching. One can go further: uncertain of his mimicking abilities, the would-be satirist may practice at home before the mirror, in which case he is not twitching, winking, or parodying, but rehearsing; though so far as what a camera, a radical behaviorist, or a believer in protocol sentences would record he is just rapidly contracting his right eyelids like all the others. Complexities are possible, if not practically without end, at least logically so. The original winker might, for example, actually have been fake-winking, say, to mislead outsiders into imagining there was a conspiracy afoot when there in fact was not, in which case our descriptions of what the parodist is parodying and the rehearser rehearsing of course shift accordingly. But the point is that between what Ryle calls the "thin description" of what the rehearser (parodist, winker, twitcher . . .) is doing ("rapidly contracting his right eyelids") and the "thick description" of what he is doing ("practicing a burlesque of a friend faking a wink to deceive an innocent into thinking a conspiracy is in motion") lies the object of ethnography: a stratified hierarchy of meaningful structures in terms of which twitches, winks, fake-winks, parodies, rehearsals of parodies are produced, perceived, and interpreted, and without which they would not (not even the zero-form twitches, which, *as a cultural category*, are as much nonwinks as winks are nontwiches) in fact exist, no matter what anyone did or didn't do with his eyelids.

Like so many of the little stories Oxford philosophers like to make up for themselves, all this winking, fake-winking, burlesque-fake-winking, rehearsed-burlesque-fake-winking, may seem a bit artificial. In way of adding a more empirical note, let me give, deliberately unprecedented by any prior explanatory comment at all, a not untypical excerpt from my own field journal to demonstrate that, however, evened off for didactic purposes, Ryle's example presents an image only too exact of the sort of piled-up structures of inference and implication through which an ethnographer is continually trying to pick his way:

> The French [the informant said] had only just arrived. They set up twenty or so small forts between here, the town, and the Marmusha area up in the middle of the mountains, placing them on promontories so they could survey the countryside. But for all this they couldn't guarantee safety, especially at night, so although the *mezrag*, trade-pact, system was supposed to be legally abolished it in fact continued as before.
>
> One night, when Cohen (who speaks fluent Berber), was up there, at Marmusha, two other Jews who were traders to a neighboring tribe came by to purchase some goods from him. Some Berbers, from yet another neighboring tribe, tried to break into Cohen's place, but he fired his rifle in the air. (Traditionally, Jews were not allowed to carry weapons; but at this period things were so unsettled many did so anyway.) This attracted the attention of the French and the marauders fled.
>
> The next night, however, they came back, one of them disguised as a woman who knocked on the door with some sort of a story. Cohen was suspicious and didn't want to let "her" in, but the other Jews said, "oh, it's all right, it's only a woman." So they opened the door and the whole lot came pouring in. They killed the two visiting Jews, but Cohen managed to barricade himself in an adjoining room. He heard the robbers planning to burn him alive in the shop after they removed his goods, and so he opened the door and, laying about him wildly with a club, managed to escape through a window.
>
> He went up to the fort, then, to have his wounds dressed, and complained to the local commandant, one Captain Dumari, saying he wanted his *'ar*—i.e., four or five times the value of the merchandise stolen from him. The robbers were from a tribe which had not yet submitted to French authority and were in open rebellion against it, and he wanted authorization to go with his *mezrag*-holder, the Marmusha tribal *sheikh*, to collect the indemnity that, under traditional rules, he had coming to him. Captain Dumari couldn't officially give him permission to do this, because of the French prohibition of the *mezrag* relationship, but he gave him verbal authorization, saying, "If you get killed, it's your problem."
>
> So the *sheikh*, the Jew, and a small company of armed Marmushans went off ten or fifteen kilometers up into the rebellious area, where there were of course no French, and, sneaking up, captured the thief-tribe's shepherd and stole its herds. The other tribe soon came riding out on horses after them, armed with rifles and ready to attack. But when they saw who the "sheep thieves" were, they thought better of it and said, "all right, we'll talk." They couldn't really deny what had happened—that some of their men had robbed Cohen and killed the two visitors—and they weren't prepared to start the serious feud with the Marmusha a scuffle with the invading party would bring on. So the two groups talked, and talked, and talked, there on the plain amid the thousands of sheep, and decided finally on five-hundred-sheep damages. The two armed Berber groups then lined up on their horses at opposite ends of the plain, with the sheep herded between them, and Cohen, in his black gown, pillbox hat, and flapping slippers, went out alone among the sheep, picking out, one by one and at his own good speed, the best ones for his payment.
>
> So Cohen got his sheep and drove them back to Marmusha. The French, up in their fort, heard them coming from some distance ("Ba, ba, ba" said Cohen, happily, recalling the image) and said, "What the hell is that?" And Cohen said, "That is my *'ar*." The French couldn't believe he had actually done what he said he had done, and accused him of being a spy for the rebellious Berbers, put him in

prison, and took his sheep. In the town, his family, not having heard from him in so long a time, thought he was dead. But after a while the French released him and he came back home, but without his sheep. He then went to the Colonel in the town, the Frenchman in charge of the whole region, to complain. But the Colonel said, "I can't do anything about the matter. It's not my problem."

Quoted raw, a note in a bottle, this passage conveys, as any similar one similarly presented would do, a fair sense of how much goes into ethnographic description of even the most elemental sort—how extraordinarily "thick" it is. In finished anthropological writings, including those collected here, this fact—that what we call our data are really our own constructions of other people's constructions of what they and their compatriots are up to—is obscured because most of what we need to comprehend a particular event, ritual, custom, idea, or whatever is insinuated as background information before the thing itself is directly examined. (Even to reveal that this little drama took place in the highlands of central Morocco in 1912—and was recounted there in 1968—is to determine much of our understanding of it.) There is nothing particularly wrong with this, and it is in any case inevitable. But it does lead to a view of anthropological research as rather more of an observational and rather less of an interpretive activity than it really is. Right down at the factual base, the hard rock, insofar as there is any, of the whole enterprise, we are already explicating: and worse, explicating explications. Winks upon winks upon winks.

Analysis, then, is sorting out the structures of signification—what Ryle called established codes, a somewhat misleading expression, for it makes the enterprise sound too much like that of the cipher clerk when it is much more like that of the literary critic—and determining their social ground and import. Here, in our text, such sorting would begin with distinguishing the three unlike frames of interpretation ingredient in the situation, Jewish, Berber, and French, and would then move on to show how (and why) at that time, in that place, their copresence produced a situation in which systematic misunderstanding reduced traditional form to social farce. What tripped Cohen up, and with him the whole, ancient pattern of social and economic relationships within which he functioned, was a confusion of tongues.

I shall come back to this too-compacted aphorism later, as well as to the details of the text itself. The point for now is only that ethnography is thick description. What the ethnographer is in fact faced with—except when (as, of course, he must do) he is pursuing the more automatized routines of data collection—is a multiplicity of complex conceptual structures, many of them superimposed upon or knotted into one another, which are at once strange, irregular, and inexplicit, and which he must contrive somehow first to grasp and then to render. And this is true at the most down-to-earth, jungle field work levels of his activity: interviewing informants, observing rituals, eliciting kin terms, tracing property lines, censusing households … writing his journal. Doing ethnography is like trying to read (in the sense of "construct a reading of") a manuscript—foreign, faded, full of ellipses, incoherencies, suspicious emendations, and tendentious commentaries, but written not in conventionalized graphs of sound but in transient examples of shaped behavior.

Culture, this acted document, thus is public, like a burlesqued wink or a mock sheep raid. Though ideational, it does not exist in someone's head; though unphysical, it is not an occult entity. The interminable, because unterminable, debate within anthropology as to whether culture is "subjective" or "objective," together with the mutual exchange of intellectual insults ("idealist!"—"materialist!"; "mentalist!"—"behaviorist!"; "impressionist!"—"positivist!") which accompanies it, is wholly misconceived. Once human behavior is seen as (most of the time; there *are* true twitches) symbolic action—action which, like phonation in speech, pigment in painting, line in writing, or sonance in music, signifies—the question as to whether culture is patterned conduct or a frame of mind, or even the two somehow mixed together, loses sense. The thing to ask about a burlesqued wink or a mock sheep raid is not what their ontological status is. It is the same as that of rocks on the one hand and dreams on the other—they are things of this world. The thing to ask is what their import is: what it is, ridicule or challenge, irony or anger, snobbery or pride, that, in their occurrence and through their agency, is getting said.

This may seem like an obvious truth, but there are a number of ways to obscure it. One is to imagine that culture is a self-contained "super-organic" reality with forces and purposes of its own; that is, to reify it. Another is to claim that it consists in the brute pattern of behavioral events we observe in fact to occur in some identifiable community or other; that is, to reduce it. But though both these confusions still exist, and doubtless will be always with us, the main source of theoretical muddlement in contemporary anthropology is a view which developed in reaction to them and is right now very widely held—namely, that, to quote Ward Goodenough, perhaps its leading proponent, "culture [is located] in the minds and hearts of men."

Variously called ethnoscience, componential analysis, or cognitive anthropology (a terminological wavering which reflects a deeper uncertainty), this school of thought holds that culture is composed of psychological structures by means of which individuals or groups of individuals guide their behavior. "A society's culture," to quote Goodenough again, this time in a passage which has become the *locus classicus* of the whole movement, "consists of whatever it is one has to know or believe in order to operate in a manner acceptable to its members." And from this view of what culture is follows a view equally assured, of what describing it is—the writing out of systematic rules, an ethnographic algorithm, which, if followed, would make it possible so to operate, to pass (physical appearance aside) for a native. In such a way, extreme subjectivism is married to extreme formalism, with the expected result: an explosion of debate as to whether particular analyses (which come in the form of taxonomies, paradigms, tables, trees, and other ingenuities) reflect what the natives "really" think or are merely clever simulations, logically equivalent but substantively different, of what they think. . . .

Culture is public because meaning is. You can't wink (or burlesque one) without knowing what counts as winking or how, physically, to contract your eyelids, and you can't conduct a sheep raid (or mimic one) without knowing what it is to steal a sheep and how practically to go about it. But to draw from such truths the conclusion that knowing how to wink is winking and knowing how to steal a sheep is sheep raiding is to betray as deep a confusion as, taking thin descriptions for thick, to identify winking with eyelid contractions or sheep raiding with chasing woolly animals out of pastures. The cognitivist fallacy—that culture consists (to quote another spokesman for the movement, Stephen Tyler) of "mental phenomena which can [he means "should"] be analyzed by formal methods similar to those of mathematics and logic"—is as destructive of an effective use of the concept as are the behaviorist and idealist fallacies to which it is a misdrawn correction. Perhaps, as its errors are more sophisticated and its distortions subtler, it is even more so.

The generalized attack on privacy theories of meaning is, since early Husserl and late

Wittgenstein, so much a part of modern thought that it need not be developed once more here. What is necessary is to see to it that the news of it reaches anthropology; and in particular that it is made clear that to say that culture consists of socially established structures of meaning in terms of which people do such things as signal conspiracies and join them or perceive insults and answer them, is no more to say that it is a psychological phenomenon, a characteristic of someone's mind, personality, cognitive structure, or whatever, than to say that Tantrism, genetics, the progressive form of the verb, the classification of wines, the Common Law, or the notion of "a conditional curse"... is. What, in a place like Morocco, most prevents those of us who grew up winking other winks or attending other sheep from grasping what people are up to is not ignorance as to how cognition works (though, especially as, one assumes, it works the same among them as it does among us, it would greatly help to have less of that too) as a lack of familiarity with the imaginative universe within which their acts are signs. As Wittgenstein has been invoked, he may as well be quoted:

> We ... say of some people that they are transparent to us. It is, however, important as regards this observation that one human being can be a complete enigma to another. We learn this when we come into a strange country with entirely strange traditions; and, what is more, even given a mastery of the country's language. We do not *understand* the people. (And not because of not knowing what they are saying to themselves.) We cannot find our feet with them.

Finding our feet, an unnerving business which never more than distantly succeeds, is what ethnographic research consists of as a personal experience; trying to formulate the basis on which one imagines, always excessively, one has found them is what anthropological writing consists of as a scientific endeavor.... We are seeking, in the widened sense of the term in which it encompasses very much more than talk, to converse with them, a matter a great deal more difficult, and not only with strangers, than is commonly recognized....

Looked at in this way, the aim of anthropology is the enlargement of the universe of human discourse. That is not, of course, its only aim—instruction, amusement, practical counsel, moral advance, and the discovery of natural order in human behavior are others; nor is anthropology the only discipline which pursues it. But it is an aim to which a semiotic concept of culture is peculiarly well adapted. As interworked systems of construable signs (what, ignoring provincial usages, I would call symbols), culture is not a power, something to which social events, behaviors, institutions, or processes can be causally attributed; it is a context, something within which they can be intelligibly—that is, thickly—described....

What it means is that descriptions of Berber, Jewish, or French culture must be cast in terms of the constructions we imagine Berbers, Jews, or Frenchmen to place upon what they live through, the formulae they use to define what happens to them. What it does not mean is that such descriptions are themselves Berber, Jewish, or French—that is, part of the reality they are ostensibly describing; they are anthropological—that is, part of a developing system of scientific analysis. They must be cast in terms of the interpretations to which persons of a particular denomination subject their experience, because that is what they profess to be descriptions of; they are anthropological because it is, in fact, anthropologists who profess them. Normally, it is not necessary to point out quite so laboriously that the object of study is one thing and the study of it another. It is clear enough that the physical world is not physics and *A Skeleton Key to Finnegan's Wake* not *Finnegan's Wake*. But, as, in the study of culture, analysis penetrates into the very body of the object—that is, *we begin with our own interpretations of what our informants are up to, or think they are up to, and then systematize those*—the line between (Moroccan) culture as a natural fact and (Moroccan) culture as a theoretical entity tends to get blurred. All the more so, as the latter is presented in the form of an actor's-eye description of (Moroccan) conceptions of everything from violence, honor, divinity, and justice, to tribe, property, patronage, and chiefship.

In short, anthropological writings are themselves interpretations, and second and third order ones to boot. (By definition, only a "native" makes first order ones: it's *his* culture.) They are, thus, fictions; fictions, in the sense that they are "something made," "something fashioned." ...

If ethnography is thick description and ethnographers those who are doing the describing, then the determining question for any given example of it, whether a field journal squib or a Malinowski-sized monograph, is whether it sorts winks from twitches and real winks from mimicked ones. It is not against a body of uninterpreted data, radically thinned descriptions, that we must measure the cogency of our explications, but against the power of the scientific imagination to bring us into touch with the lives of strangers. It is not worth it, as Thoreau said, to go round the world to count the cats in Zanzibar. ...

Cultural systems must have a minimal degree of coherence, else we would not call them systems; and, by observation, they normally have a great deal more. But there is nothing so coherent as a paranoid's delusion or a swindler's story. The force of our interpretations cannot rest, as they are now so often made to do, on the tightness with which they hold together, or the assurance with which they are argued. Nothing has done more, I think, to discredit cultural analysis than the construction of impeccable depictions of formal order in whose actual existence nobody can quite believe.

If anthropological interpretation is constructing a reading of what happens, then to divorce it from what happens—from what, in this time or that place, specific people say, what they do, what is done to them, from the whole vast business of the world—is to divorce it from its applications and render it vacant. A good interpretation of anything—a poem, a person, a history, a ritual, an institution, a society—takes us into the heart of that of which it is the interpretation. When it does not do that, but leads us instead somewhere else—into an admiration of its own elegance, of its author's cleverness, or of the beauties of Euclidean order—it may have its intrinsic charms; but it is something else than what the task at hand—figuring out what all that rigamarole with the sheep is about—calls for.

The rigamarole with the sheep—the sham theft of them, the reparative transfer of them, the political confiscation of them—is (or was) essentially a social discourse, even if, as I suggested earlier, one conducted in multiple tongues and as much in action as in words. ...

The ethnographer "inscribes" social discourse; *he writes it down*. In so doing, he turns it from a passing event, which exists only in its own moment of occurrence, into an account, which exists in its inscriptions and can be reconsulted. ...

"What does the ethnographer do?"—he writes. This, too, may seem a less than startling discovery, and to someone familiar with the current "literature," an implausible one. But as the standard answer to our question has been, "He observes, he records, he analyzes"—a kind of *veni, vidi, vici* conception of the matter—it may have more deep-going consequences than are at first apparent, not the least of which is that distinguishing these three phases of knowledge-seeking may not, as a matter of fact, normally be possible; and, indeed, as autonomous "operations" they may not in fact exist.

The situation is even more delicate, because, as already noted, what we inscribe (or try to) is not raw social discourse, to which, because, save very marginally or very specially, we are not actors, we do not have direct access, but only that small part of it which our informants can lead us into understanding. This is not as fatal as it sounds, for, in fact, not all Cretans are liars, and it is not necessary to know everything in order to understand something. But it does make the view of anthropological analysis as the conceptual manipulation of discovered facts, a logical reconstruction of a mere reality, seem rather lame. To set forth symmetrical crystals of significance, purified of the material complexity in which they were located, and then attribute their existence to autogenous principles of order, universal properties of the human mind, or vast, a priori *weltanschauungen*, is to pretend a science that does not exist and imagine a reality that cannot be found. Cultural analysis is (or should be) guessing at meanings, assessing the guesses, and drawing explanatory conclusions from the better guesses, not discovering the Continent of Meaning and mapping out its bodiless landscape.

So, there are three characteristics of ethnographic description: it is interpretive; what it is interpretive of is the flow of social discourse; and the interpreting involved consists in trying to rescue the "said" of such discourse from its perishing occasions and fix it in perusable terms. . .

But there is, in addition, a fourth characteristic of such description, at least as I practice it: it is microscopic.

This is not to say that there are no large-scale anthropological interpretations of whole societies, civilizations, world events, and so on. Indeed, it is such extension of our analyses to wider contexts that, along with their theoretical implications, recommends them to general attention and justifies our constructing them. . . .

History may have its unobtrusive turning points, "great noises in a little room"; but this little go-round was surely not one of them.

It is merely to say that the anthropologist characteristically approaches such broader interpretations and more abstract analyses from the direction of exceedingly extended acquaintances with extremely small matters. He confronts the same grand realities that others—historians, economists, political scientists, sociologists—confront in more fateful settings: Power, Change, Faith, Oppression, Work, Passion, Authority, Beauty, Violence, Love, Prestige; but he confronts them in contexts obscure enough . . . to take the capital letters off them. These all-too-human constancies, "those big words that make us all afraid," take a homely form in such homely contexts. But that is exactly the advantage. There are enough profundities in the world already.

Yet, the problem of how to get from a collection of ethnographic miniatures on the order of our sheep story—an assortment of remarks and anecdotes—to wall-sized culturescapes of the nation, the epoch, the continent, or the civilization is not so easily passed over with vague allusions to the virtues of concreteness and the down-to-earth mind. For a science born in Indian tribes, Pacific islands, and African lineages and subsequently seized with grander ambitions, this has come to be a major methodological problem, and for the most part a badly handled one. The models that anthropologists have themselves worked out to justify their moving from local truths to general visions have been, in fact, as responsible for undermining the effort as anything their critics—sociologists obsessed with sample sizes, psychologists with measures, or economists with aggregates—have been able to devise against them.

Of these, the two main ones have been: the Jonesville-is-the-USA "microcosmic" model; and the Easter-Island-is-a-testing-case "natural experiment" model. . . .

The notion that one can find the essence of national societies, civilizations, great religions, or whatever summed up and simplified in so-called "typical" small towns and villages is palpable nonsense. What one finds in small towns and villages is (alas) small-town or village life. If localized, microscopic studies were really dependent for their greater relevance upon such a premise—that they captured the great world in the little—they wouldn't have any relevance.

The "natural laboratory" notion has been equally pernicious, not only because the analogy is false—what kind of a laboratory is it where *none* of the parameters are manipulable?—but because it leads to a notion that the data derived from ethnographic studies are purer, or more fundamental, or more solid, or less conditioned (the most favored word is "elementary") than those derived from other sorts of social inquiry. The great natural variation of cultural forms is, of course, not only anthropology's great (and wasting) resource, but the ground of its deepest theoretical dilemma: how is such variation to be squared with the biological unity of the human species? But it is not, even metaphorically, experimental variation, because the context in which it occurs varies along with it, and it is not possible (though there are those who try) to isolate the *y*'s from *x*'s to write a proper function.

The famous studies purporting to show that the Oedipus complex was backwards in the Trobriands, sex roles were upside down in Tchambuli, and the Pueblo Indians lacked aggression (it is characteristic that they were all negative—"but not in the South"), are, whatever their empirical validity may or may not be, not "scientifically tested and approved" hypotheses. They are interpretations, or misinterpretations, like any others, arrived at in the same way as any others, and as inherently inconclusive as any others, and the attempt to invest them with the authority of physical experimentation is but methodological sleight of hand. Ethnographic findings are not privileged, just particular: another country heard from. To regard them as anything more (*or anything less*) than that distorts both them and their implications, which are far profounder than mere primitivity, for social theory.

The methodological problem which the microscopic nature of ethnography presents is both real and critical. But it is not to be resolved by regarding a remote locality as the world in a teacup or as the sociological equivalent of a cloud chamber. It is to be resolved—or, anyway, decently kept at bay—by realizing that social actions are comments on more than themselves; that where an interpretation comes from does not determine where it can be impelled to go. Small facts speak to large issues, winks to epistemology, or sheep raids to revolution, because they are made to.

Which brings us, finally, to theory. The besetting sin of interpretive approaches to anything—literature, dreams, symptoms, culture—is that they tend to resist, or to be permitted to resist, conceptual articulation and thus to escape systematic modes of assessment. You either grasp an interpretation or you do not, see the point of it or you do not, accept it or you do not. Imprisoned in the immediacy of its own detail, it is presented as self-validating, or, worse, as validated by the supposedly developed sensitivities of the person who presents it; any attempt to cast what it says in terms other than its own is regarded as a travesty—as, the anthropologist's severest term of moral abuse, ethnocentric.

For a field of study which, however timidly (though I, myself, am not timid about the matter at all), asserts itself to be a science, this just will not do. There is no reason why the conceptual structure of a cultural interpretation should be any less formulable, and thus less susceptible to explicit canons of appraisal, than that of, say, a biological observation or a physical experiment—no reason except that the terms in which such formulations can be cast are if not wholly nonexistent, very nearly so. We are reduced to insinuating theories because we lack the power to state them.

At the same time, it must be admitted that there are a number of characteristics of cultural interpretation which make the theoretical development of it more than usually difficult. The first is the need for theory to stay rather closer to the ground than tends to be the case in sciences more able to give themselves over to imaginative abstraction. Only short flights of ratiocination tend to be effective in anthropology; longer ones tend to drift off into logical dreams, academic bemusements with formal symmetry. The whole point of a semiotic approach to culture is, as I have said, to aid us in gaining access to the conceptual world in which our subjects live so that we can, in some extended sense of the term, converse with them. The tension between the pull of this need to penetrate an unfamiliar universe of symbolic action and the requirements of technical advance in the theory of culture, between the need to grasp and the need to analyze, is, as a result, both necessarily great and essentially irremovable. Indeed, the further theoretical development goes, the deeper the tension gets. This is the first condition for cultural theory: it is not its own master. As it is unseverable from the immediacies thick description presents, its freedom to shape itself in terms of its internal logic is rather limited. What generality it contrives to achieve grows out of the delicacy of its distinctions, not the sweep of its abstractions.

And from this follows a peculiarity in the way, as a simple matter of empirical fact, our knowledge of culture ... cultures ... a culture ... grows: in spurts. Rather than following a rising curve of cumulative findings, cultural analysis breaks up into a disconnected yet coherent sequence of bolder and bolder sorties. Studies do build on other studies, not in the sense that they take up where the others leave off, but in the sense that, better informed and better conceptualized, they plunge more deeply into the same things. Every serious cultural analysis starts from a sheer beginning and ends where it manages to get before exhausting its intellectual impulse. Previously discovered facts are mobilized, previously developed concepts used, previously formulated hypotheses tried out; but the movement is not from already proven theorems to newly proven ones, it is from an awkward fumbling for the most elementary understanding to a supported claim that one has achieved that and surpassed it. A study is an advance if it is more incisive—whatever that may mean—than those that preceded it; but it less stands on their shoulders than, challenged and challenging, runs by their side.

[B]ut one cannot write a "General Theory of Cultural Interpretation." Or, rather, one can, but there appears to be little profit in it, because the essential task of theory building here is not to codify abstract regularities but to make thick description possible, not to generalize across cases but to generalize within them.

To generalize within cases is usually called, at least in medicine and depth psychology, clinical inference. Rather than beginning with a set of observations and attempting to subsume them under a governing law, such inference begins with a set of (presumptive) signifiers and attempts to place them within an intelligible frame. Measures are matched to theoretical predictions, but symptoms (even when they are measured) are scanned for theoretical peculiarities—that is, they are diagnosed. In the study of culture the signifiers are not symptoms or clusters of symptoms, but symbolic acts or clusters of symbolic acts, and the aim is not therapy but the analysis of social discourse. But the way in which theory is used—to ferret out the unapparent import of things—is the same.

Thus we are lead to the second condition of cultural theory: it is not, at least in the strict meaning of the term, predictive. The diagnostician doesn't predict measles; he decides that someone has them, or at the very most *anticipates* that someone is rather likely shortly to get them. But this limitation, which is real enough, has commonly been both misunderstood and exaggerated, because it has been taken to mean that cultural interpretation is merely post facto: that, like the peasant in the old story, we first shoot the holes in the fence and then paint the bull's-eyes around them. It is hardly to be denied that there is a good deal of that sort of thing around, some of it in prominent places. It is to be denied, however, that it is the inevitable outcome of a clinical approach to the use of theory.

It is true that in the clinical style of theoretical formulation, conceptualization is directed toward the task of generating interpretations of matters already in hand, not toward projecting outcomes of experimental manipulations or deducing future states of a determined system. But that does not mean that theory has only to fit (or, more carefully, to generate cogent interpretations of) realities past; it has also to survive—intellectually survive—realities to come. Although we formulate our interpretation of an outburst of winking or an instance of sheep-raiding after its occurrence, sometimes long after, the theoretical framework in terms of which such an interpretation is made must be capable of continuing to yield defensible interpretations as new social phenomena swim into view. Although one starts any effort at thick description, beyond the obvious and superficial, from a state of general bewilderment as to what the devil is going on—trying to find one's feet—one does not start (or ought not) intellectually empty-handed. Theoretical ideas are not created wholly anew in each study; as I have said, they are adopted from other, related studies, and, refined in the process, applied to new interpretive problems. If they cease being useful with respect to such problems, they tend to stop being used and are more or less abandoned. If they continue being useful, throwing up new understandings, they are further elaborated and go on being used.

Such a view of how theory functions in an interpretive science suggests that the distinction, relative in any case, that appears in the experimental or observational sciences between "description" and "explanation" appears here as one, even more relative, between "inscription" ("thick description") and "specification" ("diagnosis")—between setting down the meaning particular social actions have for the actors whose actions they are, and stating, as explicitly as we can manage, what the knowledge thus attained demonstrates about the society in which it is found, and beyond that, about social life as such. Our double task is to uncover the conceptual structures that inform our subjects' acts, the "said" of social discourse, and to construct a system of analysis in whose terms what is generic to those structures, what belongs to them because they are what they are, will stand out against the other determinants of human behavior. In ethnography, the office of theory is to provide a vocabulary in which what symbolic action has to say about itself—that is, about the role of culture in human life—can be expressed.

Aside from a couple of orienting pieces concerned with more foundational matters, it is in such a manner that theory operates in the essays collected here. A repertoire of very general, made-in-the-academy concepts and systems of concepts—"integration," "rationalization," "symbol," "ideology," "ethos," "revolution," "identity," "metaphor," "structure," "ritual," "world view," "actor," "function," "sacred," and, of course, "culture" itself—is woven into the body of thick-description ethnography in the hope of rendering mere occurrences scientifically eloquent. The aim is to draw large conclusions from small, but very densely textured facts; to support broad assertions about the role of culture in the construction of collective life by engaging them exactly with complex specifics.

Thus it is not only interpretation that goes all the way down to the most immediate observational level: the theory upon which such interpretation conceptually depends does so also. My interest in Cohen's story, like Ryle's in winks, grew out of some very general notions indeed. The "confusion of tongues" model—the view that social conflict is not something that happens when, out of weakness, indefiniteness, obsolescence, or neglect, cultural forms cease to operate, but rather something which happens when, like burlesqued winks, such forms are pressed by unusual situations or unusual intentions to operate in unusual ways—is not an idea I got from Cohen's story. It is one, instructed by colleagues, students, and predecessors, I brought to it.

Our innocent-looking "note in a bottle" is more than a portrayal of the frames of meaning of Jewish peddlers, Berber warriors, and French proconsuls, or even of their mutual interference. It is an argument that to rework the pattern of social relationships is to rearrange the coordinates of the experienced world. Society's forms are culture's substance.

There is an Indian story—at least I heard it as an Indian story—about an Englishman who, having been told that the world rested on a platform which rested on the back of an elephant which rested in turn on the back of a turtle, asked (perhaps he was an ethnographer; it is the way they behave), what did the turtle rest on? Another turtle. And that turtle? "Ah, Sahib, after that it is turtles all the way down."

Cultural analysis is intrinsically incomplete. And, worse than that, the more deeply it goes the less complete it is. It is a strange science whose most telling assertions are its most tremulously based, in which to get somewhere with the matter at hand is to intensify the suspicion, both your own and that of others, that you are not quite getting it right. But that, along with plaguing subtle people with obtuse questions, is what being an ethnographer is like.

The fact is that to commit oneself to a semiotic concept of culture and an interpretive approach to the study of it is to commit oneself to a view of ethnographic assertion as, to borrow W. B. Gallie's by now famous phases, "essentially contestable." Anthropology, or at least interpretive anthropology, is a science whose progress is marked less by a perfection of consensus than by a refinement of debate. What gets better is the precision with which we vex each other.

This is very difficult to see when one's attention is being monopolized by a single party to the argument. Monologues are of little value here, because there are no conclusions to be reported; there is merely a discussion to be sustained. Insofar as the essays here collected have any importance, it is less in what they say than what they are witness to: an enormous increase in interest, not only in anthropology, but in social studies generally, in the role of symbolic forms in human life. Meaning, that elusive and ill-defined pseudoentity we were once more than content to leave philosophers and literary critics to fumble with, has now come back into the heart of our discipline. Even Marxists are quoting Cassirer; even positivists, Kenneth Burke.

My own position in the midst of all this has been to try to resist subjectivism on the one hand and cabbalism on the other, to try to keep the analysis of symbolic forms as closely tied as I could to concrete social events and occasions, the public world of common life, and to organize it in such a way that the connections between theoretical formulations and descriptive interpretations were unobscured by appeals to dark sciences. I have never been impressed by the argument that, as complete objectivity is impossible in these matters (as, of course, it is), one might as well let one's sentiments run loose. As Robert Solow has remarked, that is like saying that as a perfectly aseptic environment is impossible, one might as well conduct surgery

Max Horkheimer and Theodor Adorno

The group known today as the Frankfurt School came together in 1923, taking its name after the city in which the activities of the *Institut für Sozialforschung* (Institute for Social Research) were initially concentrated. The Institute was established to provide a setting in which certain historical and theoretical issues not addressed in the university could be openly discussed, such as the unexpected developments undergone by Marxism and socialism in the aftermath of the First World War. Socialism had been defeated in Germany immediately during and after that nation's capitulation to the Allies in 1918, and Bolshevism had trimphed only a short time before 1912 in the new Soviet Union. These historical events led to an effort to theorize the direction Marxist thought should take. The process of theoretical re-evaluation generated some of this century's most influential social theories, and the roster of those at one time or another associated with the School is impressive: Hannah Arendt, Walter Benjamin, Ernst Cassirer, Erich Fromm, Georg Lukács, Herbert Marcuse, to name a few of the most prominent. As the interwar period drew to a close, however, the Frankfurt School was increasingly menaced. Composed as it was of leftist, almost uniformly Jewish intellectuals, the combined contributions of such an array of thinkers quickly fell into disfavor after Hitler's rise to power in 1933.

Many of the members of the Frankfurt School wound up in American exile during the 1930s and 1940s. They were not alone: fortunates from across occupied Europe found refuge in the United States, from Albert Einstein to Bertold Brecht, to the logical positivist philosopher Rudolph Carnap. In New York, where the Frankfurt School established makeshift operations after the fall of Europe, Lévi-Strauss dined with Franz Boas, and heard lectures by Czech structural linguist Roman Jackobson. Surrealist André Breton, conductor Arturo Toscanini, and many others made up a population of emigrés of which Adorno and Horkheimer were to form a part.

The work from which the following selection was taken, however, was written not in New York, but in Southern California. As a result, much of the passionate criticism of modern culture entitled *Dialectic of the Enlightenment* (1944) derives its sense of urgency from the juxtaposition of two intellectuals, for whom the threat and presence of fascism were primary categories of daily experience, with what they viewed as the anesthetizing culture of the

American film industry. Acknowledged as a criticism of limited historical extension by its authors in later years, much of the essence of what Horkheimer and Adorno concluded concerning the relationship of Enlightenment to domination nevertheless set the tone for later postmodern treatments of culture, media, and power.

The work's central thesis is that the Enlightenment as represented by Kant, the essence of which the authors discern as far back in history as Homer's epic story *The Odyssey,* contains within itself the seeds of the sort of mass alienation that made possible the totalitarian politics of the fascist state. For Horkheimer and Adorno, the manipulation of media images in the Hollywood era of the censorship board and the studio system were tools of tyranny, only lacking in implementation. What the administrative rationalization of capitalist society had accomplished, by means of such an infant "culture industry," and the exaltation of a science that would brook no utopian speculation, was to convince the victims of social injustice to consent to their misfortune as part of the unalterable status quo.

The ethical poverty of Enlightenment, conceived of as exclusively analytical reason, is the common denominator by which Horkheimer and Adorno group together such apparently diverse writers as Kant, de Sade, and Nietzsche, none of whom, the authors argue, were able to satisfactorily justify resistance to domination in terms of reason alone. It is the demoralizing effect of deterministic science and the economic system built around it that are the greatest, and ultimately most disastrous, shortcomings of Enlightenment reason.

MAX HORKHEIMER AND
THEODOR ADORNO
(1944)

Dialectic of the

Enlightenment

When we began this work, the first samples of which we dedicate to Friedrich Pollock, we had hoped to be able to have the finished whole ready for his fiftieth birthday. But the more intensively we pursued our task, the clearer it became that our own powers were disproportionate to it. It turned out, in fact, that we had set ourselves nothing less than the discovery of why mankind, instead of entering into a truly human condition, is sinking into a new kind of barbarism. We underestimated the difficulties of interpretation, because we still trusted too much in the modern consciousness. Even though we had known for many years that the great discoveries of applied science are paid for with an increasing diminution of theoretical awareness, we still thought that in regard to scientific activity our contribution could be restricted to the criticism or extension of specialist axioms. Thematically, at any rate, we were to keep to the traditional disciplines: to sociology, psychology, and epistemology.

However, the fragments united in this volume show that we were forced to abandon this conviction. If the assiduous maintenance and verification of the scientific heritage are an essential part of knowledge (especially where zealous positivists have treated it as useless ballast and consigned it to oblivion), in the present collapse of bourgeois civilization not only the pursuit but the meaning of science has become problematical in that regard. What the brazen Fascists hypocritically laud and pliable humanist experts naïvely put into practice—the indefatigable self-destructiveness of enlightenment—requires philosophy to discard even the last vestiges of innocence in regard to the habits and tendencies of the spirit of the age. When public opinion has reached a state in which thought inevitably becomes a commodity, and language the

English translation, pp. xi–xvii, 3–17. © 1972 by Herder and Herder, Inc. Reprinted by permission of the Continuum Publishing Group.

means of promoting that commodity, then the attempt to trace the course of such depravation has to deny any allegiance to current linguistic and conceptual conventions, lest their world-historical consequences thwart it entirely.

If it were only a question of the obstacles resulting from the self-oblivious instrumentalization of science, then a critique of social problems could at least attach itself to trends opposed to the accepted scientific mode; yet even these are affected by the total process of production. They have changed no less than the ideology to which they referred. They suffer what triumphant thought has always suffered. If it willingly emerges from its critical element to become a mere means at the disposal of an existing order, then despite itself it tends to convert the positive it elected to defend into something negative and destructive. The philosophy which put the fear of death into infamy in the eighteenth century, despite all the book-burnings and piles of corpses, chose to serve that very infamy under Napoleon. Ultimately, Comte's school of apologetic usurped the succession to the inflexible Encyclopedists, and joined hands with everything that the latter had formerly rejected. The metamorphoses of criticism into affirmation do not leave the theoretical content untouched, for its truth evaporates. Now, of course, a mechanized history outstrips such intellectual developments, and the official apologists—who have other concerns—liquidate the history that helped them to their place in the sun, before it can prostitute itself.

When examining its own guilty conscience, thought has to forgo not only the affirmative use of scientific and everyday conceptual language, but just as much that of the opposition. There is no longer any available form of linguistic expression which has not tended toward accommodation to dominant currents of thought; and what a devalued language does not do automatically is proficiently executed by societal mechanisms. There are analogies in all areas for the censors voluntarily maintained by film companies faced otherwise with the threat of increased overheads. The process which a literary text has to undergo, if not in the anticipatory maneuvers of its author, then certainly in the combined efforts of readers, editors, subeditors and ghost writers in and outside publishing houses, exceeds any censorship in thoroughness. To make its functions wholly superfluous would seem to be the ambition of the educational system, despite all salutary reforms. Believing that without strict limitation to the verification of facts and probability theory, the cognitive spirit would prove all too susceptible to charlatanism and superstition, it makes a parched ground ready and avid for charlatanism and superstition. Just as prohibition has always offered access to the poisonous product, so the obstruction of the theoretical faculty paved the way for political error and madness. And even so far as men have not yet succumbed to political delusion, the mechanisms of censorship—both internal and external—will deprive them of the means of resistance.

The dilemma that faced us in our work proved to be the first phenomenon for investigation: the self-destruction of the Enlightenment. We are wholly convinced—and therein lies our *petitio principii*—that social freedom is inseparable from enlightened thought. Nevertheless, we believe that we have just as clearly recognized that the notion of this very way of thinking, no less than the actual historic forms—the social institutions—with which it is interwoven, already contains the seed of the reversal universally apparent today. If enlightenment does not accommodate reflection on this recidivist element, then it seals its own fate. If consideration of the destructive aspect of progress is left to its enemies, blindly pragmatized thought loses its transcending quality and, its relation to truth. In the enigmatic readiness of the technologically educated masses to fall under the sway of any despotism, in its self-destructive affinity to popular paranoia, and in all uncomprehended absurdity, the weakness of the modern theoretical faculty is apparent.

We believe that these fragments will contribute to the health of that theoretical understanding, insofar as we show that the prime cause of the retreat from enlightenment into mythology is not to be sought so much in the nationalist, pagan and other modern mythologies manufactured precisely in order to contrive such a reversal, but in the Enlightenment itself when paralyzed by fear of the truth. In this respect, both concepts are to be understood not merely as historico-cultural (*geistesgeschichtlich*) but as real. Just as the Enlightenment expresses the actual movement of civil society as a whole in the aspect of its idea as embodied in individuals and institutions, so truth is not merely the rational consciousness but equally the form that consciousness assumes in actual life. The dutiful child of modern civilization is possessed by a fear of departing from the facts which, in the very act of perception, the dominant conventions of science, commerce, and politics—cliché-like—have already molded; his anxiety is none other than the fear of social deviation. The same conventions define the notion of linguistic and conceptual clarity which the art, literature and philosophy of the present have to satisfy. Since that notion declares any negative treatment of the facts or of the dominant forms of thought to be obscurantist formalism or—preferably—alien, and therefore taboo, it condemns the spirit to increasing darkness. It is characteristic of the sickness that even the best-intentioned reformer who uses an impoverished and debased language to recommend renewal, by his adoption of the insidious mode of categorization and the bad philosophy it conceals, strengthens the very power of the established order he is trying to break. False clarity is only another name for myth; and myth has always been obscure and enlightening at one and the same time: always using the devices of familiarity and straightforward dismissal to avoid the labor of conceptualization.

The fallen nature of modern man cannot be separated from social progress. On the one hand the growth of economic productivity furnishes the conditions for a world of greater justice; on the other hand it allows the technical apparatus and the social groups which administer it a disproportionate superiority to the rest of the population. The individual is wholly devalued in relation to the economic powers, which at the same time press the control of society over nature to hitherto unsuspected heights. Even though the individual disappears before the apparatus which he serves, that apparatus provides for him as never before. In an unjust state of life, the impotence and pliability of the masses grow with the quantitative increase in commodities allowed them. The materially respectable and socially deplorable rise in the living standard of the lower classes is reflected in the simulated extension of the spirit. Its true concern is the negation of reification; it cannot survive where it is fixed as a cultural commodity and doled out to satisfy consumer needs. The flood of detailed information and candy-floss entertainment simultaneously instructs and stultifies mankind.

The issue is not that of culture as a value, which is what the critics of civilization, Huxley, Jaspers, Ortega y Gasset and others, have in mind. The point is rather that the Enlightenment *must consider itself*, if men are not to be wholly betrayed. The task to be accomplished is not the conservation of the past, but the redemption of the hopes of the past. Today, however, the past is preserved as the destruction of the past. Whereas a worthwhile education was a privilege until the nineteenth century, and one paid for by the increased suffering of the uneducated, in the twentieth century factory space has been purchased by melting down all cultural values in a gigantic crucible. Perhaps that would not be so high a price as the defenders of culture suppose, if the selling-out of culture did not contribute to the conversion of economic triumphs into their opposite.

Under existing conditions the gifts of fortune themselves become elements of misfortune. Their quantity, in default of a social subject, operated during the internal economic crises of times past as so-called "surplus production"; today, because of the enthronement of power-groups as that social subject, it produces the international threat of Fascism: progress becomes regression. That the hygienic shop-floor and everything that goes with it, the Volkswagen or the sportsdrome, leads to an insensitive liquidation of metaphysics, would be irrelevant; but that in the social whole they themselves become a metaphysics, an ideological curtain behind which the real evil is concentrated, is not irrelevant. This is the starting-point of our deliberations.

The first study, which provides the theoretical basis for the second, is an attempt to focus understanding more clearly upon the nexus of rationality and social actuality, and upon what is inseparable therefrom—that of nature and the mastery of nature. The accompanying critique of enlightenment is intended to prepare the way for a positive notion of enlightenment which will release it from entanglement in blind domination....

The second excursus is concerned with Kant, Sade, and Nietzsche, who mercilessly elicited the implications of the Enlightenment. Here we show how the submission of everything natural to the autocratic subject finally culminates in the mastery of the blindly objective and natural. This tendency evens out all the antinomies of bourgeois thought—even that of moral rigor and absolute amorality.

The essay on the "culture industry" demonstrates the regression of enlightenment to ideology which finds its typical expression in cinema and radio. Here enlightenment consists above all in the calculation of effectiveness and of the techniques of production and distribution; in accordance with its content, ideology expends itself in the idolization of given existence and of the power which controls technology. In the treatment of this contradiction the culture industry is taken more seriously than it would implicitly require. But since its appeal to its own properly commercial nature, its acknowledgement of a qualified truth, has long been a subterfuge that it uses to evade responsibility for lies, our analysis keeps to the products' objectively inherent claim to be aesthetic images which accordingly embody truth, and demonstrates the nullity of social being in the nihilism of that claim. The section on the "culture industry" is even more fragmentary than the others.

The argument and thesis of "Elements of Anti-Semitism" is concerned with the actual reversion of enlightened civilization to barbarism. Not merely the ideal but the practical tendency to self-destruction has always been characteristic of rationalism, and not only in the stage in which it appears undisguised. In this sense we offer the main lines of a philosophical prehistory of anti-Semitism. Its "irrationalism" is deduced from the nature of the dominant *ratio* itself, and the world which corresponds to its image. This chapter is directly related to empirical research carried out at the Institut für Sozialforschung, the foundation established and maintained by Felix Weil, and without which not merely our studies but a good part of the theoretical work of German emigrants that continued despite Hitler would not have been possible.

THE CONCEPT OF ENLIGHTENMENT

In the most general sense of progressive thought, the Enlightenment has always aimed at liberating men from fear and establishing their sovereignty. Yet the fully enlightened earth radiates disaster triumphant. The program of the Enlightenment was the disenchantment of the world; the dissolution of myths and the substitution of knowledge for fancy. Bacon, the "father of experimental philosophy," had defined its motives. He looked down on the masters of tradition, the "great reputed authors" who first "believe that others know that which they know not; and after themselves know that which they know not. But indeed facility to believe, impatience to doubt, temerity to answer, glory to know, doubt to contradict, end to gain, sloth to search, seeking things in words, resting in part of nature; these and the like have been the things which have forbidden the happy match between the mind of man and the nature of things; and in place thereof have married it to vain notions and blind experiments: and what the posterity and issue of so honorable a match may be, it is not hard to consider. Printing, a gross invention; artillery, a thing that lay not far out of the way; the needle, a thing partly known before: what a change have these three things made in the world in these times; the one in state of learning, the other in the state of war, the third in the state of treasure, commodities, and navigation! And those, I say, were but stumbled upon and lighted upon by chance. Therefore, no doubt, the sovereignty of man lieth hid in knowledge; wherein many things are reserved, which kings with their treasure cannot buy, nor with their force command; their spials and intelligencers can give no news of them, their seamen and discoverers cannot sail where they grow: now we govern nature in opinions, but we are thrall unto her in necessity: but if we would be led by her in invention, we should command her by action."

Despite his lack of mathematics, Bacon's view was appropriate to the scientific attitude that prevailed after him. The concordance between the mind of man and the nature of things that he had in mind is patriarchal: the human mind, which overcomes superstition, is to hold sway over a disenchanted nature. Knowledge, which is power, knows no obstacles: neither in the enslavement of men nor in compliance with the world's rulers. As with all the ends of bourgeois economy in the factory and on the battlefield, origin is no bar to the dictates of the entrepreneurs: kings, no less directly than businessmen, control technology; it is as democratic as the economic system with which it is bound up. Technology is the essence of this knowledge. It does not work by concepts and images, by the fortunate insight, but refers to method, the exploitation of others' work, and capital. The "many things" which, according to Bacon, "are reserved," are themselves no more than instrumental: the radio as a sublimated printing press, the dive bomber as a more effective form of artillery, radio control as a more reliable compass. What men want to learn from nature is how to use it in order wholly to dominate it and other men. That is the only aim. Ruthlessly, in despite of itself, the Enlightenment has extinguished any trace of its own self-consciousness. The only kind of thinking that is sufficiently hard to shatter myths is ultimately self-destructive. In face of the present triumph of the factual mentality, even Bacon's nominalist credo would be suspected of a metaphysical bias and come under the same verdict of vanity that he pronounced on scholastic philosophy. Power and knowledge are synonymous. For Bacon as for Luther, "knowledge that tendeth but to satisfaction, is but as a courtesan, which is for pleasure, and not for fruit or generation." Not "satisfaction, which men call truth," but "operation," "to do the business," is the "right mark": for "... what is the true end, scope, or office of knowledge, which I have set down to consist not in any plausible, delectable, reverend or admired discourse, or any satisfactory arguments, but in effecting and working, and in discovery of particulars not revealed before, for the better endowment and help of man's life." There is to be no mystery—which means, too, no wish to reveal mystery.

The disenchantment of the world is the extirpation of animism. Xenophanes derides the multitude of deities because they are but replicas of the men who produced them, together with all that is contingent and evil in mankind; and the most recent school of logic denounces—for the impressions they bear—the words of language, holding them to be false coins better replaced by neutral counters. The world becomes chaos, and synthesis salvation. There is said to be no difference between the totemic animal, the dreams of the ghost-seer, and the absolute Idea. On the road to modern science, men renounce any claim to meaning. They substitute formula for concept, rule and probability for cause and motive. Cause was only the last philosophic concept which served as a yardstick for scientific criticism: so to speak because it alone among the old ideas still seemed to offer itself to scientific criticism, the latest secularization of the creative principle. Substance and quality, activity and suffering, being and existence: to define these concepts in a way appropriate to the times was a concern of philosophy after Bacon—but science managed without such categories. They were abandoned as *idola theatri* of the old metaphysics, and assessed as being even then memorials of the elements and powers of the prehistory for which life and death disclosed their nature in myths and became interwoven in them. The categories by which Western philosophy defined its everlasting natural order marked the spots once occupied by Oncus and Persephone, Ariadne and Nereus. The pre-Socratic cosmologies preserve the moment of transition. The moist, the indivisible, air, and fire, which they hold to be the primal matter of nature, are already rationalizations of the mythic mode of apprehension. Just as the images of generation from water and earth, which came from the Nile to the Greeks, became here hylozoistic principles, or elements, so all the equivocal multitude of mythical demons were intellectualized in the pure form of ontological essences. Finally, by means of the Platonic ideas, even the patriarchal gods of Olympus were absorbed in the philosophical *logos*. The Enlightenment, however, recognized the old powers in the Platonic and Aristotelian aspects of metaphysics, and opposed as superstition the claim that truth is predicable of universals. It asserted that in the authority of universal concepts, there was still discernible fear of the demonic spirits which men sought to portray in magic rituals, hoping thus to influence nature. From now on, matter would at last be mastered without any illusion of ruling or inherent powers, of hidden qualities. For the Enlightenment, whatever does not conform to the rule of computation and utility is suspect. So long as it can develop undisturbed by any outward repression, there is no holding it. In the process, it treats its own ideas of human rights exactly as it does the older universals. Every spiritual resistance it encounters serves merely to increase its strength. Which means that enlightenment still recognizes itself even in myths. Whatever myths the resistance may appeal to, by virtue of the very fact that they become arguments in the process of opposition, they acknowledge the principle of dissolvent rationality for which they reproach the Enlightenment. Enlightenment is totalitarian.

Enlightenment has always taken the basic principle of myth to be anthropomorphism, the projection onto nature of the subjective. In this view, the supernatural, spirits and demons, are mirror images of men who allow themselves to be frightened by natural phenomena. Consequently the many mythic figures can all be brought to a common denominator, and reduced to the human subject. Oedipus' answer to the Sphinx's riddle: "It is man!" is the Enlightenment stereotype repeatedly offered as information, irrespective of whether it is faced with a piece of objective intelligence, a bare schematization, fear of evil powers, or hope of redemption. In advance, the Enlightenment recognizes as being and occurrence only what can be apprehended in unity: its ideal is the system from which all and everything follows. Its rationalist and empiricist versions do not part company on that point. Even though the individual schools may interpret the axioms differently, the structure of scientific unity has always been the same. Bacon's postulate of *una scientia universalis*, whatever the number of fields of research, is as inimical to the unassignable as Leibniz's *mathesis universalis* is to discontinuity. The multiplicity of forms is reduced to position and arrangement, history to fact, things to matter. According to Bacon, too, degrees of universality provide an unequivocal logical connection between first principles and observational judgments. De Maistre mocks him for haboring *"une idole d'échelle."* Formal logic was the major school of unified science. It provided the Enlightenment thinkers with the schema of the calculability of the world. The mythologizing equation of Ideas with numbers in Plato's last writings expresses the longing of all demythologization: number became the canon of the Enlightenment. The same equations dominate bourgeois justice and commodity exchange. Is not the rule, *'Si inaequalibus aequalia addas, omnia erunt inaequalia,'* an axiom of justice as well as of the mathematics? And is there not a true coincidence between commutative and distributive justice, and arithmetical and geometrical proportion? Bourgeois society is ruled by equivalence. It makes the dissimilar comparable by reducing it to abstract quantities. To the Enlightenment, that which does not reduce to numbers, and ultimately to the one, becomes illusion; modern positivism writes it off as literature. Unity is the slogan from Parmenides to Russell. The destruction of gods and qualities alike is insisted upon.

Yet the myths which fell victim to the Enlightenment were its own products. In the scientific calculation of occurrence, the computation is annulled which thought had once transferred from occurrence into myths. Myth intended report, naming, the narration of the Beginning; but also presentation, confirmation, explanation: a tendency that grew stronger with the recording and collection of myths. Narrative became didactic at an early stage. Every ritual includes the idea of activity as a determined process which magic can nevertheless influence. This theoretical element in ritual won independence in the earliest national epics. The myths, as the tragedians came upon them, are already characterized by the discipline and power that Bacon celebrated as the "right mark." In place of the local spirits and demons there appeared heaven and its hierarchy; in place of the invocations of the magician and the tribe the distinct gradation of sacrifice and the labor of the unfree mediated through the word of command. The Olympic deities are no longer directly identical with elements, but signify them. In Homer, Zeus represents the sky and the weather, Apollo controls the sun, and Helios and Eos are already shifting to an allegorical function. The gods are distinguished from material elements as their quintessential concepts. From now on, being divides into the *logos* (which with the progress of philosophy contracts to the monad, to a mere point of reference), and into the mass of all things and creatures without. This single distinction between existence proper and reality engulfs all others. Without regard to distinctions, the world becomes subject to man. In this the Jewish creation narrative and the religion of Olympia are at one: ". . . and let them have dominion over the fish of the sea, and over the fowl of the air, and over the cattle, and over all the earth, and over every creeping thing that creepeth upon the earth." "O Zeus, Father Zeus, yours is the dominion of the heavens, and you oversee the works of man, both wicked and just, and even the wantonness of the beasts; and righteousness is your concern." "For so it is that one atones straightaway, and another later; but should one escape and the threatening decree of the gods not reach him, yet it will certainly be visited at last, if not upon him then upon his children or another generation." Only he who always submits survives in the face of the gods. The awakening of the self is paid for by the acknowledgement of power as the principle of all relations. In view of the unity of this *ratio*, the divorcement between God and man dwindles to the degree of irrelevancy to which unswervable reason has drawn attention since even the earliest critique of Homer. The creative god and the systematic spirit are alike as rulers of nature. Man's likeness to God consists in sovereignty over existence, in the countenance of the lord and master, and in command.

Myth turns into enlightenment, and nature into mere objectivity. Men pay for the increase of their power with alienation from that over which they exercise their power. Enlightenment behaves toward things as a dictator toward men. He knows them in so far as he can manipulate them. The man of science knows things in so far as he can make them. In this way their potentiality is turned to his own ends. In the metamorphosis the nature of things, as a substratum of domination, is revealed as always the same. This identity constitutes the unity of nature. It is a presupposition of the magical invocation as little as the unity of the subject. The shaman's rites were directed to the wind, the rain, the serpent without, or the demon in the sick man, but not to materials or specimens. Magic was not ordered by one, identical spirit: it changed like the cultic masks which were supposed to accord with the various spirits. Magic is utterly untrue, yet in it domination is not yet negated by transforming itself into the pure truth and acting as the very ground of the world that has become subject to it. The magician imitates demons; in order to frighten them or to appease them, he behaves frighteningly or makes gestures of appeasement. Even though his task is impersonation, he never conceives of himself as does the civilized man for whom the unpretentious preserves of the happy hunting-grounds become the unified cosmos, the inclusive concept for all possibilities of plunder. The magician never interprets himself as the image of the invisible power; yet this is the very image in which man attains to the identity of self that cannot disappear through identification with another, but takes possession of itself once and for all as an impenetrable mask. It is the identity of the spirit and its correlate, the unity of nature, to which the multiplicity of qualities falls victim. Disqualified nature becomes the chaotic matter of mere classification, and the all-powerful self becomes mere possession—abstract identity. In magic there is specific representation. What happens to the enemy's spear, hair or name, also happens to the individual; the sacrificial animal is massacred instead of the god. Substitution in the course of sacrifice marks a step toward discursive logic. Even though the hind offered up for the daughter, and the lamb for the first-born, still had to have specific qualities, they already represented the species. They already exhibited the non-specificity of the example. But the holiness of the *hic et nunc*, the uniqueness of the chosen one into which the representative enters, radically marks it off, and makes it unfit for exchange. Science prepares the end of this state of affairs. In science there is no specific representation: and if there are no sacrificial animals there is no god. Representation is exchanged for the fungible—universal interchangeability. An atom is smashed not in representation but as a specimen of matter, and the rabbit does not represent but, as a mere example, is subsumed in the same matter, the scientific object is petrified, and the fixed ritual of former times appears flexible because it attributed the other to the one. The world of magic retained distinctions whose traces have disappeared even in linguistic form. The multitudinous affinities between existents are suppressed by the single relation between the subject who bestows meaning and the meaningless object, between rational significance and the chance vehicle of significance. On the magical plane, dream and image were not mere signs for the thing in question, but were bound up with it by similarity or names. The relation is one not of intention but of relatedness. Like science, magic pursues aims, but seeks to achieve them by mimesis—not by progressively distancing itself from the object. It is not grounded in the "sovereignty of ideas," which the primitive, like the neurotic, is said to ascribe to himself; there can be no "over-evaluation of mental processes as against reality" where there is no radical distinction between thoughts and reality. The "unshakable confidence in the possibility of world domination," which Freud anachronistically ascribes to magic, corresponds to realistic world domination only in terms of a more skilled science. The replacement of the milieu-bound practices of the medicine man by all-inclusive industrial technology required first of all the autonomy of ideas in regard to objects that was achieved in the reality-adjusted ego.

As a linguistically expressed totality, whose claim to truth suppresses the older mythic belief, the national religion or patriarchal solar myth is itself an Enlightenment with which the philosophic form can compare itself on the same level. And now it has its requital. Mythology itself set off the unending process of enlightenment in which ever and again, with the inevitability of necessity, every specific theoretic view succumbs to the destructive criticism that it is only a belief—until even the very notions of spirit, of truth and, indeed, enlightenment itself, have become animistic magic. The principle of fatal necessity, which brings low the heroes of myth and derives as a logical consequence from the pronouncement of the oracle, does not merely, when refined to the stringency of formal logic, rule in every rationalistic system of Western philosophy, but itself dominates the series of systems which begins with the hierarchy of the gods and, in a permanent twilight of the idols, hands down an identical content: anger against insufficient righteousness. Just as the myths already realize enlightenment, so enlightenment with every step becomes more deeply engulfed in mythology. It receives all its matter from the myths, in order to destroy them; and even as a judge it comes under the mythic curse. It wishes to extricate itself from the process of fate and retribution, while exercising retribution on that process. In the myths everything that happens must atone for having happened. And so it is in enlightenment: the fact becomes null and void, and might as well not have happened. The doctrine of the equivalence of action and reaction asserted the power of repetition over reality, long after men had renounced the illusion that by repetition they could identify themselves with the repeated reality and thus escape its power. But as the magical illusion fades away, the more relentlessly in the name of law repetition imprisons man in the cycle—that cycle whose objectification in the form of natural law he imagines will ensure his action as a free subject. The principle of immanence, the explanation of every event as repetition, that the Enlightenment upholds against mythic imagination, is the principle of myth itself. That arid wisdom, that holds there is nothing new under the sun, because all the pieces in the meaningless game have been played, and all the great thoughts have already been thought, and because all possible discoveries can be construed in advance and all men are decided on adaptation as the means to self-preservation—that dry sagacity merely reproduces the fantastic wisdom that it supposedly rejects: the sanction of fate that in retribution relentlessly remakes what has already been. What was different is equalized. That is the verdict which critically determines the limits of possible experience. The identity of everything with everything else is paid for in that nothing may at the same time be identical with itself. Enlightenment dissolves the injustice of the old inequality—unmediated lordship and mastery—but at the same time perpetuates it in universal mediation, in the relation of any one existent to any other. It does what Kierkegaard praises his Protestant ethic for, and what in the Heraclean epic cycle is one of the primal images of mythic power; it excises the incommensurable. Not only are qualities dissolved in thought, but men are brought to actual conformity.

The blessing that the market does not enquire after one's birth is paid for by the barterer, in that he models the potentialities that are his by birth on the production of the commodities that can be bought in the market. Men were given their individuality as unique in each case, different to all others, so that it might all the more surely be made the same as any other. But because the unique self never wholly disappeared, even after the liberalistic epoch, the Enlightenment has always sympathized with the social impulse. The unity of the manipulated collective consists in the negation of each individual: for individuality makes a mockery of the kind of society which would turn all individuals to the one collectivity. The horde which so assuredly appears in the organization of the Hitler Youth is not a return to barbarism but the triumph of repressive equality, the disclosure through peers of the parity of the right to injustice. The phony Fascist mythology is shown to be the genuine myth of antiquity, insofar as the genuine one saw retribution, whereas the false one blindly doles it out to the sacrifices. Every attempt to break the natural thralldom, because nature is broken, enters all the more deeply into that natural enslavement. Hence the course of European civilization. Abstraction, the tool of enlightenment, treats its objects as did fate, the notion of which it rejects: it liquidates them. Under the leveling domination of abstraction (which makes everything in nature repeatable), and of industry (for which abstraction ordains repetition), the freedom themselves finally came to form that "herd" which Hegel has declared to be the result of the Enlightenment.

The distance between subject and object, a presupposition of abstraction, is grounded in the distance from the thing itself which the master achieved through the mastered. The lyrics of Homer and the hymns of the Rig-Veda date from the time of territorial dominion and the secure locations in which a dominant warlike race established themselves over the mass of vanquished natives. The first god among the gods arose with this civil society in which the king, as chieftain of the armsbearing nobility, holds down the conquered to the earth, whereas physicians, soothsayers, craftsmen and merchants see to social intercourse. With the end of a nomadic existence, the social order is created on a basis of fixed property. Mastery and labor are divided. A proprietor like Odysseus "manages from a distance a numerous, carefully graded staff of cowherds, shepherds, swineherds and servants. In the evening, when he has seen from his castle that the countryside is illumined by a thousand fires, he can compose himself for sleep with a quiet mind: he knows that his upright servants are keeping watch lest wild animals approach, and to chase thieves from the preserves which they are there to protect. The universality of ideas as developed by discursive logic, domination in the conceptual sphere, is raised up on the basis of actual domination. The dissolution of the magical heritage, of the old diffuse ideas, by conceptual unity, expresses the hierarchical constitution of life determined by those who are free. The individuality that learned order and subordination in the subjection of the world, soon wholly equated truth with the regulative thought without whose fixed distinctions universal truth cannot exist. Together with mimetic magic, it tabooed the knowledge which really concerned the object. Its hatred was extended to the image of the vanquished former age and its imaginary happiness. The chthonic gods of the original inhabitants are banished to the hell to which, according to the sun and light religion of Indra and Zeus, the earth is transformed.

Heaven and hell, however, hang together. Just as the name of Zeus, in non-exclusive cults, was given to a god of the underworld as well as to a god of light; just as the Olympian gods had every kind of commerce with the chthonic deities: so the good and evil powers, salvation and disaster, were not unequivocally distinct. They were linked together like coming up and passing away, life and death, summer and winter. The gloomy and indistinct religious principle that was honored as *mana* in the earliest known stages of humanity, lives on in the radiant world of Greek religion. Everything unknown and alien is primary and undifferentiated: that which transcends the confines of experience; whatever in things is more than their previously known reality. What the primitive experiences in this regard is not a spiritual as opposed to a material substance, but the intricacy of the Natural in contrast to the individual. The gasp of surprise which accompanies the experience of the unusual becomes its name. It fixes the transcendence of the unknown in relation to the known, and therefore terror as sacredness. The dualization of nature as appearance and sequence, effort and power, which first makes possible both myth and science, originates in human fear, the expression of which becomes explanation. It is not the soul which is transposed to nature, as psychologism would have it; *mana*, the moving spirit, is no projection, but the echo of the real supremacy of nature in the weak souls of primitive men. The separation of the animate and the inanimate, the occupation of certain places by demons and deities, first arises from this pre-animism, which contains the first lines of the separation of subject and object. When the tree is no longer approached merely as tree, but as evidence for an Other, as the location of *mana*, language expresses the contradiction that something is itself and at one and the same time something other than itself, identical and not identical. Through the deity, language is transformed from tautology to language. The concept, which some would see as the sign-unit for whatever is comprised under it, has from the beginning been instead the product of dialectical thinking in which everything is always that which it is, only because it becomes that which it is not. That was the original form of objectifying definition, in which concept and thing are separated. The same form which is already far advanced in the Homeric epic and confounds itself in modern positivist science. But this dialectic remains impotent to the extent that it develops from the cry of terror which is the duplication, the tautology, of terror itself. The gods cannot take fear away from man, for they bear its petrified sound with them as they bear their names. Man imagines himself free from fear when there is no longer anything unknown. That determines the course of demythologization, of enlightenment, which compounds the animate with the inanimate just as myth compounds the inanimate with the animate. Enlightenment is mythic fear turned radical. The pure immanence of positivism, its ultimate product, is no more than a so to speak universal taboo. Nothing at all may remain outside, because the mere idea of outsideness is the very source of fear. The revenge of the primitive for death, when visited upon one of his kin, was sometimes appeased by reception of the murderer into his own family; this, too, signified the infusion of alien blood into one's own, the generation of immanence. The mythic dualism does not extend beyond the environs of existence. The world permeated by *mana* and even the world of Indian and Greek myth know no exits, and are eternally the same. Every birth is paid for with death, every fortune with misfortune. Men and gods may try in their short space to assess fate in other terms than the blind course of destiny, but in the end existence triumphs over them. Even their justice, which is wrested from fatality, bears the marks of fatality: it corresponds to the look which men—primitives, Greeks and barbarians alike—cast from a society of pressure and misery on the circumambient world. Hence, for mythic and enlightened justice, guilt and atonement, happiness and unhappiness were sides of an equation. Justice is subsumed in law. The shaman wards off danger by means of its image. Equivalence is his instrument; and equivalence regulates punishment and reward in civilization. The mythic representations can also be traced back in their entirety to natural conditions. Just as the Gemini—the constellation of

Castor and Pollux—and all other symbols of duality refer to the inevitable cycle of nature, which itself has its ancient sign in the symbol of the egg from which they came, the balance held by Zeus, which symbolizes the justice of the entire patriarchal world, refers back to mere nature. The step from chaos to civilization, in which natural conditions exert their power no longer directly but through the medium of the human consciousness, has not changed the principle of equivalence. Indeed, men paid for this very step by worshipping what they were once in thrall to only in the same way as all other creatures. Before, the fetishes were subject to the law of equivalence. Now equivalence itself has become a fetish. The blindfold over Justitia's eyes does not only mean that there should be no assault upon justice, but that justice does not originate in freedom.

Thomas Kuhn

In the years following the publication of *The Structure of Scientific Revolutions*, by Princeton professor of History Thomas Kuhn, his work has been read and taken very seriously by scholars in almost every discipline from physics to political science. Before Kuhn, the popular perception of scientific practice was rooted in Enlightenment rationalism. Scientists were viewed as neutral observers of concrete phenomena. Knowledge was the cumulative result of individual efforts to know the truth, and it was a central tenet of modern faith that individuals would increasingly be able to know and control the world around them. Kuhn shattered this understanding of science by demonstrating that far from being an individualistic enterprise, science took place among a community of practitioners whose research goals and conclusions were validated through consensus.

Kuhn argued that scientific research takes place within a paradigm, a set of shared understandings that dictates what research is important and which problems need to be solved. An example of a paradigm is Newtonian physics which is based on the following assumptions: (1) time and space are objective realities that exist independently of the observer; (2) the universe is a machine that obeys the laws of cause and effect; (3) the atom is the basic unit of matter; (4) heated bodies emit radiation in continuous waves, and; (5) investigation will eventually lead to complete knowledge of the universe. In the course of practicing normal science, researchers run up against anomalies—empirical data which will not fit into a paradigm. For example, the discovery of the electron in 1897 undermined the notion of the atom as the basic unit of matter and further research into the sub-atomic world revealed that laws of cause and effect did not always apply. When enough anomalies have accrued, a paradigm shift occurs which is able to include in its explanation the data which was anomalous in an earlier paradigm. Einstein's theory of relativity is often viewed as an example of this type of shift because Einstein was able to explain phenomena not covered by Newtonian physics by abandoning the assumption that time and space are separate and objective entities. Further, Kuhn argues that the terms of analysis, the methodology of the scientist and the types of questions scientists ask are incommensurable across paradigms. A new paradigm represents an entirely new way of looking at the world.

Underneath this fairly straightforward description of how science works are several assumptions that give those of us involved in scholarly inquiry cause for concern. If paradigms are the product of consensus within a group, it is difficult to establish any outside criteria that determine why one paradigm is better or more true than any other, that Einstein is any more right than Newton. Furthermore the notion that scientific paradigms can shift in such a revolutionary fashion serves to undermine the belief in the orderly and progressive nature of scientific practice. One historian of science has suggested that Kuhn's conclusions lead to the view that science is practiced by "mob rule."

One of the broadest conclusions which can be drawn from Kuhn's study is the notion that truth is relative to time and place. This is an historicist conception of knowledge which chips at the foundations of modern thought even as it preserves the modern affinity for constant change.

THOMAS KUHN
(1962)

The Structure

of Scientific

Revolutions

History, if viewed as a repository for more than anecdote or chronology, could produce a decisive transformation in the image of science by which we are now possessed. That image has previously been drawn, even by scientists themselves, mainly from the study of finished scientific achievements as these are recorded in the classics and, more recently, in the textbooks from which each new scientific generation learns to practice its trade. Inevitably, however, the aim of such books is persuasive and pedagogic; a concept of science drawn from them is no more likely to fit the enterprise that produced them than an image of a national culture drawn from a tourist brochure or a language text. This essay attempts to show that we have been misled by them in fundamental ways. Its aim is a sketch of the quite different concept of science that can emerge from the historical record of the research activity itself.

Even from history, however, that new concept will not be forthcoming if historical data continue to be sought and scrutinized mainly to answer questions posed by the unhistorical stereotype drawn from science texts. Those texts have, for example, often seemed to imply that the content of science is uniquely exemplified by the observations, laws, and theories described in their pages. Almost as regularly, the same books have been read as saying that scientific methods are simply the ones illustrated by the manipulative techniques used in gathering textbook data, together with the logical operations employed when relating those data to the textbook's theoretical generalizations. The result has been a concept of science with profound implications about its nature and development.

If science is the constellation of facts, theories, and methods collected in current texts, then scientists are the men who, successfully or not, have striven to contribute one or another element to that particular constellation. Scientific development becomes the piecemeal process by which these items have been added, singly and in combination, to the ever growing stockpile that constitutes scientific technique and knowledge. And history of science becomes the discipline that chronicles both these successive increments and the obstacles that have inhibited their accumulation. Concerned with scientific development, the historian then appears to have two main tasks. On the one hand, he must determine by what man and at what point in time each contemporary scientific fact, law, and theory was discovered or invented. On the other, he must describe and explain the congeries of error, myth, and superstition that have inhibited the more rapid accumulation of the constituents of the modern science text. Much research has been directed to these ends, and some still is.

In recent years, however, a few historians of science have been finding it more and more difficult to fulfill the functions that the concept of development-by-accumulation assigns to them. As chroniclers of an incremental process, they discover that additional research makes it harder, not easier, to answer questions like: When was oxygen discovered? Who first conceived of energy conservation? Increasingly, a few of them suspect that these are simply the wrong sorts of questions to ask. Perhaps science does not develop by the accumulation of individual discoveries and inventions. Simultaneously, these same historians confront growing difficulties in distinguishing the "scientific" component of past observation and belief from what their predecessors had readily labeled "error" and "superstition." The more carefully they study, say, Aristotelian dynamics, phlogistic chemistry, or caloric thermodynamics, the more certain they feel that those once current views of nature were, as a whole, neither less scientific nor more the product of human idiosyncrasy than those current today. If these out-of-date beliefs are to be called myths, then myths can be produced by the same sorts of methods and held for the same sorts of reasons that now lead to scientific knowledge. If, on the other hand, they are to be called science, then science has included bodies of belief quite incompatible with the ones we hold today. Given these alternatives, the historian must choose the latter. Out-of-date theories are not in principle unscientific because they have been discarded. That choice, however, makes it difficult to see scientific development as a process of accretion. The same historical research that displays the difficulties in isolating individual inventions and discoveries gives ground for profound doubts about the cumulative process through which these individual contributions to science were thought to have been compounded.

The result of all these doubts and difficulties is a historiographic revolution in the study of science, though one that is still in its early stages. Gradually, and often without entirely realizing they are doing so, historians of science have begun to ask new sorts of questions and to trace different, and often less than cumulative, developmental lines for the sciences. Rather than seeking the permanent contributions of an older science to our present vantage, they attempt to display the historical integrity of that science in its own time. They ask, for example, not about the relation of Galileo's views to those of modern science, but rather about the relationship between his views and those of his group i.e., his teachers, contemporaries, and immediate successors in the sciences. Furthermore, they insist upon studying the opinions of that group and other similar ones from the viewpoint—usually very different from that of modern science—that gives those opinions the maximum internal coherence and the closest possible fit to nature. Seen through the works that result, works perhaps best exemplified in the writings of Alexandre Koyré, science does not seem altogether the same enterprise as the one discussed by writers in the older historio-graphic tradition. By implication, at least, these historical studies suggest the possibility of a new image of science. This essay aims to delineate that image by making explicit some of the new historiography's implications. . . .

In this essay, 'normal science' means research firmly based upon one or more past scientific achievements, achievements that some particular scientific community acknowledges for a time as supplying the foundation for its further practice. Today such achievements are recounted, though seldom in their original form, by science textbooks, elementary and advanced. These textbooks expound the body of accepted theory, illustrate many or all of its successful applications, and compare these applications with exemplary observations and experiments. Before such books became popular early in the nineteenth century (and until even more recently in the newly matured sciences), many of the famous classics of science fulfilled a similar function. Aristotle's *Physica*, Ptolemy's *Almagest*, Newton's *Principia* and *Opticks*, Franklin's *Electricity*, Lavoisier's *Chemistry*, and Lyell's *Geology*—these and many other works served for a time implicitly to define the legitimate problems and methods of a research field for succeeding generations of practitioners. They were able to do so because they shared two essential characteristics. Their achievement was sufficiently unprecedented to attract an enduring group of adherents away from competing modes of scientific activity. Simultaneously, it was sufficiently open-ended to leave all sorts of problems for the redefined group of practitioners to resolve.

Achievements that share these two characteristics I shall henceforth refer to as 'paradigms,' a term that relates closely to 'normal science.' By choosing it, I mean to suggest that some accepted examples of actual scientific practice—examples which include law, theory, application, and instrumentation together—provide models from which spring particular coherent traditions of scientific research. These are the traditions which the historian describes under such rubrics as 'Ptolemaic astronomy' (or 'Copernican'), 'Aristotelian dynamics' (or 'Newtonian'), 'corpuscular optics' (or 'wave optics'), and so on. The study of paradigms, including many that are far more specialized than those named illustratively above, is what mainly prepares the student for membership in the particular scientific community with which he will later practice. Because he there joins men who learned the bases of their field from the same concrete models, his subsequent practice will seldom evoke overt disagreement over fundamentals. Men whose research is based on shared paradigms are committed to the same rules and standards for scientific practice. That commitment and the apparent consensus it produces are prerequisites for normal science, i.e., for the genesis and continuation of a particular research tradition. . . .

What then is the nature of the more professional and esoteric research that a group's reception of a single paradigm permits? If the paradigm represents work that has been done once and for all, what further problems does it leave the united group to resolve? Those questions will seem even more urgent if we now note one respect in which the terms used so far may be misleading. In its established usage, a paradigm is an accepted model or pattern, and that aspect of its meaning has enabled me, lacking a better word, to appropriate 'paradigm' here. But it will shortly be clear that the sense of 'model' and 'pattern' that permits the appropriation is not quite the one usual in defining 'paradigm.' In grammar, for example, *'amo, amas, amat'* is a paradigm because it displays the pattern to be used in conjugating a large number of other Latin verbs, e.g., in producing 'laudo, laudas, laudat.' In this standard application, the paradigm functions by permitting the replication of examples any one of which could in principle serve to replace it. In a science, on the other hand, a paradigm is rarely an object for replication. Instead, like an accepted judicial decision in the common law, it is an object for further articulation and specification under new or more stringent conditions.

To see how this can be so, we must recognize how very limited in both scope and precision a paradigm can be at the time of its first appearance. Paradigms gain their status because they are more successful than their competitors in solving a few problems that the group of practitioners has come to recognize as acute. To be more successful is not, however, to be either completely successful with a single problem or notably successful with any large number. The success of a paradigm—whether Aristotle's analysis of motion, Ptolemy's computations of planetary position, Lavoisier's application of the balance, or Maxwell's mathematization of the electromagnetic field—is at the start largely a promise of success discoverable in selected and still incomplete examples. Normal science consists in the actualization of that promise, an actualization achieved by extending the knowledge of those facts that the paradigm displays as particularly revealing, by increasing the extent of the match between those facts and the paradigm's predictions, and by further articulation of the paradigm itself.

Few people who are not actually practitioners of a mature science realize how much mop-up work of this sort a paradigm leaves to be done or quite how fascinating such work can prove in the execution. And these points need to be understood. Mopping-up operations are what engage most scientists throughout their careers. They constitute what I am here calling normal science. Closely examined, whether historically or in the contemporary laboratory, that enterprise seems an attempt to force nature into the preformed and relatively inflexible box that the paradigm supplies. No part of the aim of normal science is to call forth new sorts of phenomena; indeed those that will not fit the box are often not seen at all. Nor do scientists normally aim to invent new theories, and they are often intolerant of those invented by others. Instead, normal-scientific research is directed to the articulation of those phenomena and theories that the paradigm already supplies.

Perhaps these are defects. The areas investigated by normal science are, of course, minuscule; the enterprise now under discussion has drastically restricted vision. But those restrictions, born from confidence in a paradigm, turn out to be essential to the development of science. By focusing attention upon a small range of relatively esoteric problems, the paradigm forces scientists to investigate some part of nature in a detail and depth that would otherwise be unimaginable. And normal science possesses a built-in mechanism that ensures the relaxation of the restrictions that bound research whenever the paradigm from which they derive ceases to function effectively. At that point scientists begin to behave differently, and the nature of their research problems changes. In the interim, however, during the period when the paradigm is successful, the profession will have solved problems that its members could scarcely have imagined and would never have undertaken without commitment to the paradigm. And at least part of that achievement always proves to be permanent....

Perhaps the most striking feature of the normal research problems we have just encountered is how little they aim to produce major novelties, conceptual or phenomenal....

But if the aim of normal science is not major substantive novelties—if failure to come near the anticipated result is usually failure as a scientist—then why are these problems undertaken at all? Part of the answer has already been developed. To scientists, at least, the results gained in normal research are significant because they add to the scope and precision with which the paradigm can be applied. That answer, however, cannot account for the enthusiasm and devotion that scientists display for the problems of normal research. No one devotes years to, say, the development of a better spectrometer or the production of an improved solution to the problem of vibrating strings simply because of the importance of the information that will be obtained. The data to be gained by computing ephemerides or by further measurements with an existing instrument are often just as significant, but those activities are regularly spurned by scientists because they are so largely repetitions of procedures that have been carried through before. That rejection provides a clue to the fascination of the normal research problem. Though its outcome can be anticipated, often in detail so great that what remains to be known is itself uninteresting, the way to achieve that outcome remains very much in doubt. Bringing a normal research problem to a conclusion is achieving the anticipated in a new way, and it requires the solution of all sorts of complex instrumental, conceptual, and mathematical puzzles. The man who succeeds proves himself an expert puzzle-solver, and the challenge of the puzzle is an important part of what usually drives him on.

The terms 'puzzle' and 'puzzle-solver' highlight several of the themes that have become increasingly prominent in the preceding pages. Puzzles are, in the entirely standard meaning here employed, that special category of problems that can serve to test ingenuity or skill in solution. Dictionary illustrations are 'jigsaw puzzle' and 'crossword puzzle,' and it is the characteristics that these share with the problems of normal science that we now need to isolate. One of them has just been mentioned. It is no criterion of goodness in a puzzle that its outcome be intrinsically interesting or important. On the contrary, the really pressing problems, e.g., a cure for cancer or the design of a lasting peace, are often not puzzles at all, largely because they may not have any solution. Consider the jigsaw puzzle whose pieces are selected at random from each of two different puzzle boxes. Since that problem is likely to defy (though it might not) even the most ingenious of men, it cannot serve as a test of skill in solution. In any usual sense it is not a puzzle at all. Though intrinsic value is no criterion for a puzzle, the assured existence of a solution is.

We have already seen, however, that one of the things a scientific community acquires with a paradigm is a criterion for choosing problems that, while the paradigm is taken for granted, can be assumed to have solutions. To a great extent these are the only problems that the community will admit as scientific or encourage its members to undertake. Other problems, including many that had previously been standard, are rejected as metaphysical, as the concern of another discipline, or sometimes as just too problematic to be worth the time. A paradigm can, for that matter, even insulate the community from those socially important problems that are not reducible to the puzzle form, because they cannot be stated in terms of the conceptual and instrumental tools the paradigm supplies. Such problems can be a distraction, a lesson brilliantly illustrated by several facets of seventeenth-century Baconianism and by some of the contemporary social sciences. One of the reasons why normal science seems to progress so rapidly is that its practitioners concentrate on problems that only their own lack of ingenuity should keep them from solving.

If, however, the problems of normal science are puzzles in this sense, we need no longer ask why scientists attack them with such passion and devotion. A man may be attracted to science for all sorts of reasons. Among them are the desire to be useful, the excitement of exploring new territory, the hope of finding order, and the drive to test established knowledge. These motives and others besides also help to determine the particular problems that will later engage him. Furthermore, though the result is occasional frustration, there is good reason why motives like these should first attract him and then lead him on. The scientific enterprise as a whole does from time to time prove useful, open up new territory, display order, and test long-accepted belief. Nevertheless, *the individual* engaged on a normal research problem *is almost never doing any one of these things*. Once engaged, his motivation is of a rather different sort. What then challenges him is the conviction that, if only he is skilful enough, he will succeed in solving a puzzle that no one before has solved or solved so well. Many of the greatest scientific minds have devoted all of their professional attention to demanding puzzles of this sort. On most occasions any particular field of specialization offers nothing else to do, a fact that makes it no less fascinating to the proper sort of addict.

Turn now to another, more difficult, and more revealing aspect of the parallelism between puzzles and the problems of normal science. It it is to classify as a puzzle, a problem must be characterized by more than an assured solution. There must also be rules that limit both the nature of acceptable solutions and the steps by which they are to be obtained. To solve a jigsaw puzzle is not, for example, merely "to make a picture." Either a child or a contemporary artist could do that by scattering selected pieces, as abstract shapes, upon some neutral ground. The picture thus produced might be far better, and would certainly be more original, than the one from which the puzzle had been made. Nevertheless, such a picture would not be a solution. To achieve that all the pieces must be used, their plain sides must be turned down, and they must be interlocked without forcing until no holes remain. Those are among the rules that govern jigsaw-puzzle solutions. Similar restrictions upon the admissible solutions of crossword puzzles, riddles, chess problems, and so on, are readily discovered.

If we can accept a considerably broadened use of the term 'rule'—one that will occasionally equate it with 'established viewpoint' or with 'preconception'—then the problems accessible within a given research tradition display something much like this set of puzzle characteristics. The man who builds an instrument to determine optical wave lengths must not be satisfied with a piece of equipment that merely attributes particular numbers to particular spectral lines. He is not just an explorer or measurer. On the contrary, he must show, by analyzing his apparatus in terms of the established body of optical theory, that the numbers his instrument produces are the ones that enter theory as wave lengths. If some residual vagueness in the theory or some unanalyzed component of his apparatus prevents his completing that demonstration, his colleagues may well conclude that he has measured nothing at all. For example, the electron-scattering maxima that were later diagnosed as indices of electron wave length had no apparent significance when first observed and recorded. Before they became measures of anything, they had to be related to a theory that predicted the wave-like behavior of matter in motion. And even after that relation was pointed out, the apparatus had to be redesigned so that the experimental results might be correlated unequivocally with theory. Until those conditions had been satisfied, no problem had been solved.

Similar sorts of restrictions bound the admissible solutions to theoretical problems. Throughout the eighteenth century those scientists who tried to derive the observed motion of the moon from Newton's laws of motion and gravitation consistently failed to do so. As a result, some of them suggested replacing the inverse square law with a law that deviated from it as small distances. To do that, however, would have been to change the paradigm, to define a new puzzle, and not to solve the old one. In the event, scientists preserved the rules until, in 1750, one of them discovered how they could successfully be applied. Only a change in the rules of the game could have provided an alternative.

The study of normal-scientific traditions discloses many additional rules, and these provide much information about the commitments that scientists derive from their paradigms. What can we say are the main categories into which these rules fall? The most obvious and probably the most binding is exemplified by the sorts of generalizations we have just noted. These are explicit statements of scientific law and about scientific concepts and theories. While they continue to be honored, such statements help to set puzzles and to limit acceptable solutions. Newton's Laws, for example, performed those functions during the eighteenth and nineteenth centuries. As long as they did so, quantity-of-matter was a fundamental ontological category for physical scientists, and the forces that act between bits of matter were a dominant topic for research. In chemistry the laws of fixed and definite proportions had, for a long time, an exactly similar force—setting the problem of atomic weights, bounding the admissible results of chemical analyses, and informing chemists what atoms and molecules, compounds and mixtures were. Maxwell's equations and the laws of statistical thermodynamics have the same hold and function today.

Less local and temporary, though still not unchanging characteristics of science, are the higher level, quasi-metaphysical commitments that historical study so regularly displays. After about 1630, for example, and particularly after the appearance of Descartes's immensely influential scientific writings, most physical scientists assumed that the universe was composed of microscopic corpuscles and that all natural phenomena could be explained in terms of corpuscular shape, size, motion, and interaction. That nest of commitments proved to be both metaphysical and methodological. As metaphysical, it told scientists what sorts of entities the universe did and did not contain: there was only shaped matter in motion. As methodological, it told them what ultimate laws and fundamental explanations must be like: laws must specify corpuscular motion and interaction, and explanation must reduce any given natural phenomenon to corpuscular action under these laws. More important still, the corpuscular conception of the universe told scientists what many of their research problems should be. For example, a chemist who, like Boyle, embraced the new philosophy gave particular attention to reactions that could be viewed as transmutations. More clearly than any others these displayed the process of corpuscular rearrangement that must underlie all chemical change. Similar effects of corpuscularism can be observed in the study of mechanics, optics, and heat.

Finally, at a still higher level, there is another set of commitments without which no man is a scientist. The scientist must, for example, be concerned to understand the world and to extend the precision and scope with which it has been ordered. That commitment must, in turn, lead him to scrutinize, either for himself or through colleagues, some aspect of nature in great empirical detail. And, if that scrutiny displays pockets of apparent disorder, then these must challenge him to a new refinement of his observational techniques or to a further articulation of his theories. Undoubtedly there are still other rules like these, ones which have held for scientists at all times.

The existence of this strong network of commitments—conceptual, theoretical, instrumental, and methodological—is a principal source of the metaphor that relates normal science to puzzle-solving. Because it provides rules that tell the practitioner of a mature specialty what both the world and his science are like, he can concentrate with assurance upon the esoteric problems that these rules and existing knowledge define for him. What then personally challenges him is how to bring the residual puzzle to a solution. In these and other respects a discussion of puzzles and of rules illuminates the nature of normal scientific practice. Yet, in another way, that illumination may be significantly misleading. Though there obviously are rules to which all the practitioners of a scientific specialty adhere at a given time, those rules may not by themselves specify all that the practice of those specialists has in common. Normal science is a highly determined activity, but it need not be entirely determined by rules. That is why, at the start of this essay, I introduced shared paradigms rather than shared rules, assumptions, and points of view as the source of coherence for normal research traditions. Rules, I suggest, derive from paradigms, but paradigms can guide research even in the absence of rules. . . .

To discover the relation between rules, paradigms, and normal science, consider first how the historian isolates the particular loci of commitment that have just been described as accepted rules. Close historical investigation of a given specialty at a given time discloses a set of recurrent and quasi-standard illustrations of various theories in their conceptual, observational, and instrumental applications. These are the community's paradigms, revealed in its textbooks, lectures, and laboratory exercises. By studying them and by practicing with them, the members of the corresponding community learn their trade. The historian, of course, will discover in addition a penumbral area occupied by achievements whose status is still in doubt, but the core of solved problems and techniques will usually be clear. Despite occasional ambiguities, the paradigms of a mature scientific community can be determined with relative ease.

The determination of shared paradigms is not, however, the determination of shared rules. That demands a second step and one of a somewhat different kind. When undertaking it, the historian must compare the community's paradigms with each other and with its current research reports. In doing so, his object is to discover what isolable elements, explicit or implicit, the members of that community may have *abstracted* from their more global paradigms and deployed as rules in their research. Anyone who has attempted to describe or analyze the evolution of a particular scientific tradition will necessarily have sought accepted principles and rules of this sort. Almost certainly, as the preceding section indicates, he will have met with at least partial success. But, if his experience has been at all like my own, he will have found the search for rules both more difficult and less satisfying than the search for paradigms. Some of the generalizations he employs to describe the community's shared beliefs will present no problems. Others, however, including some of those used as illustrations above, will seem a shade too strong. Phrased in just that way, or in any other way he can imagine, they would almost certainly have been rejected by some members of the group he studies. Nevertheless, if the coherence of the research tradition is to be understood in terms of rules, some specification of common ground in the corresponding area is needed. As a result, the search for a body of rules competent to constitute a given normal research tradition becomes a source of continual and deep frustration.

Recognizing that frustration, however, makes it possible to diagnose its source. Scientists can agree that a Newton, Lavoisier, Maxwell, or Einstein has produced an apparently permanent solution to a group of outstanding problems and still disagree, sometimes without being aware of it, about the particular abstract characteristics that make those solutions permanent. They can, that is, agree in their *identification* of a paradigm without agreeing on, or even attempting to produce, a full *interpretation* or *rationalization* of it. Lack of a standard interpretation or of an agreed reduction to rules will not prevent a paradigm from guiding research. Normal science can be determined in part by the direct inspection of paradigms, a process that is often aided by but does not depend upon the formulation of rules and assumptions. Indeed, the existence of a paradigm need not even imply that any full set of rules exists.

Inevitably, the first effect of those statements is to raise problems. In the absence of a competent body of rules, what restricts the scientist to a particular normal-scientific tradition? What can the phrase 'direct inspection of paradigms' mean? Partial answers to questions like these were developed by the the late Ludwig Wittgenstein, though in a very different context. Because that context is both more elementary and more familiar, it will help to consider his form of the argument first. What need we know, Wittgenstein asked, in order that we apply terms like 'chair,' or 'leaf,' or 'game' unequivocally and without provoking argument.

That question is very old and has generally been answered by saying that we must know, consciously or intuitively, what a chair, or leaf, or game *is*. We must, that is, grasp some set of attributes that all games and that only games have in common. Wittgenstein, however, concluded that, given the way we use language and the sort of world to which we apply it, there need be no such set of characteristics. Though a discussion of *some* of the attributes shared by a *number* of games or chairs or leaves often helps us learn how to employ the corresponding term, there is no set of characteristics that is simultaneously applicable to all members of the class and to them alone. Instead, confronted with a previously unobserved activity, we apply the term 'game' because what we are seeing bears a close "family resemblance" to a number of the activities that we have previously learned to call by that name. For Wittgenstein, in short, games, and chairs, and leaves are natural families, each constituted by a network of overlapping and crisscross resemblances. The existence of such a network sufficiently accounts for our success in identifying the corresponding object or activity. Only if the families we named over-lapped and merged gradually into one another—only that is, if there were no *natural* families—would our success in identifying and naming provide evidence for a set of common characteristics corresponding to each of the class names we employ.

Something of the same sort may very well hold for the various research problems and tech-niques that arise within a single normal-scientific tradition. What these have in common is not that they satisfy some explicit or even some fully discoverable set of rules and assumptions that gives the tradition its character and its hold upon the scientific mind. Instead, they may relate by resemblance and by modeling to one or another part of the scientific corpus which the commu-nity in question already recognizes as among its established achievements. Scientists work from models acquired through education and through subsequent exposure to the literature often without quite knowing or needing to know what characteristics have given these models the status of community paradigms. And because they do so, they need no full set of rules. The coherence displayed by the research tradition in which they participate may not imply even the existence of an underlying body of rules and assumptions that additional historical or philo-sophical investigation might uncover. That scientists do not usually ask or debate what makes a particular problem or solution legitimate tempts us to suppose that, at least intuitively, they know the answer. But it may only indicate that neither the question nor the answer is felt to be relevant to their research. Paradigms may be prior to, more binding, and more complete than any set of rules for research that could be unequivocally abstracted from them. . . .

Normal science, the puzzle-solving activity we have just examined, is a highly cumulative enterprise, eminently successful in its aim, the steady extension of the scope and precision of scientific knowledge. In all these respects it fits with great precision the most usual image of scientific work. Yet one standard product of the scientific enterprise is missing. Normal science does not aim at novelties of fact or theory and, when successful, finds none. New and unsuspected phenomena are, however, repeatedly uncovered by scientific research, and radical new theories have again and again been invented by scientists. History even suggests that the scientific enterprise has developed a uniquely powerful technique for producing surprises of this sort. If this characteristic of science is to be reconciled with what has already been said, then research under a paradigm must be a particularly effective way of inducing paradigm change. That is what fundamental novelties of fact and theory do. Produced inadvertently by a game played under one set of rules, their assimilation requires the elaboration of another set. After they have become parts of science, the enterprise, at least of those specialists in whose particular field the novelties lie, is never quite the same again.

We must now ask how changes of this sort can come about, considering first discoveries, or novelties of fact, and then inventions, or novelties of theory. That distinction between discovery and invention or between fact and theory will, however, immediately prove to be exceedingly artificial. Its artificiality is an important clue to several of this essay's main theses. Examining selected discoveries in the rest of this section, we shall quickly find that they are not isolated events but extended episodes with a regularly recurrent structure. Discovery commences with the awareness of anomaly, i.e., with the recognition that nature has somehow violated the paradigm-induced expectations that govern normal science. It then continues with a more or less extended exploration of the area of anomaly. And it closes only when the paradigm theory has been adjusted so that the anomalous has become the expected. Assimilating a new sort of fact demands a more than additive adjustment of theory, and until that adjustment is completed—until the scientist has learned to see nature in a different way—the new fact is not quite a scientific fact at all. . . .

If awareness of anomaly plays a role in the emergence of new sorts of phenomena, it should surprise no one that a similar but more profound awareness is prerequisite to all acceptable changes of theory. On this point historical evidence is, I think, entirely unequivocal. The state of Ptolemaic astronomy was a scandal before Copernicus' announcement. Galileo's contributions to the study of motion depended closely upon difficulties discovered in Aristotle's theory by scholastic critics. Newton's new theory of light and color originated in the discovery that none of the existing pre-paradigm theories would account for the length of the spectrum, and the wave theory that replaced Newton's was announced in the midst of growing concern about anomalies in the relation of diffraction and polarization effects to Newton's theory. Thermodynamics was born from the collision of two existing nineteenth-century physical theories, and quantum mechanics from a variety of difficulties surrounding black-body radiation, specific heats, and the photoelectric effect. Furthermore in all these cases except that of Newton the awareness of anomaly had lasted so long and penetrated so deep that one can appropriately describe the fields affected by it as in a state of growing crisis. Because it demands large-scale paradigm destruction and major shifts in the problems and techniques of normal science, the emergence of new theories is generally preceded by a period of pronounced professional insecurity. As one might expect, that insecurity is generated by the persistent failure of the puzzles of normal science to come out as they should. Failure of existing rules is the prelude to a search for new ones. . . .

How, then, to return to the initial question, do scientists respond to the awareness of an anomaly in the fit between theory and nature? What has just been said indicates that even a discrepancy unaccountably larger than that experienced in other applications of the theory need not draw any very profound response. There are always some discrepancies. Even the most stubborn ones usually respond at last to normal practice. Very often scientists are willing to wait, particularly if there are many problems available in other parts of the field. We have already noted, for example, that during the sixty years after Newton's original computation, the predicted motion of the moon's perigee remained only half of that observed. As Europe's best mathematical physicists continued to wrestle unsuccessfully with the well-known discrepancy, there were occasional proposals for a modification of Newton's inverse square law. But no one took these proposals very seriously, and in practice this patience with a major anomaly proved justified. . . .

It follows that if an anomaly is to evoke crisis, it must usually be more than just an anomaly. There are always difficulties somewhere in the paradigm-nature fit; most of them are set right sooner or later, often by processes that could not have been foreseen. The scientist who pauses to examine every anomaly he notes will seldom get significant work done. We therefore have to ask what it is that makes an anomaly seem worth concerted scrutiny, and to that question there is probably no fully general answer. The cases we have already examined are characteristic but scarcely prescriptive. Sometimes an anomaly will clearly call into question explicit and fundamental generalizations of the paradigm, as the problem of ether drag did for those who accepted Maxwell's theory. Or, as in the Copernican revolution, an anomaly without apparent fundamental import may evoke crisis if the applications that it inhibits have a particular practical importance, in this case for calendar design and astrology. Or, as in eighteenth-century chemistry, the development of normal science may transform an anomaly that had previously been only a vexation into a source of crisis: the problem of weight relations had a very different status after the evolution of pneumatic-chemical techniques. Presumably there are still other circumstances that can make an anomaly particularly pressing, and ordinarily several of these will combine. We have already noted, for example, that one source of the crisis that confronted Copernicus was the mere length of time during which astronomers had wrestled unsuccessfully with the reduction of the residual discrepancies in Ptolemy's system.

When, for these reasons or others like them, an anomaly comes to seem more than just another puzzle of normal science, the transition to crisis and to extraordinary science has begun. The anomaly itself now comes to be more generally recognized as such by the profession. More and more attention is devoted to it by more and more of the field's most eminent men. If it still continues to resist, as it usually does not, many of them may come to view its resolution as *the* subject matter of their discipline. For them the field will no longer look quite the same as it had earlier. Part of its different appearance results simply from the new fixation point of scientific scrutiny. An even more important source of change is the divergent nature of the numerous partial solutions that concerted attention to the problem has made available. The early attacks upon the resistant problem will have followed the paradigm rules quite closely. But with continuing resistance, more and more of the attacks upon it will have involved some minor or not so minor articulation of the paradigm, no two of them quite alike, each partially successful, but none sufficiently so to be accepted as paradigm by the group. Through this proliferation of divergent articulations (more and more frequently they will come to be described as *ad hoc* adjustments), the rules of normal science become increasingly blurred. Though there still is a paradigm, few practitioners prove to be entirely agreed about what it is. Even formerly standard solutions of solved problems are called in question. . . .

All crises begin with the blurring of a paradigm and the consequent loosening of the rules for normal research. In this respect research during crisis very much resembles research during the pre-paradigm period, except that in the former the locus of difference is both smaller and more clearly defined. And all crises close in one of three ways. Sometimes normal science ultimately proves able to handle the crisis-provoking problem despite the despair of those who have seen it as the end of an existing paradigm. On other occasions the problem resists even apparently radical new approaches. Then scientists may conclude that no solution will be forthcoming in the present state of their field. The problem is labeled and set aside for a future generation with more developed tools. Or, finally, the case that will most concern us here, a crisis may end with the emergence of a new candidate for paradigm and with the ensuing battle over its acceptance. This last mode of closure will be considered at length in later sections, but we must anticipate a bit of what will be said there in order to complete these remarks about the evolution and anatomy of the crisis state.

The transition from a paradigm in crisis to a new one from which a new tradition of normal science can emerge is far from a cumulative process, one achieved by an articulation or extension of the old paradigm. Rather it is a reconstruction of the field from new fundamentals, a reconstruction that changes some of the field's most elementary theoretical generalizations as well as many of its paradigm methods and applications. During the transition period there will be a large but never complete overlap between the problems that can be solved by the old and by the new paradigm. But there will also be a decisive difference in the modes of solution. When the transition is complete, the profession will have changed its view of the field, its methods, and its goals. One perceptive historian, viewing a classic case of a science's reorientation by paradigm change, recently described it as "picking up the other end of the stick," a process that involves "handling the same bundle of data as before, but placing them in a new system of relations with one another by giving them a different framework." Others who have noted this aspect of scientific advance have emphasized its similarity to a change in visual gestalt: the marks on paper that were first seen as a bird are now seen as an antelope, or vice versa. That parallel can be misleading. Scientists do not see something *as* something else; instead, they simply see it. We have already examined some of the problems created by saying that Priestley saw oxygen as dephlogisticated air. In addition, the scientist does not preserve the gestalt subject's freedom to switch back and forth between ways of seeing. Nevertheless, the switch of gestalt, particularly because it is today so familiar, is a useful elementary prototype for what occurs in full-scale paradigm shift. . . .

The resulting transition to a new paradigm is scientific revolution, a subject that we are at long last prepared to approach directly. . . .

These characteristic shifts in the scientific community's conception of its legitimate problems and standards would have less significance to this essay's thesis if one could suppose that they always occurred from some methodologically lower to some higher type. In that case their effects, too, would seem cumulative. No wonder that some historians have argued that the history of science records a continuing increase in the maturity and refinement of man's conception of the nature of science. Yet the case for cumulative development of science's problems and standards is even harder to make than the case for cumulation of theories. The attempt to explain gravity, though fruitfully abandoned by most eighteenth-century scientists, was not directed to an intrinsically illegitimate problem; the objections to innate forces were neither inherently unscientific nor metaphysical in some pejorative sense. There are no external standards to permit a judgment of that sort. What occurred was neither a decline nor a raising of standards, but simply a change demanded by the adoption of a new paradigm. Furthermore, that change has since been reversed and could be again. In the twentieth century Einstein succeeded in explaining gravitational attractions, and that explanation has returned science to a set of canons and problems that are, in this particular respect, more like those of Newton's predecessors than of his successors. Or again, the development of quantum mechanics has reversed the methodological prohibition that originated in the chemical revolution. Chemists now attempt, and with great success, to explain the color, state of aggregation, and other qualities of the substances used and produced in their laboratories. A similar reversal may even be underway in electromagnetic theory. Space, in contemporary physics, is not the inert and homogenous substratum employed in both Newton's and Maxwell's theories; some of its new properties are not unlike those once attributed to the ether; we may someday come to know what an electric displacement is.

By shifting emphasis from the cognitive to the normative functions of paradigms, the preceding examples enlarge our understanding of the ways in which paradigms give form to the scientific life. Previously, we had principally examined the paradigm's role as a vehicle for scientific theory. In that role it functions by telling the scientist about the entities that nature does and does not contain and about the ways in which those entities behave. That information provides a map whose details are elucidated by mature scientific research. And since nature is too complex and varied to be explored at random, that map is as essential as observation and experiment to science's continuing development. Through the theories they embody, paradigms prove to be constitutive of the research activity. They are also, however, constitutive of science in other respects, and that is now the point. In particular, our most recent examples show that paradigms provide scientists not only with a map but also with some of the directions essential for map-making. In learning a paradigm the scientist acquires theory, methods, and standards together, usually in an inextricable mixture. Therefore, when paradigms change, there are usually significant shifts in the criteria determining the legitimacy both of problems and of proposed solutions.

That observation returns us to the point from which this section began, for it provides our first explicit indication of why the choice between competing paradigms regularly raises questions that cannot be resolved by the criteria of normal science. To the extent, as significant as it is incomplete, that two scientific schools disagree about what is a problem and what a solution, they will inevitably talk through each other when debating the relative merits of their respective paradigms. In the partially circular arguments that regularly result, each paradigm will be shown to satisfy more or less the criteria that it dictates for itself and to fall short of a few of those dictated by its opponent. There are other reasons, too, for the incompleteness of logical contact that consistently characterizes paradigm debates. For example, since no paradigm ever solves all the problems it defines and since no two paradigms leave all the same problems unsolved, paradigm debates always involve the question: Which problems is it more significant to have solved? Like the issue of competing standards, that question of values can be answered only in terms of criteria that lie outside of normal science altogether, and it is that recourse to external criteria that most obviously makes paradigm debates revolutionary. Something even more fundamental than standards and values is, however, also at stake. I have so far argued only that paradigms are constitutive of science. Now I wish to display a sense in which they are constitutive of nature as well. . . .

We have already seen several reasons why the proponents of competing paradigms must fail to make complete contact with each other's viewpoints. Collectively these reasons have been described as the incommensurability of the pre- and postrevolutionary normal-scientific traditions, and we need only recapitulate them briefly here. In the first place, the proponents of competing paradigms will often disagree about the list of problems that any candidate for paradigm must resolve. Their standards or their definitions of science are not the same. Must a theory of motion explain the cause of the attractive forces between particles of matter or may it simply note the existence of such forces? Newton's dynamics was widely rejected because, unlike both Aristotle's and Descartes's theories, it implied the latter answer to the question. When Newton's theory had been accepted, a question was therefore banished from science. That question, however, was one that general relativity may proudly claim to have solved. Or again, as disseminated in the nineteenth century, Lavoisier's chemical theory inhibited chemists from asking why the metals were so much alike, a question that phlogistic chemistry had both asked and answered. The transition to Lavoisier's paradigm had, like the transition to Newton's, meant a loss not only of a permissible question but of an achieved solution. That loss was not, however, permanent either. In the twentieth century questions about the qualities of chemical substances have entered science again, together with some answers to them.

More is involved, however, than the incommensurability of standards. Since new paradigms are born from old ones, they ordinarily incorporate much of the vocabulary and apparatus, both conceptual and manipulative, that the traditional paradigm had previously employed. But they seldom employ these borrowed elements in quite the traditional way. Within the new paradigm, old terms, concepts, and experiments fall into new relationships one with the other. The inevitable result is what we must call, though the term is not quite right, a misunderstanding between the two competing schools. The laymen who scoffed at Einstein's general theory of relativity because space could not be "curved"—it was not that sort of thing—were not simply wrong or mistaken. Nor were the mathematicians, physicists, and philosophers who tried to develop a Euclidean version of Einstein's theory. What had previously been meant by space was necessarily flat, homogeneous, isotropic, and unaffected by the presence of matter. If it had not been, Newtonian physics would not have worked. To make the transition to Einstein's universe, the whole conceptual web whose strands are space, time, matter, force, and so on, had to be shifted and laid down again on nature whole. Only men who had together undergone or failed to undergo that transformation would be able to discover precisely what they agreed or disagreed about. Communication across the revolutionary divide is inevitably partial. . . .

In its normal state, then, a scientific community is an immensely efficient instrument for solving the problems or puzzles that its paradigms define. Furthermore, the result of solving those problems must inevitably be progress. There is no problem here. Seeing that much, however, only highlights the second main part of the problem of progress in the sciences. Let us therefore turn to it and ask about progress through extraordinary science. Why should progress also be the apparently universal concomitant of scientific revolutions? Once again, there is much to be learned by asking what else the result of a revolution could be. Revolutions close with a total victory for one of the two opposing camps. Will that group ever say that the result of its victory has been something less than progress? That would be rather like admitting that they had been wrong and their opponents right. To them, at least, the outcome of revolution must be progress, and they are in an excellent position to make certain that future members of their community will see past history in the same way. . . .

Though science surely grows in depth, it may not grow in breadth as well. If it does so, that breadth is manifest mainly in the proliferation of scientific specialties, not in the scope of any single specialty alone. Yet despite these and other losses to the individual communities, the nature of such communities provides a virtual guarantee that both the list of problems solved by science and the precision of individual problem-solutions will grow and grow. At least, the nature of the community provides such a guarantee if there is any way at all in which it can be provided. What better criterion than the decision of the scientific group could there be?

These last paragraphs point the directions in which I believe a more refined solution of the problem of progress in the sciences must be sought. Perhaps they indicate that scientific progress is not quite what we had taken it to be. But they simultaneously show that a sort of progress will inevitably characterize the scientific enterprise so long as such an enterprise survives. In the sciences there need not be progress of another sort. We may, to be more precise, have to relinquish the notion, explicit or implicit, that changes of paradigm carry scientists and those who learn from them closer and closer to the truth.

It is now time to notice that until the last very few pages the term 'truth' had entered this essay only in a quotation from Francis Bacon. And even in those pages it entered only as a source for the scientist's conviction that incompatible rules for doing science cannot coexist except during revolutions when the profession's main task is to eliminate all sets but one. The developmental process described in this essay has been a process of evolution *from* primitive beginnings—a process whose successive stages are characterized by an increasingly detailed and refined understanding of nature. But nothing that has been or will be said makes it a process of evolution *toward* anything. Inevitably that lacuna will have disturbed many readers. We are all deeply accustomed to seeing science as the one enterprise that draws constantly nearer to some goal set by nature in advance.

But need there be any such goal? Can we not account for both science's existence and its success in terms of evolution from the community's state of knowledge at any given time? Does it really help to imagine that there is some one full, objective, true account of nature and that the proper measure of scientific achievement is the extent to which it brings us closer to that ultimate goal? If we can learn to substitute evolution-from-what-we-do-know for evolution-toward-what-we-wish-to-know, a number of vexing problems may vanish in the process. . . .

I have argued that the parties to such debates inevitably see differently certain of the experimental or observational situations to which both have recourse. Since the vocabularies in which they discuss such situations consist, however, predominantly of the same terms, they must be attaching some of those terms to nature differently, and their communication is inevitably only partial. As a result, the superiority of one theory to another is something that cannot be proved in the debate. Instead, I have insisted, each party must try, by persuasion, to convert the other. Only philosophers have seriously misconstrued the intent of these parts of my argument. A number of them, however, have reported that I believe the following: . . . the proponents of incommensurable theories cannot communicate with each other at all; as a result, in a debate over theory-choice there can be no recourse to *good* reasons; instead theory must be chosen for reasons that are ultimately personal and subjective; some sort of mystical apperception is responsible for the decision actually reached. More than any other parts of the book, the passages on which these misconstructions rest have been responsible for charges of irrationality. . . .

Briefly put, what the participants in a communication breakdown can do is recognize each other as members of different language communities and then become translators. Taking the differences between their own intra- and inter-group discourse as itself a subject for study, they can first attempt to discover the terms and locations that, used unproblematically within each community, are nevertheless foci of trouble for inter-group discussions. (Locations that present no such difficulties may be homophonically translated.) Having isolated such areas of difficulty in scientific communication, they can next resort to their shared everyday vocabularies in an effort further to elucidate their troubles. Each may, that is, try to discover what the other would see and say when presented with a stimulus to which his own verbal response would be different. If they can sufficiently refrain from explaining anomalous behavior as the consequence of mere error or madness, they may in time become very good predictors of each other's behavior. Each will have learned to translate the other theory and its consequences into his own language and simultaneously to describe in his language the world to which that theory applies. That is what the historian of science regularly does (or should) when dealing with out-of-date scientific theories.

Since translation, if pursued, allows the participants in a communication breakdown to experience vicariously something of the merits and defects of each other's points of view, it is a potent tool both for persuasion and for conversion. But even persuasion need not succeed, and, if it does, it need not be accompanied or followed by conversion. The two experiences are not the same, an important distinction that I have only recently fully recognized. . . .

The conversion experience that I have likened to a gestalt switch remains, therefore, at the heart of the revolutionary process. Good reasons for choice provide motives for conversion and a climate in which it is more likely to occur. Translation may, in addition, provide points of entry for the neural reprogramming that, however inscrutable at this time, must underlie conversion. But neither good reasons nor translation constitute conversion, and it is that process we must explicate in order to understand an essential sort of scientific change. . . .

Alasdair MacIntyre

Alasdair MacIntyre's essay is included here as an example of the types of responses to Kuhn's work made by those resistant to an entirely historicist position. MacIntyre, a contemporary philosopher, argues against Kuhn's notion of paradigms as completely incommensurable. He suggests that epistemological crises (Kuhn's build-up of anomalies) are resolved when one is able to construct a narrative. A narrative in this sense means a story which goes beyond the period of crisis. Through narrative we are able to explain where we are intellectually by talking about how we got there. Thus an old way of thinking is never entirely foreign to people who have passed beyond it. For MacIntyre the fact that we continually construct and reconstruct scientific narratives does not mean that science is not progressive. Rather, MacIntyre suggests that narratives become more and more adequate representations of the phenomena we hope to explain. In this perspective, historicism, putting truth in context, does not necessarily undermine the modern project but rescues it.

ALASDAIR MACINTYRE
(1974)

Epistemological Crises,

Dramatic Narrative,

and the Philosophy of Science

What is an epistemological crisis? Consider, first, the situation of ordinary agents who are thrown into such crises. Someone who has believed that he was highly valued by his employers and colleagues is suddenly fired; someone proposed for membership of a club whose members were all, so he believed, close friends is blackballed. Or someone falls in love and needs to know what the loved one *really* feels; someone falls out of love and needs to know how he or she can possibly have been so mistaken in the other. For all such persons the relationship of *seems* to *is* becomes crucial. It is in such situations that ordinary agents who have never learned anything about academic philosophy are apt to rediscover for themselves versions of the other-minds problem and the problem of the justification of induction. They discover, that is, that there is a problem about the rational justification of inferences from premises about the behaviour of other people to conclusions about their thoughts, feelings, and attitudes and of inferences from premises about how individuals have acted in the past to conclusions expressed as generalizations about their behaviour—generalizations which would enable us to make reasonably reliable predications about their future behaviour. What they took to be evidence pointing unambiguously in some one direction now turns out to have been equally susceptible of rival interpretations. Such a discovery is often paralysing, and were we all of us all of the time to have to reckon with the multiplicity of possible interpretations open to us, social life as we know it could scarcely continue. For social life is sustained by the assumption that we are, by and large, able to construe each others' behaviour—that error, deception, self-deception, irony, and ambiguity, although omnipresent in social life, are not so

Reprinted from *The Monist* 60 (1977), pp. 453–71 © 1977, *The Monist*, La Salle, Illinois 61301. Reprinted by permission.

pervasive as to render reliable reasoning and reasonable action impossible. But can this assumption in any way be vindicated?

Consider what it is to share a culture. It is to share schemata which are at one and the same time constitutive of and normative for intelligible action by myself and are also means for my interpretations of the actions of others. My ability to understand what you are doing and my ability to act intelligibly (both to myself and to others) are one and the same ability. It is true that I cannot master these schemata without also acquiring the means to deceive, to make more or less elaborate jokes, to exercise irony and utilize ambiguity, but it is also, and even more importantly, true that my ability to conduct any successful transactions depends on my presenting myself to most people most of the time in unambiguous, unironical, undeceiving, intelligible ways. It is these schemata which enable inferences to be made from premises about past behaviour to conclusions about future behaviour and present inner attitudes. They are not, of course, empirical generalisations; they are prescriptions for interpretation. But while it is they which normally preserve us from the pressure of the other-minds problem and the problem of induction, it is precisely they which can in certain circumstances thrust those very problems upon us.

For it is not only that an individual may rely on the schemata which have hitherto informed all his interpretations of social life and find that he or she has been led into radical error or deception, so that for the first time the schemata are put in question—perhaps for the first time they also in this moment become visible to the individual who employs them—but it is also the case that the individual may come to recognise the possibility of systematically different possibilities of interpretation, of the existence of alternative and rival schemata which yield mutually incompatible accounts of what is going on around him. Just this is the form of epistemological crisis encountered by ordinary agents and it is striking that there is not a single account of it anywhere in the literature of academic philosophy. Perhaps this is an important symptom of the condition of that discipline. But happily we do possess one classic study of such crises. It is Shakespeare's *Hamlet*.

Hamlet arrives back from Wittenberg with too many schemata available for interpreting the events at Elsinore of which already he is a part. There is the revenge schema of the Norse sagas; there is the renaissance courtier's schema; there is a Machiavellian schema about competition for power. But he not only has the problem of which schema to apply, he also has the other ordinary agents' problem: whom now to believe? His mother? Rosencrantz and Guildenstern? His father's ghost? Until he has adopted some schema he does not know what to treat as evidence; until he knows what to treat as evidence he cannot tell which schema to adopt. Trapped in this epistemological circularity the general form of his problem is: 'what is going on here?' Thus Hamlet's problem is close to that of the literary critics who have asked: "What is going on in *Hamlet*?" And it is close to that of directors who have asked: "What should be cut and what should be included in my production so that the audience may understand what is going on in *Hamlet*?"

The resemblance between Hamlet's problem and that of the critics and directors is worth noticing; for it suggests that both are asking a question which could equally well be formulated as: 'what is going on in *Hamlet*?' or 'how ought the narrative of these events to be constructed?' Hamlet's problems arise because the dramatic narrative of his family and of the kingdom of Denmark through which he identified his own place in society and his relationships to others has been disrupted by radical interpretative doubts. His task is to reconstitute, to rewrite that in a sewer. Nor, on the other hand, have I been impressed with claims that structural linguistics, computer engineering, or some other advanced form of thought is going to enable us to understand men without knowing them. Nothing will discredit a semiotic approach to culture more quickly than allowing it to drift into a combination of intuitionism and alchemy, no matter how elegantly the intuitions are expressed or how modern the alchemy is made to look.

The danger that cultural analysis, in search of all-too-deep-lying turtles, will lose touch with the hard surfaces of life—with the political, economic, stratificatory realities within which men are everywhere contained—and with the biological and physical necessities on which those surfaces rest, is an ever-present one. The only defense against it, and against, thus, turning cultural analysis into a kind of sociological aestheticism, is to train such analysis on such realities and such necessities in the first place. It is thus that I have written about nationalism, about violence, about identity, about human nature, about legitimacy, about revolution, about ethnicity, about urbanization, about status, about death, about time, and most of all about particular attempts by particular peoples to place these things in some sort of comprehensible, meaningful frame.

To look at the symbolic dimensions of social action—art, religion, ideology, science, law, mortality, common sense—is not to turn away from the existential dilemmas of life for some empyrean realm of de-emotionalized forms; it is to plunge into the midst of them. The essential vocation of interpretive anthropology is not to answer our deepest questions, but to make available to us answers that others, guarding other sheep in other valleys, have given, and thus to include them in the consultable record of what man has said.

narrative, reversing his understanding of past events in the light of present responses to his probing. This probing is informed by two ideals, truth and intelligibility, and the pursuit of both is not always easily coherent. The discovery of an hitherto unsuspected truth is just what may disrupt an hitherto intelligible account. And of course while Hamlet tries to discover a true and intelligible narrative of the events involving his parents and Claudius, Gertrude and Claudius are trying to discover a true and intelligible narrative of Hamlet's investigation. To be unable to render onself intelligible is to risk being taken to be mad, is, if carried far enough, to be mad. And madness or death may always be the outcomes which prevent the resolution of an epistemological crisis, for an epistemological crisis is always a crisis in human relationships.

When an epistemological crisis is resolved, it is by the construction of a new narrative which enables the agent to understand *both* how he or she could intelligibly have held his or her original beliefs *and* how he or she could have been so drastically misled by them. The narrative in terms of which he or she at first understood and ordered experiences is itself made into the subject of an enlarged narrative. The agent has come to understand how the criteria of truth and understanding must be reformulated. He has had to become epistemologically self-conscious and at a certain point he may have come to acknowledge two conclusions: the first is that his new forms of understanding may themselves in turn come to be put in question at any time; the second is that, because in such crises the criteria of truth, intelligibility, and rationality may always themselves be put in question—as they are in *Hamlet*—we are never in a position to claim that now we possess the truth or now we are fully rational. The most that we can claim is that this is the best account which anyone has been able to give so far, and that our beliefs about what the marks of 'a best account so far' are will themselves change in what are at present unpredictable ways. . . .

One further aspect of narratives and their role in epistemological crises remains to be noticed. I have suggested that epistemological progress consists in the construction and reconstruction of more adequate narratives and forms of narrative and that epistemological crises are occasions for such reconstruction. But if this were really the case then two kinds of questions would need to be answered. The first would be of the form: how does this progress begin? What are the narratives from which we set out? The second would be of the form: how is it, then, that narrative is not only given so little place by thinkers from Descartes onwards, but has so often before and after been treated as a merely aesthetic form? The answers to these questions are not entirely unconnected.

We begin from myth, not only from the myths of primitive peoples, but from those myths or fairy stories which are essential to a well-ordered childhood. Bruno Bettelheim has written: "Before and well into the oedipal period (roughly, the ages between three and six or seven), the child's experience of the world is chaotic. . . . During and because of the oedipal struggles, the outside world comes to hold more meaning for the child and he begins to try to make some sense of it . . . As a child listens to a fairy tale, he gets ideas about how he may create order out of the chaos that is his inner life." It is from fairy tales, so Bettelheim argues, that the child learns how to engage himself with and perceive an order in social reality; and the child who is deprived of the right kind of fairy tale at the right age later on is apt to have to adopt strategies to evade a reality he has not learned how to interpret or to handle.

"The child asks himself, 'Who am I? Where did I come from? How did the world come into being? Who created man and all the animals? What is the purpose of life?' . . . He wonders who or what brings adversity upon him and what can protect him against it. Are there benevolent powers in addition to his parents? *Are* his parents benevolent powers? How should he form himself, and why? Is there hope for him, though he may have done wrong? Why did all this happen to him? What will it mean to his future?" The child originally requires answers that are true to his own experience, but of course the child comes to learn the inadequacy of that experience. Bettelheim points out that the young child told by adults that the world is a globe suspended in space and spinning at incredible speeds may feel bound to repeat what they say, but would find it immensely more plausible to be told that the earth is held up by a giant. But in time the young child learns that what the adults told him is indeed true. And such a child may well become a Descartes, one who feels that all narratives are misleading fables when compared with what he now takes to be the solid truth of physics.

Yet to raise the question of truth need not entail rejecting myth or story as the appropriate and perhaps the only appropriate form in which certain truths can be told. The child may become not a Descartes, but a Vico or a Hamann who writes a story about how he had to escape from the hold which the stories of his childhood and the stories of the childhood of the human race originally had upon him in order to discover how stories can be true stories. Such a narrative will be itself a history of epistemological transitions and this narrative may well be brought to a point at which questions are thrust upon the narrator which make it impossible for him to continue to use it as an instrument of interpretation. Just this, of course, happens to Descartes, who having abjured history as a means to truth, recounts to us his own history as the medium through which the search for truth is to be carried on. For Descartes and for others this moment is that at which an epistemological crisis occurs. And all those questions which the child has asked of the teller of fairy tales arise in a new adult form. Philosophy is now set the same task that had once been set for myth.

Descartes's description of his own epistemological crisis has, of course, been uniquely influential. Yet Descartes radically misdescribes his own crisis and thus has proved a highly misleading guide to the nature of epistemological crises in general. The agent who is plunged into an epistemological crisis knows something very important: that a schema of interpretation which he has trusted so far has broken down irremediably in certain highly specific ways. So it is with Hamlet. Descartes, however, starts from the assumption that he knows nothing whatsoever until he can discover a presuppositionless first principle on which all else can be founded. Hamlet's doubts are formulated against a background of what he takes to be—rightly—well-founded beliefs; Descartes's doubt is intended to lack any such background. It is to be context-less doubt. Hence also that tradition of philosophical teaching arises which presupposes that Cartesian doubts can be entertained by anyone at any place or time. But of course someone who really believed that he knew nothing would not even know how to begin on a course of radical doubt; for he would have no conception of what his task might be, of what it would be to settle his doubts and to acquire well-founded beliefs. Conversely, anyone who knows enough to know *that* does indeed possess a set of extensive epistemological beliefs which he is not putting in doubt at all.

Descartes's failure is complex. First of all he does not recognise that among the features of the universe which he is not putting in doubt is his own capacity not only to use the French and the Latin languages, but even to express the same thought in both languages; and as a consequence he does not put in doubt what he has inherited in and with these languages, namely, a way of ordering both thought and the world expressed in a set of meanings. These meanings have a history; seventeenth-century Latin bears the marks of having been the language of scholasticism, just as scholasticism was itself marked by the influence of twelfth- and thirteenth-century Latin. It was perhaps because the presence of his languages was invisible to the Descartes of the *Discours* and the *Meditationes* that he did not notice either what Gilson pointed out in detail, how much of what he took to be the spontaneous reflections of his own mind was in fact a repetition of sentences and phrases from his school textbooks. Even the *Cogito* is to be found in Saint Augustine.

What thus goes unrecognised by Descartes is the presence not only of languages, but of a tradition—a tradition that he took himself to have successfully disowned. It was from this tradition that he inherited his epistemological ideals. For at the core of this tradition was a conception of knowledge as analogous to vision: the mind's eye beholds its objects by the light of reason. At the same time this tradition wishes to contrast sharply knowledge and sense-experience, including visual experience. Hence there is metaphorical incoherence at the heart of every theory of knowledge in this Platonic and Augustinian tradition, an incoherence which Descartes unconsciously reproduces. Thus Descartes also cannot recognise that he is responding not only to the timeless demands of scepticism, but to a highly specific crisis in one particular social and intellectual tradition.

One of the signs that a tradition is in crisis is that its accustomed ways for relating *seems* and *is* begin to break down. Thus the pressures of scepticism become more urgent and attempts to do the impossible, to refute scepticism once and for all, become projects of central importance to the culture and not mere private academic enterprises. Just this happens in the late middle ages and the sixteenth century. Inherited modes of ordering experience reveal too many rival possibilities of interpretation. It is no accident that there are a multiplicity of rival interpretations of both the thought and the lives of such figures as Luther and Machiavelli in a way that there are not for such equally rich and complex figures as Abelard and Aquinas. Ambiguity, the possibility of alternative interpretations, becomes a central feature of human character and activity. *Hamlet* is Shakespeare's brilliant mirror to the age, and the difference between Shakespeare's account of epistemological crises and Descartes's is now clear. For Shakespeare invites us to reflect on the crisis of the self as a crisis in the tradition which has formed the self; Descartes by his attitude to history and to fable has cut himself off from the possibility of recognising himself; he has invented an unhistorical self-endorsed self-consciousness and tries to describe his epistemological crisis in terms of it. Small wonder that he misdescribes it.

Consider by contrast Galileo. When Galileo entered the scientific scene, he was confronted by much more than the conflict between the Ptolemaic and Copernican astronomies. The Ptolemaic system was itself inconsistent both with the widely accepted Platonic requirements for a true astronomy and with the perhaps even more widely accepted principles of Aristotelian physics. These latter were in turn inconsistent with the findings over two centuries of scholars at Oxford, Paris, and Padua about motion. Not surprisingly, instrumentalism flourished as a philosophy of science and Osiander's instrumentalist reading of Copernicus was no more than the counterpart to earlier instrumentalist interpretations of the Ptolemaic system. Instrumentalism, like attempts to refute scepticism, is characteristically a sign of a tradition in crisis.

Galileo resolves the crisis by a threefold strategy. He rejects instrumentalism; he reconciles astronomy and mechanics; and he redefines the place of experiment in natural science. The old mythological empiricist view of Galileo saw him as appealing to the facts against Ptolemy and

Aristotle; what he actually did was to give a new account of what an appeal to the facts had to be. Wherein lies the superiority of Galileo to his predecessors? The answer is that he, for the first time, enables the work of all his predecessors to be evaluated by a common set of standards. The contributions of Plato, Aristotle, the scholars at Merton College, Oxford, and at Padua, the work of Copernicus himself at last all fall into place. Or, to put matters in another and equivalent way: the history of late medieval science can finally be cast into a coherent narrative. Galileo's work implies a rewriting of the narrative which constitutes the scientific tradition. For it now became retrospectively possible to identify those anomalies which had been genuine counterexamples to received theories from those anomalies which could justifiably be dealt with by ad hoc explanatory devices or even ignored. It also became retrospectively possible to see how the various elements of various theories had fared in their encounters with other theories and with observations and experiments, and to understand how the form in which they had survived bore the marks of those encounters. A theory always bears the marks of its passage through time and the theories with which Galileo had to deal were no exception.

Let me cast the point which I am trying to make about Galileo in a way which, at first sight, is perhaps paradoxical. We are apt to suppose that because Galileo was a peculiarly great scientist, therefore he has his own peculiar place in the history of science. I am suggesting instead that it is because of his peculiarly important place in the history of science that he is accounted a particularly great scientist. The criterion of a successful theory is that it enables us to understand its predecessors in a newly intelligible way. It, at one and the same time, enables us to understand precisely why its predecessors have to be rejected or modified and also why, without and before its illumination, past theory could have remained credible. It introduces new standards for evaluating the past. It recasts the narrative which constitutes the continuous reconstruction of the scientific tradition.

This connection between narrative and tradition has hitherto gone almost unnoticed, perhaps because tradition has usually been taken seriously only by conservative social theorists. Yet those features of tradition which emerge as important when the connection between tradition and narrative is understood are ones which conservative theorists are unlikely to attend to. For what constitutes a tradition is a conflict of interpretations of that tradition, a conflict which itself has a history susceptible of rival interpretations. If I am a Jew, I have to recognise that the tradition of Judaism is partly constituted by a continuous argument over what it means to be a Jew. Suppose I am an American: the tradition is one partly constituted by continuous argument over what it means to be an American and partly by continuous argument over what it means to have rejected tradition. If I am an historian, I must acknowledge that the tradition of historiography is partly, but centrally, constituted by arguments about what history is and ought to be, from Hume and Gibbon to Namier and Edward Thompson. Notice that all three kinds of tradition—religious, political, intellectual—involve epistemological debate as a necessary feature of their conflicts. For it is not merely that different participants in a tradition disagree; they also disagree as to how to characterize their disagreements and as to how to resolve them. They disagree as to what constitutes appropriate reasoning, decisive evidence, conclusive proof.

A tradition then not only embodies the narrative of an argument, but is only to be recovered by an argumentative retelling of that narrative which will itself be in conflict with other argumentative retellings. Every tradition therefore is always in danger of lapsing into incoherence, and when a tradition does so lapse it sometimes can only be recovered by a revolutionary reconstitution. Precisely such a reconstitution of a tradition which had lapsed into incoherence was the work of Galileo.

It will now be obvious why I introduced the notion of tradition by alluding negatively to the viewpoint of conservative theorists. For they, from Burke onwards, have wanted to counterpose tradition and reason and tradition and revolution. Not reason, but prejudice; not revolution, but inherited precedent; these are Burke's key oppositions. Yet if the present arguments are correct it is traditions which are the bearers of reason, and traditions at certain periods actually require and need revolutions for their continuance. Burke saw the French Revolution as merely the negative overthrow of all that France had been and many French conservatives have agreed with him, but later thinkers as different as Péguy and Hilaire Belloc were able retrospectively to see the great revolution as reconstituting a more ancient France, so that Jeanne D'Arc and Danton belong within the same single, if immensely complex, tradition.

Conflict arises, of course, not only within but between traditions, and such a conflict tests the resources of each contending tradition. It is yet another mark of a degenerate tradition that it has contrived a set of epistemological defences which enable it to avoid being put in question or at least to avoid recognising that it is being put in question by rival traditions. This is, for example, part of the degeneracy of modern astrology, of some types of psychoanalytic thought, and of liberal Protestantism. Although, therefore, any feature of any tradition, any theory, any practice, any belief can always under certain conditions be put in question, the practice of putting in question, whether within a tradition or between traditions, itself always requires the context of a tradition. Doubting is a more complex activity than some sceptics have realised. To say to oneself or to someone else "Doubt all your beliefs here and now" without reference to historical or autobiographical context is not meaningless; but it is an invitation not to philosophy, but to mental breakdown, or rather to philosophy as a means of mental breakdown. Descartes concealed from himself, as we have seen, an unacknowledged background of beliefs which rendered what he was doing intelligible and sane to himself and to others. But suppose that he had put that background in question too—what would have happened to him then?

> We are not without clues, for we do have the record of the approach to breakdown in the life of one great philosopher. "For I have already shown," wrote Hume, that the understanding, when it acts alone, and according to its most general principles, entirely subverts itself, and leaves not the lowest degree of evidence in any proposition, either in philosophy or common life.... The *intense* view of these manifold contradictions and imperfections in human reason has so wrought upon me, and heated my brain, that I am ready to reject all belief and reasoning, and can look upon no opinion even as more probable or likely than another. Where am I, or what? from what causes do I derive my existence, and to what condition shall I return? Whose favour shall I court, and whose anger must I dread? What beings surround me? and on whom have I any influence? I am confronted with all these questions, and begin to fancy myself in the most deplorable condition imaginable, inviron'd with the deepest darkness and utterly depriv'd of the use of every member and faculty.

We may note three remarkable features of Hume's cry of pain. First, like Descartes, he has set a standard for the foundations of his beliefs which could not be met; hence all beliefs founder equally. He has not asked if he can find good reasons for preferring in respect of the best criteria of reason and truth available some among others of the limited range of possibilities of belief which actually confront him in his particular cultural situation. Secondly, he is in consequence thrust back without any answers or possibility of answers upon just that range of questions that, according to Bettelheim, underlie the whole narrative enterprise in early childhood. There is indeed the most surprising and illuminating correspondence between the questions which Bettelheim ascribes to the child and the questions framed by the adult, but desperate, Hume. For Hume by his radical scepticism has lost any means of making himself—or others—intelligible to himself, let alone, to others. His very scepticism itself becomes unintelligible.

There is perhaps a possible world in which 'empiricism' would have become the name of a mental illness, while 'paranoia' would be the name of a well-accredited theory of knowledge. For in this world empiricists would be consistent and unrelenting—unlike Hume—and they would thus lack any means to order their experience of other people or of nature. Even a knowledge of formal logic would not help them; for until they knew how to order their experiences they would possess neither sentences to formalize nor reasons for choosing one way of formalizing them rather than another. Their world would indeed be reduced to that chaos which Bettelheim perceives in the child at the beginning of the oedipal phase. Empiricism would lead not to sophistication, but to regression. Paranoia by contrast would provide considerable resources for living in the world. The empiricist maxims 'Believe only what can be based upon sense-experience' or Occam's razor, would leave us bereft of all generalizations and therefore of all attitudes towards the future (or the past). They would isolate us in a contentless present. But the paranoid maxims 'Interpret everything which happens as an outcome of envious malice' and 'Everyone and everything will let you down' receive continuous confirmation for those who adopt them. Hume cannot answer the question: "What beings surround me?" But Kafka knew the answer to this very well: "In fact the clock has certain personal relationships to me, like many things in the room, save that now, particularly since I gave notice—or rather since I was given notice...—they seem to be beginning to turn their backs on me, above all the calendar.... Lately it is as if it had been metamorphosed. Either it is absolutely uncommunicative—for example, you want its advice, you go up to it, but the only thing it says is 'Feast of the Reformation'—which probably has a deeper significance, but who can discover it?—or, on the contrary, it is nastily ironic."

So in this possible world they will speak of Hume's Disease and of Kafka's Theory of Knowledge. Yet is this possible world so different from that which we inhabit? What leads us to segregate at least some types of mental illness from ordinary, sane behaviour is that they presuppose and embody ways of interpreting the natural and social world which are radically discordant with our customary and, as we take it, justified modes of interpretation. That is, certain types of mental illness seem to presuppose rival theories of knowledge. Conversely every theory of knowledge offers us schemata for accepting some interpretations of the natural and social world rather than others. As Hamlet discovered earlier, the categories of psychiatry and of epistemology must be to some extent interdefinable....

For I shall want to reinforce my thesis that dramatic narrative is the crucial form for the understanding of human action and I shall want to argue that natural science can be a rational form of enquiry if and only if the writing of a true dramatic narrative—that is, of history understood in a particular way—can be a rational activity. Scientific reason turns out to be subordinate to, and intelligible only in terms of, historical reason. And if this is true of the natural sciences, *a fortiori* it will be true also of the social sciences. . . .

What Kuhn originally presented was an account of epistemological crises in natural science which is essentially the same as the Cartesian account of epistemological crises in philosophy. . . .

Kuhn did of course recognise very fully how a scientific tradition may lapse into incoherence. And he must have (with Feyerabend) the fullest credit for recognising in an original way the significance and character of incommensurability. But the conclusions which he draws, namely that "proponents of competing paradigms must fail to make complete contact with each other's viewpoints" and that the transition from one paradigm to another requires a "conversion experience" do not follow from his premises concerning incommensurability. These last are threefold: adherents of rival paradigms during a scientific revolution disagree about what set of problems provide the test for a successful paradigm in that particular scientific situation; their theories embody very different concepts; and they "see different things when they look from the same point in the same direction." Kuhn concludes that "just because it is a transition between incommensurables" the transition cannot be made step by step; and he uses the expression "gestalt switch" as well as "conversion experience." What is important is that Kuhn's account of the transition requires an additional premise. It is not just that the adherents of rival paradigms disagree, but that *every* relevant area of rationality is invaded by that disagreement. It is not just that threefold incommensurability is present but rationality apparently cannot be present in any other form. . . .

What follows from the position thus formulated? It is that scientific revolutions are epistemological crises understood in a Cartesian way. Everything is put in question simultaneously. There is no rational continuity between the situation at the time immediately preceding the crisis and any situation following it. To such a crisis the language of evangelical conversion would indeed be appropriate. We might indeed begin to speak with the voice of Pascal, lamenting that the highest achievement of reason is to learn what reason cannot achieve. But of course, as we have already seen, the Cartesian view of epistemological crises is false; it can never be the case that everything is put in question simultaneously. That would indeed lead to large and unintelligible lacunas not only in the history of practices, such as those of the natural sciences, but also in the personal biographies of scientists.

Moreover Kuhn does not distinguish between two kinds of transition experience. The experience which he is describing seems to be that of the person who having been thoroughly educated into practices defined and informed by one paradigm has to make the transition to a form of scientific practice defined and informed by some radically different paradigm. Of this kind of person what Kuhn asserts may well on occasion be true. But such a scientist is always being invited to make a transition that has already been made by others; the very characterization of his situation presupposes that the new paradigm is already operative while the old still retains some power. But what of the very different type of transition made by those scientists who first invented or discovered the new paradigm? Here Kuhn's divergences from Polanyi ought to have saved him from his original Polanyi-derived conclusion. For Kuhn does recognise very fully and insightfully how traditions lapse into incoherence. What some, at least, of those who are educated into such a tradition may come to recognise is the gap between its *own* epistemological ideals and its actual practices. Of those who recognise this some may tend towards scepticism and some towards instrumentalism. Just this, as we have already seen, characterised late medieval and sixteenth-century science. What the scientific genius, such as

Galileo, achieves in his transition, then, is not only a new way of understanding nature, but also and inseparably a new way of understanding the old science's way of understanding nature. It is because only from the standpoint of the new science can the inadequacy of the old science be characterized that the new science is taken to be more adequate than the old. It is from the standpoint of the new science that the continuities of narrative history are reestablished.

Kuhn has of course continuously modified his earlier formulations and to some degree his position. He has in particular pointed out forcefully to certain of his critics that it is they who have imputed to him the thesis that scientific revolutions are nonrational or irrational events, a conclusion which he has never drawn himself. His own position is "that, if history or any other empirical discipline leads us to believe that the development of science depends essentially on behavior that we have previously thought to be irrational, then we should conclude not that science is irrational, but that our notion of rationality needs adjustment here and there.". . .

What is carried over from one paradigm to another are epistemological ideals and a correlative understanding of what constitutes the progress of a single intellectual life. Just as Descartes's account of his own epistemological crisis was only possible by reason of Descartes's ability to recount his own history, indeed to live his life as a narrative about to be cast into a history—an ability which Descartes himself could not recognise without falsifying his own account of epistemological crises. . . .

Kuhn interestingly denies any notion of truth to natural science other than that truth which attaches to solutions to puzzles and to concrete predictions. In particular he wants to deny that a scientific theory can embody a true ontology, that it can provide a true representative of what is 'really there'. "There is, I think no theory-independent way to reconstruct phrases like 'really there'; the notion of a match between the ontology of a theory and its 'real' counterpart in nature now seems to me illusive in principle."

This is very odd; because science has certainly shown us decisively that some existence-claims are false just because the entities in question are *not* really there—whatever *any* theory may say. Epicurean atomism is not true, there are no humours, nothing with negative weight exists; phlogiston is one with the witches and the dragons. But other existence-claims have survived exceptionally well through a succession of particular theoretical positions: molecules, cells, electrons. Of course our beliefs about molecules, cells, and electrons are by no means what they once were. But Kuhn would be put into a very curious position if he adduced this as a ground for denying that some existence-claims still have excellent warrant and others do not.

What however, worries Kuhn is something else: "in some important respects, though by no means in all, Einstein's general theory of relativity is closer to Aristotle's mechanics than either of them is to Newton's." He therefore concludes that the superiority of Einstein to Newton is in puzzle solving and not in an approach to a true ontology. But what an Einstein ontology enables us to understand is why *from the standpoint of an approach to truth* Newtonian mechanics is superior to Aristotelian. For Aristotelian mechanics as it lapsed into incoherence could never have led us to the special theory; construe them how you will, the Aristotelian problems about time will not yield the questions to which special relativity is the answer. A history which moved from Aristotelianism directly to relativistic physics is not an imaginable history.

What Kuhn's disregard for ontological truth neglects is the way in which the progress toward truth in different sciences is such that they have to converge. The easy reductionism of some positivist programs for science was misleading here, but the rejection of such a reductionism must not blind us to the necessary convergence of physics, chemistry, and biology. Were it not for a concern for ontological truth the nature of our demand for a coherent and convergent relationship between all the sciences would be unintelligible.

Kuhn's view may, of course, seem attractive simply because it seems consistent with a fallibilism which we have every reason to accept. *Perhaps* Einsteinian physics will one day be overthrown just as Newtonian was; perhaps, as Lakatos in his more colourfully rhetorical moments used to suggest, all our scientific beliefs are, always have been, and always will be false. But it seems to be a presupposition of the way in which we do natural science that fallibilism has to be made consistent with the regulative ideal of an approach to a true account of the fundamental order of things and not vice versa. If this is so, Kant is essentially right; the notion of an underlying order—the kind of order that we would expect if the ingenious, unmalicious god of Newton and Einstein had created the universe—*is* a regulative ideal of physics. We do not need to understand this notion quite as Kant did, and our antitheological beliefs may make us uncomfortable in adopting it. But perhaps discomfort at this point is a sign of philosophical progress.

I am suggesting, then, that the best account that can be given of why some scientific theories are superior to others presupposes the possibility of constructing an intelligible dramatic narrative which can claim historical truth and in which such theories are the subject of successive episodes. It is because and only because we can construct better and worse histories of this kind, histories which can be rationally compared with each other, that we can compare theories rationally too. Physics presupposes history and history of a kind that invokes just those concepts of tradition, intelligibility, and epistemological crises for which I argued earlier. It is this that enables us to understand why Kuhn's account of scientific revolutions can in fact be rescued from the charges of irrationalism. . . .

A final thesis can now be articulated. When the connection between narrative and tradition on the one hand, and theory and method on the other, is lost sight of, the philosophy of science is set insoluble problems. Any set of finite observations is compatible with any one out of an infinite set of generalizations. Any attempt to show the rationality of science, once and for all, by providing a rationally justifiable set of rules for linking observations and generalizations breaks down. . . .

It is only when theories are located in history, when we view the demands for justification in highly particular contexts of a historical kind, that we are freed from either dogmatism or capitulation to scepticism. It therefore turns out that the program which dominated the philosophy of science from the eighteenth century onwards, that of combining empiricism and natural science was bound either at worst to break down in irrationalism or at best in a set of successively weakened empiricist programs whose driving force was a deep desire not to be forced into irrationalist conclusions. Hume's Disease is, however, incurable and ultimately fatal and even backgammon (or that type of analytical philosophy which is often the backgammon of the professional philosopher) cannot stave off its progress indefinitely. It is, after all, Vico, and neither Descartes nor Hume, who has turned out to be in the right in approaching the relationship between history and physics.

Paul Ricoeur

Hermeneutics refers to the criticism of texts, and it became an important part of the battle between *philosophes* and churchmen in the eighteenth century. Originally involving the study of word derivations and the tracing of references in a given text, hermeneutics has come to refer to the science of interpretation, a scholarly pursuit of meaning not totally dissimilar to the anthropologist's study of symbolic systems. In this essay, "The Model of the Text: Meaningful Action Considered as a Text," French philosopher Paul Ricoeur (1913–   ), makes an argument that hermeneutics should be used as a model for the social sciences, because social action can be fruitfully approached as a text. A philosopher and linguist, Ricoeur has done more than anyone to reveal the linkages of hermeneutics with both phenomenology and structuralism, and, in the process, has revealed its power in eliciting meaning.

PAUL RICOEUR
(1971)

The Model of the Text:

Meaningful Action

Considered as a Text

My aim in this paper is to test an hypothesis which I will expound briefly.

I assume that the primary sense of the word "hermeneutics" concerns the rules required for the interpretation of the written documents of our culture. In assuming this starting point I am remaining faithful to the concept of *Auslegung* as it was stated by Wilhelm Dilthey; whereas *Verstehen* (understanding, comprehension) relies on the recognition of what a foreign subject means or intends on the basis of all kinds of signs in which psychic life expresses itself (*Lebensausserungen*), *Auslegung* (interpretation, exegesis) implies something more specific: it covers only a limited category of signs, those which are fixed by writing, including all the sorts of documents and monuments which entail a fixation similar to writing.

Now my hypothesis is this: if there are specific problems which are raised by the interpretation of texts because they are texts and not spoken language, and if these problems are the ones which constitute hermeneutics as such, then the human sciences may be said to be hermeneutical (1) inasmuch as their *object* displays some of the features constitutive of a text as text, and (2) inasmuch as their *methodology* develops the same kind of procedures as those of *Auslegung* or text-interpretation.

Hence the two questions to which my paper will be devoted are: (1) To what extent may we consider the notion of text as a good paradigm for the so-called object of the social sciences? (2) To what extent may we use the methodology of text-interpretation as a paradigm for interpretation in general in the field of human sciences? . . .

This article originally appeared in *Social Research* 38 (Autumn, 1971), pp. 529–62, published by the New School for Social Research, New York. Reprinted by permission.

In discourse, we said—and this was the second differential trait of discourse in relation to language—the sentence designates its speaker by diverse indicators of subjectivity and personality. In spoken discourse, this reference by discourse to the speaking subject presents a character of immediacy that we can explain in the following way. The subjective intention of the speaking subject and the meaning of the discourse overlap each other in such a way that it is the same thing to understand what the speaker means and what his discourse means. The ambiguity of the French expression *vouloir-dire*, the German *meinen*, and the English "to mean," attests to this overlapping. It is almost the same thing to ask "What do you mean?" and "What does that mean?" With written discourse, the author's intention and the meaning of the text cease to coincide. This dissociation of the verbal meaning of the text and the mental intention is what is really at stake in the inscription of discourse. Not that we can conceive of a text without an author; the tie between the speaker and the discourse is not abolished, but distended and complicated. The dissociation of the meaning and the intention is still an adventure of the reference of discourse to the speaking subject. But the text's career escapes the finite horizon lived by its author. What the text says now matters more than what the author meant to say, and every exegesis unfolds its procedures within the circumference of a meaning that has broken its moorings to the psychology of its author. Using Plato's expression again, written discourse cannot be "rescued" by all the processes by which spoken discourse supports itself in order to be understood—intonation, delivery, mimicry, gestures. In this sense, the inscription in "external marks," which first appeared to alienate discourse, marks the actual spirituality of discourse. Henceforth, only the meaning "rescues" the meaning, without the contribution of the physical and psychological presence of the author. But to say that the meaning rescues the meaning is to say that only interpretation is the "remedy" for the weakness of discourse which its author can no longer "save." . . .

The event is surpassed by the meaning a third time. Discourse, we said, is what refers to the world, to *a* world. In spoken discourse this means that what the dialogue ultimately refers to is the *situation* common to the interlocutors. This situation in a way surrounds the dialogue, and its landmarks can all be shown by a gesture, or by pointing a finger, or designated in an ostensive manner by the discourse itself through the oblique reference of those other indicators which are the demonstratives, the adverbs of time and place, and the tense of the verb. In oral discourse, we are saying, reference is *ostensive*. What happens to it in written discourse? Are we saying that the text no longer has a reference? This would be to confound reference and monstration, world and situation. Discourse cannot fail to be about something. In saying this, I am separating myself from any ideology of an absolute text. Only a few sophisticated texts satisfy this ideal of a text without reference. They are texts where the play of the signifier breaks away from the signified. But this new form is only valuable as an exception and cannot give the key to all other texts which in one manner or another speak about the world. But what then is the subject of texts when nothing can be shown? Far from saying that the text is then without a world, I will now say without paradox that only man *has a world* and not just a situation. In the same manner that the text frees its meaning from the tutelage of the mental intention, it frees its reference from the limits of ostensive reference. For us, the world is the ensemble of references opened up by the texts. Thus we speak about the "world" of Greece, not to designate any more what were the situations for those who lived them, but to designate the non-situational references which outlive the effacement of the first and which henceforth are offered as possible modes of being, as symbolic dimensions of our being-in-the-world. For me, this is the referent of all literature; no longer the *Umwelt* of the ostensive references of dialogue, but the *Welt* projected by the non-ostensive references of every text that we have read, understood, and loved. To understand a text is at the same time to light up our own situation, or, if you will, to interpolate among the predicates of our situation all the significations which make a *Welt* of our *Umwelt*. It is this enlarging of the *Umwelt* into the *World* which permits us to speak of the references *opened up* by the text—it would be better to say that the references *open up* the world. Here again the spirituality of discourse manifests itself through writing, which frees us from the visibility and limitation of situations by opening up a world for us, that is, new dimensions of our being-in-the-world.

In this sense, Heidegger rightly says—in his analysis of *verstehen* in *Being and Time*—that what we understand first in a discourse is not another person, but a project, that is, the outline of a new being-in-the-world. Only writing, in freeing itself, not only from its author, but from the narrowness of the dialogical situation, reveals this destination of discourse as projecting a world. . . .

But it is perhaps with the fourth trait that the accomplishment of discourse in writing is most exemplary. Only discourse, not language, is addressed to someone. This is the foundation of communication. But it is one thing for discourse to be addressed to an interlocutor equally present to the discourse situation, and another to be addressed, as is the case in virtually every piece of writing, to whoever knows how to read. The narrowness of the dialogical relation explodes. Instead of being addressed just to you, the second person, what is written is addressed to the audience that it creates itself. This, again, marks the spirituality of writing, the counterpart of its materiality and of the alienation which it imposes upon discourse. The *vis-à-vis* of the written is just whoever knows how to read. The co-presence of dialoguing subjects ceases to be the model for every "understanding." The relation writing-reading ceases to be a particular case of the relation speaking-hearing. But at the same time, discourse is revealed as discourse in the universality of its address. In escaping the momentary character of the event, the bounds lived by the author, and the narrowness of ostensive reference, discourse escapes the limits of being face to face. It no longer has a visible auditor. An unknown, invisible reader has become the unprivileged addressee of the discourse.

To what extent may we say that the object of the human sciences conforms to the paradigm of the text? Max Weber defines this object as *sinnhaft orientiertes Verhalten*, as meaningfully oriented behavior. To what extent may we replace the predicate "meaningfully oriented" by what I would like to call *readability-characters* derived from the preceding theory of the text? . . .

My claim is that action itself, action as meaningful, may become an object of science, without losing its character of meaningfulness, through a kind of objectification similar to the fixation which occurs in writing. By this objectification, action is no longer a transaction to which the discourse of action would still belong. It constitutes a delineated pattern which has to be interpreted according to its inner connections.

This objectification is made *possible* by some inner traits of the action which are similar to the structure of the speech-act and which make doing a kind of utterance. In the same way as the fixation by writing is made possible by a dialectic of intentional exteriorization immanent to the speech-act itself, a similar dialectic within the process of transaction prepares the detachment of the *meaning* of the action from the *event* of the action.

First an action has the structure of a locutionary act. It has a *propositional* content which can be identified and re-identified as the same. This "propositional" structure of the action has been clearly and demonstratively expounded by Antony Kenny in *Action, Emotion and Will*. The verbs of action constitute a specific class of predicates which are similar to relations and which, like relations, are irreducible to all the kinds of predicates which may follow the copula "is." The class of action predicates, in its turn, is irreducible to the relations and constitutes a specific set of predicates. Among other traits, the verbs of action allow a plurality of "arguments" capable of complementing the verb, ranging from no argument (Plato taught) to an indeterminate number of arguments (Brutus killed Caesar in the Curia, on the Ides of March, with a . . . , with the help of . . .). This variable polydicity of the predicative structure of the action-sentences is typical of the propositional structure of action. Another trait which is important for the transposition of the concept of fixation from the sphere of discourse to the sphere of action concerns the ontological status of the "complements" of the verbs of action. Whereas relations hold between terms equally existing (or nonexisting), certain verbs of action have a topical subject which is identified as existing and to which the sentence refers, and complements which do not exist. Such is the case with the "mental acts" (to believe, to think, to will, to imagine, etc.). . . . I should like to speak here of the noematic structure of action. It is this noematic structure which may be fixed and detached from the process of interaction and become an object to interpret.

We may now say that an action, like a speech-act, may be identified not only according to its propositional content, but also according to its illocutionary force. Both constitute its "sense-content." Like the speech-act, the action-event (if we may coin this analogical expression) develops a similar dialectic between its temporal status as an appearing and disappearing event, and its logical status as having such-and-such identifiable meaning or "sense-content." But if the "sense-content" is what makes possible the "inscription" of the action-event, what makes it real? In other words, what corresponds to writing in the field of action?

Let us return to the paradigm of the speech-act. What is fixed by writing, we said, is the *noema* of the speaking, the saying as *said*. To what extent may we say that what is *done* is inscribed? Certain metaphors may be helpful at this point. We say that such-and-such event *left its mark* on its time. We speak of marking events. Are not there "marks" on time, the kind of thing which calls for a reading, rather than for a hearing? But what is meant by this metaphor of the printed mark?

The three other criteria of the text will help us to make the nature of this fixation more precise.

In the same way that a text is detached from its author, an action is detached from its agent and develops consequences of its own. This autonomization of human action constitutes the *social* dimension of action. An action is a social phenomenon not only because it is done by several agents in such a way that the role of each of them cannot be distinguished from the role of the others, but also because our deeds escape us and have effects which we did not intend. One of the meanings of the notion of "inscription" appears here. The kind of distance which we found between the intention of the speaker and the verbal meaning of a text occurs also between the agent and its action. It is this distance which makes the ascription of responsibility a specific problem. We do not ask, who smiled? who raised his hand? The doer is present to his doing in the same way as the speaker is present to his speech. With simple actions like those which require no previous action in order to be done, the meaning (*noema*) and the intention (*noesis*) coincide or overlap. With complex actions some segments are so remote from the initial simple segments, which can be said to express the intention of the doer, that the ascription of these actions or action-segments constitutes a problem as difficult to solve as that of authorship in some cases of literary criticism. The assignation of an author becomes a mediate inference well known to the historian who tries to isolate the role of an historical character in the course of events.

We just used the expression "the course of events." Could we not say that what we call the course of events plays the role of the material thing which "rescues" the vanishing discourse when it is written? As we said in a metaphorical way, some actions are events which imprint their mark on their time. But on what did they imprint their mark? Is it not in something spatial that discourse is inscribed? How could an event be printed on something temporal? Social time, however, is not only something which flees; it is also the place of durable effects, of persisting patterns. An action leaves a "trace," it makes its "mark" when it contributes to the emergence of such patterns which become the *documents* of human action.

Another metaphor may help us to delineate this phenomenon of the social "imprint": the metaphor of the "record" or of the "registration." Joel Feinberg, in *Reason and Responsibility*, introduces this metaphor in another context, that of responsibility, in order to show how an action may be submitted to blame. Only actions, he says, which can be "registered" for further notice, placed as an entry on somebody's "record," can be blamed. And when there are no formal records (such as those which are kept by institutions like employment offices, schools, banks, and the police), there is still an informal analogue of these formal records which we call reputation and which constitutes a basis for blaming. I would like to apply this interesting metaphor of a record and reputation to something other than the quasi-judicial situations of blaming, charging, crediting, or punishing. Could we not say that history is itself the record of human action? History is this quasi-"thing" *on* which human action leaves a "trace," puts its mark. Hence the possibility of "archives." Before the archives which are intentionally written down by the memorialists, there is this continuous process of "recording" human action which is history itself as the sum of "marks," the fate of which escapes the control of individual actors. Henceforth history may appear as an autonomous entity, as a play with players who do not know the plot. This hypostasis of history may be denounced as a fallacy, but this fallacy is well entrenched in the process by which human action becomes social action when written down in the archives of history. Thanks to this sedimentation in social time, human deeds become "institutions," in the sense that their meaning no longer coincides with the logical intentions of the actors. The meaning may be "depsychologized" to the point where the *meaning* resides in the work itself. In the words of P. Winch, in *The Idea of Social Science*, the object of the social sciences is a "rule-governed behavior." But this rule is not superimposed; it is the meaning as articulated from within these sedimented or instituted works.

Such is the kind of "objectivity" which proceeds from the "social fixation" of meaningful behavior.

According to our third criterion of what a text is, we could say that a meaningful action is an action the *importance* of which goes "beyond" its *relevance* to its initial situation. This new trait is very similar to the way in which a text breaks the ties of discourse to all the ostensive references. As a result of this emancipation from the situational context, discourse can develop non-ostensive references which we called a "world," in the sense in which we speak of the Greek "world," not in the cosmological sense of the word, but as an ontological dimension.

What would correspond in the field of action to the non-ostensive references of a text?

We opposed, in introducing the present analysis, the *importance* of an action to its *relevance* as regards the situation to which it wanted to respond. An important action, we could say, develops meanings which can be actualized or fulfilled in situations other than the one in which this action occurred. To say the same thing in different words, the meaning of an important event exceeds, overcomes, transcends, the social conditions of its production and may be reenacted in new social contexts. Its importance is its durable relevance and, in some cases, its omnitemporal relevance.

This third trait has important implications as regards the relation between cultural phenomena and their social conditions. Is it not a fundamental trait of the great works of culture to overcome the conditions of their social production, in the same way as a text develops new references and constitutes new "worlds"? It is in this sense that Hegel spoke, in *The Philosophy of Right*, of the institutions (in the largest sense of the word) which "actualize" freedom as a *second nature* in accordance with freedom. This "realm of actual freedom" is constituted by the deeds and works capable of receiving relevance in new historical situations. If this is true, this way of overcoming one's own conditions of production is the key to the puzzling problem raised by Marxism concerning the status of the "superstructures." The autonomy of superstructures as regards their relation to their own infrastructures has its paradigm in the non-ostensive references of a text. A work does not only mirror its time, but it opens up a world which it bears within itself.

Finally, according to our fourth criterion of the text as text, the meaning of human action is also something which is *addressed* to an indefinite range of possible "readers." The judges are not the contemporaries, but, as Hegel said, history itself. *Weltgeschichte ist Weltgericht*. That means that, like a text, human action is an open work, the meaning of which is "in suspense." It is because it "opens up" new references and receives fresh relevance from them, that human deeds are also waiting for fresh interpretations which decide their meaning. All significant events and deeds are, in this way, opened to this kind of practical interpretation through present *praxis*. Human action, too, is opened to anybody who *can read*. In the same way that the meaning of an event is the sense of its forthcoming interpretations, the interpretation by the contemporaries has no particular privilege in this process.

This dialectic between the work and its interpretations will be the topic of the *methodology of interpretation* that we shall now consider. . . .

I want now to show the fruitfulness of this analogy of the text at the level of methodology.

The main implication of our paradigm, as concerns the methods of the social sciences, is that it offers a fresh approach to the question of the relation between *erklären* (explanation) and *verstehen* (understanding, comprehension) in the human sciences. As is well known, Dilthey gave this relation the meaning of a dichotomy. For him, any model of explanation is borrowed from a different region of knowledge, that of the natural sciences with their inductive logic. Thereafter, the autonomy of the so-called *Geisteswissenschaften* is preserved only by recognizing the irreducible factor of understanding a foreign psychic life on the basis of the signs in which this life is immediately exteriorized. But, if *verstehen* is separated from *erklären* by this logical gap, how can the human sciences be scientific at all? Dilthey kept wrestling with this paradox. He discovered more and more clearly, mainly after having read Husserl's *Logical Investigations*, that the *Geisteswissenschaften* are sciences inasmuch as the expressions of life undergo a kind of objectification which makes possible a scientific approach somewhat similar to that of the natural sciences, in spite of the logical gap between *Natur* and *Geist*, factual knowledge and knowledge by signs. In this way the mediation offered by these objectifications appeared to be more important, for a scientific purpose, than the immediate meaningfulness of the expressions of life for everyday transactions.

My own interrogation starts from this last perplexity in Dilthey's thought. And my hypothesis is that the kind of objectification implied in the status of discourse as text provides a better answer to the problem raised by Dilthey. This answer relies on the dialectical character of the relation between *erklären* and *verstehen* as it is displayed in reading.

Our task therefore will be to show to what extent the paradigm of reading, which is the counterpart of the paradigm of writing, provides a solution for the methodological paradox of the human sciences.

The dialectic involved in reading expresses the originality of the relation between writing and reading and its irreducibility to the dialogical situation based on the immediate reciprocity between speaking and hearing. There is a dialectic between explaining and comprehending *because* the writing/reading situation develops a problematic of its own which is not merely an extension of the speaking/hearing situation constitutive of dialogue.

It is here, therefore, that our hermeneutic is most critical as regards the Romanticist tradition in hermeneutics which took the dialogical situation as the standard for the hermeneutical operation applied to the text. My contention is that it is this operation, on the contrary, which reveals the meaning of what is already hermeneutical in dialogical understanding. Then, if the dialogical relation does not provide us with the paradigm of reading, we have to build it as an original paradigm, as a paradigm of its own.

This paradigm draws its main features from the status of the text itself as characterized by (1) the fixation of the meaning, (2) its dissociation from the mental intention of the author, (3) the display of non-ostensive references, and (4) the universal range of its addressees. These four traits taken together constitute the "objectivity" of the text. From this "objectivity" derives a possibility of *explaining* which is not derived in any way from another field, that of natural events, but which is congenial to this kind of objectivity. Therefore there is no transfer from one region of reality to another—let us say, from the sphere of facts to the sphere of signs. It is within the same sphere of signs that the process of objectification takes place and gives rise to explanatory procedures. And it is within the same sphere of signs that explanation and comprehension are confronted.

I propose that we consider this dialectic in two different ways: (1) as proceeding from comprehension to explanation, and (2) as proceeding from explanation to comprehension. The exchange and the reciprocity between both procedures will provide us with a good approximation of the dialectical character of the relation.

At the end of each half of this demonstration I shall try to indicate briefly the possible extension of the paradigm of reading to the whole sphere of the human sciences.

This first dialectic—or rather this first figure of a unique dialectic—may be conveniently introduced by our contention that to understand a text is not to rejoin the author. The disjunction of the meaning and the intention creates an absolutely original situation which engenders the dialectic of *erklären* and *verstehen*. If the objective meaning is something other than the subjective intention of the author, it may be construed in various ways. The problem of the right understanding can no longer be solved by a simple return to the alleged intention of the author.

This construction necessarily takes the form of a process. As Hirsch says in his book *Validity in Interpretation*, there are no rules for making good guesses. But there are methods for validating guesses. This dialectic between guessing and validating constitutes one figure of our dialectic between comprehension and explanation.

In this dialectic both terms are decisive. Guessing corresponds to what Schleiermacher called the "divinatory," validation to what he called the "grammatical." My contribution to the theory of this dialectic will be to link it more tightly to the theory of the text and text-reading.

Why do we need an art of guessing? Why do we have to "construe" the meaning?

Not only—as I tried to say a few years ago—because language is metaphorical and because the double meaning of metaphorical language requires an art of deciphering which tends to unfold the several layers of meaning. The case of the metaphor is only a particular case for a general theory of hermeneutics. In more general terms, a text has to be construed because it is not a mere sequence of sentences, all on an equal footing and separately understandable. A text is a whole, a totality. The relation between whole and parts—as in a work of art or in an animal—requires a specific kind of "judgment" for which Kant gave the theory in the Third Critique. Correctly, the whole appears as a hierarchy of topics, or primary and subordinate topics. The reconstruction of the text as a whole necessarily has a circular character, in the sense that the presupposition of a certain kind of whole is implied in the recognition of the parts. And reciprocally, it is in construing the details that we construe the whole. There is no necessity and no evidence concerning what is important and what is unimportant, what is essential and what is unessential. The judgment of importance is a guess.

To put the difficulty in other terms, if a text is a whole, it is once more an individual like an animal or a work of art. As an individual it can only be reached by a process of narrowing the scope of generic concepts concerning the literary genre, the class of text to which this text belongs, the structures of different kinds which intersect in this text. The localization and the individualization of this unique text is still a guess. . . .

At the same time, we are prepared to give an acceptable meaning to the famous concept of a *hermeneutical circle*. Guess and validation are in a sense circularly related as subjective and objective approaches to the text. But this circle is not a vicious circularity. It would be a cage if we were unable to escape the kind of "self-confirmability" which, according to Hirsch, threatens this relation between guess and validation. To the procedures of validation also belong procedures of invalidation similar to the criteria of falsifiability emphasized by Karl Popper in his *Logic of Scientific Discovery*. The role of falsification is played here by the conflict between competing interpretations. An interpretation must not only be probable, but more probable than another. There are criteria of relative superiority which may easily be derived from the logic of subjective probability.

In conclusion, if it is true that there is always more than one way of construing a text, it is not true that all interpretations are equal and may be assimilated to so-called "rules of thumb." The text is a limited field of possible constructions. The logic of validation allows us to move between the two limits of dogmatism and skepticism. It is always possible to argue for or against an interpretation, to confront interpretations, to arbitrate between them, and to seek for an agreement, even if this agreement remains beyond our reach.

To what extent is this dialectic between guessing and validating paradigmatic for the whole field of the human sciences?

That the meaning of human actions, of historical events, and of social phenomena may be *construed* in several different ways is well known by all experts in the human sciences. What is less known and understood is that this methodological perplexity is founded in the nature of the object itself and, moreover, that it does not condemn the scientist to oscillate between dogmatism and skepticism. As the logic of text-interpretation suggests, there is a *specific plurivocity* belonging to the meaning of human action. Human action, too, is a limited field of possible constructions.

A trait of human action which has not yet been emphasized in the preceding analysis may provide an interesting link between the specific plurivocity of the text and the analogical plurivocity of human action. This trait concerns the relation between the purposive and the motivational dimensions of action. As many philosophers in the new field of Action Theory have shown, the purposive character of an action is fully recognized when the answer to the question "what" is explained in terms of an answer to the question "why." I *understand* what you intended to do, if you are able to *explain* to me why you did such-and-such an action. Now, what kinds of answer to the question "why" make sense? Only those answers which afford a motive understood as a reason for—and not as a cause. And what is a reason for —which is not a cause? It is, in the terms of E. Anscombe and A. I. Meldon, an expression, or a phrase, which allows us to consider the action *as* this or that. If you tell me that you did this or that because of jealousy or in a spirit of revenge, you are asking me to put your action in the light of this category of feelings or dispositions. By the same token, you claim to make sense with your action. You claim to make it understandable for others and for yourself. This attempt is particularly helpful when applied to what E. Anscombe calls the "desirability-character" of wanting. Wants and beliefs have the character not only of being *forces* which make people act in such-and-such ways, but of making sense as a result of the apparent good which is the correlate of their desirability-character. I may have to answer the question, *as* what do you want this? On the basis of these desirability-characters, and the apparent good which corresponds to them, it is possible to *argue* about the meaning of an action, to argue for or against this or that interpretation. In this way the account of motives already foreshadows a logic of argumentation procedures. Could we not say that what can be (and must be) *construed* in human action is the motivational basis of this action, i.e., the set of desirability-characters which may explain it? And could we not say that the process of *arguing* linked to the explanation of action by its motives unfolds a kind of plurivocity which makes action similar to a text?

What seems to legitimate this extension from guessing the meaning of a text to guessing the meaning of an action is that in arguing about the meaning of an action I put my wants and my beliefs at a distance and submit them to a concrete dialectic of confrontation with opposite points of view. This way of putting my action at a distance in order to make sense of my own motives paves the way for the kind of distanciation which occurs with what we called the social *inscription* of human action and to which we applied the metaphor of the "record." The same actions which may be put into "records" and henceforth "recorded" may also be *explained* in different ways according to the multivocity of the arguments applied to their motivational background.

If we are correct in extending to action the concept of "guess" which we took as a synonym for *verstehen*, we may also extend to the field of action the concept of "validation" in which we saw an equivalent of *erklären*.

Here, too, the modern theory of action provides us with an intermediary link between the procedures of literary criticism and those of the social sciences. Some thinkers have tried to elucidate the way in which we *impute* actions to agents in the light of the juridical procedures by which a judge or a tribunal validates a decision concerning a contract or a crime. In a famous article, "The Ascription of Responsibility and Rights," H. L. A. Hart shows in a very convincing way that juridical reasoning does not at all consist in applying general laws to particular cases, but each time in construing uniquely referring decisions. These decisions terminate a careful refutation of the excuses and defenses which could "defeat" the claim or the accusation. In saying that human actions are fundamentally "defeatible" and that juridical reasoning is an argumentative process which comes to grips with the different ways of "defeating" a claim or an accusation, Hart has paved the way for a general theory of validation in which juridical reasoning would be the fundamental link between validation in literary criticism and validation in the social sciences.... Only in the tribunal is there a moment when the procedures of appeal are exhausted. But it is because the decision of the judge is implemented by the force of public power. Neither in literary criticism, nor in the social sciences, is there such a last word. Or, if there is any, we call that violence.

The same dialectic between comprehension and understanding may receive a new meaning if taken in the reverse way, from explanation to understanding. This new *Gestalt* of the dialectic proceeds from the nature of the referential function of the text. This referential function, as we said, exceeds the mere ostensive designation of the situation common to both speaker and hearer in the dialogical situation. This abstraction from the surrounding world gives rise to two opposite attitudes. As readers, we may either remain in a kind of state of suspense as regards any kind of referred-to world, or we may actualize the potential non-ostensive references of the text in a new situation, that of the reader. In the first case, we treat the text as a worldless entity; in the second, we create a new ostensive reference through the kind of "execution" which the art of reading implies. These two possibilities are equally entailed by the act of reading, conceived as their dialectical interplay. . . .

I want now to show in what way "explanation" (*erklären*) requires "understanding" (*verstehen*) and brings forth in a new way the inner dialectic which constitutes "interpretation" as a whole.

As a matter of fact, nobody stops with a conception of myths and of narratives as formal as this algebra of constitutive units. This can be shown in different ways. First, even in the most formalized presentation of myths by Lévi-Strauss, the units which he calls "mythemes" are still expressed as sentences which bear meaning and reference. Can anyone say that their meaning as such is neutralized when they enter into the "bundle of relations" which alone is taken into account by the "logic" of the myth? Even this bundle of relations, in its turn, must be written in the form of a sentence. Finally, the kind of language game which the whole system of oppositions and combinations embodies, would lack any kind of significance if the oppositions themselves, which, according to Lévi-Strauss, the myth tends to mediate, were not meaningful oppositions concerning birth and death, blindness and lucidity, sexuality and truth. Beside these existential conflicts there would be no contradictions to overcome, no logical function of the myth as an attempt to solve these contradictions. Structural analysis does not exclude, but presupposes, the opposite hypothesis concerning the myth, i.e., that it has a meaning as a narrative of the origins. Structural analysis merely represses this function. But it cannot suppress it. The myth would not even function as a logical operator if the propositions which it combines did not point toward boundary situations. Structural analysis, far from getting rid of this radical questioning, restores it at a level of higher radicality.

If this is true, could we not say that the function of structural analysis is to lead from a surface-semantics, that of the narrated myth, to a depth-semantics, that of the boundary situations which constitute the ultimate "referent" of the myth?

I really believe that if such were not the function of structural analysis, it would be reduced to a sterile game, a divisive algebra, and even the myth would be bereaved of the function which Lévi-Strauss himself assigns to it, that of making men aware of certain oppositions and of tending toward their progressive mediation. To eliminate this reference to the *aporias* of existence around which mythic thought gravitates would be to reduce the theory of myth to the necrology of the meaningless discourses of mankind. If, on the contrary, we consider structural analysis as a stage—and a necessary one—between a naive interpretation and a critical interpretation, between a surface-interpretation and a depth-interpretation, then it would be possible to locate explanation and understanding at two different stages of a unique *hermeneutical arc*. It is this depth-semantics which constitutes the genuine object of understanding and which requires a specific affinity between the reader and the kind of things the text is *about*.

But we must not be misled by this notion of personal *affinity*. The depth-semantics of the text is not what the author intended to say, but what the text is about, i.e., the non-ostensive reference of the text. And the non-ostensive reference of the text is the kind of world opened up by the depth-semantics of the text.

Therefore what we want to understand is not something hidden behind the text, but something disclosed in front of it. What has to be understood is not the initial situation of discourse but what points toward a possible world. Understanding has less than ever to do with the author and his situation. It wants to grasp the world-propositions opened up by the references of the text. To understand a text is to follow its movement from sense to reference, from what it says, to what it talks about. In this process the *mediating* role played by structural analysis constitutes both the justification of this objective approach and the rectification of the subjective approach. We are definitely prevented from identifying understanding with some kind of intuitive grasping of the intention underlying the text. What we have said about the depth-semantics which structural analysis yields invites us rather to think of the sense of the text as an injunction starting from the text, as a new way of looking at things, as an injunction to think in a certain manner.

Such is the reference born of depth-semantics. The text speaks of a possible world and of a possible way of orientating oneself within it. The dimensions of this world are properly opened up by, disclosed by, the text. Disclosure is the equivalent for written language of ostensive reference for spoken language.

If, therefore, we preserve the language of Romanticist hermeneutics when it speaks of overcoming the distance, of making "one's own," of appropriating what was distant, other, foreign, it will be at the price of an important corrective. That which we make our own— *Aneignung* in German—that which we appropriate, is not a foreign experience, but the power of disclosing a world which constitutes the reference of the text.

This link between disclosure and appropriation is, to my mind, the cornerstone of a hermeneutic which would claim both to overcome the shortcomings of historicism and to remain faithful to the original intention of Schleiermacher's hermeneutics. To understand an author better than he could understand himself is to display the power of disclosure implied in his discourse beyond the limited horizon of his own existential situation. The process of distanciation, of atemporalization, to which we connected the phrase of *Erklärung*, is the fundamental presupposition for this enlarging of the horizon of the text.

This second figure or *Gestalt* of the dialectic between explanation and comprehension has a strong paradigmatic character which holds for the whole field of the human sciences. I want to emphasize three points.

First, the structural model, taken as a paradigm for explanation, may be extended beyond textual entities to all social phenomena because it is not limited in its application to linguistic signs, but applies to all kinds of signs which are analogous to linguistic signs. The intermediary link between the model of the text and social phenomena is constituted by the notion of semiological systems. A linguistic system, from the point of view of semiology, is only a species within the semiotic genre, although this species has the privilege of being a paradigm for the other species of the genre. We can say therefore that a structural model of explanation can be generalized as far as all social phenomena which may be said to have a semiological character, i.e., as far as it is possible to define the typical relations of a semiological system at their level: the general relation between code and message, relations among the specific units of the code, the relation between signifier and signified, the typical relation within and among social messages, the structure of communication as an exchange of messages, etc. Inasmuch as the semiological model holds, the semiotic or symbolic function, i.e., the function of substituting signs for things and of representing things by the means of signs, appears to be more than a mere effect in social life. It is its very foundation. We should have to say, according to this generalized function of the semiotic, not only that the symbolic function is social, but that social reality is fundamentally symbolic.

If we follow this suggestion, then the kind of explanation which is implied by the structural model appears to be quite different from the classical causal model, especially if causation is interpreted in Humean terms as a regular sequence of antecedents and consequents with no inner logical connection between them. Structural systems imply relations of a quite different kind, correlative rather than sequential or consecutive. If this is true, the classical debate about motives and causes which has plagued the theory of action these last decades loses its importance. If the search for correlations within semiotic systems is the main task of explanation, then we have to reformulate the problem of motivation in social groups in new terms. But it is not the aim of this paper to develop this implication.

Secondly, the second paradigmatic factor in our previous concept of text-interpretation proceeds from the role which we assigned to depth-semantics *between* structural analysis and appropriation. This mediating function of depth-semantics must not be overlooked, since the appropriation's losing its psychological and subjective character and receiving a genuine epistemological function depends on it.

Is there something similar to the depth-semantics of a text in social phenomena?

I should tend to say that the search for correlations within and between social phenomena treated as semiotic entities would lose importance and interest if it would not yield *something like* a depth-semantics. In the same way as linguistic games are forms of life, according to the famous aphorism of Wittgenstein, social structures are also attempts to cope with existential perplexities, human predicaments and deep-rooted conflicts. In this sense, these structures, too, have a referential dimension. They point toward the *aporias* of social existence, the same *aporias* around which mythical thought gravitates. And this analogical function of reference develops traits very similar to what we called the non-ostensive reference of a text, i.e., the display of a *Welt* which is no longer an *Umwelt*, the projection of a world which is more than a situation. May we not say that in social science, too, we proceed from naive interpretations to critical interpretations, from surface-interpretations to depth-interpretations *through* structural analysis? But it is depth-interpretation which gives meaning to the whole process.

This last remark leads us to our third and last point.

If we follow the paradigm of the dialectic between explanation and understanding to its end, we must say that the meaningful patterns which a depth-interpretation wants to grasp cannot be understood without a kind of personal commitment similar to that of the reader who grasps the depth-semantics of the text and makes it his "own." Everybody knows the objection which an extension of the concept of appropriation to the social sciences is exposed to. Does it not legitimate the intrusion of personal prejudices, of subjective bias into the field of scientific inquiry? Does it not introduce all the paradoxes of the hermeneutical circle into the human sciences? In other words, does not the paradigm of disclosure *plus* appropriation destroy the very concept of a human science? The way in which we introduced this pair of terms within the framework of text-interpretation provides us not only with a paradigmatic problem, but with a paradigmatic solution. This solution is not to deny the role of personal commitment in understanding human phenomena, but to quality it.

As the model of text-interpretation shows, understanding has nothing to do with an *immediate* grasping of a foreign psychic life or with an *emotional* identification with a mental intention. Understanding is entirely *mediated* by the whole of explanatory procedures which precede it and accompany it. The counterpart of this personal appropriation is not something which can be *felt*, it is the dynamic meaning released by the explanation which we identified earlier with the reference of the text, i.e., its power of disclosing a world.

The paradigmatic character of text-interpretation must be applied down to this ultimate implication. This means that the conditions of an authentic appropriation, as they were displayed in relation to texts, are themselves paradigmatic. Therefore we are not allowed to exclude the final act of personal commitment from the whole of objective and explanatory procedures which mediate it.

This qualification of the notion of personal commitment does not eliminate the "hermeneutical circle." This circle remains an insuperable structure of knowledge when it is applied to human things, but this qualification prevents it from becoming a vicious circle.

Ultimately, the correlation between explanation and understanding, between understanding and explanation, is the "hermeneutical circle."

Postmodernist Thought

The De[con]struction

of Modernity

Introduction

The adjective "postmodern" was first popularized during the 1970s in reference to a new sensibility in the world of the arts and architecture. Postmodern architects rejected the high modern architectural project—the construction of rational and pragmatic buildings which could lead to the progressive amelioration of the human condition. Postmodernists also broke with the modernist credo that took reason as the first principle of all design efforts. One of the greatest modern architects of public housing, Le Corbusier, embraced the benevolent effects of technology and the universal, international truths of the proletariat. His utilitarian high-rise structures were meant to bring "Man" adequate light, space, and plumbing, and thus ensure a better existence for their inhabitants.

However "enlightened" functional modern structures appeared on blueprint, postmodernists have often interpreted their ultimate effect as alienating and misguided. For those interested in a precise chronology, the postmodern architectural critic Charles Jencks dates the death of modernism, and subsequently the emergence of "postmodernism" as a cultural aesthetic, to the demolition of a "technologically-perfect" housing development in 1972. Although envisioned as *the* solution to inner-city squalor, the award-winning Pruitt-Igoe housing structure of St. Louis, a clone of Le Corbusier's dream of modern life, had simply become uninhabitable. Despite the grandiose ideological intentions of urban planning, the "rational" Pruitt-Igo structure created an unintended final reality, an impersonal, even hostile environment which may have increased levels of violence.[1]

Having recognized an incapacity of building to better the human lot, postmodern architects now produce an eclectic mixture of styles which speak not of the elitist project of saving humanity, but of a far less serious goal, that of amusing people of different cultures. For the postmodernist, structures need no longer be symbolic of the progressive ideals of Western civilization. Postmodern architects construct corporate palaces and shopping malls which exhibit "dual coding" or speak two languages: buildings recount our illustrious heritage through historical references, but also speak the "commercial slang of the street."[2] This innovative aesthetic can be viewed in Charles Moore's Piazza d'Italia in New Orleans. The building is composed of disjointed classical Greek and Roman architectural formulas, but its use of history has no meaning for our present. It is a theatrical and fragmented site to which all American immigrants are invited to amuse themselves and, of course, to purchase.

If rationalism was the ideological foundation of modernist urban planning, postmodernist urban *design* has dispensed with such an unattainable and hegemonic precept. Postmodern architects favor "dual coding" or schizophrenia, a word which for them has no pejorative connotation. For the postmodernist, the pursuit of universality and homogeneous truths produced tenements, that is, the Enlightenment project inspired projects (and here the negative connotation rests intact) such as the Pruitt-Igoe housing development. As a result, postmodern buildings tempt us to abandon thoughts of progress, and enjoy heterogeneous messages. They suggest that logocentrism, the belief in the existence of universal and homogeneous truths, is an ideological house of cards. We should now seek endless play with multiple decks—the disparate truths of advanced consumer capitalism.

Postmodernism describes more than architectural innovation. The new architectural "style" is a metaphor for a new condition; in the late twentieth century, social scientists and artists alike have found themselves alienated from what they view as the "empty" promises of modernity. Postmodernism is a general rubric that encompasses many aesthetic undertakings and critical methods, all of which hint at the fact that we may be witnessing a major reconfiguration of cultural and philosophical paradigms. Postmodernism is not, however, a new imperative with strictly defined limitations and prescriptions. Postmodernism hints at pluralism, the proliferation of various means of fashioning and viewing reality. But it does not presume to proselytize us into a global, albeit alternative, religion.

The characteristics of postmodernist thought are the subject of intense debate, and therefore the thinkers who have generated it do not lend themselves to concise categorization. Some radical postmodernists appear hopeless about the future, while others display more tempered attitudes. The postmodernists featured in this section belong to this latter group. While they may be critical of dominant discourses, they are not pessimistic. On the contrary they are ecstatic, holding the demise of Western metanarratives to be cause for celebration. Release from epistemological and cultural norms offers endless possibilities for creative activity. Who are these postmodernists, the "prophets of extremity"[3] as one historian calls them, who contest faith in the doctrines of modernity? Michel Foucault, Hayden White, Jacques Derrida, and Richard Rorty, whose writings are featured in this section, represent a range of postmodern concerns.[4]

White, an American historian, once published conventional intellectual histories. He is now the foremost American critic of the modern historiographical tradition, demanding that his colleagues question the formulaic structures with which they represent the past. Derrida is a French philosopher, literary critic, and spokesperson for postmodernism. The most radical of the thinkers studied here, he dispenses with the "established" categorizations of human knowledge and consciousness. Through an intensified focus upon the inherent contradictions within language and the text, Derrida interprets the inconsistencies rather than what are commonly held to be coherent messages within the spoken language and written canon. Rorty, an American professor of philosophy, contests those philosophical traditions which claim to establish the foundations of knowledge and interpretation. He prefers a "pragmatic" search for social consensus which circumvents the, in his opinion, pointless pursuit for ultimate, foundational categories such as "just" versus "unjust."

The work of Foucault has had the most influential impact upon the social sciences, especially the historical profession. Like White, Rorty, and Derrida, Foucault has attacked the basic foundations of social scientific theory in critiquing the assumptions inherent within modern thought. He reformulated "great" philosophical questions and turned the generic epistemological query "what is knowledge?" on its head. Foucault achieved this end through tracing how broad conceptual categories such as madness, sexuality, and humanity, hitherto taken for granted as "natural," function as mechanisms of power. For Foucault, sexuality, madness, and many other all-encompassing categories are the sites of knowledge-production within specific social contexts. Through his "genealogies of power/knowledge," Foucault demonstrated how knowing constitutes a locus of power.

As we have seen, the most famous, and perhaps infamous, postmodernist thinkers are French, yet postmodernism is a cultural and intellectual phenomenon whose influence has been most pervasive in the United States. We cannot simplistically claim that postmodern ideas emerged from the European and American "debacles" of the Sixties and Seventies, nor can we attribute it to the cyclical return of a nihilism and cultural despair of yet another fin-de-siècle. Nevertheless, the following events may suggest why postmodernism has been received with such enthusiasm in many quarters.

The failure of the student revolts of the Sixties to effect other than cursory transformations of the "Establishment" may account for the bitter tone of some postmodernist attitudes towards agency and progress. Protest initially led to drastic changes in public policy, the Civil Rights movement and the decision to withdraw from Vietnam being the most important and memorable examples in the United States. Despite the legacy of Martin Luther King, Jr., legislative reform, and progressive ideals, racism still mars the present. The Los Angeles riots of April 1992 and the situation in the nation once known as Yugoslavia confirm this truth. The continued existence of xenophobic and prejudiced cultural viewpoints is only one facet of what postmodernists refer to as a dismal modern record. The perpetuation of inegalitarian economic and political systems and the destruction of the environment in the name of progress are also cited. The reverence in which technology and science are held, some postmodernists remark, made possible the world wars of this century, Hiroshima, efforts at racial cleansing, and the potential for nuclear holocaust.

The above events and trends are but a smattering of causes for the moral and cultural malaise of our collective present. Postmodernist thought can be categorized as an attempt to displace the quasi-religious metanarratives which are held responsible for the questionable modern record. Postmodern thinkers have lost their faith in what they refer to as the dogma of modernity. For them the Enlightenment successfully challenged the tyrannical authority of Christianity, but it merely replaced religion with an equally hegemonic set of prerogatives. Postmodernists reject these Enlightenment scriptures because they are totalizing metanarratives. A metanarrative is a legitimizing discourse which draws upon a long-term story (narrative) such as the Enlightenment "emancipation of the subject" from evil incarnate—ignorance. Postmodernists have identified three Enlightenment metanarratives as targets: namely the subject or rational human agent, the notion of secular salvation or progress, and science in its broadest sense, including an entire constellation of philosophical and metaphysical foundations. For them, these modern scriptures—the subject, secular salvation, and science—no longer offer convincing or valid justification for the activities we undertake in our contemporary world.

The demise of the subject or "Man" is at first glance the most disturbing reassessment of the modern condition. Postmodernists believe "Man," or humanity, was a concept created during the Enlightenment, as humans transferred the power previously attributed to an omniscient God to their own faculties. The moderns appropriated God's grammatical capital (letter) to become deified "Man." The articulation of categories such as consciousness and objectivity provided the epistemological foundation for belief in an autonomous and universal human subject, a subject whose existence, once verified, the postmodernists note, became the focus of control, discipline, and subjection.

Postmodernism is not the first philosophical strain which has contested certain aspects of the subject. Romantic poets sought to revalorize the spiritual and irrational elements within human consciousness. The late nineteenth-century anti-positivist Friedrich Nietzsche found that a strict focus on human rationality engendered weakness, and argued for a more instinctual and formless "will-to-power." Postmodernists go beyond a critique of the elements composing the subject's constitution, to posit the very death of the subject. Human consciousness, either logical and reasoned or intuitive and emotional, is no longer the point of contention. Through a renewed focus upon linguistic structure, language, rather than the powers of the human being, is seen as the focal point of the human world.

Ferdinand de Saussure and succeeding generations of structural linguists had attacked the notion of language as representative of a fixed reality. In simpler terms, earlier strains of thought such as rationalism and empiricism held that the individual subject speaks a language, molding private marks to meet his or her own purposes. Poststructuralist linguistic theory posits a different reality, in which utterances do not simply "represent" truths. Words, if perceived as floating signs, are rendered meaningful only through shared usage by groups rather than mere isolated individuals. This shift has invalidated the autonomous and private thoughts of the individual, and emphasized the hegemony of public group activities.

Linguistic indeterminacy renders the notion of a powerful individual human subject problematic. It contests the existence of autonomous persons who construct their own reality through use of their "free will" and reason. We do not speak language and create our own reality. Language speaks through us and follows a group-determined order which implies that our own personal use of words is relatively insignificant.

The eclipse of the rational autonomous subject behind linguistic relativism has repercussions for modern conceptions of secular salvation, familiar to us as the narrative of progress. Some postmodernists hail the death of this progress, as it has been told by conventional history. The "death of history" may sound like an absurd and ludicrous slogan, or perhaps, may already be familiar to you. Friedrich Nietzsche denounced the malevolent effects of history in many of his works, as a cultural affliction which deprives both the individual and society at large of volition. Many postmodernists depart from Nietzsche's warnings about history, to a blatant rejection of it altogether, known as an "End-of-History" philosophy. This allows some critics to liken them to the caricatural man in the street proclaiming the end of the world on a placard. Not mere prophets of doom, through the deconstruction of past methods of history, postmodernists seek to divulge the sources, and unearth the mythical nature, of historical storytelling.

Postmodernists object that the moderns have conceptualized time and space as fixed, linear, and measurable. But more importantly, modern historians have recounted only those narratives which are a testimonial to the success of the Western world. In short, the historical profession has privileged the telling of a peculiarly Occidental success story. History has told only the "right" stories in the past: if the central character of the Western story is the rational white male, the plot is this autonomous individual's correct preference for progress, its vindicatory rationale of utilitarianism, and its means, scientific technology.

Postmodernists have dissected the historical metanarrative known as progress. The radical postmodernist Jean-François Lyotard has coined the term "performativity," which refers to the modern cultural belief that scientific productivity is the highest of human aspirations. Increased technological and industrial output is achieved only through knowledge. Knowledge, usually culled from empirical and statistical bases, and then rationalized through philosophical justification, becomes power. "Power-knowledge," as Michel Foucault called it, has only been perpetuated through prejudiced focus upon the winners in history, or those who utilized technological know-how to the fullest. For postmodernists, progress has too long provided the plot for historical narratives, and the knowledge which founds our belief in secular salvation must also be deconstructed.

If the moderns told the story of the strong, autonomous individual and his use of technology to better the world, postmodernists see science as this individual's most potent means of self-justification. According to the radical postmodernist Lyotard, the very word "modern" refers to any science which "legitimates itself . . . [by] making an explicit appeal to some grand narrative, such as the dialectics of Spirit, the Hermeneutics of meaning, the emancipation of the rational or working subject, or the creation of wealth."[5] Postmodernists attack knowledge-accumulation in all of its realms, especially the most hallowed of modern endeavors, science (which here refers to *all* sciences including philosophy).

According to Derrida, philosophy has dominated the center of the Modern stage, playing a presumptuous role. One particular branch of philosophy known as "epistemology," which examines the origins, methods, and limits of knowledge, has been endowed with the status of a "privileged" discourse. Epistemology strictly defined transcendent categories of "objectivity," thought to be capable of representing and duplicating reality. The French structuralists, in the Fifties and Sixties, attempted to bypass the constraints of epistemology. Claude Lévi-Strauss diminished the value of science through likening it to the much vilified competitor-magic. In this sense, structuralism sought to make philosophical speculation unnecessary. Postmodernists believe structuralism did not go far enough, as it still relied upon binary metaphysical oppositions, in this case a simple reversal of the hierarchical view of science, and the restitution of its competitor, magic.

Postmodernist philosophers Derrida and Rorty believe that structuralism "failed" because it remained persistent about assigning a final "meaning" to any object of study. Derrida and Rorty, therefore, have followed paths toward a Nietzschean "beyond-philosophy." They focus upon multiple interpretations, often called a radical hermeneutic, containing no pretense to ultimate truth. Unlike their predecessors, Derrida and Rorty find it absurd that any discipline or field should claim a monopoly over objective truths. Through innovative conceptual methods such as Derridean "deconstruction," they search for conflictual tendencies within thought. Deconstruction tears a text apart, searching for its internal inconsistencies. While structuralism shared this focus upon inconsistency, it often forced closure upon apparent contradictions, assigning them a final, universal meaning. Rather than constructing final and unified "Truths," postmodernists delineate contradictory notions of truth.

The disruption of the scientific endeavor is not the final stage of some unidentified and unfinished Western teleology. However, it does suggest a philosophical trajectory. If the Enlightenment thinkers first queried, "what is knowledge?", nineteenth-century social theorists added, "what is knowledge *good for*?" Poststructuralists such as Foucault reformulated such generic questions, asking "how does knowledge work?" Derrida goes one step further, searching for what is beyond knowledge and meaning. He asks the radical question "do knowledge and its supposed corollary, meaning, truly exist?"

Another radical postmodernist prophet recently claimed that the "secret of theory is, indeed, that truth doesn't exist."[6] Such apparently devastating remarks have led critics to denounce postmodernist thought as "creative destruction" run amok. Reactions to postmodernism have been harsh. Critics charge it with relativism, an appalling lack of ethics, or a pervasive cynicism. Some claim postmodernism harbors menacing anarchical implications, making politics into a rhetorical device devoid of any means of effecting change. The nihilistic strains of postmodernism, these opponents claim, obviate any need to pay more than cursory attention to its precepts: the political and ethical irresponsibility of postmodernist thought destroys any novelty of perception which it may offer. More humorous critics such as David Harvey and Terry Eagleton believe we should take postmodernism with a grain of salt. Rather than attempting to make sense of it, we should realize it is merely a means of making "cents" since "pomo" ideas have been appropriated by the media, consumer culture, and the academic Establishment.

Yet if concepts such as nature, science, and objectivity are no longer representative of a concrete reality, where do postmodernists suggest we go from a here which may already be nowhere? As Jencks wryly notes, "Very convenient this slippery word [post], it simply states where you've left, not arrived."[7] Although the subject, secular salvation, and science may be but mere components of an "inflated rhetoric,"[8] the postmodern individual can still avoid a pointless and absurd existence. Postmodernism does indeed seek to evade the eternal return of conjecture about the ultimate nature of reality, through proffering heterogeneity as an alternative. Rather than positing the preference of one bipolar opposite over another, postmodernism bends traditional antinomies such as good and bad. Implicit hierarchies are rearranged and new pairings do not suggest the superiority of one element in the pair. Rather than debate the dualism, objectivity versus subjectivity, the postmodernist cultivates an interest in something considered irrelevant by modern terms, or forgotten, undervalued, peripheral, or silenced.

For example, postmodern culture revels in the notion of "kitsch," toppling the traditional binary distinction between elite (valuable) and popular (debased). The paintings of Andy Warhol are exemplary of this new aesthetic; one particularly famous canvas utilizes the motif of cheap imitation of a commodified star (Marilyn Monroe) as art form. While the nineteenth-century modernist *avant-garde* predicated its success upon shocking the spectator, the regnant artistic credo known as *épater le bourgeois*, postmodernist art cannot be bothered. It does not seek the elitist status of newness, but ruthlessly and unabashedly recycles the old.

Postmodern film reappropriates "classic" pictures and recycles their motifs, employing the concept of intertextuality, in which two previously incommensurable symbolic worlds are mixed together at random, neither taking precedence. This effect can be achieved through an anachronistic mixture of chronological setting and costume. The director David Lynch in *Blue Velvet* (1986) combines the two moral worlds of middle-class suburban "purity" and its supposed evil twin, the violent underworld of drugs and dementia. In conventional modern film, one of these worlds is deemed more valuable than the other at fade-away, but Lynch gives both equal airtime, depriving spectators of a perspective on which world is "right." We, as spectators, must achieve our own closure. Our apologies to the late Sergio Leone, but for Lynch, both "good" and "bad" are "ugly."

Postmodern literature also plays with lack of closure, utilizing non-linear plots in which characters are fractured, dispersed, and undeveloped. The reader is given neither hero nor anti-hero, the dualism offered by the modern literary canon. The omniscient narrative voice, the most hegemonic of modernist literary devices, is traded for a plurality of voices. These new voices may be those of previously marginalized groups such as women, non-Western peoples, gays and lesbians, and the mentally ill. This unconventional approach has also reached into the community of professional historians. Foucault, for example, assembled nineteenth-century documentation on "deviants" such as hermaphrodites and parricides.[9] His intentions were twofold; to contest the supposed clarity of dualisms such as normal and abnormal and to highlight, with irony, the idea that an unbiased collection of historical artifacts is in and of itself fictitious.

Postmodernism undermines the cultural dominance of metanarratives. It trades totalizing discourses for the creation of local narratives, popular lore in the vernacular form. While this may include the "thick" cultural interpretation associated with Geertzian anthropology, it differs in leaving out the enforced enlightened insertion of "meaning" onto these local dialogues. Postmodernism, drawing from terminology of literary criticism, gives us what are called "writerly" rather than "readerly" texts, with which we as readers are expected to make our own active reinterpretation of the words before our eyes. We are no longer allowed the luxury of the passive, albeit instructive, reading which furnishes us with an accurate representation of the world. In short, postmodernism privileges fractured and non-uniform perspectives. While this may appear to be a privileging of the "underdog," postmodernism does not seek to invert hierarchy by investing marginality and difference with moral superiority. Nor does postmodernism have one distinct "message" for the contemporary individual. In distinct contrast to some of its predecessors, postmodernism is not a quasi-political alliance, with goals, agendas and projects. Deconstruction, the Derridean method of textual analysis, refuses to force closure upon any text. This text will respect that goal, and decline to make any final judgement upon the validity of postmodernism. That is the task of the reader, and we hope it will be done in play.

NOTES

1   Charles A. Jencks, *The Language of Post-Modern Architecture* (London: Academy Editions, 1977; reprint, New York: Rizzoli, 1977), p. 9.

2   *Ibid.*, p. 8.

3   Allan Megill, *Prophets of Extremity* (Berkeley: University of California Press, 1985).

4   Michel Foucault and Jacques Derrida are often referred to as "poststructuralists," the name given to those French theorists who built upon and went beyond structuralism, the philosophical critique generated by Claude Lévi-Strauss, Jacques Lacan, and Roland Barthes. For our present purposes, poststructuralism differs only minimally from postmodernism.

5   Jean-François Lyotard, *The Postmodern Condition: A Report on Knowledge*, trans. by Geoff Bennington and Brian Massumi (Minneapolis: University of Minnesota Press, 1984), p. xxiii. These metanarratives are those of course envisioned and articulated by well-known modern thinkers including G. W. F. Hegel, Sigmund Freud, Karl Marx, and Adam Smith.

6   Jean Baudrillard, "Forgetting Baudrillard," *Social Text* 15 (Fall 1986), p. 141.

7   Charles Jencks, *The Language of Post-Modern Architecture*, p. 7.

8   Michel Foucault, *Discipline and Punish: The Birth of the Prison*, trans. by Alan Sheridan (New York: Vintage Books, 1979), p. 7.

9   See *Herculine Barbin: being the recently discovered memoirs of a nineteenth-century French hermaphrodite* (New York: Pantheon Books, 1980) and *I, Pierre Rivière, having slaughtered my mother, my sister and my brother ... a case of parricide in the nineteenth-century* (New York: Pantheon Books, 1975).

Hayden White

Hayden White is a professor of the History of Consciousness at the University of California at Santa Cruz. He is the only postmodernist considered here who works within the academic discipline of history. White wrote traditional works of intellectual history such as *The Emergence of Liberal Humanism* (co-written with Wilson Coates in 1966) early in his career. Only since the historical profession made the "linguistic turn" has White become known as the foremost critic of the modern historiographical tradition. While his predecessors focused upon historical *methodology*, White questions the very forms of language in which history is written.

In the following essay, White undertakes a critique similar to that of Thomas Kuhn in *The Structure of Scientific Revolutions* (1962). Kuhn described the gradual accumulation of doubt and anomalies in normal science which eventually culminate in a "paradigm" shift, or revolutionary changes in the formulation of basic scientific questions. White lobbies for a similar epistemological revolution within the social sciences. While science has undertaken a rigorous analysis of its own inherent biases, White says that the social sciences are still trapped within positivistic nineteenth-century representative models. Drawing from the language of literary criticism, White suggests that historians effect their own paradigm shift. In the seventeenth century René Descartes claimed that mathematical methods, those now associated with the hard sciences, could more reliably access reality than the methods of the humanities. White intimates that we might dispense with the opposition between scientific precision and fictional narrative.

According to White, historians display an unfounded confidence in a conventional form of written expression—the narrative. The supposedly detached and objective form of narrative called irony, is viewed as the most accurate means of representing reality. Irony is only superior to the other literary tropes, Romance, Comedy, and Tragedy, by consensus among historians. In short, historians have treated the narrative as a mere mirror reflection, or representation, of historical "reality." Since the nineteenth century, history, as a professional discipline which must legitimize its ability to make "truth claims," has imprisoned itself within the sanctified trope of irony in an effort to emulate the scientific community.

For White, history and all social sciences in general are based upon an overly strict distinction between facts (*episteme*) and mere fiction or opinion (*doxa*). White suggests that science has been more flexible in its approach to "normative" procedure, and more importantly, willing to reflect upon its own vocabulary. Social scientists, if unwilling to debunk "objectivity" as the goal of the historical profession, should at least dissect their own normative procedure, which entails unquestioned use of the generic and formulaic ironic narrative. As White claims, "narrative is not merely a neutral discursive form."[1]

White presents contemporary debates between postmodernism and traditional historiography which reflect the larger-scale epistemological crisis of "representation." White divulges the pretense to neutrality of the ironic narrative, and through this endeavor, hopes to liberate history from the gilded cage of narrativity.

1   *The Content of the Form: Narrative Discourse and Historical Representation* (Baltimore: The Johns Hopkins University Press, 1987), p. ix.

HAYDEN WHITE
(1987)

The Value of

Narrativity in the

Representation of Reality

To raise the question of the nature of narrative is to invite reflection on the very nature of culture and, possibly, even on the nature of humanity itself. So natural is the impulse to narrate, so inevitable is the form of narrative for any report on the way things really happened, that narrativity could appear problematical only in a culture in which it was absent—or, as in some domains of contemporary Western intellectual and artistic culture, programmatically refused. Considered as panglobal facts of culture, narrative and narration are less problems than simply data. As the late (and profoundly missed) Roland Barthes remarked, narrative "is simply there like life itself . . . international, transhistorical, transcultural." Far from being a problem, then, narrative might well be considered a solution to a problem of general human concern, namely, the problem of how to translate knowing into telling, the problem of fashioning human experience into a form assimilable to structures of meaning that are generally human rather than culture-specific. We may not be able fully to comprehend specific thought patterns of another culture, but we have relatively less difficulty understanding a story coming from another culture, however exotic that culture may appear to us. As Barthes says, "narrative is *translatable* without fundamental damage," in a way that a lyric poem or a philosophical discourse is not.

This suggests that far from being one code among many that a culture may utilize for endowing experience with meaning, narrative is a meta-code, a human universal on the basis of which transcultural messages about the nature of a shared reality can be transmitted. Arising, as Barthes says, between our experience of the world and our efforts to describe that experience

Reprinted from *The Content of the Form* by Hayden White (Baltimore: Johns Hopkins University Press, 1987), pp. 1–25, by permission of the Johns Hopkins University Press.

in language, narrative "ceaselessly substitutes meaning for the straightforward copy of the events recounted." And it would follow that the absence of narrative capacity or a refusal of narrative indicates an absence or refusal of meaning itself.

But what kind of meaning is absent or refused? The fortunes of narrative in the history of historical writing give us some insight into this question. Historians do not have to report their truths about the real world in narrative form. They may choose other, nonnarrative, even anti-narrative modes of representation, such as the meditation, the anatomy, or the epitome. Tocqueville, Burckhardt, Huizinga, and Braudel, to mention only the most notable masters of modern historiography, refused narrative in certain of their historiographical works, presumably on the assumption that the meaning of the events with which they wished to deal did not lend itself to representation in the narrative mode. They refused to tell a story about the past, or rather, they did not tell a story with well-marked beginning, middle, and end phases; they did not impose upon the processes that interested them the form that we normally associate with storytelling. While they certainly narrated their accounts of the reality that they perceived, or thought they perceived, to exist within or behind the evidence they had examined, they did not narrativize that reality, did not impose upon it the form of a story. And their example permits us to distinguish between a historical discourse that narrates and a discourse that narrativizes, between a discourse that openly adopts a perspective that looks out on the world and reports it and a discourse that feigns to make the world speak itself and speak itself as a story.

The idea that narrative should be considered less as a form of representation than as a manner of speaking about events, whether real or imaginary, has been recently elaborated within a discussion of the relationship between discourse and narrative that has arisen in the wake of Structuralism and is associated with the work of Jakobson, Benveniste, Genette, Todorov, and Barthes. Here narrative is regarded as a manner of speaking characterized, as Genette expresses it, "by a certain number of exclusions and restrictive conditions" that the more "open" form of discourse does not impose upon the speaker. According to Genette, Benveniste showed that certain grammatical forms like the pronoun "I" (and its implicit reference "thou"), the pronominal "indicators" (certain demonstrative pronouns), the adverbial indicators (like "here," "now," "yesterday," "today," "tomorrow," etc.) and, at least in French, certain verb tenses like the present, the present perfect, and the future, find themselves limited to discourse, while narrative in the strictest sense is distinguished by the exclusive use of the third person and of such forms as the preterite and the pluperfect.

This distinction between discourse and narrative is, of course, based solely on an analysis of the grammatical features of two modes of discourse in which the "objectivity" of the one and the "subjectivity" of the other are definable primarily by a "linguistic order of criteria." The "subjectivity" of the discourse is given by the presence, explicit or implicit, of an "ego" who can be defined "only as the person who maintains the discourse." By contrast, the "objectivity of narrative is defined by the absence of all reference to the narrator." In the narrativizing discourse, then, we can say, with Benveniste, that "truly there is no longer a 'narrator.' The events are chronologically recorded as they appear on the horizon of the story. No one speaks. The events seem to tell themselves."

What is involved in the production of a discourse in which "events seem to tell themselves," especially when it is a matter of events that are explicitly identified as real rather than imaginary, as in the case of historical representations? In a discourse having to do with manifestly imaginary events, which are the "contents" of fictional discourses, the question poses few problems. For why should not imaginary events be represented as "speaking themselves"? Why should not, in the domain of the imaginary, even the stones themselves speak—like Memnon's column when touched by the rays of the sun? But real events should not speak, should not tell themselves. Real events should simply be; they can perfectly well serve as the referents of a discourse, can be spoken about, but they should not pose as the subjects of a narrative. The lateness of the invention of historical discourse in human history and the difficulty of sustaining it in times of cultural breakdown (as in the early Middle Ages) suggest the artificiality of the notion that real events could "speak themselves" or be represented as "telling their own story." Such a fiction would have posed no problems before the distinction between real and imaginary events was imposed upon the storyteller; storytelling becomes a problem only after two orders of events dispose themselves before the storyteller as possible components of stories and storytelling is compelled to exfoliate under the injunction to keep the two orders unmixed in discourse. What we wish to call mythic narrative is under no obligation to keep the two orders of events, real and imaginary, distinct from one another. Narrative becomes a problem only when we wish to give to real events the form of story. It is because real events do not offer themselves as stories that their narrativization is so difficult.

What is involved, then, in that finding of the "true story," that discovery of the "real story" within or behind the events that come to us in the chaotic form of "historical records"? What wish is enacted, what desire is gratified, by the fantasy that real events are properly represented when they can be shown to display the formal coherency of a story? In the enigma of this wish, this desire, we catch a glimpse of the cultural function of narrativizing discourse in general, an intimation of the psychological impulse behind the apparently universal need not only to narrate but to give to events an aspect of narrativity.

Historiography is an especially good ground on which to consider the nature of narration and narrativity because it is here that our desire for the imaginary, the possible, must contest with the imperatives of the real, the actual. If we view narration and narrativity as the instruments with which the conflicting claims of the imaginary and the real are mediated, arbitrated, or resolved in a discourse, we begin to comprehend both the appeal of narrative and the grounds for refusing it. If putatively real events are represented in a nonnarrative form, what kind of reality is it that offers itself, or is conceived to offer itself, to perception in this form? What would a nonnarrative representation of historical reality look like? In answering this question, we do not necessarily arrive at a solution to the problem of the nature of narrative, but we do begin to catch a glimpse of the basis for the appeal of narrativity as a form for the representation of events construed to be real rather than imaginary.

Fortunately, we have examples aplenty of representations of historical reality that are nonnarrative in form. Indeed, the *doxa* of the modern historiographical establishment has it that there are three basic kinds of historical representation—the annals, the chronicle, and the history proper—the imperfect "historicality" of two of which is evidenced in their failure to attain to full narrativity of the events of which they treat. Needless to say, narrativity alone does not permit the distinction of the three kinds. In order for an account of events, even of past events or of past real events, to count as a proper history, it is not enough that it display all of the features of narrativity. In addition, the account must manifest a proper concern for the judicious handling of evidence, and it must honor the chronological order of the original occurrence of the events of which it treats as a baseline not to be transgressed in the classification of any given event as either a cause or an effect. But by common consent, it is not enough that an historical account deal in real, rather than merely imaginary, events; and it is not enough that the account represents events in its order of discourse according to the chronological sequence in which they originally occurred. The events must be not only registered within the chronological framework of their original occurrence but narrated as well, that is to say, revealed as possessing a structure, an order of meaning, that they do not possess as mere sequence.

Needless to say, also, the annals form lacks completely this narrative component, since it consists only of a list of events ordered in chronological sequence. The chronicle, by contrast, often seems to wish to tell a story, aspires to narrativity, but typically fails to achieve it. More specifically, the chronicle usually is marked by a failure to achieve narrative closure. It does not so much conclude as simply terminate. It starts out to tell a story but breaks off *in media res*, in the chronicler's own present; it leaves things unresolved, or rather, it leaves them unresolved in a storylike way.

While annals represent historical reality as if real events did not display the form of story, the chronicler represents it as if real events appeared to human consciousness in the form of unfinished stories. And the official wisdom has it that however objective a historian might be in his reporting of events, however judicious he has been in his assessment of evidence, however punctilious he has been in his dating of *res gestae*, his account remains something less than a proper history if he has failed to give to reality the form of a story. Where there is no narrative, Croce said, there is no history. And Peter Gay, writing from a perspective directly opposed to the relativism of Croce, puts it just as starkly: "Historical narration without analysis is trivial, historical analysis without narration is incomplete." Gay's formulation calls up the Kantian bias of the demand for narration in historical representation, for it suggests, to paraphrase Kant, that historical narratives without analysis are empty, while historical analyses without narrative are blind. Thus we may ask, What kind of insight does narrative give into the nature of real events? What kind of blindness with respect to reality does narrativity dispell?

In what follows I treat the annals and chronicle forms of historical representation, not as the imperfect histories they are conventionally conceived to be, but rather as particular products of possible conceptions of historical reality, conceptions that are alternatives to, rather than failed anticipations of, the fully realized historical discourse that the modern history form is supposed to embody. This procedure will throw light on the problems of both historiography and narration alike and will illuminate what I conceive to be the purely conventional nature of the relationship between them. What will be revealed, I think, is that the very distinction between real and imaginary events that is basic to modern discussions of both history and fiction presupposes a notion of reality in which "the true" is identified with "the real" only insofar as it can be shown to possess the character of narrativity.

When we moderns look at an example of a medieval annals, we cannot but be struck by the apparent naïveté of the annalist; and we are inclined to ascribe this naïveté to the annalist's apparent refusal, inability, or unwillingness to transform the set of events ordered vertically as a file of annual markers into the elements of a linear/horizontal process. In other words, we are likely to be put off by the annalist's apparent failure to see that historical events dispose themselves to the percipient eye as stories waiting to be told, waiting to be narrated. But surely a genuinely historical interest would require that we ask not how or why the annalist failed to write a "narrative" but rather what kind of notion of reality led him to represent in the annals form what, after all, he took to be real events. If we could answer this question, we might be able to understand why, in our own time and cultural condition, we could conceive of narrativity itself as a problem.

Volume 1 of the *Monumenta Germaniae Historica*, in the *Scriptores* series, contains the text of the *Annals of Saint Gall*, a list of events that occurred in Gaul during the eighth, ninth, and tenth centuries of our era. Although this text is "referential" and contains a representation of temporality—Ducrot and Todorov's definition of what can count as a narrative—it possesses none of the characteristics that we normally attribute to a story: no central subject, no well-marked beginning, middle, and end, no peripeteia, and no identifiable narrative voice. In what are, for us, the theoretically most interesting segments of the text, there is no suggestion of any necessary connection between one event and another. Thus, for the period 709-34, we have the following entries:

709.	Hard winter. Duke Gottfried died.
710.	Hard year and deficient in crops.
711.	
712.	Flood everywhere.
713.	
714.	Pippin, mayor of the palace, died.
715.	
716.	
717.	
718.	Charles devastated the Saxon with great destruction.
719.	
720.	Charles fought against the Saxons.
721.	Theudo drove the Saracens out of Aquitaine.
722.	Great crops.
723.	
724.	
725.	Saracens came for the first time.
726.	
727.	
728.	
729.	
730.	
731.	Blessed Bede, the presbyter, died.
732.	Charles fought against the Saracens at Poiters on Saturday.
733.	
734.	

This list immediately locates us in a culture hovering on the brink of dissolution, a society of radical scarcity, a world of human groups threatened by death, devastation, flood, and famine. All of the events are extreme, and the implicit criterion for selecting them for remembrance is their liminal nature. Basic need—food, security from external enemies, political and military leadership—and the threat of their not being provided are the subjects of concern; but the connection between basic needs and the conditions for their possible satisfaction is not explicitly commented on. Why "Charles fought against the Saxons" remains as unexplained as why one year yielded "great crops" and another produced "flood everywhere." Social events are apparently as incomprehensible as natural events. They seem to have the same order of importance or unimportance. They seem merely to have occurred, and their importance seems to be indistinguishable from the fact that they were recorded. In fact, it seems that their importance consists in nothing other than their having been recorded.

And by whom they were recorded we have no idea; nor do we have any idea of when they were recorded. The entry for 725—"Saracens came for the *first* time"—suggests that this event at least was recorded after the Saracens had come a second time and set up what we might consider to be a genuine narrativist expectation; but the coming of the Saracens and their repulsion is not the subject of this account. Charles's fight "against the Saracens at Poitiers on Saturday" is recorded, but the outcome of the battle is not. And that "Saturday" is disturbing, because the month and day of the battle are not given. There are too many loose ends—no plot in the offing—and this is frustrating, if not disturbing, to the modern reader's story expectations as well as his desire for specific information.

We note further that this account is not really inaugurated. It simply begins with the "title" (is it a title?) *Anni domini*, which stands at the head of two columns, one of dates, the other of events. Visually, at least, this title links the file of dates in the left-hand column with the file of events in the right-hand column in a promise of signification that we might be inclined to take for mythical were it not for the fact that *Anni domini* refers us both to a cosmological story given in Scripture and to a calendrical convention that historians in the West still use to mark the units of their histories. We should not too quickly refer the meaning of the text to the mythic framework it invokes by designating the "years" as being "of the Lord," for these "years" have a regularity that the Christian mythos, with its clear hypotactical ordering of the events it comprises (Creation, Fall, Incarnation, Resurrection, Second Coming), does not possess. The regularity of the calendar signals the "realism" of the account, its intention to deal in real rather than imaginary events. The calendar locates events, not in the time of eternity, not in *kairotic* time, but in chronological time, in time as it is humanly experienced. This time has no high points or low points; it is, we might say, paratactical and endless. It has no gaps. The list of times is full even if the list of events is not.

Finally, the annals do not conclude; they simply terminate. The last entries are the following:

1045. 1046. 1047. 1048. 1049. 1050. 1051. 1052. 1053. 1054. 1055.

1056.   The Emperor Henry died; and his son Henry succeeded to the rule.

1057. 1058. 1059. 1060. 1061. 1062. 1063. 1064. 1065. 1066. 1067. 1068. 1069. 1070. 1071. 1072.

The continuation of the list of years at the end of the account does, to be sure, suggest a continuation of the series ad infinitum, or rather, until the Second Coming. But there is no story conclusion. How could there be, since there is no central subject about which a story could be told?

Nonetheless, there must be a story, since there is surely a plot—if by plot we mean a structure of relationships by which the events contained in the account are endowed with a meaning by being identified as parts of an integrated whole. Here, however, I am referring, not to the myth of the Fall and Redemption (of the just parts of humankind) contained in the Bible, but to the list of dates of the years given in the left-hand file of the text, which confers coherence and fullness on the events by registering them under the years in which they occurred. To put it another way, the list of dates can be seen as the signified of which the events given in the right-hand column are the signifiers. The meaning of the events is their registration in this kind of list. This is why, I presume, the annalist would have felt little of the anxiety that the modern scholar feels when confronted with what appear to be gaps, discontinuities, and lack of causal connections between the events recorded in the text. The modern scholar seeks fullness and continuity in an order of events; the annalist has both in the sequence of the years. Which is the more "realistic" expectation?

Recall that we are dealing with neither oneiric nor infantile discourse. It may even be a mistake to call it discourse at all, but it has something discursive about it. The text summons up a "substance," operates in the domain of memory rather than in that of dream or fantasy, and unfolds under the sign of "the real" rather than that of "the imaginary." In fact, it seems eminently rational and, on the face of it, rather prudent in its manifest desire to record only those events about which there could be little doubt as to their occurrence and in its resolve not to interpellate facts on speculative grounds or to advance arguments about how the events are really connected to one another.

Modern commentators have remarked on the fact that the annalist recorded the Battle of Poitiers of 732 but failed to note the Battle of Tours which occurred in the same year and which, as every schoolboy knows, was one of "the ten great battles of world history." But even if the annalist had known of Tours, what principle or rule of meaning would have required him to record it? It is only from our knowledge of the subsequent history of Western Europe that we can presume to rank events in terms of their world-historical significance, and even then that significance is less world historical than simply Western European, representing a tendency of modern historians to rank events in the record hierarchically from within a perspective that is culture-specific, not universal at all.

It is this need or impulse to rank events with respect to their significance for the culture or group that is writing its own history that makes a narrative representation of real events possible. It is surely much more "universalistic" simply to record events as they come to notice. And at the minimal level on which the annals unfold, what gets put into the account is of much greater theoretical importance for the understanding of the nature of narrative than what gets left out. But this does raise the question of the function in this text of the recording of those years in which "nothing happened." Every narrative, however seemingly "full," is constructed on the basis of a set of events that might have been included but were left out; this is as true of imaginary narratives as it is of realistic ones. And this consideration permits us to ask what kind of notion of reality authorizes construction of a narrative account of reality in which continuity rather than discontinuity governs the articulation of the discourse.

If we grant that this discourse unfolds under a sign of a desire for the real, as we must do in order to justify the inclusion of the annals form among the types of historical representation, we must conclude that it is a product of an image of reality according to which the social system, which alone could provide the diacritical markers for ranking the importance of events, is only minimally present to the consciousness of the writer, or rather, is present as a factor in the composition of the discourse only by virtue of its absence. Everywhere it is the forces of disorder, natural and human, the forces of violence and destruction, that occupy the forefront of attention. The account deals in qualities rather than agents, figuring forth a world in which things happen to people rather than one in which people do things. It is the hardness of the winter of 709, the hardness of the year 710 and the deficiency of the crops of that year, the flooding of the waters in 712 and the imminent presence of death that recur with a frequency and regularity lacking in the representation of acts of human agency. Reality for this observer wears the face of adjectives that override the capacity of the nouns they modify to resist their determinancy. Charles does manage to devastate the Saxons, to fight against them, and Theudo even manages to drive the Saracens out of Aquitaine, but these actions appear to belong to the same order of existence as the natural events which bring either "great" crops or "deficient" harvests, and are as seemingly incomprehensible.

The absence of a principle for assigning importance or significance to events is signaled above all in the gaps in the list of events in the right-hand file, for example in the year 711, in which, it seems, "nothing happened." The overabundance of the waters noted for the year 712 is preceded and followed by years in which also "nothing happened." Which puts one in mind of Hegel's remark that periods of human happiness and security are blank pages in history. But the presence of these blank years in the annalist's account permits us to perceive, by way of contrast, the extent to which narrative strains for the effect of having filled in all the gaps, of having put an image of continuity, coherency, and meaning in place of the fantasies of emptiness, need, and frustrated desire that inhabit our nightmares about the destructive power of time. In fact, the annalist's account calls up a world in which need is everywhere present, in which scarcity is the rule of existence, and in which all of the possible agencies of satisfaction are lacking or absent or exist under imminent threat of death.

The notion of possible gratification is, however, implicitly present in the list of dates that make up the left-hand column. The fullness of this list attests to the fullness of time, or at least to the fullness of the "years of the Lord." There is no scarcity of the years: they descend regularly from their origin, the year of the Incarnation, and roll relentlessly on to their potential end, the Last Judgment. What is lacking in the list of events to give it a similar regularity and fullness is a notion of a social center by which to locate them with respect to one another and to charge them with ethical or moral significance. It is the absence of any consciousness of a social center that prohibits the annalist from ranking the events he treats as elements of a historical field of occurrence. And it is the absence of such a center that precludes or undercuts any impulse he might have had to work up his discourse into the form of a narrative. Without such a center, Charles's campaigns against the Saxons remain simply fights, the invasion of the Saracens simply a coming, and the fact that the Battle of Poitiers was fought on a Saturday as important as the fact that the battle was even fought at all. All this suggests to me that Hegel was right when he opined that a genuinely historical account had to display not only a certain form, namely, the narrative, but also a certain content, namely, a politicosocial order. . . .

And this raises the suspicion that narrative in general, from the folktale to the novel, from the annals to the fully realized "history," has to do with the topics of law, legality, legitmacy, or, more generally, authority. And indeed, when we look at what is supposed to be the next stage in the evolution of historical representation after the annals form, namely, the chronicle, this suspicion is borne out. The more historically self-conscious the writer of any form of historiography, the more the question of the social system and the law that sustains it, the authority of this law and its justification, and threats to the law occupy his attention. If, as Hegel suggests, historicality as a distinct mode of human existence is unthinkable without the presupposition of a system of law in relation to which a specifically legal subject could be constituted, then historical self-consciousness, the kind of consciousness capable of imagining the need to represent reality as a history, is conceivable only in terms of its interest in law, legality, and legitimacy, and so on.

Interest in the social system, which is nothing other than a system of human relationships governed by law, creates the possibility of conceiving the kinds of tensions, conflicts, struggles, and their various kinds of resolutions that we are accustomed to find in any representation of reality presenting itself to us as a history. This permits us to speculate that the growth and development of historical consciousness, which is attended by a concomitant growth and development of narrative capability (of the sort met with in the chronicle as against the annals form), has something to do with the extent to which the legal system functions as a subject of concern. . . .

And this suggests that narrativity, certainly in factual storytelling and probably in fictional storytelling as well, is intimately related to, if not a function of, the impulse to moralize reality, that is, to identify it with the social system that is the source of any morality that we can imagine.

The annalist of Saint Gall shows no concern about any system of merely human morality or law. The entry for 1056, "The Emperor Henry died; and his son Henry succeeded to the rule," contains in embryo the elements of a narrative. Indeed, it is a narrative, and its narrativity, in spite of the ambiguity of the connection between the first event (Henry's death) and the second (Henry's succession) suggested by the particle *and*, achieves closure by its tacit invocation of the legal system, the rule of genealogical succession, which the annalist takes for granted as a principle rightly governing the passing of authority from one generation to another. But this small narrative element, this "narreme," floats easily on the sea of dates that figures succession itself as a principle of cosmic organization. Those of us who know what was awaiting the younger Henry in his conflicts with his nobles and with the popes during the period of the Investiture Struggle, in which the issue of precisely where final authority on earth was located was fought out, may be irritated by the economy with which the annalist recorded an event so fraught with future moral and legal implications. The years 1057-72, which the annalist simply lists at the end of his record, provided more than enough "events" prefiguring the onset of this struggle, more than enough conflict to warrant a full narrative account of its inception. But the annalist simply ignored them. He apparently felt that he had done his duty solely by listing the dates of the years themselves. What is involved, we might ask, in this refusal to narrate? . . .

Now, the capacity to envision a set of events as belonging to the same order of meaning requires some metaphysical principle by which to translate difference into similarity. In other words, it requires a "subject" common to all of the referents of the various sentences that register events as having occurred. If such a subject exists, it is the "Lord" whose "years" are treated as manifestations of His power to cause the events that occur in them. The subject of the account, then, does not exist in time and could not therefore function as the subject of a narrative. Does it follow that in order for there to be a narrative, there must be some equivalent of the Lord, some sacral being endowed with the authority and power of the Lord, existing in time? If so, what could such an equivalent be?

The nature of such a being, capable of serving as the central organizing principle of meaning of a discourse that is both realistic and narrative in structure, is called up in the mode of historical representation known as the chronicle. By common consensus among historians of historical writing, the chronicle is a "higher" form of historical conceptualization and represents a mode of historiographical representation superior to the annals form. Its superiority consists in its greater comprehensiveness, its organization of materials "by topics and reigns," and its greater narrative coherency. The chronicle also has a central subject—the life of an individual, town, or region; some great undertaking, such as a war or crusade; or some institution, such as a monarchy, episcopacy, or monastery. The link of the chronicle with the annals is perceived in the perseverance of the chronology as the organizing principle of the discourse, and this is what makes the chronicle something less than a fully realized "history." Moreover, the chronicle, like the annals but unlike the history, does not so much conclude as simply terminate; typically it lacks closure, that summing up of the "meaning" of the chain of events with which it deals that we normally expect from the well-made story. The chronicle typically promises closure but does not provide it—which is one of the reasons why the nineteenth-century editors of the medieval chronicles denied them the status of genuine "histories."

Suppose that we look at the matter differently. Suppose we grant, not that the chronicle is a "higher" or more sophisticated representation of reality than the annals, but that it is merely a different kind of representation, marked by a desire for a kind of order and fullness in an account of reality that remains theoretically unjustified, a desire that is, until shown otherwise, purely gratuitous. What is involved in the imposition of this order and the provision of this fullness (of detail) which mark the differences between the annals and the chronicle?

I take as an example of the chronicle type of historical representation the *History of France* by one Richerus of Rheims, written on the eve of the year A.D. 1000 (ca. 998). We have no difficulty recognizing this text as a narrative. It has a central subject ("the conflicts of the French"); a proper geographical center (Gaul) and a proper social center (the archepiscopal see of Rheims, beset by a dispute over which of two claimants to the office of archbishop is the legitimate occupant); and a proper beginning in time (given in a synoptic version of the history of the world from the Incarnation down to the time and place of Richerus's own writing of his account). But the work fails as a proper history, at least according to the opinion of later commentators, by virtue of two considerations. First, the order of the discourse follows the order of chronology; it presents events in the order of their occurrence and cannot, therefore, offer the kind of meaning that a narratologically governed account can be said to provide. Second, probably owing to the "annalistic" order of the discourse, the account does not so much conclude as simply terminate; it merely breaks off with the flight of one of the disputants for the office of archishop and throws onto the reader the burden for retrospectively reflecting on the linkages between the beginning of the account and its ending. The account comes down to the writer's own "yesterday," adds one more fact to the series that began with the Incarnation, and then simply ceases. As a result, all of the normal narratological expectations of the reader (this reader) remain unfulfilled. The work appears to be unfolding a plot but then belies its own appearance by merely stopping *in medias res*, with the cryptic notation "Pope Gregory authorizes Arnulfus to assume provisionally the episcopal functions, while awaiting the legal decision that would either confer these upon him or withdraw the right to them" (2:133).

And yet Richerus is a self-conscious narrator. He explicitly says at the outset of his account that he proposes "especially to preserve in writing [ad memoriam recuere scripto specialiter propositum est]" the "wars," "troubles," and "affairs" of the French and, moreover, to write them up in a manner superior to other accounts, especially that of one Flodoard, an earlier scribe of Rheims who had written an annals on which Richerus has drawn for information. Richerus notes that he has drawn freely on Flodoard's work but that he has often "put other words" in the place of the original ones and "modified completely the style of the presentation [pro aliis longe diversissimo orationis scemate disposuisse]" (1:4). He also situates himself in a tradition of historical writing by citing such classics as Caesar, Orosius, Jerome, and Isidore as authorities for the early history of Gaul and suggests that his own personal observations gave him insight into the facts he is recounting that no one else could claim. All of this suggests a certain self-consciouness about his own discourse that is manifestly lacking in the writer of the *Annals of Saint Gall*. Richerus's discourse is a fashioned discourse, the narrativity of which, compared with that of the annalist, is a function of the self-consciousness with which this fashioning activity is entered upon.

Paradoxically, however, it is this self-conscious fashioning activity, an activity that gives to Richerus's work the aspect of a historical narrative, that decreases its "objectivity" as a historical account—or so the consensus of modern analysts of the text has it. For example, a modern editor of the text, Robert Latouche, indicts Richerus's pride in the originality of his style as the cause of his failure to write a proper history. "Ultimately," Latouche notes, "the *History* of Richerus is not, properly speaking [*proprement parler*], a history but a work of rhetoric composed by a monk ... who sought to imitate the techniques of Salluste." And he adds, "What interested him was not the material [*matière*], which he molded to fit his fancy, but the form" (1:xi).

The problem of authority pervades the text written by Richerus in a way that cannot be ascribed to the text written by the annalist of Saint Gall. For the annalist there is no need to claim the authority to narrate events, since there is nothing problematical about their status as manifestations of a reality that is being contested. Since there is no "contest," there is nothing to narrativize, no need for them to "speak themselves" or be represented as if they could "tell their own story." It is necessary only to record them in the order that they come to notice, for since there is no contest, there is no story to tell. It is because there was a contest that there is something to narrativize for Richerus. But it is not because the contest was not resolved that the quasi narrative produced by Richerus has no closure; for in fact the contest *was* resolved— by the flight of Gerbert to the court of King Otto and the installation of Arnulfus as archbishop of Rheims by Pope Gregory.

What was lacking for a proper discursive resolution, a narrativizing resolution, was the moral principle in light of which Richerus might have judged the resolution as either just or unjust. Reality itself has judged the resolution by resolving it as it has done. To be sure, there is the suggestion that a kind of justice was provided for Gerbert by King Otto, who, "having recognized Gerbert's learning and genius, installs him as bishop of Ravenna." But that justice is located at another place and is disposed by another authority, another king. The end of the discourse does not cast its light back over the events originally recorded in order to redistribute the force of a meaning that was immanent in all of the events from the beginning. There is no justice, only force, or, rather, only an authority that presents itself as different kinds of forces.

I do not offer these reflections on the relation between historiography and narrative as aspiring to anything other than an attempt to illuminate the distinction between story elements and plot elements in the historical discourse. Common opinion has it that the plot of a narrative imposes a meaning on the events that make up its story level by revealing at the end a structure that was immanent in the events all along. What I am trying to establish is the nature of this immanence in any narrative account of real events, events that are offered as the proper content of historical discourse. These events are real not because they occurred but because, first, they were remembered and, second, they are capable of finding a place in a chronologically ordered sequence. In order, however, for an account of them to be considered a historical account, it is not enough that they be recorded in the order of their original occurrence. It is the fact that they can be recorded otherwise, in an order of narrative, that makes them, at one and the same time, questionable as to their authenticity and susceptible to being considered as tokens of reality. In order to qualify as historical, an event must be susceptible to at least two narrations of its occurrence. Unless at least two versions of the same set of events can be imagined, there is no reason for the historian to take upon himself the authority of giving the true account of what really happened. The authority of the historical narrative is the authority of reality itself; the historical account endows this reality with form and thereby makes it desirable by the imposition upon its processes of the formal coherency that only stories possess.

The history, then, belongs to the category of what might be called "the discourse of the real," as against the "discourse of the imaginary" or "the discourse of desire." The formulation is Lacanian, obviously, but I do not wish to push its Lacanian aspects too far. I merely wish to suggest that we can comprehend the appeal of historical discourse by recognizing the extent to which it makes the real desirable, makes the real into an object of desire, and does so by its imposition, upon events that are represented as real, of the formal coherency that stories possess. Unlike that of the annals, the reality represented in the historical narrative, in "speaking itself," speaks to us, summons us from afar (this "afar" is the land of forms), and displays to us a formal coherency to which we ourselves aspire. The historical narrative, as against the chronicle, reveals to us a world that is putatively "finished," done with, over, and yet not dissolved, not falling apart. In this world, reality wears the mask of a meaning, the completeness and fullness of which we can only imagine, never experience. Insofar as historical stories can be completed, can be given narrative closure, can be shown to have had a plot all along, they give to reality the odor of the ideal. This is why the plot of a historical narrative is always an embarrassment and has to be presented as "found" in the events rather than put there by narrative techniques. . . .

This puts us close to a possible characterization of the demand for closure in the history, for the want of which the chronicle form is adjudged to be deficient as a narrative. The demand for closure in the historical story is a demand, I suggest, for moral meaning, a demand that sequences of real events be assessed as to their significance as elements of a moral drama. Has any historical narrative ever been written that was not informed not only by moral awareness but specifically by the moral authority of the narrator? It is difficult to think of any historical work produced during the nineteenth century, the classic age of historical narrative, that was not given the force of a moral judgment on the events it related. . . .

But on what other grounds could a narrative of real events possibly conclude? When it is a matter of recounting the concourse of real events, what other "ending" could a given sequence of such events have than a "moralizing" ending? What else could narrative closure consist of than the passage from one moral order to another? I confess that I cannot think of any other way of "concluding" an account of real events, for we cannot say, surely, that any sequence of real events actually comes to an end, that reality itself disappears, that events of the order of the real have ceased to happen. Such events could only seem to have ceased to happen when meaning is shifted, and shifted by narrative means, from one physical or social space to another. Where moral sensitivity is lacking, as it seems to be in an annalistic account of reality, or is only potentially present, as it appears to be in a chronicle, not only meaning but the means to track such shifts of meaning, that is, narrativity, appears to be lacking also. Where, in any account of reality, narrativity is present, we can be sure that morality or a moralizing impulse is present too. There is no other way that reality can be endowed with the kind of meaning that both displays itself in its consummation and withholds itself by its displacement to another story "waiting to be told" just beyond the confines of "the end."

What I have been working around to is the question of the value attached to narrativity itself, especially in representations of reality of the sort embodied in historical discourse. It may be thought that I have stacked the cards in favor of my thesis—that narrativizing discourse serves the purpose of moralizing judgments—by my use of exclusively medieval materials. And perhaps I have, but it is the modern historiographical community that has distinguished between the annals, chronicle, and history forms of discourse on the basis of their attainment of narrative fullness or failure to attain it and this same scholarly community has yet to account for the fact that just when, by its own account, historiography was transformed into an "objective" discipline, it was the narrativity of the historical discourse that was celebrated as one of the signs of its maturation as a fully "objective" discipline—a science of a special sort but a science nonetheless. It is historians themselves who have transformed narrativity from a manner of speaking into a paradigm of the form that reality itself displays to a "realistic" consciousness. It is they who have made narrativity into a value, the presence of which in a discourse having to do with "real" events signals at once its objectivity, its seriousness, and its realism.

What I have sought to suggest is that this value attached to narrativity in the representation of real events arises out of a desire to have real events display the coherence, integrity, fullness, and closure of an image of life that is and can only be imaginary. The notion that sequences of real events possess the formal attributes of the stories we tell about imaginary events could only have its origin in wishes, daydreams, reveries. Does the world really present itself to perception in the form of well-made stories, with central subjects, proper beginnings, middles, and ends, and a coherence that permits us to see "the end" in every beginning? Or does it present itself more in the forms that the annals and chronicle suggest, either as mere sequence without beginning or end or as sequences of beginnings that only terminate and never conclude? And does the world, even the social world, ever really come to us as already narrativized, already "speaking itself" from beyond the horizon of our capacity to make scientific sense of it? Or is the fiction of such a world, capable of speaking itself and of displaying itself as a form of a story, necessary for the establishment of that moral authority without which the notion of a specifically social reality would be unthinkable? If it were only a matter of realism in representation, one could make a pretty good case for both the annals and chronicle forms as paradigms of ways that reality offers itself to perception. Is it possible that their supposed want of objectivity, manifested in their failure to narrativize reality adequately, has to do, not at all with the modes of perception that they presuppose, but with their failure to represent the moral under the aspect of the aesthetic? And could we answer that question without giving a narrative account of the history of objectivity itself, an account that would already prejudice the outcome of the story we would tell in favor of the moral in general? Could we ever narrativize without moralizing?

Michel Foucault

Michel Foucault died in 1984, leaving followers and critics endlessly debating the validity and merit of his works. His works defy synthesis; neither conventionally historical nor purely philosophical, they utilize and subvert the terminologies of both disciplines at will. Sympathetic historians are willing to forgive Foucault for his sins against careful documentation: he was truly a philosopher, they claim, and thus not subject to the rigorous requirements of orthodox fact-gathering. Hostile historians feel Foucault's blatant disregard for "proper" evidence disqualifies his philosophy from historical contests. As if defying the parameters of academic disciplines were not enough, Foucault wrote difficult prose punctuated by obscure references and recurrent neologisms. Nonetheless, Foucault's works have had a phenomenal impact upon many social scientific disciplines.

Foucault's thought underwent several transformations during his lifetime, so the question "Which Foucault?" must be asked each time reference is made to him. Early in his career, Foucault traced the historical development of the dualism sanity/madness as well as the birth of the "human" sciences. While many claim these works are examples of structuralism, Foucault denied allegiance to any mainstream academic or intellectual current. He criticized structuralism for its perpetuation of general epistemological questions, and naive belief in the representative power of words. Hayden White credits Foucault with divulging "[t]he illusion on which all of the modern human sciences have been founded ... that 'words' enjoy a privileged status among 'the order of things' as transparent icons, as value-neutral instruments of representation."[1] In *The Order of Things* (1970), Foucault sought to unearth the layers of historical accumulation which led up to the creation of the notion of "humanity." Foucault calls the static period of sensibility or definition an *episteme*, a neologism very similar to a Kuhnian "paradigm."

Two recurrent motifs can be found within the corpus of Foucault's works. Firstly, he demonstrates how a concept which we take for granted as "in the order of things," ("Man," for example) is a social construction; this construction becomes a lens through which we view and order all phenomena. This particular aspect of Foucault's analysis was not so novel: similar claims can be found within Nietzschean critiques of democracy and Christianity, and Foucault openly avowed his debt to this philosopher.

In his later works, Foucault broke with mere critique and reformulated generic episte-mological queries such as "What is Sanity?" (only one of the cultural constructions he stud-ied, the others being humanity, sexuality, and "humane" forms of punishment), and "How do we know it exists?" Foucault posed more interpretive questions, illuminating how dualisms such as sanity/madness function within society as powerful constructors of human individuality and differentiation. In his attempt to historicize these "grand abstractions," Foucault debated their supposed neutrality.

For Foucault, some Enlightenment metanarratives have successfully veiled their true function, the operation of minute mechanisms of power over the human body and soul. While all dominant metanarratives have been vaunted as benevolent and progressive, Foucault suggests they are oppressive. One such "stifling" notion may be the idea of the human individual, as only in being declared an "individual" can one be subjected to norms, rules, and discipline. In the following texts, Foucault discusses the "natural and neutral" human attribute, sexuality, and reevaluates the philosophical event known as the Enlightenment.

1   Hayden White, "Foucault Decoded," in *Tropics of Discourse: Essays in Cultural Criticism* (Baltimore: Johns Hopkins University Press, 1978), p. 232.

MICHEL FOUCAULT
(1984)

What Is

Enlightenment?

Today when a periodical asks its readers a question, it does so in order to collect opinions on some subject about which everyone has an opinion already; there is not much likelihood of learning anything new. In the eighteenth century, editors preferred to question the public on problems that did not yet have solutions. I don't know whether or not that practice was more effective; it was unquestionably more entertaining.

In any event, in line with this custom, in November 1784 a German periodical, *Berlinische Monatschrift*, published a response to the question: *Was ist Aufklärung?* And the respondent was Kant.

A minor text, perhaps. But it seems to me that it marks the discreet entrance into the history of thought of a question that modern philosophy has not been capable of answering but that it has never managed to get rid of, either. And one that has been repeated in various forms for two centuries now. From Hegel through Nietzsche or Max Weber to Horkheimer or Habermas, hardly any philosophy has failed to confront this same question, directly or indirectly. What, then, is this event that is called the *Aufklärung* and that has determined, at least in part, what we are, what we think, and what we do today? Let us imagine that the *Berlinische Monatschrift* still exists and that it is asking its readers the question: What is modern philosophy? Perhaps we could respond with an echo: modern philosophy is the philosophy that is attempting to answer the question raised so imprudently two centuries ago: *Was ist Aufklärung?*

Let us linger a few moments over Kant's text. It merits attention for several reasons. . . .

In itself and within the Christian tradition, Kant's text poses a new problem.

It was certainly not the first time that philosophical thought had sought to reflect on its own present. But, speaking schematically, we may say that this reflection had until then taken three main forms.

The present may be represented as belonging to a certain era of the world, distinct from the others through some inherent characteristics, or separated from the others by some dramatic event. Thus, in Plato's *The Statesman* the interlocutors recognize that they belong to one of those revolutions of the world in which the world is turning backwards, with all the negative consequences that may ensue.

The present may be interrogated in an attempt to decipher in it the heralding signs of a forthcoming event. Here we have the principle of a kind of historical hermeneutics of which Augustine might provide an example.

The present may also be analyzed as a point of transition toward the dawning of a new world. That is what Vico describes in the last chapter of *La Scienza Nuova*; what he sees "today" is "a complete humanity ... spread abroad through all nations, for a few great monarchs rule over this world of peoples"; it is also "Europe ... radiant with such humanity that it abounds in all the good things that make for the happiness of human life."

Now the way Kant poses the question of *Aufklärung* is entirely different: it is neither a world era to which one belongs, nor an event whose signs are perceived, nor the dawning of an accomplishment. Kant defines *Aufklärung* in an almost entirely negative way, as an *Ausgang*, an "exit," a "way out." In his other texts on history, Kant occasionally raises questions of origin or defines the internal teleology of a historical process. In the text on *Aufklärung*, he deals with the question of contemporary reality alone. He is not seeking to understand the present on the basis of a totality or of a future achievement. He is looking for a difference: What difference does today introduce with respect to yesterday?

I shall not go into detail here concerning this text, which is not always very clear despite its brevity. I should simply like to point out three or four features that seem to me important if we are to understand how Kant raised the philosophical question of the present day.

Kant indicates right away that the "way out" that characterizes Enlightenment is a process that releases us from the status of "immaturity." And by "immaturity," he means a certain state of our will that makes us accept someone else's authority to lead us in areas where the use of reason is called for. Kant gives three examples: we are in a state of "immaturity" when a book takes the place of our understanding, when a spiritual director takes the place of our conscience, when a doctor decides for us what our diet is to be. (Let us note in passing that the register of these three critiques is easy to recognize, even though the text does not make it explicit.) In any case, Enlightenment is defined by a modification of the preexisting relation linking will, authority, and the use of reason.

We must also note that this way out is presented by Kant in a rather ambiguous manner. He characterizes it as a phenomenon, an ongoing process; but he also presents it as a task and an obligation. From the very first paragraph, he notes that man himself is responsible for his immature status. Thus it has to be supposed that he will be able to escape from it only by a change that he himself will bring about in himself. Significantly, Kant says that this Enlightenment has a *Wahlspruch*: now a *Wahlspruch* is a heraldic device, that is, a distinctive feature by which one can be recognized, and it is also a motto, an instruction that one gives oneself and proposes to others. What, then, is this instruction? *Aude sapere*: "dare to know," "have the courage, the audacity, to know." Thus Enlightenment must be considered both as a process in which men participate collectively and as an act of courage to be accomplished personally. Men are at once elements and agents of a single process. They may be actors in the process to the extent that they participate in it; and the process occurs to the extent that men decide to be its voluntary actors. *man & society both create (k)*

A third difficulty appears here in Kant's text, in his use of the word "mankind," *Menschheit*. The importance of this word in the Kantian conception of history is well known. Are we to understand that the entire human race is caught up in the process of Enlightenment? In that case, we must imagine Enlightenment as a historical change that affects the political and social existence of all people on the face of the earth. Or are we to understand that it involves a change affecting what constitutes the humanity of human beings? But the question then arises of knowing what this change is. Here again, Kant's answer is not without a certain ambiguity. In any case, beneath its appearance of simplicity, it is rather complex.

Kant defines two essential conditions under which mankind can escape from its immaturity. And these two conditions are at once spiritual and institutional, ethical and political.

The first of these conditions is that the realm of obedience and the realm of the use of reason be clearly distinguished. Briefly characterizing the immature status, Kant invokes the familiar expression: "Don't think, just follow orders"; such is, according to him, the form in which military discipline, political power, and religious authority are usually exercised. Humanity will reach maturity when it is no longer required to obey, but when men are told: "Obey, and you will be able to reason as much as you like." We must note that the German word used here is *räsonieren*; this word, which is also used in the *Critiques*, does not refer to just any use of reason, but to a use of reason in which reason has no other end but itself: *räsonieren* is to reason for reasoning's sake. And Kant gives examples, these too being perfectly trivial in appearance: paying one's taxes, while being able to argue as much as one likes about the system of taxation, would be characteristic of the mature state; or again, taking responsibility for parish service, if one is a pastor, while reasoning freely about religious dogmas.

We might think that there is nothing very different here from what has been meant, since the sixteenth century, by freedom of conscience: the right to think as one pleases so long as one obeys as one must. Yet it is here that Kant brings into play another distinction, and in a rather surprising way. The distinction he introduces is between the private and public uses of reason. But he adds at once that reason must be free in its public use, and must be submissive in its private use. Which is, term for term, the opposite of what is ordinarily called freedom of conscience.

But we must be somewhat more precise. What constitutes, for Kant, this private use of reason? In what area is it exercised? Man, Kant says, makes a private use of reason when he is "a cog in a machine"; that is, when he has a role to play in society and jobs to do: to be a soldier, to have taxes to play, to be in charge of a parish, to be a civil servant, all this makes the human being a particular segment of society; he finds himself thereby placed in a circumscribed position, where he has to apply particular rules and pursue particular ends. Kant does not ask that people practice a blind and foolish obedience, but that they adapt the use they make of their reason to these determined circumstances; and reason must then be subjected to the particular ends in view. Thus there cannot be, here, any free use of reason.

On the other hand, when one is reasoning only in order to use one's reason, when one is reasoning as a reasonable being (and not as a cog in a machine), when one is reasoning as a member of reasonable humanity, then the use of reason must be free and public. Enlightenment is thus not merely the process by which individuals would see their own personal freedom of thought guaranteed. There is Enlightenment when the universal, the free, and the public uses of reason are superimposed on one another. | (R)eason (R) when used by public.

Now this leads us to a fourth question that must be put to Kant's text. We can readily see how the universal use of reason (apart from any private end) is the business of the subject himself as an individual; we can readily see, too, how the freedom of this use may be assured in a purely negative manner through the absence of any challenge to it; but how is a public use of that reason to be assured? Enlightenment, as we see, must not be conceived simply as a general process affecting all humanity; it must not be conceived only as an obligation prescribed to individuals: it now appears as a political problem. The question, in any event, is that of knowing how the use of reason can take the public form that it requires, how the audacity to know can be exercised in broad daylight, while individuals are obeying as scrupulously as possible. And Kant, in conclusion, proposes to Frederick II, in scarcely veiled terms, a sort of contract— what might be called the contract of rational despotism with free reason: the public and free use of autonomous reason will be the best guarantee of obedience, on condition, however, that the political principle that must be obeyed itself be in conformity with universal reason.

Let us leave Kant's text here. I do not by any means propose to consider it as capable of constituting an adequate description of Enlightenment; and no historian, I think, could be satisfied with it for an analysis of the social, political, and cultural transformations that occurred at the end of the eighteenth century.

Nevertheless, notwithstanding its circumstantial nature, and without intending to give it an exaggerated place in Kant's work, I believe that it is necessary to stress the connection that exists between this brief article and the three *Critiques*. Kant in fact describes Enlightenment as the moment when humanity is going to put its own reason to use, without subjecting itself to any authority; now it is precisely at this moment that the critique is necessary, since its role is that of defining the conditions under which the use of reason is legitimate in order to determine what can be known, what must be done, and what may be hoped. Illegitimate uses of reason are what give rise to dogmatism and heteronomy, along with illusion; on the other hand, it is when the legitimate use of reason has been clearly defined in its principles that its autonomy can be assured. The critique is, in a sense, the handbook of reason that has grown up in Enlightenment; and, conversely, the Enlightenment is the age of the critique.

It is also necessary, I think, to underline the relation between this text of Kant's and the other texts he devoted to history. These latter, for the most part, seek to define the internal teleology of time and the point toward which history of humanity is moving. Now the analysis of Enlightenment, defining this history as humanity's passage to its adult status, situates contemporary reality with respect to the overall movement and its basic directions. But at the same time, it shows how, at this very moment, each individual is responsible in a certain way for that overall process.

The hypothesis I should like to propose is that this little text is located in a sense at the crossroads of critical reflection and reflection on history. It is a reflection by Kant on the contemporary status of his own enterprise. No doubt it is not the first time that a philosopher has given his reasons for undertaking his work at a particular moment. But it seems to me that it is the first time that a philosopher has connected in this way, closely and from the inside, the significance of his work with respect to knowledge, a reflection on history and a particular analysis of the specific moment at which he is writing and because of which he is writing. It is in the reflection on "today" as difference in history and as motive for a particular philosophical task that the novelty of this text appears to me to lie.

And, by looking at it in this way, it seems to me we may recognize a point of departure: the outline of what one might call the attitude of modernity.

I know that modernity is often spoken of as an epoch, or at least as a set of features characteristic of an epoch; situated on a calendar, it would be preceded by a more or less naive or archaic premodernity, and followed by an enigmatic and troubling "postmodernity." And then we find ourselves asking whether modernity constitutes the sequel to the Enlightenment and its development, or whether we are to see it as a rupture or a deviation with respect to the basic principles of the eighteenth century.

Thinking back on Kant's text, I wonder whether we may not envisage modernity rather as an attitude than as a period of history. And by "attitude," I mean a mode of relating to contemporary reality; a voluntary choice made by certain people; in the end, a way of thinking and feeling; a way, too, of acting and behaving that at one and the same time marks a relation of belonging and presents itself as a task. A bit, no doubt, like what the Greeks called an *ethos*. And consequently, rather than seeking to distinguish the "modern era" from the "premodern" or "postmodern," I think it would be more useful to try to find out how the attitude of modernity, ever since its formation, has found itself struggling with attitudes of "countermodernity."

To characterize briefly this attitude of modernity, I shall take an almost indispensable example, namely, Baudelaire; for his consciousness of modernity is widely recognized as one of the most acute in the nineteenth century.

Modernity is often characterized in terms of consciousness of the discontinuity of time: a break with tradition, a feeling of novelty, of vertigo in the face of the passing moment. And this is indeed what Baudelaire seems to be saying when he defines modernity as "the ephemeral, the fleeting, the contingent." But, for him, being modern does not lie in recognizing and accepting this perpetual movement; on the contrary, it lies in adopting a certain attitude with respect to this movement; and this deliberate, difficult attitude consists in recapturing something eternal that is not beyond the present instant, nor behind it, but within it. Modernity is distinct from fashion, which does no more than call into question the course of time; modernity is the attitude that makes it possible to grasp the "heroic" aspect of the present moment. Modernity is not a phenomenon of sensitivity to the fleeting present; it is the will to "heroize" the present.

I shall restrict myself to what Baudelaire says about the painting of his contemporaries. Baudelaire makes fun of those painters who, finding nineteenth-century dress excessively ugly, want to depict nothing but ancient togas. But modernity in painting does not consist, for Baudelaire, in introducing black clothing onto the canvas. The modern painter is the one who can show the dark frock-coat as "the necessary costume of our time," the one who knows how to make manifest, in the fashion of the day, the essential, permanent, obsessive relation that our age entertains with death. "The dress-coat and frock-coat not only possess their political beauty, which is an expression of universal equality, but also their poetic beauty, which is an expression of the public soul—an immense cortège of undertaker's mutes (mutes in love, political mutes, bourgeois mutes . . .). We are each of us celebrating some funeral." To designate this attitude of modernity, Baudelaire sometimes employs a litotes that is highly significant because it is presented in the form of a precept: "You have no right to despise the present."

This heroization is ironical, needless to say. The attitude of modernity does not treat the passing moment as sacred in order to try to maintain or perpetuate it. It certainly does not involve harvesting it as a fleeting and interesting curiosity. That would be what Baudelaire would call the spectator's posture. The *flâneur*, the idle, strolling spectator, is satisfied to keep his eyes open, to pay attention and to build up a storehouse of memories. In opposition to the *flâneur*, Baudelaire describes the man of modernity: "Away he goes, hurrying, searching.... Be very sure that this man ... —this solitary, gifted with an active imagination, ceaselessly journeying across the great human desert—has an aim loftier than that of a mere *flâneur*, an aim more general, something other than the fugitive pleasure of circumstance. He is looking for that quality which you must allow me to call 'modernity'.... He makes it his business to extract from fashion whatever element it may contain of poetry within history." As an example of modernity, Baudelaire cites the artist Constantin Guys. In appearance a spectator, a collector of curiosities, he remains "the last to linger wherever there can be a glow of light, an echo of poetry, a quiver of life or a chord of music; wherever a passion can *pose* before him, wherever natural man and conventional man display themselves in a strange beauty, wherever the sun lights up the swift joys of the *depraved animal*."

But let us make no mistake. Constantin Guys is not a *flâneur*; what makes him the modern painter *par excellence* in Baudelaire's eyes is that, just when the whole world is falling asleep, he begins to work, and he transfigures that world. His transfiguration does not entail an annulling of reality, but a difficult interplay between the truth of what is real and the exercise of freedom; "natural" things become "more than natural," "beautiful" things become "more than beautiful," and individual objects appear "endowed with an impulsive life like the soul of [their] creator." For the attitude of modernity, the high value of the present is indissociable from a desperate eagerness to imagine it, to imagine it otherwise than it is, and to transform it not by destroying it but by grasping it in what it is. Baudelairean modernity is an exercise in which extreme attention to what is real is confronted with the practice of a liberty that simultaneously respects this reality and violates it.... Modern man, for Baudelaire, is not the man who goes off to discover himself, his secrets and his hidden truth; he is the man who tries to invent himself. This modernity does not "liberate man in his own being"; it compels him to face the task of producing himself.

Let me add just one final word. This ironic heroization of the present, this transfiguring play of freedom with reality, this ascetic elaboration of the self—Baudelaire does not imagine that these have any place in society itself, or in the body politic. They can only be produced in another, a different place, which Baudelaire calls art.

I do not pretend to be summarizing in these few lines either the complex historical event that was the Enlightenment, at the end of the eighteenth century, or the attitude of modernity in the various guises it may have taken on during the last two centuries.

I have been seeking, on the one hand, to emphasize the extent to which a type of philosophical interrogation—one that simultaneously problematizes man's relation to the present, man's historical mode of being, and the constitution of the self as an autonomous subject—is rooted in the Enlightenment. On the other hand, I have been seeking to stress that the thread that may connect us with the Enlightenment is not faithfulness to doctrinal elements, but rather the permanent reactivation of an attitude—that is, of a philosophical ethos that could be described as a permanent critique of our historical era. I should like to characterize this ethos very briefly.

This ethos implies, first, the refusal of what I like to call the "blackmail" of the Enlightenment. I think that the Enlightenment, as a set of political, economic, social, institutional, and cultural events on which we still depend in large part, constitutes a privileged domain for analysis. I also think that as an enterprise for linking the progress of truth and the history of liberty in a bond of direct relation, it formulated a philosophical question that remains for us to consider. I think, finally, as I have tried to show with reference to Kant's text, that it defined a certain manner of philosophizing.

But that does not mean that one has to be "for" or "against" the Enlightenment. It even means precisely that one has to refuse everything that might present itself in the form of a simplistic and authoritarian alternative: you either accept the Enlightenment and remain within the tradition of its rationalism (this is considered a positive term by some and used by others, on the contrary, as a reproach); or else you criticize the Enlightenment and then try to escape from its principles of rationality (which may be seen once again as good or bad). And we do not break free of this blackmail by introducing "dialectical" nuances while seeking to determine what good and bad elements there may have been in the Enlightenment.

We must try to proceed with the analysis of ourselves as beings who are historically determined, to a certain extent, by the Enlightenment. Such an analysis implies a series of historical inquiries that are as precise as possible; and these inquiries will not be oriented retrospectively toward the "essential kernel of rationality" that can be found in the Enlightenment and that would have to be preserved in any event; they will be oriented toward the "contemporary limits of the necessary," that is, toward what is not or is no longer indispensable for the constitution of ourselves as autonomous subjects. . . .

Yet while taking these precautions into account, we must obviously give a more positive content to what may be a philosophical ethos consisting in a critique of what we are saying, thinking, and doing, through a historical ontology of ourselves.

This philosophical ethos may be characterized as a *limit-attitude*. We are not talking about a gesture of rejection. We have to move beyond the outside-inside alternative; we have to be at the frontiers. Criticism indeed consists of analyzing and reflecting upon limits. But if the Kantian question was that of knowing what limits knowledge has to renounce transgressing, it seems to me that the critical question today has to be turned back into a positive one: in what is given to us as universal, necessary, obligatory, what place is occupied by whatever is singular, contingent, and the product of arbitrary constraints? The point, in brief, is to transform the critique conducted in the form of necessary limitation into a practical critique that takes the form of a possible transgression.

This entails an obvious consequence: that criticism is no longer going to be practiced in the search for formal structures with universal value, but rather as a historical investigation into the events that have led us to constitute ourselves and to recognize ourselves as subjects of what we are doing, thinking, saying. In that sense, this criticism is not transcendental, and its goal is not that of making a metaphysics possible: it is genealogical in its design and archaeological in its method. Archaeological—and not transcendental—in the sense that it will not seek to identify the universal structures of all knowledge or of all possible moral action, but will seek to treat the instances of discourse that articulate what we think, say, and do as so many historical events. And this critique will be genealogical in the sense that it will not deduce from the form of what we are what it is impossible for us to do and to know; but it will separate out, from the contingency that has made us what we are, the possibility of no longer being, doing, or thinking what we are, do, or think. It is not seeking to make possible a metaphysics that has finally become a science; it is seeking to give new impetus, as far and wide as possible, to the undefined work of freedom.

But if we are not to settle for the affirmation or the empty dream of freedom, it seems to me that this historico-critical attitude must also be an experimental one. I mean that this work done at the limits of ourselves must, on the one hand, open up a realm of historical inquiry and, on the other, put itself to the test of reality, of contemporary reality, both to grasp the points where change is possible and desirable, and to determine the precise form this change should take. This means that the historical ontology of ourselves must turn away from all projects that claim to be global or radical. In fact we know from experience that the claim to escape from the system of contemporary reality so as to produce the overall programs of another society, of another way of thinking, another culture, another vision of the world, has led only to the return of the most dangerous traditions. . . .

A brief summary, to conclude and to come back to Kant.

I do not know whether we will ever reach mature adulthood. Many things in our experience convince us that the historical event of the Enlightenment did not make us mature adults, and we have not reached that stage yet. However, it seems to me that a meaning can be attributed to that critical interrogation on the present and on ourselves which Kant formulated by reflecting on the Enlightenment. It seems to me that Kant's reflection is even a way of philosophizing that has not been without its importance or effectiveness during the last two centuries. The critical ontology of ourselves has to be considered not, certainly, as a theory, a doctrine, nor even as a permanent body of knowledge that is accumulating; it has to be conceived as an attitude, an ethos, a philosophical life in which the critique of what we are is at one and the same time the historical analysis of the limits that are imposed on us and an experiment with the possibility of going beyond them.

This philosophical attitude has to be translated into the labor of diverse inquiries. These inquiries have their methodological coherence in the at once archaeological and genealogical study of practices envisaged simultaneously as a technological type of rationality and as strategic games of liberties; they have their theoretical coherence in the definition of the historically unique forms in which the generalities of our relations to things, to others, to ourselves, have been problematized. They have their practical coherence in the care brought to the process of putting historico-critical reflection to the test of concrete practices. I do not know whether it must be said today that the critical task still entails faith in Enlightenment; I continue to think that this task requires work on our limits, that is, a patient labor giving form to our impatience for liberty.

MICHEL FOUCAULT
(1976)

Selections from

The History

of Sexuality

For a long time, the story goes, we supported a Victorian regime, and we continue to be dominated by it even today. Thus the image of the imperial prude is emblazoned on our restrained, mute, and hypocritical sexuality.

At the beginning of the seventeenth century a certain frankness was still common, it would seem. Sexual practices had little need of secrecy; words were said without undue reticence, and things were done without too much concealment; one had a tolerant familiarity with the illicit. Codes regulating the coarse, the obscene, and the indecent were quite lax compared to those of the nineteenth century. It was a time of direct gestures, shameless discourse, and open transgressions, when anatomies were shown and intermingled at will, and knowing children hung about amid the laughter of adults: it was a period when bodies "made a display of themselves."

But twilight soon fell upon this bright day, followed by the monotonous nights of the Victorian bourgeoisie. Sexuality was carefully confined; it moved into the home. The conjugal family took custody of it and absorbed it into the serious function of reproduction. On the subject of sex, silence became the rule. The legitimate and procreative couple laid down the law. The couple imposed itself as model, enforced the norm, safeguarded the truth, and reserved the right to speak while retaining the principle of secrecy. A single locus of sexuality was acknowledged in social space as well as at the heart of every household, but it was a utilitarian and fertile one: the parents' bedroom. The rest had only to remain vague; proper

The History of Sexuality: An Introduction, vol. 1, trans. by Robert Hurley (New York: Vintage, 1978). pp. 3–7, 17–18, 20–35, 38–39, 46–47, 54–57, 68–69, 92–93. Reprinted by permission of Georges Borchardt, Inc.

demeanor avoided contact with other bodies, and verbal decency sanitized one's speech. And sterile behavior carried the taint of abnormality; if it insisted on making itself too visible, it would be designated accordingly and would have to pay the penalty.

Nothing that was not ordered in terms of generation or transfigured by it could expect sanction or protection. Nor did it merit a hearing. It would be driven out, denied, and reduced to silence. Not only did it not exist, it had no right to exist and would be made to disappear upon its least manifestation—whether in acts or in words. Everyone knew, for example, that children had no sex, which was why they were forbidden to talk about it, why one closed one's eyes and stopped one's ears whenever they came to show evidence to the contrary, and why a general and studied silence was imposed. These are the characteristic features attributed to repression, which serve to distinguish it from the prohibitions maintained by penal law: repression operated as a sentence to disappear, but also as an injunction to silence, an affirmation of nonexistence, and, by implication, an admission that there was nothing to say about such things, nothing to see, and nothing to know. Such was the hypocrisy of our bourgeois societies with its halting logic. It was forced to make a few concessions, however. If it was truly necessary to make room for illegitimate sexualities, it was reasoned, let them take their infernal mischief elsewhere: to a place where they could be reintegrated, if not in the circuits of production, at least in those of profit. The brothel and the mental hospital would be those places of tolerance: the prostitute, the client, and the pimp, together with the psychiatrist and his hysteric—those "other Victorians," as Steven Marcus would say—seem to have surreptitiously transferred the pleasures that are unspoken into the order of things that are counted. Words and gestures, quietly authorized, could be exchanged there at the going rate. Only in those places would untrammeled sex have a right to (safely insularized) forms of reality, and only to clandestine, circumscribed, and coded types of discourse. Everywhere else, modern puritanism imposed its triple edict of taboo, nonexistence, and silence.

But have we not liberated ourselves from those two long centuries in which the history of sexuality must be seen first of all as the chronicle of an increasing repression? Only to a slight extent, we are told. Perhaps some progress was made by Freud; but with such circumspection, such medical prudence, a scientific guarantee of innocuousness, and so many precautions in order to contain everything, with no fear of "overflow," in that safest and most discrete of spaces, between the couch and discourse: yet another round of whispering on a bed. And could things have been otherwise? We are informed that if repression has indeed been the fundamental link between power, knowledge, and sexuality since the classical age, it stands to reason that we will not be able to free ourselves from it except at a considerable cost: nothing less than a transgression of laws, a lifting of prohibitions, an irruption of speech, a reinstating of pleasure within reality, and a whole new economy in the mechanisms of power will be required. For the least glimmer of truth is conditioned by politics. Hence, one cannot hope to obtain the desired results simply from a medical practice, nor from a theoretical discourse, however rigorously pursued. . . .

This discourse on modern sexual repression holds up well, owing no doubt to how easy it is to uphold. A solemn historical and political guarantee protects it. By placing the advent of the age of repression in the seventeenth century, after hundreds of years of open spaces and free expression, one adjusts it to coincide with the development of capitalism: it becomes an integral part of the bourgeois order. The minor chronicle of sex and its trials is transposed into the ceremonious history of the modes of production; its trifling aspect fades from view. A principle of explanation emerges after the fact: if sex is so rigorously repressed, this is because it is incompatible with a general and intensive work imperative. At a time when labor capacity was being systematically exploited, how could this capacity be allowed to dissipate itself in pleasurable pursuits, except in those—reduced to a minimum—that enabled it to reproduce itself? Sex and its effects are perhaps not so easily deciphered; on the other hand, their repression, thus reconstructed, is easily analyzed. And the sexual cause—the demand for sexual freedom, but also for the knowledge to be gained from sex and the right to speak about it—becomes legitimately associated with the honor of a political cause: sex too is placed on the agenda for the future. A suspicious mind might wonder if taking so many precautions in order to give the history of sex such an impressive filiation does not bear traces of the same old prudishness: as if those valorizing correlations were necessary before such a discourse could be formulated or accepted.

But there may be another reason that makes it so gratifying for us to define the relationship between sex and power in terms of repression: something that one might call the speaker's benefit. If sex is repressed, that is, condemned to prohibition, nonexistence, and silence, then the mere fact that one is speaking about it has the appearance of a deliberate transgression. A person who holds forth in such language places himself to a certain extent outside the reach of power; he upsets established law; he somehow anticipates the coming freedom. This explains the solemnity with which one speaks of sex nowadays. When they had to allude to it, the first demographers and psychiatrists of the nineteenth century thought it advisable to excuse themselves for asking their readers to dwell on matters so trivial and base. But for decades now, we have found it difficult to speak on the subject without striking a different pose: we are conscious of defying established power, our tone of voice shows that we know we are being subversive, and we ardently conjure away the present and appeal to the future, whose day will be hastened by the contribution we believe we are making. Something that smacks of revolt, of promised freedom, of the coming age of a different law, slips easily into this discourse on sexual oppression. Some of the ancient functions of prophecy are reactivated therein. Tomorrow sex will be good again. Because this repression is affirmed, one can discreetly bring into coexistence concepts which the fear of ridicule or the bitterness of history prevents most of us from putting side by side: revolution and happiness; or revolution and a different body, one that is newer and more beautiful; or indeed, revolution and pleasure. What sustains our eagerness to speak of sex in terms of repression is doubtless this opportunity to speak out against the powers that be, to utter truths and promise bliss, to link together enlightenment, liberation, and manifold pleasures; to pronounce a discourse that combines the fervor of knowledge, the determination to change the laws, and the longing for the garden of earthly delights. This is perhaps what also explains the market value attributed not only to what is said about sexual repression, but also to the mere fact of lending an ear to those who would eliminate the effects of repression. Ours is, after all, the only civilization in which officials are paid to listen to all and sundry impart the secrets of their sex: as if the urge to talk about it, and the interest one hopes to arouse by doing so, have far surpassed the possibilities of being heard, so that some individuals have even offered their ears for hire.

But it appears to me that the essential thing is not this economic factor, but rather the existence in our era of a discourse in which sex, the revelation of truth, the overturning of global laws, the proclamation of a new day to come, and the promise of a certain felicity are linked together. Today it is sex that serves as a support for the ancient form—so familiar and important in the West—of preaching. A great sexual sermon—which has had its subtle theologians and its popular voices—has swept through our societies over the last decades....

The seventeenth century, then, was the beginning of an age of repression emblematic of what we call the bourgeois societies, an age which perhaps we still have not completely left behind. Calling sex by its name thereafter became more difficult and more costly. As if in order to gain mastery over it in reality, it had first been necessary to subjugate it at the level of language, control its free circulation in speech, expunge it from the things that were said, and extinguish the words that rendered it too visibly present. And even these prohibitions, it seems, were afraid to name it. Without even having to pronounce the word, modern prudishness was able to ensure that one did not speak of sex, merely through the interplay of prohibitions that referred back to one another: instances of muteness which, by dint of saying nothing, imposed silence. Censorship.

Yet when one looks back over these last three centuries with their continual transformations, things appear in a very different light: around and apropos of sex, one sees a veritable discursive explosion. We must be clear on this point, however. It is quite possible that there was an expurgation—and a very rigorous one—of the authorized vocabulary. It may indeed be true that a whole rhetoric of allusion and metaphor was codified. Without question, new rules of propriety screened out some words: there was a policing of statements. A control over enunciations as well: where and when it was not possible to talk about such things became much more strictly defined; in which circumstances, among which speakers, and within which social relationships. Areas were thus established, if not of utter silence, at least of tact and discretion: between parents and children, for instance, or teachers and pupils, or masters and domestic servants. This almost certainly constituted a whole restrictive economy, one that was incorporated into that politics of language and speech—spontaneous on the one hand, concerted on the other—which accompanied the social redistributions of the classical period.

At the level of discourses and their domains, however, practically the opposite phenomenon occurred. There was a steady proliferation of discourses concerned with sex—specific discourses, different from one another both by their form and by their object: a discursive ferment that gathered momentum from the eighteenth century onward. Here I am thinking not so much of the probable increase in "illicit" discourses, that is, discourses of infraction that crudely named sex by way of insult or mockery of the new code of decency; the tightening up of the rules of decorum likely did produce, as a countereffect, a valorization and intensification of indecent speech. But more important was the multiplication of discourses concerning sex in the field of exercise of power itself: an institutional incitement to speak about it, and to do so more and more; a determination on the part of the agencies of power to hear it spoken about, and to cause *it* to speak through explicit articulation and endlessly accumulated detail....

For this was an evil that afficted the whole man, and in the most secret of forms: "Examine diligently, therefore, all the faculties of your soul: memory, understanding, and will. Examine with precision all your senses as well.... Examine, moreover, all your thoughts, every word you speak, and all your actions. Examine even unto your dreams, to know if, once awakened, you did not give them your consent. And finally, do not think that in so sensitive and perilous a matter as this, there is anything trivial or insignificant." Discourse, therefore, had to trace the meeting line of the body and the soul, following all its meanderings: beneath the surface of the sins, it would lay bare the unbroken nervure of the flesh. Under the authority of a language that had been carefully expurgated so that it was no longer directly named, sex was taken charge of, tracked down as it were, by a discourse that aimed to allow it no obscurity, no respite.

It was here, perhaps, that the injunction, so peculiar to the West, was laid down for the first time, in the form of a general constraint. I am not talking about the obligation to admit to violations of the laws of sex, as required by traditional penance; but of the nearly infinite task of telling—telling oneself and another, as often as possible, everything that might concern the interplay of innumerable pleasures, sensations, and thoughts which, through the body and the soul, had some affinity with sex. This scheme for transforming sex into discourse had been devised long before in an ascetic and monastic setting. The seventeenth century made it into a rule for everyone. It would seem in actual fact that it could scarcely have applied to any but a tiny elite; the great majority of the faithful who only went to confession on rare occasions in the course of the year escaped such complex prescriptions. But the important point no doubt is that this obligation was decreed, as an ideal at least, for every good Christian. An imperative was established: Not only will you confess to acts contravening the law, but you will seek to transform your desire, your every desire, into discourse. Insofar as possible, nothing was meant to elude this dictum, even if the words it employed had to be carefully neutralized. The Christian pastoral prescribed as a fundamental duty the task of passing everything having to do with sex through the endless mill of speech. The forbidding of certain words, the decency of expressions, all the censorings of vocabulary, might well have been only secondary devices compared to that great subjugation: ways of rendering it morally acceptable and technically useful.

One could plot a line going straight from the seventeenth-century pastoral to what became its projection in literature, "scandalous" literature at that. "Tell everything," the directors would say time and again: "not only consummated acts, but sensual touchings, all impure gazes, all obscene remarks ... all consenting thoughts." Sade takes up the injunction in words that seem to have been retranscribed from the treatises of spirtual direction: "Your narrations must be decorated with the most numerous and searching details; the precise way and extent to which we may judge how the passion you describe relates to human manners and man's character is determined by your willingness to disguise no circumstance; and what is more, the least circumstance is apt to have an immense influence upon the procuring of that kind of sensory irritation we expect from your stories." And again at the end of the nineteenth century, the anonymous author of *My Secret Life* submitted to the same prescription; outwardly, at least, this man was doubtless a kind of traditional libertine; but he conceived the idea of complementing his life—which he had almost totally dedicated to sexual activity—with a scrupulous account of every one of its episodes. He sometimes excuses himself by stressing his concern to educate young people, this man who had eleven volumes published, in a printing of only a few copies, which were devoted to the least adventures, pleasures, and sensations of his sex. It is best to take him at his word when he lets into his text the voice of a pure imperative: "I recount the facts, just as they happened, insofar as I am able to recollect them; this is all that I can do"; "a secret life must not leave out anything; there is nothing to be ashamed of ... one can never know too much concerning human nature." The solitary author of *My Secret Life* often says, in order to justify his describing them, that his strangest practices undoubtedly were shared by thousands of men on the surface of the earth. But the guiding principle for the strangest of these practices, which was the fact of recounting them all, and in detail, from day to day, had been lodged in the heart of modern man for over two centuries. Rather than seeing in this singular man a courageous fugitive from a "Victorianism" that would have compelled him to silence, I am inclined to think that, in an epoch dominated by (highly prolix) directives enjoining discretion and modesty, he was the most direct and in a way the most naive representative of a plurisecular injunction to talk about sex. The historical accident would consist rather of the reticences of "Victorian puritanism"; at any rate, they were a digression, a refinement, a tactical diversion in the great process of transforming sex into discourse.

This nameless Englishman will serve better than his queen as the central figure for a sexuality whose main features were already taking shape with the Christian pastoral. Doubtless, in contrast to the latter, for him it was a matter of augmenting the sensations he experienced with the details of what he said about them; like Sade, he wrote "for his pleasure alone," in the strongest sense of the expression; he carefully mixed the editing and rereading of his text with erotic scenes which those writer's activities repeated, prolonged, and stimulated. But after all, the Christian pastoral also sought to produce specific effects on desire, by the mere fact of transforming it —fully and deliberately—into discourse: effects of mastery and detachment, to be sure, but also an effect of spiritual reconversion, of turning back to God, a physical effect of blissful suffering from feeling in one's body the pangs of temptation and the love that resists it. This is the essential thing: that Western man has been drawn for three centuries to the task of telling everything concerning his sex; that since the classical age there has been a constant optimization and an increasing valorization of the discourse on sex; and that this carefully analytical discourse was meant to yield multiple effects of displacement, intensification, reorientation, and modification of desire itself. Not only were the boundaries of what one could say about sex enlarged, and men compelled to hear it said; but more important, discourse was connected to sex by a complex organization with varying effects, by a deployment that cannot be adequately explained merely by referring it to a law of prohibition. A censorship of sex? There was installed rather an apparatus for producing an ever greater quantity of discourse about sex, capable of functioning and taking effect in its very economy.

This technique might have remained tied to the destiny of Christian spirituality if it had not been supported and relayed by other mechanisms. In the first place, by a "public interest." Not a collective curiosity or sensibility; not a new mentality; but power mechanisms that functioned in such a way that discourse on sex—for reasons that will have to be examined— became essential. Toward the beginning of the eighteenth century, there emerged a political, economic, and technical incitement to talk about sex. And not so much in the form of a general theory of sexuality as in the form of analysis, stocktaking, classification, and specification, of quantitative or causal studies. This need to take sex "into account," to pronounce a discourse on sex that would not derive from morality alone but from rationality as well, was sufficiently new that at first it wondered at itself and sought apologies for its own existence. How could a discourse based on reason speak of *that?* "Rarely have philosophers directed a steady gaze to these objects situated between disgust and ridicule, where one must avoid both hypocrisy and scandal." And nearly a century later, the medical establishment, which one might have expected to be less surprised by what it was about to formulate, still stumbled at the moment of speaking: "The darkness that envelops these facts, the shame and disgust they inspire, have always repelled the observer's gaze. . . . For a long time I hesitated to introduce the loathsome picture into this study." What is essential is not in all these scruples, in the "moralism" they betray, or in the hypocrisy one can suspect them of, but in the recognized necessity of overcoming this hesitation. One had to speak of sex; one had to speak publicly and in a manner that was not determined by the division between licit and illicit, even if the speaker maintained the distinction for himself (which is what these solemn and preliminary declarations were intended to show): one had to speak of it as of a thing to be not simply condemned or tolerated but managed, inserted into systems of utility, regulated for the greater good of all, made to function according to an optimum. Sex was not something one simply judged; it was a thing one administered. It was in the nature of a public potential; it called for management procedures; it had to be taken charge of by analytical discourses. In the eighteenth century, sex became a "police" matter—in the full and strict sense given the term at the time: not the repression of disorder, but an ordered maximization of collective and individual forces: "We must consolidate and augment, through the wisdom of its regulations, the internal power of the state; and since this power consists not only in the Republic in general, and in each of the members who constitute it, but also in the faculties and talents of those belonging to it, it follows that the police must concern themselves with these means and make them serve the public welfare. And they can only obtain this result through the knowledge they have of those different assets." A policing of sex: that is, not the rigor of a taboo, but the necessity of regulating sex through useful and public discourses.

A few examples will suffice. One of the great innovations in the techniques of power in the eighteenth century was the emergence of "population" as an economic and political problem: population as wealth, population as manpower or labor capacity, population balanced between its own growth and the resources it commanded. Governments perceived that they were not dealing simply with subjects, or even with a "people," but with a "population," with its specific phenomena and its peculiar variables: birth and death rates, life expectancy, fertility, state of health, frequency of illnesses, patterns of diet and habitation. All these variables were situated at the point where the characteristic movements of life and the specific effects of institutions intersected: "States are not populated in accordance with the natural progression of propagation, but by virtue of their industry, their products, and their different institutions.... Men multiply like the yields from the ground and in proportion to the advantages and resources they find in their labors." At the heart of this economic and political problem of population was sex: it was necessary to analyze the birthrate, the age of marriage, the legitimate and illegitimate births, the precocity and frequency of sexual relations, the ways of making them fertile or sterile, the effects of unmarried life or of the prohibitions, the impact of contraceptive practices—of those notorious "deadly secrets" which demographers on the eve of the Revolution knew were already familiar to the inhabitants of the countryside.

Of course, it had long been asserted that a country had to be populated if it hoped to be rich and powerful; but this was the first time that a society had affirmed, in a constant way, that its future and its fortune were tied not only to the number and the uprightness of its citizens, to their marriage rules and family organization, but to the manner in which each individual made use of his sex. Things went from ritual lamenting over the unfruitful debauchery of the rich, bachelors, and libertines to a discourse in which the sexual conduct of the population was taken both as an object of analysis and as a target of intervention; there was a progression from the crudely populationist arguments of the mercantilist epoch to the much more subtle and calculated attempts at regulation that tended to favor or discourage—according to the objectives and exigencies of the moment—an increasing birthrate. Through the political economy of population there was formed a whole grid of observations regarding sex. There emerged the analysis of the modes of sexual conduct, their determinations and their effects, at the boundary line of the biological and the economic domains. There also appeared those systematic campaigns which, going beyond the traditional means—moral and religious exhortations, fiscal measures—tried to transform the sexual conduct of couples into a concerted economic and political behavior. In time these new measures would become anchorage points for the different varieties of racism of the nineteenth and twentieth centuries. It was essential that the state know what was happening with its citizens' sex, and the use they made of it, but also that each individual be capable of controlling the use he made of it. Between the state and the individual, sex became an issue, and a public issue no less; a whole web of discourses, special knowledges, analyses, and injunctions settled upon it.

The situation was similar in the case of children's sex. It is often said that the classical period consigned it to an obscurity from which it scarcely emerged before the *Three Essays* or the beneficent anxieties of Little Hans. It is true that a longstanding "freedom" of language between children and adults, or pupils and teachers, may have disappeared. No seventeenth-century pedagogue would have publicly advised his disciple, as did Erasmus in his *Dialogues*, on the choice of a good prostitute. And the boisterous laughter that had accompanied the precocious sexuality of children for so long—and in all social classes, it seems—was gradually stifled. But this was not a plain and simple imposition of silence. Rather, it was a new regime of discourses. Not any less was said about it; on the contrary. But things were said in a different way; it was different people who said them, from different points of view, and in order to obtain different results. Silence itself—the things one declines to say, or is forbidden to name, the discretion that is required between different speakers—is less the absolute limit of discourse, the other side from which it is separated by a strict boundary, than an element that functions alongside the things said, with them and in relation to them within over-all strategies. There is no binary division to be made between what one says and what one does not say; we must try to determine the different ways of not saying such things, how those who can and those who cannot speak of them are distributed, which type of discourse is authorized, or which form of discretion is required in either case. There is not one but many silences, and they are an integral part of the strategies that underlie and permeate discourses.

Take the secondary schools of the eighteenth century, for example. On the whole, one can have the impression that sex was hardly spoken of at all in these institutions. But one only has to glance over the architectural layout, the rules of discipline, and their whole internal organization: the question of sex was a constant preoccupation. The builders considered it explicitly. The organizers took it permanently into account. All who held a measure of authority were placed in a state of perpetual alert, which the fixtures, the precautions taken, the interplay of punishments and responsibilities, never ceased to reiterate. The space for classes, the shape of the tables, the planning of the recreation lessons, the distribution of the dormitories (with or without partitions, with or without curtains), the rules for monitoring bedtime and sleep periods—all this referred, in the most prolix manner, to the sexuality of children. What one might call the internal discourse of the institution—the one it employed to address itself, and which circulated among those who made it function—was largely based on the assumption that this sexuality existed, that it was precocious, active, and ever present. But this was not all: the sex of the schoolboy became in the course of the eighteenth century—and quite apart from that of adolescents in general—a public problem. Doctors counseled the directors and professors of educational establishments, but they also gave their opinions to families; educators designed projects which they submitted to the authorities; schoolmasters turned to students, made recommendations to them, and drafted for their benefit books of exhortation, full of moral and medical examples. Around the schoolboy and his sex there proliferated a whole literature of precepts, opinions, observations, medical advice, clinical cases, outlines for reform, and plans for ideal institutions. . . .

It would be less than exact to say that the pedagogical institution has imposed a ponderous silence on the sex of children and adolescents. On the contrary, since the eighteenth century it has multiplied the forms of discourse on the subject; it has established various points of implantation for sex; it has coded contents and qualified speakers. Speaking about children's sex, inducing educators, physicians, administrators, and parents to speak of it, or speaking to them about it, causing children themselves to talk about it, and enclosing them in a web of discourses which sometimes address them, sometimes speak about them, or impose canonical bits of knowledge on them, or use them as a basis for constructing a science that is beyond their grasp—all this together enables us to link an intensification of the interventions of power to a multiplication of discourse. The sex of children and adolescents has become, since the eighteenth century, an important area of contention around which innumerable institutional devices and discursive strategies have been deployed. It may well be true that adults and children themselves were deprived of a certain way of speaking about sex, a mode that was disallowed as being too direct, crude, or coarse. But this was only the counterpart of other discourses, and perhaps the condition necessary in order for them to function, discourses that were interlocking, hierarchized, and all highly articulated around a cluster of power relations.

One could mention many other centers which in the eighteenth or nineteenth century began to produce discourses on sex. First there was medicine, via the "nervous disorders"; next psychiatry, when it set out to discover the etiology of mental illnesses, focusing its gaze first on "excess," then onanism, then frustration, then "frauds against procreation," but especially when it annexed the whole of the sexual perversions as its own province; criminal justice, too, which had long been concerned with sexuality, particularly in the form of "heinous" crimes and crimes against nature, but which, toward the middle of the nineteenth century, broadened its jurisdiction to include petty offenses, minor indecencies, insignificant perversions; and lastly, all those social controls, cropping up at the end of the last century, which screened the sexuality of couples, parents and children, dangerous and endangered adolescents—undertaking to protect, separate, and forewarn, signaling perils everywhere, awakening people's attention, calling for diagnoses, piling up reports, organizing therapies. These sites radiated discourses aimed at sex, intensifying people's awareness of it as a constant danger, and this in turn created a further incentive to talk about it.

One day in 1867, a farm hand from the village of Lapcourt, who was somewhat simpleminded, employed here then there, depending on the season, living hand-to-mouth from a little charity or in exchange for the worst sort of labor, sleeping in barns and stables, was turned in to the authorities. At the border of a field, he had obtained a few caresses from a little girl, just as he had done before and seen done by the village urchins round about him; for, at the edge of the wood, or in the ditch by the road leading to Saint-Nicolas, they would play the familiar game called "curdled milk." So he was pointed out by the girl's parents to the mayor of the village, reported by the mayor to the gendarmes, led by the gendarmes to the judge, who indicted him and turned him over first to a doctor, then to two other experts who not only wrote their report but also had it published. What is the significant thing about this story? The pettiness of it all; the fact that this everyday occurrence in the life of village sexuality, these inconsequential bucolic pleasures, could become, from a certain time, the object not only of a collective intolerance but of a judicial action, a medical intervention, a careful clinical examination, and an entire theoretical elaboration. The thing to note is that they went so far as to measure the brainpan, study the facial bone structure, and inspect for possible signs of degenrescence the anatomy of this personage who up to that moment had been an integral part of village life; that they made him talk; that they questioned him concerning his thoughts, inclinations, habits, sensations, and opinions. And then, acquitting him of any crime, they decided finally to make him into a pure object of medicine and knowledge—an object to be shut away till the end of his life in the hospital at Maréville, but also one to be made known to the world of learning through a detailed analysis. One can be fairly certain that during this same period the Lapcourt schoolmaster was instructing the little villagers to mind their language and not talk about all these things aloud. But this was undoubtedly one of the conditions enabling the institutions of knowledge and power to overlay this everyday bit of theater with their solemn discourse. So it was that our society—and it was doubtless the first in history to take such measures—assembled around these timeless gestures, these barely furtive pleasures between simple-minded adults and alert children, a whole machinery for speechifying, analyzing, and investigating.

Between the licentious Englishman, who earnestly recorded for his own purposes the singular episodes of his secret life, and his contemporary, this village halfwit who would give a few pennies to the little girls for favors the older ones refused him, there was without doubt a profound connection: in any case, from one extreme to the other, sex became something to say, and to say exhaustively in accordance with deployments that were varied, but all, in their own way, compelling. Whether in the form of a subtle confession in confidence or an authoritarian interrogation, sex—be it refined or rustic—had to be put into words. A great polymorphous injunction bound the Englishman and the poor Lorrainese peasant alike.

Since the eighteenth century, sex has not ceased to provoke a kind of generalized discursive erethism. And these discourses on sex did not multiply apart from or against power, but in the very space and as the means of its exercise. Incitements to speak were orchestrated from all quarters, apparatuses everywhere for listening and recording, procedures for observing, questioning, and formulating. Sex was driven out of hiding and constrained to lead a discursive existence. From the singular imperialism that compels everyone to transform their sexuality into a perpetual discourse, to the manifold mechanisms which, in the areas of economy, pedagogy, medicine, and justice, incite, extract, distribute, and institutionalize the sexual discourse, an immense verbosity is what our civilization has required and organized. Surely no other type of society has ever accumulated—and in such a relatively short span of time—a similar quantity of discourses concerned with sex. It may well be that we talk about sex more than anything else; we set our minds to the task; we convince ourselves that we have never said enough on the subject, that, through inertia or submissiveness, we conceal from ourselves the blinding evidence, and that what is essential always eludes us, so that we must always start out once again in search of it. It is possible that where sex is concerned, the most long-winded, the most impatient of societies is our own.

But as this first overview shows, we are dealing less with *a* discourse on sex than with a multiplicity of discourses produced by a whole series of mechanisms operating in different institutions. The Middle Ages had organized around the theme of the flesh and the practice of penance a discourse that was markedly unitary. In the course of recent centuries, this relative uniformity was broken apart, scattered, and multiplied in an explosion of distinct discursivities which took form in demography, biology, medicine, psychiatry, psychology, ethics, pedagogy, and political criticism. More precisely, the secure bond that held together the moral theology of concupiscence and the obligation of confession (equivalent to the theoretical discourse on sex and its first-person formulation) was, if not broken, at least loosened and diversified: between the objectification of sex in rational discourses, and the movement by which each individual was set to the task of recounting his own sex, there has occurred, since the eighteenth century, a whole series of tensions, conflicts, efforts at adjustment, and attempts at retranscription. So it is not simply in terms of a continual extension that we must speak of this discursive growth; it should be seen rather as a dispersion of centers from which discourses emanated, a diversification of their forms, and the complex deployment of the network connecting them. Rather than the uniform concern to hide sex, rather than a general prudishness of language, what distinguishes these last three centuries is the variety, the wide dispersion of devices that were invented for speaking about it, for having it be spoken about, for inducing it to speak of itself, for listening, recording, transcribing, and redistributing what is said about it: around sex, a whole network of varying, specific, and coercive transpositions into discourse. Rather than a massive censorship, beginning with the verbal proprieties imposed by the Age of Reason, what was involved was a regulated and polymorphous incitement to discourse.

The objection will doubtless be raised that if so many stimulations and constraining mechanisms were necessary in order to speak of sex, this was because there reigned over everyone a certain fundamental prohibition; only definite necessities—economic pressures, political requirements—were able to lift this prohibition and open a few approaches to the discourse on sex, but these were limited and carefully coded; so much talk about sex, so many insistent devices contrived for causing it to be talked about—but under strict conditions: does this not prove that it was an object of secrecy, and more important, that there is still an attempt to keep it that way? But this often-stated theme, that sex is outside of discourse and that only the removing of an obstacle, the breaking of a secret, can clear the way leading to it, is precisely what needs to be examined. Does it not partake of the injunction by which discourse is provoked? Is it not with the aim of inciting people to speak of sex that it is made to mirror, at the outer limit of every actual discourse, something akin to a secret whose discovery is imperative, a thing abusively reduced to silence, and at the same time difficult and necessary, dangerous and precious to divulge? We must not forget that by making sex into that which, above all else, had to be confessed, the Christian pastoral always presented it as the disquieting enigma: not a thing which stubbornly shows itself, but one which always hides, the insidious presence that speaks in a voice so muted and often disguised that one risks remaining deaf to it. Doubtless the secret does not reside in that basic reality in relation to which all the incitements to speak of sex are situated—whether they try to force the secret, or whether in some obscure way they reinforce it by the manner in which they speak of it. It is a question rather of a theme that forms part of the very mechanics of these incitements: a way of giving shape to the requirement to speak about the matter, a fable that is indispensable to the endlessly proliferating economy of the discourse on sex. What is peculiar to modern societies, in fact, is not that they consigned sex to a shadow existence, but that they dedicated themselves to speaking of it *ad infinitum*, while exploiting it as *the* secret.

Breaking the rules of marriage or seeking strange pleasures brought an equal measure of condemnation. On the list of grave sins, and separated only by their relative importance, there appeared debauchery (extramarital relations), adultery, rape, spiritual or carnal incest, but also sodomy, or the mutual "caress." As to the courts, they could condemn homosexuality as well as infidelity, marriage without parental consent, or bestiality. What was taken into account in the civil and religious jurisdictions alike was a general unlawfulness. Doubtless acts "contrary to nature" were stamped as especially abominable, but they were perceived simply as an extreme form of acts "against the law"; they were infringements of decrees which were just as sacred as those of marriage, and which had been established for governing the order of things and the plan of beings. Prohibitions bearing on sex were essentially of a juridical nature. The "nature" on which they were based was still a kind of law. For a long time hermaphrodites were criminals, or crime's offspring, since their anatomical disposition, their very being, confounded the law that distinguished the sexes and prescribed their union.

The discursive explosion of the eighteenth and nineteenth centuries caused this system centered on legitimate alliance to undergo two modifications. First, a centrifugal movement with respect to heterosexual monogamy. Of course, the array of practices and pleasures continued to be referred to it as their internal standard; but it was spoken of less and less, or in any case with a growing moderation. Efforts to find out its secrets were abandoned; nothing further was demanded of it than to define itself from day to day. The legitimate couple, with its regular sexuality, had a right to more discretion. It tended to function as a norm, one that was stricter, perhaps, but quieter. On the other hand, what came under scrutiny was the sexuality of children, mad men and women, and criminals; the sensuality of those who did not like the opposite sex; reveries, obsessions, petty manias, or great transports of rage. It was time for all these figures, scarcely noticed in the past, to step forward and speak, to make the difficult confession of what they were. No doubt they were condemned all the same; but they were listened to; and if regular sexuality happened to be questioned once again, it was through a reflux movement, originating in these peripheral sexualities.

Whence the setting apart of the "unnatural" as a specific dimension in the field of sexuality. This kind of activity assumed an autonomy with regard to the other condemned forms such as adultery or rape (and the latter were condemned less and less): to marry a close relative or practice sodomy, to seduce a nun or engage in sadism, to deceive one's wife or violate cadavers, became things that were essentially different. The area covered by the Sixth Commandment began to fragment. Similarly, in the civil order, the confused category of "debauchery," which for more than a century had been one of the most frequent reasons for administrative confinement, came apart. From the debris, there appeared on the one hand infractions against the legislation (or morality) pertaining to marriage and the family, and on the other, offenses against the regularity of a natural function (offenses which, it must be added, the law was apt to punish). Here we have a likely reason, among others, for the prestige of Don Juan, which three centuries have not erased. Underneath the great violator of the rules of marriage—stealer of wives, seducer of virgins, the shame of families, and an insult to husbands and fathers—another personage can be glimpsed: the individual driven, in spite of himself, by the somber madness of sex. Underneath the libertine, the pervert. He deliberately breaks the law, but at the same time, something like a nature gone awry transports him far from all nature; his death is the moment when the supernatural return of the crime and its retribution thwarts the flight into counternature...

[P]leasures, that is [are], both sought after and searched out; compartmental sexualities that are tolerated or encouraged; proximities that serve as surveillance procedures, and function as mechanisms of intensification; contacts that operate as inductors. This is the way things worked in the case of the family, or rather the household, with parents, children, and in some instances, servants. Was the nineteenth-century family really a monogamic and conjugal cell? Perhaps to a certain extent. But it was also a network of pleasures and powers linked together at multiple points and according to transformable relationships. The separation of grown-ups and children, the polarity established between the parents' bedroom and that of the children (it became routine in the course of the century when working-class housing construction was undertaken), the relative segregation of boys and girls, the strict instructions as to the care of nursing infants (maternal breast-feeding, hygiene), the attention focused on infantile sexuality, the supposed dangers of masturbation, the importance attached to puberty, the methods of surveillance suggested to parents, the exhortations, secrets, and fears, the presence—both valued and feared—of servants: all this made the family, even when brought down to its smallest dimensions, a complicated network, saturated with multiple, fragmentary, and mobile sexualities. To reduce them to the conjugal relationship, and then to project the latter, in the form of a forbidden desire, onto the children, cannot account for this apparatus which, in relation to these sexualities, was less a principle of inhibition than an inciting and multiplying mechanism. Educational or psychiatric institutions, with their large populations, their hierarchies, their spatial arrangements, their surveillance systems, constituted, alongside the family, another way of distributing the interplay of powers and pleasures; but they too delineated areas of extreme sexual saturation, with privileged spaces or rituals such as the classroom, the dormitory, the visit, and the consultation. The forms of a nonconjugal, nonmonogamous sexuality were drawn there and established.

Nineteenth-century "bourgeois" society—and it is doubtless still with us—was a society of blatant and fragmented perversion. And this was not by way of hypocrisy, for nothing was more manifest and more prolix, or more manifestly taken over by discourses and institutions. Not because, having tried to erect too rigid or too general a barrier against sexuality, society succeeded only in giving rise to a whole perverse outbreak and a long pathology of the sexual instinct. At issue, rather, is the type of power it brought to bear on the body and on sex. In point of fact, this power had neither the form of the law, nor the effects of the taboo. On the contrary, it acted by multiplication of singular sexualities. It did not set boundaries for sexuality; it extended the various forms of sexuality, pursuing them according to lines of indefinite penetration. It did not exclude sexuality, but included it in the body as a mode of specification of individuals. It did not seek to avoid it; it attracted its varieties by means of spirals in which pleasure and power reinforced one another. It did not set up a barrier; it provided places of maximum saturation. It produced and determined the sexual mosaic. Modern society is perverse, not in spite of its puritanism or as if from a backlash provoked by its hypocrisy; it is in actual fact, and directly, perverse.

In actual fact. The manifold sexualities—those which appear with the different ages (sexualities of the infant or the child), those which become fixated on particular tastes or practices (the sexuality of the invert, the gerontophile, the fetishist), those which, in a diffuse manner, invest relationships (the sexuality of doctor and patient, teacher and student, psychiatrist and mental patient), those which haunt spaces (the sexuality of the home, the school, the prison)— all form the correlate of exact procedures of power. We must not imagine that all these things that were formerly tolerated attracted notice and received a pejorative designation when the time came to give a regulative role to the one type of sexuality that was capable of reproducing labor power and the form of the family. . . .

It thus became associated with an insistent and indiscreet medical practice, glibly proclaiming its aversions, quick to run to the rescue of law and public opinion, more servile with respect to the powers of order than amenable to the requirements of truth.... [I]t assumed other powers; it set itself up as the supreme authority in matters of hygienic necessity, taking up the old fears of venereal affliction and combining them with the new themes of asepsis, and the great evolutionist myths with the recent institutions of public health; it claimed to ensure the physical vigor and the moral cleanliness of the social body; it promised to eliminate defective individuals, degenerate and bastardized populations. In the name of a biological and historical urgency, it justified the racisms of the state, which at the time were on the horizon. It grounded them in "truth."

When we compare these discourses on human sexuality with what was known at the time about the physiology of animal and plant reproduction, we are struck by the incongruity. Their feeble content from the standpoint of elementary rationality, not to mention scientificity, earns them a place apart in the history of knowledge. They form a strangely muddled zone. Throughout the nineteenth century, sex seems to have been incorporated into two very distinct orders of knowledge: a biology of reproduction, which developed continuously according to a general scientific normativity, and a medicine of sex conforming to quite different rules of formation. From one to the other, there was no real exchange, no reciprocal structuration; the role of the first with respect to the second was scarcely more than as a distant and quite fictitious guarantee: a blanket guarantee under cover of which moral obstacles, economic or political options, and traditional fears could be recast in a scientific-sounding vocabulary. It is as if a fundamental resistance blocked the development of a rationally formed discourse concerning human sex, its correlations, and its effects. A disparity of this sort would indicate that the aim of such a discourse was not to state the truth but to prevent its very emergence. Underlying the difference between the physiology of reproduction and the medical theories of sexuality, we would have to see something other and something more than an uneven scientific development or a disparity in the forms of rationality; the one would partake of that immense will to knowledge which has sustained the establishment of scientific discourse in the West, whereas the other would derive from a stubborn will to nonknowledge.

This much is undeniable: the learned discourse on sex that was pronounced in the nineteenth century was imbued with age-old delusions, but also with systematic blindnesses: a refusal to see and to understand; but further—and this is the crucial point—a refusal concerning the very thing that was brought to light and whose formulation was urgently solicited. For there can be no misunderstanding that is not based on a fundamental relation to truth. Evading this truth, barring access to it, masking it: these were so many local tactics which, as if by superimposition and through a last-minute detour, gave a paradoxical form to a fundamental petition to know. Choosing not to recognize was yet another vagary of the will to truth. Let Charcot's Salpêtrière serve as an example in this regard: it was an enormous apparatus for observation, with its examinations, interrogations, and experiments, but it was also a machinery for incitement, with its public presentations, its theater of ritual crises, carefully staged with the help of ether or amyl nitrate, its interplay of dialogues, palpations, laying on of hands, postures which the doctors elicited or obliterated with a gesture or a word, its hierarchy of personnel who kept watch, organized, provoked, monitored, and reported, and who accumulated an immense pyramid of observations and dossiers. It is in the context of this continuous incitement to discourse and to truth that the real mechanisms of misunderstanding (*méconnaissance*) operated: thus

Charcot's gesture interrupting a public consultation where it began to be too manifestly a question of "that"; and the more frequent practice of deleting from the succession of dossiers what had been said and demonstrated by the patients regarding sex, but also what had been seen, provoked, solicited by the doctors themselves, things that were almost entirely omitted from the published observations. The important thing, in this affair, is not that these men shut their eyes or stopped their ears, or that they were mistaken; it is rather that they constructed around and apropos of sex an immense apparatus for producing truth, even if this truth was to be masked at the last moment. The essential point is that sex was not only a matter of sensation and pleasure, of law and taboo, but also of truth and falsehood, that the truth of sex became something fundamental, useful, or dangerous, precious or formidable: in short, that sex was constituted as a problem of truth. What needs to be situated, therefore, is not the threshold of a new rationality whose discovery was marked by Freud—or someone else—but the progressive formation (and also the transformations) of that "interplay of truth and sex" which was bequeathed to us by the nineteenth century, and which we may have modified, but, lacking evidence to the contrary, have not rid ourselves of. Misunderstandings, avoidances, and evasions were only possible, and only had their effects, against the background of this strange endeavor: to tell the truth of sex. An endeavor that does not date from the nineteenth century, even if it was then that a nascent science lent it a singular form. It was the basis of all the aberrant, naïve, and cunning discourses where knowledge of sex seems to have strayed for such a long time.

Historically, there have been two great procedures for producing the truth of sex.

On the one hand, the societies—and they are numerous: China, Japan, India, Rome, the Arabo-Moslem societies—which endowed themselves with an *ars erotica*. In the erotic art, truth is drawn from pleasure itself, understood as a practice and accumulated as experience; pleasure is not considered in relation to an absolute law of the permitted and the forbidden, nor by reference to a criterion of utility, but first and foremost in relation to itself; it is experienced as pleasure, evaluated in terms of its intensity, its specific quality, its duration, its reverberations in the body and the soul. Moreover, this knowledge must be deflected back into the sexual practice itself, in order to shape it as though from within and amplify its effects. In this way, there is formed a knowledge that must remain secret, not because of an element of infamy that might attach to its object, but because of the need to hold it in the greatest reserve, since, according to tradition, it would lose its effectiveness and its virtue by being divulged. . . . Paradoxically, the *scientia sexualis* that emerged in the nineteenth century kept as its nucleus the singular ritual of obligatory and exhaustive confession, which in the Christian West was the first technique for producing the truth of sex. Beginning in the sixteenth century, this rite gradually detached itself from the sacrament of penance, and via the guidance of souls and the direction of conscience—the *ars artium*—emigrated toward pedagogy, relationships between adults and children, family relations, medicine, and psychiatry. In any case, nearly one hundred and fifty years have gone into the making of a complex machinery for producing true discourses on sex: a deployment that spans a wide segment of history in that it connects the ancient injunction of confession to clinical listening methods. It is this deployment that enables something called "sexuality" to embody the truth of sex and its pleasures.

"Sexuality": the correlative of that slowly developed discursive practice which constitutes the *scientia sexualis*. The essential features of this sexuality are not the expression of a representation that is more or less distorted by ideology, or of a misunderstanding caused by taboos; they correspond to the functional requirements of a discourse that must produce its truth.

Situated at the point of intersection of a technique of confession and a scientific discursivity, where certain major mechanisms had to be found for adapting them to one another (the listening technique, the postulate of causality, the principle of latency, the rule of interpretation, the imperative of medicalization), sexuality was defined as being "by nature": a domain susceptible to pathological processes, and hence one calling for therapeutic or normalizing interventions; a field of meanings to decipher; the site of processes concealed by specific mechanisms; a focus of indefinite causal relations; and an obscure speech (*parole*) that had to be ferreted out and listened to. The "economy" of discourses—their intrinsic technology, the necessities of their operation, the tactics they employ, the effects of power which underlie them and which they transmit—this, and not a system of representations, is what determines the essential features of what they have to say. The history of sexuality—that is, the history of what functioned in the nineteenth century as a specific field of truth—must first be written from the viewpoint of a history of discourses.

Let us put forward a general working hypothesis. The society that emerged in the nineteenth century—bourgeois, capitalist, or industrial society, call it what you will—did not confront sex with a fundamental refusal of recognition. On the contrary, it put into operation an entire machinery for producing true discourses concerning it. Not only did it speak of sex and compel everyone to do so; it also set out to formulate the uniform truth of sex. As if it suspected sex of harboring a fundamental secret. As if it needed this production of truth. As if it was essential that sex be inscribed not only in an economy of pleasure but in an ordered system of knowledge. Thus sex gradually became an object of great suspicion; the general and disquieting meaning that pervades our conduct and our existence, in spite of ourselves; the point of weakness where evil portents reach through to us; the fragment of darkness that we each carry within us: a general signification, a universal secret, an omnipresent cause, a fear that never ends. And so, in this "question" of sex (in both senses: as interrogation and problematization, and as the need for confession and integration into a field of rationality), two processes emerge, the one always conditioning the other: we demand that sex speak the truth (but, since it is the secret and is oblivious to its own nature, we reserve for ourselves the function of telling the truth of its truth, revealed and deciphered at last), and we demand that it tell us our truth, or rather, the deeply buried truth of that truth about ourselves which we think we possess in our immediate consciousness. . .

Hence the objective is to analyze a certain form of knowledge regarding sex, not in terms of repression or law, but in terms of power. But the word *power* is apt to lead to a number of misunderstandings—misunderstandings with respect to its nature, its form, and its unity. By power, I do not mean "Power" as a group of institutions and mechanisms that ensure the subservience of the citizens of a given state. By power, I do not mean, either, a mode of subjugation which, in contrast to violence, has the form of the rule. Finally, I do not have in mind a general system of domination exerted by one group over another, a system whose effects, through successive derivations, pervade the entire social body. The analysis, made in terms of power, must not assume that the sovereignty of the state, the form of the law, or the over-all unity of a domination are given at the outset; rather, these are only the terminal forms power takes. It seems to me that power must be understood in the first instance as the multiplicity of force relations immanent in the sphere in which they operate and which constitute their own organization; as the process which, through ceaseless struggles and confrontations, transforms, strengthens, or reverses them; as the support which these force relations find in one another, thus forming a chain or a system, or on the contrary, the disjunctions and contradictions which isolate them from one another; and lastly, as the strategies in which they take effect, whose general design or institutional crystallization is embodied in the state apparatus, in the formulation of the law, in the various social hegemonies. Power's condition of possibility, or in any case the viewpoint which permits one to understand its exercise, even in its more "peripheral" effects, and which also makes it possible to use its mechanisms as a grid of intelligibility of the social order, must not be sought in the primary existence of a central point, in a unique source of sovereignty from which secondary and descendent forms would emanate; it is the moving substrate of force relations which, by virtue of their inequality, constantly engender states of power, but the latter are always local and unstable. The omnipresence of power: not because it has the privilege of consolidating everything under its invincible unity, but because it is produced from one moment to the next, at every point, or rather in every relation from one point to another. Power is everywhere; not because it embraces everything, but because it comes from every-where. And "Power," insofar as it is permanent, repetitious, inert, and self-reproducing, is simply the over-all effect that emerges from all these mobilities, the concatenation that rests on each of them and seeks in turn to arrest their movement. One needs to be nominalistic, no doubt: power is not an institution, and not a structure; neither is it a certain strength we are endowed with; it is the name that one attributes to a complex strategical situation in a particu-lar society....

Jacques Derrida

Jacques Derrida is either heir-apparent or pretender to the French intellectual throne recently vacated by Michel Foucault, depending upon one's sympathy, or lack thereof, to postmodernism. Like Foucault, Derrida has been hailed as one of the preeminent philosophers of the twentieth century. This fact is in and of itself ironic as Derrida oftentimes ridicules the traditional precepts of philosophy. Through a sophisticated method of textual analysis, he undermines logocentric attempts to establish the foundations of human consciousness. For Derrida, the creation of an epistemology of knowledge or a hermeneutic of meaning is a futile endeavor. These rather lofty ideals have been associated with philosophy for centuries, and to a certain extent, he merely carries on the critique of Western metaphysics undertaken by Friedrich Nietzsche and Martin Heidegger. Derrida's originality lies in the extent to which he subverts and distorts the traditional goals and methods of critique. As Richard Rorty has noted, "[Derrida] has played all the authority figures, and all the descriptions of himself which these figures might be imagined as giving, off against each other, with the result that the very notion of 'authority' loses application in reference to his work."[1]

An innovative critic, Derrida has developed his own personal "philosophical" vocabulary including the neologisms "*différance*" and "*grammatology*." These concepts are part of his greater critical method called deconstruction. *Différance*, for example, is a decentering motif that allows us, presumably, to go beyond mere bipolar oppositions. The creation of such novel manipulative heuristic devices should be familiar from descriptions of Foucault's "geneaology of power/knowledge." The conceptual tool *différance* neutralizes archetypal binary oppositions, from the obviously subjective "good" versus "bad," to even the apparently concrete "male" versus "female." According to Derrida, such dualisms are the bane of Western metaphysics: we should no longer waste our energy in affirming or denying subjectivity, and revel in marginality, alterity, and antinomy.

In the first of the following articles, Derrida deconstructs works by structural anthropologist Claude Lévi-Strauss and structural linguist Ferdinand de Saussure. Derrida acknowledges both individuals' attempts to go beyond over-inflated notions of man such as humanism. He objects, however, that both thinkers retain latent metaphysical oppositions which imprison them within the hermeneutic circle of Western metaphysics. In the second text,

Derrida "deconstructs" the American Declaration of Independence, emphasizing the tauto-logical and circular nature of its argument about the rights of man.

For Derrida, epistemological assumptions are like the myth of Sisyphus. Unless one rejects inscribed philosophical dualisms, and embraces conflictual and alternative textual readings, one is doomed, like the mythical king of Corinth, to perpetual and ineffectual labor. As Sisyphus rolled his boulder to the mountaintop, lost control over it, and started again, Western philosophers re-pose the query "What is truth?" in myriad and ineffectual fashions. Derrida does not dispense with "truth," he simply claims that a multiplicity of truths can be discovered within any given text. It is just that no one truth can claim precedence over any other: a hierarchy of truth-value cannot be etched in stone.

1 Richard Rorty, *Contingency, Irony, and Solidarity* (New York: Cambridge University Press, 1989), p. 137.

JACQUES DERRIDA
(1978)

Structure, Sign, and Play

in the Discourse

of the Human Sciences

Perhaps something has occurred in the history of the concept of structure that could be called an "event," if this loaded word did not entail a meaning which it is precisely the function of structural—or structuralist—thought to reduce or to suspect. Let us speak of an "event," nevertheless, and let us use quotation marks to serve as a precaution. What would this event be then? Its exterior form would be that of a *rupture* and a redoubling.

It would be easy enough to show that the concept of structure and even the word "structure" itself are as old as the *epistēmē*—that is to say, as old as Western science and Western philosophy—and that their roots thrust deep into the soil of ordinary language, into whose deepest recesses the *epistēmē* plunges in order to gather them up and to make them part of itself in a metaphorical displacement. Nevertheless, up to the event which I wish to mark out and define, structure—or rather the structurality of structure—although it has always been at work, has always been neutralized or reduced, and this by a process of giving it a center or of referring it to a point of presence, a fixed origin. The function of this center was not only to orient, balance, and organize the structure—one cannot in fact conceive of an unorganized structure—but above all to make sure that the organizing principle of the structure would limit what we might call the *play* of the structure. By orienting and organizing the coherence of the system, the center of a structure permits the play of its elements inside the total form. And even today the notion of a structure lacking any center represents the unthinkable itself.

Nevertheless, the center also closes off the play which it opens up and makes possible. As

From Jacques Derrida, *Writing and Difference*, trans. by Alan Bass (Chicago: University of Chicago Press, 1978), pp. 278–93. By permission of the Press.

center, it is the point at which the substitution of contents, elements, or terms is no longer possible. At the center, the permutation or the transformation of elements (which may of course be structures enclosed within a structure) is forbidden. At least this permutation has always remained *interdicted* (and I am using this word deliberately). Thus it has always been thought that the center, which is by definition unique, constituted that very thing within a structure which while governing the structure, escapes structurality. This is why classical thought concerning structure could say that the center is, paradoxically, *within* the structure and *outside it*. The center is at the center of the totality, and yet, since the center does not belong to the totality (is not part of the totality), the totality *has its center elsewhere*. The center is not the center. The concept of centered structure—although it represents coherence itself, the condition of the *epistēmē* as philosophy or science—is contradictorily coherent. And as always, coherence in contradiction expresses the force of a desire. The concept of centered structure is in fact the concept of a play based on a fundamental ground, a play constituted on the basis of a fundamental immobility and a reassuring certitude, which itself is beyond the reach of play. And on the basis of this certitude anxiety can be mastered, for anxiety is invariably the result of a certain mode of being implicated in the game, of being caught by the game, of being as it were at stake in the game from the outset. And again on the basis of what we call the center (and which, because it can be either inside or outside, can also indifferently be called the origin or end, *archē* or *telos*), repetitions, substitutions, transformations, and permutations are always *taken* from a history of meaning [*sens*]—that is, in a word, a history—whose origin may always be reawakened or whose end may always be anticipated in the form of presence. This is why one perhaps could say that the movement of any archaeology, like that of any eschatology, is an accomplice of this reduction of the structurality of structure and always attempts to conceive of structure on the basis of a full presence which is beyond play.

If this is so, the entire history of the concept of structure, before the rupture of which we are speaking, must be thought of as a series of substitutions of center for center, as a linked chain of determinations of the center. Successively, and in a regulated fashion, the center receives different forms or names. The history of metaphysics, like the history of the West, is the history of these metaphors and metonymies. Its matrix—if you will pardon me for demonstrating so little and for being so elliptical in order to come more quickly to my principal theme—is the determination of Being as *presence* in all senses of this word. It could be shown that all the names related to fundamentals, to principles, or to the center have always designated an invariable presence—*eidos, archē, telos, energeia, ousia* (essence, existence, substance, subject) *alētheia*, transcendentality, consciousness, God, man, and so forth.

The event I called a rupture, the disruption I alluded to at the beginning of this paper, presumably would have come about when the structurality of structure had to begin to be thought, that is to say, repeated, and this is why I said that this disruption was repetition in every sense of the word. Henceforth, it became necessary to think both the law which somehow governed the desire for a center in the constitution of structure, and the process of signification which orders the displacements and substitutions for this law of central presence—but a central presence which has never been itself, has always already been exiled from itself into its own substitute. The substitute does not substitute itself for anything which has somehow existed before it. Henceforth, it was necessary to begin thinking that there was no center, that the center could not be thought in the form of a present-being, that the center had no natural site, that it was not a fixed locus but a function, a sort of nonlocus in which an infinite number of sign-substitutions came into play. This was the moment when language invaded the universal problematic, the moment when, in the absence of a center or origin, everything became discourse—provided we can agree on this word—that is to say, a system in which the central signified, the original or transcendental signified, is never absolutely present outside a system of differences. The absence of the transcendental signified extends the domain and the play of signification infinitely.

Where and how does this decentering, this thinking the structurality of structure, occur? It would be somewhat naïve to refer to an event, a doctrine, or an author in order to designate this occurrence. It is no doubt part of the totality of an era, our own, but still it has always already begun to proclaim itself and begun to *work*. Nevertheless, if we wished to choose several "names," as indications only, and to recall those authors in whose discourse this occurrence has kept most closely to its most radical formulation, we doubtless would have to cite the Nietzschean critique of metaphysics, the critique of the concepts of Being and truth, for which were substituted the concepts of play, interpretation, and sign (sign without present truth); the Freudian critique of self-presence, that is, the critique of consciousness, of the subject, of self-identity and of self-proximity or self-possession; and, more radically, the Heideggerean destruction of metaphysics, of onto-theology, of the determination of Being as presence. But all these destructive discourses and all their analogues are trapped in a kind of circle. This circle is unique. It describes the form of the relation between the history of metaphysics and the destruction of the history of metaphysics. There is no sense in doing without the concepts of metaphysics in order to shake metaphysics. We have no language—no syntax and no lexicon—which is foreign to this history; we can pronounce not a single destructive proposition which has not already had to slip into the form, the logic, and the implicit postulations of precisely what it seeks to contest. To take one example from many: the metaphysics of presence is shaken with the help of the concept of *sign*. But, as I suggested a moment ago, as soon as one seeks to demonstrate in this way that there is no transcendental or privileged signified and that the domain or play of signification henceforth has no limit, one must reject even the concept and word "sign" itself—which is precisely what cannot be done. For the signification "sign" has always been understood and determined, in its meaning, as sign-of, a signifier referring to a signified, a signifier different from its signified. If one erases the radical difference between signifier and signified, it is the word "signifier" itself which must be abandoned as a metaphysical concept. When Lévi-Strauss says in the preface to *The Raw and the Cooked* that he has "sought to transcend the opposition between the sensible and the intelligible by operating from the outset at the level of signs," the necessity, force, and legitimacy of his act cannot make us forget that the concept of the sign cannot in itself surpass this opposition between the sensible and the intelligible. The concept of the sign, in each of its aspects, has been determined by this opposition throughout the totality of its history. It has lived only on this opposition and its system. But we cannot do without the concept of the sign, for we cannot give up this metaphysical complicity without also giving up the critique we are directing against this complicity, or without the risk of erasing difference in the self-identity of a signified reducing its signifier into itself or, amounting to the same thing, simply expelling its signifier outside itself. . . .

What is the relevance of this formal schema when we turn to what are called the "human sciences"? One of them perhaps occupies a privileged place—ethnology. In fact one can assume that ethnology could have been born as a science only at the moment when a decentering had come about: at the moment when European culture—and, in consequence, the history of metaphysics and of its concepts—had been *dislocated*, driven from its locus, and forced to stop considering itself as the culture of reference. This moment is not first and foremost a moment of philosophical or scientific discourse. It is also a moment which is political, economic, technical, and so forth. One can say with total security that there is nothing fortuitous about the fact that the critique of ethnocentrism—the very condition for ethnology—should be systematically and historically contemporaneous with the destruction of the history of metaphysics. Both belong to one and the same era. Now, ethnology—like any science—comes about within the element of discourse. And it is primarily a European science employing traditional concepts, however much it may struggle against them. Consequently, whether he wants to or not—and this does not depend on a decision on his part—the ethnologist accepts into his discourse the premises of ethnocentrism at the very moment when he denounces them. This necessity is irreducible; it is not a historical contingency. We ought to consider all its implications very carefully. But if no one can escape this necessity, and if no one is therefore responsible for giving in to it, however little he may do so, this does not mean that all the ways of giving in to it are of equal pertinence. The quality and fecundity of a discourse are perhaps measured by the critical rigor with which this relation to the history of metaphysics and to inherited concepts is thought. Here it is a question both of a critical relation to the language of the social sciences and a critical responsibility of the discourse itself. It is a question of explicitly and systematically posing the problem of the status of a discourse which borrows from a heritage the resources necessary for the deconstruction of that heritage itself. A problem of *economy* and *strategy*.

If we consider, as an example, the texts of Claude Lévi-Strauss, it is not only because of the privilege accorded to ethnology among the social sciences, nor even because the thought of Lévi-Strauss weighs heavily on the contemporary theoretical situation. It is above all because a certain choice has been declared in the work of Lévi-Strauss and because a certain doctrine has been elaborated there, and precisely, in a *more or less explicit manner*, as concerns both this critique of language and this critical language in the social sciences.

In order to follow this movement in the text of Lévi-Strauss, let us choose as one guiding thread among others the opposition between nature and culture. Despite all its rejuvenations and disguises, this opposition is congenital to philosophy. It is even older than Plato. It is at least as old as the Sophists. Since the statement of the opposition *physis/nomos*, *physis/technē*, it has been relayed to us by means of a whole historical chain which opposes "nature" to law, to education, to art, to technics—but also to liberty, to the arbitrary, to history, to society, to the mind, and so on. Now, from the outset of his researches, and from his first book (*The Elementary Structures of Kinship*) on, Lévi-Strauss simultaneously has experienced the necessity of utilizing this opposition and the impossibility of accepting it. In the *Elementary Structures*, he begins from this axiom or definition: that which is *universal* and spontaneous, and not dependent on any particular culture or on any determinate norm, belongs to nature. Inversely, that which depends upon a system of *norms* regulating society and therefore is capable of *varying* from one social structure to another, belongs to culture. These two definitions are of the traditional type. But in the very first pages of the *Elementary Structures* Lévi-Strauss, who has begun by giving credence to these concepts, encounters what he calls a *scandal*, that is to say, something which no longer tolerates the nature/culture opposition he has accepted, something which *simultaneously* seems to require the predicates of nature and of culture. This scandal is the *incest prohibition*. The incest prohibition is universal; in this sense one could call it natural.

But it is also a prohibition, a system of norms and interdicts; in this sense one could call it cultural:

> Let us suppose then that everything universal in man relates to the natural order, and is character-
> ized by spontaneity, and that everything subject to a norm is cultural and is both relative and
> particular. We are then confronted with a fact, or rather, a group of facts, which, in the light of
> previous definitions, are not far removed from a scandal: we refer to that complex group of beliefs,
> customs, conditions and institutions described succinctly as the prohibition of incest, which
> presents, without the slightest ambiguity, and inseparably combines, the two characteristics in
> which we recognize the conflicting features of two mutually exclusive orders. It constitutes a rule,
> but a rule which, alone among all the social rules, possesses at the same time a universal character.

Obviously there is no scandal except within a system of concepts which accredits the difference between nature and culture. By commencing his work with the *factum* of the incest prohibition, Lévi-Strauss thus places himself at the point at which this difference, which has always
been assumed to be self-evident, finds itself erased or questioned. For from the moment when
the incest prohibition can no longer be conceived within the nature/culture opposition, it can
no longer be said to be a scandalous fact, a nucleus of opacity within a network of transparent
significations. The incest prohibition is no longer a scandal one meets with or comes up against
in the domain of traditional concepts; it is something which escapes these concepts and
certainly precedes them—probably as the condition of their possibility. It could perhaps be
said that the whole of philosophical conceptualization, which is systematic with the
nature/culture opposition, is designed to leave in the domain of the unthinkable the very thing
that makes this conceptualization possible: the origin of the prohibition of incest.

This example, too cursorily examined, is only one among many others, but nevertheless it
already shows that language bears within itself the necessity of its own critique. Now this
critique may be undertaken along two paths, in two "manners." Once the limit of the
nature/culture opposition makes itself felt, one might want to question systematically and
rigorously the history of these concepts. This is a first action. Such a systematic and historic
questioning would be neither a philological nor a philosophical action in the classic sense of
these words. To concern oneself with the founding concepts of the entire history of philosophy, to deconstitute them, is not to undertake the work of the philologist or of the classic
historian of philosophy. Despite appearances, it is probably the most daring way of making the
beginnings of a step outside of philosophy. The step "outside philosophy" is much more difficult to conceive than is generally imagined by those who think they made it long ago with
cavalier ease, and who in general are swallowed up in metaphysics in the entire body of
discourse which they claim to have disengaged from it.

The other choice (which I believe corresponds more closely to Lévi-Strauss's manner), in
order to avoid the possibly sterilizing effects of the first one, consists in conserving all these old
concepts within the domain of empirical discovery while here and there denouncing their
limits, treating them as tools which can still be used. No longer is any truth value attributed to
them; there is a readiness to abandon them, if necessary, should other instruments appear more
useful. In the meantime, their relative efficacy is exploited, and they are employed to destroy
the old machinery to which they belong and of which they themselves are pieces. This is how
the language of the social sciences criticizes *itself*. Lévi-Strauss thinks that in this way he can

separate *method* from *truth*, the instruments of the method and the objective significations envisaged by it. One could almost say that this is the primary affirmation of Lévi-Strauss; in any event, the first words of the *Elementary Structures* are: "Above all, it is beginning to emerge that this distinction between nature and society ('nature' and 'culture' seem preferable to us today), while of no acceptable historical significance, does contain a logic, fully justifying its use by modern sociology as a methodological tool."

Lévi-Strauss will always remain faithful to this double intention: to preserve as an instrument something whose truth value he criticizes.

On the one hand, he will continue, in effect, to contest the value of the nature/culture opposition. More than thirteen years after the *Elementary Structures*, *The Savage Mind* faithfully echoes the text I have just quoted: "The opposition between nature and culture to which I attached much importance at one time ... now seems to be of primarily methodological importance." And this methodological value is not affected by its "ontological" nonvalue (as might be said, if this notion were not suspect here): "However, it would not be enough to reabsorb particular humanities into a general one. This first enterprise opens the way for others which ... are incumbent on the exact natural sciences: the reintegration of culture in nature and finally of life within the whole of its physico-chemical conditions."

On the other hand, still in *The Savage Mind*, he presents as what he calls *bricolage* what might be called the discourse of this method. The *bricoleur*, says Lévi-Strauss, is someone who uses "the means at hand," that is, the instruments he finds at his disposition around him, those which are already there, which had not been especially conceived with an eye to the operation for which they are to be used and to which one tries by trial and error to adapt them, not hesitating to change them whenever it appears necessary, or to try several of them at once, even if their form and their origin are heterogeneous—and so forth....

If one calls *bricolage* the necessity of borrowing one's concepts from the text of a heritage which is more or less coherent or ruined, it must be said that every discourse is *bricoleur*. The engineer, whom Lévi-Strauss opposes to the *bricoleur*, should be the one to construct the totality of his language, syntax, and lexicon. In this sense the engineer is a myth. A subject who supposedly would be the absolute origin of his own discourse and supposedly would construct it "out of nothing," "out of whole cloth," would be the creator of the verb, the verb itself. The notion of the engineer who supposedly breaks with all forms of *bricolage* is therefore a theological idea; and since Lévi-Strauss tells us elsewhere that *bricolage* is mythopoetic, the odds are that the engineer is a myth produced by the *bricoleur*. As soon as we cease to believe in such an engineer and in a discourse which breaks with the received historical discourse, and as soon as we admit that every finite discourse is bound by a certain *bricolage* and that the engineer and the scientist are also species of *bricoleurs*, then the very idea of *bricolage* is menaced and the difference in which it took on its meaning breaks down.

This brings us to the second thread which might guide us in what is being contrived here.

Lévi-Strauss describes *bricolage* not only as an intellectual activity but also as a mythopoetical activity. One reads in *The Savage Mind*, "Like *bricolage* on the technical plane, mythical reflection can reach brilliant unforeseen results on the intellectual plane. Conversely, attention has often been drawn to the mythopoetical nature of *bricolage*."

But Lévi-Strauss's remarkable endeavor does not simply consist in proposing, notably in his most recent investigations, a structural science of myths and of mythological activity. His endeavor also appears—I would say almost from the outset—to have the status which he accords to his own discourse on myths, to what he calls his "mythologicals." It is here that his discourse on the myth reflects on itself and criticizes itself. And this moment, this critical period, is evidently of concern to all the languages which share the field of the human sciences. What does Lévi-Strauss say of his "mythologicals"? It is here that we rediscover the mythopoetical virtue of *bricolage*. In effect, what appears most fascinating in this critical search for a new status of discourse is the stated abandonment of all reference to a *center*, to a *subject*, to a privileged *reference*, to an origin, or to an absolute *archia*. The theme of this decentering could be followed throughout the "Overture" to his last book, *The Raw and the Cooked*. I shall simply remark on a few key points.

1. From the very start, Lévi-Strauss recognizes that the Bororo myth which he employs in the book as the "reference myth" does not merit this name and this treatment. The name is specious and the use of the myth improper. This myth deserves no more than any other its referential privilege: "In fact, the Bororo myth, which I shall refer to from now on as the key myth, is, as I shall try to show, simply a transformation, to a greater or lesser extent, of other myths originating either in the same society or in neighboring or remote societies. I could, therefore, have legitimately taken as my starting point any one representative myth of the group. From this point of view, the key myth is interesting not because it is typical, but rather because of its irregular position within the group."

2. There is no unity or absolute source of the myth. The focus or the source of the myth are always shadows and virtualities which are elusive, unactualizable, and nonexistent in the first place. Everything begins with structure, configuration, or relationship. The discourse on the acentric structure that myth itself is, cannot itself have an absolute subject or an absolute center. It must avoid the violence that consists in centering a language which describes an acentric structure if it is not to shortchange the form and movement of myth. Therefore it is necessary to forego scientific or philosophical discourse, to renounce the *epistémē* which absolutely requires, which is the absolute requirement that we go back to the source, to the center, to the founding basis, to the principle, and so on. In opposition to *epistemic* discourse, structural discourse on myths—*mythological* discourse—must itself be *mythomorphic*. It must have the form of that of which it speaks. This is what Lévi-Strauss says in the *The Raw and the Cooked*, from which I would now like to quote a long and remarkable passage:

> The study of myths raises a methodological problem, in that it cannot be carried out according to the Cartesian principle of breaking down the difficulty into as many parts as may be necessary for finding the solution. There is no real end to methodological analysis, no hidden unity to be grasped once the breaking-down process has been completed. Themes can be split up *ad infinitum*. Just when you think you have disentangled and separated them, you realize that they are knitting together again in response to the operation of unexpected affinities. Consequently the unity of the myth is never more than tendential and projective and cannot reflect a state or a particular moment of the myth. It is a phenomenon of the imagination, resulting from the attempt at interpretation; and its function is to endow the myth with synthetic form and to prevent its disintegration into a confusion of opposites. The science of myths might therefore be termed "anaclastic," if we take this old term in the broader etymological sense which includes the study of both reflected rays and broken rays. But unlike philosophical reflection, which aims to go back to its own source, the reflections we are dealing with here concern rays whose only source is hypothetical. . . . And in seeking to imitate the spontaneous movement of mythological thought, this essay, which is

also both too brief and too long, has had to conform to the requirements of that thought and to respect its rhythm. It follows that this book on myths is itself a kind of myth.

This statement is repeated a little farther on: "As the myths themselves are based on secondary codes (the primary codes being those that provide the substance of language), the present work is put forward as a tentative draft of a tertiary code, which is intended to ensure the reciprocal translatability of several myths. This is why it would not be wrong to consider this book itself as a myth: it is, as it were, the myth of mythology." The absence of a center is here the absence of a subject and the absence of an author: "Thus the myth and the musical work are like conductors of an orchestra, whose audience becomes the silent performers. If it is now asked where the real center of the work is to be found, the answer is that this is impossible to determine. Music and mythology bring man face to face with potential objects of which only the shadows are actualized. . . . Myths are anonymous." The musical model chosen by Lévi-Strauss for the composition of his book is apparently justified by this absence of any real and fixed center of the mythical or mythological discourse.

Thus it is at this point that ethnographic *bricolage* deliberately assumes its mythopoetic function. But by the same token, this function makes the philosophical or epistemological requirement of a center appear as mythological, that is to say, as a historical illusion.

Nevertheless, even if one yields to the necessity of what Lévi-Strauss has done, one cannot ignore its risks. If the mythological is mythomorphic, are all discourses on myths equivalent? Shall we have to abandon any epistemological requirement which permits us to distinguish between several qualities of discourse on the myth? A classic, but inevitable question. It cannot be answered—and I believe that Lévi-Strauss does not answer it—for as long as the problem of the relations between the philosopheme or the theorem, on the one hand, and the mytheme or the mythopoem, on the other, has not been posed explicitly, which is no small problem. For lack of explicitly posing this problem, we condemn ourselves to transforming the alleged transgression of philosophy into an unnoticed fault within the philosophical realm. Empiricism would be the genus of which these faults would always be the species. Transphilosophical concepts would be transformed into philosophical naivetés. Many examples could be given to demonstrate this risk: the concepts of sign, history, truth, and so forth. What I want to emphasize is simply that the passage beyond philosophy does not consist in turning the page of philosophy (which usually amounts to philosophizing badly), but in continuing to read philosophers *in a certain way*. The risk I am speaking of is always assumed by Lévi-Strauss, and it is the very price of this endeavor. I have said that empiricism is the matrix of all faults menancing a discourse which continues, as with Lévi-Strauss in particular, to consider itself scientific. If we wanted to pose the problem of empiricism and *bricolage* in depth, we would probably end up very quickly with a number of absolutely contradictory propositions concerning the status of discourse in structural ethnology. On the one hand, structuralism justifiably claims to be the critique of empiricism. But at the same time there is not a single book or study by Lévi-Strauss which is not proposed as an empirical essay which can always be completed or invalidated by new information. The structural schemata are always proposed as hypotheses resulting from a finite quantity of information and which are subjected to the proof of experience. Numerous texts could be used to demonstrate this double postulation. Let us turn once again to the "Overtune" of *The Raw and the Cooked*, where it seems clear that if this postulation is double, it is because it is a question here of a language on language:

If critics reproach me with not having carried out an exhaustive inventory of South American myths before analyzing them, they are making a grave mistake about the nature and function of these documents. The total body of myth belonging to a given community is comparable to its speech. Unless the population dies out physically or morally, this totality is never complete. You might as well criticize a linguist for compiling the grammar of a language without having complete records of the words pronounced since the language came into being, and without knowing what will be said in it during the future part of its existence. Experience proves that a linguist can work out the grammar of a given language from a remarkably small number of sentences. . . . And even a partial grammar or an outline grammar is a precious acquisition when we are dealing with unknown languages. Syntax does not become evident only after a (theoretically limitless) series of events has been recorded and examined, because it is itself the body of rules governing their production. What I have tried to give is an outline of the syntax of South American mythology. Should fresh data come to hand, they will be used to check or modify the formulation of certain grammatical laws, so that some are abandoned and replaced by new ones. But in no instance would I feel constrained to accept the arbitrary demand for a total mythological pattern, since, as has been shown, such a requirement has no meaning.

Totalization, therefore, is sometimes defined as *useless*, and sometimes as *impossible*. This is no doubt due to the fact that there are two ways of conceiving the limit of totalization. And I assert once more that these two determinations coexist implicitly in Lévi-Strauss's discourse. Totalization can be judged impossible in the classical style: one then refers to the empirical endeavor of either a subject or a finite richness which it can never master. There is too much, more than one can say. But nontotalization can also be determined in another way: no longer from the standpoint of a concept of finitude as relegation to the empirical, but from the standpoint of the concept of *play*. If totalization no longer has any meaning, it is not because the infiniteness of a field cannot be covered by a finite glance or a finite discourse, but because the nature of the field—that is, language and a finite language—excludes totalization. This field is in effect that of *play*, that is to say, a field of infinite substitutions only because it is finite, that is to say, because instead of being an inexhaustible field, as in the classical hypothesis, instead of being too large, there is something missing from it: a center which arrests and grounds the play of substitutions. One could say—rigorously using that word whose scandalous signification is always obliterated in French—that this movement of play, permitted by the lack or absence of a center or origin, is the movement of *supplementarity*. One cannot determine the center and exhaust totalization because the sign which replaces the center, which supplements it, taking the center's place in its absence—this sign is added, occurs as a surplus, as a *supplement*. The movement of signification adds something, which results in the fact that there is always more, but this addition is a floating one because it comes to perform a vicarious function, to supplement a lack on the part of the signified. Although Lévi-Strauss in his use of the word "supplementary" never emphasizes, as I do here, the two directions of meaning which are so strangely compounded within it, it is not by chance that he uses this word twice in his "Introduction to the Work of Marcel Mauss," at one point where he is speaking of the "overabundance of signifier, in relation to the signifieds to which this overabundance can refer":

In his endeavor to understand the world, man therefore always has at his disposal a surplus of signification (which he shares out amongst things according to the laws of symbolic thought—

which is the task of ethnologists and linguists to study). This distribution of a *supplementary* allowance [*ration supplémentaire*]—if it is permissible to put it that way—is absolutely necessary in order that on the whole the available signifier and the signified it aims at may remain in the relationship of complementarity which is the very condition of the use of symbolic thought."

(It could no doubt be demonstrated that this *ration supplémentaire* of signification is the origin of the *ratio* itself.) The word reappears a little further on, after Lévi-Strauss has mentioned "this floating signifier, which is the servitude of all finite thought":

> In other words—and taking as our guide Mauss's precept that all social phenomena can be assimilated to language—we see in *mana*, *Wakau*, *oranda* and other notions of the same type, the conscious expression of a semantic function, whose role it is to permit symbolic thought to operate in spite of the contradiction which is proper to it. In this way are explained the apparently insoluble antinomies attached to this notion. . . . At one and the same time force and action, quality and state, noun and verb; abstract and concrete, omnipresent and localized—*mana* is in effect all these things. But is it not precisely because it is none of these things that *mana* is a simple form, or more exactly, a symbol in the pure state, and therefore capable of becoming charged with any sort of symbolic content whatever? In the system of symbols constituted by all cosmologies, *mana* would simply be a zero symbolic value, that is to say, a sign marking the necessity of a symbolic content *supplementary* [my italics] to that with which the signified is already loaded, but which can take on any value required, provided only that this value still remains part of the available reserve and is not, as phonologists put it, a group-term."

Lévi-Strauss adds the note: "Linguists have already been led to formulate hypotheses of this type. For example: 'A zero phoneme is opposed to all the other phonemes in French in that it entails no differential characters and no constant phonetic value. On the contrary, the proper function of the zero phoneme is to be opposed to phoneme absence.' . . . Similarly, if we schematize the conception I am proposing here, it could almost be said that the function of notions like *mana* is to be opposed to the absence of signification, without entailing by itself any particular signification."

The *overabundance* of the signifier, its *supplementary* character, is thus the result of a finitude, that is to say, the result of a lack which must be *supplemented*.

It can now be understood why the concept of play is important in Lévi-Strauss. His references to all sorts of games, notably to roulette, are very frequent, especially in his *Conversations*, in *Race and History*, and in *The Savage Mind*. Further, the reference to play is always caught up in tension.

Tension with history, first of all. This is a classical problem, objections to which are now well worn. I shall simply indicate what seems to me the formality of the problem: by reducing history, Lévi-Strauss has treated as it deserves a concept which has always been in complicity with a teleological and eschatological metaphysics, in other words, paradoxically, in complicity with that philosophy of presence to which it was believed history could be opposed. The thematic of historicity, although it seems to be a somewhat late arrival in philosophy, has always been required by the determination of Being as presence. With or without etymology, and despite the classic antagonism which opposes these significations throughout all of classical thought, it could be shown that the concept of *epistēmē* has always called forth that of *historia*, if history is always the unity of a becoming, as the tradition of truth or the development of science or knowledge oriented toward the appropriation of truth in presence and self-presence, toward knowledge in consciousness-of-self. History has always been conceived as the movement of a resumption of history, as a detour between two presences. But if it is legitimate to suspect this concept of history, there is a risk, if it is reduced without an explicit statement of the problem I am indicating here, of falling back into an ahistoricism of a classical type, that is to say, into a determined moment of the history of metaphysics. Such is the algebraic formality of the problem as I see it. More concretely, in the work of Lévi-Strauss it must be recognized that the respect for structurality, for the internal originality of the structure, compels a neutralization of time and history. For example, the appearance of a new structure, of an original system, always comes about—and this is the very condition of its structural specificity—by a rupture with its past, its origin, and its cause. Therefore one can describe what is peculiar to the structural organization only by not taking into account, in the very moment of this description, its past conditions: by omitting to posit the problem of the transition from one structure to another, by putting history between brackets. In this "structuralist" moment, the concepts of chance and discontinuity are indispensable. And Lévi-Strauss does in fact often appeal to them, for example, as concerns that structure of structures, language, of which he says in the "Introduction to the Work of Marcel Mauss" that it "could only have been born in one fell swoop":

> Whatever may have been the moment and the circumstances of its appearance on the scale of animal life, language could only have been born in one fell swoop. Things could not have set about acquiring signification progressively. Following a transformation the study of which is not the concern of the social sciences, but rather of biology and psychology, a transition came about from a stage where nothing had a meaning to another where everything possessed it.

This standpoint does not prevent Lévi-Strauss from recognizing the slowness, the process of maturing, the continuous toil of factual transformations, history (for example, *Race and History*. But, in accordance with a gesture which was also Rousseau's and Husserl's, he must "set aside all the facts" at the moment when he wishes to recapture the specificity of a structure. Like Rousseau, he must always conceive of the origin of a new structure on the model of catastrophe—an overturning of nature in nature, a natural interruption of the natural sequence, a setting aside *of* nature.

Besides the tension between play and history, there is also the tension between play and presence. Play is the disruption of presence. The presence of an element is always a signifying and substitutive reference inscribed in a system of differences and the movement of a chain. Play is always play of absence and presence, but if it is to be thought radically, play must be conceived of before the alternative of presence and absence. Being must be conceived as presence or absence on the basis of the possibility of play and not the other way around. If Lévi-Strauss, better than any other, has brought to light the play of repetition and the repetition of play, one no less perceives in his work a sort of ethic of presence, an ethic of nostalgia for origins, an ethic of archaic and natural innocence, of a purity of presence and self-presence in speech—an ethic, nostalgia, and even remorse, which he often presents as the motivation of the ethnological project when he moves toward the archaic societies which are exemplary societies in his eyes. These texts are well known.

Turned towards the lost or impossible presence of the absent origin, this structuralist thematic of broken immediacy is therefore the saddened, *negative*, nostalgic, guilty, Rousseauistic side of the thinking of play whose other side would be the Nietzschean *affirmation*, that is the joyous affirmation of the play of the world and of the innocence of becoming, the affirmation of a world of signs without fault, without truth, and without origin which is offered to an active interpretation. *This affirmation then determines the noncenter otherwise than as loss of the center.* And it plays without security. For there is a *sure* play: that which is limited to the *substitution* of *given* and *existing*, *present*, pieces. In absolute chance, affirmation also surrenders itself to *genetic* indetermination, to the *seminal* adventure of the trace.

There are thus two interpretations of interpretation, of structure, of sign, of play. The one seeks to decipher, dreams of deciphering a truth or an origin which escapes play and the order of the sign, and which lives the necessity of interpretation as an exile. The other, which is no longer turned toward the origin, affirms play and tries to pass beyond man and humanism, the name of man being the name of that being who, throughout the history of metaphysics or of ontotheology—in other words, throughout his entire history—has dreamed of full presence, the reassuring foundation, the origin and the end of play. The second interpretation of interpretation, to which Nietzsche pointed the way, does not seek in ethnography, as Lévi-Strauss does, the "inspiration of a new humanism" (again citing the "Introduction to the Work of Marcel Mauss").

There are more than enough indications today to suggest we might perceive that these two interpretations of interpretation—which are absolutely irreconcilable even if we live them simultaneously and reconcile them in an obscure economy—together share the field which we call, in such a problematic fashion, the social sciences.

For my part, although these two interpretations must acknowledge and accentuate their difference and define their irreducibility, I do not believe that today there is any question of *choosing*—in the first place because here we are in a region (let us say, provisionally, a region of historicity) where the category of choice seems particularly trivial; and in the second, because we must first try to conceive of the common ground, and the *différance* of this irreducible difference. Here there is a kind of question, let us still call it historical, whose *conception*, *formation*, *gestation*, and *labor* we are only catching a glimpse of today. I employ these words, I admit, with a glance toward the operations of childbearing—but also with a glance toward those who, in a society from which I do not exclude myself, turn their eyes away when faced by the as yet unnamable which is proclaiming itself and which can do so, as is necessary whenever a birth is in the offing, only under the species of the nonspecies, in the formless, mute, infant, and terrifying form of monstrosity.

JACQUES DERRIDA
(1986)

Declarations of Independence

It is better that you know right away: I am not going to keep my promise.

I beg your pardon, but it will be impossible for me to speak to you this afternoon, even in an indirect style, about what I was engaged to deal with. Very sincerely, I would have liked to be able to do it.

But as I'd rather not simply remain silent about what I should have spoken about to you, I will say a word about it in the form of an excuse. I will speak to you, then, a little, about what I won't speak about, and about what I would have wanted—because I ought—to have spoken about.

Still, it remains that I fully intend to discuss with you—at least you will be able to confirm this—the promise, the contract, engagement, the signature, and even about what always presupposes them, in a strange way: the presentation of excuses.

In honoring me with his invitation, Roger Shattuck proposed that I try, here of all places, a "textual" analysis, at once philosophical and literary, of the Declaration of Independence and the Declaration of the Rights of Man. In short, an exercise in comparative literature, which would treat unusual objects for specialized departments in this improbable discipline of "comparative literature."

At first, I was astonished. An intimidating proposition. Nothing had prepared me for it. No previous work had led me along the path of such analyses, whose interest and necessity obviously impose themselves. On reflection, I said to myself that if I had the time and the strength to do it, I'd like to try the experiment, at least in order to put to the test here those conceptual

Jacques Derrida, "Declarations of Independence," *New Political Science* 15 (1986), pp. 7–15. Reprinted by permission of the author.

schemes—such as a critical problematic of "speech acts," a theory of "performative" writing, of the signature, of the contract, of the proper name, of political and academic institutions— which had already proved useful elsewhere, with what are called other "objects," whether "philosophical" or "literary" texts. Basically, I said to myself, if I had the time or the strength, I would have liked, if not to try a juridico-political study of the two texts and the two events which are marked there—a task inaccessible to me—then at least to sharpen, in a preliminary way and using these texts as an example, some questions which have been elaborated else-where, on an apparently less political corpus. And out of all these questions, the only one I will retain for the occasion, this afternoon, at a university in Virginia—which has just celebrated, more appropriately than anywhere else, the bicentennial of the Declaration of Independence (which already sets the tone for the celebration of another anniversary or birthday around which we will turn shortly)—is this one: *who signs, and with what so-called proper name, the declarative act which founds an institution?*

Such an act does not come back to a constative or descriptive discourse. It performs, it accomplishes, it does what it says it does: that at least would be its intentional structure. Such an act does not have the same relation to its presumed signer—to whatever subject, individual or collective, engages itself in producing it—as a text of the "constative" type, if in all rigor there are any "constative" texts and if one could come across them in "science," in "philoso-phy," or in "literature." The declaration which founds an institution, a constitution or a State requires that a signer engage him- or herself. The signature maintains a link with the instituting act, as an act of language and of writing, a link which has absolutely nothing of the empirical accident about it. This attachment does not let itself be reduced, not as easily in any case as it does in a scientific text, where the value of the utterance is separated or cuts itself off from the name of its author without essential risk and, indeed, even has to be able to do so in order for it to pretend to objectivity. Although in principle an institution—in its history and in its tradi-tion, in its offices [*permanence*] and thus in its very institutionality—has to render itself indepen-dent of the empirical individuals who have taken part in its production, although it has in a certain way to mourn them or resign itself to their loss [*faire son deuil*], even and especially if it commemorates them, it turns out, precisely by reason of the structure of instituting language, that the founding act of an institution—the act as archive as well as the act as performance— *has to maintain within itself the signature.*

But just whose signature exactly? Who is the actual signer of such acts? And what does actual [*effectif*] mean? The same question spreads or propagates itself in a chain reaction through all the concepts affected by the same rumbling: act, performative, signature, the "present" "I" and "we," etc.

Prudence imposes itself here, as does attention to detail. Let us distinguish between the several instances within the moment of your Declaration. Take, for example, Jefferson, the "draftsman [*rédacteur*]" of the project or draft [*projet*] of the Declaration, of the "Draft," the facsimile of which I have before my eyes. No one would take him for the true signer of the Declaration. *By right*, he writes but he does not sign. Jefferson represents the representatives who have delegated to him the task of drawing up [*rédiger*] what they knew *they* wanted to say. He was not responsible for *writing*, in the productive or initiating sense of the term, only for *drawing up*, as one says of a secretary that he or she draws up a *letter* of which the spirit has been breathed into him or her, or even the content dictated. Moreover, after having thus drawn up a project or a draft, a sketch, Jefferson had to submit it to those whom, for a time, he *represented* and who are themselves *representatives*, namely the "representatives of the United States in General Congress assembled." These "representatives," of whom Jefferson represents a sort of advance-pen, will have the right to revise, to correct and to ratify the project or draft of the Declaration.

Shall we say, for all that, that they are the ultimate signers?

You know what scrutiny and examination this letter, this literal declaration in its first state, underwent, how long it remained and deferred, undelivered, in sufferance between all those representative instances, and with what suspense or suffering Jefferson paid for it. As if he had secretly dreamed of signing all alone.

As for the "representatives" themselves, they don't sign either. In principle at least, because the right is divided here. In fact, they sign; by right, they sign for themselves but also "for" others. They have been delegated the proxies, the power of attorney, for signing [*Ils ont délégation ou procuration de signature*]. They speak, "declare," declare themselves and sign "in the name of...": "We, therefore, the representatives of the United State of America in General Congress assembled, do in the name and by the authority of the good people of these [...] that as free and independent states...".

By right, the signer is thus the people, the "good" people (a decisive detail because it guarantees the value of the intention and of the signature, but we will see further along on what and on whom such a guarantee is founded or founds itself). It is the "good people" who declare themselves free and independent by the relay of their representatives and of their representatives of representatives. One cannot decide—and that's the interesting thing, the force and the coup of force of such a declarative act—whether independence is stated or produced by this utterance. We have not finished following the chain of these representatives of representatives, and doing so further complicates this necessary undecidability. Is it that the good people have already freed themselves in fact and are only stating the fact of this emancipation in [*par*] the Declaration? Or is it rather that they free themselves at the instant of and by [*par*] the signature of this Declaration? It is not a question here of an obscurity or of a difficulty of interpretation, of a problematic on the way to its (re)solution. It is not a question of a difficult analysis which would fail in the face of the structure of the acts involved and the overdetermined temporality of the events. This obscurity, this undecidability between, let's say, a performative structure and a constative structure, is *required* in order to produce the sought-after effect. It is essential to the very positing or position of a right as such, whether one is speaking here of hypocrisy, of equivocation, of undecidability, or of fiction. I would even go so far as to say that every signature finds itself thus affected.

Here then is the "good people" who engage themselves and engage only themselves in signing, in having their own declaration signed. The "we" of the declaration speaks "in the name of the people."

But this people does not exist. They do *not* exist as an entity, it does *not exist, before* this declaration, not *as such*. If it gives birth to itself, as free and independent subject, as possible signer, this can hold only in the act of the signature. The signature invents the signer. This signer can only authorize him- or herself to sign once he or she has come to the end [*parvenu au vout*], if one can say this, of his or her own signature, in a sort of fabulous retroactivity. That first signature authorizes him or her to sign. This happens every day, but it is fabulous—every time I evoke this type of event I think of Francis Ponge's "Fable": "By the word *by* begins thus this text/Of which the first line says the truth. [*Par le mot par commence donc ce text/Dont la première ligne dit la vérité...*]."

In signing, the people say—and do what they say they do, but in differing or deferring themselves through [*différant par*] the intervention of their representatives whose representativity is fully legitimated only by the signature, thus after the fact or the coup [*après coup*]—henceforth, I have the right to sign, in truth I will already have had it since I was able to give it to myself. I will have given myself a name and an "ability" or a "power," understood in the sense of power or ability-to-sign by delegation of signature. But this future perfect, the proper tense for this coup of right (as one would say coup of force), should not be declared, mentioned, taken into account. It's as though it didn't exist.

There was no signer, by right, before the text of the Declaration which itself remains the producer and guarantor of its own signature. By this fabulous event, by this fable which implies the structure of the trace and is only in truth possible thanks to [*par*] the inadequation to itself of a present, a signature gives itself a name. It opens *for itself* a line of credit, *its* own credit, for itself *to* itself. The *self* surges up here in all cases (nominative, dative, accusative) as soon as a signature gives or extends credit to itself, in a single coup of force, which is also a coup of writing, as the right to writing. The coup of force makes right, founds right or the law, gives right, *brings the law to the light of day, gives both birth and day to the law* [donne le jour à la loi]. Brings the law to the light of day, gives both birth and day to the law: read "The Madness of the Day," by Maurice Blanchot.

That this unheard-of thing should also be an everday occurrence should not make us forget the singular context of this act. In this case, another state signature had to be effaced in "dissolving" the links of colonial paternity or maternity. One will confirm it in reading: this "dissolution" too involves both constation and performance, indissociably mixed. The signature of every American citizen today depends, in fact and by right, on this indispensable confusion. The constituttion and the laws of your country somehow guarantee the signature, as they guarantee your passport and the circulation of subjects and of seals foreign to this country, of letters, of promises, of marriages, of checks—all of which may be given occasion or asylum or right.

And yet. And yet another instance still holds itself back behind the scenes. Another "subjectivity" is still coming to sign, in order to guarantee it, this production of signature. In short, there are only countersignatures in this process. There is a differential process here because there is a countersignature, but everything should concentrate itself in the *simulacrum of the instant*. It is still "in the name of" that the "good people" of America call *themselves* and declare *themselves* independent, at the instant in which they invent (for) themselves a signing identity. They sign in the name of the laws of nature and in the name of God. They *pose or posit* their institutional laws on the foundation of natural laws and by the same coup (the interpretive coup of force) in the name of God, creator of nature. He comes, in effect, to guarantee the rectitude of popular intentions, the unity and goodness of the people. He founds natural laws and thus the whole game which tends to present performative utterances *as* constative utterances.

Do I dare, here, in Charlottesville, recall the *incipit* of your Declaration? "When in the course of human events it becomes necessary for one people to dissolve the political bands which have connected them with another, and to assume among the powers of the earth the separate and equal station to which the laws of Nature and of Nature's God entitle them, a decent respect to the opinions of mankind requires that they should declare the causes which impel them to the separation. We hold these truths to be self-evident; that all men are created equal; that they are endowed by their creator with inalienable Rights [. . .]." And finally: "We therefore the Representatives of the United States of America, in General Congress assembled, appealing to the Supreme Judge of the world for the rectitude of our intentions, do in the Name and by the authority of the good People of these Colonies solemnly *publish* and *declare*, that these united Colonies are and of right ought to be *free and independant states* [. . .]."

"Are and ought to be"; the "and" articulates and conjoins here the two discursive modalities, the to be and the ought to be, the constation and the prescription, the fact and the right. *And* is God: at once creator of nature and judge, supreme judge of what is (the state of the world) and of what relates to what ought to be (the rectitude of our intentions). The instance of judgment, at the level of the supreme judge, is the last instance for saying the fact *and* the law. One can understand this Declaration as a vibrant act of faith, as a hypocrisy indispensable to a politico-military-economic, etc. coup of force, or, more simply, more economically, as the analytic and consequential deployment of a tautology: for this Declaration to have a meaning *and* an effect, there must be a last instance. God is the name, the best one, for this last instance and this ultimate signature. Not only the best one in a determined context (such and such a nation, such and such a religion, etc.), but the name of the best name in general. Now, this (best) name also *ought to be* a proper name. God is the best proper name, the proper name the best [*Dieu est le nom propre le meilleur*]. One could not replace "God" by "the best proper name [*le meilleur nom propre*]."

Jefferson knew it.

Secretary and draftsman, he represents. He represents the "representatives" who are the representatives of the people in whose name they speak, the people themselves authorizing themselves and authorizing their representatives (in addition to the rectitude of their intentions) in the name of the laws of nature which inscribe themselves in the name of God, judge and creator,

If he knew all this, why did he suffer? What did he suffer from, this representative of representatives who themselves represent, *to infinity*, up to God, other representative instances?

Apparently he suffered because he clung to his text. It was very hard for him to see it, to see *himself*, corrected, emended, "improved," shortened, especially by his colleagues. A feeling of wounding and of mutilation should be inconceivable for someone who knows not to write in his own name, his proper name, but *simply by representation* and in place of another. If the wound does not efface itself in the delegation, that is because things aren't so simple, neither the structure of the representation nor the procuration of the signature.

Someone, let's call him Jefferson (but why not God?), desired that the institution of the American people should be, by the same coup, the erection of his proper name. A name of State.

Did he succeed? I would not venture to decide.

You heard the story before I did. Franklin wants to console Jefferson about the "mutilation" (the word is not my own). He tells him a story about a hatter. He (the hatter) had first imagined a sign-board for his shop: the image of a hat and, beneath it, an inscription: "John Thompson, hatter, makes and sells hats for ready money." A friend suggests that he efface "hatter": what good is it, anyway, since "makes hats" is explicit enough? Another friend proposes that he suppress "makes hats," since the buyer couldn't care less who makes the hats as long as he likes them. This "deletion" is particularly interesting—it effaces the signing mark of the producer The third friend—it's always friends who urge the effacement—suggests that he economize on "for ready money," because custom at that time demanded that one pay "cash";

then, in the same movement, that he erase "sells hats," as only an idiot would believe that the hats are to be given away. Finally, the sign-board bears only an image and, under the iconic sign in the shape of a hat, a proper name, John Thompson. Nothing else. One might just as well have imagined other businesses, and the proper name inscribed under an umbrella, or even on some shoes.

The legend says nothing about Jefferson's reaction. I imagine it as strongly undecided. The story [*récit*] reflected his unhappiness but also his greatest desire. Taken as a whole, a complete and total effacement of his text would have been better, leaving in place, under a map of the United States, only the nudity of his proper name: instituting text, founding act and signing energy. Precisely in the place of the last instance where God—who had nothing to do with any of this and, having represented god knows whom or what in the interest of all those nice people, doubtless doesn't give a damn [*s'en moque*]—alone will have signed. His own declaration of independence. In order, neither more nor less, to make a state-ment of it [*en faire état*].

The question remains. How is a State made or founded, how does a State make or found itself? And an independence? And the autonomy of one which both gives itself, and signs, its own law? Who signs all these authorizations to sign?

I won't, in spite of my promise, engage myself on this path, today.

Making it easier on myself, falling back on subjects which are closer, if not more familiar, to me, I will speak to you of Nietzsche: of his names, of his signatures, of the thoughts he had for the institution, the State, academic and state apparatuses, "academic freedom," declarations of independence, signs, sign-boards, and teaching assignments [*signes, enseignes, et enseignements*], Nietzsche today, in short, in Charlottesville, to celebrate some birthdays.

Richard Rorty

Richard Rorty is the University Professor of Humanities at the University of Virginia. In the following essays Rorty attempts to lay out his ideas concerning a visionary postmodernism, which dispenses with distinctions between knowledge and opinion. Rorty's aim is to demonstrate that rather than a pointless search for metaphysical truths, we should undertake an effort to be more "pragmatic" after the philosopher John Dewey and soften the distinction between subjective and objective. Although detractors claim this leads Rorty to politically relativistic conclusions, Rorty forges ahead to assert that only by dispensing with our iron-clad beliefs in the superiority of science, objectivity, and "hard" truth, can we move beyond epistemological muddle and hermeneutic mire. Rorty believes this can be done through a simplistic ascription to an "Ironist" perspective, in which we remain skeptical of "final vocabularies." Although his critics claim he is naively optimistic, Rorty adheres to numerous open-ended perspectives: pragmatism, realism, nominalism, and historicism. It is only through these perspectives that one can cease to have false faith in epistemological "truth claims." For Rorty, liberal hope is a condition which the ironist can achieve if only "reciprocal loyalty" can be implemented. Along this vein Rorty's thought resembles that of one of the most acerbic critics of postmodernity, Jürgen Habermas. Both philosophers work with the notion of a shared community, in which the creation of consensus is the ultimate goal. Rorty believes that humans can achieve a certain measure of solidarity, and thus a "just" and benevolent form of government, through consensus. An affirmative postmodernist, Rorty wishes to circumvent the eternal return of foundational, epistemological queries.

RICHARD RORTY
(1990)

Private Irony

and Liberal Hope

All human beings carry about a set of words which they employ to justify their actions, their beliefs, and their lives. These are the words in which we formulate praise of our friends and contempt for our enemies, our long-term projects, our deepest self-doubts and our highest hopes. They are the words in which we tell, sometimes prospectively and sometimes retrospectively, the story of our lives. I shall call those words a person's "final vocabulary."

It is "final" in the sense that if doubt is cast on the worth of these words, their user has no noncircular argumentative recourse. Those words are as far as he can go with language; beyond them there is only helpless passivity or a resort to force. A small part of a final vocabulary is made up of thin, flexible, and ubiquitous terms such as "true," "good," "right," and "beautiful." The larger part contains thicker, more rigid, and more parochial terms, for example, "Christ," "England," "professional standards," "decency," "kindness," "the Revolution," "the Church," "progressive," "rigorous," "creative." The more parochial terms do most of the work.

I shall define an "ironist" as someone who fulfills three conditions: (1) She has radical and continuing doubts about the final vocabulary she currently uses, because she has been impressed by other vocabularies, vocabularies taken as final by people or books she has encountered; (2) she realizes that argument phrased in her present vocabulary can neither underwrite nor dissolve these doubts; (3) insofar as she philosophizes about her situation, she does not think that her vocabulary is closer to reality than others, that it is in touch with a power not herself. Ironists who are inclined to philosophize see the choice between vocabularies as made neither within a

Richard Rorty, "Private Irony and Liberal Hope" in *Contingency, Irony, and Solidarity*, (Cambridge: Cambridge University Press, 1990), pp. 73–95. © Cambridge University Press, 1991. Reprinted with the permission of Cambridge University Press.

neutral and universal metavocabulary nor by an attempt to fight one's way past appearances to the real, but simply by playing the new off against the old.

I call people of this sort "ironists" because their realization that anything can be made to look good or bad by being redescribed, and their renunciation of the attempt to formulate criteria of choice between final vocabularies, puts them in the position which Sartre called "metastable": never quite able to take themselves seriously because always aware that the terms in which they describe themselves are subject to change, always aware of the contingency and fragility of their final vocabularies, and thus of their selves. Such people take naturally to the line of thought developed in the first two chapters of this book. If they are also liberals—people for whom (to use Judith Shklar's definition) "cruelty is the worst thing they do"—they will take naturally to the views offered in the third chapter.

The opposite of irony is common sense. For that is the watchword of those who unselfconsciously describe everything important in terms of the final vocabulary to which they and those around them are habituated. To be commonsensical is to take for granted that statements formulated in that final vocabulary suffice to describe and judge the beliefs, actions and lives of those who employ alternative final vocabularies. . . .

When common sense is challenged, its adherents respond at first by generalizing and making explicit the rules of the language game they are accustomed to play (as some of the Greek Sophists did, and as Aristotle did in his ethical writings). But if no platitude formulated in the old vocabulary suffices to meet an argumentative challenge, the need to reply produces a willingness to go beyond platitudes. At that point, conversation may go Socratic. The question "What is x?" is now asked in such a way that it cannot be answered simply by producing paradigm cases of x-hood. So one may demand a definition, an essence.

To make such Socratic demands is not yet, of course, to become an ironist in the sense in which I am using this term. It is only to become a "metaphysician," in a sense of that term which I am adapting from Heidegger. In this sense, the metaphysician is someone who takes the question "What is the intrinsic nature of (e.g., justice, science, knowledge, Being, faith, morality, philosophy)?" at face value. He assumes that the presence of a term in his own final vocabulary ensures that it refers to something which *has* a real essence. The metaphysician is still attached to common sense, in that he does not question the platitudes which encapsulate the use of a given final vocabulary, and in particular the platitude which says there is a single permanent reality to be found behind the many temporary appearances. He does not redescribe but, rather, analyzes old descriptions with the help of other old descriptions.

The ironist, by contrast, is a nominalist and a historicist. She thinks nothing has an intrinsic nature, a real essence. So she thinks that the occurrence of a term like "just" or "scientific" or "rational" in the final vocabulary of the day is no reason to think that Socratic inquiry into the essence of justice or science or rationality will take one much beyond the language games of one's time. The ironist spends her time worrying about the possibility that she has been initiated into the wrong tribe, taught to play the wrong language game. She worries that the process of socialization which turned her into a human being by giving her a language may have given her the wrong language, and so turned her into the wrong kind of human being. But she cannot give a criterion of wrongness. So, the more she is driven to articulate her situation in philosophical terms, the more she reminds herself of her rootlessness by constantly using terms like "Weltanschauung," "perspective," "dialectic," "conceptual framework," "historical epoch," "language game," "redescription," "vocabulary," and "irony.". . .

For a metaphysician, "philosophy," as defined by reference to the canonical Plato-Kant sequence, is an attempt to know about certain things—quite general and important things. For the ironist, "philosophy," so defined, is the attempt to apply and develop a particular antecedently chosen final vocabulary—one which revolves around the appearance-reality distinction. The issue between them is, once again, about the contingency of our language—about whether what the common sense of our own culture shares with Plato and Kant is a tip-off to the way the world is, or whether it is just the characteristic mark of the discourse of people inhabiting a certain chunk of space-time. The metaphysician assumes that our tradition can raise no problems which it cannot solve—that the vocabulary which the ironist fears may be merely "Greek" or "Western" or "bourgeois" is an instrument which will enable us to get at something universal. The metaphysician agrees with the Platonic Theory of Recollection, in the form in which this theory was restated by Kierkegaard, namely, that we have the truth within us, that we have built-in criteria which enable us to recognize the right final vocabulary when we hear it. The cash value of this theory is that our contemporary final vocabularies are close enough to the right one to let us converge upon it—to formulate premises from which the right conclusions will be reached. The metaphysician thinks that although we may not have all the answers, we have already got criteria for the right answers. So he thinks "right" does not merely mean "suitable for those who speak as we do" but has a stronger sense—the sense of "grasping real essence."...

The rise of literary criticism to preeminence within the high culture of the democracies—its gradual and only semiconscious assumption of the cultural role once claimed (successively) by religion, science, and philosophy—has paralleled the rise in the proportion of ironists to metaphysicians among the intellectuals. This has widened the gap between the intellectuals and the public. For metaphysics is woven into the public rhetoric of modern liberal societies. So is the distinction between the moral and the "merely" aesthetic—a distinction which is often used to relegate "literature" to a subordinate position within culture and to suggest that novels and poems are irrelevant to moral reflection. Roughly speaking, the rhetoric of these societies takes for granted most of the oppositions which ... have become impediments to the culture of liberalism.

This situation has led to accusations of "irresponsibility" against ironist intellectuals. Some of these accusations come from know-nothings—people who have not read the books against which they warn others, and are just instinctively defending their own traditional roles. The know-nothings include religious fundamentalists, scientists who are offended at the suggestion that being "scientific" is not the highest intellectual virtue, and philosophers for whom it is an article of faith that rationality requires the deployment of general moral principles of the sort put forward by Mill and Kant. But the same accusations are made by writers who know what they are talking about, and whose views are entitled to respect. As I have already suggested, the most important of these writers is Habermas, who has mounted a sustained, detailed, carefully argued polemic against critics of the Enlightenment (e.g., Adorno, Foucault) who seem to turn their back on the social hopes of liberal societies. In Habermas's view, Hegel (and Marx) took the wrong tack in sticking to a philosophy of "subjectivity"—of self-reflection—rather than attempting to develop a philosophy of intersubjective communication....

I want to defend ironism....

Habermas, and other metaphysicians who are suspicious of a merely "literary" conception of philosophy, think that liberal political freedoms require some consensus about what is universally human. We ironists who are also liberals think that such freedoms require no consensus on any topic more basic than their own desirability. From our angle, all that matters for liberal politics is the widely shared conviction that ... we shall call "true" or "good" whatever is the outcome of free discussion—that if we take care of political freedom, truth and goodness will take care of themselves.

"Free discussion" here does not mean "free from ideology," but simply the sort which goes on when the press, the judiciary, the elections, and the universities are free, social mobility is frequent and rapid, literacy is universal, higher education is common, and peace and wealth have made possible the leisure necessary to listen to lots of different people and think about what they say....

The social glue holding together the ideal liberal society ... consists in little more than a consensus that the point of social organization is to let everybody have a chance at self-creation to the best of his or her abilities, and that that goal requires, besides peace and wealth, the standard "bourgeois freedoms." This conviction would not be based on a view about universally shared human ends, human rights, the nature of rationality, the Good for Man, nor anything else. It would be a conviction based on nothing more profound than the historical facts which suggest that without the protection of something like the institutions of bourgeois liberal society, people will be less able to work out their private salvations, create their private self-images, reweave their webs of belief and desire in the light of whatever new people and books they happen to encounter. In such an ideal society, discussion of public affairs will revolve around (1) how to balance the needs for peace, wealth, and freedom when conditions require that one of these goals be sacrificed to one of the others and (2) how to equalize opportunities for self-creation and then leave people alone to use, or neglect, their opportunities.

The suggestion that this is all the social glue liberal societies need is subject to two main objections. The first is that as a practical matter, this glue is just not thick enough—that the (predominantly) metaphysical rhetoric of public life in the democracies is essential to the continuation of free institutions. The second is that it is psychologically impossible to be a liberal ironist—to be someone for whom "cruelty is the worst thing we do," and to have no metaphysical beliefs about what all human beings have in common.

The first objection is a prediction about what would happen if ironism replaced metaphysics in our public rhetoric. The second is a suggestion that the public-private split I am advocating will not work: that no one can divide herself up into a private self-creator and a public liberal, that the same person cannot be, in alternate moments, Nietzsche and J. S. Mill.

I want to dismiss the first of these objections fairly quickly, in order to concentrate on the second. The former amounts to the prediction that the prevalence of ironist notions among the public at large, the general adoption of antimetaphysical, antiessentialist views about the nature of morality and rationality and human beings, would weaken and dissolve liberal societies. It is possible that this prediction is correct, but there is at least one excellent reason for thinking it false. This is the analogy with the decline of religious faith. That decline, and specifically the decline of people's ability to take the idea of postmortem rewards seriously, has not weakened liberal societies, and indeed has strengthened them....

The idea that liberal societies are bound together by philosophical beliefs seems to me ludicrous. What binds societies together are common vocabularies and common hopes. The vocabularies are, typically, parasitic on the hopes—in the sense that the principal function of the vocabularies is to tell stories about future outcomes which compensate for present sacrifices.

Modern, literate, secular societies depend on the existence of reasonably concrete, optimistic, and plausible *political* scenarios, as opposed to scenarios about redemption beyond the grave. To retain social hope, members of such a society need to be able to tell themselves a story about how things might get better, and to see no insuperable obstacles to this story's coming true. If social hope has become harder lately, this is not because the clerks have been committing treason but because, since the end of World War II, the course of events has made it harder to tell a convincing story of this sort. The cynical and impregnable Soviet Empire, the continuing shortsightedness and greed of the surviving democracies, and the exploding, starving populations of the Southern Hemisphere make the problems our parents faced in the 1930s—Fascism and unemployment—look almost manageable. People who try to update and rewrite the standard social democratic scenario about human equality, the scenario which their grandparents wrote around the turn of the century, are not having much success. The problems which metaphysically inclined social thinkers believe to be caused by our failure to find the right sort of theoretical glue—a philosophy which can command wide assent in an individualistic and pluralistic society—are, I think, caused by a set of historical contingencies. These contingencies are making it easy to see the last few hundred years of European and American history—centuries of increasing public hope and private ironism—as an island in time, surrounded by misery, tyranny, and chaos. As Orwell put it, "The democratic vistas seem to end in barbed wire.". . .

For the moment, I am simply trying to disentangle the public question "Is absence of metaphysics politically dangerous?" from the private question "Is ironism compatible with a sense of human solidarity?" To do so, it may help to distinguish the way nominalism and historicism look at present, in a liberal culture whose public rhetoric—the rhetoric in which the young are socialized—is still metaphysical, from the way they might look in a future whose public rhetoric is borrowed from nominalists and historicists. We tend to assume that nominalism and historicism are the exclusive property of intellectuals, of high culture, and that the masses cannot be so blasé about their own final vocabularies. But remember that once upon a time atheism, too, was the exclusive property of intellectuals.

In the ideal liberal society, the intellectuals would still be ironists, although the nonintellectuals would not. The latter would, however, be commonsensically nominalist and historicist. So they would see themselves as contingent through and through, without feeling any particular doubts about the contingencies they happened to be. They would not be bookish, nor would they look to literary critics as moral advisers. But they would be commonsensical nonmetaphysicians, in the way in which more and more people in the rich democracies have been commonsensical nontheists. . . . Such a person would not need a justification for her sense of human solidarity, for she was not raised to play the language game in which one asks and gets justifications for that sort of belief. Her culture is one in which doubts about the public rhetoric of the culture are met not by Socratic requests for definitions and principles, but by Deweyan requests for concrete alternatives and programs. Such a culture could, as far as I can see, be every bit as self-critical and every bit as devoted to human equality as our own familiar, and still metaphysical, liberal culture—if not more so.

But even if I am right in thinking that a liberal culture whose public rhetoric is nominalist and historicist is both possible and desirable, I cannot go on to claim that there could or ought to be a culture whose public rhetoric is *ironist*. I cannot imagine a culture which socialized its youth in such a way as to make them continually dubious about their own process of socialization. Irony seems inherently a private matter. On my definition, an ironist cannot get along without the contrast between the final vocabulary she inherited and the one she is trying to create for herself. Irony is, if not intrinsically resentful, at least reactive. Ironists have to have something to have doubts about, something from which to be alienated.

This brings me to the second of the two objections I listed above, and thus to the idea that there is something about being an ironist which unsuits one for being a liberal, and that a simple split between private and public concerns is not enough to overcome the tension.

One can make this claim plausible by saying that there is at least a prima facie tension between the idea that social organization aims at human equality and the idea that human beings are simply incarnated vocabularies. The idea that we all have an overriding obligation to diminish cruelty, to make human beings equal in respect to their liability to suffering, seems to take for granted that there is something within human beings which deserves respect and protection quite independently of the language they speak. It suggests that a nonlinguistic ability, the ability to feel pain, is what is important, and that differences in vocabulary are much less important.

Metaphysics—in the sense of a search for theories which will get at real essence—tries to make sense of the claim that human beings are something more than centerless webs of beliefs and desires. The reason many people think such a claim essential to liberalism is that if men and women were, indeed, nothing more than sentential attitudes—nothing more than the presence or absence of dispositions toward the use of sentences phrased in some historically conditioned vocabulary—then not only human nature, but human *solidarity*, would begin to seem an eccentric and dubious idea. For solidarity with all possible vocabularies seems impossible. Metaphysicians tell us that unless there is some sort of common ur-vocabulary, we have no "reason" not to be cruel to those whose final vocabularies are very unlike ours. A universalistic ethics seems incompatible with ironism, simply because it is hard to imagine stating such an ethic without some doctrine about the nature of man. Such an appeal to real essence is the antithesis of ironism.

So the fact that greater openness, more room for self-creation, is the standard demand made by ironists on their societies is balanced by the fact that this demand seems to be merely for the freedom to speak a kind of ironic theoretical metalanguage which makes no sense to the man in the street . . . Ironism, as I have defined it results from awareness of the power of redescription. But most people do not want to be redescribed. They want to be taken on their own terms— taken seriously just as they are and just as they talk. The ironist tells them that the language they speak is up for grabs by her and her kind. . . .

The redescribing ironist, by threatening one's final vocabulary, and thus one's ability to make sense of oneself in one's own terms rather than hers, suggests that one's self and one's world are futile, obsolete, *powerless*. Redescription often humiliates.

But notice that redescription and possible humiliation are no more closely connected with ironism than with metaphysics. The metaphysician also redescribes, even though he does it in the name of reason rather than in the name of the imagination. Redescription is a generic trait of the intellectual, not a specific mark of the ironist. So why do ironists arouse *special* resentment? We get a clue to an answer from the fact that the metaphysician typically backs up his redescription with argument—or, as the ironist redescribes the process, disguises his redescription under the cover of argument. But this in itself does not solve the problem, for argument, like redescription, is neutral between liberalism and antiliberalism. Presumably the relevant difference is that to offer an argument in support of one's redescription amounts to telling the audience that they are being *educated*, rather than simply reprogrammed—that the Truth was already in them and merely needed to be drawn out into the light. Redescription which presents itself as uncovering the interlocutor's true self, or the real nature of a common public world which the speaker and the interlocutor share, suggests that the person being redescribed is being empowered, not having his power diminished.

The metaphysician, in short, thinks that there is a connection between redescription and power, and that the right redescription can make us free. The ironist offers no similar assurance. She has to say that our chances of freedom depend on historical contingencies which are only occasionally influenced by our self-redescriptions. She knows of no power of the same size as the one with which the metaphysician claims acquaintance. When she claims that her redescription is better, she cannot give the term "better" the reassuring weight the metaphysician gives it when he explicates it as "in better correspondence with reality."

So I conclude that what the ironist is being blamed for is not an inclination to humiliate but an inability to empower. There is no reason the ironist cannot be a liberal, but she cannot be a "progressive" and "dynamic" liberal in the sense in which liberal metaphysicians sometimes claim to be. For she cannot offer the same sort of social hope as metaphysicians offer. She cannot claim that adopting her redescription of yourself or your situation makes you better able to conquer the forces which are marshaled against you. On her account, that ability is a matter of weapons and luck, not a matter of having truth on your side, or having detected the "movement of history."

There are, then, two differences between the liberal ironist and the liberal metaphysician. The first concerns their sense of what redescription can do for liberalism; the second, their sense of the connection between public hope and private irony. The first difference is that the ironist thinks that the *only* redescriptions which serve liberal purposes are those which answer the question "What humiliates?" whereas the metaphysician also wants to answer the question "Why should I avoid humiliating?" The liberal metaphysician wants our *wish to be kind* to be bolstered by an argument, one which entails a self-redescription which will highlight a common human essence, an essence which is something more than our shared ability to suffer humiliation. The liberal ironist just wants our *chances of being kind*, of avoiding the humiliation of others, to be expanded by redescription. She thinks that recognition of a common susceptibility to humiliation is the *only* social bond that is needed. Whereas the metaphysician takes the morally relevant feature of the other human beings to be their relation to a larger shared power—rationality, God, truth, or history, for example—the ironist takes the morally relevant definition of a person, a moral subject, to be "something that can be humiliated." Her sense of human solidarity is based on a sense of a common danger, not on a common possession or a shared power.

What, then, of the point I made earlier; that people want to be described in their own terms? As I have already suggested, the liberal ironist meets this point by saying that we need to distinguish between redescription for private and for public purposes. For my private purposes, I may redescribe you and everybody else in terms which have nothing to do with my attitude toward your actual or possible suffering. My private purposes, and the part of my final vocabulary which is not relevant to my public actions, are none of your business. But as I am a liberal, the part of my final vocabulary which is relevant to such actions requires me to become aware of all the various ways in which other human beings whom I might act upon can be humiliated. So the liberal ironist needs as much imaginative acquaintance with alternative final vocabularies as possible, not just for her own edification, but in order to understand the actual and possible humiliation of the people who use these alternative final vocabularies.

The liberal metaphysician, by contrast, wants a final vocabulary with an internal and organic structure, one which is not split down the middle by a public-private distinction, not just a patchwork. He thinks that acknowledging that everybody wants to be taken on their own terms commits us to finding a least common denominator of those terms, a single description which will suffice for both public and private purposes, for self-definition and for one's relations with others. He prays, with Socrates, that the inner and the outer man will be as one—that irony will no longer be necessary. . . .

But that distinction between a central, shared, obligatory portion and a peripheral, idiosyncratic, optional portion of one's final vocabulary is just the distinction which the ironist refuses to draw. She thinks that what unites her with the rest of the species is not a common language but *just* susceptibility to pain and in particular to that special sort of pain which the brutes do not share with the humans—humiliation. On her conception, human solidarity is not a matter of sharing a common truth or a common goal but of sharing a common selfish hope, the hope that one's world—the little things around which one has woven into one's final vocabulary—will not be destroyed. For public purposes, it does not matter if everybody's final vocabulary is different, as long as there is enough overlap so that everybody has some words with which to express the desirability of entering into other people's fantasies as well as into one's own. But those overlapping words—words like "kindness" or "decency" or "dignity"—do not form a vocabulary which all human beings can reach by reflection on their natures. Such reflection will not produce anything except a heightened awareness of the possibility of suffering. It will not produce a *reason to care* about suffering. What matters for the liberal ironist is not finding such a reason but making sure that she *notices* suffering when it occurs. Her hope is that she will not be limited by her own final vocabulary when faced with the possibility of humiliating someone with a quite different final vocabulary. . . .

The suspicion that ironism in philosophy has not helped liberalism is quite right, but that is not because ironist philosophy is inherently cruel. It is because liberals have come to expect philosophy to do a certain job—namely, answering questions like "Why not be cruel?" and "Why be kind?"—and they feel that any philosophy which refuses this assignment must be heartless. But that expectation is a result of a metaphysical upbringing. If we could get rid of the expectation, liberals would not ask ironist philosophy to do a job which it cannot do, and which it defines itself as unable to do.

The metaphysician's association of theory with social hope and of literature with private perfection is, in an ironist liberal culture, reversed. Within a liberal metaphysical culture the disciplines which were charged with penetrating behind the many private appearances to the one general common reality—theology, science, philosophy—were the ones which were expected to bind human beings together, and thus to help eliminate cruelty. Within an ironist culture, by contrast, it is the disciplines which specialize in thick description of the private and idiosyncratic which are assigned this job. In particular, novels and ethnographies which sensitize one to the pain of those who do not speak our language must do the job which demonstrations of a common human nature were supposed to do. Solidarity has to be constructed out of little pieces, rather than found already waiting, in the form of an ur-language which all of us recognize when we hear it.

Conversely, within our increasingly ironist culture, philosophy has become more important for the pursuit of private perfection rather than for any social task. . . .

RICHARD RORTY
(1987)

Science as
Solidarity

In our culture, the notions of "science," "rationality," "objectivity," and "truth" are bound up with one another. Science is thought of as offering "hard," "objective" truth: truth as correspondence to reality, the only sort of truth worthy of the name. Humanists like philosophers, theologians, historians, and literary critics have to worry about whether they are being "scientific"—whether they are entitled to think of their conclusions, no matter how carefully argued, as worthy of the term "true." We tend to identify seeking "objective truth" with "using reason," and so we think of the natural sciences as paradigms of rationality. We also think of rationality as a matter of following procedures laid down in advance, of being "methodical." So we tend to use "methodical," "rational," "scientific," and "objective" as synonyms.

Worries about "cognitive status" and "objectivity" are characteristic of a secularized culture in which the scientist replaces the priest. The scientist is now seen as the person who keeps humanity in touch with something beyond itself. As the universe was depersonalized, beauty (and, in time, even moral goodness) came to be thought of as "subjective." So truth is now thought of as the only point at which human beings are responsible to something nonhuman. A commitment to "rationality" and to "method" is thought to be a recognition of this responsibility. The scientist becomes a moral exemplar, one who selflessly exposes himself again and again to the hardness of fact.

One result of this way of thinking is that any academic discipline which wants a place at the trough, but is unable to offer the predictions and the technology provided by the natural

John S. Nelson, Allan Megill, Donald N. McClockey, eds., *The Rhetoric of Human Sciences: Language and Argument in Scholarship and Public Affairs* (Madison: University of Wisconsin Press, 1987), pp. 38–52. ©The University of Wisconsin Press, 1987. By permission of the Press.

sciences, must either pretend to imitate science or find some way of obtaining "cognitive status" without the necessity of discovering facts. Practitioners of these disciplines must either affiliate themselves with this quasi-priestly order by using terms like "behavioral sciences" or else find something other than "fact" to be concerned with. People in the humanities typically choose the latter strategy. They either describe themselves as concerned with "value" as opposed to facts, or as developing and inculcating habits of "critical reflection."

Neither sort of rhetoric is very satisfactory. No matter how much humanists talk about "objective values," the phrase always sounds vaguely confused. It gives with one hand what it takes back with the other. The distinction between the objective and the subjective was designed to parallel that between fact and value, so an objective value sounds as vaguely mythological as a winged horse. Talk about the humanists' special skill at critical reflection fares no better. Nobody really believes that philosophers or literary critics are better at critical thinking, or at taking big broad views of things, than theoretical physicists or microbiologists. So society tends to ignore both these kinds of rhetoric. It treats humanities as on a par with the arts, and thinks of both as providing pleasure rather than truth. Both are, to be sure, thought of as providing "high" rather than "low" pleasures. But an elevated and spiritual sort of pleasure is still a long way from the grasp of a truth.

These distinctions between hard facts and soft values, truth and pleasure, and objectivity and subjectivity are awkward and clumsy instruments. They are not suited to dividing up culture; they create more difficulties than they resolve. It would be best to find another vocabulary, to start afresh. But in order to do so, we first have to find a new way of describing the natural sciences. It is not a question of debunking or downgrading the natural scientist, but simply of ceasing to see him as a priest. We need to stop thinking of science as the place where the human mind confronts the world, and of the scientist as exhibiting proper humility in the face of superhuman forces. We need a way of explaining why scientists are, and deserve to be, moral exemplars which does not depend on a distinction between objective fact and something softer, squishier, and more dubious.

To get such a way of thinking, we can start by distinguishing two senses of the term "rationality." In one sense, the one I have already discussed, to be rational is to be methodical: that is, to have criteria for success laid down in advance. We think of poets and painters as using some faculty other than "reason" in their work because, by their own confession, they are not sure of what they want to do before they have done it. They make up new standards of achievement as they go along. By contrast, we think of judges as knowing in advance what criteria a brief will have to satisfy in order to invoke a favorable decision, and of business people as setting well-defined goals and being judged by their success in achieving them. Law and business are good examples of rationality, but the scientist, knowing in advance what would count as disconfirming his hypothesis and prepared to abandon that hypothesis as a result of the unfavourable outcome of a single experiment, seems a truly heroic example. Further, we seem to have a clear criterion for the success of a scientific theory—namely, its ability to predict, and thereby to enable us to control some portion of the world. If to be rational means to be able to lay down criteria in advance, then it is plausible to take natural science as the paradigm of rationality.

The trouble is that in this sense of "rational" the humanities are never going to qualify as rational activities. If the humanities are concerned with ends rather than means, then there is no way to evaluate their success in terms of antecedently specified criteria. If we already knew what criteria we wanted to satisfy, we would not worry about whether we were pursuing the right ends. If we thought we knew the goals of culture and society in advance, we would have no use for the humanities—as totalitarian societies in fact do not. It is characteristic of democratic and pluralistic societies to continually redefine their goals. But if to be rational means to satisfy criteria, then this process of redefinition is bound to be nonrational. So if the humanities are to be viewed as rational activities, rationality will have to be thought of as something other than the satisfaction of criteria which are statable in advance.

Another meaning for "rational" is, in fact, available. In this sense, the word means something like "sane" or "reasonable" rather than "methodical." It names a set of moral virtues tolerance, respect for the opinions of those around one, willingness to listen, reliance on persuasion rather than force. These are the virtues which members of a civilized society must possess if the society is to endure. In this sense of "rational," the word means something more like "civilized" than like "methodical." When so construed, the distinction between the rational and the irrational has nothing in particular to do with the difference between the arts and the sciences. On this construction, to be rational is simply to discuss any topic religious, literary, or scientific—in a way which eschews dogmatism, defensiveness, and righteous indignation.

There is no problem about whether, in this latter, weaker, sense, the humanities are "rational disciplines." Usually humanists display the moral virtues in question. Sometimes they don't, but then sometimes scientists don't either. Yet these moral virtues are felt to be not enough. Both humanists and the public hanker after rationality in the first, stronger sense of the term: a sense which is associated with objective truth, correspondence to reality, and method, and criteria.

We should not try to satisfy this hankering, but rather try to eradicate it. No matter what one's opinion of the secularization of culture, it was a mistake to try to make the natural scientist into a new sort of priest, a link between the human and the nonhuman. So was the idea that some sorts of truths are "objective" whereas others are merely "subjective or "relative"—the attempt to divide up the set of true sentences into "genuine knowledge" and "mere opinion," or into the "factual" and "judgmental." So was the idea that the scientist has a special method which, if only the humanists would apply it to ultimate values, would give us the same kind of self-confidence about the moral ends as we now have about technological means. I think that we should content ourselves with the second, "weaker" conception of rationality, and avoid the first, "stronger" conception. We should avoid the idea that there is some special virtue in knowing in advance what criteria you are going to satisfy, in having standards by which to measure progress.

One can make these issues somewhat more concrete by taking up the current controversy among philosophers about the "rationality of science." For some twenty years, ever since the publication of Thomas Kuhn's book *The Structure of Scientific Revolutions*, philosophers have been debating whether science is rational. Attacks on Kuhn for being an "irrationalist" are now as frequent and as urgent as were, in the thirties and forties, attacks on the logical positivists for saying that moral judgments were "meaningless." We are constantly being warned of the danger of "relativism," which will beset us if we give up our attachment to objectivity, and to the idea of rationality as obedience to criteria.

Whereas Kuhn's enemies routinely accuse him of reducing science to "mob psychology," and pride themselves on having (by a new theory of meaning, or reference, or verisimilitude) vindicated the "rationality of science," his pragmatist friends (such as myself) routinely congratulate him on having softened the distinction between science and nonscience. It is fairly easy for Kuhn to show that the enemies are attacking a straw man. But it is harder for him to save himself from his friends. For he has said that "there is no theory-independent way to reconstruct phrases like 'really there.'" He has asked whether it really helps "to imagine that there is some one full, objective, true account of nature and that the proper measure of scientific achievement is the extent to which it brings us closer to that ultimate goal." We pragmatists quote these passages incessantly in the course of our effort to enlist Kuhn in our campaign to drop the objective-subjective distinction altogether.

What I am calling "pragmatism" might also be called "left-wing Kuhnianism." It has been also rather endearingly called (by one of its critics, Clark Glymour) the "new fuzziness," because it is an attempt to blur just those distinctions between the objective and the subjective and between fact and value which the criterial conception of rationality has developed. We fuzzies would like to substitute the idea of "unforced agreement" for that of "objectivity." We should like to put all of culture on an epistemological level—or, to put it another way, we would like to get rid of the idea of "epistemological level" or "cognitive status." We would like to disabuse social scientists and humanists of the idea that there is something called "scientific status" which is a desirable goal. On our view, "truth" is a univocal term. It applies equally to the judgments of lawyers, anthropologists, physicists, philologists, and literary critics. There is no point in assigning degrees of "objectivity" or "hardness" to such disciplines. For the presence of unforced agreement in all of them gives us everything in the way of "objective truth" which one could possibly want: namely, intersubjective agreement.

As soon as one says that objectivity is intersubjectivity, one is likely to be accused of being a relativist. That is the epithet traditionally applied to pragmatists. But this epithet is ambiguous. It can name any of three different views. The first is the silly and self-refuting view that every belief is as good as every other. The second is the wrong-headed view that "true" is an equivocal term, having as many meanings as there are contexts of justification. The third is the ethnocentric view that there is nothing to be said about either truth or rationality apart from descriptions of the familiar procedures of justification which a given society—*ours*—uses in one or another area of inquiry. The pragmatist does hold this third, ethnocentric, view. But he does not hold the first or the second.

But "relativism" is not an appropriate term to describe this sort of ethnocentrism. For we pragmatists are not holding a positive theory which says that something is relative to something else. Instead, we are making the purely *negative* point that we would be better off without the traditional distinctions between knowledge and opinion, construed as the distinction between truth as correspondence to reality and truth as a commendatory term for well-justified belief. Our opponents calls this negative claim "relativistic" because they cannot imagine that anybody would seriously deny that truth has an intrinsic nature. So when we say that there is nothing to be said about truth save that each of us will commend as true those beliefs which he or she finds good to believe, the realist is inclined to interpret this as one more positive theory about the nature of truth: a theory according to which truth is simply the contemporary opinion of a chosen individual or group. Such a theory would, of course, be self-refuting. But we pragmatists do not have a theory of truth, much less a relativistic one. As partisans of solidarity, our account of the value of cooperative human inquiry has only an ethical base, not an epistemological or metaphysical one.

To say that we must be ethnocentric may sound suspicious, but this will only happen if we identify ethnocentrism with pig-headed refusal to talk to representatives of other communities.

In my sense of ethnocentrism, to be ethnocentric is simply to work by our own lights. The defense of ethnocentrism is simply that there are no other lights to work by. Beliefs suggested by another individual or another culture must be tested by trying to weave them together with beliefs which we already have. We *can* so test them, because everything which we can identify as a human being or as a culture will be something which shares an enormous number of beliefs with us. (If it did not, we would simply not be able to recognize that it was speaking a language, and thus that it had any beliefs at all.)

This way of thinking runs counter to the attempt, familiar since the eighteenth century, to think of political liberalism as based on a conception of the nature of man. To most thinkers of the Enlightenment, it seemed clear that the access to Nature which physical science had provided should now be followed by the establishment of social, political, and economic institutions which were "in accordance with Nature." Ever since, liberal social thought has centered on social reform as made possible by objective knowledge of what human beings are like—not knowledge of what Greeks or Frenchmen or Chinese are like, but of humanity as such. This tradition dreams of a universal human community which will exhibit a nonparochial solidarity because it is the expression of an ahistorical human nature.

Philosophers who belong to this tradition, who wish to ground solidarity in objectivity, have to construe truth as correspondence to reality. So they must construct an epistemology which had room for a kind of justification which is not merely social but natural, springing from human nature itself, and made possible by a link between that part of nature and the rest of nature. By contrast, we pragmatists, who wish to reduce objectivity to solidarity, do not require either a metaphysics or an epistemology. We do not need an account of a relation between beliefs and objects called "correspondence," nor an account of human cognitive abilities which ensures that our species is capable of entering into that relation. We see the gap between truth and justification not as something to be bridged by isolating a natural and transcultural sort of rationality which can be used to criticize certain cultures and praise others, but simply as the gap between the actual good and the possible better. From a pragmatist point of view, to say that what is rational for us now to believe may not be *true* is simply to say that somebody may come up with a better idea.

On this pragmatist view of rationality as civility, inquiry is a matter of continually reweaving a web of beliefs rather than the application of criteria to cases. Criteria change in just the way other beliefs change, and there is no touchstone which can preserve any criterion from possible revision. That is why the pragmatist is not frightened by the specter of "cultural relativism." Our interchange with other communities and cultures is not to be thought of as a clash between irreconcilable systems of thought, deductively inferred from incompatible first premises. Alternative cultures should not be thought of on the model of alternative geometries—as irreconcilable because they have axiomatic structures and contradictory axioms. Such geometries are *designed* to be irreconcilable. Individual and cultural webs of belief are not so designed, and do not have axiomatic structures.

Cultures can, indeed, protect themselves by institutionalizing knowledge-claims and making people suffer who do not hold certain beliefs. But such institutional backups take the form of bureaucrats and policemen, not of "rules of language" or "criteria of rationality." The criterial conception of rationality has suggested that every distinct culture comes equipped with certain unchallengeable axioms, "necessary truths," and that these form barriers to communication between cultures. So it has seemed as if there could be no conversation between cultures but only subjugation by force. On the pragmatic conception of rationality, there are no such barriers. The distinction between different cultures differs only in degree from the distinction between theories held by members of a single culture. The Tasmanian aborigines and the British colonies, for example, had trouble in communicating, but this trouble was different only in extent from the difficulties in communication experienced by Gladstone and Disraeli. The trouble in all such cases is just the difficulty of explaining why other people disagree with us, and of reweaving our beliefs so as to fit the fact of disagreement together with the other beliefs we hold. The same pragmatist (and, more specifically, Quinean) arguments which dispose of the positivist's distinction between analytic and synthetic truths dispose of the anthropologists' distinction between the intercultural and the intracultural.

Another reason for describing us as "relativistic" is that we pragmatists drop the idea that inquiry is destined to converge to a single point—that truth is out there waiting for human beings to arrive at it. This idea seems to us an unfortunate attempt to carry a religious conception over into a culture. All that is worth preserving of the claim that rational inquiry will converge to a single point is the claim to be able to explain why past false views were held in the past, and explain how we go about reeducating our benighted ancestors. To teach that we think we are heading in the right direction is just to say, with Kuhn, that we can, by hindsight, tell the story of the past as a story of progress.

But the fact that we can trace such a direction and tell such a story does not mean that we have gotten closer to a goal which is out there waiting for us. We cannot, I think, imagine a moment at which the human race could settle back and say, "Well, now that we've finally arrived at the Truth we can relax." Paul Feyerabend is right in suggesting that we should discard the metaphor of inquiry, and human activity generally, as converging rather than proliferating, becoming more unified rather than more diverse. On the contrary, we should relish the thought that the sciences as well as the arts will *always* provide a spectacle of fierce competition between alternative theories, movements, and schools. The end of human activity is not rest, but rather richer and better human activity. We should think of human progress as making it possible for human beings to do more interesting things and be more interesting people, not as heading toward a place which has somehow been prepared for us in advance. To drop the criterial conception of rationality in favor of the pragmatist conception would be to give up the idea of Truth as something to which we were responsible. Instead we should think of "true" as a word which applies to those beliefs upon which we are able to agree, as roughly synonymous with "justified." To say that beliefs can be agreed upon without being true is, once again, merely to say that somebody might come up with a better idea.

Another way of characterizing this line of thought is to say that pragmatists would like to drop the idea that human beings are responsible to a nonhuman power. We hope for a culture in which questions about the "objectivity of value" or the "rationality of science" would seem equally unintelligible. Pragmatists would like to replace the desire for objectivity—the desire to be in touch with a reality which is more than some community with which we identify ourselves—with the desire for solidarity with that community. They think that the habits of relying on persuasion rather than force, of respect for the opinions of colleagues, of curiosity and eagerness for new data and ideas, are the *only* virtues which scientists have. They do not think that there is an intellectual virtue called "rationality" over and above these moral virtues.

On this view there is no reason to praise scientists for being more "objective" or "logical" or "methodical" or "devoted to truth" than other people. But there is plenty of reason to praise the institutions they have developed and within which they work, and to use these as models for the rest of culture. For these institutions give concreteness and detail to the idea of "unforced agreement." Reference to such institutions fleshes out the idea of "a free and open encounter"— the sort of encounter in which truth cannot fail to win. On this view, to say that truth will win in such an encounter is not to make a metaphysical claim about the connection between human reason and the nature of things. It is merely to say that the best way to find out what to believe is to listen to as many suggestions and arguments as you can.

My rejection of traditional notions of rationality can be summed up by saying that the only sense in which science is exemplary is that it is a model of human solidarity. We should think of the institutions and practices which make up various scientific communities as providing suggestions about the way in which the rest of culture might organize itself. When we say that our legislatures are "unrepresentative" or "dominated by special interests," or that the art world is dominated by "fashion," we are contrasting these areas of culture with areas which seem to be in better order. The natural sciences strike us as being such areas. But, on this view, we shall not explain this better order by thinking of the scientists as having a "method" which the rest of us would do well to imitate, nor as benefiting from the desirable hardness of their subjects compared with the undesirable softness of other subjects. If we say that sociology or literary criticism "is not a science," we shall mean merely that the amount of agreement among sociologists or literary critics on what counts as significant work, work which needs following up, is less than among, say, microbiologists.

Pragmatists will not attempt to explain this latter phenomenon by saying that societies or literary texts are squishier than molecules, or than the human sciences cannot be as "value-free" as the natural sciences, or that the sociologists and critics have not yet found their paradigms. Nor will they assume that "a science" is necessarily something which we want sociology to be. One consequence of their view is the suggestion that perhaps "the human sciences" *should* look quite different from the natural sciences. This suggestion is not based on epistemological or metaphysical considerations which show that inquiry into societies must be different from inquiry into things. Instead, it is based on the observation that natural scientists are interested primarily in predicting and controlling the behavior of things, and that prediction and control may not be what we want from our sociologists and our literary critics.

Despite the encouragement he has given it, however, Kuhn draws back from this pragmatist position. He does so when he asks for an explanation of "why science works." The request for such an explanation binds him together with his opponents and separates him from his left-wing friends. Anti-Kuhnians tend to unite in support of the claim that "merely psychological or sociological reasons" will not explain why natural science is so good at predicting. Kuhn joins them when he says that he shares "Hume's itch"—the desire for "an explanation of the viability of the whole language game that involves 'induction' and underpins the form of life we live."

Pragmatists think that one will suffer from Hume's itch only if one has been scratching oneself with what has sometimes been called "Hume's fork"—the distinction between "relations of ideas" and "matters of fact." This distinction survives in contemporary philosophy as the distinction between "questions of language" and "questions of fact." We pragmatists think that philosophers of language such as Wittgenstein, Quine, Goodman, Davidson, and others have shown us how to get along without these distinctions. Once one has lived without them for a while, one learns to live without those between knowledge and opinion, or between subjective and objective, as well. The purposes served by the latter distinctions come to be served by the unproblematic sociological distinction between areas in which unforced agreement is relative infrequent and areas in which it is relatively frequent. So we do not itch for an explanation of the success of recent Western science any more than for the success of recent Western politics. That is why we fuzzies applaud Kuhn when he says that "one does not know what a person who denies the rationality of learning from experience is trying to say," but are aghast when he goes on to ask *why* "we have no rational alternatives to learning from experience."

On the pragmatist view, the contrast between "relations of ideas" and "matters of fact" is a special case of the bad seventeenth-century contrasts between being "in us" and being "out there," between subject and object, between our beliefs and what those beliefs (moral, scientific, theological, etc.) are trying to get right. Pragmatists avoid this latter contrast by instead contrasting our beliefs with proposed alternative beliefs. They recommend that we worry only about the choice between two hypotheses, rather than about whether there is something which "makes" either true. To take this stance would rid us of questions about the objectivity of value, the rationality of science, and the causes of the viability of our language games. All such theoretical questions would be replaced with practical questions about whether we ought to keep our present values, theories, and practices or try to replace them with others. Given such a replacement, there would be nothing to be responsible to except ourselves.

This may sound like solipsistic fantasy, but the pragmatist regards it as an alternative in account of the nature of intellectual and moral responsibility. He is suggesting that instead of invoking anything like the idea-fact or language fact, or mind-word, or subject-object distinctions to explicate our intuition that there is something out there to be responsible to, we just drop that intuition. We should drop it in favor of the thought that we might be better than we presently are—in the sense of being better scientific theorists, or citizens or friends. The backup for this intuition would be the actual or imagined existence of other human beings who were already better (utopian fantasies, or actual experience, of superior individuals or societies). On this account, to be responsible is a matter of what Peirce called "contrite fallibilism" rather than of respect for something beyond. The desire for "objectivity" boils down to a desire to acquire beliefs which will eventually receive unforced agreement in the course of a free and open encounter with people holding other beliefs.

Pragmatists interpret the goal of inquiry (in any sphere of culture) as the attainment of an appropriate mixture of unforced agreement with tolerant disagreement (where what counts as appropriate is determined, within that sphere by trial and error). Such a reinterpretation of our sense of responsibility would, if carried through, gradually make unintelligible the subject-object model of inquiry; the child-parent model of moral obligation, and the correspondence theory of truth. A world in which these models, and that theory, no longer had any intuitive appeal would be a pragmatist's paradise.

When Dewey urged that we try to create such paradise, he was said to be irresponsible for, it was said, he left us bereft of weapons to use against our enemies he gave us nothing with which to "answer the Nazis." When we new fuzzies try to revive Dewey's repudiation of criteriology, we are said to be "relativistic." We must, people say, believe that every coherent view is as good as every other, since we have no "outside" touchstone for choice among such views. We are said to leave the general public defenseless against the witch doctor, the defender of creationism or anyone else who is clever and patient enough to deduce a consistent and wide-ranging set of theorems from his "alternative first principles."

Nobody is convinced when we fuzzies say that we can be just as morally indignant as the new philosopher. We are suspected of being contritely fallibilist when righteous fury is called for. Even when we actually display appropriate emotions we get nowhere, for we are told that we have no *right* to these emotions. When we suggest that one of the few things we know about (or need to know) about truth is that it is what wins in a free and open encounter, we are told that we have defined "true" as "satisfies the standards of our community." But we pragmatists do not hold this relativist view. We do not infer from "there is no way to step outside communities to a neutral standpoint" that "there is no rational way to justify liberal communities over totalitarian communities." For that inference involves just the notion of "rationality" as a set of ahistorical principles which pragmatists abjure. What we in fact infer is that there is no way to beat totalitarians in argument by appealing to shared common premises, and no point in pretending that a common human nature makes the totalitarians unconsciously hold such premises.

The claim that we fuzzies have no right to be furious at moral evil, no right to commend our views as true unless we simultaneously refute ourselves by claiming that there are objects out there which *make* those views true, begs all the theoretical questions. But it gets to the practical and moral heart of the matter. This is the question of whether notions like "unforced agreement" and "free and open encounter"—descriptions of social situations—can take the place in our moral lives of notions like "the world," "the will of God," "the moral law," "what our beliefs are trying to represent accurately," and "what makes our beliefs true." All the philosophical presuppositions which make Hume's fork seem inevitable are ways of suggesting that human communities must justify their existence by striving to attain a nonhuman goal. To suggest that we can forget about Hume's fork, forget about being responsible to what is "out there," is to suggest that human communities can only justify their existence by comparisons with other actual and possible human communities.

I can make this contrast a bit more concrete by asking whether free and open encounters, and the kind of community which permits and encourages such encounters, are for the sake of truth and goodness, or whether "the quest for truth and goodness" is simply the quest for that kind of community. Is the sort of community which is exemplified by groups of scientific inquirers and by democratic political institutions a means to an end, or is the formation of such communities the only goal we need? Dewey thought that it was the only goal we needed, and I think he was right. But whether he was or not, this question is the one to which the debates about Kuhn's "irrationalism" and the new fuzzies "relativism" will eventually boil down.

Dewey was accused of blowing up the optimism and flexibility of a parochial and jejune way of life (the American) into a philosophical system. So he did, but his reply was that *any* philosophical system is only to be an attempt to express the ideals of *some* community's *way* of life. He was quite ready to admit that the virtue of his philosophy was, indeed, nothing more than the virtue of the way of life which it commended. On his view, philosophy does not justify affiliation with a community in the light of something ahistorical called "reason" or "transcultural principles." It simply expatiates on the special advantages of that community over other communities. Dewey's best argument for doing philosophy this way is also the best argument we partisans of solidarity have against partisans of objectivity: it is Nietzsche's argument that the traditional Western metaphysico-epistemological way of firming up our habits is not working anymore.

What would it be like to be less fuzzy and parochial than this? I suggest that it would be to become less genial, tolerant, open-minded, and fallibilist than we are now. In the nontrivial, pejorative sense of "ethnocentric," the sense in which we congratulate ourselves on being less ethnocentric now than our ancestors were three hundred years ago, the way to avoid ethno-centrism is precisely to abandon the sort of thing we fuzzies are blamed for abandoning. It is to have only the most tenuous and cursory formulations of criteria for changing our beliefs, only the loosest and most flexible standards. Suppose that for the last three hundred years we had been using an explicit algorithm for determining how just a society was, and how good a phys-ical theory was. Would we have developed either parliamentary democracy or relativity physics? Suppose that we had the sort of "weapons" against the fascists of which Dewey was said to deprive us—firm, unrevisable, moral principles which were not merely "ours" but "universal" and "objective." How could we avoid having these weapons turn in our hands and bash all the genial tolerance out of our own heads?

Imagine, to use another example, that a few years from now you open your copy of the *New York Times* and read that the philosophers, in convention assembled, have unanimously agreed that values are objective, science rational, truth a matter of correspondence to reality, and so on. Recent breakthroughs in semantics and meta-ethics, the report goes on, have caused the last remaining noncognitivists in ethics to recant. Similar breakthroughs in philosophy of science have led Kuhn formally to abjure his claim that there is no theory-independent way to reconstruct statements about what is "really there." All the new fuzzies have repudiated all their former views. By way of making amends for the intellectual confusion which the philosophical profession has recently caused, the philosophers have adopted a short, crisp, set of standards of rationality and morality. Next year the convention is expected to adopt the report of the committee charged with formulating a standard of aesthetic taste.

Surely the public reaction to this would not be "Saved!" but rather "Who on earth do these philosophers think they *are?*" It is one of the best things about the form of intellectual life we Western liberals lead that this *would* be our reaction. No matter how much we moan about the disorder and confusion of the current philosophical scene, about the treason of the clerks, we do not really want things any other way. What prevents us from relaxing and enjoying the new fuzziness is perhaps no more than cultural lag, the fact that the rhetoric of the Enlightenment praised the emerging natural sciences in a vocabulary which was left over from a less liberal and tolerant era. This rhetoric enshrined all the old philosophical oppositions between mind and world, appearance and reality, subject and object, truth and pleasure. Dewey thought that it was the continued prevalence of such oppositions which prevented us from seeing that modern science was a new and promising invention, a way of life which had not existed before and which ought to be encouraged and imitated, something which required a new rhetoric rather than justification by an old one.

Suppose that Dewey was right about this, and that eventually we learn to find the fuzzi-ness which results from breaking down such oppositions spiritually conforting rather than morally offensive. What would the rhetoric of the culture, and in particular of the humanities, sound like? Presumably it would be more Kuhnian, in the sense that it would mention particu-lar concrete achievements—paradigms—more, and "method" less. There would be less talk about rigor and more about originality. The image of the great scientist would not be of some-body who got it right but of somebody who made it new. The new rhetoric would draw more on the vocabulary of Romantic poetry and socialist politics, and less on that of Greek meta-physics, religious morality, or Enlightenment scientism. A scientist would rely on a sense of solidarity with the rest of her profession, rather than a picture of herself as battling through the veils of illusion, guided by the light of reason.

If all this happened, the term "science," and thus the oppositions between the humanities, the arts, and the sciences, might gradually fade away. Once "science" was deprived of an honorific sense, we might not need it for taxonomy. We might feel no more need for a term which groups together paleontology, physics, anthropology, and psychology than we do for one which groups together engineering, law, social work, and medicine. The people now called "scientists" would no longer think of themselves as a member of a quasi-priestly order, nor would the public think of themselves as in the care of such an order.

In this situation, "the humanities" would no longer think of themselves as such, nor would they share a common rhetoric. Each of the disciplines which now fall under that rubric would worry as little about its method or cognitive status as do mathematics, civil engineering, and sculpture. It would worry as little about its philosophical foundations. For terms which denoted disciplines would not be thought to divide "subject-matters," chunks of the world which had "interfaces" with each other. Rather, they would be thought to denote communities whose boundaries were as fluid as the interests of their members. In this heyday of the fuzzy, there would be as little reason to be self-conscious about the nature and status of one's discipline as, in the ideal democratic community, about the nature and status of one's race or sex. For one's ultimate loyalty would be to the larger community which permitted and encouraged this kind of freedom and insouciance. This community would serve no higher end than its own preservation and self improvement, the preservation and enhancement of civilization. It would identify rationality with that effort, rather than with the desire for objectivity. So it would feel no need for a foundation more solid than reciprocal loyalty.

Cornel West

Cornel West, born in 1953, has distinguished himself during the 1980s and 90s as a public intellectual and powerful spokesman for the African-American community. A professor of both Afro-American studies and the philosophy of religion at Harvard University, West has ranged broadly over the scholarly terrain in order to map out a course of thought and action for American blacks. His writings speak to the widest possible audience. More an essayist than a writer of treatises, West uses philosophy to root contemporary issues in a conceptual matrix. Coming under the influence of philosopher Richard Rorty while a graduate student at Princeton, West has taken in the postmodernist perspective without yielding to its linguistic emphasis. In this selection drawn from his first book, *Prophecy Deliverance! An Afro-American Revolutionary Christianity*, West embeds Western European thinking about race in the very foundations of the scientific tradition that triumphed with the Enlightenment.

CORNEL WEST
(1982)

A Geneaology
of Modern Racism

The notion that black people are human beings is a relatively new discovery in the modern West. The idea of black equality in beauty, culture, and intellectual capacity remains problematic and controversial within prestigious halls of learning and sophisticated intellectual circles. The Afro-American encounter with the modern world has been shaped first and foremost by the doctrine of white supremacy, which is embodied in institutional practices and enacted in everyday folkways under varying circumstances and evolving conditions.

My aim in this chapter is to give a brief account of the way in which the idea of white supremacy was constituted as an object of modern discourse in the West, without simply appealing to the objective demands of the prevailing mode of production, the political interests of the slaveholding class, or the psychological needs of the dominant white racial group. Despite the indispensable role these factors would play in a full-blown explanatory model to account for the emergence and sustenance of modern racism in the West, I try to hold these factors constant and focus solely on a neglected variable in past explanatory models—namely, the way in which the very structure of modern discourse *at its inception* produced forms of rationality, scientificity, and objectivity as well as aesthetic and cultural ideals which require the constitution of the idea of white supremacy.

This requirement follows from a logic endemic to the very structure of modern discourse. This logic is manifest in the way in which the controlling metaphors, notions, and categories of modern discourse produce and prohibit, develop and delimit, specific conceptions of truth and knowledge, beauty and character, so that certain ideas are rendered incomprehensible and

Reprinted from *Prophesy Deliverance! An Afro-American Revolutionary Christianity* by Cornel West. 1982 Cornel West. Used by permission of Westminster John Knox Press.

unintelligible. I suggest that one such idea that cannot be brought within the epistemological field of the initial modern discourse is that of black equality in beauty, culture, and intellectual capacity. This act of discursive exclusion, of relegating this idea to silence, does not simply correspond to (or is not only reflective of) the relative powerlessness of black people at the time. It also reveals the evolving internal dynamics of the structure of modern discourse in the late seventeenth and eighteenth centuries in western Europe—or during the Enlightenment. The concrete effects of this exclusion and the intellectual traces of this silence continue to haunt the modern West: on the nondiscursive level, in ghetto streets, and on the discursive level, in methodological assumptions in the disciplines of the humanities.

I shall argue that the initial structure of modern discourse in the West "secretes" the idea of white supremacy. I call this "secretion"—the underside of modern discourse—a particular logical consequence of the quest for truth and knowledge in the modern West. To put it crudely, my argument is that the authority of science, undergirded by a modern philosophical discourse guided by Greek ocular metaphors and Cartesian notions, promotes and encourages the activities of observing, comparing, measuring, and ordering the physical characteristics of human bodies. Given the renewed appreciation and appropriation of classical antiquity, these activities are regulated by classical aesthetic and cultural norms. The creative fusion of scientific investigation, Cartesian epistemology, and classical ideals produced forms of rationality, scientificity, and objectivity which, though efficacious in the quest for truth and knowledge, prohibited the intelligibility and legitimacy of the idea of black equality in beauty, culture, and intellectual capacity. In fact, to "think" such an idea was to be deemed irrational, barbaric, or mad. . . .

I call this inquiry a "genealogy" because, following the works of Friedrich Nietzsche and Michel Foucault, I am interested in the emergence (*Entstehung*) or the "moment of arising" of the idea of white supremacy within the modern discourse in the West. This genealogy tries to address the following questions: What are the discursive conditions for the possibility of the intelligibility and legitimacy of the idea of white supremacy in modern discourse? How is this idea constituted within the epistemological field of modern discourse? What is the complex configuration of metaphors, notions, categories, and norms which produces and promotes such an object of modern discourse?

My genealogical approach subscribes to a conception of power that is neither simply based on individual subjects—e.g., heroes or great personages as in traditional historiography—nor on collective subjects—e.g., groups, elites, or classes as in revisionist and vulgar Marxist historiography. Therefore I do not believe that the emergence of the idea of white supremacy in the modern West can be fully accounted for in terms of the psychological needs of white individuals and groups or the political and economic interests of a ruling class. I will try to show that the idea of white supremacy emerges partly because of the powers within the structure of modern discourse—powers to produce and prohibit, develop and delimit, forms of rationality, scientificity, and objectivity which set perimeters and draw boundaries for the intelligibility, availability, and legitimacy of certain ideas. . . .

I understand "the structure of modern discourse" to be the controlling metaphors, notions, categories, and norms that shape the predominant conceptions of truth and knowledge in the modern West. These metaphors, notions, categories, and norms are circumscribed and determined by three major historical processes: the scientific revolution, the Cartesian transformation of philosophy, and the classical revival.

The scientific revolution is usually associated with the pioneering breakthroughs of Copernicus and Kepler in astronomy, Galileo and Newton in physics, and Descartes and Leibnitz in mathematics. These breakthroughs were pre-Enlightenment, most of them occurring during the seventeenth century; the so-called Age of Genius. The scientific revolution is noteworthy (to say the least) primarily because it signified the authority of science. This authority justified new modes of knowledge and new conceptions of truth and reality; it arose at the end of the era of pagan Christianity and set the framework for the advent of modernity. . . .

For our purposes, the scientific revolution is significant because it highlights two fundamental ideas: *observation* and *evidence*. These two ideas have played, in an isolated manner, a role in previous paradigms of knowledge in the West (since the times of Aristotle and Aristarchus). But the scientific revolution brought these ideas together in such a way that they have become the two foci around which much of modern discourse evolves. The modern concepts of hypothesis, fact, inference, validation, confirmation, and verification cluster around the ideas of observation and evidence.

The major proponents of the scientific revolution, or, more specifically, of the authority of science, were two philosophers, Francis Bacon and René Descartes. Bacon is noteworthy primarily because of his metaphilosophical honesty. For him, the aim of philosophy was to give humankind mastery over nature by means of scientific discoveries and inventions. He then promoted the philosophical importance of the inductive method as a means of arriving at general laws to facilitate this human mastery. . . .

Descartes is highly significant because his thought provided the controlling notions of modern discourse: *the primacy of the subject and the preeminence of representation*. Descartes is widely regarded as the founder of modern philosophy not simply because his philosophical outlook was profoundly affected by the scientific revolution but, more important, because he associated the scientific aim of predicting and explaining the world with the philosophical aim of picturing and representing the world. In this view, the fruits of scientific research do not merely provide more useful ways for human beings to *cope* with reality; such research also yields a true *copy* of reality. Descartes's conception of philosophy as a tortuous move from the subject to objects, from the veil of ideas to the external world, from immediate awareness to extended substances, from self-consciousness to things in space, and ultimately from doubt to certainty was motivated primarily by an attempt to provide a theoretical basis for the legitimacy of modern science. Martin Heidegger made this crucial connection between Cartesian philosophy and modern science in his famous essay, "The Age of the World View":

> We are reflecting on the nature of modern science in order to find its metaphysical basis. What conception of the existent and what concept of truth cause science to become research?
>
> Understanding as research holds the existent to account on the question of how and how far it can be put at the disposal of available "representation." Research has the existent at its disposal if it can either calculate it in advance, in its future course, or calculate it afterwards as past. Nature and history become the object of expository representation. . . .
>
> This objectification of the existent takes place in a re-presentation which aims at presenting whatever exists to itself in such a way that the calculating person can be secure, that is, certain of the existent. Science as research is produced when and only when truth has been transformed into such certainty of representation. In the metaphysics of Descartes the existent was defined for the first time as objectivity of representation, and truth as certainty of representation.

Bacon and Descartes had basic differences: Bacon inductive orientation and Descartes the deductive viewpoint; Bacon the empiricist outlook and Descartes the rationalist (mathematical) perspective. Despite these differences, both of these propagandists of modern science agreed that scientific method provides a new paradigm of knowledge and that observation and evidence is at the center of scientific method. In *The New Organon*, Bacon likened his ideal natural philosopher to the bee, which collects "its material from the flowers of the garden and of the field" and digests it "by a power of its own." In his *Discourse on Method*, Descartes set forth as a rule that "observations" become "the more necessary the further we advance in knowledge." And, as D'Alembert acknowledged in *The Encyclopedia*, both Bacon and Descartes "introduced the spirit of experimental science."

The last major historical process that circumscribed and determined the metaphors, notions, categories, and norms of modern discourse was the classical revival. This classical revival—in response to medieval mediocrity and religious dogmatism—was initiated in the Early Renaissance (1300-1500), principally with humanist studies in Roman art and Latin literature, such as Giotto in painting, Petrarch in letters, and Dufay in music. This revival intensified during the High Renaissance (1500-1530), with Da Vinci, Raphael, Bramante, and the early Michelangelo in the arts; Ariosto, Rabelais, and Erasmus in literature; and Josquin and Lassus in music. . . .

For our purposes, the classical revival is important because it infuses Greek ocular metaphors and classical ideals of beauty, proportion, and moderation into the beginnings of modern discourse. Greek ocular metaphors—Eye of the Mind, Mind as Mirror of Nature, Mind as Inner Arena with its Inner Observer—dominate modern discourse in the West. Coupled with the Cartesian notion of knowledge as inner representation, modern philosophical inquiry is saddled with the epistemological model of intellect (formerly Plato's and Aristotle's Nous, now Descartes's Inner Eye) inspecting entities modeled on retinal images, with the Eye of the Mind viewing representations in order to find some characteristic that would testify to their fidelity.

The creative fusion of scientific investigation, Cartesian philosophy, Greek ocular metaphors, and classical aesthetic and cultural ideals constitutes the essential elements of modern discourse in the West. In short, modern discourse rests upon a conception of truth and knowledge governed by an ideal value-free subject engaged in observing, comparing, ordering, and measuring in order to arrive at evidence sufficient to make valid inferences, confirm speculative hypotheses, deduce error-proof conclusions, and verify true representations of reality.

The recovery of classical antiquity in the modern West produced what I shall call a "normative gaze," namely, an ideal from which to order and compare observations. This ideal was drawn primarily from classical aesthetic values of beauty, proportion, and human form and classical cultural standards of moderation, self-control, and harmony. The role of classical aesthetic and cultural norms in the emergence of the idea of white supremacy as an object of modern discourse cannot be underestimated.

These norms were consciously projected and promoted by many influential Enlightenment writers, artists, and scholars, of whom the most famous was J. J. Winckelmann. In his widely read book, *History of Ancient Art*, Winckelmann portrayed ancient Greece as a world of beautiful bodies. He laid down rules—in art and aesthetics—that should govern the size of eyes and eyebrows, of collar-bones, hands, feet, and especially noses. He defined beauty as noble simplicity and quiet grandeur. In a celebrated passage he wrote:

As the depth of the ocean always remains calm however much the surface may be agitated, so does the expression in the figures of the Greeks reveal a great and composed soul in the midst of passions.

Although Winckelmann was murdered in middle life, never set foot in Greece, and saw almost no original Greek art (only one exhibition of Greek art in Munich), he viewed Greek beauty and culture as the ideal or standard against which to measure other peoples and cultures.

Winthrop Jordan and Thomas Gossett have shown that there are noteworthy premodern racist viewpoints aimed directly and indirectly at nonwhite, especially black, people. For example, in 1520 Paracelus held that black and primitive peoples had a separate origin from Europeans. In 1591, Giordano Bruno made a similar claim, but had in mind principally Jews and Ethiopians. And Lucilio Vanini posited that Ethiopians had apes for ancestors and had once walked on all fours. Since theories of the separate origin of races were in disagreement with the Roman Catholic Church, Bruno and Vanini underwent similar punishment: both were burned at the stake. Of course, biblically based accounts of racial inferiority flourished, but the authority of the church prohibited the proliferation of nonreligious, that is, protomodern, accounts of racial inferiority.

What is distinctive about the role of classical aesthetic and cultural norms at the advent of modernity is that they provided an acceptable authority for the idea of white supremacy, an acceptable authority that was closely linked with the major authority on truth and knowledge in the modern world, namely, the institution of science. In order to see how this linkage took place, let us examine the categories and aims of the major discipline that promoted this authority, that is, those of natural history.

The principal aim of natural history is to observe, compare, measure, and order animals and human bodies (or classes of animals and human bodies) *based on visible, especially physical, characteristics.* These characteristics permit one to discern identity and difference, equality and inequality, beauty and ugliness among animals and human bodies.

The governing categories of natural history are preeminently *classificatory* categories—that is, they consist of various taxonomies in the form of tables, catalogs, indexes, and inventories which impose some degree of order or representational schema on a broad field of visible characteristics. *Observation* and *differentness* are the essential guiding notions in natural history. Foucault wrote:

> Natural history has as a condition of its possibility the common affinity of things and language with representation; but it exists as a task only in so far as things and language happen to be separate. It must therefore reduce this distance between them so as to bring language as close as possible to the observing gaze, and the things observed as close as possible to words. Natural history is nothing more than the nomination of the visible. . . .
>
> Natural history . . . covers a series of complex operations that introduce the possibility of a constant order into a totality of representations. It constitutes a whole domain of empiricity as at the same time describable and orderable.

The initial basis for the idea of white supremacy is to be found in the classificatory categories and the descriptive, representational, order-imposing aims of natural history. The captivity of natural history to what I have called the "normative gaze" signifies the first stage of the emergence of the idea of white supremacy as an object of modern discourse. More specifically (and as Ashley Montagu has tirelessly argued), the genealogy of racism in the modern West is inseparable from the appearance of the classificatory category of race in natural history.

The category of race—denoting primarily skin color—was first employed as a means of classifying human bodies by Francois Bernier, a French physician, in 1684. He divided humankind into basically four races: Europeans, Africans, Orientals, and Lapps. The first authoritative racial division of humankind is found in the influential *Natural System* (1735) of the most preeminent naturalist of the eighteenth century, Carolus Linnaeus. For Linnaeus, species were fixed in number and kind; they were immutable prototypes. Varieties, however, were members of a species that might change in appearance. The members of a species produced fertile offspring; interfertility was the test for the division of species. There were variations of kind within a species; the races were a prime example. For Linnaeus, there were four races: Homo Europaeus, Homo Asiaticus, Homo Afer, and Homo Americanus.

Winthrop Jordan has argued that Linnaeus did not subscribe to a hierarchical ranking of races but rather to "one chain of universal being." Jordan states:

> It was one thing to classify all living creation and altogether another to arrange it in a single great hierarchy; and when Linnaeus undertook the first of these tasks he was not thereby forced to attempt the latter. In the many editions of the *Systema Naturae* he duly catalogued the various kinds of men, yet never in a hierarchic manner.

Yet it is quite apparent that Linnaeus implicitly evaluated the observable characteristics of the racial classes of people, especially those pertaining to character and disposition. For example, compare Linnaeus' description of the European with the African:

> European. White, Sanguine, Brawny. Hair abundantly flowing. Eyes blue. Gentle, acute, inventive. Covered with close vestments. Governed by customs.
> African. Black, Phlegmatic, Relaxed. Hair black, frizzled. Skin silky. Nose flat. Lips tumid. Women's bosom a matter of modesty. Breasts give milk abundantly. Crafty, indolent. Negligent. Anoints himself with grease. Governed by caprice.

Linnaeus' use of evaluative terms revealed, at the least, an implicit hierarchy by means of personal preference. It also is important to note that he included some remarks about the African woman, but that he said nothing about the European woman (nor the American and Asiatic woman). It also is significant that in the 1750s when he first acknowledged that hybridization of species occurs, he chose black people and apes as the probable candidates, while restricting such unions to black women and male apes.

Georges Louis Leclerc de Buffon accepted hybridization without question in his famous *Natural History of Man* (1778). Although Buffon, like Linnaeus, viewed races as mere chance variations, he held that white was "the real and natural color of man." Black people and other races were variations of this natural color, yet somehow not members of a different species. He remained uncertain about the objective reality of species. Buffon believed that black skin was caused by hot climate and would change if the climate became colder. Although he was a fervent antislavery advocate, he claimed that black people had "little genius" and then added, "The unfortunate negroes are endowed with excellent hearts, and possess the seeds of every human virtue."

In the works of Johann Friedrich Blumenbach, one of the founders of modern anthropology, the aesthetic criteria and cultural ideals of Greece began to come to the forefront. Like Linnaeus and Buffon, Blumenbach held that all human beings belonged to the same species and that races were merely varieties. Yet contrary to the claims by Winthrop Jordan, Ashley Montagu, and Thomas Gossett concerning Blumenbach's opposition to hierarchic racial ranking or irritation at those who use aesthetic standards for such ranking, Blumenbach praised the symmetrical face as the most beautiful of human faces precisely because it approximated the "divine" works of Greek art, and specifically the proper anatomical proportions found in Greek sculpture. Applying the classical ideal of moderation, he claimed that the more moderate the climate, the more beautiful the face. The net result was that since black people were farthest from the Greek ideal and located in extremely hot climates, they were, by implication, inferior in beauty to Europeans.

The second stage of the emergence of the idea of white supremacy as an object of modern discourse primarily occurred in the rise of phrenology (the reading of skulls) and physiognomy (the reading of faces). These new disciplines—closely connected with anthropology—served as an open platform for the propagation of the idea of white supremacy not principally because they were pseudosciences, but, more important, because these disciplines acknowledged the European value-laden character of their observations. This European value-laden character was based on classical aesthetic and cultural ideals.

Pieter Camper, the Dutch anatomist, made aesthetic criteria the pillar of his chief discovery: the famous "facial angle." Camper claimed that the "facial angle"—a measure of prognathism—permitted a comparison of heads of human bodies by way of cranial and facial measurements. For Camper, the ideal "facial angle" was a 100-degree angle which was achieved only by the ancient Greeks. He openly admitted that this ideal conformed to Winckelmann's classical ideal of beauty. Following Winckelmann, Camper held that Greek proportions and stature exemplified beauty and embodied perfection. Camper further held that a beautiful face, beautiful body, beautiful nature, beautiful character, and beautiful soul were inseparable. He tried to show that the "facial angle" of Europeans measured about 97 degrees and those of black people between 60 and 70 degrees, closer to the measurements of apes and dogs than to human beings.

Although many anthropologists readily accepted the "facial angle" as a scientific notion, Camper made it clear that his aim was not simply to contribute to the new discipline of anthropology but also to promote the love of classical antiquity to young artists and sculptors. As George Mosse has noted, historians of race theories often overlook the fact that Camper and many subsequent theoreticians of race and racism were trained as artists and writers. Camper was a painter by training and, in fact, won the gold medal of the Amsterdam School of Art two years before he published his work on the "facial angle."

Johann Kaspar Lavater, the father of physiognomy, explicitly acknowledged that the art of painting was the mother of his new discipline. Moreau, an early editor of Lavater's work, clearly noted that the true language of physiognomy was painting, because it spoke through images, equally to the eye and to the spirit. This new discipline linked particular visible characteristics of human bodies, especially those of the face, to the character and capacities of human beings. This discipline openly articulated what many of the early naturalists and anthropologists tacitly assumed: *the classical ideals of beauty, proportion, and moderation regulated the classifying and ranking of groups of human bodies.* In short, physiognomy brought the "normative gaze" into daylight.

Lavater believed that the Greek statues were the models of beauty. His description of the desirable specimen—blue eyes, horizontal forehead, bent back, round chin, and short brown hair—resembled the beautiful person preferred by Camper. . . .

Lavater's promotion of what I call the "normative gaze" consisted no longer of detailed measurements, as was the case with the naturalists, but rather of the visual glance. He wrote: "Trust your first quick impression, for it is worth more than what is usually called observation." Therefore it is not surprising that Lavater put forth an elaborate theory of noses, the most striking member of the face. Neither is it surprising that subsequent classifications of noses, based on Lavater's formulations, associate Roman and Greek noses with conquerors and persons of refinement and taste.

The next and last step we shall consider in this genealogy of racism in late-seventeenth- and eighteenth-century Europe is the advent of phrenology, the new discipline which held that human character could be read through the shape of the human head. Franz Joseph Gall, a highly regarded German physician, argued in 1796 that the inner workings of the brain could be determined by the shape of the skull. For example, he associated an arched forehead with a penchant for metaphysical speculation; a skull arched at the rear with love of fame; and a skull large at the base with a criminal disposition. In the nineteenth century, when racist ideology was systematized, this new discipline took on a life of its own with Johann Kaspar Spurzheim, Anders Retzius, Carl Gustav Carus, and others; it also aided in allying modern racism with nationalism and repressed sexuality in bourgeois morality.

A major example of the way in which the restrictive powers of modern discourse delimit theoretical alternatives and strategic options in regard to the idea of white supremacy is seen in writings of radical environmentalists of the period—those one would expect to be open to the idea of black equality in beauty, culture, and intellectual capacity. Yet even these progressive antislavery advocates remain captive to the "normative gaze."

The major opponent of predominant forms of a hierarchic ranking of races and the outspoken proponent of intermarriage in the United States during this era, Samuel Stanhope Smith, illustrates this captivity. In his day Smith stood at the pinnacle of American academia. He was president of Princeton University and an honorary member of the American Philosophical Society. He was awarded honorary degrees from Harvard and Yale. In his well-known *Essays* of 1787 (and revised in 1810) Smith argued that humankind constituted one species and that human variations could be accounted for in reference to three natural causes: "climate," "state of society," and "habits of living." He believed "that colour may be justly considered as an universal freckle."

The "normative gaze" operative in Smith's viewpoint is located, as in Buffon, in the assumption that physical, especially racial, variations are always degenerate ones from an ideal state. For Smith, this ideal state consisted of highly civilized white people. As Winthrop Jordan notes, "Smith treated the complexion and physiognomy of the white man not merely as indication of superiority but as the hallmark of civilization." Smith justified this ideal standard and legitimized his "normative gaze" by appealing to the classical ideals of beauty. In a patriotic footnote he wrote:

> It may perhaps gratify my countrymen to reflect that the United States occupy those latitudes that have ever been most favourable to the beauty of the human form. When time shall have accommodated the constitution of its new state, and cultivation shall have meliorated the climate,

the beauties of Greece and Circasia may be renewed in America; as there are not a few already who rival those of any quarter of the globe.

Smith's radical environmentalism (along with his adherence to Greek aesthetic ideals) led him to adopt the most progressive and sympathetic alternative which promotes the welfare of black people permissible within the structure of modern discourse: integration which *uplifts* black people, assimilation which *civilizes* black people, intermarriage which *ensures less Negroid features* in the next generation. For example, Smith wrote:

> The great difference between the domestic and field slaves gives reason to believe that, if they were perfectly free, enjoyed property, and were admitted to a liberal participation of the society rank and privileges of their masters, they would change their African peculiarities much faster.

This theoretical alternative was taken to its logical consequence by the distinguished American antislavery advocate, publicizer of talented black writers, and eminent physician, Benjamin Rush. This logical consequence was the elimination of the skin color of black people. In a paper entitled "Observations Intended to Favour a Supposition that the Black Color (As it is called) of the Negroes is Derived From the Leprosy," Rush denounced the idea of white supremacy, then stated: "Is the color of Negroes a disease? Then let science and humanity combine their efforts and endeavor to discover a remedy for it." In one bold stroke, Rush provided grounds for promoting abolitionism, opposing intermarriage (who wants to marry diseased persons!), and supporting the Christian unity of humankind. In his opinion, his view-point also maximized the happiness of black and white people:

> To encourage attempts to cure this disease of the skin in Negroes, let us recollect that succeeding in them, we shall produce a large portion of happiness in the world. . . .
>   Secondly, we shall add greatly to their happiness, for however well they appear to be satisfied with their color, there are many proofs of their preferring that of the white people.

The intellectual legitimacy of the idea of white supremacy, though grounded in what we now consider marginal disciplines (especially in its second stage), was pervasive. This legiti-macy can be illustrated by the extent to which racism permeated the writings of the major figures of the Enlightenment. It is important to note that the idea of white supremacy not only was accepted by these figures, but, more important, it was accepted by them *without their having to put forward their own arguments to justify it.* Montesquieu and Voltaire of the French Enlightenment, Hume and Jefferson of the Scotch and the American Enlightenment, and Kant of the German Enlightenment not merely held racist views; they also uncritically—during this age of criticism—believed that the *authority* for these views rested in the domain of naturalists, anthropologists, physiognomists, and phrenologists.

Montesquieu's satirical remarks in *Spirit of the Laws* about black people (and his many revi-sions of these remarks) may seem to suggest an equivocal disposition toward the idea of white supremacy. Yet his conclusion leaned toward support of the idea:

> It is impossible for us to suppose that these beings should be men; because if we supposed them to be men, one would begin to believe we ourselves were not Christians.

Voltaire's endorsement of the idea of white supremacy was unequivocal. In his essay "The People of America," he claimed that black people (and Indians) were distinct species from Europeans:

> The Negro race is a species of men as different from ours as the breed of spaniels is from that of grey-hounds. The mucous membrane, or network, which nature has spread between the muscles and the skin, is white in us and black or copper-colored in them....
>
> If their understanding is not of a different nature form ours, it is at least greatly inferior. They are not capable of any great application or association of ideas, and seemed formed neither for the advantages nor the abuses of philosophy.

Hume's racism was notorious; it served as a major source of proslavery arguments and antiblack education propaganda. In his famous footnote to his essay "Of National Characteristics," he stated:

> I am apt to suspect the negroes, and in general all the other species of men (for there are four or five different kinds) to be naturally inferior to the whites. There never was a civilized nation of any other complexion than white, nor even any individual eminent either in action or speculation. No inge-nious manufactures amongst them, no arts, no sciences....
>
> In Jamaica indeed they talk of one negroe as a man of parts and learning; but 'tis likely he is admired for very slender accomplishments, like a parrot, who speaks a few words plainly.

Jefferson arrived at mildly similar conclusions in his *Notes on Virginia*. Regarding the intel-lectual capacities of black people, he wrote:

> Comparing them by their faculties of memory, reason, and imagination, it appears to me, that in memory they are equal to the whites; in reason much inferior ... and that in imagination they are dull, tasteless and anomalous.... Never yet could I find that a black had uttered a thought above the level of plain narration; never see even an elementary trait of painting or sculpture.

Finally, Kant, whose views were based heavily on Hume's claims, held that "the negroes of Africa have by nature no feeling that rises above the trifling." In his *Observations on the Feeling of the Beautiful and Sublime*, Kant noted:

> Mr. Hume challenges anyone to cite a simple example in which a negro has shown talents, and asserts that among the hundreds of thousands of blacks who are transported elsewhere from their countries, although many of them have even been set free, still not a single one was ever found who presented anything great in art or science or any other praiseworthy quality, even though among the whites some continually rise aloft from the lowest rabble, and through superior gifts earn respect in the world. So fundamental is the difference between the two races of man, and it appears to be as great in regard to mental capacities as in color.

Kant further revealed his racist views when, in reply to advice that a black person gave to Father Labat, he wrote,

> And it might be that there was something in this which perhaps deserved to be considered; but in short, this fellow was quite black from head to foot, a clear proof that what he said was stupid.

The emergence of the idea of white supremacy as an object of modern discourse seems inevitable in that, besides the practical need to justify nonwhite domination (especially in the early nineteenth century), the only available theoretical alternative for the unhampered search for truth and knowledge in the modern West consisted of detailed observation, measurement, comparison, and ordering of the natural and human kingdom by autonomous subjects in the light of the aesthetic and cultural ideals of classical antiquity. . . .

The emergence of the idea of white supremacy as an object of modern discourse seems contingent, in that there was no iron necessity at work in the complex configuration of metaphors, notions, categories, and norms that produce and promote this idea. There is an accidental character to the discursive emergence of modern racism, a kind of free play of discursive powers which produce and prohibit, develop and delimit the legitimacy and intelligibility of certain ideas within a discursive space circumscribed by the attractiveness of classical antiquity.

Yet even such claims about the contingency of the emergence of the idea of white supremacy in the modern West warrant suspicion. This is so because, as we noted earlier, this genealogical approach *does not purport to be an explanation of the rise of modern racism, but rather a theoretical inquiry into a particular neglected variable, i.e., the discursive factor, within a larger explanatory model.* This variable is significant because it not only precludes reductionist treatments of modern racism; it also highlights the cultural and aesthetic impact of the idea of white supremacy on black people. This inquiry accents the fact that the everyday life of black people is shaped not simply by the exploitative (oligopolistic) capitalist system of production but also by cultural attitudes and sensibilities, including alienating ideals of beauty.

The idea of white supremacy is a major bowel unleashed by the structure of modern discourse, a significant secretion generated from the creative fusion of scientific investigation, Cartesian philosophy, and classical aesthetic and cultural norms. Needless to say, the odor of this bowel and the fumes of this secretion continue to pollute the air of our postmodern times.

Responding

to

Postmodernism

Introduction

The postmodern attack on Enlightenment reason and the modern ideals of continual progress and individual liberation from superstition, convention and false belief, has been astonishingly successful. We are now familiar, possibly even comfortable, with Hayden White's assertions that history is merely a narrative fiction written for self-interested purposes and with Richard Rorty's claims that truth is entirely dependent on context, and thus one should never impose one's own truth upon another. While we may not always agree with Jacques Derrida that there is nothing outside the text, he does evoke a nod of understanding when we look around and see that the major events of our time appear scripted and staged, and that a good deal of what constitutes our "reality" is not in fact real, but rather the product of an entertainment industry and advertising culture which produces images we all see and refer to in every day discussion. The fact that what often unites people across continents is the simultaneous viewing of events like the Gulf War, during which media images combined to give the impression of a "clean" war and directed our attention to the evaluation of the performance of high tech weapons systems over and above the actual causes and effects of the war itself, gives strength to the assertion that our world is something we "construct" versus something that "is." And hence the feeling that we still inhabit a world of false pretenses and slavish belief; that the modern project of human liberation through reason has indeed failed. The spread of this postmodern sensibility during the last two decades, however, has provoked a critical re-assessment of the political, ideological and philosophical positions which adherence to postmodern modes of thinking may engender. This unit addresses the issues raised by those who, despite their diverse back-grounds and agendas, share an unwillingness to accept uncritically this postmodern state of affairs.

One of the earliest critics of postmodernism in American society was the sociologist Daniel Bell. Bell's early assessment of postmodernism took place before the term gained the wide currency and usage it has today. Writing in 1978, Bell reflected on the social and political upheavals of the 1960s and argued that they must be viewed as consequences of inherent contradictions within capitalism. On the one hand, Bell saw the success of American capitalism rooted in Weber's "Protestant ethic" which valued work for work's sake, delayed gratification and extolled a spirited individualism which prompted entrepreneurial risk-taking and innovation. On the other hand, Bell noted that the success of American capitalism was equally rooted in a mass consumption market which, since the 1920s, has been premised on the extension of credit, delayed payment, and the ability of advertisers to stimulate consumer demand over and above the satisfaction of "needs" by creating "wants." For Bell it was the shift to a consumerism based on wants which ultimately undermined the moral basis for capitalist behavior within the United States. This decline in the "Protestant ethic," in particular, and religious sensibility in general, led to a rise in the power of culture, specifically modernist culture, to influence the tastes, behavior, and lifestyle choices of American citizens.

According to Bell, modernist culture, or modernism, had always taken a critical stance towards modernity; often reflected in its "rage" against the order of bourgeois society and articulated through the use of multiple perspectives. Pablo Picasso's *Guernica* is a case in point. Produced in 1937 in protest to the bombing of the town of Guernica during the Spanish Civil War, Picasso evoked the violence of the event by disrupting the linear lines of traditional painting and juxtaposing a series of perspectives. Despite Picasso and other modern artists' determination to play with perspective in order to describe the anxiety-ridden condition of the modern individual, modernism was similarly marked by its concern with form and unity, its celebration of constant change, its conception of the work of art as a unified whole, and of the artist as a social critic.

Bell witnessed with alarm the increasing pervasiveness of modernist values at the mass level throughout the 1960s. Horrified by the "happenings" or "spectacles," in which theatre left the stage and painting left the frame, Bell saw art on a canvas as something entirely different from art in the streets where, he argued, modernism encouraged and legitimated the hedonistic and politically bankrupt mass nihilism of the 60s counter-culture. For Bell, postmodernism was modernism perverted through its democratization. Bell's discussion of postmodernism as the diffusion of modernist values within society and as a crisis within high art, both of which he linked to the changes in the structure of capitalism, succeeded in raising many of the issues later critics of the postmodern phenomena would explore.

More than a decade after Bell, the British geographer David Harvey examined the "condition of postmodernity" and insisted that the essential questions students of culture and society must ask themselves are: Does postmodernism represent a radical break with modernism or a revolt within modernism against a certain form of high modernism? Is postmodernism a style or merely a periodizing concept? Does postmodernism have a revolutionary potential by virtue of its opposition to all forms of metanarrative and its attention to the "other" or is it simply the commercialization and domestication of modernism? Does it undermine or integrate with neo-conservative politics? And finally, should we link its rise to the radical restructuring of capitalism?[1] To some extent all of these questions were addressed in Bell's work.

Taking a cue from Bell, David Harvey attempts to discredit postmodern pretensions to revolutionary potential by systematically examining the nature and degree of change which capitalism has undergone since the beginning of the twentieth century. Harvey's work details the many ways in which the present is a postindustrial society by citing the shift in occupational structure from industry to service professions, the internationalization of capital markets, the growth of economies of scope over economies of scale, the acceleration of turnover time in product development, and the geographic mobility of capital and labor. Central to this transition from an industrial to a postindustrial economy is an enormous degree of "space-time" compression as the world becomes a "global village" and decisions made in Tokyo, New York, or London reverberate instantaneously all over the world. Harvey argues that just as modernism was a cultural reaction to the first round of space-time compression produced by the technological breakthroughs of modernity, postmodernism is a similar response to a new round of space-time compression produced by the economic realities of late capitalism. Thus while postmodernism indicates the existence of a radically new organization of social, economic, and political relationships in the late twentieth century, it is not the initiator of these changes, but merely their reflection in the realm of culture.

Leaving aside the question of whether or not we inhabit a postindustrial world, British intellectual Christopher Norris attacks postmodernist thought by arguing that postmodern theory is fundamentally "uncritical." He notes that by claiming that we are unable to distinguish between fictional narrative and other types of narrative, Hayden White, Michel Foucault, and Richard Rorty have dissolved the line between life and art, making activism based on knowledge almost impossible. The dissolution of the boundary between life and art has been termed by some theorists the "aestheticization of politics," and characterized as a condition in which rhetoric takes precedence over substance, style over content, and image over reality. Examples of this phenomena include the impact of television on the 1960 presidential campaign when viewers of a televised debate between Republican candidate Richard Nixon and Democratic candidate John Fitzgerald Kennedy thought Nixon was less credible because of his heavy five o'clock shadow. Thinkers including Bell, Norris, and Harvey find the aestheticization of politics inherently dangerous, in part because they view this phenomena as having occurred at previous points in the past, specifically when myths of Aryan supremacy became popularized in Nazi Germany. Following this line of thought, critics of postmodernism are quick to point out that the deconstructionist Paul de Man once collaborated with the Nazis as did the philosopher Martin Heidegger who figures prominently as a source of inspiration for many postmodern theorists.

The German philosopher Jürgen Habermas is another thinker who criticizes postmodernism for what he believes are its neo-conservative tendencies, although he bases his criticisms on the philosophical precepts of postmodern thinking more than the political backgrounds of individual theorists. Habermas has sought to undermine postmodernism by delineating the outlines of a methodology by which rational debate, reasoned inquiry, and the Enlightenment project might be sustained through the development of a theory of communicative action. Turning away from the textualism which has undergirded so many postmodern arguments, Habermas has concentrated on speech as it is practiced in daily life. Arguing that much of our daily communication takes place in an uncoerced and consensual fashion, as individuals seek to convey information and practice mutual understanding, Habermas distinguishes between communicative reason, where individuals have the opportunity to clarify questions and misunderstandings through gestures and speech, and the instrumental reason of positive science which requires empirical proof. Some thinkers see Habermas's distinction between types of reason as a breakthrough on which new universalist theories of truth can be developed.

Many feminist theorists have also been highly critical of postmodernist thought. The anthropologists Frances Mascia-Lees, Patricia Sharpe, and Colleen Ballerino Cohen suggest that postmodernism is a double-edged sword which serves to undermine the status of the subject, the autonomous individual actor celebrated by the Enlightenment, at the precise moment when women and non-Western peoples are beginning to claim the status of subject for themselves.[2] Hayden White's poststructural theories of historical narratives are one example. While the notion that history is a creative fiction lends support to those critical of traditional histories which write minorities and women out of the historical record, they similarly undermine the claims of revisionist historians that their work has substantive validity.

Thinkers on the left of the political spectrum share with feminists a concern with the postmodern attack on the concept of a coherent subject. Central to the Marxist critique of capitalist social relations is the concept of alienation and alienated labor which presupposes an autonomous individual worker. The work of Foucault and Derrida has done much to destroy the concept of the autonomous individual actor by arguing that individuals can only act and think within discourses which they create as part of a community of users.

While many of the criticisms discussed above take issue with several tendencies within postmodern thinking, there are a variety of more "local" criticisms which have been raised as well. Taking a position which might seem more familiar to those of us versed in academic debates, Christopher Norris has argued that postmodernism is intellectually flawed because it has both ignored and misread many of the thinkers whose work it claims to further. Norris has pointed out that there has been a good deal of work in linguistic analysis that postmodernists ignore when they trace their heritage directly to the early twentieth century linguist Ferdinand de Saussure. Equally distressing to Norris is the wholesale transfer of a paradigm developed for the study of language to the study of other forms of social interaction.

While the criticisms leveled against postmodernist thought are as varied as the work produced and the arguments advanced by postmodern thinkers themselves, many postmodern ideas have been incorporated into a variety of academic disciplines. In many ways the collective work of our postmodern thinkers may be seen as legitimating the changes in college curriculum which have taken place since Bell's turbulent 1960s, including the growth of women's and ethnic studies departments. By attacking traditional historical narratives (Hayden White), stressing the importance of individual experience in defining truth (Richard Rorty), and problematizing objects of inquiry (Michel Foucault), postmodern thought has opened up new research agendas and facilitated the efforts of marginalized groups to deconstruct the totalizing histories of modernity. Yet many of the thinkers who value the ways in which postmodernism has deconstructed traditional academic canons and curricula have had to grapple with the ways in which it undermines the possibility of constructing new ones to take their place. To some extent we are all left with the task of figuring out how the insights of postmodernist thought can be used to construct, as well as deconstruct, our postmodern reality.

NOTES

1   David Harvey, *The Condition of Postmodernity* (Cambridge: Basil Blackwell, 1989), p. 42.
2   Frances Mascia-Lees, Patricia Sharpe, and Colleen Ballerino Cohen, "The Postmodernist Turn in Anthropology: Cautions from a Feminist Perspective," *Signs* 15 (1989), p. 4.

David Harvey

The "postmodern" intellectuals sampled in previous sections produced their most widely-known works in the decade of the 1970s, before the term "postmodern" itself came to signify anything outside the realm of the arts and architecture. It was left to a small group of texts, clustering together between the end of the 70s and the early 80s, to announce the emergence of the postmodern as not merely an aesthetic school but as a new periodization in Western history. That Jacques Derrida, minority identity politics, and economic restructuring should all be taken together to represent a new, distinct historical epoch was not immediately apparent before the presentation of these arguments in the late 70s.

Daniel Bell wrote vaguely of the contradictions in capitalism and the dominance of the culture industry in 1976; Jean-François Lyotard termed The Postmodern Condition the peculiar course that science and politics had taken in tandem since 1979; followed in the subsequent year by David Harvey's critical downplaying of postmodernism as an unsurpassable rupture with modernity. Differing in this respect with Lyotard, Harvey argues for a "condition" preceding anything postmodern, rather than vice versa; and it is in this that the crux of his argument lies.

The criticism of Marxism strongly voiced in the 1970s, at precisely the time when postmodern theory was becoming increasingly influential, was its insufficient appreciation of all that has been loosely associated with "culture": religion, ideology, and belief. David Harvey sees this preference given to culture as a politically dangerous privileging of the irrational, exactly the sort of thing a revamped Marxism could be capable of remedying. Thus, to bring the prophets of postmodernity to heel, Harvey sets out to demonstrate the compatibility of the geographical category of "space" with basic Marxist economic principles.

Our senses of the flow of time, and the nature of the space around us, are basic categories of experience. They are also historically variable. If Harvey can show that capitalism is something that not only powerfully shapes and alters our sense of time and space in its very operations, but also that it is dependent upon space in a way that Marx did not fully describe, then he will have laid the foundation for a materialist understanding of culture, having deflated the postmodern dragon with one and the same stroke.

DAVID HARVEY
(1980)

The

Condition

of Postmodernity

TIME-SPACE COMPRESSION AND THE POSTMODERN CONDITION

How have the uses and meanings of space and time shifted with the transition from Fordism to flexible accumulation? I want to suggest that we have been experiencing, these last two decades, an intense phase of time-space compression that has had a disorienting and disruptive impact upon political-economic practices, the balance of class power, as well as upon cultural and social life. While historical analogies are always dangerous, I think it no accident that post-modern sensibility evidences strong sympathies for certain of the confused political, cultural, and philosophical movements that occurred at the beginning of this century (in Vienna for example) when the sense of time-space compression was also peculiarly strong. I also note the revival of interest in geopolitical theory since around 1970, the aesthetics of place, and a revived willingness (even in social theory) to open the problem of spatiality to a general reconsideration.

The transition to flexible accumulation was in part accomplished through the rapid deployment of new organizational forms and new technologies in production. Though the latter may have originated in the pursuit of military superiority, their application had everything to do with bypassing the rigidities of Fordism and accelerating turnover time as a solution to the grumbling problems of Fordism-Keynesianism that erupted into open crisis in 1973. Speed-up was achieved in production by organizational shifts towards vertical disintegration—outsourcing, etc.—that reversed the sub-contracting, Fordist tendency towards vertical integration and

From *The Condition of Postmodernity: An Inquiry into the Origins of Cultural Change* (Oxford: Basil Blackwell, 1980), pp. 284–307. By permission of Basil Blackwell.

produced an increasing roundaboutness in production even in the face of increasing financial centralization. Other organizational shifts—such as the 'just-in-time' delivery system that reduces stock inventories—when coupled with the new technologies of electronic control, small-batch production, etc., all reduced turnover times in many sectors of production electronic, machine tools, automobiles, construction, clothing, etc.). For the labourers this all implied an intensification (speed-up) in labour processes and an acceleration in the de-skilling and re-skilling required to meet new labour needs.

Accelerating turnover time in production entails parallel accelerations in exchange and consumption. Improved systems of communication and information flow, coupled with rationalizations in techniques of distribution (packaging, inventory control, containerization, market feed-back, etc.), made it possible to circulate commodities through the market system with greater speed. Electronic banking and plastic money were some of the innovations that improved the speed of the inverse flow of money. Financial services and markets (aided by computerized trading) likewise speeded up, so as to make, as the saying has it, 'twenty-four hours a very long time' in global stock markets. . . .

Of the innumerable consequences that have flowed from this general speed-up in the turnover times of capital, I shall focus on those that have particular bearing on postmodern ways of thinking, feeling, and doing.

The first major consequence has been to accentuate volatility and ephemerality of fashions, products, production techniques, labour processes, ideas and ideologies, values and established practices. The sense that 'all that is solid melts into air' has rarely been more pervasive (which probably accounts for the volume of writing on that theme in recent years). The effect of this on labour markets and skills has already been considered. My interest here is to look at the more general society-wide effects.

In the realm of commodity production, the primary effect has been to emphasize the values and virtues of instantaneity (instant and fast foods, meals, and other satisfactions) and of disposability (cups, plates, cutlery, packaging, napkins, clothing, etc.). The dynamics of a 'throwaway' society, as writers like Alvin Toffler (1970) dubbed it, began to become evident during the 1960s. It meant more than just throwing away produced goods (creating a monumental waste-disposal problem), but also being able to throw away values, life-styles, stable relationships, and attachments to things, buildings, places, people, and received ways of doing and being. These were the immediate and tangible ways in which the 'accelerative thrust in the larger society' crashed up against 'the ordinary daily experience of the individual' (Toffler, p. 40). Through such mechanisms (which proved highly effective from the standpoint of accelerating the turnover of goods in consumption) individuals were forced to cope with disposability, novelty, and the prospects for instant obsolescence. 'Compared to the life in a less rapidly changing society, more situations now flow through the channel in any given interval of time—and this implies profound changes in human psychology.' This transience, Toffler goes on to suggest, creates 'a temporariness in the structure of both public and personal value systems' which in turn provides a context for the 'crack-up of consensus' and the diversification of values within a fragmenting society. The bombardment of stimuli, simply on the commodity front, creates problems of sensory overload that make Simmel's dissection of the problems of modernist urban living at the turn of the century seem to pale into insignificance by comparison. Yet, precisely because of the relative qualities of the shift, the psychological responses exist roughly within the range of those which Simmel identified—the blocking out of sensory stimuli, denial, and cultivation of the blasé attitude, myopic specialization, reversion to images of a lost past (hence the importance of mementoes, museums, ruins), and excessive simplification (either in the presentation of self or in the interpretation of events). In this regard, it is instructive to see how Toffler, at a much later moment of time-space compression, echoes the thinking of Simmel, whose ideas were shaped at a moment of similar trauma more than seventy years before.

The volatility, of course, makes it extremely difficult to engage in any long-term planning. Indeed, learning to play the volatility right is now just as important as accelerating turnover time. This means either being highly adaptable and fast-moving in response to market shifts, or masterminding the volatility. The first strategy points mainly towards short-term rather than long-term planning, and cultivating the art of taking short-term gains wherever they are to be had. This has been a notorious feature of US management in recent times. The average tenure of company executive officers has come down to five years, and companies nominally involved in production frequently seek short-term gains through mergers, acquisitions, or operations in financial and currency markets. The tension of managerial performance in such an environment is considerable, producing all kinds of side-effects, such as the so-called 'yuppie flu' (a psychological stress condition that paralyses the performance of talented people and produces long-lasting flu-like symptoms) of the frenzied life-style of financial operators whose addiction to work, long hours, and the rush of power makes them excellent candidates for the kind of schizophrenic mentality that Jameson depicts.

Mastering or intervening actively in the production of volatility, on the other hand, entails manipulation of taste and opinion, either through being a fashion leader or by so saturating the market with images as to shape the volatility to particular ends. This means, in either case, the construction of new sign systems and imagery, which is itself an important aspect of the postmodern condition—one that needs to be considered from several different angles. To begin with, advertising and media images have come to play a very much more integrative role in cultural practices and now assume a much greater importance in the growth dynamics of capitalism. Advertising, moreover, is no longer built around the idea of informing or promoting in the ordinary sense, but is increasingly geared to manipulating desires and tastes through images that may or may not have anything to do with the product to be sold. If we stripped modern advertising of direct reference to the three themes of money, sex, and power there would be very little left. Furthermore, images have, in a sense, themselves become commodities. This phenomenon has led Baudrillard (1981) to argue that Marx's analysis of commodity production is outdated because capitalism is now predominantly concerned with the production of signs, images, and sign systems rather than with commodities themselves. The transition he points to is important, though there are in fact no serious difficulties in extending Marx's theory of commodity production to cope with it. To be sure, the systems of production and marketing of images (like markets for land, public goods, or labour power) do exhibit some special features that need to be taken into account. The consumer turnover time of certain images can be very short indeed (close to that ideal of the 'twinkling of an eye' that Marx saw as optimal from the standpoint of capital circulation). Many images can also be mass-marketed instantaneously over space. Given the pressures to accelerate turnover time (and to overcome spatial barriers), the commodification of images of the most ephemeral sort would seem to be a godsend from the standpoint of capital accumulation, particularly when other paths to relieve over-accumulation seem blocked. Ephemerality and instantaneous communicability over space then become virtues to be explored and appropriated by capitalists for their own purposes.

But images have to perform other functions. Corporations, governments, political and intellectual leaders, all value a stable (though dynamic) image as part of their aura of authority and power. The mediatization of politics has now become all pervasive. This becomes, in effect, the fleeting, superficial, and illusory means whereby an individualistic society of transients sets forth its nostalgia for common values. The production and marketing of such images of permanence and power require considerable sophistication, because the continuity and stability of the image have to be retained while stressing the adaptability, flexibility, and dynamism of whoever or whatever is being imaged. Moreover, image becomes all-important in competition, not only through name-brand recognition but also because of various associations of 'respectability,' 'quality,' 'prestige,' 'reliability,' and 'innovation.' Competition in the image-building trade becomes a vital aspect of inter-firm competition. Success is so plainly profitable that investment in image-building (sponsoring the arts, exhibitions, television productions, new buildings, as well as direct marketing) becomes as important as investment in new plant and machinery. The image serves to establish an identity in the market place. This is also true in labour markets. The acquisition of an image (by the purchase of a sign system such as designer clothes and the right car) becomes a singularly important element in the presentation of self in labour markets and, by extension, becomes integral to the quest for individual identity, self-realization, and meaning. Amusing yet sad signals of this sort of quest abound. A California firm manufactures imitation car telephones, indistinguishable from the real ones, and they sell like hot cakes to a populace desperate to acquire such a symbol of importance. Personal image consultants have become big business in New York City, the *International Herald Tribune* has reported, as a million or so people a year in the city region sign up for courses with firms called Image Assemblers, Image Builders, Image Crafters, and Image Creators. 'People make up their minds about you in around one tenth of a second these days,' says one image consultant. 'Fake it till you make it,' is the slogan of another.

It has always been the case, of course, that symbols of wealth, status, fame, and power as well as of class have been important in bourgeois society, but probably nowhere near as widely in the past as now. The increasing material affluence generated during the post-war Fordist boom posed the problem of converting rising incomes into an effective demand that satisfied the rising aspirations of youth, women, and the working class. Given the ability to produce images as commodities more or less at will, it becomes feasible for accumulation to proceed at least in part on the basis of pure image production and marketing. The ephemerality of such images can then be interpreted in part as a struggle on the part of the oppressed groups of whatever sort to establish their own identity (in terms of street culture, musical styles, fads and fashions made up for themselves) and the rush to convert those innovations to commercial advantage (Carnaby Street in the late 1960s proved an excellent pioneer). The effect is to make it seem as if we are living in a world of ephemeral created images. The psychological impacts of sensory overload, of the sort that Simmel and Toffler identify, are thereby put to work with a redoubled effect.

The materials to produce and reproduce such images, if they were not readily at hand, have themselves been the focus for innovation—the better the replication of the image, the greater the mass market for image making could become. This is in itself an important issue and it brings us more explicitly to consider the role of the 'simulacrum' in postmodernism. By 'simulacrum' is meant a state of such near perfect replication that the difference between the original and the copy becomes almost impossible to spot. The production of images as simulacra is relatively easy, given modern techniques. Insofar as identity is increasingly dependent upon images, this means that the serial and recursive replications of identities (individual, corporate, institutional, and political) becomes a very real possibility and problem. We can certainly see it at work in the realm of politics as the image makers and the media assume a more powerful role in the shaping of political identities. But there are many more tangible realms where the simulacrum has a heightened role. With modern building materials it is possible to replicate ancient buildings with such exactitude that authenticity or origins can be put into doubt. The manufacture of antiques and other art objects becomes entirely possible, making the high-class forgery a serious problem in the art collection business. We not only possess, therefore, the capacity to pile images from the past or from other places eclectically and simultaneously upon the television screen, but even to transform those images into material simulacra in the form of built environments, events and spectacles, and the like, which become in many respects indistinguishable from the originals. What happens to cultural forms when the imitations become real, and the real takes on many of the qualities of an imitation, is a question to which we shall return. . . .

The popularity of a work like Alvin Toffler's *Future Shock* lay precisely in its prescient appreciation of the speed with which the future has come to be discounted into the present. Out of that, also, comes a collapse of cultural distinctions between, say, 'science' and 'regular' fiction (in the works of, for example, Thomas Pynchon and Doris Lessing), as well as a merging of the cinema of distraction with the cinema of futuristic universes. We can link the schizophrenic dimension to postmodernity which Jameson emphasizes with accelerations in turnover times in production, exchange, and consumption that produce, as it were, the loss of a sense of the future except and insofar as the future can be discounted into the present. Volatility and ephemerality similarly make it hard to maintain any firm sense of continuity. Past experience gets compressed into some overwhelming present. Italo Calvino (1981, 8) reports the effect on his own craft of novel writing this way:

> long novels written today are perhaps a contradiction: the dimension of time had been shattered, we cannot live or think except in fragments of time each of which goes off along its own trajectory and immediately disappears. We can rediscover the continuity of time only in the novels of that period when time no longer seemed stopped and did not yet seem to have exploded, a period that lasted no more than a hundred years.

Baudrillard (1986), never afraid to exaggerate, considers the United States as a society so given over to speed, motion, cinematic images, and technological fixes as to have created a crisis of explanatory logic. It represents, he suggests, 'the triumph of effect over cause, of instantaneity over time as depth, the triumph of surface and of pure objectivization over the depth of desire.' This, of course, is the kind of environment in which deconstructionism can flourish. If it is impossible to say anything of solidity and permanence in the midst of this ephemeral and fragmented world, then why not join in the [language] game? Everything, from novel writing and philosophizing to the experience of labouring or making a home, has to face the challenge of accelerating turnover time and the rapid write-off of traditional and historically acquired values. The temporary contract in everything, as Lyotard remarks, then becomes the hallmark of postmodern living.

But, as so often happens, the plunge into the maelstrom of ephemerality has provoked an explosion of opposed sentiments and tendencies. To begin with, all sorts of technical means arise to guard against future shocks. Firms sub-contract or resort to flexible hiring practices to discount the potential unemployment costs of future market shifts. Futures markets in everything, from corn and pork bellies to currencies and government debt, coupled with the 'securitization' of all kinds of temporary and floating debts, illustrate techniques for discounting the future into the present. Insurance hedges of all kinds against future volatility become much more widely available.

Deeper questions of meaning and interpretation also arise. The greater the ephemerality, the more pressing the need to discover or manufacture some kind of eternal truth that might lie therein. The religious revival that has become much stronger since the late sixties, and the search for authenticity and authority in politics (with all of its accoutrements of nationalism and localism and of admiration for those charismatic and 'protean' individuals with their Nietzschian 'will to power') are cases in point. The revival of interest in basic institutions (such as the family and community), and the search for historical roots are all signs of a search for more secure moorings and longer-lasting values in a shifting world. Rochberg-Halton (1986, 173), in a sample study of North Chicago residents in 1977, finds, for example, that the objects actually valued in the home were not the 'pecuniary trophies' of a materialist culture which acted as 'reliable indices of one's socio-economic class, age, gender and so on,' but the artefacts that embodied 'ties to loved ones and kin, valued experiences and activities, and memories of significant life events and people.' Photographs, particular objects (like a piano, a clock, a chair), and events (the playing of a record of a piece of music, the singing of a song) become the focus of a contemplative memory, and hence a generator of a sense of self that lies outside the sensory overloading of consumerist culture and fashion. The home becomes a private museum to guard against the ravages of time-space compression. At the very time, furthermore, that postmodernism proclaims the 'death of the author' and the rise of anti-auratic art in the public realm, the art market becomes ever more conscious of the monopoly power of the artist's signature and of questions of authenticity and forgery (no matter that the Rauschenberg is itself a mere reproduction montage). It is, perhaps, appropriate that the postmodernist developer building, as solid as the pink granite of Philip Johnson's AT & T building, should be debt-financed, built on the basis of fictitious capital, and architecturally conceived of, at least on the outside, more in the spirit of fiction than of function.

The spatial adjustments have been no less traumatic. The satellite communications systems deployed since the early 1970s have rendered the unit cost and time of communication invariant with respect to distance. It costs the same to communicate over 500 miles as it does over 5,000 via satellite. Air freight rates on commodities have likewise come down dramatically, while containerization has reduced the cost of bulk sea and road transport. It is now possible for a large multinational corporation like Texas Instruments to operate plants with simultaneous decision-making with respect to financial, market, input costs, quality control, and labour process conditions in more than fifty different locations across the globe (Dicken, 1986, 110-13). Mass television ownership coupled with satellite communication makes it possible to experience a rush of images from different spaces almost simultaneously, collapsing the world's spaces into a series of images on a television screen. The whole world can watch the Olympic Games, the World Cup, the fall of a dictator, a political summit, a deadly tragedy . . . while mass tourism, films made in spectacular locations, make a wide range of simulated or vicarious experiences of what the world contains available to many people. The image of places and spaces becomes as open to production and ephemeral use as any other.

We have, in short, witnessed another fierce round in that process of annihilation of space through time that has always lain at the center of capitalism's dynamic. Marshall McLuhan described how he thought the 'global village' had now become a communications reality in the mid-1960s:

> After three thousand years of explosion, by means of fragmentary and mechanical technologies, the Western World is imploding. During the mechanical ages we had extended our bodies in space. Today, after more than a century of electronic technology, we have extended our central nervous system itself in a global embrace, abolishing both space and time as far as our planet is concerned.

But the collapse of spatial barriers does not mean that the significance of space is decreasing. Not for the first time in capitalism's history, we find the evidence pointing to the converse thesis. Heightened competition under conditions of crisis has coerced capitalists into paying much closer attention to relative locational advantages, precisely because diminishing spatial barriers give capitalists the power to exploit minute spatial differentiations to good effect. Small differences in what the space contains in the way of labour supplies, resources, infrastructures, and the like become of increased significance. Superior command over space becomes an even more important weapon in class struggle. It becomes one of the means to enforce speed-up and the redefinition of skills on recalcitrant work forces. Geographical mobility and decentralization are used against a union power which traditionally concentrated in the factories of mass production. Capital flight, deindustrialization of some regions, and the industrialization of others, the destruction of traditional working-class communities as power bases in class struggle, become leitmotifs of spatial transformation under more flexible conditions of accumulation (Martin and Rowthorn, 1986; Bluestone and Harrison, 1982; Harrison and Bluestone, 1988).

As spatial barriers diminish so we become much more sensitized to what the world's spaces contain. Flexible accumulation typically exploits a wide range of seemingly contingent geographical circumstances, and reconstitutes them as structured internal elements of its own encompassing logic. For example, geographical differentiations in the mode and strengths of labour control together with variations in the quality as well as the quantity of labour power assume a much greater significance in corporate locational strategies. New industrial ensembles arise, sometimes out of almost nothing (as the various silicon valleys and glens) but more often on the basis of some pre-existing mix of skills and resources. The 'Third Italy' (Emilia-Romagna) builds upon a peculiar mix of co-operative entrepreneurialism, artisan labour, and local communist administrations anxious to generate employment, and inserts its clothing products with incredible success into a highly competitive world economy. Flanders attracts outside capital on the basis of a dispersed, flexible, and reasonably skilled labour supply with a deep hostility to unionism and socialism. Los Angeles imports the highly successful patriarchal labour systems of South-East Asia through mass immigration, while the celebrated paternalistic labour control system of the Japanese and Taiwanese is imported into California and South Wales. The story in each case is different, making it appear as if the uniqueness of this or that geographical circumstance matters more than ever before. Yet it does so, ironically, only because of the collapse of spatial barriers.

While labour control is always central, there are many other aspects of geographical organization that have risen to a new prominence under conditions of more flexible accumulation. The need for accurate information and speedy communication has emphasized the role of so-called 'world cities' in the financial and corporate system (centres equipped with teleports, airports, fixed communication links, as well as a wide array of financial, legal, business, and infrastructural services). The diminution of spatial barriers results in the reaffirmation and realignment of hierarchy within what is now a global urban system. The local availability of material resources of special qualities, or even at marginally lower costs, starts to be ever more important, as do local variations in market taste that are today more easily exploited under conditions of small-batch production and flexible design. Local differences in entrepreneurial ability, venture capital, scientific and technical know-how, social attitudes, also enter in, while the local networks of influence and power, the accumulation strategies of local ruling elites (as opposed to nation state policies) also become more deeply implicated in the regime of flexible accumulation.

But this then raises another dimension to the changing role of spatiality in contemporary society. If capitalists become increasingly sensitive to the spatially differentiated qualities of which the world's geography is composed, then it is possible for the peoples and powers that command those spaces to alter them in such a way as to be more rather than less attractive to highly mobile capital. Local ruling elites can, for example, implement strategies of local labour control, of skill enhancement, of infrastructural provision, of tax policy, state regulation, and so on, in order to attract development within their particular space. The qualities of place stand thereby to be emphasized in the midst of the increasing abstractions of space. The active production of places with special qualities becomes an important stake in spatial competition between localities, cities, regions, and nations. Corporatist forms of governance can flourish in such spaces, and themselves take on entrepreneurial roles in the production of favourable business climates and other special qualities. And it is in this context that we can better situate the striving . . . for cities to forge a distinctive image and to create an atmosphere of place and tradition that will act as a lure to both capital and people 'of the right sort' (i.e. wealthy and influential). Heightened inter-place competition should lead to the production of more variegated spaces within the increasing homogeneity of international exchange. But to the degree that this competition opens up cities to systems of accumulation, it ends up producing what Boyer (1988) calls a 'recursive' and 'serial' monotony, 'producing from already known patterns or molds places almost identical in ambience from city to city: New York's South Street Seaport, Boston's Quincy Market, Baltimore's Harbor Place.'

We thus approach the central paradox: the less important the spatial barriers, the greater the sensitivity of capital to the variations of place within space, and the greater the incentive for places to be differentiated in ways attractive to capital. The result has been the production of fragmentation, insecurity, and ephemeral uneven development within a highly unified global space economy of capital flows. The historic tension within capitalism between centralization and decentralization is now being worked out in new ways. Extraordinary decentralization and proliferation of industrial production ends up putting Benetton or Laura Ashley products in almost every serially produced shopping mall in the advanced capitalist world. Plainly, the new round of time-space compression is fraught with as many dangers as it offers possibilities for survival of particular places or for a solution to the overaccumulation problem.

The geography of devaluation through deindustrialization, rising local unemployment, fiscal retrenchment, write-offs of local assets, and the like, is indeed a sorry picture. But we can

at least see its logic within the frame of the search for a solution to the overaccumulation problem through the push into flexible and more mobile systems of accumulation. But there are
also a priori reasons to suspect (as well as some material evidence to support the idea) that
regions of maximum churning and fragmentation are also regions that seem best set to survive
the traumas of devaluation in the long run. There is more than a hint that a little devaluation
now is better than massive devaluation later in the scramble for local survival in the world of
severely constrained opportunities for positive growth. Reindustrializing and restructuring
cannot be accomplished without deindustrializing and devaluing first.

None of these shifts in the experience of space and time would make the sense or have the
impact they do without a radical shift in the manner in which value gets represented as money.
Though long dominant, money has never been a clear or unambiguous representation of value,
and on occasion it becomes so muddled as to become itself a major source of insecurity and
uncertainty. Under the terms of the postwar settlement, the question of world money was put
on a fairly stable basis. The US dollar became the medium of world trade, technically backed
by a fixed convertibility into gold, and backed politically and economically by the overwhelming power of the US productive apparatus. The space of the US production system
became, in effect, the guarantor of international value. But, as we have seen, one of the signals
of the breakdown of the Fordist-Keynesian system was the breakdown of the Bretton Woods
agreement, of convertibility of US dollars to gold, and the shift to a global system of floating
exchange rates. The breakdown in part occurred because of the shifting dimensionalities of
space and time generated out of capital accumulation. Rising indebtedness (particularly within
the United States), and fiercer international competition from the reconstructed spaces of the
world economy under conditions of growing accumulation, had much to do with undermining
the power of the US economy to operate as an exclusive guarantor of world money.

The effects have been legion. The question of how value should now get represented,
what form money should take, and the meaning that can be put upon the various forms of
money available to us, has never been far from the surface of recent concerns. Since 1973,
money has been 'de-materialized' in the sense that it no longer has a formal or tangible link to
precious metals (though the latter have continued to play a role as one potential form of
money among many others), or for that matter to any other tangible commodity. Nor does it
rely exclusively upon productive activity within a particular space. The world has come to rely,
for the first time in its history, upon immaterial forms of money—i.e. money of account
assessed quantitatively in numbers of some designated currency (dollars, yen, Deutsch Marks,
sterling, etc.). Exchange rates between the different currencies of the world have also been
extremely volatile. Fortunes could be lost or made simply by holding the right currency during
the right phases. The question of which currency I hold is directly linked to which place I put
my faith in. That may have something to do with the competitive economic position and
power of different national systems. That power, given the flexibility of accumulation over
space, is itself a rapidly shifting magnitude. The effect is to render the spaces that underpin the
determination of value as unstable as value itself. This problem is compounded by the way that
speculative shifts bypass actual economic power and performance, and then trigger self-fulfill-
ing expectations. The de-linking of the financial system from active production and from any
material monetary base calls into question the reliability of the basic mechanism whereby value
is supposed to be represented.

These difficulties have been most powerfully present in the process of devaluation of money, the measure of value, through inflation. The steady inflation rates of the Fordist-Keynesian era (usually in the 3 per cent range, and rarely above 5 per cent) gave way from 1969 onwards, and then accelerated in all the major capitalist countries during the 1970s into double-digit rates.... Worse still, inflation became highly unstable, between as well as within countries, leaving everyone in doubt as to what the true value (the buying power) of a particular money might be in the near future. Money consequently became useless as a means of storing value for any length of time (the real rate of interest, measured as the money rate of interest minus the rate of inflation, was negative for several years during the 1970s, so dispossessing savers of the value they were seeking to store). Alternative means had to be found to store value effectively. And so began the vast inflation in certain kinds of asset prices—collectibles, art objects, antiques, houses, and the like. Buying a Degas or Van Gogh in 1973 would surely outstrip almost any other kind of investment in terms of capital gain. Indeed it can be argued that the growth of the art market (with its concern for authorial signature) and the strong commercialization of cultural production since around 1970 have had a lot to do with the search to find alternative means to store value under conditions where the usual money forms were deficient. Commodity and general price inflation, though to some degree brought under control in the advanced capitalist countries during the 1980s, has by no means diminished as a problem. It is rampant in countries like Mexico, Argentina, Brazil, and Israel (all with recent rates in hundreds of per cent), and the prospect of generalized inflation looms in the advanced capitalist countries, where it is in any case arguable that the inflation of asset prices (housing, works of art, antiques, etc.) has taken over where commodity and labour market inflation left off in the early 1980s.

The breakdown of money as a secure means of representing value has itself created a crisis of representation in advanced capitalism. It has also been reinforced by, and added its very considerable weight to, the problems of time-space compression which we earlier identified. The rapidity with which currency markets fluctuate across the world's spaces, the extraordinary power of money capital flow in what is now a global stock and financial market, and the volatility of what the purchasing power of money might represent, define, as it were, a high point of that highly problematic intersection of money, time, and space as interlocking elements of social power in the political economy of postmodernity.

It is, furthermore, not hard to see how all of this might create a more general crisis of representation. The central value system, to which capitalism has always appealed to validate and gauge its actions, is dematerialized and shifting, time horizons are collapsing, and it is hard to tell exactly what space we are in when it comes to assessing causes and effects, meanings or values. The intriguing exhibition at the Pompidou Centre in 1985 on 'The Immaterial' (an exhibition for which none other than Lyotard acted as one of the consultants) was perhaps a mirror image of the dissolution of the material representations of value under conditions of more flexible accumulation, and of the confusions as to what it might mean to say, with Paul Virilio, that time and space have disappeared as meaningful dimensions to human thought and action.

There are, I would submit, more tangible and material ways than this to go about assessing the significance of space and time for the condition of postmodernity. It should be possible to consider how, for example, the changing experience of space, time, and money has formed a distinctive material basis for the rise of distinctive systems of interpretation and representation, as well as opening a path through which the aestheticization of politics might once more reassert itself. If we view culture as that complex of signs and significations (including language) that mesh into codes of transmission of social values and meanings, then we can at least begin upon the task of unravelling its complexities under present-day conditions by recognizing that money and commodities are themselves the primary bearers of cultural codes. Since money and commodities are entirely bound up with the circulation of capital, it follows that cultural forms are firmly rooted in the daily circulation process of capital. It is, therefore, with the daily experience of money and the commodity that we should begin, no matter if special commodities or even whole sign systems may be extracted from the common herd and made the basis of 'high' culture or that specialized 'imaging' which we have already had cause to comment upon. . . .

The whole world's cuisine is now assembled in one place in almost exactly the same way that the world's geographical complexity is nightly reduced to a series of images on a static television screen. This same phenomenon is exploited in entertainment palaces like Epcott and Disneyworld; it becomes possible, as the US commercials put it, 'to experience the Old World for a day without actually having to go there.' The general implication is that through the experience of everything from food, to culinary habits, music, television, entertainment, and cinema, it is now possible to experience the world's geography vicariously, as a simulacrum. The interweaving of simulacra in daily life brings together different worlds (of commodities) in the same space and time. But it does so in such a way as to conceal almost perfectly any trace of origin, of the labour processes that produced them, or of the social relations implicated in their production.

The simulacra can in turn become the reality. Baudrillard (1986) in L'Amérique even goes so far, somewhat exaggeratedly in my view, to suggest that US reality is now constructed as a giant screen: 'the cinema is everywhere, most of all in the city, incessant and marvellous film and scenario.' Places portrayed in a certain way, particularly if they have the capacity to attract tourists, may begin to 'dress themselves up' as the fantasy images prescribe. Mediaeval castles offer mediaeval weekends (food, dress, but not of course the primitive heating arrangements). Vicarious participation in these various worlds has real effects on the ways in which these worlds get ordered. Jencks (1984, 127) proposes that the architect should be an active participant in this:

> Any middle class urbanite in any large city from Teheran to Tokyo is bound to have a well-stocked, indeed over-stocked 'image bank' that is continually restuffed by travel and magazines. His *museé imaginaire* may mirror the pot-pourri of the producers but it is nonetheless natural to his way of life. Barring some kind of totalitarian reduction in the heterogeneity of production and consumption, it seems to be desirable that architects learn to use this inevitable heterogeneity of languages. Besides, it is quite enjoyable. Why, if one can afford to live in different ages and cultures, restrict oneself to the present, the locale? Eclecticism is the natural evolution of a culture with choice.

Much the same can be said of popular music styles. Commenting on how collage and eclecticism have recently come to dominate, Chambers (1987) goes on to show how oppositional and subcultural musics like reggae, Afro-American and Afro-Hispanic have taken their place 'in the museum of fixed symbolic structures' to form a flexible collage of 'the already seen, the already worn, the already played, the already heard.' A strong sense of 'the Other' is replaced, he suggests, by a weak sense of 'the others.' The loose hanging together of divergent street cultures in the fragmented spaces of the contemporary city re-emphasizes the contingent and accidental aspects of this 'otherness' in daily life. This same sensibility exists in postmodern fiction. It is, says McHale (1987), concerned with 'ontologies,' with a potential as well as an actual plurality of universes, forming an eclectic and 'anarchic landscape of worlds in the plural.' Dazed and distracted characters wander through these worlds without a clear sense of location, wondering, 'Which world am I in and which of my personalities do I deploy?' Our postmodern ontological landscape, suggests McHale, 'is unprecedented in human history—at least in the degree of its pluralism.' Spaces of very different worlds seem to collapse upon each other, much as the world's commodities are assembled in the supermarket and all manner of sub-cultures get juxtaposed in the contemporary city. Disruptive spatiality triumphs over the coherence of perspective and narrative in postmodern fiction, in exactly the same way that imported beers coexist with local brews, local employment collapses under the weight of foreign competition, and all the divergent spaces of the world are assembled nightly as a collage of images upon the television screen.

There seem to be two divergent sociological effects of all of this in daily thought and action. The first suggests taking advantage of all of the divergent possibilities, much as Jencks recommends, and cultivating a whole series of simulacra as milieux of escape, fantasy, and distraction:

> All around us—on advertisement hoardings, bookshelves, record covers, television screens—these miniature escape fantasies present themselves. This, it seems, is how we are destined to live, as split personalities in which the private life is disturbed by the promise of escape routes to another reality. (Cohen and Taylor, 1978, quoted in McHale, 1987, 38)

From this standpoint I think we have to accept McHale's argument that postmodern fiction is mimetic of something, much as I have argued that the emphasis upon ephemerality, collage, fragmentation, and dispersal in philosophical and social thought mimics the conditions of flexible accumulation. And it should not be surprising either to see how all of this fits in with the emergence since 1970 of a fragmented politics of divergent special and regional interest groups.

But it is exactly at this point that we encounter the opposite reaction that can best be summed up as the search for personal or collective identity, the search for secure moorings in a shifting world. Place-identity, in this collage of superimposed spatial images that implode in upon us, becomes an important issue, because everyone occupies a space of individuation (a body, a room, a home, a shaping community, a nation), and how we individuate ourselves shapes identity. Furthermore, if no one 'knows their place' in this shifting collage world, then how can a secure social order be fashioned or sustained?

There are two elements within this problem that deserve close consideration. First, the capacity of most social movements to command place better than space puts a strong emphasis upon the potential connection between place and social identity. This is manifest in political action. The defensiveness of municipal socialism, the insistence on working-class community, the localization of the fight against capital, become central features of working-class struggle within an overall patterning of uneven geographical development. The consequent dilemmas of socialist or working-class movements in the face of a universalizing capitalism are shared by other oppositional groups—racial minorities, colonized peoples, women, etc.—who are relatively empowered to organize in place but disempowered when it comes to organizing over space. In clinging, often of necessity, to a place-bound identity, however, such oppositional movements become a part of the very fragmentation which a mobile capitalism and flexible accumulation can feed upon. 'Regional resistances,' the struggle for local autonomy, place-bound organization, may be excellent bases for political action, but they cannot bear the burden of radical historical change alone. 'Think globally and act locally' was the revolutionary slogan of the 1960s. It bears repeating.

The assertion of any place-bound identity has to rest at some point on the motivational power of tradition. It is difficult, however, to maintain any sense of historical continuity in the face of all the flux and ephemerality of flexible accumulation. The irony is that tradition is now often preserved by being commodified and marketed as such. The search for roots ends up at worst being produced and marketed as an image, as a simulacrum or pastiche (imitation communities constructed to evoke images of some folksy past, the fabric of traditional working-class communities being taken over by an urban gentry). The photograph, the document, the view, and the reproduction become history precisely because they are so overwhelmingly present. The problem, of course, is that none of these are immune from tampering or downright faking for present purposes. At best, historical tradition is reorganized as a museum culture, not necessarily of high modernist art, but of local history, of local production, of how things once upon a time were made, sold, consumed, and integrated into a long-lost and often romanticized daily life (one from which all trace of oppressive social relations may be expunged). Through the presentation of a partially illusory past it becomes possible to signify something of local identity and perhaps to do it profitably.

The second reaction to the internationalism of modernism lies in the search to construct place and its meanings qualitatively. Capitalist hegemony over space puts the aesthetics of place very much back on the agenda. But this, as we have seen, meshes only too well with the idea of spatial differentiations as lures for a peripatetic capital that values the option of mobility very highly. Isn't this place better than that place, not only for the operations of capital but also for living in, consuming well, and feeling secure in a shifting world? The construction of such places, the fashioning of some localized aesthetic image, allows the construction of some limited and limiting sense of identity in the midst of a collage of imploding spatialities. . . .

This should alert us to the acute geopolitical dangers that attach to the rapidity of time-space compression in recent years. The transition from Fordism to flexible accumulation, such as it has been, ought to imply a transition in our mental maps, political attitudes, and political institutions. But political thinking does not necessarily undergo such easy transformations, and is in any case subject to the contradictory pressures that derive from spatial integration and differentiation. There is an omni-present danger that our mental maps will not match current realities. The serious diminution of the power of individual nation states over fiscal and monetary policies, for example, has not been matched by any parallel shift towards an internationalization of politics. Indeed, there are abundant signs that localism and nationalism have become stronger precisely because of the quest for the security that place always offers in the midst of all the shifting that flexible accumulation implies. The resurgence of geopolitics and of faith in charismatic politics (Thatcher's Falklands War, Reagan's invasion of Grenada) fits only too well with a world that is increasingly nourished intellectually and politically by a vast flux of ephemeral images.

Time-space compression always exacts its toll on our capacity to grapple with the realities unfolding around us. Under stress, for example, it becomes harder and harder to react accurately to events. The erroneous identification of an Iranian airbus, ascending within an established commercial flight corridor, with a fighter-bomber descending towards a targeted US warship—an incident that resulted in many civilian deaths—is typical of the way that reality gets created rather than interpreted under conditions of stress and time-space compression. The parallel with Kern's account of the outbreak of World War I . . . is instructive. If 'seasoned negotiators cracked under the pressure of tense confrontations and sleepless nights, agonizing over the probable disastrous consequences of their snap judgements and hasty actions,' then how much more difficult must decision-making now be? The difference this time is that there is not even time to agonize. And the problems are not confined to the realms of political and military decision-making, for the world's financial markets are on the boil in ways that make a snap judgement here, an unconsidered word there, and a gut reaction somewhere else the slip that can unravel the whole skein of fictitious capital formation and of interdependency.

The conditions of postmodern time-space compression exaggerate in many respects the dilemmas that have from time to time beset capitalist procedures of modernization in the past (1848 and the phase just before the First World War spring particularly to mind). While the economic, cultural, and political responses may not be exactly new, the range of those responses differs in certain important respects from those which have occurred before. The intensity of time-space compression in Western capitalism since the 1960s, with all of its congruent features of excessive ephemerality and fragmentation in the political and private as well as in the social realm, does seem to indicate an experiential context that makes the condition of postmodernity somewhat special. But by putting this condition into its historical context, as part of a history of successive waves of time-space compression generated out of the pressures of capital accumulation with its perpetual search to annihilate space through time and reduce turnover time, we can at least pull the condition of postmodernity into the range of a condition accessible to historical materialist analysis and interpretation.

Jürgen Habermas

An exact contemporary of Jacques Derrida and Michel Foucault, Jürgen Habermas, born in 1929, has played a similar role as a public intellectual in his native Germany. Linking dense philosophical learning to public discussions of higher education and civic life in his writings and speeches, Habermas made his profound commitment to democracy most evident in the student movements of the 1960s. Throughout his career he has argued against positivist definitions of knowledge and spoken publicly on behalf of a theory of knowledge built upon social practice. His best known work, *The Structural Transformation of the Public Sphere*, did not appear in an American translation until 1989, twenty-seven years after its German publication. In it Habermas argued for the importance of deliberative politics and analyzed the corrupting impact of mass communication upon them. It is this recommitment to the Enlightenment goal of bringing reason to bear upon public issues which has made Habermas a counterweight to postmodernist views about knowledge and power. His position is exemplified in the selection here, "Philosophy as Stand-in and Interpreter."

JÜRGEN HABERMAS
(1987)

Philosophy as Stand-In and Interpreter

Master thinkers have fallen on hard times. This has been true of Hegel ever since Popper unmasked him in the forties as an enemy of the open society. It has also been true—intermittently—of Marx. The last to denounce him as a false prophet were the New Philosophers in the seventies. Today even Kant is affected by this decline. If I am correct, he is being viewed for the first time as a *maître penseur*, that is, as the magician of a false paradigm from the intellectual constraints of which we have to escape. Whereas among a philosophical audience there may still be a majority of scholars whose image of Kant has stayed the same, in the world outside his reputation is being eclipsed, and not for the first time, by Nietzsche.

Historically, Kantian philosophy marks the birth of a new mode of justification. Kant felt that the physics of his time and the growth of knowledge brought by it were important developments to which the philosopher had to respond. For Kant, the new science represented, not some philosophically indifferent fact of life, but proof of man's capacity to know. Specifically, the challenge Newtonian physics posed for philosophy was to explain how empirical knowledge is at all possible, an explanation that could not itself be empirical but had to be transcendental. What Kant calls "transcendental" is an inquiry into the a priori conditions of what makes experience possible. The specific upshot of Kant's transcendental inquiry is that those conditions are identical with the conditions of possible objects of experience. The first job for the philosopher, then, is to analyze the concepts of objects as we "always already" intuitively use them. Transcendental analysis is a nonempirical reconstruction of the a priori achievements

Reprinted from *After Philosophy: End or Transformation?* ed. by K. Baynes, James Bohman, and T. McCarthy (Cambridge: MIT Press, 1987), pp. 296–314. © Massachusetts Institute of Technology. Reprinted by permission of the Press.

of the cognizing subject, achievements for which there is no alternative: No experience shall be thought possible under *different* conditions. Transcendental justification has nothing to do with deduction from first principles. Rather, the hallmark of the transcendental justification is the notion that we can prove the nonsubstitutability of certain mental operations that we always already (intuitively) perform in accordance with rules.

As a master thinker, Kant fell into disfavor because he used transcendental justification to found the new discipline of epistemology. In so doing he redefined the task, or vocation if you like, of philosophy in a more demanding way. There are two principal reasons why the Kantian view of philosophy's vocation has a dubious ring today.

The first reason has directly to do with the foundationalism of epistemology. In championing the idea of a cognition *before* cognition, Kantian philosophy sets up a domain between itself and the sciences, arrogating authority to itself. It wants to clarify the foundations of the sciences once and for all, defining, the limits of what can and cannot be experienced. This is tantamount to an act of ushering the sciences to their proper place. I think philosophy cannot and should not try to play the role of usher.

The second reason lies in the fact that transcendental philosophy refuses to be confined to epistemology. Above and beyond analyzing the bases of cognition, the critique of pure reason is also supposed to enable us to criticize the abuses of this cognitive faculty, which is limited to phenomena. Kant replaces the substantive concept of reason found in traditional metaphysics with a concept of reason the moments of which have undergone differentiation, to the point where their unity, is merely formal. He sets up practical reason, judgment, and theoretical cognition in isolation from each other, giving each a foundation unto itself, with the result that philosophy is cast in the role of the highest arbiter for all matters, including culture as a whole. Kantian philosophy differentiates what Weber was to call the "value spheres of culture" (science and technology, law and morality, art and art criticism), while at the same time legitimating them within their respective limits. Thus Kant's philosophy poses as the highest court of appeal vis-à-vis the sciences and culture as a whole.

There is a necessary link between the Kantian foundationalism in epistemology, which nets philosophy the unenviable role of usher, and the ahistoricity of the conceptual system Kant superimposes on culture, which nets philosophy the equally undesirable role of judge, parceling out separate areas of jurisdiction to science, morality, and art.

> Without the Kantian assumption that the philosopher can decide *questions juris* concerning the rest of culture, this self-image collapses.... To drop the notion of the philosopher as knowing something about knowing which nobody else knows so well would be to drop the notion that his voice always has an overriding claim on the attention of the other participants in the conversation. It would also be to drop the notion that there is something called "philosophical method" or "philosophical technique" or "the philosophical point of view" which enables the professional philosopher, *ex officio*, to have interesting views about, say, the respectability of psychoanalysis, the legitimacy of certain dubious laws, the resolution of moral dilemmas, the soundness of schools of historiography or literary criticism, and the like.

Richard Rorty's impressive critique of philosophy assembles compelling metaphilosophical arguments in support of the view that the roles Kant the master thinker had envisaged for philosophy, namely those of usher and judge, are too big for it. While I find myself in agreement with much of what Rorty says, I have trouble accepting his conclusion, which is that if philosophy forswears these two roles, it must also surrender the function of being the "guardian of rationality." If I understand Rorty, he is saying that the new modesty of philosophy involves the abandonment of any claim to reason—the very claim that has marked philosophical thought since its inception. Rorty not only argues for the demise of philosophy. He also unflinchingly accepts the end of the belief that ideas like truth or the unconditional with their transcending power are a necessary condition of humane forms of collective life.

Implied by Kant's conception of formal, differentiated reason is a theory of modernity. Modernity is characterized by a rejection of the substantive rationality typical of religious and metaphysical worldviews and by a belief in procedural rationality and its ability to give credence to our views in the three areas of objective knowledge, moral-practical insight, and aesthetic judgment. What I am asking myself is this: Is it true that this (or a similar) concept of modernity becomes untenable when you dismiss the claims of a foundationalist theory of knowledge?

What follows is an attempt to narrate a story that might help put Rorty's criticism of philosophy in perspective. Granted, by going this route I cannot settle the controversy. What I can do is throw light on some of its presuppositions. . . . I will argue that philosophy, while well advised to withdraw from the problematic roles of usher (*Platzanweiser*) and judge, can and ought to retain its claim to reason, provided it is content to play the more modest roles of stand-in (*Platzhalter*) and interpreter.

1. Hegel fashioned his dialectical mode of justification in deliberate opposition to the transcendental one of Kant. Hegel—and I can only hint at this here—agrees with those who charge that in the end Kant failed to justify or ground the pure concepts of the understanding, for he merely culled them from the table of forms of judgment, unaware of their historical specificity. Thus he failed, in Hegel's eyes, to prove that the a priori conditions of what makes experience possible are truly necessary. In his *Phenomenology of Spirit* Hegel proposes to correct this flaw by taking a genetic approach. What Kant regarded as a unique (Copernican) turn to transcendental reflection becomes, in Hegel, a general mechanism for turning consciousness back upon itself. This mechanism has been switched on and off time and time again in the development of spirit. As the subject becomes conscious of itself, it destroys one form of consciousness after another. This process epitomizes the subjective experience that what initially appears to the subject as a being in itself acquires content only by virtue of the form imparted to it by the subject. The transcendental philosopher's experience is thus, according to Hegel, reenacted naively by every in-itself as it becomes a for-itself. What Hegel calls "dialectical" is the reconstruction of this recurrent experience and its assimilation by the subject, which is faced with ever more complex structures. In sum, Hegel goes beyond the particular manifestation of consciousness Kant analyzed, focusing instead on knowledge that has become autonomous—that is, absolute knowledge. This highest vantage point, absolute knowledge, enables Hegel to witness the genesis of structures of consciousness that Kant had assumed to be timeless.

Hegel, it should be noted, exposes himself to a criticism similar to the one he levels against Kant. Reconstructing successive forms of consciousness is one thing. Proving the necessity of their succession is quite another. Hegel is not unaware of this gap, and he tries to close it by logical means, thereby laying the basis for a philosophical absolutism that claims an even grander role for philosophy than did Kant. In Hegel's *Logic* philosophy's role is to effect an encyclopedic conceptual synthesis of the diffuse chunks of content thrown up by the sciences. In addition Hegel picks up Kant's latent theory of modernity, making it explicit and developing it into a critique of the diremptive, self-contradictory features of modernity. It is this peculiar twist that gave philosophy a new world-historical relevance in relation to culture as a whole. And this is the stuff of which the suspect image of Hegel as a master thinker is made.

The metaphilosophical attack on the *maîtres penseurs*, whether its target be Hegel's absolutism or Kant's foundationalism, is a recent phenomenon. Antecedents of it can be found in the strands of self-criticism that have run through Kantianism and Hegelianism for quite some time. I shall comment briefly on two lines of self-criticism that I think complement each other in an interesting way.

2. In reference to Kant's transcendental philosophy there are today three distinct critical positions: the analytic one of Strawson, the constructivist one of Lorenzen, and the critical-rationalist one of Popper.

Analytic philosophy appropriates Kant by jettisoning any claim to ultimate justification (*Letztbegründung*). From the very outset it drops the objective Kant had in mind when he deduced the pure concepts of the understanding from the unity of self-consciousness. The analytic reception of Kant is confined to comprehending those concepts and rules that underlie experience, to the degree to which they can be couched in elementary propositions. The analysis focuses on general, indispensable, conceptual preconditions that make experience possible. Unable to prove the objective validity of its basic concepts and presuppositions, this analysis nevertheless makes a universalistic claim. Redeeming it involves changing Kant's transcendental strategy of justification into a testing procedure. If the hypothetically reconstructed conceptual system underlying experience as such is valid, then not a single intelligible alternative to it can possibly exist. This means any alternative proposal will be scrutinized with a view to proving its derivative character, that is, with a view to showing that the alleged alternative inevitably utilizes portions of the very hypothesis it seeks to supplant. A strategy of argumentation like this tries to prove that the concepts and presuppositions it singles out as fundamental cannot be dispensed with. Turned modest, the transcendental philosopher of the analytic variety takes on the role of the skeptic who keeps trying to find counterexamples that might invalidate his theories. In short, he acts like a hypothesis-testing scientist.

The *constructivist position* tried to compensate for the justificatory shortfall that has now opened up from the perspective of transcendental philosophy in the following way. It concedes from the start that the basic conceptual organization of experience is conventional, while at the same time putting a constructivist critique of language in the service of epistemology.

Those conventions are considered valid that are generated methodically and therefore transparently. It should be clear that this approach lays—rather than uncovers—the foundations of cognition.

On the face of it, the *critical-rationalist position* breaks completely with transcendentalism. It holds that the three horns of the "Münchhausen trilemma"—logical circularity, infinite regress, and recourse to absolute certitude—can only be avoided if one gives up any hope of grounding or justifying whatsoever. Here the notion of justification is being dislodged in favor of the concept of critical testing, which becomes the critical rationalist's equivalent for justification. In this connection I would argue that criticism is itself a procedure whose employment is never presuppositionless. That is why I think that critical rationalism, by clinging to the idea of irrefutable rules of criticism, allows a weak version of the Kantian justificatory mode to sneak into its inner precincts through the back door.

Self-criticism in the Hegelian tradition has become differentiated along similar lines as self-criticism among Kantians. Again, three distinct positions might be said to be represented by the young Lukács and his materialist critique of epistemology, which restricts the claim to justification of dialectics to the man-made world and excludes nature; by K. Korsch's and H. Freyer's practicism, wherein the classical relation of theory and practice is stood on its head and the "interested" perspective of creating a society of the future informs the theoretical reconstruction of social development; and finally by the negativism of Adorno, who clings to a comprehensive logic of development for the sole purpose of proving that it is impossible to break the spell of instrumental reason gone mad.

I cannot examine these positions here. All I shall do is point out certain interesting parallels between the Hegelian and Kantian strands of self-criticism. The self-criticism that begins by doubting the Kantian transcendental deduction and the self-criticism that begins by doubting Hegel's passage to absolute knowledge have this in common: They reject the claim that the categorical makeup and the pattern of development of the human spirit, respectively, can be proved to be necessary. With regard to constructivism and practicism, a similar convergence occurs: Both are involved in a shift from rational reconstruction to creative praxis where theory is viewed as an after-thought of praxis. Critical rationalism and negativism, for their part, share something too, which is that they reject both transcendental and dialectical means of cognition while at the same time using them in a paradoxical way. In short, one way of viewing them is to say that they represent attempts at radical negation which show that these two modes of justification cannot be abolished except on penalty of self-contradiction.

Our comparison between parallel self-critical strategies to restrict the justificatory claims of transcendental and dialectical philosophies gives rise to the following question: Do these self-limiting tendencies merely reinforce each other, encouraging the skeptic to reject justification all the more roundly? Or does the retrenchment on either side to a position of diminished justificatory objectives and strategies represent a precondition for viewing them, not as opposites, but as supplementing each other? I think the second possibility deserves serious consideration. The genetic structuralism of Jean Piaget provides an instructive model along these lines, instructive I think for all philosophers but particularly those who want to remain philosophers. Piaget conceives "reflective abstraction" as that learning mechanism which explains the transition between cognitive stages in ontogenetic development. The end point of this development is a decentered understanding of the world. Reflective abstraction is similar to transcendental reflection in that it brings out the formal elements hidden in the cognitive content, identifies them as the schemata that underlie the knowing subject's action, differentiates them, and reconstructs them at the next highest stage of reflection. Seen from a different perspective, the same learning mechanism has a function similar to Hegel's power of negation which dialectically supersedes self-contradictory forms of consciousness.

3. The aforementioned six positions in the tradition of Kant and Hegel stick to a claim to reason, however small in scope, however cautious in formulation. It is this final intention that sets off Popper and Lakatos from a Feyerabend, Horkheimer and Adorno from a Foucault. They still say *something* about the indispensable conditions of claims to the validity of those

opinions we hold to be justified, claims that transcend all restrictions of time and place. Now, any attack on the master thinkers questions this residual claim to reason, thus in essence making a plea for the abolition of philosophy. I can explain this radical turn by talking briefly about a wholly different criticism, one that has been raised against Kant *and* Hegel jointly.

Its proponents can be found in *pragmatism* and *hermeneutic philosophy*. Their doubts concerning the justificatory and self-justificatory potential of philosophy operate at a more profound level than do the self-criticisms within the Kantian and Hegelian traditions. They step resolutely outside the parameters set by the philosophy of consciousness and its cognitive paradigm, which stresses the perception and representation of objects. Pragmatism and hermeneutics oust the traditional notion of the solitary subject that confronts objects and becomes reflective only by turning itself into an object. In its place they put an idea of cognition that is mediated by language and linked to action. Moreover, they emphasize the web of everyday life and communication surrounding "our" cognitive achievements. The latter are intrinsically intersubjective and cooperative. Just how this web is conceptualized, whether as "form of life," "life world," "practice," "linguistically mediated interaction," "language game," "convention," "cultural background," "tradition," "effective history," or what have you, is unimportant. The important thing is that these commonsensical ideas, though they may function quite differently, attain a status that used to be reserved for the basic concepts of epistemology. Pragmatism and hermeneutics, then, accord a higher position to acting and speaking than to knowing. But there is more to it than that. Purposive action and linguistic communication play a qualitatively different role from that of self-reflection in the philosophy of consciousness. They have no justificatory function any more save one: to expose the need for foundational knowledge as unjustified.

Charles S. Peirce doubted that radical doubt is possible. His intentions were the same as those of Dilthey, who doubted that neutrality in interpretive understanding is possible. For Peirce, problems always arise in a specific situation. They come to us, as it were. We do not go to them, for we do not fully control the totality of our practical existence. In a similar vein, Dilthey argues that we cannot grasp a symbolic expression unless we have an intuitive preunderstanding of its context, for we do not have unlimited freedom to convert the unproblematic background knowledge of our own culture into explicit knowledge. Every instance of problem solving and every interpretation depend on a web of myriad presuppositions. Since this web is holistic and particularistic at the same time, it can never be grasped by an abstract, general analysis. It is from this standpoint that the myth of the given—that is, the distinctions between sensuality and intellect, intuition and concept, form and content—can be debunked, along with the distinctions between analytical and synthetic judgments, between a priori and a posteriori. These Kantian dualisms are all being dissolved, a fact that is vaguely reminiscent of Hegel's metacritique. Of course, a full-fledged return to Hegel is made impossible by the contextualism and historicism to which the pragmatist and hermeneutic approaches subscribe.

There is no denying that pragmatism and hermeneutics represent a gain. Instead of focusing introspectively on consciousness, these two points of view look outside: at objectifications of action and language. Gone is the fixation on the cognitive function of consciousness. Gone too is the emphasis on the representational function of language and the visual metaphor of the "mirror of nature." What takes their place is the notion of justified opinion, spanning the whole spectrum of what can be said—what Wittgenstein and Austin call illocutionary force—rather than just the contents of fact-stating discourses. "Saying things is not always saying how things are."

Do these considerations strengthen Rorty's interpretation of pragmatism and hermeneutics, which argues for the abnegation, by philosophical thought, of any claim to rationality, indeed for the abnegation of philosophy per se? Or do they mark the beginning of a new paradigm that, while discarding the mentalistic language game of the philosophy of consciousness, retains the justificatory modes of that philosophy in the modest, self-critical form in which I have presented them? I cannot answer this question directly for want of compelling and simple arguments. Once again the answer I will give is a narrative one.

4. Marx wanted to supersede (*aufheben*) philosophy by realizing it—so convinced was he of the truth of Hegelian philosophy, whose only fault was that concept and reality cleaved unbearably, a fault that Hegel studiously overlooked. The corresponding, though fundamentally different, present-day attitude to philosophy is the dismissive goodbye and good riddance. These farewells take many forms, three of which are currently in vogue. For simplicity's sake I will call them the therapeutic, the heroic, and the salvaging farewell.

Wittgenstein championed the notion of a *therapeutic* philosophy, therapeutic in the specific sense of self-healing, for philosophy was sick to the core. Wittgenstein's diagnosis was that philosophy had disarrayed language games that function perfectly well in everyday life. The weakness of this particular farewell to philosophy is that it leaves the world as it is. For the standards by which philosophy is being criticized are taken straight from the self-sufficient, routinized forms of life in which philosophy happens to survive for now. And what about possible successors? Field research in cultural anthropology seems to be the strongest candidate to succeed philosophy after its demise. Surely, the history of philosophy will henceforth be interpreted as the unintelligible doings of some outlandish tribe that today is fortunately extinct. (Perhaps Rorty will one day be celebrated as the path-breaking Thucydides of this new approach, which incidentally could only get under way after Wittgenstein's medicine had proven effective.)

There is a sharp contrast between the soft-spoken farewell of the therapeutic philosopher and the noisy demolition undertaken by someone like Georges Bataille or Heidegger. Their goodbye is *heroic*. From their perspective too, the false habits of living and thinking are concentrated in elevated forms of philosophical reflection. But instead of blaming philosophy for homely category mistakes or simple disruptions of everyday life, their deconstruction of metaphysics and repressive thought has a more incisive, epochal quality. This more dramatic farewell to philosophy does not promise a cure. Rather, it resembles Hölderlin's pathos-laden idea of a rescue attempt *in extremis*. The devalued and discredited philosophical tradition, rather than being replaced by something even more valueless than itself, is supposed to give way to a *different* medium that makes possible a return to the immemorial—to Bataille's sovereignty or Heidegger's being.

Least conspicuous, finally, is the *salvaging* type of farewell to philosophy. Contemporary neo-Aristotelians best exemplify this type, insofar as they do exegeses that are informed by hermeneutics. Some of their work is unquestionably significant. But all too often it departs from pure interpretation in an effort to salvage some old truth or other. At any rate, this farewell to philosophy has a disingenuous ring: While the salvager keeps invoking the need to preserve philosophy, he wants to have nothing to do with its systematic claims. He does not try to make the ancients relevant to the discussion of some subject matter. Nor does he present the classics as a cultural treasure prepared by philosophy and history. What he does is to appropriate by assimilation texts that were once thought to embody knowledge, treating them instead as sources of illumination and edification.

Let us return for a moment to the critique of Kant, the master thinker, in particular his foundationalism in epistemology. Clearly, present-day philosophies of the sort just described wisely sidestep the Kantian trap. The last thing they think they can do is usher the natural sciences to their proper seat. Contemporary poststructuralist, late-pragmatist, and neohistoricist tendencies share a narrow objectivistic conception of science. Over against scientific cognition they carve out a sphere where thought can be illuminating or awakening instead of being objective. These tendencies prefer to sever all links with general, criticizable claims to validity. They would rather make do without notions like consensus, incontrovertible results, and justified opinions. Paradoxically enough, whereas they make these (unnecessary) sacrifices, they somehow keep believing in the authority and superiority of philosophical insights: their own. In terms of their views on science, the philosophers of the definitive farewell agree with the existentialist proposal (Jaspers, Sartre, Kolakowski) for a division of labor that puts science radically to one side and ends up equating philosophy with belief, life, existential freedom, myth, education, or what have you. All these juxtapositions are identical in structure. Where they differ is in their assessment of what Max Weber termed the cultural relevance of science, which may range from negative to neutral to positive. As is well known, Continental philosophy has a penchant for dramatizing the dangers of objectivism and instrumental reason, whereas Anglo-American philosophy takes a more relaxed view of them.

With his distinction between normal and abnormal discourse, Richard Rorty has come up with an interesting variation on the above theme. In times of widely acknowledged theoretical progress, normality takes hold of the established sciences. This means methods become available that make problem solving and dispute settling possible. What Rorty calls commensurable discourses are those discourses that operate with reliable criteria of consensus building. In contrast, discourses are incommensurable or abnormal when basic orientations are contested. Generally, abnormal conversations tend to pass over into normal ones, their ultimate purpose being to annul themselves and to bring about universal agreement. Occasionally, however, abnormal discourses stop short of taking this self-transcending step and are content with "interesting and fruitful disagreement." That is, they become *sufficient unto themselves*. It is at this point that abnormal discourses take on the quality that Rorty calls "edifying." According to him, philosophy as a whole verges on edifying conversation once it has sloughed off all pretensions to problem solving. Such philosophical edification enjoys the benefits of all three types of farewell: therapeutic relief, heroic overcoming, and hermeneutic reawakening. It combines the inconspicuously subversive force of leisure with an elitist notion of creative linguistic imagination and with the wisdom of the ages. The desire for edification, however, works to the detriment of the desire for truth: "Edifying philosophers can never end philosophy, but they can help prevent it from attaining the secure path of a science."

I am partly sympathetic to Rorty's allocation of roles, for I agree that philosophy has no business playing the part of the highest arbiter in matters of science and culture. I find his argument unconvincing all the same. For even after pragmatism and hermeneutics have done their work and curtailed the scope of philosophy, the latter, though reduced to edifying conversation, can never find a niche *beyond* the sciences. Philosophical conversation cannot but gravitate toward argumentation and justificatory dispute. There is no alternative.

The existentialist or, if you like, exclusive division of labor between philosophy and science is untenable. This is borne out by the particular version of discourse theory Rorty proposes. Ultimately there is only one criterion by which opinions can be judged valid, and that is that they are based on agreement reached by argumentation. This means that *everything* whose validity is at all disputable rests on shaky foundations. It matters little if the ground underfoot shakes a bit less for those who debate problems of physics than for those who debate problems of morals and aesthetics. The difference is a matter of degree only, as the postempiricist philosophy of science has shown. Normalization of discourse is not a sufficiently trenchant criterion for distinguishing science from edifying philosophical conversation.

5. To those who advocate a cut-and-dried division of labor, research traditions representing a blend of philosophy and science have always been particularly offensive. Marxism and psychoanalysis are cases in point. They cannot, on this view, help being pseudosciences because they straddle normal and abnormal discourse, refusing to fall on either side of the dividing line. . . .

What I have said lies mainly in the realm of speculative conjecture. But unless I am completely mistaken, it makes sense to suggest that philosophy, instead of just dropping the usher role and being left with nothing, ought to exchange it for the part of stand-in (*Platzhalter*). Whose seat would philosophy be keeping, what would it be standing in for? Empirical theories with strong universalistic claims. As I have indicated, fertile minds have surfaced and will continue to surface in nonphilosophical disciplines, who will give such theories a try. The chance for their emergence is greatest in the reconstructive sciences. Starting primarily from the intuitive knowledge of competent subjects—competent in terms of judgment, action, and language—and secondarily from systematic knowledge handed down by culture, the reconstructive sciences explain the presumably universal bases of rational experience and judgment, as well as of action and linguistic communication. Marked down in price, the venerable transcendental and dialectical modes of justification may still come in handy. All they can fairly be expected to furnish, however, is reconstructive hypotheses for use in empirical settings. Telling examples of a successful cooperative integration of philosophy and science can be seen in the development of a theory of rationality. This is an area where philosophers work as suppliers of ideas without raising foundationalist or absolutist claims à la Kant or Hegel. Fallibilistic in orientation, they reject the dubious faith in philosophy's ability to do things single-handedly, hoping instead that the success that has for so long eluded it might come from an auspicious matching of different theoretical fragments. From the vantage point of my own research interests, I see such a cooperation taking shape between philosophy of science and history of science; between speech act theory and empirical approaches to pragmatics of language; between a theory of informal argumentation and empirical approaches to natural argumentation; between philosophical theories of action and the ontogenetic study of action competences.

If it is true that philosophy has entered upon a phase of cooperation with the sciences of man, does it not run the risk of losing its identity? . . . In defense, one might argue that a philosophy that contributes something important to an analysis of the rational foundations of knowing, acting, and speaking does retain at least a thematic connection with the whole. But is this enough? What becomes of the theory of modernity, what of the window on the totality of culture that Kant and Hegel opened with their foundational and hypostatizing concepts of reason? Down to Husserl's *Crisis of the European Sciences*, philosophy not only usurped the part of supreme judge, it also played a directing role. Again, what happens when it surrenders the role of judge in matters of science as well as culture? Does this mean philosophy's relation to the totality is severed? Does this mean it can no longer be the guardian of rationality?

The situation of culture as a whole is no different from the situation of science as a whole. As totalities, neither needs to be grounded or justified or given a place by philosophy. Since the dawn of modernity in the eighteenth century, culture has generated those structures of rationality that Max Weber and Emil Lask conceptualized as cultural value spheres. Their existence calls for description and analysis, not philosophical justification.

Reason has split into three moments—modern science; positive law and posttraditional ethics; autonomous art and institutionalized art criticism—but philosophy had precious little to do with this disjunction. Ignorant of sophisticated critiques of reason, the sons and daughters of modernity have progressively learned to differentiate their cultural tradition in terms of these three aspects of rationality such that they deal with issues of truth, justice, and taste discretely, never simultaneously. At a different level, this shift toward differentiation produces the following phenomena: (1) The sciences disgorge more and more elements of religion, thus renouncing their former claim to being able to interpret nature and history as one whole. (2) Cognitivist moral theories disgorge issues of the good life, focusing instead strictly on deontological, generalizable aspects of ethics, so that all that remains of "the good" is the just. (3) With art it is likewise. Since the turn to autonomy, art has striven mightily to mirror one basic aesthetic experience, which is the increasing decentration of subjectivity. It occurs as the subject leaves the spatio-temporal structures of everyday life behind, freeing itself from the conventions of everyday perception, of purposive behavior, and of the imperatives of work and utility.

I repeat, these eminent trends toward compartmentalization, constituting as they do the hallmark of modernity, can do very well without philosophical justification. But they do pose problems of mediation. First, how can reason, once it has been thus sundered, go on being a unity on the level of culture? And second, how can expert cultures, which are being pushed more and more to the level of rarefied, esoteric forms, be made to stay in touch with everyday communication? To the extent to which philosophy keeps at least one eye trained on the topic of rationality, that is, to the extent to which it keeps inquiring into the conditions of the unconditional, to that extent it will not dodge the demand for these two kinds of efforts at mediation.

The first type of problem of mediation arises within the spheres of science, morals, and art. In this area we witness the rise of countermovements. For example, in human sciences nonobjective approaches bring moral and aesthetic criticism into play without undermining the primacy of issues of truth. Another example is the way in which the debate about ethics of responsibility versus ethics of ultimate ends (to the degree to which it emphasizes utilitarian motifs within moral cognitivism) assimilates notions like risk taking, need interpretation, and so on, notions that lie clearly in the field of the cognitive and expressive rather than the moral. Let us finally look at postmodern art as our third example. It is characterized by a strange simultaneity of realistic, politically committed schools, on the one hand, and authentic followers of that classical modernism to which we owe the crystallization of the specific meaning of the aesthetic, on the other. In realistic and politically committed art, elements of the cognitive and the moral-practical come into play once again, but at the level of the wealth of forms unloosed by the avant-garde. To that extent they act as agents of mediation. Counterdevelopments like these, it seems, mitigate the rigid compartmentalization of reason, pointing to reason's unity. In this regard, everyday life is a more promising medium for regaining the lost unity of reason than are today's expert cultures or yesteryear's classical philosophy of reason.

In everyday communication cognitive interpretations, moral expectations, expressions, and evaluations cannot help overlapping and interpenetrating. Reaching understanding in the lifeworld requires a cultural tradition that ranges across *the whole spectrum*, not just the fruits of science and technology. As far as philosophy is concerned, it might do well to refurbish its link with the totality by taking on the role of interpreter on behalf of the lifeworld. It might then be able to help set in motion the interplay between the cognitive-instrumental, moral-practical, and aesthetic-expressive dimensions that has come to a standstill today, like a tangled mobile. This simile at least helps identify the issue philosophy will face when it stops playing the part of the arbiter who inspects culture and instead starts playing the part of a mediating interpreter. That issue is how to overcome the isolation of science, morals, and art and their respective expert cultures. How can they be joined to the impoverished traditions of the life-world, and how can this be done without detriment to their regional rationality? How can a new balance between the separated moments of reason be established in communicative every-day life?

The critic of the master thinkers will likely express his alarm one more time. What in the world, he will ask, gives the philosopher the right to offer his services as a translator mediating between the everyday world and cultural modernity with its autonomous sectors, when he is already more than busy trying to carve out a space for ambitious theoretical strategies within the system of the sciences? I think pragmatism and hermeneutics have joined forces to answer this question, by attributing epistemic authority to the community of all who cooperate and speak with one another. Everyday communication makes possible a kind of understanding that is based on claims to validity, thus furnishing the only real alternative to exerting influence on one another, which is always more or less coercive. The validity claims that we raise in conver-sation—that is, when we say something with conviction—transcend this specific conversa-tional context, pointing to something beyond the spatio-temporal ambit of the occasion. Every agreement, whether produced for the first time or reaffirmed, is based on (controvertible) grounds or reasons. Grounds have a special property: They force us into yes or no positions. Built into the structure of action-oriented-to-reaching-understanding is therefore an element of unconditionality. And it is this unconditional element that makes the validity (*Gültigkeit*) we claim for our views different from the mere de facto acceptance (*Geltung*) of habitual practices. From the perspective of first persons, what we consider justified is not a function of life styles but a question of justification or grounding. That is why philosophy is "rooted in the urge to see social practices of justification as more than just such practices." The same urge is at work when people like me stubbornly cling to the notion that philosophy is the guardian of rationality.

Craig Calhoun

Craig Calhoun, a professor of sociology and history at the University of North Carolina at Chapel Hill, explores in this essay the significance of some of Jürgen Habermas's most intriguing concepts. Originally published in German in 1962, Habermas's *The Structural Transformation of the Public Sphere* was not published in English until 1989. For many social critics, Habermas's idea of a public sphere provides a direct challenge to radical elements in postmodernist thought. Instead of discourses intrinsically tied to power structures or language paralyzed by the possibility of infinite interpretation, Habermas attempts to describe a set of conditions in which individuals might assert positions, make truth-claims, and arrive at uncoerced agreement through rational argument.

The public sphere Habermas discusses is historically specific. As Calhoun notes, Habermas focuses on seventeenth- and eighteenth-century bourgeois communities in Western Europe made up of educated, independent, wealthy, and propertied men. Free from economic or personal contraints and undivided by status distinctions, the elite discussed literature and politics in ways that promoted the practice of free, intelligent argument as the arbiter of divisive issues. But the conditions required for that process did not last. As the state took on a larger role in shaping private lives and large corporations and industries restricted individual control over work rhythms and families, the independence of mind and identity required for a select, enlightened public to arrive at truth gradually dissolved. Instead of a center for rational critical debate, the public sphere of this century became an arena for advertising and a mass culture based on thoughtless consumption. As Calhoun points out, Habermas cannot seem to find an institutional basis in advanced capitalist society that would enable reason to play its older role.

In Habermas's thought, however, many still find profound implications for both democracy and epistemology. Unlike postmodernist thinkers, Habermas's theory goes beyond discussing contextual truths and attempts to identify an applied reason that might bring about human emancipation. Although today's society does not appear to lend itself to the creation of a public sphere, some hold that argument in small communities might still produce reasoned evaluations of the environment surrounding us. Where others appear ready to reject the possibility of human communication or embrace relativism, Habermas maintains and strives to defend a faith in the potential of the Enlightenment project.

CRAIG CALHOUN
(1992)

Habermas and
the Public Sphere

> If we attend to the course of conversation in mixed companies consisting not merely of scholars and subtle reasoners but also of business people or women, we notice that besides storytelling and jesting they have another entertainment, namely, arguing.
>
> — *Immanuel Kant*

Jürgen Habermas's important early book *The Structural Transformation of the Public Sphere* asks when and under what conditions the arguments of mixed companies could become authoritative bases for political action. The question, Habermas shows, is a crucial one for democratic theory. What are the social conditions, he asks, for a rational-critical debate about public issues conducted by private persons willing to let arguments and not statuses determine decisions? This is an inquiry at once into normative ideals and actual history. It focuses upon the bourgeois political life of the seventeenth through mid twentieth centuries, yet it aims to reach beyond the flawed realities of this history to recover something of continuing normative importance. This something is an institutional location for practical reason in public affairs and for the accompanying valid, if often deceptive, claims of formal democracy.

Habermas's social theory is often interpreted as moving over the years from a Hegelian-Marxist orientation to a sort of Kantian orientation. Though not without truth, this view underestimates the unity in his intellectual project. Kant occupies a central place in *Structural Transformation* as the theorist who offered the fullest articulation of the ideal of the bourgeois public sphere. In this public sphere, practical reason was institutionalized through norms of reasoned discourse in which arguments, not statuses or traditions, were to be decisive. Though Habermas rejects Kantian epistemology and its corollary ahistorical exaltation of philosophy as arbiter and foundation of all science and culture, in his recent work he nonetheless argues that something remains crucial from the Kantian view of modernity. Above all else, this is a notion of "procedural rationality and its ability to give credence to our views in the three areas

Craig Calhoun, introduction to *Habermas and the Public Sphere* (Cambridge, Mass.: MIT Press, 1992). © Massachusetts Institute of Technology. Reprinted by permission of the Press.

of objective knowledge, moral-practical insight, and aesthetic judgment." This procedural rationality is fundamentally a matter of basing judgment on reasons.

Habermas's task in *Structural Transformation* is to develop a critique of this category of bourgeois society showing both (1) its internal tensions and the factors that led to its transformation and partial degeneration and (2) the element of truth and emancipatory potential that it contained despite its ideological misrepresentation and contradictions. The key issues are implicit, if rather lightly expressed, in the quotation above from Kant. In a nutshell, a public sphere adequate to a democratic polity depends upon both quality of discourse and quantity of participation. Habermas develops the first requirement in elaborating how the classical bourgeois public sphere of the seventeenth and eighteenth centuries was constituted around rational critical argument, in which the merits of arguments and not the identities of arguers were crucial. The key point to draw from Kant, then, is the ubiquity of argument; this exercise of reason was the valuable kernel in the flawed ideology of the bourgeois public sphere. Kant betrayed a certain elitism in the way he noted that mere business people and even women might argue, but the emphasis can be put on the positive, since participation in argument is a means of education capable of overcoming the debilities that make some arguers inferior (and thus it is a very different matter from ascribed statuses that permanently exclude some people). On the other hand, reading Kant more negatively, we see that businesspeople and women were not "subtle reasoners," and we come across the dialectic leading to the decline of the public sphere.

The early bourgeois public spheres were composed of narrow segments of the European population, mainly educated, propertied men, and they conducted a discourse not only exclusive of others but prejudicial to the interests of those excluded. Yet the transformations of the public sphere that Habermas describes turn largely on its continual expansion to include more and more participants (as well as on the development of large scale social organizations as mediators of individual participation). He suggests that ultimately this inclusivity brought degeneration in the quality of discourse, but he contends that both the requirements of democracy and the nature of contemporary large-scale social organization mean that it is impossible to progress today by going back to an elitist public sphere.

1

The Structural Transformation of the Public Sphere was born in controversy and is likely to continue to spark controversy. It originated as Habermas's *Habilitationschrift* (thesis for the post-doctoral qualification required of German professors) and was intended for submission to Max Horkheimer (and Theodor Adorno) at Frankfurt. Horkheimer and Adorno, however, apparently thought it at once insufficiently critical of the illusions and dangerous tendencies of an Enlightenment conception of democratic public life, especially in mass society, and too radical in its politically focused call for an attempt to go beyond liberal constitutional protections in pursuit of truer democracy.... The book remains extraordinarily suggestive, still the most significant modern work on its subject.

That subject is the historically specific phenomenon of the bourgeois public sphere created out of the relations between capitalism and the state in the seventeenth and eighteenth centuries. Habermas sets out to establish what the category of public meant in bourgeois society and how its meaning and material operation were transformed in the centuries after its constitution. The motivation for this lies largely in an attempt to revive the progressive potential in "formal" democracy and law and thus to counterbalance their neglect in the Marxist tradition. More specifically, it is part of Habermas's lifelong effort to reground the Frankfurt School project of critical theory in order to get out of the pessimistic cul de sac in which Horkheimer and Adorno found themselves in the postwar era. In a nutshell, the attempt to ground a vision of societal transformation and human emancipation on the proletariat had foundered. The experience of fascism and the rise of the cultural industry and "engineered consent" seemed to indicate that there was no historical subject on which critics might pin their hopes for transcending capitalism. Habermas turned away from the search for such a subject and developed an account of intersubjective communicative processes and their emancipatory potential in place of any philosophy (or politics) of the subject. At the same time Habermas sought to incorporate into his theory a full appreciation of the implications of changes that had occurred in both capitalism and state structures through the period of Western modernity. The rise of the large corporation, the problematization of consumption (as a response to successful increases in productive capacity), the development of the social-welfare state and mass democracy all altered both the conditions that framed the view of classical Marxism and the conditions of bourgeois society itself. In this respect, *Structural Transformation* also parallels much of the older Frankfurt School's analysis of the transition from liberal to "organized" capitalism.

The importance of the public sphere lies in its potential as a mode of societal integration. Public discourse (and what Habermas later and more generally calls communicative action) is a possible mode of coordination of human life, as are state power and market economies. But money and power are non-discursive modes of coordination, as Habermas's later theory stresses; they offer no intrinsic openings to the identification of reason and will, and they suffer from tendencies toward domination and reification. State and economy are thus both crucial topics for rivals of the democratic public sphere.

Structural Transformation approaches these concerns first by trying to develop a historically specific understanding of the modern category of publicness. The bourgeois public sphere is "a category that is typical of an epoch. It cannot be abstracted from the unique developmental history of that 'civil society' (buürgerliche Gesellschaft) originating in the European High Middle Ages; nor can it be transferred, ideal typically generalized, to any number of historical situations that represent formally similar constellations." The Enlightenment category thus is different from its classical Greek ancestor, just as it is different from its transformed contemporary descendant. Greek thought made a strong division between public and private affairs. But in the private realm of the *oikos*, the Greek head of a household confronted only necessity. Freedom was to be found in public, though of course the public realm of autonomous citizens rested on the private autonomy of each as master of a household (most of whose members were excluded from the public). The bourgeois public sphere that Habermas explores shares some features with this picture, but it reverses a key element. It is defined as the public of *private* individuals who join in debate of issues bearing on state authority. Unlike the Greek conception, individuals are here understood to be formed primarily in the private realm, including the family. Moreover, the private realm is understood as one of freedom that has to be defended against the domination of the state.

The seventeenth- and eighteenth-century notion developed alongside the rise and transformation of the modern state, as well as on the basis of capitalist economic activity. The modern state constituted the public as a specific realm again (as had the Greek polis). In the middle ages, publicness had been more of a "status attribute." It was a characteristic of the ruler, borne even by his person. In a world of kings who could say "L'etat, c'est moi," the public of a country did not exist apart from a king and his court. This was the heyday of "representative publicity," and lordship was represented "not for but 'before' the people." Gradually, however, court society developed into the new sort of sociability of eighteenth-century salons. Aristocrats played leading roles in the early bourgeois public sphere. Habermas does not mean to suggest that what made the public sphere bourgeois was simply the class composition of its members. Rather, it was *society* that was bourgeois, and bourgeois society produced a certain form of public sphere. The new sociability, together with the rational-critical discourse that grew in the salons (and coffee houses and other places), depended on the rise of national and territorial power states on the basis of the early capitalist commercial economy. This process led to an idea of society separate from the ruler (or the state) and of a private realm separate from the public.

This notion of civil society is basic to Habermas's account of the public sphere, and his account in turn offers a great deal of richness to current discussions of civil society that come close to equating it with the private market. Civil society, in the seventeenth and eighteenth centuries, developed as "the genuine domain of private autonomy [that] stood opposed to the state." Capitalist market economies formed the basis of this civil society, but it included a good deal more than that. It included institutions of sociability and discourse only loosely related to the economy. Transformations of the economy nonetheless produced transformations in all of civil society.

Habermas shows the intimate involvement of print media in the early extensions of market economies beyond local arenas. Long-distance trade, for example, meant a traffic in news almost as immediately as a traffic in commodities. Merchants needed information about prices and demand, but the newsletters that supplied those needs very quickly began to carry other sorts of information as well. The same processes helped to engender both a more widespread literacy and an approach to the printed word as a source of currently significant "public" information. These developments became revolutionary in the era of mercantilism, when town economies were extended into national territories and the modern state grew up to administer these territories. The development of the state bureaucracies as agents of permanent administration, buttressed by standing armies, created a new sphere of public authority. "Now continuous state activity corresponded to the continuity of contact among those trafficking in commodities and news (stock market, press)." Public authority thus was consolidated into a palpable object distinct from the representative publicity of the ruler and the older estates as well as from the common people, who were excluded from it. "'Public' in this narrower sense was synonymous with 'state-related'." But the public sphere was not coterminous with the state apparatus, for it included all those who might join in a discussion of the issues raised by the administration of the state. The participants in this discussion included agents of the state and private citizens.

The public sphere, like civil society in general, could only be conceptualized in this full sense once the state was constituted as an *impersonal* locus of authority. Unlike the ancient notion of the public, therefore, the modern notion depended on the possibility of counterposing state and society. Here Habermas joins with Arendt in stressing how a private sphere of society could take on a public relevance. "Civil society came into existence as the corollary of a depersonalized state authority."

It became possible to recognize society in the relationships and organizations created for sustaining life and to bring these into public relevance by bringing them forward as interests for a public discussion and/or the action of the state. In this way a certain educated elite came to think of itself as constituting the public and thereby transformed the abstract notion of the *publicum* as counterpart to public authority into a much more concrete set of practices. The members of this elite public began to see themselves through this category not just as the object of state actions but as the opponent of public authority.

> Because, on the one hand, the society now confronting the state clearly separated a private domain from public authority and because, on the other hand, it turned the reproduction of life into something transcending the confines of private domestic authority and becoming a subject of public interest, that zone of continuous administrative contact became "critical" also in the sense that it provoked the critical judgment of a public making use of its reason.

The last phrase of the quote is crucial. The bourgeois public sphere institutionalized, according to Habermas, not just a set of interests and an opposition between state and society but a practice of rational-critical discourse on political matters. Thus, for example, critical reasoning entered the press in the early eighteenth century, supplementing the news with learned articles and quickly creating a new genre of periodical. The very idea of the public was based on the notion of a general interest sufficiently basic that discourse about it need not be distorted by particular interests (at least in principle) and could be a matter of rational approach to an objective order, that is to say, of truth.

> The bourgeois public sphere may be conceived above all as the sphere of private people come together as a public; they soon claimed the public sphere regulated from above against the public authorities themselves, to engage them in a debate over the general rules governing relations in the basically privatized but publicly relevant sphere of commodity exchange and social labor. The medium of this political confrontation was peculiar and without historical precedent: people's public use of their reason.

2

With the general category of public sphere established, we can now look at several of Habermas's more specific arguments about its transformations. After its introductory section, *Structural Transformation* is organized as a repeated series of themes: social structure, political functions, and ideology are analyzed first for the constitution of the classical sphere and then for its degenerative transformation.

Two processes helped to institutionalize the public sphere as it developed out of court society and urban corporations in the early modern era. First, the family was reconstituted as an intimate sphere that grounded both the evaluative affirmation of ordinary life and of economic activity alluded to above and the participation of its patriarchal head in the public sphere. Second, the public sphere was initially constituted in the world of letters, which paved the way for that oriented to politics. The two processes were intertwined. For example, early novels helped to circulate a vision of intimate sentimentality, communicating to the members of the literary public spheres just how they should understand the heart of private life.

The intimate sphere figures importantly in Habermas's account: "The public's understanding of the public use of reason was guided specifically by such private experiences as grew out of the audience-oriented subjectivity of the conjugal family's intimate domain. Historically, the latter was the source of privateness in the modern sense of a saturated and free interiority." In the new conjugal family, "private" meant not merely the burden of necessity, as in classical Greece, and not only the property-owning privacy of economic control either. Rather, the family was understood as at least partially differentiated from material reproduction. Just as state and society were split, so economy and family (the intimate sphere) were distinguished within the private realm. The subjectivity the family nurtured was "audience-oriented" because it was played out in dramas staged for the other members of the family (mirroring the ideal types offered by the sentimental literature of the period).

In this way the reconceived family helped lead to a reconceptualization of humanity itself. It emphasized, first off, the autonomy of its head. This rested on the private ownership of property, but the notion of the intimate family excluded that from its core, thus providing a key element of the false consciousness of the bourgeois. The family was believed to be independent of the market, "whereas in truth it was profoundly caught up in the requirements of the market. The ambivalence of the family as an agent of society yet simultaneously as the anticipated emancipation from society manifested itself in the situation of the family members: on the one hand, they were held together by patriarchal authority; on the other, they were bound to one another by human closeness. As a privatized individual, the bourgeois was two things in one: owner of goods and persons and one human being among others, i.e., *bourgeois* and *homme*." The family was idealized as the purely human realm of "intimate relationships between human beings who, under the aegis of the family, were nothing more than human." At the same time, the intimacy of the family promised a liberation from the constraints of what existed, from necessity, because it was a realm of pure interiority following its own laws and not any external purpose. "In this specific notion of humanity a conception of what existed was promulgated within the bourgeois world which promised redemption from the constraint of what existed without escaping into a transcendental realm. This conception's transcendence of what was immanent was the element of truth that raised bourgeois ideology above ideology itself, most fundamentally in that area where the experience of 'humanity' originated." The family thus provided a crucial basis for the immanent critique of the bourgeois public sphere itself, for it taught that there was something essential to humanness that economic or other status could not take away.

Literature of the period, especially sentimental early novels like Richardson's *Pamela*, relied on and reinforced this same sense of humanness. This was a matter not just of their content but of the author-reader relationship developed by the genre: "The relations between author, work, and public changed. They became intimate mutual relationships between privatized individuals who were psychologically interested in what was 'human,' in self-knowledge, and in empathy." At the same time, the literary public sphere helped to develop the distinctively modern idea of culture as an autonomous realm: "Inasmuch as culture became a commodity and thus finally evolved into 'culture' in the specific sense (as something that pretends to exist merely for its own sake), it was claimed as the ready topic of a discussion through which an audience-oriented subjectivity communicated with itself."

Beyond this subjectivity, the greatest contributions of the literary public sphere to the political sphere lay in the development of institutional bases. These ranged from meeting places to journals to webs of social relationships. Thus early British businessmen met in coffee houses to discuss matters of trade, including the "news," which was coming into ever-wider circulation. London had 3,000 coffee houses by the first decade of the eighteenth century, each with a core of regulars. The conversation of these little circles branched out into affairs of state administration and politics. Journals of opinion were created, which linked the thousands of smaller circles in London and throughout the country. These were often based at particular coffee houses and replicated in their contents the style of convivial exchange. In France, salons, pubic institutions located in private homes, played a crucial role, bridging a literary public sphere dominated by aristocrats with the emergent bourgeois political public sphere. In Germany, table societies drew together especially academics but also other sorts of people. The public outside these institutions was very small.

In all these instances, several features were crucial. The first and perhaps most basic was "a kind of social intercourse that, far from presupposing the equality of status, disregarded status altogether." Of course, this was not fully realized, but the idea had an importance of its own. This "mutual willingness to accept the given roles and simultaneously to suspend their reality was based on the justifiable trust that within the public—presupposing its shared class inter-est—friend-or-foe relations were in fact impossible." The notion of common interest in truth or right policy thus undergirded the "bracketing" of status differences. This was in turn linked to a second crucial feature, the notion that rational argument was the sole arbiter of any issue. However often the norm was breached, the idea that the best rational argument and not the identity of the speaker was supposed to carry the day was institutionalized as an available claim. Third, "discussion within such a public presupposed the problematization of areas that until then had not been questioned." All sorts of topics over which church and state authorities had hitherto exercised a virtual monopoly of interpretation were opened to discussion, inas-much as the public defined its discourse as focusing on all matters of common concern. Fourth, the emerging public established itself as inclusive in principle. Anyone with access to cultural products—books, plays, journals—had at least a potential claim on the attention of the culture-debating public. "However exclusive the public might be in any given instance, it could never close itself off entirely and become consolidated as a clique; for it always understood and found itself immersed within a more inclusive public of all private people, persons who— insofar as they were propertied and educated—as readers, listeners, and spectators could avail themselves via the market of the objects that were subject to discussion."

This literary public sphere produced the practice of literary criticism. The division between critics and "mere readers" was not initially sharp, for "when reviewers of the caliber of Schiller and Schlegel did not regard themselves as too good for voluminous incidental activity of this sort, the lay judgment of the private people with an interest in literature had been insti-tutionalized." It thus institutionalized a form of rational-critical discourse about objects of common concern that could be carried over directly into political discussion: "The process in which the state-governed public sphere was appropriated by the public of private people making use of their reason and was established as a sphere of criticism of public authority was one of functionally converting the public sphere in the world of letters already equipped with institutions of the public and with forums for discussion." A central topic for the transforma-tional discourse was the question of absolute sovereignty versus the rule of general, abstract, depersonalized laws. The new public sphere of civil society made its initial political mark through commitment to the latter, and assertion of "itself (i.e., public opinion) as the only legit-imate source of this law."

3

This argument is most famously that between Hobbes and those, such as Locke and Montesquieu, who would limit or qualify absolute sovereignty. Its primary locus was Britain, and indeed, Britain serves Habermas as the model case of the development of the public sphere. It was there, for example, that the elimination of the institution of censorship first marked a new stage in the development of public discourse. The free provision of information was, alongside education, crucial to putting the public in a position to arrive at a considered, rather than merely a common, opinion. It was in Britain too, after the Glorious Revolution, that national-level political opposition shifted away from resort to violence, so that "through the critical debate of the public, it took the form of a permanent controversy between the governing party and the opposition."

In France a public that critically debated political issues arose only near the middle of the eighteenth century. Even then it lacked the capacity to institutionalize its critical impulses until the Revolution. There was nothing like the British Parliament, with its attendant political press, nor was the state amenable to any notion of a "loyal opposition." Only in the years just before the Revolution did the philosophes turn their critical attention from art, literature, and religion to politics. The founding of clubs and journals focused on economic policy toward English inspiration in the 1770s. The physiocrats were central, and they were the first to combine activity in this public discourse and membership in the government—a sign that public opinion was becoming effective. The occasion for this, as for the summoning of the Estates General, was the government's growing financial crisis. Revolution followed quickly, and from the beginning it was a matter of bourgeois public discourse as much as mob action. The clubs played a central role, and almost overnight an extraordinary range of publications sprang up. The Constitution of 1791 declared that "the free communication of ideas and opinions is one of the most precious rights of man."

Germany lagged behind France. There "the public's rational-critical debate of political matters took place predominantly in the private gatherings of the bourgeoisie." The nobility remained completely dependent on the courts and thus failed to develop strong enough lines of communication with bourgeois intellectuals to participate in creating a strong civil society separate from the state. Nonetheless, journals with political content proliferated and were debated in reading societies, even if the political efficacy of this public remained limited.

In all three settings some degree of institutional basis for a public sphere was established. Habermas stresses the economic foundations: "The social precondition for this 'developed' bourgeois public sphere was a market that, tending to be liberalized, made affairs in the sphere of social reproduction as much as possible a matter of private people left to themselves and so finally completed the privatization of civil society." This institutionalization of a new and stronger sense of privacy as free control of productive property was a crucial contribution of capitalism to the public sphere. It was reflected on the Continent in the codification of civil law, where basic private freedoms were guaranteed. At the same time a fundamental parity among persons was established, corresponding to that among owners of commodities in the market and among educated individuals in the public sphere. Though not all people were full legal subjects, all such legal subjects were joined in a more or less undifferentiated category of persons. The extension of these notions into the doctrines of laissez-faire and even free trade among nations brought the development of "civil society as the private sphere emancipated from public authority" to its fullest extent, though it lasted only for "one blissful moment in the long history of capitalist development."

Conceptually, from the physiocrats through classical economists, it was crucial that the laws of the market were seen as a natural order. Hence, civil society could be understood as neutral regarding power and domination, and its discourse only a matter of discovering the right policies for allowing its full development: "The constitutional state predicated on civil rights pretended, on the basis of an effective public sphere, to be an organization of public power ensuring the latter's subordination to the needs of a private sphere itself taken to be neutralized as regards power and domination. Thus the constitutional norms implied a model of civil society that by no means corresponded to its reality." This contradiction would in time become transformative. In this period of its classical flowering, however, the public still understood itself as using its critical debate not to achieve compromises or to exercise power, but rather to discover laws immanent to its form of society. "The 'domination' of the public, according to its own idea, was an order in which domination itself was dissolved.... Public debate was supposed to transform *voluntas* into a *ratio* that in the public competition of private arguments came into being as the consensus about what was practically necessary in the interest of all." Here we see reflected not only economic conditions but also the idea of formless or pure humanity developed out of the bourgeois family's conjugal sphere.

The public sphere in this era remained rooted in the world of letters even as it assumed political functions. It took that older, elite public as constitutive of the whole relevant citizenry. Education and property ownership were its two criteria for admission. Restrictions of the franchise did not have to be viewed as restrictions of the public sphere but could be interpreted rather as "mere legal ratification of a status attained economically in the private sphere." These qualifications defined a "man," that is, the fully capable and autonomous person competent to enter into the rational-critical discourse about the general interest. "For the private person, there was no break between *homme* and *citoyen*, as long as the *homme* was simultaneously an owner of private property who as *citoyen* was to protect the stability of the property order as a private one." So central was this phenomenon that Habermas (echoing stresses of the young Marx) sees in it the origin of ideology itself, in the strong sense that grounds immanent critique as well as describes false consciousness:

> If ideologies are not only manifestations of the socially necessary consciousness in its essential falsity, if there is an aspect to them that can lay a claim to truth inasmuch as it transcends the status quo in utopian fashion, even if only for purposes of justification, then ideology exists at all only from this period on. Its origin would be the identification of "property owner" with "human being as such" in the role accruing to private people as members of the public in the political public sphere of the bourgeois constitutional state.

4

In chapter 4 Habermas turns to ideology, especially in the realm of the most "advanced" ideas and greatest thinkers of the time. Here the movement is essentially from Hobbes through Locke, the physiocrats, and Rousseau to Kant and then on to Hegel, Marx, Mill, and Tocqueville. What is being developed and then critiqued is a conception of public opinion as a reasoned form of access to truth. This replaces the notions of public opinion as the "mere opinion" (or arbitrary views) of isolated individuals taken in the aggregate, the reputation that emerges in the mirror of dispersed opinions, and the opinion of the "common" sort of people. Rather, public opinion comes to refer more positively to the views held by those who join in rational-critical debate on an issue.

Despite his unpublic doctrine of absolute sovereignty, Hobbes did bring new respect to opinion by identifying it with conscience (and consciousness). His very devaluation of religious conviction meant a corresponding upward revaluation of other opinion. But it was Locke who fully freed opinion from the taint of pure prejudice. Reason and criticism constructed an educated opinion that was fundamentally different from the "mere" opinion that had been seen as so vulgar. The physiocrats moved still further along this path of separating critique from opinion, at least for the enlightened public.

Rousseau, of course, was more complicated. "The physiocrats spoke out in favor of an absolutism complemented by a public sphere that was a place of critical activity; Rousseau wanted democracy without public debate." The general will was nonetheless a sort of public opinion, a consensus of hearts rather than arguments. However polarized in substance, both sides followed Guizot's injunction "to seek after truth, and to tell it to power." Since truth was the object of critical reflection and the general will alike, these could be interpreted as in a sense apolitical. The task was to rationalize politics in the name of morality as well as truth, not simply to engage in it.

In this pursuit, Kant became the paradigmatic voice, following Rousseau on the idea of the will of the whole people but the *philosophes* and the British Enlightenment thinkers on the centrality of critical reason. His was the most fully developed philosophy of the bourgeois public sphere. By themselves, Kant reasoned in "What Is Enlightenment?" individuals would have a hard time working their way out of tutelage, the inability to make use of understanding without external direction. Enlightenment became more possible in free public discourse. "In regard to enlightenment, therefore, thinking for oneself seemed to coincide with thinking aloud and the use of reason with its public use." Communication and criticism were central. Thus even Kantian notions of universality, cosmopolitanism, and science were constituted in the communication of rational beings. When Kant called on Enlightenment thinkers to address the "world," or to be men of the world, the public sphere was essential to its definition; the very unity and dignity of the human species was revealed, in part, by its capacity to join in public discourse: "'World' here pointed to humanity as a species, but in that guise in which its unity presented itself in appearance: the world of a critically debating reading public that at the time was just evolving within the broader bourgeois strata." Engagement in the public sphere was the means by which the conflicting private wills of rational people could be brought into harmony. This could happen because society, particularly the private economy, necessarily gave rise to the conditions for turning politics into morality. *Bourgeois* could be conflated with *homme* because the private economy was a natural order, so constructed that justice was immanent in free commerce.

If Kant offered the fullest philosophy of bourgeois publicness, Hegel offered the first critique, denouncing the public of civil society as ideology. Public opinion had the form of common sense; it was dispersed among people in the form of prejudices, not true knowledge; it took the fortuitous for the permanent. "Hegel took the teeth out of the idea of the public sphere of civil society; for anarchic and antagonistic civil society did not constitute the public sphere, emancipated from domination and insulated from the interference of power, in which autonomous private people related to one another." This did not provide the basis for transforming political authority into rational authority, force or interest into reason. Civil society could not dispense with domination but on the contrary required it because of a tendency toward disintegration.

It was only a short step to Marx's denunciation of public opinion as a mask for bourgeois class interests. "The public sphere with which Marx saw himself confronted contradicted its own principle of universal accessibility—the public could no longer claim to be identical with the nation, civil society with all of society." Similarly, of course, property owners could not be seen as equivalent to human beings in general. Indeed, the very division of state and society entailed an alienating division of the person into public and private. The private realm did not offer true respite from public tensions, for the realm did not offer true respite from public tensions, for the family and the intimate sphere in general were marked by the necessity of labor, patriarchal property ownership, and domination. In Marx's vision, the state would be absorbed into society, and rational planning would enable the development of "an intimate sphere set free from economic functions." In this vision, interaction would be emancipated from the demands of social labor, and private relationships would be freed from the need for any legal regulations. Behind the Marxist view, however, was still the idea of a natural order—Marx disagreed not with the general idea but only with the claim that bourgeois civil society constituted the natural order that could give rise to harmonious human relationships.

Liberals like Mill and Tocqueville were willing, Habermas suggests, to take the step of discarding the notion of an underlying natural order adequate to ground a philosophy of history in which politics would become morality. Accepting the disharmony of much of capitalist civil society, the liberalism they developed sought protections and ameliorations, relative not perfect freedom. The political public sphere, in their account, did not rest on any natural basis, though some form of the bourgeois public sphere did need to be defended through common sense, prudence, and realism. The key issue that they confronted was how to maintain the virtues of public life while its size increased and its composition changed. This democratization of the public sphere was an inevitable result of the tension between its original class limitations and its principled openness. "Electoral reform was the topic of the nineteenth century: no longer the principle of publicity as such, as had been true in the eighteenth century, but of the enlargement of the public." As the public was enlarged, however, public opinion itself came to seem a threat, particularly when it seemed to involve a compulsion toward conformity more than critical discourse. Thus it was that both Mill and Tocqueville worried, for example, about protecting minorities from persecution by majorities. This was actually a matter, in part, of protecting the possibility of free, critical thought from public opinion itself. Here we clearly see an initial theoretical response to the structural transformation of the public sphere.

Mill and Tocqueville thus accepted an individualism without a comparable notion of the whole and resigned themselves to a more imperfect world.

> This resignation before the inability to resolve rationally the competition of interests in the public
> sphere was disguised as perspectivist epistemology: because the particular interests were no longer
> measured against the general, the opinions into which they were ideologically transposed
> possessed an irreducible kernel of faith.... The unity of reason and of public opinion lacked the
> objective guarantee of a concordance of interests existing in society, the rational demonstrability
> of a universal interest as such.

The "principle" of the public sphere, critical public discourse, seemed to lose in strength in proportion as it extended as a sphere, partly because its very foundations in the private realm were undermined.

5

The undermining of the foundations of the public sphere came about, Habermas suggests, through a "refeudalization" of society. "The model of the bourgeois public sphere presupposed strict separation of the public from the private realm in such a way that the public sphere, made up of private people gathered together as a public and articulating the needs of society with the state, was itself considered part of the private realm." Structural transformation came about, however, as private organizations began increasingly to assume public power on the one hand, while the state penetrated the private realm on the other. State and society, once distinct, became interlocked. The public sphere was necessarily transformed as the distinction between public and private realms blurred, the equation between the intimate sphere and private life broke down with a polarization of family and economic society, rational-critical debate gave way to the consumption of culture.

The blurring of relations between private and public involved centrally the loss of the notion that private life (family, economy) created autonomous, relatively equal persons who in public discourse might address the general or public interest. First, the inequalities always present in civil society ceased to be "bracketed" and became instead the basis of discussion and action. This happened both because these inequalities grew greater (as in the case of giant corporations) and because the inclusion of more people in the public sphere made it impossible to escape addressing the class divisions of civil society (because, for example, some of these people were excluded from the franchise or lacked the private ownership of the means of production that were the basis of the putative autonomy of *bourgeois* and *homme*). Second and relatedly, the notion of an objective general interest was replaced, even ideally, with one of a fairly negotiated compromise among interests. The functioning of the public sphere thus shifted from rational-critical debate to negotiation. "The process of the politically relevant exercise and equilibration of power now takes place directly between the private bureaucracies, special-interest associations, parties, and public administration. The public as such is included only sporadically in this circuit of power, and even then it is brought in only to contribute its acclamation." This second process marked the beginning of the movement toward the welfare state as interest groups in civil society used the public sphere to demand "social rights"—the services or protection of the state. Attempts were made, in other words, to transfer to a political level those conflicts, e.g., between workers and employers, that were not resolvable in the private sphere alone. "The more society became transparent as a mere nexus of coercive constraints, the more urgent became the need for a strong state." But "the occupation of the political public sphere by the unpropertied masses led to an interlocking of state and society which [contrary to Marx's expectations] removed from the new public sphere its former basis without supplying a new one."

Civil society was changed also by the establishment of a world of work as a sphere of its own right between the public and private realms. Large organizations, both public and private, played the central role in separating work from the purely private sphere of the household or the paternalistically managed workplace. The private sphere in turn was reduced to the family. An "externalization of what is declared to be the inner life" occurred. "To the extent that private people withdrew from their socially controlled roles as property owners into the purely 'personal' ones of their noncommittal use of leisure time, they came directly under the influence of semi-public authorities, without the protection of an institutionally respected domestic domain."

At the same time, and largely as a consequence of these trends, the public sphere was turned into a sham semblance of its former self. The key tendency was to replace the shared, critical activity of public discourse by a more passive culture consumption on the one hand and an apolitical sociability on the other. Habermas's account here is typical of the critique of mass culture in which members of the Frankfurt School had already played a prominent role.... Thus participants in social gatherings lost the sense of the pleasures and virtues of argument that Kant and the members of the eighteenth-century public sphere had made central to public life: "In the course of our century, the bourgeois forms of sociability have found substitutes that have one tendency in common despite their regional and national diversity: abstinence from literary and political debate. On the new model the convivial discussion among individuals gave way to more or less noncommittal group activities." This did not mean that there was not a sharing of culture, only that it was a joint consumption rather than a more active participation in mutual critique (and production). "Individual satisfaction of needs might be achieved in a public fashion, namely, in the company of many others; but a public sphere itself did not emerge from such a situation.... Rational-critical debate had a tendency to be replaced by consumption, and the web of public communication unraveled into acts of individuated reception, however uniform in mode." Where works of literature, for example, had previously been appropriated not just through individual reading but through group discussion and the critical discourse of literary publications, the modern media and the modern style of appropriation "removed the ground for a communication about what has been appropriated." Thus, "the world fashioned by the mass media is a public sphere in appearance only."

What happened was that in the expansion of access, the form of participation was fatally altered. Innovations that opened economic access to the public sphere and the realm of "high" culture, e.g., cheaper editions of books (not to mention higher incomes of readers), are worthy of praise. But alongside these there has been a psychological facilitation of access by lowering the threshold capacity required for appreciation or participation. "Serious involvement with culture produces facility, while the consumption of mass culture leaves no lasting trace; it affords a kind of experience which is not cumulative but regressive." The distinction between "serious involvement" and "consumption of mass culture" is perhaps overdrawn, if familiar; that between economically opening access and psychologically facilitating it is clearer. It is surprising, however, that Habermas does not consider the various ways in which access was opened that do not fall into either category—the extension of public education and mass literacy, for example, or the increase in working-class leisure time. In any case, what he is charting is simultaneously the depoliticization of the public sphere and its impoverishment by removal of critical discourse. "In relation to the expansion of the news-reading public, therefore, the press that submitted political issues to critical discussion in the long run lost its influence. Instead, the culture-consuming public whose inheritance derived from the public sphere in the world of letters more than from that in the political realm attained a remarkable dominance."

The eighteenth-century public sphere had been constituted in the discourse of private persons but was based on a distinction between the private activities that formed them for public life and provided its motivations and that public life itself. By contrast, "the sphere generated by the mass media has taken on the traits of a secondary realm of intimacy." We experience radio, film, and television communication with an immediacy far greater than that characteristic of the printed word. One of the effects of this on public discourse is that "bracketing" personal attributes and concentrating on the rational-critical argument becomes more difficult. This feeds into a more general "sentimentality toward persons and corresponding cynicism toward institutions," which curtails "subjective capacity for rational criticism of public authority, even where it might objectively still be possible." A personalized politics revives representative publicity by making candidates into media stars. At the same time the new public-relations industry finds it easy to engineer consent among the consumers of mass culture. Even states must address citizens as consumers when they, like private corporations or political candidates, seek to cultivate an "uncommitted friendly disposition." This of course involves an element of false consciousness in which the degenerate mass public sphere understands itself on the model of its more effective predecessor: "The awakened readiness of the consumers involves the false consciousness that as critically reflecting private people they contribute responsibly to public opinion." Even legislatures are affected, as they become arenas for staged displays aimed at persuading the masses rather than forums for critical debate among their members. The mass-consumption mentality substitutes a pursuit of acclamation for the development of rational-critical consensus.

The weakening of the public is not just a matter of new (lower class) entrants being mere consumers or substandard participants. On the contrary, Habermas asserts (with some empirical evidence), the consumption of mass culture increases with wealth, status, and urbanization. The most that can be said is that the consumption levels are highest for those whose wealth has outstripped their education. And the result is that the public sphere as a whole is transformed, not just diluted around the edges.

This transformation involves a literal disintegration. With the loss of a notion of general interest and the rise of a consumption orientation, the members of the public sphere lose their common ground. The consumption orientation of mass culture produces a proliferation of products designed to please various tastes. Not only are these not subjected, according to Habermas, to much critical discussion; none of them reaches the whole of the public. "Of Richardson's *Pamela* it could be said that it was read by the entire public, that is, by 'everyone' who could read at all." Nothing attains such general currency today. This break involves not only segmentation of audiences but transformation of the once intimate relationship between cultural producers and consumers. It is, Habermas argues, precisely with this break that intellectuals begin to form a distinct stratum of those who produce culture and its critical commentaries. Once they are so distinguished, they have to explain to themselves their isolation from the public of the educated bourgeoisie. The ideology of the free-floating intelligentsia responds to precisely this predicament. At the same time, however, even the elite of producers and critics undergoes a specialization that undercuts its public function. "The sounding board of an educated stratum tutored in the public use of reason has been shattered; the public is split apart into minorities of specialists [e.g., lawyers, academics] who put their reason to use nonpublicly and the great mass of consumers whose receptiveness is public but uncritical."

6

By means of these transformations, the public sphere has become more an arena for advertising than a setting for rational-critical debate. Legislators stage displays for constituents. Special-interest organizations use publicity work to increase the prestige of their own positions, without making the topics to which those positions refer subjects of genuine public debate. The media are used to create occasions for consumers to identify with the public positions or personas of others. All this amounts to the return of a version of representative publicity, to which the public responds by acclamation, or the withholding of acclamation, rather than critical discourse. In this respect, the latter sections of *Structural Transformation* directly foreshadow Habermas's arguments in *Legitimation Crisis* (1975). The public sphere becomes a setting for states and corporate actors to develop legitimacy not by responding appropriately to an independent and critical public but by seeking to instill in social actors motivations that conform to the needs of the overall system dominated by those states and corporate actors. The only difference is that in the earlier book Habermas implies that organized capitalism has a more successful legitimation regime.

Even political parties reflect the transformation of the public sphere. From the nineteenth century these ceased to be groups of voters so much as bureaucratic organizations aimed at motivating voters and attracting their psychological identification and acclamation by voting. Modern parties "in the proper sense" are thus "organized supralocally and with a bureaucratic apparatus and aimed at the ideological integration and the political mobilization of the broad voting masses." Their attention is focused on attracting the votes of those not yet committed (and in some cases motivating those whose opinions, but not actual participation, they can count on). Such parties attempt to move people to offer their acclamation without providing political education or remedies for the "political immaturity" of voters. Plebiscites replace public discourse. When parties were constituted as groups of voters, they were simultaneously groups of participants in the rational-critical public sphere. Legislators were given free mandates, the argument went, because they, *like their constituents*, were autonomous parties to the public sphere with parity of standing in its rational-critical debate; they could not be bound to a position in advance of the discourse. But with the consumption orientation of mass culture and the interpenetration of state and society through organized interest groups and corporations, legislators become agents (or principals) of parties. Instead of joining with their constituents in rational-critical debate, they attempt to garner the support not just of independent constituents (as anachronistic liberal theory has it) but also of special-interest groups. They do this not through rational-critical debate but through offering to represent those interests in bargaining. "Direct mutual contact between the members of the public was lost in the degree that the parties, having become integral parts of a system of special-interest associations under public law, had to transmit and represent at any given time the interests of several such organizations that grew out of the private sphere into the public sphere.

As parties dominate politics and as state and society are generally intertwined, the material conditions for the old sort of public sphere disappear. The new version of representative publicity responds to a "democratic" broadening of the constituency of the public, but at the cost of its internally democratic functioning. No attempt to go back to the old bourgeois public sphere can be progressive, for social change has made its contradictory foundations manifest. "Any attempt at restoring the liberal public sphere through the reduction of its plebiscitarily expanded form will only serve to weaken even more the residual functions genuinely remaining within it." The struggle instead must be to find a form of democratic public discourse that can salvage critical reason in an age of largescale institutions and fuzzy boundaries between state and society. The answer, Habermas suggests, lies in what in the 1960s came sometimes to be called "the long march through the institutions." That is, parties, parastatal agencies, and bureaucracies of all sorts must themselves be internally democratized and subjected to critical publicity. In the case of the media, for example, some mechanism for insuring more democratic access and selection is needed as a response to the concentration of ownership and increasing scale of media organizations. There may be no alternative to a politics based on negotiation of interests among organized groups. But the trend for these organizations to become less open to rational-critical discourse can be reversed. "To be able to satisfy these functions in the sense of democratic opinion and consensus formation their inner structure must first be organized in accord with the principle of publicity and must institutionally permit an intraparty or intra-association democracy—to allow for unhampered communication and public rational-critical debate."

The struggle to transform institutions and reclaim the public sphere, to make good on the kernel of truth in the ideology of the bourgeois public sphere, is a struggle to make publicity a source of reasoned, progressive consensus formation rather than an occasion for the manipulation of popular opinion. Only thereby can the public realm become an authority for politics rather than merely its playing field: "'Public opinion' takes on a different meaning depending on whether it is brought into play as a critical authority in connection with the normative mandate that the exercise of political and social power be subject to publicity or as the object to be molded in connection with a staged display of, and manipulative propagation of, publicity in the service of persons and institutions, consumer goods, and programs." The often touted democratic potential of plebiscites and public-opinion research is minimal, because neither in itself offers an occasion for discursive will formation. "Publicity was, according to its very idea, a principle of democracy not because anyone could in principle announce, with equal opportunity, his personal inclinations, wishes, and convictions—opinions; it could only be realized in the measure that these personal opinions could evolve through the rational-critical debate of a public into public opinion." Public-opinion research is more akin to the simultaneously developed field of group psychology than to democratic practice; it is an auxiliary science to public administration rather than a basis or substitute for true public discourse.

The ideal of the public sphere calls for social integration to be based on rational-critical discourse. Integration, in other words, is to be based on communication rather than domination. "Communication" in this context means not merely sharing what people already think or know but also a process of potential transformation in which reason is advanced by debate itself. This goal cannot be realized by a denial of the implications of large-scale social organization, by imagining a public sphere occupied only by autonomous private individuals, with no large organizations and with no cleavages of interest inhibiting the identification of the general good, as liberal theory suggests. "Institutionalized in the mass democracy of the social-welfare state, ... the idea of publicity ... is today realizable only as a rationalization ... of the exercise of societal and political power under the mutual control of rival organizations themselves committed to publicity as regards both their internal structure and their interaction with one another and with the state." The rationalization is limited, just as it was in the bourgeois public sphere of critical debate among private people, but it is rationalization nonetheless.

7

The second half of *Structural Transformation* is less satisfying than the first. If the early chapters succeed in recovering a valuable critical ideal from the classical bourgeois public sphere, Habermas ultimately cannot find a way to ground his hopes for its realization very effectively in his account of the social institutions of advanced or organized capitalism. While his idea of intraorganizational publicity and democracy is important, in the absence of a unifying general interest, it can only improve representation in compromise, not achieve the identification of the political with the moral through the agency of rational-critical debate. At the center of this impasse is Habermas's inability to find in advanced capitalist societies an institutional basis for an effective political public sphere corresponding in character and function to that of early capitalism and state formation but corresponding in scale and participation to the realities of later capitalism and states.

Habermas responds to this problem in three ways. First, especially in *Legitimation Crisis*, he addresses the consequences of extensive state intervention into the economy. This, as I noted above, is shown in *Structural Transformation* to undermine the bases in civil society for the development of a public sphere as a part of the private realm. Habermas's next move is to argue that this state intervention effectively prevents a focus on the contradictions of capital as such and thus orients political action away from the bases of potential fundamental transformation and toward the state itself. Welfare state democracy demands that states legitimate themselves by demonstrating that their policies serve the overall interests of their constituents. This is a result not only of state intervention as such (which is functionally required to maintain stable socioeconomic function) but also of the transformation of the public sphere into an arena in which a wide range of social interests vie for state action. Because those interests conflict, states are left to face a crisis in which they are unable simultaneously to produce adequate motivation for work and loyalty to the existing regime.

Second, Habermas takes up the division between system and lifeworld. He argues that advanced capitalist society cannot be conceptualized as a social totality, because it is split into separate realms integrated on different bases. The lifeworld is the realm of personal relationships and (at its best) communicative action. But to it is counterposed a system ordered on the basis of nonlinguistic steering media (money and power), integrating society impersonally through functional or cybernetic feedback. This split cannot be overcome, Habermas argues, because there is no immanent logic of capitalism to produce its dialectical transcendence and because large-scale modern society would be impossible without such systemic integration (and dreams of doing away with such large-scale societal integration are not only romantic but dangerous because reduction in scale can come about only in catastrophic ways). Nonetheless, the lifeworld is the locus for basic human values and is undergoing rationalization processes of its own; it needs to be defended against the continual encroachment of systemic media.

Third, Habermas shifted his attention from the institutional construction of a public sphere as the basis for democratic will formation to the validity claims universally implicit in all speech. In the latter he finds the basis for a progressive rationalization of communication and the capacity for noninstrumental organization of interpersonal relationships. Habermas thus turns away from historically specific grounding for democracy (though the public sphere remains the institutional locus for democratic political practice) toward reliance on a transhistorical capacity of human communication. Communicative action thus provides an alternative to money and power as a basis for societal integration. On the one hand, Habermas idealizes the directly interpersonal relations of the lifeworld as counterpoint to systemic integration with its dehumanization and reification. On the other hand, especially in more recent work, he explores the capacity of specific institutionalized discourses like law to develop communicative action as a means of societal rationalization and integration. More generally, "a radical-democratic change in the process of legitimation aims at a new balance between the forces of societal integration so that the social-integrative power of solidarity—the 'communicative force of production'—can prevail over the powers of the other two control resources, i.e., money and administrative power, and therewith successfully assert the practically oriented demands of the lifeworld."

Habermas thus continues to seek a way to recover the normative ideal of formal democracy from early bourgeois political theory and practice and to develop a basis for discerning the social directions by which it might progress. More specifically, he continues to see the development of welfare state capitalism as producing impasses (rather than crises born of a dialectic, which will resolve them) but destroying earlier bases for addressing them through utopian collective action. However, where *Structural Transformation* located the basis for the application of practical reason to politics in the historically specific social institutions of the public sphere, the theory of communicative action locates them in transhistorical, evolving communicative capacities or capacities of reason conceived intersubjectively as in its essence a matter of communication. The public sphere remains an ideal, but it becomes a contingent product of the evolution of communicative action, rather than its basis.

What happened in *Structural Transformation* to make these moves seem necessary? More precisely, did Habermas have to abandon the more historically specific and social-institutional strategy of *Structural Transformation* to locate bases for the simultaneous rationalization and democratization of politics? I think the answer lies in the last chapters of the book. In a sense, Habermas himself seems to have been persuaded more by his account of the degeneration of the public sphere than by his suggestions of its revitalization through intraorganizational reforms and the application of norms of publicity to interorganizational relations. He seems to have seen no bases for progress in social institutions as such, either those of capitalism and civil society or those of the state, and so turned elsewhere to look for them. The crucial question was what might underpin the development and recognition of a truly general interest. No longer believing in the capacity of either the public sphere as such or of socialist transformation of civil society to meet this need, Habermas sought a less historical, more transcendental basis for democracy. This is what he found in an evolutionary account of human communicative capacity that stressed the potentials implicit in all speech. This gave him the basis for revitalizing Kantian ideals, and more generally democratic ideals, in a world still torn asunder and subjected to domination by capitalism and bureaucratic power.

Seyla Benhabib

Seyla Benhabib is a professor of political science and philosophy at Harvard University. In her book *Situating the Self*, Benhabib attempts to define the concept "interactive universalism." This abstract notion is meant to evade both the hegemony of Enlightenment certainty concerning epistemology and human reason and the more nihilistic postmodernist precepts that deny the human agent any causality whatsoever. Benhabib claims that "the crucial insights of the universalist tradition in practical philosophy can be reformulated today without committing oneself to the metaphysical illusions of the Enlightenment."[1]

Benhabib undertakes an analysis of the tenuous alliance between postmodernism and feminism, departing from the shared attribute of both intellectual currents, circumspection regarding Enlightenment metanarratives. Benhabib notes, however, that if the feminist theorist accepts the strong variants of postmodernist critiques of "Man, History, and Metaphysics," feminism becomes deprived of the very critical stance which may enable it to effect some change in social and political theory.

1   *Situating the Self* (New York: Routledge, 1992), p. 4.

SEYLA BENHABIB
(1992)

Feminism and the Question of Postmodernism

Perhaps no other text has marked the contemporary discussion concerning the complex cultural, intellectual, artistic, social and political phenomena which we have come to designate as "post-modernism" as much as Jean-François Lyotard's short treatise on *The Postmodern Condition: A Report on Knowledge*. Written at the request of the president of the Conseil des Universités of the government of Quebec as a report on knowledge "in the most highly developed societies," or as a sociology of knowledge under late capitalism, Lyotard's treatise soon became the central text for the philosophical and literary discussions of postmodernism. For feminist debates on postmodernism as well, Lyotard's presentation and conceptualization of the "postmodern problematic" has been crucial.

This chapter will consider the contemporary alliance between feminism and postmodernism. Viewed from within the intellectual and academic culture of western capitalist democracies, feminism and postmodernism have emerged as two leading currents of our time, and each is in its own way profoundly critical of the principles and meta-narratives of western Enlightenment and modernity. Although exactly what constitutes such Enlightenment and modernity, and what those principles and meta-narratives are to which we should bid farewell is by no means clear. Feminism and postmodernism are often mentioned as if they were allies; yet certain other characterizations of postmodernism should make us rather ask "feminism or postmodernism?" At issue, of course, are not merely terminological quibbles. Both feminism and postmodernism are not merely descriptive categories: they are constitutive and evaluative terms, informing and helping define the very practices which they attempt to describe. As cate-

Reprinted from *Situating the Self: Gender, Community and Postmodernism in Contemporary Ethics*, pp. 203–30 (New York, 1992) by permission of Routledge, Inc.

gories of the present, they project modes of thinking about the future and evaluating the past. Here I will consider the complex relationship between feminism and postmodernism with an eye to one issue in particular: are the meta-philosophical premises of the positions referred to as "postmodernism" compatible with the normative content of feminism, not just as a theoretical position but as a theory of women's struggle for emancipation? I would like first to consider the "demise of the episteme of representation." Both feminism and postmodernism are theoretical movements growing out of the demise of this modernist episteme. Depending though on how we conceptualize the intellectual movements and currents leading to this transformation, different epistemic options and normative visions become available to us.

THE END OF THE EPISTEME OF REPRESENTATION

Modern philosophy began with the loss of the world. The decision of the autonomous bourgeois subject to take nothing and no authority for granted whose content and strictures had not been subjected to rigorous examination, and that had not withstood the test of "clarity and distinctness," began with the withdrawal from the world. The question of classical epistemology from Descartes to Hume, from Locke to Kant was how to make congruous the order of representations in consciousness with the order of representations outside the self. Caught in the prisonhouse of its own consciousness, the modern epistemological subject tried to recover the world it had well lost. The options were not many: either one reassured onself that the world would be gained by the direct and immediate evidence of the senses (empiricism) or one insisted that the rationality of the creator or the harmony of mind and nature would guarantee the correspondence between the two orders of representations (rationalism).

Whether empiricist or rationalist, modern epistemologists agreed that the task of knowledge, whatever its origins, was to build an adequate representation of things. In knowledge, mind had to "mirror" nature.

Actually, modern epistemology operated with a threefold distinction: the order of representations in our consciousness (ideas and sensations); the signs through which these "private" orders were made public, namely words, and that of which our representations were representations, and to which they referred. In this tradition, meaning was defined as "designation;" the meaning of a word was what it designates, while the primary function of language was denotative, namely to inform us about objectively existing states of affairs. The classical episteme of representation presupposed a spectator conception of the knowing self, a designative theory of meaning, and a denotative theory of language.

Already in the nineteenth century three directions of critique of the classical episteme, leading to its eventual rejection, developed. Stylizing somewhat, the first can be described as the critique of the modern epistemic subject, the second as the critique of the modern epistemic object, and the third as the critique of the modern concept of the sign. The critique of the Cartesian, spectator conception of the subject begins with German Idealism, and continues with Marx and Freud to Horkheimer in 1937, and to Habermas in *Knowledge and Human Interests*. This tradition substitutes for the spectator model of the self the view of an active, producing, fabricating humanity, creating the conditions of objectivity by forming nature through its own historical activity. The Hegelian and Marxist tradition also shows that the Cartesian ego is not a self-transparent entity and that the epistemic self cannot reach full autonomy as long as the historical origin and social constitution of the "clear and distinct" ideas it contemplates remain a mystery. At this point this critique joins hands with the Freudian one which likewise shows that the self is not "transparent" to itself, for it is not "master in its own house" (*Herr im eigenen Haus*). It is controled by desires, needs and forces whose effects upon it shape both the contents of its clear and distinct ideas, as well as its capacity to organize them. The historical and psychoanalytic critique of the Cartesian ego sees the task of reflection neither as the with-drawal from the world nor as access to clarity and distinctness, but as the rendering conscious of those unconscious forces of history and society which have shaped the human psyche. Although generated by the subject, these forces necessarily escape its memory, control and conduct. The goal of reflection is emancipation from self-incurred bondage.

The second line of criticism can be most closely associated with the names of Nietzsche, Heidegger, and Adorno and Horkheimer in *Dialectic of Enlightenment*. The modern episteme is viewed as an episteme of domination. For Nietzsche modern science universalizes Cartesian doubt. Modern knowledge divides the world into the realm of appearance on the one hand, and that of essence or things-in-themselves on the other. This dualistic vision is internalized by the subject of knowledge who in turn is split into body and mind, the senses and the concep-tual faculty. Nietzsche has no difficulty in showing that in this sense modern science signifies the triumph of Platonism. Heidegger drives the error underlying the modern episteme of representation further back than its Platonic origins, to a conception of being as presence, as what is available and present to the consciousness of the subject. This conception of being as "presence-to" reduces the manyness of the appearances by presenting them as "things" available to and disposable by a sovereign consciousness. By reducing appearances to what is present to the sovereign self, consciousness attains the option of controlling them. In a spirit that is quite akin to Heidegger's, in the *Dialectic of Enlightenment* Adorno and Horkheimer argue that it is the "concept," the very unit of thought in the western tradition that imposes homogeneity and identity upon the heterogeneity of material. This drive for identity of conceptual thought culminates in the technical triumph of western *ratio*, which can only know things in that it comes to dominate them. "The Enlightenment relates to things as the dictator to humans."

The third tradition of criticism is initiated by Ferdinand de Saussure and Charles Sanders Peirce, and given sharper contours by Frege and Wittgenstein in our century. They argue that it is impossible to make sense of meaning, reference and language in general when the view of linguistic signs as "private marks" prevails. Instead, the public and shared character of language is a beginning point. Both de Saussure and Peirce point out that there is no natural relation between a sound, the word it represents in a language, and the content it refers to. For Peirce, the relation of the sign, of which words are but one species, to the signified is mediated by the interpretant. For de Saussure, it is within a system of differential relations that certain sounds get arbitrarily frozen to stand for words. Language is that sedimented set of relations which stands ideally behind the set of enunciations, called "parole." This move in the analysis of language from the private to the public, from consciousness to sign, from the individual word to a system of relations among linguistic signs, is followed by Frege and Wittgenstein, insofar as they too argue that the unit of reference is not the word but the sentence (Frege), and that meaning can only be understood by analyzing the multiple contexts of use (Wittgenstein).

The epistemological juncture at which Lyotard operates is characterized by the triumph of this third tradition. Whether in analytic philosophy, or in contemporary hermeneutics, or in French post-structuralism, *the paradigm of language has replaced the paradigm of consciousness*. This shift has meant that the focus is no longer on the epistemic subject or on the private contents of its consciousness but on the public, signifying activities of a collection of subjects. Not only has there been a shift in the size of the interrogated epistemic unit from idea, sensation and concept to the threefold character of the sign as signifier, signified and interpretant (Peirce), to language and parole (Saussure) or to language games as "forms of life" (Wittgenstein). The identity of the epistemic subject has changed as well: the bearer of the sign cannot be an isolated self—there is no private language, as Wittgenstein has observed; the epistemic subject is either the community of selves whose identity extends as far as their horizon of interpretations (Gadamer) or it is a social community of actual language users (Wittgenstein). This enlargement of the relevant epistemic subject is one option. A second option, followed by French structuralism and poststructuralism, is to deny that in order to make sense of the epistemic object one need appeal to an epistemic subject at all. The subject is replaced by a system of structures, oppositions and differences which, to be intelligible, need not be viewed as products of a living subjectivity at all.

Lyotard wants to convince that the destruction of the episteme of representation allows only one option, namely a recognition of the irreconcilability and incommensurability of language games, and the acceptance that only local and context-specific criteria of validity can be formulated. One must accept, in other words, an "agonistics" of language: "to speak is to fight, in the sense of playing, and speech-acts fall within the domain of a general agonistics." This cognitive option yields a "polytheism of values," and a politics of justice beyond consensus, characterized by Lyotard vaguely as the "temporary contract." . . .

Faced with these debates about the "end" or "transformation" of philosophy and the emergence of a postmodernist agonistics of language, feminists feel ambivalent: on the one hand, they want to extract from the postmodernism debate only those intellectual conclusions which will aid us in the task of thinking and rethinking the western intellectual tradition and creating a new one of our own in the light of the question of gender; on the other hand, in allying themselves with postmodernist positions, feminists, willy-nilly, are getting embroiled in this dispute and entangled in a set of assumptions which go well beyond research interest centering on gender as a "useful category" to the heart of contemporary philosophical thought. Many feminists share an impulse on this issue which is quite like the "constructivist" vein of John Rawls's later writings on justice in democratic societies. Inasmuch as Rawls wants to articulate principles of justice on the basis of presuppositions "common to the democratic culture" of advanced capitalist democracies, thus avoiding philosophically controversial concepts of self and society, so too many contemporary feminists want to adopt postmodernist premises without getting embroiled in the philosophical argumentation necessary to establish the cogency of these premises. But is their position tenable? Can feminists become postmodernists and claim to develop a theory in the interests of women's emancipation?

Let us begin by considering one of the more comprehensive characterizations of the "postmodern moment" provided by a feminist theorist. In the following discussion, I shall attempt to show that just as Lyotard is right in marking the end of the episteme of representation and in searching for alternative cognitive and normative options to this no longer convincing intellectual paradigm, so too, feminist friends of postmodernism are correct in noting the profound alliances between the postmodernist critique of western thought and their own positions. Where Lyotard as well as the feminist friends of postmodernism go wrong is in their assumption that the end of meta-narratives, or the death of Man, History and Metaphysics (Jane Flax), allow only one set of conceptual and normative options. By sorting out from one another the strong and weak versions of these theses, I shall argue that the strong postmodernist position is incompatible with and in fact renders incoherent feminism as a theoretical articulation of a struggling social movement.

FEMINIST FRIENDS OF POSTMODERNISM

In her recently published book, *Thinking Fragments: Psychoanalysis, Feminism and Postmodernism in the Contemporary West*, Jane Flax characterizes the postmodern position as subscription to the theses of the death of Man, of History and of Metaphysics.

Consider for the time being how, like postmodernism, feminist theory as well has created its own versions of the three theses concerning the death of Man, History and Metaphysics.

The feminist counterpoint to the postmodernist theme of the *Death of Man* can be named the "Demystification of the Male Subject of Reason." Whereas postmodernists substitute for Man, or the sovereign subject of the theoretical and practical reason of the tradition, the study of contingent, historically changing and culturally variable social, linguistic and discursive practices, feminists claim that "gender" and the various practices contributing to its constitution are one of the most crucial contexts in which to situate the purportedly neutral and universal subject of reason. The western philosophical tradition articulates the deep structures of the experiences and consciousness of a self which it claims to be representative for humans as such. The deepest categories of western philosophy obliterate differences of gender as these shape and structure the experience and subjectivity of the self. Western reason posits itself as the discourse of the one self-identical subject, thereby blinding us to and in fact delegitimizing the presence of otherness and difference which do not fit into its categories. From Plato over Descartes to Kant and Hegel western philosophy thematizes the story of the male subject of reason.

The feminist counterpoint to the *Death of History* would be the "Engendering of Historical Narrative." If the subject of the western intellectual tradition has usually been the white, propertied, Christian, male head of household, then History as hitherto recorded and narrated has been "his story." Furthermore, the various philosophies of history which have dominated since the Enlightenment have forced historical narrative into unity, homogeneity and linearity with the consequence that fragmentation, heterogeneity and above all the varying pace of different temporalities as experienced by different groups have been obliterated. We need only remember Hegel's belief that Africa has no history. Until very recently neither did women have their own history, their own narrative with different categories of periodization and with different structural regularities.

The feminist counterpoint to the *Death of Metaphysics* would be "Feminist Skepticism Toward the Claims of Transcendent Reason." If the subject of reason is not a suprahistorical and context-transcendent being, but the theoretical and practical creations and activities of this subject bear in every instance the marks of the context out of which they emerge, then the subject of philosophy is inevitably embroiled with knowledge-governing interests which mark and direct its activities. For feminist theory, the most important "knowledge-guiding interest" in Habermas's terms, or disciplinary matrix of truth and power in Foucault's terms, are gender relations and the social, economic, political and symbolic constitution of gender differences among human beings.

Despite this "elective affinity" between feminism and postmodernism, each of the three theses enumerated above can be interpreted to permit if not contradictory then at least radically divergent theoretical strategies. And for feminists which set of theretical claims they adopt as their own cannot be a matter of indifference. As Linda Alcoff has recently observed, feminist theory is undergoing a profound identity crisis at the moment. The postmodernist position(s) thought through to their conclusions may eliminate not only the specificity of feminist theory but place in question the very emancipatory ideals of the women's movements altogether.

FEMINIST SKEPTICISM TOWARD POSTMODERNISM

The following discussion will formulate two versions of the three theses enumerated above with the goal of clarifying once more the various conceptual options made available with the demise of the episteme of representations. Put in a nutshell, my argument is that strong and weak versions of the theses of the death of Man, of History and of Metaphysics are possible. Whereas the weak versions of these theses entail premises around which critical theorists as well as postmodernists and possibly even liberals and communitarians can unite, their strong versions undermine the possibility of normative criticism at large. Feminist theory can ally itself with this strong version of postmodernism only at the risk of incoherence and self-contradictoriness.

(a) Let us begin by considering the thesis of the Death of Man for a closer understanding of the conceptual option(s) allowed by the end of the episteme of representation. The weak version of this thesis would *situate* the subject in the context of various social, linguistic and discursive practices. This view would by no means question the desirability and theoretical necessity of articulating a more adequate, less deluded and less mystified vision of subjectivity than those provided by the concepts of the Cartesian cogito, the "transcendental unity of apperception," "Geist and consciousness," or "das Man" (the they). The traditional attributes of the philosophical subject of the West, like self-reflexivity, the capacity for acting on principles, rational accountability for one's actions and the ability to project a life-plan into the future, in short, some form of autonomy and rationality, could then be reformulated by taking account of the radical situatedness of the subject.

The strong version of the thesis of the Death of the Man is perhaps best captured in Flax's own phrase that "Man is forever caught in the web of fictive meaning, in chains of signification, *in which the subject is merely another position in language.*" The subject thus dissolves into the chain of significations of which it was supposed to be the initiator. Along with this dissolution of the subject into yet "another position in language" disappear of course concepts of intentionality, accountability, self-reflexivity and autonomy. The subject that is but another position in language can no longer master and create that distance between itself and the chain of significations in which it is immersed such that it can reflect upon them and creatively alter them.

The strong version of the Death of the Subject thesis is not compatible with the goals of feminism. Surely, a subjectivity that would not be structured by language, by narrative and by the symbolic codes of narrative available in a culture is unthinkable. We tell of who we are, of the "I" that we are, by means of a narrative. "I was born on such and such a date, as the daughter of such and such..." etc. These narratives are deeply colored and structured by the codes of expectable and understandable biographies and identities in our cultures. We can concede all that, but nevertheless we must still argue that we are not merely extensions of our histories, that vis-a-vis our own stories we are in the position of author and character at once. The situated and gendered subject is heteronomously determined but still strives toward autonomy. I want to ask how in fact the very project of female emancipation would be thinkable without such a regulative ideal of enhancing the agency, autonomy and selfhood of women.

Feminist appropriations of Nietzsche on this question can only be incoherent. In her recent book, *Gender Trouble: Feminism and the Subversion of Identity*, Judith Butler wants to extend the limits of reflexivity in thinking about the self beyond the dichotomy of "sex" and "gender." Her convincing and original arguments rejecting this dichotomous reasoning within which feminist theory has operated until recently get clouded, however, by the claim that to reject this dichotomy would mean subscribing to the view that the "gendered self" does not exist; all that the self is, is a series of performances. "Gender," writes Butler, "is not to culture as sex is to nature; gender is also the discursive/cultural means by which 'sexed nature' or a 'natural sex' is produced and established as 'prediscursive,' prior to culture, a politically neutral surface *on which* culture acts." For Butler the myth of the already sexed body is the epistemological equivalent of the myth of the given: just as the given can only be identified within a discursive framework, so too it is the culturally available codes of gender that "sexualize" a body and that construct the directionality of that body's sexual desire.

But Butler also maintains that to think beyond the univocality and dualisms of gender categories, we must bid farewell to the "doer behind the deed," to the self as the subject of a life-narrative. "In an application that Nietzsche himself would not have anticipated or condoned, we might state as a corollary: There is no gender identity behind the expressions of gender; that identity is performatively constituted by the very 'expressions' that are said to be its results." Yet if this view of the self is adopted, is there any possibility of transforming those "expressions" which constitute us? If we are no more than the sum total of the gendered expressions we perform, is there ever any chance to stop the performance for a while, to pull the curtain down, and only let it rise if one can have a say in the production of the play itself? Isn't this what the struggle over gender is all about? Surely we can criticize the "metaphysical presuppositions of identity politics" and challenge the supremacy of heterosexist positions in the women's movement. Yet is such a challenge only thinkable via a complete debunking of any concepts of selfhood, agency and autonomy? What follows from this Nietzschean position is a vision of the self as a masquerading performer, except of course we are now asked to believe that there is no self behind the mask. Given how fragile and tenuous women's sense of selfhood is in many cases, how much of a hit-and-miss affair their struggles for autonomy are, this reduction of female agency to a "doing without the doer" at best appears to me to be making a virtue out of necessity.

The view that gendered identity is constituted by "deeds without the doer," or by performances without a subject, not only undermines the normative vision of feminist politics and theory. It is also impossible to get rid of the subject altogether and claim to be a fully accountable participant in the community of discourse and inquiry: the strong thesis of the death of the subject undermines the discourse of the theorist herself. If the subject who produces discourse is but a product of the discourse it has created, or better still is but "another position in language," then the responsibility for this discourse cannot be attributed to the author but must be attributable to some fictive "authorial position," constituted by the intersection of "discursive planes." (I am tempted to add that in geometry the intersection of planes produces a line!) Butler entertains this possibility in the introduction to her work: "Philosophy is the predominant disciplinary mechanism that currently mobilizes this author-subject." The "subject" here means also the "object of the discourse," not the one who utilizes the discourse but the one who is utilized by the discourse itself. Presumably that is why Butler uses the language of "a discourse mobilizing an author/subject." The center of motility is not the thinking, acting and feeling self but "discourses," "systems of signification," "chains of signs," etc. But how then should we read *Gender Trouble?*

The kind of reading I am engaging here presupposes that there is a thinking author who has produced this text, who has intentions, purposes and goals in communicating with me; that the task of theoretical reflection begins with the attempt to understand what the author meant. Certainly, language always says much more than what the author means; there will always be a discrepancy between what we mean and what we say; but we engage in communication, theoretical no less than everyday communication, to gain some basis of mutual understanding and reasoning. The view that the subject is not reducible to "yet another position in language," but that no matter how constituted by language the subject retains a certain autonomy and ability to rearrange the significations of language, is a regulative principle of all communication and social action. Not only feminist politics, but also coherent theorizing becomes impossible if the speaking and thinking self is replaced by "authorial positions," and if the self becomes a ventriloquist for discourses operating through her or "mobilizing" her.

Perhaps I have overstated the case against Butler. Perhaps Butler does not want, any more than Flax herself, to dispense with women's sense of selfhood, agency and autonomy. In the concluding reflections to *Gender Trouble* Butler returns to questions of agency, identity and politics. She writes:

> The question of locating "agency" is usually associated with the viability of the "subject," where the subject is understood to have some stable existence prior to the cultural field that it negotiated. Or, if the subject is culturally constructed, it is nevertheless vested with an agency, usually figured as the capacity for reflexive mediation, that remains intact regardless of its cultural embeddedness. On such a model, "culture" and "discourse" *mire* the subject, but do not constitute that subject. This move to qualify and to enmire the preexisting subject has appeared necessary to establish a point of agency that is not fully *determined* by that culture and discourse. And yet, this kind of reasoning falsely presumes (a) agency can only be established through recourse to a prediscursive "I," even if that "I" is found in the midst of a discursive convergence, and (b) that to be *constituted* by discourse is to be *determined* by discourse, where determination forecloses the possibility of agency.

Butler rejects that identity can only be established through recourse to an "'I' that preexists signification." She points out that "the enabling conditions for an assertion of 'I' are provided by the structure of signification, the rules that regulate the legitimate and illegitimate invocation of that pronoun, the practices that establish the terms of intelligibility by which that pronoun can circulate." The narrative codes of a culture then define the content with which this pronoun will be invested, the appropriate instances when it can be invoked, by whom and how. Yet one can agree with all that and still maintain that no individual is merely a blank slate upon whom are inscribed the codes of a culture, a kind of Lockean tabula rasa in latter-day Foucaultian garb! The historical and cultural study of diverse codes of the constitution of subjectivity, or the historical study of the formation of the individual, does not answer the question: what mechanisms and dynamics are involved in the developmental process through which the human infant, a vulnerable and dependent body, becomes a distinct self with the ability to speak its language and the ability to participate in the complex social processes which define its world? Such dynamics and mechanisms enabled the children of the ancient Egyptians to become members of that cultural community no less than they enabled Hopi children to become social individuals. The study of culturally diverse codes which define individuality is not the same as an answer to the question as to *how* the human infant becomes the social self, regardless of the cultural and normative content which defines selfhood. In the latter case we are studying *structural processes and dynamics of socialization and individuation;* in the former, historical processes of signification and meaning constitution. Indeed, as Butler observes, "to be constituted by discourse is not to be determined by discourse." We have to explain how a human infant can become the speaker of an infinitely meaningful number of sentences in a given natural language, how it acquires, that is, the competence to become a linguistic being; furthermore, we have to explain how every human infant can become the initiator of a unique life-story, of a meaningful tale—which certainly is only meaningful if we know the cultural codes under which it is constructed—but which we cannot predict even if we knew these cultural codes.

Butler writes "that 'agency' then is to be located within the possibility of a variation on that repetition" (the repetition of gender performances). But where are the resources for that variation derived from? What is it that enables the self to "vary" the gender codes? to resist hegemonic discourses? What psychic, intellectual or other sources of creativity and resistance must we attribute to subjects for such variation to be possible?

The answers to these questions, even if they were fully available to me at this point, which they are not, would go beyond the boundaries of this essay. Yet we have reached an important conclusion: the issues generated by the complex interaction between feminism and postmodernism around concepts of the self and subjectivity cannot be captured by bombastic proclamations of the "Death of the Subject." The central question is how we must understand the phrase: "the I although constituted by discourse is not determined by it." To embark upon a meaningful answer to this query from where we stand today involves not yet another decoding of metaphors and tropes about the self, but a serious interchange between philosophy and the social sciences like sociolinguistics, social interactionist psychology, socialization theory, psychoanalysis and cultural history among others. To put it bluntly: the thesis of the Death of the Subject presupposes a remarkably crude version of individuation and socialization processes when compared with currently available social-scientific reflections on the subject. But neither the fundamentalist models of inquiry of the tradition, which privilege the reflective I reflecting upon the conditions of its reflexive or non-reflexive existence, nor the postmodernist decoding of the subject into bodily surfaces "that are enacted *as* the natural, so [that] these surfaces can become the site of a dissonant and denaturalized performance" (Butler) will suffice in the task of explaining how the individual can be "constituted by discourse and yet not be determined by it." The analysis of gender once more forces the boundaries of disciplinary discourses toward a new integration of theoretical paradigms.

(b) Consider now the thesis of the Death of History. Of all positions normally associated with postmodernism this particular one appears to me to be the least problematical. Disillusionment with the ideals of progress, awareness of the atrocities committed in this century in the name of technological and economic progress, the political and moral bankruptcy of the natural sciences which put themselves in the service of the forces of human and planetary destruction—these are the shared sentiments of our century. Intellectuals and philosophers in the twentieth century are to be distinguished from one another less as being friends and opponents of the belief in progress but more in terms of the following: whether the farewell from the "meta-narratives of the Enlightenment" can be exercised in terms of a continuing belief in the power of rational reflection or whether this farewell is but a prelude to a departure from such reflection.

Interpreted as a *weak* thesis, the Death of History could mean two things: theoretically, this could be understood as a call to end the practice of "grand narratives" which are essentialist and monocausal. It is futile, let us say, to search for an essence of "motherhood," as a cross-cultural universal; just as it is futile to seek to produce a single grand theory of female oppression and male dominance across cultures and societies—be such a theory psychoanalytic, anthropological or biological. Politically, the end of such grand narratives would mean rejecting the hegemonial claims of any group or organization to "represent" the forces of history, to be moving with such forces, or to be acting in their name. The critique of the various totalitarian and totalizing movements of our century from National Socialism and Fascism to Stalinism and other forms of authoritarianism is certainly one of the most formative political experiences of postmodernist intellectuals like Lyotard, Foucault and Derrida. This is also what makes the Death of History thesis interpreted as the end of "grand narratives" so attractive to feminist theorists. Nancy Fraser and Linda Nicholson write, for example:

> The practice of feminist politics in the 1980s has generated a new set of pressures which have worked against metanarratives. In recent years, poor and working-class women, women of color, and lesbians have finally won a wider hearing for their objections to feminist theories which fail to illuminate their lives and address their problems. They have exposed the earlier quasi-metanarratives, with their assumptions of universal female dependence and confinement to the domestic sphere, as false extrapolations from the experience of the white, middle-class, heterosexual women who dominated the beginnings of the second wave.... Thus, as the class, sexual, racial and ethnic awareness of the movement has altered, so has the preferred conception of theory. It has become clear that quasi-metanarratives hamper rather than promote sisterhood, since they elide differences among women and among the forms of sexism to which different women are differentially subject.

The *strong* version of the thesis of the Death of History would imply, however, a prima facie rejection of any historical narrative that concerns itself with the long durée and that focusses on macro-rather than on micro-social practices. Nicholson and Fraser also warn against this "nominalist" tendency in Lyotard's work. I agree with them that it would be a mistake to interpret the death of "grand narratives" as sanctioning in the future local stories as opposed to global history. The decision as to how local or global a historical narrative or piece of social-scientific research need be cannot be determined by epistemological arguments extraneous to the task at hand. It is the empirical researcher who should answer this question; the philosopher has no business legislating the scope of research to the empirical scientist. To the extent that Lyotard's version of postmodernism seems to sanctify the "small" or "local narrative" over the grand one, he engages in unnecessary a priorism with regard to open-ended questions of scientific inquiry.

The more difficult question suggested by the strong thesis of the "death of history" appears to me to be different: even while we dispense with grand narratives, how can we rethink the relationship between politics, historiography and historical memory? Is it possible for struggling groups not to interpret history in light of a moral-political imperative, namely, the imperative of the future interest in emancipation? Think for a moment not only of the way in which feminist historians in the last two decades have discovered women and their hitherto invisible lives and work, but of the manner in which they have also revalorized and taught us to see with different eyes such traditionally female and previously denigrated activities like gossip, quilt-making, and even forms of typically female sickness like headaches, hysteria and taking to bed during menstruation. In this process of the "feminist transvaluation of values" our *present* interest in women's strategies of survival and historical resistance has led us to imbue these *past* activities, which were wholly uninteresting from the standpoint of the traditional historian, with new meaning and significance.

While it is no longer possible or desirable to produce "grand narratives" of history, the "death of history" thesis occludes the epistemological interest in history and in historical narrative which accompany the aspirations of all struggling historical actors. Once this "interest" in recovering the lives and struggles of those "losers" and "victims" of history are lost, can we produce engaged feminist theory?

Defenders of "postmodern historiography" like Fraser and Nicholson who issue calls for a "postmodern-feminist theory" look away from these difficulties in part because what they mean by this kind of theorizing is less "postmodernist" but more "neopragmatist." By "postmodern feminist theory" they mean a theory that would be pragmatic and fallibilistic, that "would tailor its method and categories to the specific task at hand, using multiple categories when appropriate and forswearing the metaphysical comfort of a single feminist method or feminist epistemology." Yet this even-handed and commonsensical approach to tailoring theory to the tasks at hand is not postmodernist. Fraser and Nicholson can reconcile their political commitments with their theoretical sympathies for postmodernism, only because they have substituted theoretical pragmatism for, in effect, the "hyper-theoretical" claims of postmodern historiography.

We see once more that the "death of history" thesis as well allows conceptual alternatives: agreement on the end of historical meta-narratives either of the Marxian sort which center around class struggle or of the liberal sort which center around a notion of progress is not sufficient. Beyond such agreement begin difficult questions on the relationship between historiography, politics and memory. Should we approach history to retrieve from it the victims' memories, lost struggles and unsuccessful resistances, or should we approach history to retrieve from it the monotonous succession of infinite "power/knowledge" complexes that materially constitute selves? Postmodernist historiography too, then, poses difficult alternatives for feminists which challenge any hasty or enthusiastic alliance between their positions.

(c) Finally, let me articulate strong and weak versions of the "death of metaphysics" thesis. In considering this point it would be important to note right at the outset that much of the postmodernist critique of western metaphysics itself proceeds under the spell of a meta-narrative, namely, the narrative first articulated by Heidegger and then developed by Derrida that "Western metaphysics has been under the spell of the 'metaphysics of presence' at least since Plato. . ." This characterization of the philosophical tradition allows postmodernists the rhetorical advantage of presenting what they are arguing against in its least defensible versions: listen again to Flax's words: "For postmodernists this quest for the Real conceals the philosophers' desire, which is to master the world" or "Just as the Real is the ground of Truth, so too philosophy as the privileged representative of the Real ..." etc. But is the philosophical tradition so mono-lithic and so essentialist as postmodernists would like to claim? Would not even Thomas Hobbes shudder at the suggestion that the "Real is the ground of Truth"? What would Kant say when confronted with the claim that "philosophy is the privileged representative of the Real"? Would not Hegel consider the view that concepts and language are one sphere and the "real" yet another merely a version of a naive correspondence theory of truth which the chapter on "Sense Certainty" in the *Phenomenology of Spirit* so eloquently dispensed with? In its strong version, the "death of metaphysics" thesis suffers not only from a subscription to a grandiose meta-narrative, but more significantly, this grandiose meta-narrative flattens out the history of modern philoso-phy and the competing conceptual schemes it contains to the point of unrecognizability. Once this history is rendered unrecognizable then the conceptual and philosophical problems involved in this bravado proclamation of the "death of metaphysics" can be neglected.

The weak version of the "death of metaphysics" thesis which is today more influential than the strong Heidegger-Derrida thesis about the "metaphysics of presence" is Richard Rorty's account. In *Philosophy and the Mirror of Nature* Rorty has shown in subtle and convincing manner that empiricist as well as rationalist projects in the modern period presupposed that philoso-phy, in contradistinction from the developing natural sciences in this period, could articulate the basis of validity of right knowledge and correct action. Rorty names this the project of "epistemology"; this is the view that philosophy is a metadiscourse of legitimation, articulating the criteria of validity presupposed by all other discourses. Once it ceases to be a discourse of justification, philosophy loses its raison d'être. This is indeed the crux of the matter. Once we have detranscendentalized, contextualized, historicized, genderized the subject of knowledge, the context of inquiry, and even the methods of justification, what remains of philosophy? Does not philosophy become a form of genealogical critique of regimes of discourse and power as they succeed each other in their endless historical monotony? Or maybe philosophy becomes a form of thick cultural narration of the sort that hitherto only poets had provided us with? Or maybe all that remains of philosophy is a form of sociology of knowledge, which instead of investigating the conditions of the validity of knowledge and action, investigates the empirical conditions under which communities of interpretation generate such validity claims?

Why is this question concerning the identity and future and maybe the possibility of philosophy of interest of feminists? Can feminist theory not flourish without getting embroiled in the arcane debates about the end or transformation of philosophy? The inclina-tion of the majority of feminist theorists at the present is to argue that we can side-step this question; even if we do not want to ignore it, we must not be committed to answer it one way or another. Fraser and Nicholson ask: "How can we conceive a version of criticism without philosophy which is robust enough to handle the tough job of analyzing sexism in all its endless variety and monotonous similarity?" My answer is that we cannot, and it is this which makes me doubt that as feminists we can adopt postmodernism as a theoretical ally. Social criticism without some form of philosophy is not possible, and without social criticism the project of a feminist theory which is at once committed to knowledge and to the emancipa-tory interests of women is inconceivable. Sabina Lovibond has articulated the dilemma of postmodernists quite well:

I think we have reason to be wary, not only of the unqualified Nietzschean vision of an end of legitimation, but also of the suggestion that it would somehow be "better" if legitimation exercises were carried out in a self-consciously parochial spirit. For if feminism aspires to be something more than a reformist movement, then it is bound sooner or later to find itself calling the parish boundaries into question. . . . So postmodernism seems to face a dilemma: either it can concede the necessity, in terms of the aims of feminism, of "turning the world upside down" in the way just outlined—thereby opening a door once again to the Enlightenment idea of a total reconstruction of society on rational lines; or it can dogmatically reaffirm the arguments already marshalled against that idea—thereby licensing the cynical thought that, here as elsewhere, "who will do what to whom under the new pluralism is depressingly predictable."

Faced with this objection, the answer of postmodernists committed both to the project of social criticism and to the thesis of the death of philosophy as a meta-narrative of legitimation will be that the "local narratives," "les petits récits," which constitute our everyday social practices or language games, are themselves reflexive and self-critical enough to pass judgments on themselves. The Enlightenment fiction of philosophical reflection, of *episteme* juxtaposed to the non-critical practice of everyday *doxa*, is precisely that, a fiction of legitimation which ignores that everyday practices and traditions also have their own criteria of legitimation and criticism. The question then would be if among the criteria made available to us by various practices, language games and cultural traditions we could not find some which would serve feminists in their task of social criticism and radical political transformation. Following Michael Walzer, such postmodernists might wish to maintain that the view of the social critic is never "the view from nowhere," but always the view of the one situated somewhere, in some culture, society and tradition.

The standpoint of "interactive universalism" defended in this book is itself very much situated within the hermeneutic horizon of modernity. *Au fond*, all criticism is situated, but differences arise regarding the construction of the context within which the thinker considers her own thought to be situated. As opposed to the retreat to small narratives and local knowledge, I see even this postmodern moment as being situated within the larger processes of modernization and rationalization which have been proceeding on a world scale since the seventeenth century, and which have truly become global realities in our own. In this sense, interactive universalism is the practice of situated criticism for a global community that does not shy away from knocking down the "parish walls."

Are we closer to resolving the question posed at the end of the previous section as to whether feminist social criticism without philosophy was possible? In considering the postmodernists' thesis of the "death of metaphysics" I suggested that the weak version of this thesis would identify the end of metaphysics with the end of philosophy as a metadiscourse of legitimation, transcending local narratives, while the strong version of the thesis would eliminate, I argued, not only meta-narratives of legitimation but the practice of context-transcending legitimation and criticism altogether. Postmodernists could then respond that this need not be the case, and that there were internal criteria of legitimation and criticism in our culture which the social critic could turn to such that social criticism without philosophy would be possible. I am now arguing that the practice of situated social criticism has two defects: first, the turn to internal criteria of legitimation appears to exempt one from the task of philosophical justification only because the postmodernists assume, inter alia, that there is one obvious set of such criteria to appeal to. But if cultures and traditions are more like competing sets of narratives and incoherent tapestries of meaning, then the social critic must herself construct out of these conflictual and incoherent accounts the set of criteria in the name of which she speaks. The "hermeneutic monism of meaning" brings no exemption from the responsibility of normative justification.

In the second place I have argued that the vocation of social criticism might require social exile, for there might be times when the immanent norms and values of a culture are so reified, dead or petrified that one can no longer speak in their name. The social critic who is in exile does not adopt the "view from nowhere" but the "view from outside the walls of the city," wherever those walls and those boundaries might be. It may indeed be no coincidence that from Hypatia to Diotima to Olympe de Gouges and to Rosa Luxemburg, the vocation of the feminist thinker and critic has led her to leave home and the city walls.

FEMINISM AND THE POSTMODERNIST RETREAT FROM UTOPIA

In the previous sections of this chapter I have disagreed with the view of some feminist theorists that feminism and postmodernism are conceptual and political allies. A certain version of postmodernism is not only incompatible with but would undermine the very possibility of feminism as the theoretical articulation of the emancipatory aspirations of women. This undermining occurs because in its strong version postmodernism is committed to three theses: the death of man understood as the death of the autonomous, self-reflective subject, capable of acting on principle; the death of history, understood as the severance of the epistemic interest in history of struggling groups in constructing their past narratives; the death of metaphysics, understood as the impossibility of criticizing or legitimizing institutions, practices and traditions other than through the immanent appeal to the self-legitimation of "small narratives." Interpreted thus, postmodernism undermines the feminist commitment to women's agency and sense of selfhood, to the reappropriation of women's own history in the name of an emancipated future, and to the exercise of radical social criticism which uncovers gender "in all its endless variety and monotonous similarity."

I dare suggest in these concluding considerations that postmodernism has produced a "retreat from utopia" within feminism. By "utopia" I do not mean the modernist vision of a wholesale restructuring of our social and political universe according to some rationally worked-out plan. These utopias of the Enlightenment have not only ceased to convince but with the self-initiated exit of previously existing "socialist utopias" from their state of grace, one of the greatest rationalist utopias of mankind, the utopia of a rationally planned economy leading to human emancipation, has come to an end. The end of these rationalistic visions of social engineering cannot dry up the sources of utopia in humanity. As the longing for the "wholly other" (*das ganz Andere*), for that which is not yet, such utopian thinking is a practical-moral imperative. Without such a regulative principle of hope, not only morality but also radical transformation is unthinkable. What scares the opponents of utopia, like Lyotard for example, is that in the name of such future utopia the present in its multiple ambiguity, plurality and contradiction will be reduced to a flat grand narrative. I share some of Lyotard's concerns insofar as utopian thinking becomes an excuse either for the crassest instrumentalism in the present—the end justifies the means—or to the extent that the coming utopia exempts the undemocratic and authoritarian practices of the present from critique. Yet we cannot deal with these political concerns by rejecting the ethical impulse of utopia but only by articulating the normative principles of democratic action and organization in the present. Will the postmodernists join us in this task or will they be content with singing the swan-song of normative thinking in general?

The retreat from utopia within feminist theory in the last decade has taken the form of debunking as "essentialist" any attempt to formulate a feminist ethic, a feminist politics, a feminist concept of autonomy and even a feminist aesthetic. The fact that the views of Gilligan or Chodorow or Sarah Ruddick (or for that matter Julia Kristeva) only articulate the sensitivities of white, middle-class, affluent, first world, heterosexual women may be true (although I even have empirical doubts about this). Yet what are we ready to offer in their place: as a project of an ethics which should guide us in the future are we able to offer a better vision than the synthesis of autonomous justice thinking and empathetic care? As a vision of the autonomous personality to aspire to in the future are we able to articulate a sense of self better than the model of autonomous individuality with fluid ego-boundaries and not threatened by otherness? As a vision of feminist politics are we able to articulate a better model for the future than a radically democratic polity which also furthers the values of ecology, non-militarism, and solidarity of peoples? Postmodernism can teach us the theoretical and political traps of why utopias and foundational thinking can go wrong, but it should not lead to a retreat from utopia altogether. For we, as women, have much to lose by giving up the utopian hope in the wholly other.

Suggestions for Further Reading

Alexander, Jeffrey C. *Theoretical Logic in Sociology*, 4 vols. Berkeley and Los Angeles: University of California Press, 1983.

Appleby, Joyce, Hunt, Lynn, and Jacob, Margaret. *Telling the Truth About History*. New York: W. W. Norton, 1994.

Baynes, Kenneth, Bohman, James, and McCarthy, Thomas, eds. *After Philosophy*. Cambridge, MA: MIT Press, 1993.

Bell, Daniel. *The Cultural Contradictions of Capitalism*. New York: Basic Books, 1976.

Benhabib, Seyla. *Situating the Self: Gender, Community, and Postmodernism in Contemporary Ethics*. New York: Routledge, 1992.

Birnbaum, Norman. *Towards a Critical Sociology*. New York: Oxford University Press, 1977.

Bonelli, M. L. Righini, and Sheas, William R., eds. *Reason, Experiment, and Mysticism in the Scientific Revolution*. London: Macmillan, 1975.

Bourdieu, Pierre. *The Logic of Practice*. Stanford: Stanford University Press, 1988.

Calhoun, Craig, ed. *Habermas and the Public Sphere*. Cambridge, MA: MIT Press, 1992.

Derrida, Jacques. *Of Grammatology*. Trans. Gayatri Chakravorty Spivak. Baltimore: Johns Hopkins University Press, 1974.

Diamond, Irene, and Quinby, Lee, eds. *Feminism and Foucault: Reflections on Resistance*. Boston: Northeastern University Press, 1988.

Dirks, Nicholas B., Eley, Geoff, and Ortner, Sherry B., eds. *Culture/Power/History: A Reader in Contemporary Social Theory*. Princeton: Princeton University Press, 1994.

Foucault, Michel. *The Order of Things*. New York: Vintage, 1970.

Fuller, Steve. "Being There With Thomas Kuhn: A Parable for Postmodern Times," *History and Theory* 31 (1992).

Gargan, Edward T. "Tocqueville and the Problems of Historical Prognosis," *American Historical Review* 68 (1963).

Geertz, Clifford. *The Interpretation of Cultures*. New York: Basic Books, 1973.

Gerth, H. H., and Mills, C. Wright, eds. *From Max Weber*. South Bend: Notre Dame University Press, 1974.

Habermas, Jürgen. *The Philosophical Discourse of Modernity*. Cambridge, MA: MIT Press, 1993.

————. *The Structural Transformation of the Public Sphere*, Trans. Thomas Burger. Cambridge, MA: MIT Press, 1993.

Heidegger, Martin. *The Question Concerning Technology and Other Essays*. Trans. William Lovitt. New York: Garland Publications, 1977.

Hont, Istvan, and Ignatieff, Michael. *Wealth and Virtue*. Cambridge: Cambridge University Press, 1983 .

Hunt, Lynn, ed. *The New Cultural History*. Berkeley and Los Angeles: The University of California Press, 1989.

Jay, Martin. *The Dialectical Imagination: A History of the Frankfurt School and the Institute of Social Research, 1923–1950*. London: Heinemann, 1973.

Keller, Evelyn Fox. *Reflections on Gender and Science*. New Haven: Yale University Press, 1985.

Kitcher, Philip. *The Advancement of Science*. New York: Oxford University Press, 1993.

Lakatos, Imre, and Musgrave, Alan, eds. *Criticism and the Growth of Knowledge*. Cambridge: Cambridge University Press, 1970.

Longino, Helen E. *Science as Social Knowledge*. Princeton: Princeton University Press, 1990.

Lyotard, Jean-François. *The Postmodern Condition: A Report on Knowledge*. Trans. Geoff Bennington and Brian Massumi. Minneapolis: University of Minnesota Press, 1984.

Megill, Allan. *Prophets of Extremity*. Berkeley and Los Angeles: University of California Press, 1985.

Merton, Robert. *Science, Technology and Society in Seventeenth-Century England*. Bruges: Saint Catherine Press, 1938.

Nicholson, Linda J., ed. *Feminism/Postmodernism*. New York: Routledge, 1990.

Norris, Christopher. *Uncritical Theory: Postmodernity, Intellectuals and the Gulf War*. London: Lawrence and Wishart, 1992.

Pangle, Thomas. *The Enobling of Democracy*. Baltimore: John Hopkins University Press, 1992.

Pocock, J. G. A. *Virtue, Commerce and History*. New York: Cambridge University Press, 1983.

Popper, Karl. *The Logic of Scientific Discovery*. New York: Harper and Row, 1959.

Porter, Theodore M. *Trust in Numbers: The Pursuit of Objectivity in Science and Public Life*. Princeton: Princeton University Press, 1995.

Rabinow, Paul, ed. *The Foucault Reader*. New York: Pantheon Books, 1984.

Rorty, Richard. *Philosophy and the Mirror of Nature*. Princeton: Princeton University Press, 1979.

Rouse, Joseph. *Knowledge and Power*. Ithaca: Cornell University Press, 1985.

de Saussure, Ferdinand. *Course in General Linguistics*. New York: Philosophical Library, 1959.

Skinner, Quentin, ed. *The Return of Grand Theory in the Human Sciences*. Cambridge: Cambridge University Press, 1985.

Stocking, George. *Race, Culture and Evolution*. New York: Free Press, 1968.

Webster, Charles, ed. *The Intellectual Revolution of the Seventeenth Century*. Boston: Routledge and Kegan Paul, 1974.

Westbrook, Robert. *John Dewey*. Ithaca: Cornell University Press, 1991.

White, Hayden. *Tropics of Discourse*. Baltimore: Johns Hopkins University Press, 1990.

Glossary

aestheticism: The philosophical doctrine that the principles of beauty and the standards used to appreciate art are primary, and that other principles of the good and the right are derived from them.

alterity: Emphasizing a subject's otherness by defining it in opposition to, or in terms of, another subject.

anthropology: The study of man.

Archimedean lever: Metaphorically, an idea powerful enough to effect fundamentals. Coming from the boast of Archimedes, third-century-B.C. Greek philosopher who claimed he could move the earth with a long enough lever.

Aristotelian: Referring to the philosophical work of the Greek thinker Aristotle, who lived in the fourth century B.C. and whose writings on nature and society, recovered in the Renaissance, became the model for logical and deductive reasoning.

artifice: Usually defined as artistic skill or style. In much of the work we are reading, artifice is used to suggest that something is constructed as opposed to natural.

Augustan Age: Early eighteenth-century England.

Buridam's ass: Imaginary donkey alleged to die of hunger when placed between two equidistant bails of hay.

capitalism: An economic system based on private property in which prices, production, and the distribution of goods and incomes are mainly determined through market exchanges.

conjectural history: Refers to eighteenth-century Scottish ideas about the stages of social development.

deconstruction: A postmodern method of analyzing texts which rests on the notion that a text is not a self-contained entity whose meaning is dictated by authorial intent, but exists in a context where the production of the text (i.e., the writing process) as well as its reception (i.e., the reading) are influenced by other texts. Deconstruction tears a text apart, revealing the contradictions and assumptions inherent in language and other systems of meaning.

de-familiarizing: A methodology that seeks to reconstruct the particularity of an event or text so as to question conventional understandings of it, as opposed to making it explicable in familiar terms.

discourse: The use of language in speech or text in which the meaning of words are specific to the community of users.

empiricism: A philosophical tradition which demands that all knowledge, except for certain logical truths and principles of mathematics, comes from sensory experience.

epistemology: The study of human knowledge, its nature, its sources, its justification.

foundationalism: The idea that certain privileged observations correspond directly with reality and serve as the basis for others.

functionalism: The study of society as a system of systems operating to sustain the whole (much like the organic functioning of the body).

hermeneutics: The discipline of the interpretation of texts. As broadly conceived by Heidegger and Gadamer, it is the "uncovering" of meaning in everyday life, the attempt to understand the signs and symbols of one's culture in juxtaposition with other cultures and traditions.

hermeticism: A magical view of nature that we now label "pre-modern." Hermeticism originated in Greek writing during A.D. 100–300. During the Renaissance, hermeticism was manifested in a concern for astrology, alchemy, and other occult sciences.

heuristic: A technique, device, or model that facilitates problem solving.

historicism: A philosophy that localizes truth and different views of reality in particular times, places, and peoples of history. It is generally linked to a strong relativist thesis that there is no truth apart from various historical commitments, but is sometimes linked to the belief that history is controlled by laws.

Hobson's choice: Choice between taking what is offered or taking nothing at all.

idealism: The metaphysical view that only minds and their ideas exist.

ideology: A socially ordered system of cultural symbols that in Marxist terms, always has implications of class power.

incommensurable: Having nothing in common, so that two ideas or visions cannot be held at the same time.

instrumentalism: An approach to reasoning which assumes that theories have the status of instruments or tools in relation to observational statements; also a social theory highlighting the use of ideas, including people, to achieve one's ends.

linguistics: The study of the principles and forms of language.

logical positivism: A philosophy that rejects all metaphysics in favor of an emphasis on the logic of scientific reasoning.

materialism: The view that only physical matter and its properties exist.

modernism: Very broadly defined, modernism is a term that retrospectively denotes a nineteenth- and twentieth-century movement in the arts and humanities which criticizes objective and unified notions of truth and reality in favor of an increased concern with subjectivity, experience, and multiple perspectives.

modernization theory: The theory that all societies pass through a series of well-defined stages of development from the simple to the complex. Western industrial society is viewed as having progressed to the most advanced and complex stage.

narrative: A form of discourse based on emplotment, where descriptions of events are structured so that there is a chain of events with a beginning, middle, and end. Implicit in this structure are the ideas of cause and effect sequences.

nominalism: The seventeenth-century view that names, and more generally words, are universal while things are endlessly singular and particular. As against realism.

non sequitur: A conclusion that does not follow logically from the preceding statement.

Occam's Razor: The principle that the fewest possible assumptions are to be made when explaining some thing.

positivism: A philosophical system that recognizes only facts and observable phenomena; a form of empiricism that reduces society to natural categories.

pragmatism: A distinctly American philosophical movement founded by Charles Saunders Peirce, based on the notion that truth is always to be determined by reference to practical outcomes. Only those metaphysical distinctions that make some difference in practice are worth considering. The defense of a belief is that it works.

Renaissance: Quattrocento (fifteenth-century) Italian movement in the arts that flowered in Northern Europe at the end of the sixteenth century. Also the revival of learning associated with the recovery of classical texts.

Romanticism: A movement in the humanities dating roughly from the late eighteenth century to the mid-nineteenth century which embraces a cluster of ideas stressing particularity and poetics in opposition to Enlightenment rationalism.

social structure: The idea that social life is organized around largely invisible structures of class, status, and politics.

solipsism: A metaphysical theory that the self is the only existent thing. Often used to denote something that is self-referential.

structuralism: Generally, a name for a group of interpretive cultural theories based on the inherent logic of language and thought, and the primacy of meaning over history.

teleology: The belief that all phenomena have a purpose and/or goal. In history, it refers to the belief in a principle determining change, such as progress or class conflict.

Whig history: Historical writing that is characteristically celebratory in nature and is usually concerned with the description of winning ideas and progressive developments.